OECD Tourism Trends and Policies 2024

OECD
BETTER POLICIES FOR BETTER LIVES

Please cite this publication as:
OECD (2024), *OECD Tourism Trends and Policies 2024*, OECD Publishing, Paris, https://doi.org/10.1787/80885d8b-en.

ISBN 978-92-64-32259-2 (print)
ISBN 978-92-64-69850-5 (PDF)
ISBN 978-92-64-77503-9 (HTML)
ISBN 978-92-64-52517-7 (epub)

OECD Tourism Trends and Policies
ISSN 2076-7765 (print)
ISSN 2076-7773 (online)

Photo credits: Cover © Archiwiz/Getty Images; © topform84/Getty Images.

Corrigenda to OECD publications may be found at: https://www.oecd.org/en/publications/support/corrigenda.html.

Foreword

OECD Tourism Trends and Policies is an international reference and biennial benchmark to support countries in driving sustainable and inclusive tourism growth. The publication brings together internationally comparable data on tourism and highlights good practices and key policy and governance reforms across 50 OECD member and partner countries. It also includes several topical and thematic chapters, and country-specific policy and statistical profiles.

The *2024 edition of OECD Tourism Trends and Policies* comes as tourism has rebounded strongly following significant declines in 2020-21 in the wake of the COVID-19 pandemic. In some countries, tourism has surpassed previous highs, demonstrating the resilience of tourism demand. However, the strength of the recovery is creating challenges in destinations that are struggling to manage demand and the impacts on local communities and the environment. Tourism can play a key role in fostering economic development that creates decent jobs, enhances social cohesion, and contributes to the shared interests of tourists, residents, and businesses. But the impacts can often be economically, socially, and environmentally unbalanced, and the benefits do not always, or automatically, accrue to local communities.

Many destinations, and governments at all levels, are now developing policies to better manage the social and environmental impacts, particularly from unplanned tourism growth, including through diversifying the tourism offer and managing visitor flows, as well as through investments in more timely and granular data to better understand the potential trade-offs. This is a core thread in this year's *OECD Tourism Trends and Policies* which builds on the recent momentum for sustainable tourism and the renewed focus on addressing unbalanced tourism development. The report considers what tourism success looks like and takes a deep dive on the sustainable development and management of tourism. It also highlights the need to accelerate efforts to develop more timely, granular data and measures tailored to the specific policy needs of destinations. A separate chapter zooms-in on tackling tourism workforce issues, particular labour shortages and related skills challenges, and discusses opportunities to address both short- and longer-term weaknesses in the sector.

This flagship publication was produced by the Centre for Entrepreneurship, SMEs, Regions and Cities (CFE) of the OECD, with co-financing from the European Union. The OECD Tourism Committee approved Chapter 1 on 2 July 2024, Chapters 2 and 3 on 10 June 2024, and the Country Profiles on 22 July 2024.

Acknowledgements

This report presents the 2024 edition of the *OECD Tourism Trends and Policies* publication. It was produced by the OECD Centre for Entrepreneurship, SMEs, Regions and Cities (CFE), led by Lamia Kamal-Chaoui, Director, as part of the programme of work of the OECD Tourism Committee. The report was undertaken in co-operation with the European Union*.

The report benefitted from significant contributions, feedback and guidance from policy makers and statisticians from OECD member and partner countries. It also benefitted from consultation and feedback from industry representatives and associations, including Business@OECD and the OECD Trade Union Advisory Committee, as well as intergovernmental organisations, including UN Tourism and the International Labour Organization. Chapter 2 focusing on strengthening the tourism workforce was informed by discussions at two workshops, including national industry associations and SMEs, as well as Hospitality Europe HOTREC, Les Roches, Pacific Asia Tourism Association, TUI Group and the World Travel and Tourism Council.

The report was co-ordinated and edited by Jane Stacey, Head of the Tourism Policy and Analysis Unit, under the supervision of Nadim Ahmad, Deputy Director (CFE). Kristen Corrie, Policy Analyst (CFE) authored Chapter 3 and co-authored Chapter 2. Antonia Jardim, Policy Analyst (CFE) and James Tops, Junior Policy Analyst (CFE), managed the preparation of the country policy profiles and also undertook substantial co-ordination, drafting and editing. Peter Haxton, Senior Policy Analyst (CFE), Julie Reimann, Junior Economist (CFE), Hannes Thees, Policy Analyst/Economist (CFE), Jasper Heslinga, Policy Analyst/Economist (CFE), Eva Katzer, Junior Policy Analyst (CFE) and Natalia Vankovic, Intern (CFE) also provided support in drafting and editing. Laetitia Reille, Statistician (CFE) and Sergio Montoya, Statistician (CFE) managed the statistical database and developed country statistical profiles and synthesis tables. Monserrat Fonbonnat, Assistant (CFE) provided administrative support. Jack Waters and Pauline Arbel (CFE) served as publication co-ordinators. The statistical component of the report is available via the OECD's statistical online platform – OECD Data Explorer.

External experts who drafted material include Jill Brightling (*Consultant*) for Chapter 1 and the country profiles, and Tom Baum (*University of Strathclyde)* and Richard Robinson (*University of Queensland*) for Chapter 2. Chapter 3 benefited from review and feedback from Susanne Becken (*Griffith University*). In addition, the report benefitted from the contributions and feedback of other OECD colleagues in the Centre for Entrepreneurship, SMEs, Regions and Cities (CFE).

Co-funded by the European Union

* This document was produced with the financial assistance of the European Union. The views expressed herein can in no way be taken to reflect the official opinion of the European Union.

Table of contents

Reader's Guide

This reader's guide provides information and methodological notes on the data sources used in this book: International Recommendations for Tourism Statistics 2008, Tourism Satellite Account: Recommended Methodological Framework 2008 and Balance of Payments and International Investment Position Manual.

The statistical data, metadata and sources in this report are accessible online in a single, consolidated source of tourism statistics https://data-explorer.oecd.org/. Individual data sets can be accessed through the following links: Domestic tourism, Inbound tourism, Outbound tourism, Enterprises and employment, Internal tourism consumption, Key indicators in percentage.

The data closely align with the main methodological references and international standards used for tourism statistics:

- International Recommendations for Tourism Statistics 2008, UN/UNWTO, *http://unstats.un.org/unsd/publication/SeriesM/seriesm_83rev1e.pdf*.
- Tourism Satellite Account: Recommended Methodological Framework 2008, UN/UNWTO/EUROSTAT/OECD, *http://unstats.un.org/unsd/publication/Seriesf/SeriesF_80rev1e.pdf*.
- Sixth Edition of the IMF's Balance of Payments and International Investment Position Manual 2010, IMF, *http://www.imf.org/external/pubs/ft/bop/2007/bopman6.htm*.

This note provides the reader with a methodological summary. For more detailed information, please refer to the above-mentioned methodological tools.

International Recommendations for Tourism Statistics (IRTS)

The International Recommendations on Tourism Statistics (IRTS) provides a common reference framework for countries to use in the compilation of tourism statistics. It presents an internally consistent system of definitions, concepts, classifications and indicators, and provides general guidance with respect to data sources and data compilation methods.

Tourism can be regarded as a social, cultural and economic phenomenon related to the movement of people outside their usual place of residence. Tourism refers to the activity of visitors.

A **visitor** is a traveller taking a trip to a main destination outside his/her usual environment, for less than a year, for any main purpose (business, leisure or other personal purpose) other than to be employed in the country or place visited.

A visitor is a **tourist** if his/her trip includes an overnight stay; otherwise, a visitor is classified as a **same-day visitor** (or excursionist).

Three basic forms of tourism can be distinguished:

- **Domestic tourism** comprises the activities of a resident visitor within the country of reference.
- **Inbound tourism** comprises the activities of a non-resident visitor within the country of reference.
- **Outbound tourism** comprises the activities of a resident visitor outside the country of reference.

Measuring the flows of visitors: both arrivals and nights are used to assess the flows of visitors. A distinction is made between arrivals at borders and in accommodation, and nights spent in accommodation. As far as overnight tourism is concerned, accommodation statistics are an important statistical source of information on domestic and inbound visitors.

Tourism Satellite Account: Recommended Methodological Framework (TSA: RMF)

The Tourism Satellite Account (TSA) is a conceptual framework for the economic measurement of tourism in its different components (domestic, inbound and outbound). It also highlights the relationship between consumption by visitors and the supply of goods and services in the economy, principally those from tourism industries. With this instrument, it is possible to estimate tourism GDP, establish the direct contribution of tourism to the economy and develop further analyses using the links between the TSA, the System of National Accounts and the Balance of Payments.

Tourism characteristic products and activities

The TSA reconciles tourism data related with supply and demand. Tourism measurement and analysis therefore require a classification of products, mainly those belonging to tourism expenditure, and productive activities that are the basis for defining tourism industries. Tourism characteristic activities are those that typically produce **tourism characteristic products**. A **tourism industry** represents the grouping of those establishments whose main activity is the same tourism characteristic activity.

The IRTS 2008 and the TSA-RMF 2008 provide the typology of tourism characteristic consumption products and activities (tourism industries):

Tourism characteristic consumption products	Tourism characteristic activities (tourism industries)
Accommodation services for visitors	Accommodation for visitors
Food- and beverage-serving services	Food- and beverage-serving activities
Railway passenger transport services	Railway passenger transport
Road passenger transport services	Road passenger transport
Water passenger transport services	Water passenger transport
Air passenger transport services	Air passenger transport
Transport equipment rental services	Transport equipment rental
Travel agencies and other reservation services	Travel agencies and other reservation services activities
Cultural services	Cultural activities
Sports and recreational services	Sports and recreational activities
Country-specific tourism characteristic goods	Retail trade of country-specific tourism characteristic goods
Country-specific tourism characteristic services	Other country-specific tourism characteristic activities

Note: for detailed information on the coverage, please see annexes 2 and 3 of the IRTS 2008.

Internal tourism consumption

The TSA Framework makes a distinction between tourism expenditure and tourism consumption. Tourism expenditure refers to monetary transactions, whereas tourism consumption also includes other transactions: services associated with vacation accommodation on own account, tourism social transfers in kind and other imputed consumption. However, the latter transactions have to be separately evaluated. Therefore, the data might refer to either consumption or expenditure, depending on the country.

Three forms of consumption are distinguished:

- **Domestic tourism consumption**: the tourism consumption of a resident visitor within the economy of reference.
- **Inbound tourism consumption**: the tourism consumption of a non-resident visitor within the economy of reference.
- **Internal tourism consumption**: the tourism consumption of both resident and non-resident visitors within the economy of reference. It is the sum of domestic tourism consumption and inbound tourism consumption.

Tourism Direct Gross Domestic Product and other aggregates

The Gross Domestic Product (GDP) of an economy is defined as the sum of the gross value added generated by all industries. Tourism GDP corresponds to the part of GDP generated by all industries in response to internal tourism consumption. A further distinction must be made between direct tourism GDP and indirect tourism GDP. Put simply, **tourism direct GDP** reflects the direct value-added generated by industries directly in contact with visitors, while indirect tourism GDP reflects all of the upstream value-added- generated by industries supplying inputs to industries directly in contact with the visitors. The TSA Framework limits its recommendations to the evaluation of direct tourism GDP. The evaluation of indirect tourism GDP would require the use of input-output techniques or adjustments (for imports) of expenditure-based measures.

Domestic, inbound and outbound tourism

A variety of different data sources are used to measure flows of visitors. Data can be collected directly from individuals about their tourism trips. These demand-side sources include visitor or border surveys to measure inbound tourism flows, and resident travel or household surveys to measure domestic and outbound tourism flows. These surveys feed into the tourism consumption (i.e. demand) tables of the TSA (Tables 1-4). Data on domestic and inbound visitors can also be collected from accommodation providers (supply-side).

Data from tourism demand surveys are presented in the country profile statistical tables. In the absence of data from these sources, or where data gaps exist, data from accommodation surveys are published.

For more detailed information on the data sources for individual countries, please refer to relevant datasets and metadata in the online tourism database https://data-explorer.oecd.org/

Balance of Payments and International Investment Position Manual – Sixth Edition

The following items of the Balance of Payments are used to assess the monetary flows of visitors.

Travel

Travel credits (**international travel receipts**) cover goods and services for own use or to give away acquired from an economy by non-residents during visits to that economy. Travel debits (**international travel expenditure**) cover goods and services for own use or to give away acquired from other economies by residents during visits to these other economies.

The goods and services may be purchased by the persons concerned or by another party on their behalf (e.g. business travel). The standard component breakdown of travel is between business and personal travel. *Business travel* covers goods and services acquired for personal use by persons whose primary purpose of travel is for business. *Personal travel* covers goods and services acquired by persons going abroad for purposes other than business, such as vacations, participation in recreational and cultural activities, visits with friends and relatives, pilgrimage, and education- and health-related purposes. This breakdown allows for closer links with tourism satellite accounts as well as supply and use tables.

Passenger services

Passenger services cover the transport of people. This category covers all services provided in the international transport of non-residents by resident carriers (credit or **international passenger transport**

receipts) and that of residents by non-resident carriers (debit or **international passenger transport expenditure**). Passenger services include fares and other expenditure related to the carriage of passengers, any taxes levied on passenger services, and fares that are a part of package tours, cruise fares, rentals, charters, and leases of vessels, aircraft, coaches, or other commercial vehicles with crews for the carriage of passengers.

Other issues

Enterprises in tourism: An establishment is an enterprise or part of an enterprise that is situated in a single location and in which only a single productive activity is carried out or in which the principal productive activity accounts for most of the value added. For the purposes of comparability across countries, unless otherwise stated, all statistics for enterprises refer to establishments.

Employment in tourism: data on employment refer to people or jobs. In the case of people, the data refer to employees only or to employees and self-employed people (employed people). Full-time equivalent employment is the number of full-time equivalent jobs, defined as total hours worked divided by average annual hours worked in full-time jobs.

Data expressed in US dollar terms: for some tables, national currency data have been converted to US dollar data. Exchanges rates are collected from the OECD database.

Metadata and sources

The vast majority of the data used in this publication are submitted by countries. All the detailed metadata and sources can be found under the right-hand side information panel in the on-line OECD database at https://data-explorer.oecd.org/

Country coverage

The OECD member countries are: Australia, Austria, Belgium, Canada, Chile, Colombia, Costa Rica, Czechia, Denmark, Estonia, Finland, France, Germany, Greece, Hungary, Iceland, Ireland, Israel, Italy, Japan, Korea, Latvia, Lithuania, Luxembourg, Mexico, the Netherlands, New Zealand, Norway, Poland, Portugal, the Slovak Republic, Slovenia, Spain, Sweden, Switzerland, Türkiye, the United Kingdom and the United States.

Other partner countries covered in this report are: Brazil, Bulgaria, Croatia, Indonesia, Malta, Montenegro, Morocco, Peru, Romania, Saudi Arabia, Serbia and South Africa.

Codes used for currencies

- AUD Australian Dollar
- BGN Bulgarian Lev
- BRL Brazilian Real
- CAD Canadian Dollar
- CHF Swiss Franc
- CLP Chilean Peso
- COP Colombian Peso
- CRC Costa Rican Colon

- CZK Czech Koruna
- DKK Danish Krone
- EUR Euro (Austria, Belgium, Estonia, Finland, France, Germany, Greece, Ireland, Italy, Latvia, Lithuania, Luxembourg, Malta, Montenegro, Netherlands, Portugal, Slovak Republic, Slovenia, Spain)
- GBP United Kingdom Pound Sterling
- HRK Croatia Kuna
- HUF Hungarian Forint
- IDR Indonesian Rupiah
- ILS Israeli Shequel
- ISK Iceland Krona
- JPY Japanese Yen
- KRW Korean Won
- MAD Moroccan Dirham
- MXN Mexican Peso
- NOK Norwegian Krone
- NZD New Zealand Dollar
- PEN Peruvian Sol
- PLN Polish Zloty
- RON Romanian Leu
- RSD Serbian Dinar
- SAR Saudi Riyal
- SEK Swedish Krona
- TRY Turkish Lira
- USD United States Dollar
- ZAR South African Rand

Symbols for missing data and abbreviations

These symbols are used in the country tables:

| Break in series

.. Data is not available

e Estimated data or data based on the use of a limited amount of data

f Forecast value

p Provisional

In some cases, due to rounding and specifics of electronic data processing technologies, slight discrepancies may occur between totals and sums of components in those tables that are based on survey information.

Executive Summary

Tourism has bounced back strongly from recent crises, supporting economic growth and well-being. However, the recovery is uneven and rising geopolitical tensions, cost-of-living pressures and climate-related events bring new challenges. Active, forward-looking policies are needed to step up efforts to build a more resilient, sustainable, and inclusive future for the sector.

Tourism trends and outlook as new challenges emerge

Tourism has rebounded strongly following sharp declines triggered by the COVID-19 pandemic that led tourism flows to plummet in 2020-21, following six decades of consistent growth. Tourism´s direct contribution to GDP had recovered to 3.9% in 2022 in OECD countries with available data, half a percentage point below 2019 levels, and the evidence suggests that the recovery has continued since. The return of international tourism demand following the lifting of travel restrictions has been a significant driver of this recovery, with tourism's share of services exports growing to 14.8% in 2022 in OECD countries. Although this was still 5.6 percentage points below pre-pandemic shares, international tourist arrivals have continued to strengthen and already exceeded pre-pandemic levels in some OECD countries in 2023.

A full global recovery is projected by the end of 2024, buoyed by positive traveller and business sentiment, and pick up in travel in Asia Pacific, including from China, with growth anticipated to return to pre-pandemic trends as demand and supply imbalances continue to unwind. However, recovery is uneven, and challenges remain. While tourism demand has proven resilient, businesses struggle to attract and retain workers and although inflation is abating, price pressures continue to impact transport, accommodation, and hospitality costs. Geopolitical tensions remain high, and the increasing frequency of wildfires, floods, heatwaves, and other extreme weather events is impacting the sector. Looking ahead to the longer term, tourism is expected to continue to grow. This creates significant opportunities but also brings renewed challenges, reinforcing the importance of policies to support a resilient, sustainable, and inclusive future.

Top policy priorities to promote sustainable development through tourism

Governments took exceptional measures to support tourism as recent crises raised awareness of the sector's importance as an economic and social force. The strong recovery is providing a new wakeup call for governments and the sector as a whole, as destinations struggle to manage demand and the impacts on the environment and local communities. This is putting pressure on the social licence for tourism and has highlighted the need to rebalance the impacts, understand the trade-offs and manage tourism sustainably, so the benefits outweigh the costs. At the same time, tourism offers untapped potential for many people, businesses, and places.

Governments, at all levels, have a role to play in shaping tourism development to respond to these challenges, capitalise on opportunities, and deliver better outcomes. Many countries have updated or developed tourism strategies to reflect the post-pandemic context and priorities. These strategies look to build on recent momentum to shift to more sustainable models of tourism, to adapt to an increasingly dynamic environment and engage stakeholders around a common vision for the future of the sector. Diversifying the tourism offer and attracting new source markets and segments to emerging destinations and outside of peak periods underpins many tourism strategies, to better spread the benefits and tourist flows. Significant investments are needed to reduce the environmental impact of tourism activities, while adapting to the impacts from climate change. Tourism destinations and businesses need support to keep pace with rapid technological developments, while resources are also required to develop the transport and other infrastructure needed to better manage tourism development. Boosting the capacity of the sector to attract, retain and develop a strong and sustainable workforce is a further area of ongoing focus.

However, implementation remains an issue and there is a risk that tourism slips down national policy agendas as the sector returns to pre-pandemic levels and growth paths. Effective governance practices and co-ordinated policy action are needed to deliver on these ambitions, supported by sufficient resources at national, regional, and local level. Action at destination level has an increasingly important role to play in driving momentum for change, guided by an overarching national vision for the future of tourism that in turn considers local needs and priorities, and supported by effective co-ordination mechanisms across levels of government. More granular, timely and robust evidence is also needed to manage and track progress on potential trade-offs, determine 'what works' and identify emerging policy impacts and risks, as well as the costs of inaction.

Key policy priorities

Promote co-ordinated action to deliver on a forward-looking sustainable tourism agenda

- Foster the development and implementation of forward-looking tourism policies to boost tourism's role in climate action and ensure the sector keeps pace with rapid technological advances.
- Encourage broad stakeholder engagement in the tourism policy process to deliver more equitable and inclusive benefits to everyone engaged in and impacted by tourism.
- Bolster co-ordination and delivery structures, including at destination level, to encourage better management of visitor flows, diversify the tourism offer and develop critical infrastructure.

Strengthening the tourism workforce

- Better integrate tourism into wider economic and community development strategies to address the specific needs of tourism workers and make tourism work a more attractive and viable option.
- Leverage private sector initiatives to address barriers to recruiting and retaining workers and implement new training and models of working to improve work conditions in the sector.
- Facilitate linkages with and between the private sector and education providers to meet the changing needs of the tourism sector and prepare for the green and digital transitions.

Building the evidence base for sustainable tourism policies

- Better define priority policy issues to identify key indicators and ensure decision makers have timely access to data to monitor these issues and balance trade-offs in the policy making process.
- Explore new opportunities to fill tourism data gaps, monitor and measure actions targeting environmental and social priorities, and accelerate shift to more sustainable models of tourism.
- Design tailored toolkits with indicators, tools, and metrics to monitor short and long-term priorities, exploring new methods, and building the capacity of decision makers at all levels to use this data.

Chapter 1. Tourism Trends and Policies

This chapter covers trends in tourism and associated developments in tourism governance and policy. It is based on responses to a policy and statistical survey of OECD member and partner countries. The chapter takes stock of the strong but uneven recovery and the outlook for the future as new challenges emerge. The role of government in supporting a more sustainable, resilient, and inclusive tourism in this environment is set out. Tourism policy priorities, reforms and developments are analysed with examples of country practices highlighted.

Recent tourism trends and future outlook as new challenges emerge

Tourism has rebounded strongly following sharp declines in 2020-21 triggered by the COVID-19 pandemic. Full recovery to pre-pandemic levels is anticipated by the end of 2024, with continued growth expected over the long term. However, while well advanced in many countries, the recovery is uneven and slow economic growth, rising geopolitical tensions, cost-of-living pressures, natural disasters, and extreme weather events have brought new challenges. At the same time, new and existing weaknesses in tourism development models and the wider tourism economy have been exposed.

Governments took exceptional measures to support the sector through recent crises, and these policies have paid off. Tourism demand has proven resilient. The strong recovery is providing a wakeup call for destinations struggling to manage demand and its impacts on the environment and local communities. At the same time tourism provides significant but still untapped potential and opportunities for many people, businesses, and places. As tourism navigates these challenges, large-scale social, economic, political, environmental, and technical trends continue to impact the sector.

Active, forward-looking tourism policies are needed to respond and build momentum for a more resilient, sustainable, and inclusive future for tourism. While the sector's role as a driver of economic prosperity and well-being has been elevated to the highest levels of government in recent years, tourism risks slipping down national policy agendas as the sector returns to pre-pandemic levels and growth paths.

Strong tourism rebound supporting wider economic growth

Tourism remains an important driver of economic growth, and plays a key role in stimulating economic activity, creating jobs, generating income and foreign exchange, promoting regional development, and supporting local communities. Before the COVID-19 pandemic, the tourism sector directly contributed 4.4% of GDP and 6.9% of employment, and tourism generated 20.4% of service -related exports in OECD countries, on average. The unprecedented shock from COVID-19 saw the average direct contribution of tourism to GDP fall to 2.5% in 2020 across OECD countries with data available, with knock-on consequences for the wider economy. By 2022, this figure had returned to 3.9% on average across this same set of countries, with four countries returning to pre-pandemic levels or above (Figure 1.1). UN Tourism reports that globally, direct tourism GDP recovered to pre-pandemic levels in 2023 (UN Tourism, 2024[1]).

This strong recovery in the tourism economy is supporting wider economic activity, including in countries where the sector has been particularly dynamic, such as Greece, Portugal, Switzerland, and Türkiye (OECD, 2024[2]). In a few countries the relative size of the tourism economy expanded as the sector has outperformed wider economy growth. In Portugal, for example, tourism directly contributed 8.9% of GVA in 2022, compared with 8.1% in 2019. This is before the significant indirect impacts of tourism are considered, reflecting the breadth and depth of linkages between tourism and other sectors (e.g. food production, agriculture, transport). These indirect impacts account for more than one-third of value added generated in the domestic economy through tourism.

Tourism is a labour-intensive sector and labour shortages and skills gaps have constrained the sector's recovery amid tight labour markets. Employment in the accommodation and food services sector remained down 5.3% in 2022 across the OECD, while job vacancy rates were higher on average than in other parts of the economy in many countries in 2023. While not all jobs in accommodation and food services are tourism jobs, the sector accounts for around a half of tourism employment and provides a partial but useful proxy. While labour markets are now easing, persistent challenges to attract, retain and develop the tourism workforce remain. The need to address these issues is discussed further in Chapter 2 – Strengthening the tourism workforce.

Figure 1.1. Direct contribution of tourism GDP to selected OECD countries, pre-COVID and 2022

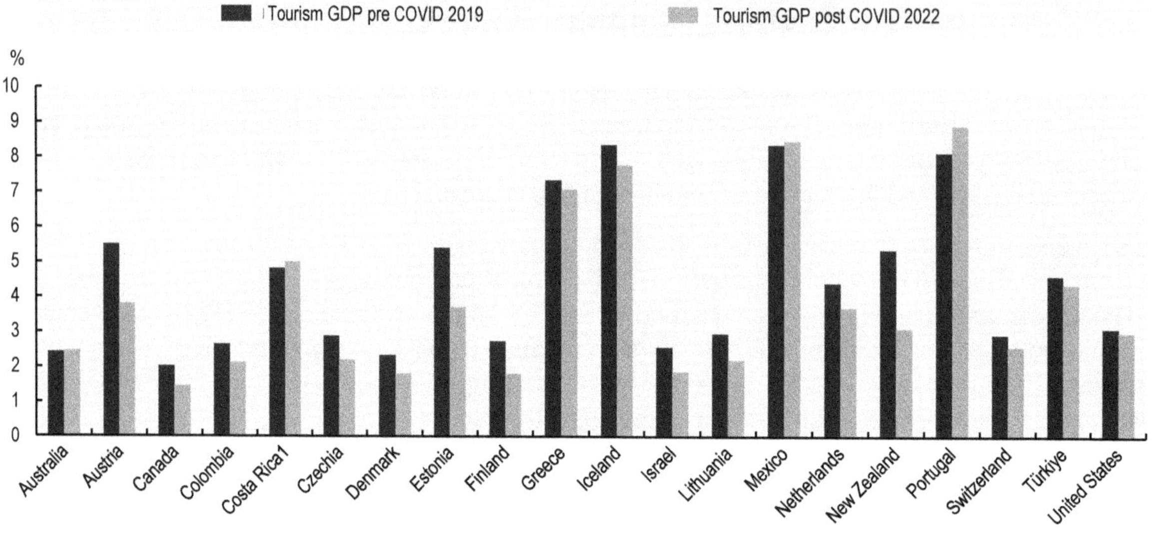

Note: Tourism Direct GDP is the preferred indicator.
Only countries with 2019 and 2022 data available are shown.
1. Tourism GDP post COVID refers to 2023.
Tourism Direct GVA is used for Canada, Colombia, Finland, Greece, Israel, Lithuania, Netherlands, New Zealand, Portugal, Switzerland, Türkiye, United States.
Source: OECD Tourism Statistics (Database).

StatLink https://stat.link/riclxm

Tourism demand has proven resilient, but recovery is uneven and challenges remain

International tourism flows have bounced back strongly and are projected to fully recover by the end of 2024. However, the recovery is uneven, and challenges remain. After falling by 68.3% in 2020 – slightly below the drop of 72.3% globally – by the end of 2022 international tourist arrivals to OECD countries had recovered to 77.3% of 2019 levels – ahead of 66.6% globally. OECD countries accounted for 65% of international tourism arrivals in 2022, up from 56% in 2019, highlighting the stronger performance compared to non-OECD countries since the pandemic. A breakdown of international tourist arrivals to OECD member countries and selected partner economies is provided in Table 1.1.

This recovery momentum has continued, driven by strong tourism demand that has proven surprisingly resilient. Globally, an estimated 1.3 billion international tourists were recorded in destinations worldwide in 2023, a recovery to 89% of pre-pandemic levels, and this is projected to reach 1.5 billion by the end of 2024 (UN Tourism, 2024[3]).

International tourist arrivals exceeded pre-pandemic levels in some OECD countries in 2023, with countries in Europe leading the way. Portugal welcomed a record 19.4 million international tourists, 12.1% more than in 2019. Other countries that saw arrivals reach or exceed pre-pandemic levels include Colombia (up 34%), Luxembourg (2.1%), Netherlands (1.4%), Norway (1.2%) and Spain (2.0%). Figure 1.2 presents the available data on international tourist arrivals to selected OECD member countries and partner economies in 2023 compared to arrivals in 2019. Countries in Europe benefited from significant intra-regional travel, while a strong US dollar boosted outbound travel from the United States to Europe.

Figure 1.2. International tourist arrivals, selected OECD and partner countries

Level in 2023 compared to 2019, %

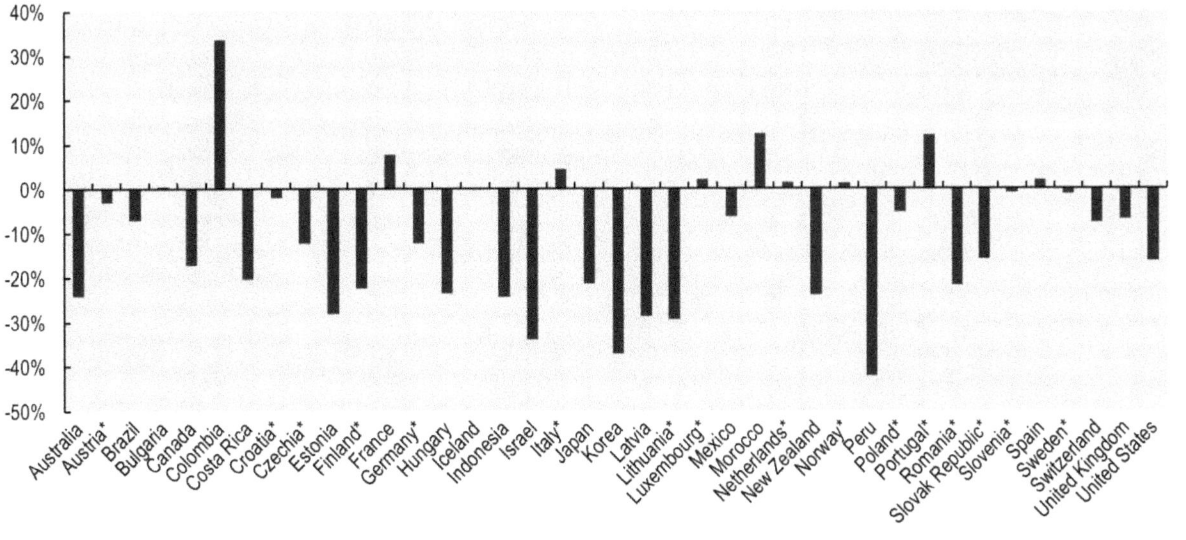

Note: *Data from supply side surveys.
Source: OECD Tourism Statistics (Database), Eurostat, National Websites and Country Profiles.

StatLink https://stat.link/mnks19

However, the road to recovery is longer for other countries. In the Asia Pacific region, this reflects in part the later opening of borders, as well as the pre-pandemic reliance on visitors from often distant source markets and the slower than anticipated return of the important People's Republic of China outbound market. This is the case as international tourist arrivals in 2023 remained below pre-pandemic levels, for example, in Australia (by 24.1%), Japan (21.4%) and New Zealand (24.0%). The pace of recovery in the region has picked up more recently, as outbound travel from China has stepped up and air capacity and connectivity has expanded to meet demand. The historically weak yen is also stimulating tourist inflows to Japan. Recovery has also picked up in other countries in the region. A continued revival of international tourism in Thailand, for example, is underpinning a steady economic recovery in the country, supported by the lifting of visa requirements for Chinese travellers (OECD, 2024[2]).

Geopolitical conflicts and tensions are also impacting tourism flows and the wider tourism economy, including Russia's war of aggression against Ukraine and evolving conflicts in the Middle East. International tourism remains down on pre-pandemic levels in Finland (by 22.3% at the end of 2023) and other countries neighbouring Russia and Ukraine. The terrorist attacks and the subsequent war have hit Israel's tourism economy hard, significantly reducing inbound tourism (down 33.9% in 2023). This is impacting service exports and economic growth in the country more widely (OECD, 2024[2]). Uncertainty about the evolution of these and other geopolitical conflicts and tensions risk impacting tourism in surrounding areas as well as denting traveller confidence more broadly, as safety and security are key conditions for tourism.

Table 1.1. International tourist arrivals in OECD and partner countries, 2019-22

	Type of indicator	2019	2020	2021	2022	Growth rate 2019 to 2020	Growth rate 2019 to 2022
		Thousand				%	
Australia	Visitors	9 466	1 828	246	3 694	-81%	-61%
Austria[1]	Tourists	31 884	15 091	12 728	26 215	-53%	-18%
Belgium[1]	Tourists	6 800	1 804	2 313	5 728	-73%	-16%
Canada	Tourists	22 145	2 960	3 062	12 824	-87%	-42%
Chile	Tourists	4 518	1 119	190	2 030	-75%	-55%
Colombia	Visitors	4 531	1 387	2 146	4 722	-69%	4%
Costa Rica	Tourists	3 139	1 012	1 347	2 350	-68%	-25%
Czechia	Tourists	14 651	3 919	3 768	10 219	-73%	-30%
Denmark	Tourists	14 725	6 229	7 555	14 190	-58%	-4%
Estonia	Tourists	3 336	1 023	801	2 166	-69%	-35%
Finland[1]	Tourists	3 290	896	807	2 127	-73%	-35%
France	Tourists	90 914	41 684	48 395	93 196	-54%	3%
Germany[1]	Tourists	39 563	12 449	11 688	28 463	-69%	-28%
Greece	Visitors	34 005	7 406	15 246	29 876	-78%	-12%
Hungary	Tourists	15 949	6 624	6 973	11 731	-58%	-26%
Iceland	Tourists	2 202	486	698	1 715	-78%	-22%
Ireland[2]	Tourists	9 353	..	..	..	..	..
Israel	Tourists	4 552	832	397	2 675	-82%	-41%
Italy	Tourists	64 513	25 190	26 888	49 811	-61%	-23%
Japan	Visitors	31 882	4 116	246	3 832	-87%	-88%
Korea	Visitors	17 503	2 519	967	3 198	-86%	-82%
Latvia	Tourists	1 946	715	442	1 139	-63%	-41%
Lithuania	Tourists	2 875	937	948	2 169	-67%	-25%
Luxembourg[1]	Tourists	1 041	525	615	1 013	-50%	-3%
Mexico	Tourists	45 024	24 284	31 860	38 326	-46%	-15%
Netherlands[1]	Tourists	20 129	7 265	6 248	16 582	-64%	-18%
New Zealand	Visitors	3 888	996	207	1 434	-74%	-63%
Norway[1]	Tourists	5 879	1 387	1 435	4 979	-76%	-15%
Poland	Tourists	21 158	8 418	9 722	15 948	-60%	-25%
Portugal[1]	Tourists	17 283	4 208	6 345	16 308	-76%	-6%
Slovak Republic[1]	Tourists	2 475	854	576	1 594	-65%	-36%
Slovenia[1]	Tourists	4 702	1 216	1 832	3 936	-74%	-16%
Spain	Tourists	83 509	18 933	31 181	71 659	-77%	-14%
Sweden	Tourists	7 616	1 957	2 990	6 629	-74%	-13%
Switzerland[1]	Tourists	11 818	3 690	4 390	9 160	-69%	-22%
Türkiye	Tourists	51 192	15 894	29 925	50 453	-69%	-1%
United Kingdom	Visitors	40 857	11 101	6 384	31 244	-73%	-24%
United States	Tourists	79 442	19 212	22 280	50 870	-76%	-36%
Brazil	Tourists	6 353	2 146	746	3 630	-66%	-43%
Bulgaria	Visitors	12 552	4 973	7 188	10 888	-60%	-13%
Croatia[1]	Tourists	17 353	5 545	10 641	15 324	-68%	-12%
Indonesia	Tourists	15 455	3 981	1 546	5 761	-74%	-63%
Malta	Tourists	2 753	659	968	2 287	-76%	-17%
Montenegro[1]	Tourists	2 510	351	1 554	2 036	-86%	-19%
Morocco	Tourists	12 933	2 778	3 722	10 869	-79%	-16%
Peru	Tourists	4 372	897	444	2 009	-79%	-54%
Romania[1]	Tourists	2 684	454	879	1 674	-83%	-38%
Saudi Arabia	Tourists	17 526	4 138	3 477	16 638	-76%	-5%

	Type of indicator	2019	2020	2021	2022	Growth rate 2019 to 2020	Growth rate 2019 to 2022
		Thousand				%	
Serbia[1]	Tourists	1 847	446	871	1 773	-76%	-4%
South Africa	Tourists	10 228	2 802	2 256	5 698	-73%	-44%
EU27		529 748	179 506	219 142	443 045	-66%	-16%
OECD members		820 401	260 164	303 843	634 204	-68%	-23%
World[2]		1 465 000	406 000	459 000	975 000	-72%	-33%

Notes: For more information, please see the country profiles.
Tourists: International tourist arrivals (excluding same-day visitors).
Visitors: International visitor arrivals (including same-day visitors).
1. Data from supply side surveys.
2. UN Tourism data (World Tourism Barometer, May 2024).
Source: OECD Tourism Statistics (Database).

The top tourism destinations and markets continue to evolve as tourism recovers. France and Spain maintain their pre-pandemic positions as most visited countries in the world in 2022, the United States returned to third position as inbound travel to the US picked up after dropping back in 2021. Türkiye takes fourth place as inbound tourism continues to perform strongly, followed by Italy. Together, these five destinations welcomed just under a third (32.0%) of global tourist arrivals in 2022 (UN Tourism, 2024[3]).

In Asia Pacific, the recovery of the tourism sector is different. While outbound travel from China has picked up and domestic tourism is expanding, inbound tourism remains significantly down on pre-pandemic levels and is constraining wider economic recovery in China (OECD, 2024[4]). China has extended visa-free travel for 11 European countries and Australia, New Zealand and Malaysia until the end of 2025. While this initiative aims to boost tourism and international ties, the availability of air capacity and ongoing flight restrictions linked with Russia's war of aggression against Ukraine may limit the uptake and impact. Outbound travel from India is emerging as a future growth engine for global tourism, with the rapid expansion of the middle classes and scaling up of air connectivity across the country.

The strong rebound in international tourist flows has been outpaced by an increase in tourism receipts in current prices, though this should be interpreted with caution given the strong inflationary pressures over the same period. International travel receipts in OECD countries had recovered to 82.3% of 2019 levels by the end of 2022, ahead of the arrivals recovery (77.3%), and accounting for 67.1% of international travel receipts in 2022, up from 61.4% in 2019 (compared with 65% and 56% of international tourism arrivals).

Table 1.2 provides a summary of international travel receipts (exports), expenditure (imports), and the travel balance for OECD and selected partner economies. Countries recording the strongest performance include Türkiye (up 39.9% on 2019 in current prices), the Netherlands (21.9%), Mexico (14.0%), Ireland (8.7%), and the United Kingdom (7.9%). Recovery was weakest in Japan (down 79.9%) and New Zealand (95.3%) where borders were closed to international tourist flows for longer.

Table 1.2. International travel receipts and expenditure in OECD and partner countries, 2019, 2022

Million USD

	Travel receipts		Travel expenditure		Travel balance	
	2019	2022	2019	2022	2019	2022
Australia	45 522	24 108	35 299	16 279	10 223	7 829
Austria	22 941	19 915	11 602	11 153	11 339	8 763
Belgium	8 837	6 934	18 686	16 298	-9 849	-9 364
Canada	29 807	24 002	35 349	24 436	-5 543	-434
Chile	2 303	1 024	2 459	1 718	-157	-695

	Travel receipts		Travel expenditure		Travel balance	
	2019	2022	2019	2022	2019	2022
Colombia	5 682	5 919	4 935	4 304	747	1 615
Costa Rica	3 989	3 137	1 036	966	2 953	2 171
Czechia	7 303	5 054	5 889	4 968	1 414	86
Denmark	8 652	8 921	10 003	8 462	-1 352	459
Estonia	1 738	1 279	1 546	1 174	192	105
Finland	3 726	2 249	5 680	4 379	-1 955	-2 129
France	63 508	59 676	50 542	41 302	12 966	18 375
Germany	41 806	31 548	93 243	89 724	-51 438	-58 176
Greece	20 351	18 614	3 072	2 027	17 279	16 587
Hungary	7 305	5 663	2 749	2 412	4 556	3 251
Iceland	2 695	2 485	1 510	1 515	1 185	970
Ireland	6 478	7 041	8 256	8 480	-1 778	-1 440
Israel	7 620	5 681	8 154	7 821	-534	-2 140
Italy	49 595	46 601	30 338	27 410	19 257	19 191
Japan	46 054	9 238	21 265	4 491	24 790	4 747
Korea	20 867	11 996	32 739	19 925	-11 872	-7 929
Latvia	1 015	1 106	749	1 011	267	95
Lithuania	1 493	1 187	1 389	1 240	104	-53
Luxembourg	5 333	5 417	3 609	3 405	1 724	2 012
Mexico	24 573	28 017	9 881	7 054	14 692	20 963
Netherlands	19 729	24 056	23 124	18 822	-3 394	5 234
New Zealand	10 533	498	4 300	284	6 233	215
Norway	5 855	5 472	16 513	14 033	-10 658	-8 560
Poland	14 013	14 497	9 286	7 681	4 727	6 816
Portugal	20 476	22 263	5 736	5 827	14 740	16 436
Slovak Republic	3 203	1 360	2 589	2 249	614	-889
Slovenia	3 183	3 130	1 679	1 825	1 504	1 305
Spain	79 670	72 891	27 778	21 920	51 892	50 971
Sweden	9 193	9 038	14 366	12 365	-5 173	-3 328
Switzerland	17 950	17 348	18 753	17 564	-803	-217
Türkiye	29 813	41 702	4 108	4 092	25 705	37 610
United Kingdom	60 637	65 406	86 605	90 939	-25 967	-25 533
United States	198 982	136 869	131 990	115 312	66 992	21 557
Brazil	5 995	4 952	17 593	12 185	-11 599	-7 233
Bulgaria	4 294	3 413	1 826	1 550	2 468	1 863
Croatia	11 798	13 810	1 763	1 460	10 035	12 350
Indonesia	16 911	6 719	11 308	6 288	5 603	431
Malta	1 897	1 841	530	476	1 367	1 365
Montenegro	1 225	1 080	58	59	1 167	1 021
Morocco	8 187	9 063	2 176	1 883	6 010	7 180
Peru	3 738	2 137	2 775	2 345	963	-208
Romania	3 578	4 704	6 001	7 762	-2 424	-3 058
Saudi Arabia	16 431	23 475	15 140	15 914	1 292	7 562
Serbia	1 604	2 592	1 806	2 459	-201	133
South Africa	8 390	4 738	3 141	2 220	5 249	2 518
EU27	424 375	395 095	343 667	306 736		
OECD members	912 430	751 339	746 807	624 862		
World[1]	1 487 000	1 120 000	1 487 000	1 120 000		

Notes: For more information, please see the country profiles.
1. UN Tourism data (World Tourism Barometer, May 2024).
Source: OECD Tourism Statistics (Database).

Tourism's share of services exports across OECD countries reached 14.8% in 2022, having fallen to 10.0% in 2020 and 9.7% in 2021, down from 20.4% in 2019 (Figure 1.3). UN Tourism reports that in 2023 export revenues from tourism reached 96% of 2019 levels in real terms (UN Tourism, 2024[1]). Continued recovery in international travel has helped support overall services trade (OECD, 2024[4]).

Figure 1.3. Contribution of tourism to service exports, 2019-22

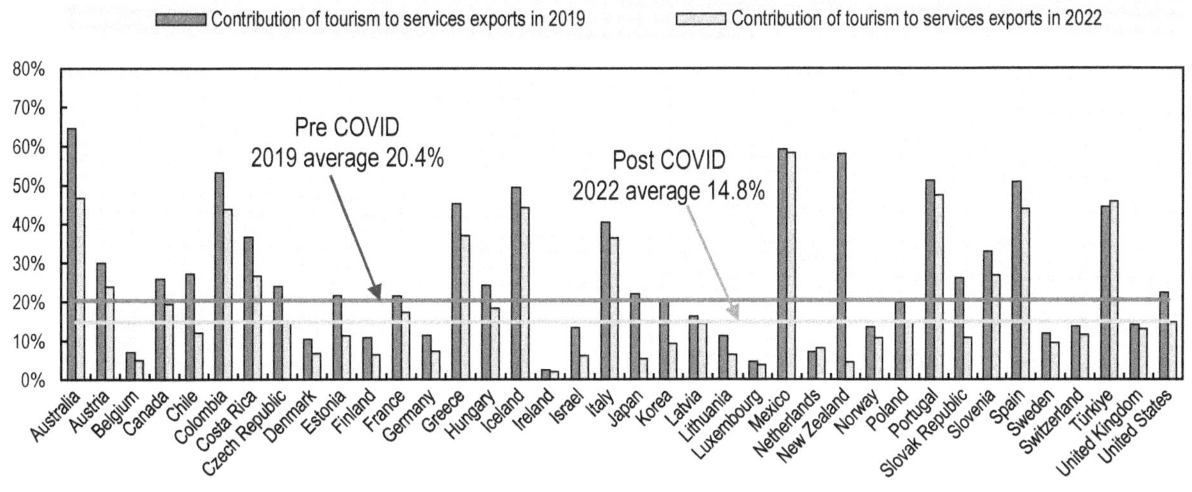

Source: OECD Trade in services by partner country (Database), extracted April 2024.

StatLink https://stat.link/8o46vf

Figure 1.4. Domestic share of tourism expenditure in selected OECD countries, 2019, 2022

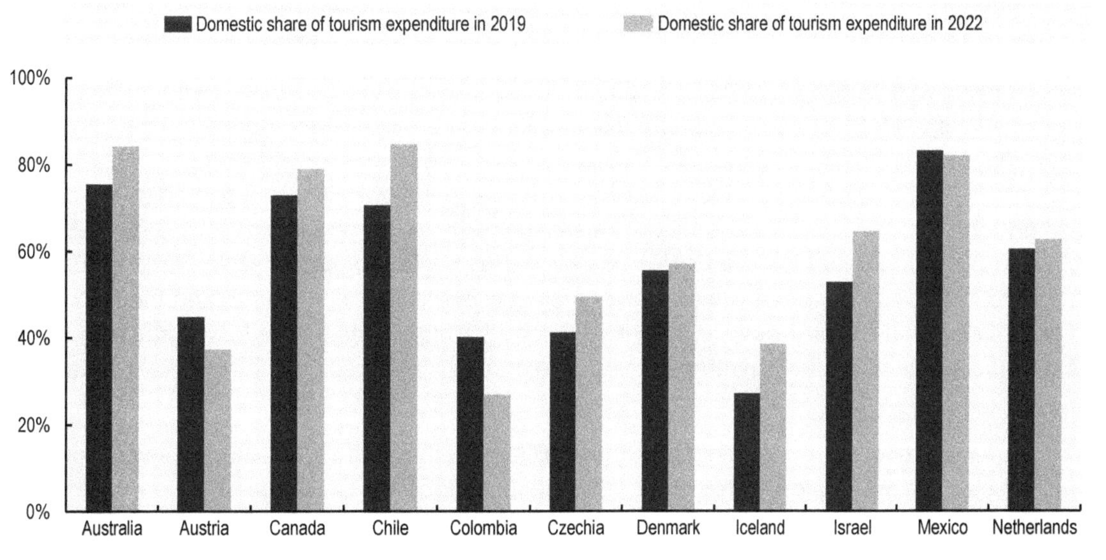

Source: OECD Tourism Statistics (Database).

StatLink https://stat.link/uqplhj

Domestic demand helped sustain the sector during the pandemic, and domestic overnight trips recovered to 90.5% of 2019 levels in 2022 among OECD countries with data1. However, its importance and the extent to which domestic tourism is helping to support recovery varies considerably by country. Some countries recorded an overall increase in domestic tourism expenditure during the pandemic, as international travel was restricted. This was the case in 2021 in Denmark (up 12.0% compared to 2019), New Zealand (12.8%), Lithuania (7.9%), Australia (6.2%), and Sweden (6.0%). In contrast, domestic tourism consumption contracted in the Slovak Republic (down 52.1% compared to 2019), Colombia (44.4%), Austria (37.4%), Hungary (27.7%), Canada (25.9%) and the Netherlands (24.6%). Figure 1.4 shows the domestic share of tourism expenditure was higher than before the pandemic in several OECD countries in 2022.

Outlook brings new challenges to adapt and manage tourism for sustainable outcomes

Looking ahead, tourism demand is expected to remain buoyant as supply and demand imbalances unwind. In the near term, the sector continues to navigate uncertainties, while unchecked longer term growth, could bring challenges for the sustainability and future of the sector.

The global economic outlook has started to brighten, though growth remains modest and the outlook differs across countries. The OECD projects steady global GDP growth of 3.1% in 2024, followed by a slight pick-up to 3.2% in 2025. Weaker outcomes are expected in many advanced economies, especially in Europe, and may dampen tourism flows from these origin countries. This may be offset by strong growth in the United States and many emerging economies. Geopolitical tensions remain a significant near-term risk, although demand growth could prove stronger than expected, if households and firms draw more fully on the savings accumulated during COVID-19 (OECD, 2024[4]).

Inflation is falling faster than initially projected, including for energy and food prices which impact strongly on transport, accommodation and hospitality costs for tourists. Real incomes are rising in many OECD countries as inflation moderates and private sector confidence is improving, which may further stimulate tourism demand. Supply and demand imbalances in labour markets are easing, with unemployment remaining at or close to record lows. This should ease the labour shortages faced by tourism businesses, but challenges remain to attract and build a strong and sustainable workforce.

Positive traveller and business sentiment points to continued strong growth momentum for tourism. Confidence levels are high among European accommodation providers with demand expected to stabilise at as pent-up demand from the pandemic dissipates (Booking.com and Statista.com, 2024[5]). Forward-bookings for flights to Europe point to a full return to pre-pandemic levels with some notable shifts in traveller preferences toward nature and city destinations. Intra-European travel is expected to remain strong, while outbound travel to Asia Pacific has picked up as European travellers venture further afield, due in part to improved connectivity, visa waivers for Europeans entering China, and the favourable euro to yen exchange rate (ForwardKeys, 2024[6]). This follows strong air passenger travel growth in Asia Pacific this year and a return to profitability across the airline industry in all regions, led by North America (IATA, 2024[7]).

The strong tourism rebound is providing a wakeup call to governments and the sector as a whole, as some destinations struggle to manage demand and its impacts on local communities and the environment. This has been exacerbated as supply has struggled to keep pace with demand. In some destinations, these capacity constraints are expected to limit further growth (OECD, 2024[4]). In other destinations, the social licence for tourism is increasingly challenged as tourism exceeds critical thresholds and is putting pressure on infrastructure, the environment and the local community, as well as on other economic sectors and the tourist experience.

Due to its strong local dimension, tourism can play a key role in fostering economic development that creates decent jobs, enhances social cohesion, and contributes to the shared interests of tourists, residents, and businesses. However, the impacts of tourism development are often economically, socially, and environmentally unbalanced. More needs to be done to manage the social impacts of tourism, particularly those cause by unplanned growth, and maximise the sector's potential to enhance well-being and promote social progress and inclusion, in traditional and emerging destinations.

As tourism resumes it growth trajectory, some popular tourism destinations are again feeling the pressures from increased visitor numbers on the local infrastructure, the environment and the host community. This has led to growing calls for more proactive policies and government action to better manage tourism development, across all levels of government, as well as a strong voice for local communities in the development of tourism. This includes taking action to diversify and diffuse the impacts of tourism temporally and spatially, and balance trade-offs to achieve more sustainable outcomes. It also involves anticipating when tourism in a destination could reach or surpass optimal levels, with detrimental impacts.

Diversifying the tourism offer and attracting new markets to emerging destinations and at different times of the year underpins wider strategies to build a strong, sustainable tourism economy. Considerable resources are devoted to developing business tourism in the form of meetings, incentives, conferences and exhibitions (MICE), in part to tackle seasonality and spread the benefits of tourism beyond traditional tourism hubs. Hosting major events can also provide a unique opportunity to rethink or reposition a destination in a period of changing global tourism dynamics. Hosting such events can help to facilitate the development of modern infrastructure (e.g. sporting and other facilities, transport, and accommodation), with mega events, such as the Olympics and Football World Cups, tending to have the longest legacy period. The Paris Olympics 2024 is looking to leverage this further with the associated Cultural Olympiad.

Accelerated climate change is impacting tourism. This has implications for structural shifts destinations and travel patterns. Warmer winters are shortening the ski season in mountain destinations, while heatwaves may reduce the attractiveness of destinations during traditional peak periods but encourage visitation at other times. Tourism businesses and destinations are adjusting the offer in response, for example by no longer scheduling hiking tours during periods when temperatures peak, while expanding the offer during traditional shoulder season periods.

The sector must also play an active role in delivering on climate goals. Wildfires, floods and heatwaves have the ability to directly impact visitors, businesses and local communities, both by the initial shock, and also from the loss of infrastructure and time it takes for tourism to recover. The world experienced unprecedented climate change impacts in 2023, and as these climate-related weather events become more extreme, losses are increasing (OECD, 2023[8]). Climate change is also expected to make incidents of severe turbulence more common for air travel.

Digital technologies, including generative Artificial Intelligence (AI), extended reality (XR) and blockchain, are fundamentally reshaping tourism and represent a powerful catalyst for innovation in the sector. Technology is changing the nature of work, business operations and service delivery, and is facilitating the adoption of innovative business models, and the shift to more sustainable tourism practices. It is also changing the way tourists plan travel and experience destinations. Digital technologies present not only an opportunity to respond to the evolving needs and desires of travellers, but also reach new consumers with novel tourism products and services (McKinsey & Company, 2024[9]). The current uptake and use of new technologies varies across countries, sectors and businesses. Small tourism enterprises with low-tech business practices face particular challenges to benefit from digital opportunities and prevent the gap widening between them and technology driven, globally connected tourism businesses.

These issues are high on the agenda of governments and the private sector and require coherent, evidence-based responses. Governments and destinations face significant challenges to access the data and information needed to understand the impacts of tourism. Such data allows policy makers to take informed decisions to rebalance the impacts of tourism, understand the trade-offs and manage tourism sustainably, so that the benefits outweigh the costs for host communities, businesses, the environment, and tourists. These issues are further discussed in Chapter 3 – Building the evidence base for sustainable tourism policies.

Governance of tourism in a complex environment

Government, at all levels, has a role to play in shaping tourism development to deliver better outcomes and shift to a more sustainable and inclusive growth path. Achieving this requires strong institutional structures, effective governance practices and co-ordinated policy action. As the world navigates successive shocks and recalibrates to moderate economic growth and geopolitical uncertainty, tourism requires integrated, adaptive, and effective governance across and between all levels of government, with the close involvement of the private sector and other stakeholders, to respond to challenges and capitalise on opportunities.

Tourism policy making is increasingly complex and highly context specific. National institutional frameworks for tourism vary from country to country, in part reflecting the different systems of government, the importance placed on the sector, and the cross-cutting nature of tourism policy. Responsibility for tourism is largely positioned within ministries responsible for economic development, trade, or industry, or in a dedicated ministry for tourism. In some countries tourism is integrated into labour or regional development ministries or alongside relevant policy sectors such as culture, sport, and transport.

While the exact institutional arrangements may differ, effective governance practices are needed to enable the planning and co-ordination of actions by key players, along with the availability of sufficient funding for their implementation. The cross-cutting nature of the sector, together with the differing national contexts, means that there is no one optimal location for tourism to be situated in national government structures.

Setting a strategic, forward-looking agenda to transform tourism post-pandemic

The OECD has long highlighted the importance for countries and destinations to develop long-term and sustainable visions for tourism, supported by forward-looking strategies and action plans. Many countries have updated or developed tourism strategies to reflect the post-pandemic context and priorities, with new strategic approaches needed to adapt to an increasingly dynamic environment and build broad stakeholder engagement around a common vision for the future of the sector. In most cases these strategies seek to balance the need to consolidate the recovery of the sector, while looking to make progress on long term priorities facing the sector.

There is evidence of sustainability being mainstreamed into the strategic direction of tourism, with an enhanced focus on developing and managing tourism sustainably. Most strategies continue to include targets to bolster visitor numbers, with 2019 considered a reference point to measure the recovery from recent shocks. However, there is a growing emphasis on the need for sustainable tourism growth and outcomes, with fewer negative externalities and greater benefits for destinations and local communities. This is reflected in the broadening of the goals and targets set out in tourism strategies and plans beyond the well-established metrics of visitor volume and expenditure to include a wider set of metrics to monitor progress and measure success differently (Box 1.1).

Strategies frequently set out concrete actions to provide future steps to meet the strategic goals and targets. A new Roadmap for the Tourism Industry in Norway, for example, aims to create a more profitable, greener and locally sustainable tourism sector. Launched in 2024, the Roadmap includes 43 actions to increase value creation through tourism, reduce the sector's climate and environmental footprint, create year-round jobs and position Norway as a competitive and sustainable destination. Initiatives range from the implementation of pilot projects to benefit from visitor contributions and support for sustainable management of natural attractions such as walking trails, to the promotion of sustainable indigenous tourism and Sámi culture.

Box 1.1. Strategic approaches to sustainable tourism development – selected country initiatives

Canada: The National Tourism Strategy, Canada 365: Welcoming the World, Every Day (launched in 2023) sets goals and actions to reduce the environmental impacts of tourism, support the sustainable development goals, enhance the sector's diversity through support to Indigenous tourism and advance Canada's gender-based analysis. Through this, Canada also aims to increase tourism GDP to CAD 61 billion and tourism-related jobs to a total of 790 000 by 2030, up from CAD 43.6 billion in GDP and 704 100 jobs in 2019.

Costa Rica: The National Tourism Development Plan 2022-27 is based on three pillars - sustainability, innovation and inclusiveness. The Plan aims to achieve a better balance between tourism development, the protection of natural resources and the distribution of profits throughout the country, so that local communities can benefit from an improved quality of life.

Czechia: The Tourism Development Strategy 2021-30 sets out a structural reform agenda focusing on sustainable tourism and the better management of tourist flows. Progress is tracked through Czechia's position in the WEF Travel and Tourism Development Index.

Iceland: The Leading in Sustainable Development, Icelandic Tourism 2030 policy framework was updated in 2023 to better align with post-pandemic priorities for the tourism sector. The updated framework has the overall ambition for tourism to enhance the quality of life and prosperity in Iceland, as a destination known for sustainable development, quality and a unique visitor experience. An increased focus on objectives for the environment and local communities is interlinked with economic ambitions to increase productivity, value creation and competitiveness, and enhance innovation, product development and the use of technology.

Italy: The Strategic Plan for Tourism 2023-27 encourages responsible travel behaviour, cultural heritage preservation, community involvement and diversification of the tourism offer to spread the impacts of tourism across the territory and across the year. It aims to promote tourism as a sustainable driver of economic development, while delivering better outcomes for destinations, local communities and the environment.

European Union: The European Agenda for Tourism 2030 sets a strategic framework for developing a sustainable, resilient, and competitive tourism sector in Europe, focusing on the green and digital transitions, enhancing the sector's resilience to crises, and fostering innovation and skills development. The Agenda calls for co-ordinated efforts among EU member states, stakeholders, and international partners to achieve these objectives and ensure the long-term sustainability and growth of European tourism. Following the Council's Conclusions calling for a European Tourism Agenda 2030-50, this document sets out potential policies and actions to meet the requirements of the Transition Pathway for Tourism. It contains a multi-year workplan for this purpose.

Increasing awareness of the social benefits of tourism has seen strategies prioritise inclusion, community involvement and regional development, and include a focus on spreading the benefits of tourism to communities throughout the territory. Colombia's Sectoral Tourism Plan 2022-26 aims to foster economic development, social inclusion, environmental protection, and peacebuilding through tourism. To achieve this goal, Colombia is increasing community-based and ethnic tourism, community protection, and the preservation of cultural heritage and values. Other countries have integrated similar objectives as central elements of their national tourism strategies, including Costa Rica, Italy, Korea, Mexico, Portugal, and the United States.

The tourism workforce has long been an area of focus for the tourism sector, but recent crises deepened labour shortages and heightening the need for co-ordinated action to address both short-term and long-term weaknesses. Morocco's Roadmap for Tourism 2023-26 aims to strengthen the tourism workforce through a training and management programme to offer better career prospects for young people in tourism. Recruiting and retaining skilled workers is one of four pillars of Germany's National Tourism Strategy which is currently under further development.

Digital transformation is another area of strategic emphasis, to increase efficiency, streamline operations, boost productivity, adapt to tourists' needs, and improve data-driven decision making. Countries like Costa Rica, Germany, Italy, Korea, Poland and Türkiye aim to modernise the tourism sector, foster innovation, and improve the overall visitor experience, by embedding digital transformation in their strategies.

As countries look to move beyond the recent crises and prepare long-term tourism strategies, they are increasingly embracing forward-looking approaches including strategic foresight and scenario planning. Such approaches recognise the dynamic and uncertain environment and different possible futures that policy makers need to consider and can inform more agile and flexible responses to future shocks and challenges. Estonia is employing strategic foresight approaches to prepare a new long-term vision for tourism to 2035, which brings together key stakeholders from across the sector to identify and analyse various potential scenarios for tourism development in the next decade (Box 1.2).

France used future-oriented techniques as part of a Horizons 2040 study to outline four potential future scenarios for the sector. These scenarios are designed to inform tourism policy development and provide useful insights for tourism stakeholders. The initiative aims to develop forward -looking approaches and strategic thinking to better anticipate factors transforming tourism and contribute to delivering the sustainable tourism goals set out in Destination France Plan 2030.

Box 1.2. Using strategic foresight to prepare a long-term vision for tourism in Estonia

Estonia is preparing a long-term vision to 2035 for tourism, to support the digitalisation and sustainable development of the sector. Recognising the cross-cutting nature of tourism and inter-connections with other sectors, a multi-level approach is being used to increase stakeholder engagement in the process, including through workshops, surveys, interviews, and validation seminars. Strategic foresight approaches have been adopted to better anticipate and prepare for potential futures and to understand the opportunities and challenges they may present. Tools employed include the STEEPLE analysis framework – Social, Technological, Economic, Environmental, Political, Legal, and Ethical factors – to help public and private sector stakeholders assess how external factors can impact tourism, and how tourism products and services should respond. Estonia plans to launch its long-term vision for tourism to 2035 in the first quarter of 2025.

Given the cross-cutting nature of tourism and need to co-ordinate across policy areas, integrating tourism as a pillar in wider national economic development plans and strategies can support a whole-of-government approach to tourism. In Lithuania, tourism is now part of a wider whole-of-economy Economic Transformation and Competitiveness Development programme, which replaces individual sectoral strategies. In addition, the tourism sector is supported by a separate National Tourism Pathway 2023, which further facilitates co-ordination across the public and private sector to deliver on tourism policy objectives.

The Council of the European Union has adopted a new European Agenda for Tourism 2030, based on its Transition Pathway for Tourism. With these initiatives, the Commission, member states and stakeholders are jointly supporting the tourism sector to navigate the green and digital transition and ensure its long-term resilience across countries in the European Union.

Furthermore, the global tourism agenda continues to be shaped by the work of a growing number of international institutions and multilateral fora. The tourism agenda of Brazil's 2024 G20 Presidency is focused on leveraging the potential of tourism to build a just and sustainable planet, while tourism is for the first time an official G7 workstream, under Italy's 2024 Presidency. Under Italy's leadership, the work will focus particularly on optimising the socio-economic impacts of tourism, human capital, employment and skills, and the implications of artificial intelligence for tourism.

Also in 2024, the Asia Pacific Economic Co-operation (APEC) Tourism Ministers issued a joint statement on innovating pathways for sustainable tourism growth, while the Association of Southeast Asian Nations (ASEAN) Tourism Ministers endorsed the Action Roadmap for Sustainable Tourism Development. International organisations and financing institutions have also expanded their activities on tourism. The Development Bank of Latin America and the Caribbean (CAF), for example, has developed a tourism strategy to promote sustainable and regenerative tourism development and strengthen regional integration and regional co-operation through tourism.

These examples build on the increased attention and expansion of activities seen in other international for a in recent years, including the OECD, UN Tourism and the World Bank. Maintaining the momentum of tourism work streams may support co-ordinated action and in turn help to keep tourism high on national policy agendas. However, ensuring strong collaboration across these fora is needed to best make use of resources and collectively advance work to build a more resilient and sustainable global tourism ecosystem.

Co-ordinating action for effective implementation of tourism plans and policies

Tourism strategies can help mobilise public and private stakeholders around a common vision and agreed goals but need to be underpinned by concrete action plans and resources, together with robust co-ordination and engagement of key stakeholders and supportive legal and regulatory frameworks to be effective. There is also a need to monitor progress and adjust policy measures where necessary, while maintaining the agility and flexibility to adapt to changes in the wider policy environment.

Countries have reported strong engagement across policy areas and levels of government, including from the private sector, to update and develop new strategies and plans since the pandemic. Maintaining this strong engagement is key to deliver on agreed actions and aspirations. However, as the sector bounces back, there is a risk that this engagement falls away as tourism slips down the list of national policy priorities, even as the strong rebound brings new challenges.

Multi-phased action plans provide one mechanism to maintain momentum and ongoing engagement for national tourism strategies. Australia's 10-year national strategy for the long-term sustainable growth of the visitor economy, THRIVE 2030, is broken down into three phases – recovery, consolidation, and acceleration. Each phase is complemented by a short-term action plan with clear targets against which progress is reviewed. Now in the consolidation phase, the focus has shifted away from driving visitation and addressing supply side issues, towards diversifying markets, investing in new products, and improving business practices and workforce capability. Implementation is further supported by an industry consultation round and institutional forums which regularly bring together tourism ministers from the Federal, State and Territory governments, as well as other relevant federal and state departments, to discuss tourism policies that can impact different sectors.

The Tourism Strategy of the Swiss Confederation presents the long-term vision for tourism in Switzerland. The main objectives are to improve the framework conditions, promote entrepreneurship, take advantage of opportunities offered by digitalisation, and enhance the attractiveness of tourism products and Switzerland's market presence. Published in 2021, each objective is supplemented by three action items, which are not final and are amended and extended as needed. This approach aims to ensure that the Strategy is agile and capable of both action and reaction.

Collaboration mechanisms help maintain a whole-of-government approach to tourism policy from strategy development to implementation phase. Canada for example has introduced a Ministerial Tourism Council to better co-ordinate efforts on tourism across the Federal Government. The Council brings together federal ministers whose responsibilities directly impact tourism (e.g. employment and skills, regional and national economic development, parks, transportation, immigration, border services, and housing). Collaboration across government can also occur to tackle specific issues. In Finland, a taskforce composed of representatives from the ministries of Economic Affairs and Employment, Justice, the Environment and Finance is working together to update and improve short-term rental legislation.

Effective tourism policy implementation requires the engagement of the private sector and other stakeholders. This includes maintaining an active and consistent voice for the private sector in government fora as well as ensuring the private sector is engaged and plays its part implementing actions and plans to deliver on a common vision for tourism. However, this can be challenging due to the fragmented nature of the sector. Some countries have created new mechanisms to encourage engagement with the private sector, also building on the legacy from the pandemic response.

Mexico launched the Mexican Tourism Planning System to enhance collaboration from public and private actors and support the Ministry of Tourism to analyse current policy programmes, identify actions that require immediate attention and propose data-driven recommendations. Germany has established a National Platform on the Future of Tourism which brings together tourism-related stakeholders, including industry representative associations, and provides a single forum for strategic dialogue with a focus on the four priority areas of climate neutrality and nature protection, recruiting and securing skilled labour, digitalisation and competitiveness.

Box 1.3. Modernising the legal framework to support tourism reform agenda in Croatia

Croatia adopted a new comprehensive Tourism Act in 2024. The law aims to drive tourism reforms and provide a supporting framework for sustainable tourism development and improved tourism management. The Act defines the institutional framework, data monitoring, analysis system and tools to preserve resources and space, and to guarantee tourist satisfaction and quality of life for local communities in tourist destinations, while ensuring the competitiveness of Croatian tourism on the international market. The Tourism Act, in co-ordination with Croatia's Sustainable Tourism Development Strategy 2030, the National Plan for the Development of Sustainable Tourism 2027 and the Action Plan for the Implementation of the National Plan 2025, sets out initiatives and approaches to encourage a more sustainable development of tourism and tackle overcrowding in destinations. They focus on promoting year-round, regionally balanced tourism, and increasing the resilience of tourism to external influences. These measures also aim to address problems associated with short-term rentals, protect the marine environment, and preserve cultural heritage sites. In addition, Croatia is working on improving the institutional and operating framework for destination management organisations to further enhance the tourism governance landscape.

Several countries have also taken steps to modernise the regulatory and legislative frameworks for tourism, to better align with the new strategies and plans and support a shift in focus to promote sustainable models of tourism development. In Greece, a new 2021 Law on Destination Management and Marketing Organisations and Model Tourism Destinations of Integrated Management has been established. It aims to advance optimal destination management through the creation of a stable co-operation framework between the public and private sectors. This legislation also acknowledges unique destination characteristics that may necessitate tailored planning and monitoring support.

Croatia modernised its legal framework, adopting a new Tourism Act in 2024 as part of a wider reform agenda to shift to a more sustainable and inclusive tourism economy. Developed in line with the national Sustainable Tourism Strategy launched in 2023, the Law establishes a structured framework for tourism development (Box 1.3).

Enhancing governance and management of tourism at regional and local level

Regional and local governments are increasingly important in developing and implementing tourism strategies and plans. Local action, guided by an overarching national vision for the future of tourism can help drive momentum for change. The regional and local dimension is also important to harness tourism's potential as a driver of economic and social development and to effectively manage tourism on the ground. Effective co-ordination across different levels of government enhances the overall impact of tourism policies, helping to align goals, use resources effectively and foster a unified approach to tourism development. It also empowers regional and local tourism bodies to create and promote tourism products and services that are bespoke and meet the economic, social, and environmental needs of places while better managing stakeholder interest for more sustainable and inclusive outcomes.

Actively involving local and regional bodies in the development of national tourism strategies helps incorporate place-based considerations and support the adaptation of actions to local needs. In Chile, for example, regional and local bodies have been involved in the development of the National Tourism Strategy 2035 through a series of regional workshops. This bottom-up participatory approach helps regional and local governments set relevant and coherent objectives while also ensuring that local needs and conditions are reflected in national strategies, and can in turn support effective implementation at destination level.

Advancing reforms to enhance co-ordination between national, regional, and local governments and strengthen destination management structures is an area of focus in many countries. Approaches vary depending on the system of government and the extent to which regional and local authorities have competence and are active on tourism development. However, there is widespread recognition of the importance of involving sub-national stakeholders, who play a key role in achieving broader tourism goals.

Streamlining and reforming destination governance structures can help to empower destinations in the strategic process of tourism development, as the focus continues to shift from marketing to management to better respond to the issues facing destinations. For example, Croatia, Estonia, Greece, Romania, and the United Kingdom have recently conducted extensive reviews of the destination governance structures and operating framework for destination management organisations, as part of wider reform agendas (Box 1.4).

Transformative destination development means destinations need to face the challenge of becoming an agent of change. As the role of destination management organisations (DMOs) continues to evolve and expand, new skills, capacities, and resources are required. DMOs are increasingly performing in similar ways as national bodies, including to address longstanding issues of seasonality by promoting the geographic and seasonal spread of tourists, however, human and financial capacity and resources are often constrained.

In Norway, as part of the National Tourism Strategy 2030, an official report on destination development and visitor management recommended that destination management teams be embedded in each region to provide strategic advice and delivery of sustainable visitor management. The aim is to help tourism develop in a more attractive manner to local communities, residents, and visitors. New Zealand has provided support for all 29 tourism destinations to develop tailored destination management plans which empower tourism stakeholders to determine the scope and approach that best serves the destination's interests and aspirations.

Destination management organisations are often better placed to more effectively partner and mobilise tourism businesses and reach a larger number of tourism SMEs in a smaller geographic footprint. Other benefits of regional and local planning include the creation of a stable and accessible co-operation framework for government and SMEs, co-ordination of activities and investments to promote tourism development, and closer integration with wider regional and local economic development policies. It can also help cross-sector initiatives that increasingly impact tourism at national level.

Box 1.4. Strengthening destination management structures – selected country examples

Estonia: A programme has been undertaken to reform and rationalise destination management structures to make DMOs more competitive, facilitate sharing of knowledge and best practice, reduce overlap and duplication, deliver national priorities around product development and address the growing performance gap between the capital city Tallinn and the rest of the country. In 2019, Estonia had approximately 40 DMOs, each employing an average of 1.5 people. By 2024, these had been consolidated into 7 DMOs capable of strategically leading the visitor economy in their areas. Long-term funding from the Government provides DMO staff with security of tenure and supports tourism development actions, but regions are expected to contribute at least half of all costs through co-financing.

Greece: A new operational framework was presented in 2023, following the passing of a Tourism Law for the establishment of destination management and marketing organisations. The operating framework aims to support local and regional authorities to develop and manage tourism sustainably, including establishing tourism observatories to enhance evidence-based policies. Key considerations have included the need to foster enhanced collaboration, ensure quality standards, and promote sustainable tourism development.

New Zealand: Collaborative Destination Management Plans (DMPs) were created to empower tourism stakeholders to determine the scope and approach to tourism that best serves each destination's interests and aspirations. The 29 DMPs aim to maintain a positive social license and establish robust local agendas for destination management. Each DMP is developed by building consensus among tourism businesses, local communities (including Māori communities), local government, and other stakeholders. The preparation of the DMPs was funded by central government, and implementation will be undertaken locally (including resourcing). Destination Management Guidelines were prepared to support stakeholders in their efforts to develop the Plans and provide suggestions on components that could be included and questions to stimulate discussion and identify gaps, opportunities, and areas for further investigation.

Resources to support sustainable tourism development

The tourism sector benefited from significant government support during the pandemic and its aftermath. This support was vital in helping the tourism sector weather the crisis and recover. Reflecting this, many countries reported an increase in the operating budget for tourism during the pandemic, while the sector also benefited from wider economic support measures not captured by tourism budgets. Many of these supports have been withdrawn as the recovery advanced, with countries reporting tourism budgets returning to similar or lower than pre-pandemic levels in 2023 and 2024.

While the withdrawal of the exceptional financial supports introduced during the pandemic is to be expected, this comes at a time when countries are setting out ambitious strategies and plans to develop and manage tourism more sustainably. Effectively implementing these strategies and delivering on anticipated policy outcomes requires sufficient resources – financial and human. However, few strategies and action plans include details on the resourcing requirements or commitments to deliver on the ambitions set out, and successfully meet the evolving demands of the sector.

Recognising this challenge, the Danish Government has allocated an additional DKK 100 million to the sector for the period 2024-27, or DKK 25 million annually, to deliver on sustainable tourism goals in the country. In Poland, tourism was allocated PLN 110.3 million, including PLN 84.5 million for the Polish Tourism Organisation, a total increase of 53% compared to 2022 to support the development of a new long-term strategy for tourism. The supplementary tourism budget in fiscal year 2023 in Japan increased to JPY 68.9 billion, which included JPY 18.4 billion to attract international visitors to local regions, JPY 20 billion to add value to tourist destinations and tourism industries, and JPY 30.5 billion to better manage tourism flows and promote sustainable tourism growth.

Significant investments are also required to reduce the environmental impact of tourism activities, while adapting to the impacts from climate change. Tourism destinations and businesses also need support to keep pace with rapid technological developments, while resources are also required to develop the infrastructure and mechanisms needed to better manage tourism development. This needs to be understood within the broader budgetary context and priorities of countries. Securing the necessary support will require a clear demonstration of the impact and effectiveness of tourism measures to promote economic growth while meeting wider policy goals and ambitions.

While national tourism budgets can serve as a practical indicator to measure the level of government support to tourism, the sector also benefits significantly from funding from other governmental bodies, including for infrastructure, transport and other tourism-related projects, and contributions can also be made to regional and local tourism authorities. Funding from international or supra-national institutions also supports tourism development. In the European Union, funds from a variety of funding sources support tourism development across member states, including through the EU Technical Support Instrument, and the European Regional Development Fund.

Building a more balanced future for tourism for more sustainable outcomes

Recognition of the need for tourism to transition towards more sustainable and resilient models of development has grown in recent years. Co-ordinated policy action across all levels of government is needed to address structural weaknesses that have impeded the sector in the past, not least to address issues linked with unbalanced tourism development and ensure jobs, resident well-being, and other benefits from tourism flow to local communities. However, preparing for the future will require accelerating mitigation and adaption measures so tourism can play its part in the low carbon transition, as well as continued progress to support digital uptake by businesses, and particularly SMEs.

Rethinking the tourism system and preparing for future shocks, while addressing long-term priorities and moving to more balanced and sustainable models of tourism development require policy makers to seize new opportunities to deploy transversal approaches that achieve multiple objectives. More granular, timely and robust evidence is needed to inform policy and business decisions, and to manage and track progress on potential trade-offs, determine 'what works', and identify emerging policy impacts and risks, as well as the costs of inaction.

Boosting the role of tourism in climate action to deliver on net zero targets

Urgent and transformative action is needed across all sectors, including tourism, if countries are to reach the target of net zero emissions by 2050 - or earlier in the case of countries that have set more ambitious targets. Tourism has an important role to play in delivering on these ambitions. Accurately estimating tourism's carbon footprint is challenging. However, a 2023 assessment of progress and gaps in critical dimensions of tourism climate action attributed 8 to 10% of global greenhouse gas emissions to tourism (Tourism Panel on Climate Change, 2023[10]). This aligns with previous estimates, with high-income countries responsible for most of these tourism-related emissions.

Tourism is also heavily exposed to multiple and often cumulative climate impacts, as evidenced in recent years with the wildfires, heatwaves, floods, and other weather events which have impacted visitors, businesses and local communities in countries around the world – both by the initial impact, but also from the loss of infrastructure and time it takes for tourism to recover.

Previous OECD Tourism Committee work has highlighted the need to accelerate the transition to a greener tourism economy, to translate commitments into real actions and outcomes, and embed environmental objectives into tourism policies and programmes. This includes promoting greener business models and destinations, encouraging consumers to make more sustainable travel choices, and the adoption of mitigation and adaptation measures along the tourism value chain. Co-ordinated action with other policy areas (e.g. transport, investment, infrastructure, skills) and across levels of government is also required to maximise the positive outcomes for tourism, while minimising unintended consequences.

Despite this widely acknowledged urgency, tourism policies to address climate mitigation and adaptation remain limited, and more needs to be done to translate net zero ambitions and related policies into action. Setting and monitoring against specific targets for tourism – or specific parts of the tourism economy – and then monitoring progress, would help to mobilise and guide action to manage and reduce the sector's carbon footprint. The complex nature of tourism, which is composed of many different sub-sectors and global value chains, makes this process challenging. challenging. Allocating emissions from international tourism, and in particular from transport, is challenging. Indicators or estimates of emissions, such as those reported in New Zealand's regular national greenhouse gas inventory, or air travel emissions in the EU Tourism Dashboard, provide guidance at the national level.

Many countries are yet to set tourism-specific greenhouse gas reduction targets and related emission budgets, even though tourism must follow national regulations and contribute to Nationally Determined Contributions to reach international targets set out in the Paris Climate Agreement. Tourism is instead often assigned to the transport or service sector. However, signatories to the Glasgow Declaration on Climate Action in Tourism commit to taking action to reduce emissions by 50% by 2030, and to reach net zero as soon as possible before 2050. This is supported by practical recommendations on how to get started with climate action (UN Tourism, 2024[11])

In recognition of tourism's contribution to the climate crisis and the need deliver on these commitments and ambitions, climate action is increasingly being integrated into national tourism strategies and plans, as shown for example by Greece, New Zealand, Norway and Slovenia. In a few cases, these strategies and plans set out specific targets to guide and monitor progress. For example, in Belgium, Visit Flanders launched a sustainability plan in 2022 to reduce emissions from tourist accommodation by 50% and tourism operators primary energy consumption by 35%, by 2030. Slovenia aims to reduce the carbon footprint of Slovenian tourism per overnight stay from 39.9 to 30.3 kgCO2eq/night, a reduction of 33% by 2028.

Beyond economy-wide climate action plans, several countries have developed tourism specific roadmaps and action plans setting out how the sector can play a more active role in achieving net zero ambitions and mobilising stakeholders to take action, including Chile, Ireland and the Netherlands (Box 1.5). These roadmaps and action plans cover a wide range of measures, including inter-ministerial and cross-sectoral workshops to build climate literacy, the launch of carbon calculators for tourists and tourism businesses, the reduction of dependence on air transport by strengthening rail infrastructure, the introduction of renewable energy programmes, climate risk analyses or the development of technical guidelines on mitigation.

Climate action roadmaps and plans recognise the role of businesses and propose concrete actions for and at the interface of different stakeholders. This includes initiating a shift in consumer behaviour away from high-emitting tourist activities, while education and climate capacity building for the tourism workforce are necessary to drive change in the sector.

Box 1.5. National roadmaps and action plans for tourism to contribute to net zero goals

Chile: The Plan for Adaptation to Climate Change in the Tourism Sector was jointly developed through extensive inter-ministerial co-ordination and adopted in 2020 to increase the resilience and sustainability of the tourism sector. It identifies tourist areas most at risk from climate change by analysing climate indicators and defining potential impacts on the tourism sector, such as changes in biodiversity and extreme weather events. Based on this assessment, the Plan sets out concrete objectives to develop the capacity and conditions to adapt and cope with the current and future impacts of climate change. The lines of action include increasing the capacity of the National Tourism Service, SERNATUR, to integrate climate change into tourism planning, public-private co-ordination, information management and communication. An update of the Plan is being undertaken in 2024 to reflect the Climate Change Framework Law.

Netherlands: Launched in 2022, the Road to Climate Neutral Tourism supports the broader Government goal for the Netherlands to be climate-neutral by 2030. With expertise from the scientific community and tourism professionals, the Roadmap outlines strategies to take action in line with the pillars of the Glasgow Declaration: measurement and research; reducing emissions; strengthening ecosystems; funding and support; and co-operation and leadership. For each measure, the Roadmap lists actions for government, businesses, branch organisations, knowledge institutes and destination management organisations. The lines of action include for example: reduce dependence on aviation, faster rollout of charging infrastructure for bicycles and cars, decrease dependence on the sea cruise industry, labels and certifications or climate neutral business as the norm.

Ireland: The National Tourism Development Agency, Fáilte Ireland, developed a Climate Action Roadmap in 2022, to help tourism and hospitality businesses reduce carbon emissions and contribute to national net zero targets. The Roadmap sets out 8 steps in the climate action journey for businesses, and provides climate action guides on water, waste and energy management, as well as carbon offsetting, biodiversity, meetings and events and festivals.

Countries also have initiatives to support tourism businesses, and SMEs in particular, to adapt and meet climate commitments, including through knowledge exchange, communication, networking and representation of specific interests in the greening of the tourism sector. SMEs as critical actors as drivers of technological change and adopters of green business models and practices to reduce their environmental footprint (OECD, 2024[12]).

In Ireland a Climate Action Programme complements Fáilte Ireland's Climate Action Roadmap and offers dedicated mentoring and investment advice to help tourism businesses reduce carbon emissions and develop tailored action plans to become more sustainable. The Programme has been oversubscribed since it was launched, reflecting strong demand from tourism businesses.

In Switzerland, the Competence Centre for Sustainability in Swiss Tourism aims to make Swiss tourism a leader in sustainability, by initiating and implementing projects and providing a central contact point for sustainability issues. It was launched in 2022 by the Swiss Tourism Federation, as part of Switzerland's

Tourism Strategy. The Swiss Parliament will soon decide on a new Law for tourist accommodation that will be implemented by the Swiss Association for Hotel Credit, to support the renovation of accommodation facilities in the Alpine region and seasonal tourist areas, with a focus on energy efficiency.

The German Climate Fund for Tourism as part of the National Climate Initiative pursues three goals: to establish an industry-wide greenhouse gas inventory, to develop climate protection measure and to develop a financing model for climate protection activities. In addition, the German association Klimalink works on the transparent presentation of the carbon footprint of travel, which has recently been joined by the tour operator association as well as companies from Austria and Switzerland. Germany has also increasingly promoting environmentally friendly tourism, including through a campaign to encourage travellers to "stay a little bit longer" as part the German National Tourist Board's sustainability strategy.

As decarbonisation measures are frequently linked to cost-intensive infrastructure improvements, various national programmes provide incentives or funding. In addition to the programmes above, Austria and Germany are among the countries with targeted support and programmes for tourism SMEs, including funding, to lead green transition initiatives and comply with climate neutrality goals (Box 1.6).

Box 1.6. Supporting tourism SMEs in the green transition – selected country examples

Austria: New funding guidelines have been launched to support investments by family-run and owner-managed tourism SMEs to strengthen sustainability and financial resilience. The scheme includes subsidised loans and guarantees, as well as a 7% sustainability bonus for investment costs up to a maximum of EUR 350 000. Eligible costs can be related to ecological, staff, regional, and digitalisation investments.

Germany: The LIFT Transformation funding is aimed at activating tourism SMEs and destinations to deal with relevant issues for the future of tourism, in line with the UN Sustainable Development Goals. The aim is to develop future-proof, applicable solutions on how tourism can be made sustainable and contribute to sustainable development. In addition, the recently established Centre of Excellence for the Green Transition of Tourism aims to support the tourism sector on its way to climate neutrality and sustainable transformation by communicating knowledge on climate-friendly and resource-saving innovations.

Balancing tourism flows with support of sustainable transport and infrastructure

The shift in focus towards more sustainable tourism development has led to a greater awareness of the role of tourism flows in destinations. Diversifying tourism to better manage the movement of visitors, both spatially and temporally, provides opportunities to strengthen destinations, build resilience to future shocks, while optimising the economic benefits and balancing the environmental and social impacts.

Efforts to sustainably disperse visitors and better spread the benefits of tourism both within and across destinations are becoming more common and are increasingly part of the strategic agenda for tourism, as is the integration of tourism into wider national and regional development agendas.

Portugal's Tourism Agenda for the Inland Territory, for example, aims to boost the tourism sector in inland Portugal to act as a catalyst for the cohesion and economic development of low-density territories. Launched in 2023, this Agenda consists of initiatives and measures aimed at connecting territories, enhancing resources, and investing in companies and the tourism offer, with a budget of around EUR 200 million.

In the United States, the Recreation Economy for Rural Communities programme has supported 25 small and rural communities in 17 states to develop strategies to increase outdoor recreation economies, help establish vibrant town centres, conserve natural resources and attract more visitors to rural areas, a key objective of the National Travel and Tourism Strategy.

Many initiatives focus on shifting tourists beyond well-established destinations to less visited or populated areas. In Korea, for example, the Digital Tourism Card initiative aims to attract Korean residents to regions facing population decline, encourage longer stays in regional areas, and foster economic growth by providing discounts on accommodation, meals, experiences, and other tourism services.

Japan's Tourism Nation Promotion Basic Plan 2023-25 focuses on attracting longer-staying and higher-spending visitors and fostering regional revitalisation by developing more offerings for high-end travellers, and funding events, tourist accommodation and facilities beyond the main tourist destinations. In 2023, 11 Model Tourist Destinations for creating Luxury Inbound Tourist Destinations were designated in regional areas with the aim of encouraging international tourists to explore Japan beyond its main cities and to attract travellers to rural areas where tourists can experience nature, history and unique culture.

The development of a more diverse tourism offer requires investments in tourism and community infrastructure to support increased visitation. Successfully encouraging tourists to visit new destinations can have significant economic and social benefits for local communities, if supported by adequate planning and resources. Hungary reintroduced the Tourism Development Contribution in 2023 to collect revenue from catering and commercial accommodation with the aim of financing new infrastructure projects to support tourism. In Iceland, the Tourist Site Protection Fund and the Icelandic Route Development Fund are both essential to support destination development and distribute tourists more evenly throughout the country. This approach aims to ease the strain on popular tourist destinations, while benefitting the sector and local communities.

The focus on balancing tourism flows has brought a renewed emphasis on the concept of carrying capacity in destinations. While the there is no clear approach or methodology for determining the carrying capacity of tourism destinations, the sector can learn from the extensive work and experience on managing visitor flows in protected areas. Improved access to data and communication with local communities can also help better understand destination capacities, balance trade-offs, and determine critical thresholds, which may differ for visitors and residents. Countries are now working with attractions, destinations, and local governments to better identify the critical thresholds for tourism.

France launched the National Strategy for Managing Tourist Flows in 2023, which includes the creation of a national Observatory for major tourist sites. The Observatory will measure the perceptions of tourist flows among locals and raise awareness about the positive and negative impacts of tourism, targeting tourists, locals and travel influencers. In Austria, the Find the Right Balance Guide supports regional decision makers to deal with imbalances in tourism and is supported by a funding call to develop tailor-made solutions to address the challenges of impacted regions.

Connecting destinations in a sustainable and accessible way is key to dispersing the benefits of tourism. The nature of tourism makes transport an integral part of the sector and creating easy-to-use and environmentally friendly transport options are typically high on the tourism policy agenda. Transport in tourism is often synonymous with aviation, which is a significant and growing contributor to global greenhouse gas emissions. The decarbonisation of air travel is therefore a priority if tourism is to have a viable and sustainable future.

At the national level, countries are working to advance sustainable aviation agendas. Australia and the United Kingdom have each convened Jet-zero councils to address sustainable aviation issues, particularly related to SAF. Air New Zealand, which is 51% owned by the Government is taking a multifaceted approach to deliver on carbon neutral by 2050 commitments, including investing in SAF, new aircraft technology and the renewal of the existing fleet, and reducing emission in ground operations.

At international level, the International Civil Aviation Organization (ICAO) Air Transport Action Group has set the ambitious target of achieving net-zero carbon emissions by 2050, however significant progress is needed to achieve this goal. The International Transport Forum (ITF) at the OECD is actively supporting this agenda, including by convening a common interest group bringing together government, private sector and other stakeholders to explore opportunities to advance policies to decarbonise aviation. One area of focus is the opportunity presented by increased use of sustainable aviation fuels (SAF). As part of this work the ITF is exploring the consequences of decarbonising aviation on travel patterns and tourism.

While the aviation sector plays an important role in the tourism sector, particularly for remote and island destinations, ground transport to and around destinations remains essential for most tourists. Reflecting this, Italy's Sustainable Tourism Fund identifies intermodal routes that leverage the use of electric means of transport with aims to mitigate overcrowding, create innovative itineraries and de-seasonalise destinations. The Fund also provides support to accommodation facilities and tourism businesses to obtain sustainability certifications, with funding of EUR 10 million available in 2024 and in 2025. Australia meanwhile is leveraging the National Electric Vehicle Strategy to give tourists more sustainable transport options, recognising the lack of a comprehensive rail system outside of capital cities.

Morocco's high-speed train has significantly impacted the tourism sector by reducing travel time between Tangier and Casablanca, making it more convenient for domestic and international tourists to travel within the country. This improvement in infrastructure, which transported over 5 million passengers in 2023, also made lesser-known cities more accessible, helping to distribute tourism benefits more broadly across the region. In 2023, the national government committed to extending the high-speed train system to other tourist destinations, such as Marrakech and Agadir.

Box 1.7. Promoting sustainable tourism and mobility across Europe

The Transport, Health and Environment Pan-European Programme (THE PEP) is an initiative launched by the World Health Organization (WHO) and the United Nations Economic Commission for Europe (UNECE). It aims to integrate environmental and health considerations into transport, mobility and urban planning to improve the quality of life for people across Europe. At the 5th THE PEP High-Level Meeting in Vienna in 2021, Ministers decided to launch a new THE PEP Partnership on Sustainable Tourism Mobility, supported by the Secretariats of UNECE and WHO. THE PEP Partnership on Sustainable Tourism Mobility, led by Austria, aims at bringing together the relevant national stakeholders responsible for mobility, climate action and tourism in a European platform in order to further promote sustainable tourism development in the pan-European region. The aim of the partnership is to raise awareness of sustainable multimodal mobility in tourism, strengthen co-operation between stakeholders and improve the institutional capacity of relevant organisations. The members of this European partnership work together on a document addressed to the national level including recommended actions and best practice examples in the following areas: foster institutional capacity, integrate sustainable tourism mobility in national strategies, understand mobility requirements of different user groups, mobility management at destinations, long-distance travel options, flexible transport systems, cycling and walking as part of the tourism experience, multimodal travel information as well as integration of sustainable mobility services into tourism packages, marketing and communication.

Sustainable mobility is becoming increasingly important as countries look to balance the need to provide adequate and diverse transport options to get to and around tourist destinations, with the need to decarbonise tourism activities themselves. Building the necessary infrastructure, reducing congestion through public transport, optimising routes and developing green transport options, like electric buses and vehicles, but also self-powered or soft mobility options such as bike-sharing programmes, and pedestrian-friendly pathways are important measures that improve the visitor experience and directly benefit local communities. In this context, the ministries responsible for climate, transport and tourism in Austria launched a pan-European partnership for sustainable tourism mobility in the framework of the Transport, Health and Environment Pan-European Programme (THE PEP) in 2021 which promotes sustainable and multimodal means of tourism mobility including public transport, active mobility (cycling, walking) and flexible transport systems (Box 1.7).

At destination level, countries are looking to promote carbon-free or low carbon transport. Luxembourg, for example, has introduced Velosummer to promote active tourism, restricting motorised transport on certain roads in August. In 2023, the initiative included 12 routes covering over 500 km, attracting almost 25 000 cyclists, and it not only reduced emissions from motorised vehicles but also encouraged greater dispersion of tourists in Luxembourg. In Italy, the Urban Trekking project in Grosseto is a regional venture to promote slow tourism, local art and history and aims to establish a network of walking and cycle paths connecting the entire province, inspiring green mobility and responsible exploration. Grosseto was awarded the 2024 European Green Pioneer of Smart Tourism.

Optimising the socio-economic value of tourism for local communities

Tourism has a key role to play to foster economic development that creates decent jobs, enhances well-being and social cohesion, and contributes to the shared interests of tourists, residents, and businesses. It also provides opportunities for SMEs to integrate into global tourism value chains. Tourism, when well-managed, can be a key driver of inclusive community development contributing to resiliency, inclusivity, and empowerment, while safeguarding natural and cultural resources (OECD, 2021[13]). However, existing models of tourism development often mean the impacts of tourism are unbalanced, with some destinations receiving visitor volumes that can place considerable strain on local communities while others seek more visitor spending to support their local economy.

Optimising the socio-economic value of tourism requires better planning, improved understanding and management of the trade-offs involved, and engagement with the local community to create a more inclusive sector where the benefits (and costs) are more widely shared. One area of increased focus is on measuring tourism acceptance, local sentiment, and the social aspect of tourism. Countries like Austria, Costa Rica, France, and New Zealand have implemented new survey approaches to measure social acceptance and the well-being of residents. This is explored in more depth in Chapter 3.

Accessibility and inclusion have become key areas of focus with countries looking to promote the potential tourism provides for inclusive growth, for tourists, the workforce, and communities (Box 1.8). This can be stimulated by enhancing accessibility for people with disabilities, providing access for vulnerable income groups, ensuring fair representation and opportunities for minority groups, and advancing gender equality in tourism-related employment and leadership.

Australia's WELCOME Framework encourages tourism businesses to view accessibility and inclusivity as a universal approach to business. Developed in 2024, the Framework brings together important aspects for tourism operators to consider in making their products and services more accessible. It guides operators to understand the needs of, and promote their business to, the accessible tourism community.

Creating liveable destinations and ensuring that the local population benefits from tourism has become a policy focus for many destinations. The impact of tourism on local communities is increasingly being integrated into national tourism strategies. In 2023, Peru implemented the Community Tourism Strategy which is accompanied by the Law for Promotion and Development of Community Tourism. Through the Strategy and Law, Peru aims to generate socio-economic dynamism and improve the quality of life of local populations through tourism.

The Slovak Republic is finalising the National Sustainable Tourism Strategy for 2035, which aims to increase the competitiveness of tourism, better use its potential, balance regional disparities, and create new jobs. A key pillar under this Strategy is to create durable destinations which can provide quality stays for visitors and quality of life for residents.

Box 1.8. Initiatives that promote more inclusive growth – selected countries

Greece: Accessible tourism is a key component of the National Strategy 2024-30. In this frame, Greece introduced the Accessible Tourism Destination and Accessible Tourism Enterprise quality labels, aiming to promote accessible tourism in Greece through the implementation of accessibility standards in tourism installations and destinations.

Italy: The Tourist Accessibility Fund was launched to promote social inclusion and diversification of the tourist offer. Additional funds are available specifically targeted to small municipalities with a tourist vocation, to encourage innovations in accessibility. These funds support the international reputation of Italy as a safe and inclusive destination, through the proposition of a diversified, inclusive, resilient, and safe offer.

Japan: A survey was undertaken to assess the prevalence of accessible tourism, identify its challenges, and evaluate market size, with the objective of promoting inclusive travel accessible to all individuals, including older people and those with a disability. Addressing the travel needs of these groups, for whom there is substantial potential demand, is crucial for stimulating travel activity and revitalising the economy with a forward-looking perspective.

United Kingdom: Actions are focused on building on existing best practice and toolkits on accessibility and inclusion, such as the National Accessible Scheme, and examining the access limitations of tourism services, based on different needs. These have been undertaken with consultation through the Tourism Industry Council Working Group on Inclusivity and Accessibility, the Disability and Accessibility Ambassador, England's Inclusive Tourism Action Group, and other stakeholders.

United States: Accessibility, diversity and inclusion is a pillar of the US National Travel and Tourism Strategy. For its implementation, the Federal Government has engaged with the Travel and Tourism Advisory Board, by installing a Private Sector Advisory Body to the Secretary of Commerce who provide recommendations on Accessibility, Sustainability, Infrastructure, and promoting diverse tourism products.

Participatory approaches which involve local communities in tourism planning and development decisions can support more balanced outcomes for residents, and in turn lead to greater acceptance of tourism. In Mexico, the Kuxatur programme aims to create sustainable tourism development zones, and integrate local communities into tourism policy development, with a focus on capacity building, so that residents can implement actions to achieve sustainable tourism targets.

Tourism can also be a catalyst for regional development, especially in rural and remote areas, and thereby increase well-being and liveability. In Korea, the Ministry of Culture, Sports and Tourism has launched an initiative to address rural and population decline in some parts of the country. Tourism plays a pivotal role to help regions realise their potential and under this initiative projects have started to stimulate digital nomadism and workcations in these areas.

Housing affordability is a well-documented issue for tourism destinations, at a time when real house purchase and rental prices have risen faster than inflation and incomes in recent decades and have disproportionately affected poorer and younger households (OECD, 2022[14]). The rise of online accommodation booking platforms and short-term rentals, second home tourism and unplanned tourism growth in some destinations have also contributed to greater housing demand, sometimes resulting in situations with residents and seasonal workers are unable to secure affordable housing. In 2024, the Council of the European Union adopted a new regulation on data collection and sharing for short-term accommodation rental services. These new obligations are not intended to regulate access to the market on these activities, but to increase transparency and support local authorities in Europe to develop and enforce policies for vacation rentals, while keeping housing accessible for residents (Box 1.9).

Box 1.9. Regulation to increase transparency and evidence on short-term rentals in the EU

In March 2024, the Council of the EU adopted a regulation on data collection and sharing for short-term accommodation rental services. It aims to help authorities produce reliable statistics and take well-informed regulatory measures to address key issues like housing affordability. The new rules introduce harmonised registration requirements for hosts and short-term rental properties, including the granting of a unique registration number to be displayed on property websites and online platforms. Local authorities and short-term rental platforms have 24 months to comply with the regulation.

Hosts need to submit simple information to obtain this registration number, which will be required to provide short-term accommodation rental services. Online platforms will be required to regularly provide information on the rental activities of their hosts (for example, number of nights sold, number of guests, address, registration number) to a single digital entry point in relevant member states.

This regulation is not intended to regulate access to the market, but rather increase transparency on these activities. Online platforms will need to ensure host information is reliable and complete, and that the registration number is clearly visible on each listing. They will also be required to conduct random information checks on hosts. Local authorities will be able to suspend registration numbers, request platforms to delete illegal listings, and sanction non-compliant platforms or hosts.

Supporting tourism SMEs to innovate with rapid technological change

Digital technologies are reshaping processes in tourism and represent a powerful catalyst for innovation in the sector. New technologies, including generative Artificial Intelligence (AI), extended reality (XR) and blockchain, are changing the way people plan and experience travel, and present opportunities to not only reach new consumers with novel tourism products and services, but also improve business operations and performance, and accelerate the transition to greener, more sustainable business models.

Despite potential benefits, SMEs lag behind larger firms in their adoption of digital technologies, and digital adoption by SMEs is to a large extent still confined to basic services, including in the tourism sector (OECD, 2021[15]). Addressing these adoption gaps, as technologies become more sophisticated, is important to a widening of the digital divide between SMEs and large, technology-driven businesses. Small tourism businesses require support to overcome key barriers to digital uptake, including a lack of digital skills, hardware costs, infrastructure gaps or adequate privacy protection (OECD, 2024[16]).

National policies can play a pivotal role in shaping the digital landscape for tourism and ensuring tourism businesses can implement new technological solutions to improve internal operations and innovate tourism services. Digital tourism strategies and plans are now being developed by countries, either dedicated to tourism, or as part of wider national digitalisation strategies and plans. These initiatives often include a tourism data space, and strategies to improve the tourist experience and digitise business models.

In Slovenia, the Digital Transformation of Slovenian Tourism 2022--26 plan aims to boost tourism competitiveness, sustainability and worker skills, through the implementation of a National Market

Intelligence Hub and introduction of smart business solutions or competence vouchers. The Spain Digital 2026 Strategy includes an initiative building on a modular platform to implement the Digital Transformation Plan for Tourist Destinations. This is complemented by the development of new tools for the Network of Smart Tourist Destinations, and a Tourism Intelligence System to integrate sources of tourism information and provide analytical services.

Tourism-specific strategies and economy-wide plans can set the strategic direction for the sector, but these need to be complemented by targeted programmes and initiatives to support SMEs through digital transformation. This includes providing support to access finance and capacity building and improving the awareness of available tools, as well as opportunities to use the data generated by tools to better tailor product and marketing strategies for tourists.

The awareness of the transformative role that AI and other technologies may have on the tourism sector is still developing. The implications of AI for tourism and tourism policymaking is a key area of focus for the G7 Tourism Working Group, under Italy's 2024 G7 Presidency. Policymakers face the challenge of keeping pace with the rapid rate of change, and to support tourism businesses to overcome barriers to the use and uptake of AI, while managing the new risks and challenges it brings for all businesses.

Countries are starting to support research and development for AI in tourism. In 2022, Spain implemented initiatives to promote AI in tourism businesses (EUR 45 million) and to foster digital development of tourism destinations (EUR 115 million) over a three-year period. As part of this funding, Spain has developed a Digitisation and Intelligence Programme for destinations and tourism businesses to develop smart destination platforms. This aims to make interoperable public and private services available to tourists.

France has encouraged tourism companies to integrate digital technology into the tourism value chain by supporting travel tech startups based on technological building blocks, including for example AI, blockchain, Internet of Things and 5G. The programme aims to support innovative start-ups and promote further innovation in the tourism sector. France has also commissioned a study on the impact and implications of AI for tourism. Korea also provides digital transformation programmes to tourism businesses including through the introduction of Innovation Vouchers for tourism SMEs (Box 1.10).

Box 1.10. Accelerating the digital transformation of tourism SMEs in Korea

To enhance the competitiveness of Korean tourism in a rapidly changing digital world, the Korean Government assists tourism businesses to embrace digital innovation. The comprehensive digital transformation programme supports tourism businesses through different stages of their lifecycle. This includes the establishment of digital infrastructure, skills enhancement for companies and workers and access to financial aid for tourism SMEs and start-ups.

Innovation Vouchers plays a key role in accelerating the digital transformation of the tourism sector. In 2024, over 150 SMEs received a voucher for digital services. Beneficiaries of the programme can access an online platform with 242 providers offering specific solutions for digitalisation, such as building a website, improving user experience, creating AI chatbots, online promotion using ads, etc.

In support of the programme, the Korea Tourism Data Lab website provides access to tourism statistics and private data, promoting granular analysis for customised tourism products and addressing issues like overcrowding.

As the digital transformation advances, there is a need to build the skills and capacity to adopt and use these technologies. Many countries have developed programmes that promote digital literacy, including through workshops, mentoring, assessment of digital maturity or concrete technical support. In Estonia, the Tourism Digital Mentoring Alongside Digitalisation Roadmap aims to increase digital literacy and uptake within tourism businesses through mentoring, which requires businesses to contribute 10% of the cost of the mentoring over a five-month period. In return, businesses receive training in digital resource management and a roadmap catered to their business needs to help achieve greater profitability and efficiency over a three-year period. Estonia also offers a support measure for tourism service providers that encourages the use of central digital solutions for resource management and makes interfaces between digital solutions in use.

In Ireland, the Digital that Delivers programme is designed to power digital transformation for visitor attractions, activity providers and day tours over a two-year period. The programme includes training and mentoring by leading digital experts and financial support, and helps businesses to become more promotable, searchable, and bookable online. The German Mittelstand-Digital Centre for Tourism provides practice-oriented knowledge on digital technologies, data systems and other digital solutions for SMEs along the entire tourism value chain. It connects businesses and digital solution providers and focuses on technology and future focused areas that are particularly relevant to the sector.

Centralised platforms can provide an entry-point for tourism businesses providing increased exposure, but also access to online tools to improve knowledge management, training and data visualisation. These initiatives often provide incentives for tourism SMEs to participate and actively use the online services but can also collect data for analysis and tailored policies. Italy has developed the Digital Tourism Hub to incentivise digital uptake. The Hub is an open and agile platform that facilitates content publication, destination promotion, and integration of public and private tourist offers. The platform helps tourists connect to the Italian tourism ecosystem better, increasing personalised experiences. The Hub has the potential, in the future, to provide the basis for strategic decision-making, informed by data processing and the incorporation of AI and machine learning.

Greece is developing My Digital Tourism, an online platform that aims to support businesses to create new products, streamline processes, and boost investment in the sector under the 2024 Action Plan. It aims to facilitate document submissions for licensing, manage tourist complaints, conduct business inspections, and gather statistical data on tourist accommodation, through a subsystem recording arrivals and departures. The platform is expected to be launched in early 2025 and benefit over 100 000 tourism businesses.

High-speed Internet access is crucial to leveraging social and economic opportunities of digitalisation, such as teleworking and new business processes and models. In 2022, on average in OECD countries people in metropolitan regions experience 40% faster Internet than those in regions far from metropolitan areas (OECD, 2022[17]). Implementing advanced technologies requires investment in the necessary digital infrastructure, particularly for tourism destinations, which are often outside of capital cities. In the United Kingdom, investments in digital connectivity across the country, such as full fibre and 5G, have helped to drive innovation in the visitor economy. This is because remaining globally competitive requires an innovative tourism sector to make full use of digital technology and data to enhance the visitor experience.

Strengthening data to guide and evaluate policy action for tourism

The rapid changes in the tourism sector have brought increased focus to the role of data in the policy-making process, and the types of data that are necessary to inform tourism decision making. As governments globally reshape their tourism strategies, and set shorter-term targets and metrics, the collection and dissemination of timely, granular, and comparable data is increasingly important to inform and evaluate tourism policy. This is particularly important to effectively navigate the dynamic and evolving landscape with often scarce resources.

The shift towards sustainable development in longer-term tourism strategies and plans has brought visibility to the lack of data beyond economic and financial measures. This requires new measures to implement and evaluate the effectiveness of efforts to shift towards more resilient, sustainable, and inclusive models of tourism. Internationally, efforts have focused on identifying potential measures, including through the recently endorsed Statistical Framework for Measuring the Sustainability of Tourism (SF-MST), led by UN Tourism. International and country initiatives to improve the tourism evidence base for sustainable tourism policies is explored in depth in Chapter 3.

An enhanced focus has been placed on monitoring and evaluating the effectiveness of tourism policies, with the incorporation of more concrete targets, indicators and goals in new strategies and plans. However, the fragmented nature of the sector, the high number of SMEs and the lagging technical capability of tourism businesses render data collection on tourism more complex. The tourism recovery has also brought an increased awareness of the role of forecasts and nowcasts for more strategic policy setting. Portugal recently conducted a feasibility study to develop a new international tourist demand forecasting model to support better informed decisions on resource allocation, marketing, and tourism development, through more accurate demand forecasts.

As decision making increasingly shifts to the sub-national and local levels, aided by more collaborative and multilevel governance practices and the evolving role of DMOs, relevant data needs to be made available at more granular levels. In response, the Slovenian Tourist Board has implemented the National Information Centre for Tourism, a platform to collect and process local, national and international tourism data. While a collaborative approach has been adopted in Denmark, integrating multiple data sources into a national data hub, to facilitate more timely decision making for DMO's and businesses (Box 1.11).

Box 1.11. Creating national data platforms to improve data access at sub-national levels

Slovenia: The National Tourism Information Centre aims to create a unique centralised data hub where local, national, and international tourism-relevant data will be collected and processed, to support data-driven decision-making. The focus of the Information Centre will be on acceleration of the green and digital transition and upgrading the Green Scheme of Slovenian tourism. The project covers two parallel phases:

- Implementing a modern digital analytical tool for measuring the impacts of tourism on all leading Slovene tourism destinations, to foster the sector's sustainable transition.
- Measuring tourism flows and determining the carrying capacity of leading destinations and the geographical distribution of tourism development in a more sustainable way.

The prototype development phase was completed in 2023 and incorporated the analysis of data sources, preparation of functional specifications, and the implementation design and architectural scheme for the Information Centre., The implementation phase commenced in 2024. Due to the complexity of the project, experts on information technology, data analytics, artificial intelligence and machine learning, will participate in the implementation phase, which is expected to be completed by the end of 2025.

Denmark: A national data platform for tourism launched in 2023 aims to provide DMOs and partners with data and tools to support decision-making. By connecting various data sources and combining data, Danish tourism stakeholders can gain new insights into the behaviour of tourists and make better business decisions. The platform combines data from both public and commercials sources (e.g, Visa, telecom companies), providing DMOs with new data options, previously unavailable at this level, as well as data on the number of nights, attractions and visitor numbers. In the long run, this platform will enable DMOs to draw on the experiences of other destinations and compare local results with new relevant benchmarks. The platform also enables DMOs to store their data securely. By the end of 2023, all Danish DMOs were connected to the platform, with companies expected to connect by 2024.

The German National Tourist Board's new Data Dashboard for Sustainable Travel Trends supports users with detailed information regarding inbound consumers sentiment towards sustainability, climate protection and interest in sustainable travel. It also provides data on perceptions of Germany as a destination, and current travel behaviour from a sustainability perspective, including the relevance of multi-destination trips, length of stay, tourism density, and CO2-equivalent emissions for transport.

The need to better monitor tourism policies and quantify results continues to prompt greater demand for alternative data sources. Traditional statistics adhere to internationally agreed methodologies and processes, ensuring cross-country comparability. However, these statistics are often released with a significant time lag and may lack detailed granularity. Conversely, alternative data sources, such as transaction and mobile positioning data, although not adhering to these same rigorous statistical standards, offer more timely and detailed insights into tourism flows and expenditure. This enables policymakers to respond more swiftly to emerging trends and developments, particularly when used to complement official statistics.

Digitalisation has opened new opportunities to obtain more granular, timely data. However, this requires policymakers to clearly communicate their data needs, and in return, data users and data makers need to clearly communicate data and insights to policymakers. This includes promoting automation to improve efficiency and reduce costs, which will require political buy-in through the allocation of resources to build and run the systems. Sweden is leading a Nordic collaboration project to integrate transaction data into the compilation of national Tourism Satellite Accounts (TSA). This method should provide more precise estimation and granularity of tourism data and allows for a shorter delivery time at a lower cost. The project, launched in 2022, is funded until the end of 2024, with hopes to secure further Nordic funding until 2025 so that the new TSA model can be fully operational in Nordic countries by 2026.

While new data sources provide new opportunities, data demand should not focus on increasing the overall volume of data collected but instead on collecting the right data, at the right time, and getting this information to decision-makers in a timely manner and in a format that is easy to understand.

References

Booking.com and Statista.com (2024), *European Accommodation Barometer 2024*, https://www.statista.com/study/168004/2024-european-accommodation-barometer/. [5]

ForwardKeys (2024), *Demand for summer travel in Europe fully recovers to pre-pandemic levels*, https://forwardkeys.com/european-summer-travel-outlook-2024/. [6]

IATA (2024), *Air Passenger Market Analysis: April 2024*, https://www.iata.org/en/iata-repository/publications/economic-reports/air-passenger-market-analysis-april-2024/. [7]

McKinsey & Company (2024), *What is the future of travel?*, https://www.mckinsey.com/featured-insights/mckinsey-explainers/what-is-the-future-of-travel. [9]

OECD (2024), *Financing SMEs and Entrepreneurs 2024: An OECD Scoreboard*, https://doi.org/10.1787/fa521246-en. [12]

OECD (2024), *OECD Economic Outlook, May 2024*, OECD Publishing, Paris, https://www.oecd.org/economic-outlook/may-2024/. [4]

OECD (2024), *OECD Economic Outlook, Volume 2024 Issue 1*, OECD Publishing, Paris, https://doi.org/10.1787/69a0c310-en. [2]

OECD (2024), *SME digitalisation in 2024 Managing shocks and transitions. An OECD D4SME Survey*, https://www.oecd.org/content/dam/oecd/en/networks/oecd-digital-for-smes-global-initiative/FINAL-D4SME-2024-Survey-Policy-Highlights.pdf/_jcr_content/renditions/original./FINAL-D4SME-2024-Survey-Policy-Highlights.pdf. [16]

OECD (2023), *The Climate Action Monitor 2023: Providing Information to Monitor Progress Towards Net-Zero*, OECD Publishing, Paris, https://doi.org/10.1787/60e338a2-en. [8]

OECD (2022), *Housing Taxation in OECD Countries*, OECD Publishing, Paris, https://doi.org/10.1787/03dfe007-en. [14]

OECD (2022), *OECD Regions and Cities at a Glance 2022*, OECD Publishing, Paris, https://doi.org/10.1787/14108660-en. [17]

OECD (2021), *G20 Rome guidelines for the future of tourism*, OECD Publishing, Paris, https://www.oecd.org/cfe/g20-rome-guidelines-for-the-future-of-tourism-d11080db-en.htm. [13]

OECD (2021), *SME's going digital: Policy challenges and recommendations*, OECD Publishing, Paris, https://doi.org/10.1787/c91088a4-en. [15]

Tourism Panel on Climate Change (2023), *Tourism and Climate Change Stocktake*, https://tpcc.info/stocktake-report/. [10]

UN Tourism (2024), *Policy Guidance to Support Climate Action by National Tourism Administrations*, UN Tourism, https://doi.org/10.18111/9789284425365. [11]

UN Tourism (2024), *UNWTO World Tourism Barometer and Statistical Annex, January 2024*, https://doi.org/10.18111/wtobarometereng. [3]

UN Tourism (2024), *UNWTO World Tourism Barometer and Statistical Annex, May 2024*, https://doi.org/10.18111/wtobarometereng. [1]

WEF (2024), *Travel & Tourism Development Index 2024*. [18]

World Travel & Tourism Council (2021), *A Net Zero Roadmap for Travel & Tourism. Proposing a new target Framework for the Travel & Tourism Sector*, https://wttc.org/Portals/0/Documents/Reports/2021/WTTC_Net_Zero_Roadmap.pdf. [19]

Note

[1] Australia, Belgium, Canada, Chile, Colombia, Denmark, Estonia, Finland, France, Germany, Greece, Hungary, Ireland, Italy, Japan, Korea, Latvia, Lithuania, Mexico, Netherlands, Norway, Poland, Portugal, Slovenia, Spain, Sweden, Türkiye, United Kingdom.

Chapter 2. Strengthening the tourism workforce

Workforce issues are a long-standing vulnerability for the tourism sector and have been exacerbated since the COVID-19 pandemic. Tackling existing and emerging workforce issues in tourism requires new and whole-of-sector responses to improve the quality of tourism jobs, strengthen the tourism offer and reduce tourism's (over)exposure to future crises. This chapter analyses policy approaches to support the sector to attract and retain talent across all skills levels and areas within the sector since the pandemic. It highlights the actions governments can take to create the right framework conditions to enable policy-led change, in collaboration with the private sector to build a more resilient tourism, considering the impacts of the green and digital transitions. Key policy considerations are identified to strengthen the tourism workforce.

Tourism is a significant employer and contributor to economic growth. Prior to the COVID-19 pandemic, tourism is estimated to have accounted for 6.9% of employment in OECD countries (OECD, 2022[1]). Tourism employment also provides important social and economic functions which are not always recognised. As an important employer of youth, women, migrants and other workers frequently marginalised from the workforce, the sector builds social capital and agency and contributes to overall social, economic and political outcomes, including in rural or remote communities.

Workforce issues are a long-standing vulnerability for the tourism sector and have been exacerbated since the COVID-19 pandemic. Tourism businesses have struggled to attract workers back into the sector amid tight labour markets and cost-of-living pressures, which deepened the impacts of the crises and further exposed tourism to labour market challenges. The interconnected nature of tourism saw shortages in one part of the tourism system have knock-on impacts throughout the sector and constrained the sectors ability to recover and cater to the post-pandemic demand for tourism services.

This has spurred a greater focus on building resilience in the tourism economy, including by addressing persistent challenges to attract, retain and develop workers. Tackling existing and emerging workforce issues in tourism requires more innovative and whole-of-sector responses to address these challenges and will in turn improve the quality of tourism jobs, strengthen the tourism offer and help avoid tourism's (over)exposure to future crises.

The chapter reviews and analyses policies and measures designed to support the sector to attract and retain talent across all skills levels and areas since the pandemic. It highlights the actions governments can take to create the right framework conditions to enable policy-led change, in collaboration with the private sector. The chapter is informed by a survey of OECD member and partner countries and two workshops, including a dialogue with the private sector. The need to tailor workforce resilience approaches to the specific policy needs of destinations is highlighted. Priority issues are identified, and considerations for policy-focused action are proposed to increase resilience across the tourism sector.

Importance of the tourism workforce for building resilience

A vibrant and sustainable workforce is key to the development of a resilient tourism system. Tourism is highly labour intensive and offers strong potential to support a job-rich economy for people of all ages and skill levels across a variety of job types and activities. At the same time, the sector is highly dependent on quality human resources to manage, develop and deliver a competitive tourism offer, and to adapt and benefit from the green and digital transitions. However, the positive aspects of jobs in tourism and the opportunities this can provide for workers to enter and move around the labour market are often lost amid wider issues, including the nature of tourism jobs and working conditions in the sector, which are frequently associated with unstable, low-wage work.

Tourism jobs can offer opportunities for people to enter the labour market and provide a stepping-stone for workers who face higher barriers to employment, such as young, low-skilled and migrant workers. Other benefits include social mobility, socially vibrant workplaces, intercultural learning, opportunities for rapid career progression, entrepreneurial prospects and the development of transferable skills. Analysis of tourism job advertisements shows that a huge diversity of skills, from more social and interpersonal skills to highly specialised and technical skills, are sought after in tourism work (CEDEFOP, 2020[2]). The interpersonal nature of tourism means that its workers often have highly developed emotional intelligence, communication and teamwork aptitudes, and it is these 'high touch' or 'interpersonal/people skills' that are highly transferable and make tourism workers desirable to other sectors. Working closely with the private sector, workers and employers organisations, policy makers can use tourism jobs as a vehicle to improve the lives of underserved populations, and the economy as a whole, by improving labour market participation.

However, there is a need to address tourism workforce issues and decent work challenges which have been a long-standing vulnerability for the sector. Many countries faced labour shortages and skills gaps in tourism before the pandemic, generated from a complex web of underlying drivers including: a lack of skilled workers; the prevalence of casual and informal work; variable and long working hours; low wages; limited access to social protection; gender-based discrimination; poor occupational safety and health practices; and the weak regulation, enforcement and organisation of labour (ILO, 2022[3]). These issues have contributed to poor perceptions of work in the tourism sector and need to be addressed to challenge attitudes that dismiss work in tourism as low skilled and dispensable (ILO, 2023[4]) while improving the quality of tourism jobs to attract and keep workers in the sector.

The COVID-19 pandemic caused significant disruption for the tourism workforce causing many workers to leave the sector for jobs elsewhere in the economy, with people in casual or informal employment disproportionately impacted. Despite a strong rebound in tourism, the sector has been unable to attract a sufficient inflow of workers to tourism jobs. This has highlighted the transferability of skills required by tourism work which are desirable to other sectors. It also brought awareness to the structural issues facing the workforce and prompted government and industry to take action to address these.

The private sector has a lead role to play to address these issues, by implementing measures to change those factors within its control while working closely with government, the role of which is to create appropriate framework conditions. The contribution of policy is to ensure co-operation across government to build better work environments and to leverage other areas of government (horizontally and vertically) to address a range of factors external to the sector (migration, housing, care, community services) that may limit the capacity of the private sector to change.

Building resilience in the tourism economy requires addressing the new and existing fragilities in a systemic way. Tourism demand has bounced back strongly, showing strong resilience amid slow economic growth and geopolitical uncertainty. However, this masks new and existing underlying structural weaknesses on the supply side that continue to impede the resilience of the tourism economy.

Beyond enabling the sector to adapt and respond to crisis, a forward-looking systemic approach is needed to mitigate emerging risks and drive resilience in preparation for future shocks. There are also opportunities to learn from other sectors that like tourism are highly reliant on services and human capital, such as the health sector where some countries have taken steps since the pandemic to offer better working conditions and build the resilience of the health workforce (ILO, 2023[4]).

Understanding the complexities of the tourism workforce

Tourism is a hugely diverse sector, and this is reflected in the employment opportunities and nature of work on offer across the tourism workforce. This diversity is reflected in the range of sub-sectors that make up tourism (Figure 2.1) as well as its dispersal across different locations and the range of businesses, from micro and SMEs through to global corporations with diverse ownership and operating models. The emergence of the platform economy in tourism has added further complexity to the sector's operating environment and nature of tourism employment.

Building resilience in tourism requires understanding of the complexity and breadth of the tourism workforce and recognition that not all areas of the tourism sector are facing the same issues. For example, while both hospitality and aviation have faced an overall workforce deficit in recent years, the reasons are different, reflecting working conditions in the former and blockages caused by problems with the costs of training, accreditation and clearances in the latter.

Figure 2.1. Share of tourism jobs in subsectors of the tourism economy in 2019, selected countries

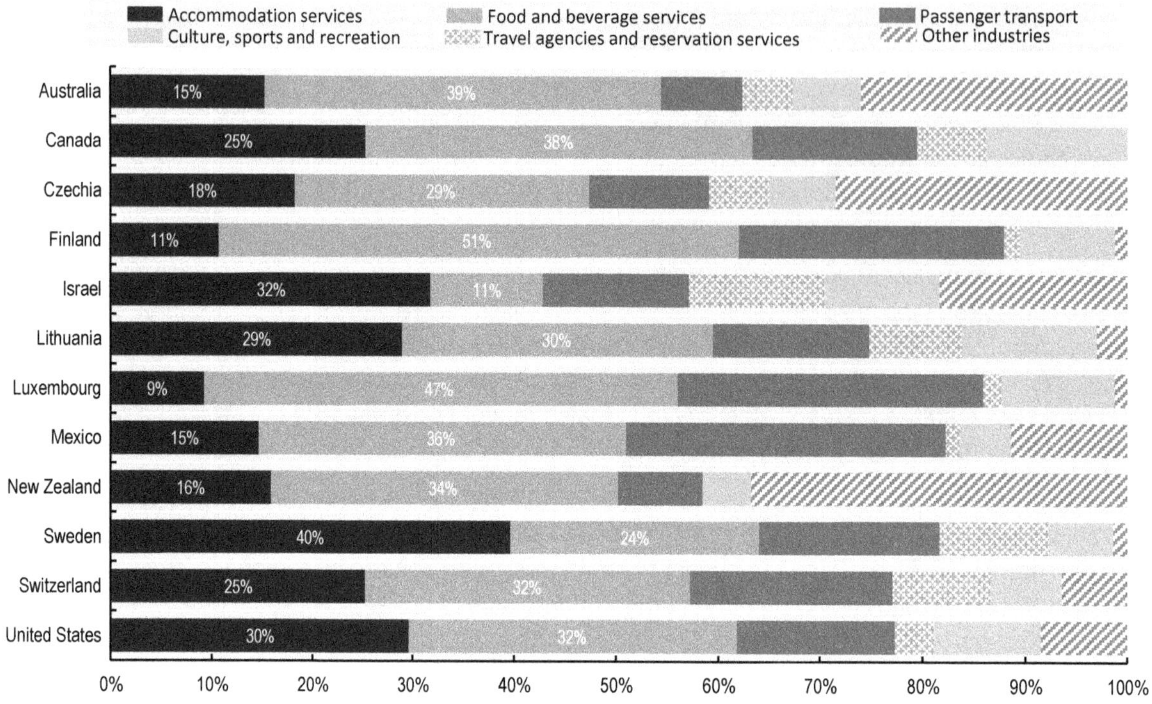

Note: The shares are shown for selected countries with available TSA data for all tourism sub-sectors in 2019. The base year 2019 was selected as it shows the breakdown of tourism employment uninterrupted by the impacts of COVID-19.
Source: OECD Tourism Statistics (Database).

StatLink https://stat.link/6ewz2d

The complexity of the sector creates significant diversity in employment opportunities and the wide range and level of skills required in the tourism workforce. Understanding the range of jobs within the sector and the different issues this brings for attracting, retaining and developing workers is an important first step to developing targeted solutions. There is no one-size-fits-all solution to workforce challenges in such a diverse and fragmented sector as tourism. However, one constant is that accommodation and food services jobs account for more than half of all tourism jobs, based on available TSA data from countries (Figure 2.1). It is also these sub-sectors that experience persistent workforce shortages across many countries – before, during, and post COVID-19 (Figure 2.2).

Supply and demand imbalances in labour markets are now easing, with unemployment remaining at or close to record lows across OECD countries (OECD, 2024[5]). Job vacancy rates, which measure the share of jobs in the economy or sector that are vacant, are falling across most countries. However, in 2023 the vacancy rates in the accommodation and food services industries were still higher than the rate for all industries, in general (Figure 2.2). While job pressures have continued to ease, job vacancy rates in the accommodation and food services industries remain higher than in 2019 and the shortage of skilled workers is a key challenge for accommodation businesses in the short term (Booking.com, Statista.com, 2024[6]). Addressing core issues in these sub-sectors to improve employment in the sector is therefore a common challenge across countries.

Figure 2.2. Job vacancy rates in tourism compared to the wider economy, selected countries

Job vacancies in accommodation and food services sectors compared to all industries in 2019 and 2023.

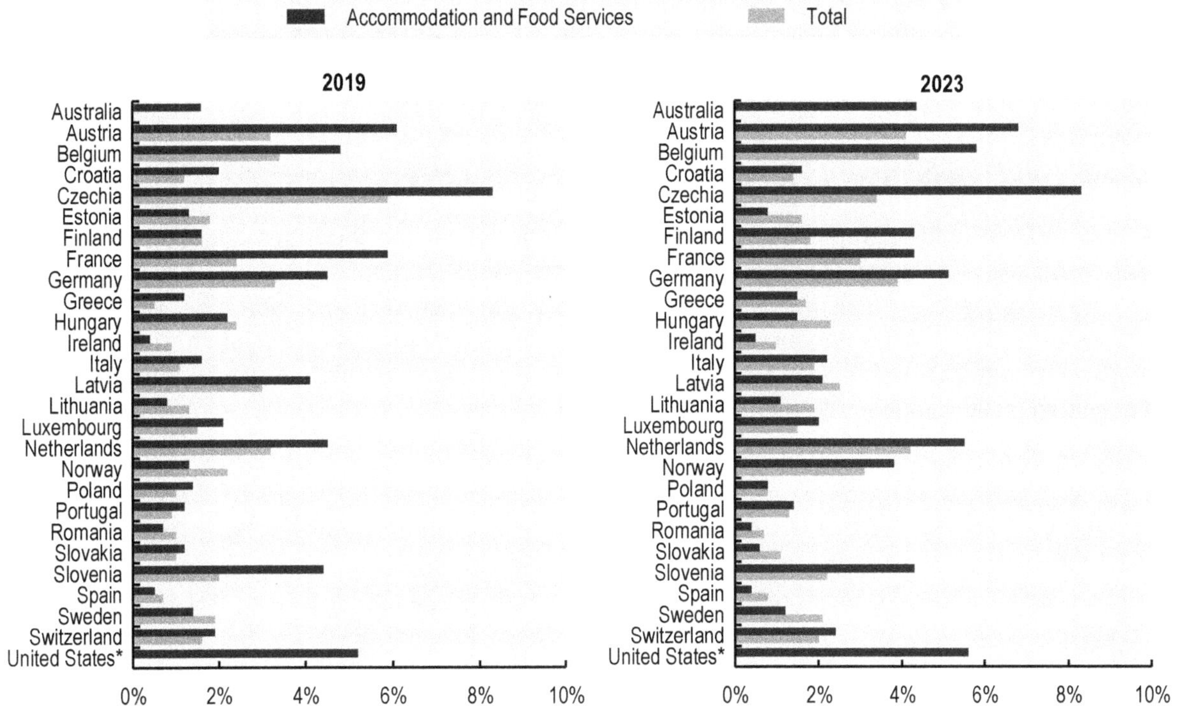

Note: Australian vacancy rates have been derived from available data. Time periods relate to Q4 of the stated year. *United States vacancy rates are seasonally adjusted.
Source: OECD calculations.

StatLink https://stat.link/v98ugi

Priority issues for a stronger tourism workforce

The extended closure and disruption caused by the COVID-19 pandemic led many workers to leave the tourism sector for job opportunities elsewhere in the economy and restricted worker mobility. The resulting labour shortages and skills gaps are not new for tourism, but have deepened since COVID-19, despite unprecedented support to maintain workers in jobs and as many workers who left the sector have not returned. The pandemic also exacerbated the early retirement of many workers in the sector and created disruptions in the education and migration pipelines for some countries. This comes on the back of historical shortages in the sector, even in countries such as Austria, where numerically the tourism workforce has recovered beyond its levels in 2019, the sector still faces labour shortages and skills gaps.

The wider economic and employment environment further exacerbated the situation. High demand for workers amid low rates of unemployment and labour shortages put tourism in direct competition with other sectors, while inflationary pressures disproportionately impacted lower paid workers. Attracting workers back to the sector to fill the existing shortages and retaining existing workers to prevent further gaps is therefore a priority for businesses and policymakers, and workforce shortages pose one of the biggest risks to making the system resilient, including for tourism (OECD, 2023[7]).

Evolving tourism and wider trends, including the green and digital transitions and ageing populations, are also changing the nature of work in the sector. This has highlighted the need to upskill and reskill the tourism workforce to adapt and respond to changing consumer and business needs. Ensuring that the workforce is equipped with the right skills to meet future needs is key to building a stronger tourism workforce. A strategic approach to skills development is necessary to create an attractive, productive and sustainable sector. Effective training and career development strategies, as well as worker satisfaction and retention, may positively impact the sectors productivity (ILO, 2022[8]).

Attracting and retaining tourism workers amid competitive labour markets

Attracting and retaining appropriately skilled workers to fill the labour shortages and skills gaps in the tourism workforce is a key priority for countries. The sector faces the challenge of a workforce deficit in a world where competition for skilled labour has intensified through a global race for talent (European Commission, 2023[9]). While labour shortages across the economy have eased in recent months, unemployment rates across the OECD remain close to historical lows (OECD, 2024[5]). Tourism therefore continues to directly compete with other sectors for workers and impacts the ability of the sector to attract workers.

Demand for flexible working conditions has also been accelerated since the pandemic, as workers across many sectors shifted by necessity to work remotely, highlighting the possibility of flexibility in many jobs. Based on evidence from the United Kingdom and Australia, the option to work from home on a regular basis is equivalent in value to workers to just over 20% of the average annual salary (OECD, 2023[10]). The challenge for tourism is how to respond to this desire for employment flexibility. The front-line nature of many tourism jobs may make it less desirable for those seeking such flexible working arrangements.

The loss of corporate knowledge and skills from workers leaving the tourism sector, either to move to other sectors or to exit the workforce, for example through early retirements, has in some cases led to inexperienced workers being promoted to fill shortages in higher level positions. This has amplified the mismatch in skills between the needs of the tourism sector and the available workforce, with consequences for maintaining the quality-of-service delivery.

Workforce competition extends beyond high skilled workers. In countries where temporary migrants are an important source of labour to fill the shortages in their tourism workforce, including international students and working holidaymakers, these pipelines and flows of workers were cut off during the pandemic. These workers are often more readily available to respond to seasonal surges in destinations during peak tourism seasons. Attracting these workers back to countries requires horizontal co-ordination across government, on visas and other issues.

Adapting to the changing needs and values of tourism workers

Post-pandemic, the employee value proposition has changed. Job seekers are increasingly looking to find more meaning in their work, with wellbeing and work-life balance now key differentiators. Competitive salaries and benefits remain important to workers but are now closely followed by the importance of work-life balance and job security (Randstad, 2022[11]). The traditional professional career model is increasingly being rejected in favour of work as a means to an economic and social end. Mobility within working lives has taken on added attraction and significance (European Commission, 2022[12]).

Adapting to more flexible ways of working can be difficult for the tourism sector, where service delivery models often require employees to interact with tourists in person, often at specific and sometimes antisocial hours. Many people entering or returning to the workforce are now opting for shorter hours and greater flexibility in their working conditions. Iceland has implemented pilot projects to shorten working hours, with over 2 500 workers moving from a 40-hour week to a 35- or 36-hour work week without a pay cut. This pilot demonstrated successful outcomes in both worker wellbeing and productivity. Similarly, a number of OECD countries have piloted a four-day working week of equivalent hours as an alternative to the traditional working week. Understanding and implementing these flexible working models will be a challenge to overcome for the tourism sector.

Rapid changes in the world of work are also associated with greater job instability across all sectors, with potential costs for companies, workers and society (OECD, 2023[10]). Across the OECD, the average length of a job held by the same worker declined by around nine months between 2012 and 2019, with the main reasons for switching jobs being low pay, feeling undervalued and lack of advancement (OECD, 2023[10]). These are core issues commonly linked to tourism jobs and can have detrimental impacts for the retention of workers.

Understanding the changing workforce environment, especially in relation to the expectations of young people entering the workforce, has led organisations to address and seek to change their workplace cultures in order to be in tune with what their existing and future employees are looking for. To address cultural issues after the pandemic, Intercontinental Hotel Group has focused on lifestyle, flexibility and wellbeing of a diverse workforce, particularly celebrating inclusion of diversity within their teams (Box 2.1).

Box 2.1. Creating an inclusive work culture at the Intercontinental Hotel Group

Intercontinental Hotels Group's (IHG) response to a challenging environment for recruitment has been to focus on creating an organisational culture that is more aligned with the expectations of the post-pandemic labour market, respecting individual needs with a focus on employee wellbeing.

In 2022, IHG launched myWellbeing, a framework to support employees across a range of important areas, including their health, lifestyle and workplace. The myWellbeing resources include an employee wellbeing handbook, wellbeing guidelines for people managers and financial education materials, designed to provide a holistic wellbeing offering, which employees can access quickly and easily.

In response to the global shift to hybrid working, IHG also took steps to create more flexible workspaces to allow employees to adopt a balance of remote and office working where practical. The 'myFlex' HR system allows employees active under the system to self-schedule their own hours at any IHG managed hotel in Australia. Employees can work as and when they want while being paid under the full terms and benefits. The new highly flexible arrangements are an effort to appeal to new and experienced workers across the accommodation and hospitality landscape and address a critical skills shortage.

Harnessing the green and digital transitions in tourism

Many aspects of contemporary tourism are shaped by the growing and transforming influence of technology. Technology drives the tourism experience for guests from searching for the initial idea, travel planning, engagement with providers and operators, financial transactions, the sharing of experiences and, increasingly, service delivery. The tourism sector is rapidly evolving due to all aspects of this digital transformation. The platform economy for example is transforming the way work is organised and performed, with new challenges emerging in ensuring that workers on platforms have access to decent work (ILO, 2024[13]). Customers of all generations now expect a seamless experience with the technology with which they interact and a consequent high level of digital maturity from service providers.

The rapid development of generative Artificial Intelligence (AI) and robotisation in the world of work and the wider digitalisation of the economy spur both innovation and productivity growth, but also changes the way that work, and production, are organised, creating in turn challenges for jobs and skills. While the adoption of AI is still relatively low, rapid progress including with generative AI, falling costs and the increasing availability of workers with AI skills suggest that OECD countries may be on the brink of an AI revolution (OECD, 2023[14]). This has important repercussions for work in the tourism sector.

Tourism is traditionally a labour-intensive sector and the digital transformation in tourism creates opportunities and challenges for the workforce. Digitalisation has already contributed to job displacement in tourism through automation and online transactions in areas such as reservations and check-in for airlines and hotels. Such trends will continue to gather pace. At the same time, some areas of tourism work may remain relatively immune to the impacts of digitalisation in the short- to medium-term, given the customer-facing nature of service delivery and centrality of people-to-people interactions as part of the tourism experience.

Small businesses, which make up the majority of operators in global tourism, face significant challenges in availing of and adopting digital transformation due to costs, budget constraints, labour shortages and complexity in implementation. Tourism SMEs will need to invest in their digitalisation to thrive in the future. This means small tourism business owners and employees need adequate skills and knowledge to take advantage of these digital tools, which can sometimes seem out of reach for SMEs.

Technological solutions can make an important contribution to a green transition in the workplace. However, digital transition also affords challenges and opportunities in the workplace as companies adopt robotisation and harness the power of AI in the delivery of tourism products, services and experiences. There is also a need for tourism to adjust to new, greener practices to comply with net-zero targets, and enabling businesses to transition towards a greener future requires new skills sets at all levels within organisations (OECD, 2023[15]).

In practical terms, the green transition will require tourism employees to upskill to understand and comply with new sustainable standards within the sector in areas such as energy use, food standards and waste management. The availability of the right skills paves the way for the transition to carbon-neutral, environmentally sustainable and socially inclusive economies and decent work (ILO, 2022[16]). This transition has implications for who is recruited into the sector, the pre-entry education and training they receive and for the upskilling needs of employees within the sector. The transition is therefore conditional on investment in training to develop skills to meet new requirements and avoid skills mismatches, particularly for smaller businesses in tourism. Forward-looking skills strategies are necessary to train young people and reskill the current tourism workforce to meet the skills needs of the new jobs generated in the transition process.

The green and digital transitions present challenges, but also opportunities for the tourism workforce. Digital technologies like AI can automate repetitive tasks that are often seen as unattractive and low paid, increasing productivity. This could lead to a redistribution of some work in the sector towards more creative and high-skilled jobs, which can in turn help to raise the average wages and make the sector more attractive. Striking the balance between increased innovation and productivity while maintaining human-centred experiences will be an ongoing challenge for the tourism sector. Coherent policies, together with social dialogue, have an important role to play in promoting a just transition (OECD, 2022[17]).

Understanding external structural factors impacting the workforce

Tourism's workforce challenges and opportunities do not exist in isolation and are not exclusively tourism issues. There is a complex inter-relationship between tourism employment and the wider economic and societal ecosystem with which the sector interacts. The resilience of tourism employment is affected by a wider range of locational, structural and infrastructure policies, practices and related factors over which tourism policymakers and wider sector interests may have limited influence.

Tourism activity often takes place in seasonal or remote locations, which may have limited other economic opportunities. Housing availability and affordability is an important issue, for example. The cumulative impacts of successive crises significantly increased the cost of living while real wages remained stagnant. Even before the COVID-19 crisis, house prices had been increasing dramatically in OECD countries, especially for renters, and the supply of affordable housing has failed to meet demand (OECD, 2024[18]).

The pipeline of resources to increase housing stocks also experienced blockages through the pandemic slowing construction. The expansion of short-term rentals has also created increased pressure on housing availability and affordability during peak season in some destinations, a time when the need for housing workers is greatest.

Tourism destinations developed to cater solely to the needs of tourists may miss the essential community services required to attract and retain a stable workforce. Some key considerations can include: public transport appropriate to the needs of work shifts; access to education and health care for dependents; childcare that suits the needs of tourism worker shift patterns as well as community infrastructure, more generally, to give tourism workers opportunities to participate fully in community life. The impact of tourism in communities often sees increases in the cost of living, making it more difficult for local residents. Integrating tourism into wider economic and regional development plans and ensuring that policymakers consider the needs of people and the community when implementing new programmes is important to address these issues.

Tackling tourism workforce issues for a more resilient tourism economy

Creating policies for a more resilient tourism economy requires addressing the current weaknesses, while also anticipating the future needs of the sector. Long-standing workforce issues within the sector have been exacerbated by the recent disruptions, compounding the challenges for the tourism sector to attract and retain workers in tight labour markets. While there is pressing need to address these issues in the short term, this should be done within the frame of longer-term changes impacting the workforce.

Immediate and short-term actions have relied on retaining the existing force and attracting new workers into the sector to fill shortages. Some countries, like Australia, Colombia and Peru, have explored strategies with older workers or people underrepresented in the workforce including women, youth, culturally diverse and indigenous workers. Australia for example has introduced a Work Bonus to increase earning potential of pensioners before impacting their income support, to help address worker demand and provide relief from the cost-of-living crisis (Box 2.2). The tourism sector has also provided employment opportunities for the influx of refugees, mainly women, from Ukraine following Russia's invasion, including in Estonia and Poland. Other initiatives included positioning tourism as a vehicle for the empowerment of women. Tourism is a prioritised sector under Mexico's Gender Parity Initiative, a public and private sector initiative to identify and reduce barriers preventing women from accessing job opportunities on equal terms.

Identifying the broader trends and what they could mean for the tourism sector, specifically the workforce, will help to better shape initiatives that are prepared for future challenges and shocks, helping to build resilience within the system. Megatrends including climate, demographic and technological change have emerged and have the potential to profoundly transform societies in the coming decades (OECD, 2023[19]). For example, shifting consumer trends in tourism, like nature tourism and digital nomads, could change the type of workers that are needed in the sector, while a greater dispersal of tourists out of popular destinations could require the workforce to live in different areas, which could require the development of new community services and infrastructure.

The private sector has a key role to play in tackling workforce issues, with government working to ensure that the right policy and regulatory frameworks are in place to support businesses, including through the education pipeline. At the same time, the trend towards values-driven work, work-life balance and wellbeing means the role of community has become increasingly important in workforce policy considerations. Continuing the good collaborative frameworks established through the COVID-19 pandemic can provide greater communication, consultation and co-ordination within government and with the private sector and education providers to create processes for smoother and well-established extensive collaboration and co-ordinated action.

Box 2.2. Leveraging economy-wide scheme for older workers for tourism vacancies in Australia

Australia identified older workers as an untapped market to address workforce shortages in the tourism sector. In September 2023, there were 90 500 less workers in the sector than in December 2019. With years of knowledge and skill to offer employers, older workers can help address the demand for workers while obtaining relief from the cost-of-living crisis. A Work Bonus incentive was introduced to increase workforce participation and provided the opportunity for pensioners to earn an additional AUD 4 000 from employment income between 1 December 2022 and 31 December 2023 before income support payments.

Implemented by the Department of Employment and Workplace Relations and the Department of Social Services, these benefits were automatically credited to eligible pensioners. This reform was not limited to tourism vacancies, but the Tourism sector has benefited significantly from this economy-wide initiative, experiencing a yearly increase of 85 600 employees as of September 2023. From 1 January 2024, all new eligible entrants to Work Bonus can earn an additional AUD 4 000 (previously AUD 0) in employment income with additional income maximum of AUD 11 800 (previously AUD 7 800).

Improving job conditions to promote a strong and skilled tourism workforce

Pay, working conditions and job quality are widely recognised issues in many parts of the tourism sector, and are key contributing factors in the long-standing skills gaps, labour shortages and high turnover rates experienced by tourism businesses in many countries. Addressing these at a policy and, where appropriate, regulatory level offers one route to change, with outcomes that can benefit attraction and retention of employees and ultimately contribute to the resilience of tourism businesses (ILO, 2017[20]).

A longstanding approach has been policy actions to promote tourism jobs while positioning the sector as a dynamic place to work and build a career to help attract talented youth workers, and similar initiatives are also being used post-pandemic. As part of France's Destination Plan launched in 2022 to strengthen the attractiveness of the tourism sector, the Tourism Careers Week initiative aims to raise awareness of tourism training and professions, promote opportunities, and attract young people and job seekers to the sector. A third edition is planned, following the edition held in 2024 which mobilised public and private stakeholders from the education and training sector at national and sub-national level to organise more than 2 300 events across the country. This included an event sponsored by Michelin-starred chef Mory Sacko, who is also an Ambassador for the French President's Make it Iconic, Choose France initiative. National campaigns have also recently been launched in Austria and Slovenia to promote careers and professions in tourism to raise the profile of hospitality and tourism professions and enhance enrolments in tourism-related education programmes.

Putting worker welfare and motivations at the forefront has become a priority to address working conditions. Promoting tourism as a place for rewarding work and careers can only succeed if the negative realities of the sector are addressed. Supporting businesses to enhance the attractiveness of the industry to prospective employees is a strategy employed by Fáilte Ireland's Employer Excellence Programme (Box 2.3).

Box 2.3. Promoting better tourism employment practices in Ireland

The national tourism development agency Fáilte Ireland created the Employer Excellence Programme to address longstanding challenges related to staff attraction and retention in the tourism sector. The Programme aims to address this by supporting tourism businesses to attract talent, drive retention, and embed a culture of quality employment practices in the sector and position the tourism and hospitality sectors as rewarding and appealing places to work.

Launched in 2022, the Programme spotlights employers over three years to profile the sector as a rewarding and attractive place to work to prospective employees. The key components of the programme are:

- A confidential employee survey and actionable insights provided by an expert in employee engagement.
- Online training in the fundamentals of people and performance management.
- Providing support to develop and implement an action plan to improve employee engagement and build the appeal of the workplace.
- Creating marketing materials to promote businesses as an Excellent Employer.
- Providing access to continuous improvement supports.

In its first year, the Programme saw 225 businesses registered and 2 100 managers completed the training. Following this positive experience, the focus is now moving to support smaller businesses with less than 20 employees in 2024.

The often unstable, irregular, and seasonal nature of tourism work remains a barrier for long-term employment in the sector. Measures to extend seasons through marketing and new product innovation can help to safeguard employment in tourism and create more stable, long-term positions in the sector, to the benefit of individuals, their employers and their communities. This is particularly important in highly seasonal destinations such as mountain and coastal destinations seeking to diversify their offer to extend the tourism season, for example through events and festivals or developing the meetings, incentives, conferences and events (MICE) market activities.

A core priority of Croatia's Sustainable Tourism Development Strategy 2030 is to extend the season through the development of tourism products with high added value and through investments in public tourist infrastructure and promotion, including through targeting domestic tourism. One key aim of the Strategy adopted in 2023 is to help reduce the number of tourism workers on short fixed-term contracts.

Modifying the tourism offer to extend the season is not viable for all destinations, and as such more creative measures are being considered. France developed a government-led 3-year plan to support and train seasonal tourism workers between 2023 and 2025 in response to raising concerns in recruiting tourism workers, especially in the lead up to the 2024 Paris Olympic Games. As part of this plan France is establishing a network of centres of excellence for training, increasing services to assist seasonal workers in their personal, administrative, and professional lives, and to offering housing solutions to meet their accommodation needs. The French Government will also work to develop local partnerships with companies interested in using or sharing the skills of seasonal workers to retain seasonal workers throughout the year.

In Finland, tourism employers have developed well-functioning co-operation between businesses operating in different high seasons to offer year-round or longer-term employment and maintain their skilled workforce. For example, employees working in a tourism safari company for the winter season have the opportunity to transfer to a hotel or a restaurant in the same location for the shoulder seasons and summer season. Similarly, the TUI Group is exploring opportunities for employee sharing across its business functions to help address seasonality issues and diversify the skills of employees. Potential exists to expand practices such as these, which remain limited in the sector.

Employee benefits, labour protections and stable employment are an ongoing area for government intervention to address structural weaknesses in the tourism workforce. Türkiye has put in place mechanisms to ensure local entrepreneurs operating SMEs in tourism comply with international labour standards and regulations ensuring a respectful, safe, and secure working environment that upholds the rights of workers. Businesses are further supported to understand and address issues and expectations related to salary levels, working conditions, and job security through employee satisfaction surveys, aiming to create a fair and respectful work environment.

The introduction of competitive collective bargaining agreements or competitive minimum wages are possible mechanisms to improve employee benefits. In Slovenia, negotiations with the trade union for tourism employees have led to an agreement on the minimum annual leave allowance and the setting of a basic minimum salary. However, it is also important to consider the impact of mandating higher wages, especially where business and labour costs are already relatively high, and the cost of living and doing business has been negatively impacted by recent crises. Collective agreements can help tourism businesses and workers find tailored and ad hoc solutions to fairly share the cost of inflation and avoid a wage-price spiral (OECD, 2022[21]).

Decent wages are central to economic and social development and to advance social justice. The idea of a living wage, which is a wage that provides workers and their families with enough income to live on at some level considered adequate, has experienced a resurgence of popularity in recent years. While a living wage is not a silver bullet to in-work poverty, which in OECD countries is often the result of underemployment rather than low pay, living wages can be useful in establishing a norm of fair pay and providing valuable information on the cost of living that firms and social partners may embed in their wage-setting processes, including in tourism (OECD, 2023[22]). In March 2024, the ILO Governing Body endorsed an agreement reached at a Meeting of Experts on the issue of the living wage and called on the ILO to continue to provide support to governments and social partners toward strengthening wage-setting processes and activities related to living wages (ILO, 2024[23]).

Individual initiatives help to improve conditions for tourism workers, but a suite of actions may be required to build a strong and stable workforce. New Zealand launched a Better Work Action Plan in 2023 which featured 14 initiatives to address key systemic issues facing the workforce including demand fluctuations, pay and conditions, firm maturity and scale and the current and future skills gap. The Plan aimed to enhance employment practices; improve the education and training system for tourism; provide for more consistent and stable employment in an industry where there is seasonality of work; improve cultural competency to build more diverse and inclusive workplaces; lift technology uptake and innovation; and showcase career pathways and people in tourism.

Promoting digital uptake to ease tourism workforce pressures

The evolution and application of new technologies are profoundly changing the way people live, work, travel and do business. It is also transforming and reshaping tourism, with implications for the nature and organisation of work in the sector. More consideration is needed on how new technologies can be adopted to improve productivity and working conditions in the tourism sector (e.g. AI, virtual reality, robotisation), and the consequences and impacts on the tourism workforce.

Rapid developments with AI in particular have the potential to drive significant further changes to work and productivity (OECD, 2023[14]). The resulting opportunities present challenges to the level playing field, including a growing gap between tech-driven and globally connected tourism businesses and traditional micro and small businesses, as well as between urban and regional destinations. Automation powered by customer data, machine learning and generative AI risks widening the technology gap for SMEs.

Embracing digitalisation throughout the tourism ecosystem is also key to building resilience, including through investing in human capital and skills to retain and develop a skilled workforce (OECD, 2021[24]). It will in turn increase demand for skills that support the development and application of such technologies by tourism businesses. Responding to the ever-increasing pace of technological advancement will require tourism workers to develop a wide range of skills, including digital skills which should interface with soft, technical and hard skills in formal and informal training (OECD, 2023[25]). Continued changes in tourism consumption patterns will have implications for experience delivery, new workplaces/spaces and the skills required. Ensuring that the workforce is equipped with the right skills to meet future needs will require working closely with the industry, including workers' and employers' organisations, and education providers.

Technology-driven innovation in tourism is led by the private sector. Airlines, travel intermediaries, tour operators and large accommodation providers have long been at the forefront of adopting new technologies in the sector, often revolutionising the interface between the consumer and service provider. Tourism providers have demonstrated innovation in the technological solutions to personalise experiences for their guests. Hilton Hotels for example has invested in digital check-in and keyless entry systems to streamline the guest experience while improving guest satisfaction scores.

The digital transformation also provides opportunities for small businesses to address their current workforce shortages. A small rural hotel in Scotland, Brambles of Inverary, invested in digital technology to maintain and improve the quality and efficiency of service delivery when faced with ongoing recruitment difficulties (Box 2.4).

For many tourism SMEs and business owners, the opportunities that digital tools present are often unknown or seem out of reach. There is a need to establish support programmes to inform and engage effectively with eligible tourism SMEs and integrate their staff development with digital uptake. The Integration and Interface Support for Tourism Sector Software initiative in Estonia looks to assist in the digitalisation and automation of work processes for tourism service providers. It supports the adoption of software, such as new resource management software which integrates with the cash register system and accounting software.

Countries are now working on policy documents and tools to support tourism stakeholders, as well as additional support in data management, the use of big data, and AI. Luxembourg's Tourism Strategy aims to drive digitalisation of the sector, including by encouraging investment and attracting qualified workers into the sector. Romania's Competences for Competitiveness Project meanwhile aims to improve the digital skills of 380 employees across the tourism and hospitality industries in specific regions to increase their professional capacities and make them more adaptable to changing sectoral needs.

Box 2.4. Using technology to address workforce shortages in a small rural hotel in Scotland

In response to the severe workforce shortages experienced in the wake of the COVID-19 pandemic, Brambles of Inveraray in Scotland have turned to digital solutions to reduce the burden on existing staff. As a small business located in a remote and highly seasonal destination, the inability to attract and retain an adequate workforce had led to concerns about the viability of the business. The goal has been to reduce labour needs by digitising and automating, without distorting the positive and organic customer experience tourists expect.

The owners, who have a background in IT and data analytics, explored alternative ways to reduce the labour need, by slowly introducing technology to match requirements of customers and staff. To date several initiatives have been implemented, including:

- QR code food and drinks ordering – introduced as an alternative to the traditional ordering style, this has become popular with those who are more digitally minded or groups who like to pay separately. It takes pressure off wait staff and there is an aim to have at least 30% of guests use this method to order.
- Revenue management app – app automates the changing of room prices to meet demand.
- Accounting and financial apps – financial apps can sync with traditional accounting systems and when working alongside an accountant takes the burden out of filing and posting administrative paperwork.
- Wellbeing apps for employees – the promotion of employee wellbeing has been a core focus. Some wellbeing apps include an Employee Assistance Program and Virtual GP and when used alongside HR support and 'coffee catchups' with management have been beneficial.

There are many existing automated systems which are yet to be adapted for a small business model. The business owners expect that when AI becomes more common place (and cheaper) there will be a positive place for it in a smaller businesses.

Better aligning training with the needs of the tourism workplace

Promoting the acquisition of skills, competencies and qualifications for tourism workers throughout their working lives is at the heart of a human-centred approach to crisis recovery and the future of work (ILO, 2022[8]). For example, skills development and lifelong learning can help workers find new jobs, develop the necessary skills for the digitalisation and greening of the sector and build resilience into long-term recovery strategies. To facilitate a flexible and future-oriented approach to emerging occupational skills, Canada has implemented a Future Skills Framework to support tourism education (Box 2.5).

A focus on education and training for tourism at all levels features in the post-pandemic responses of many countries. Many introduced free online training platforms to help tourism employees to upskill through shutdowns, which they have continued to develop and adapt.

Costa Rica launched a free virtual training platform, ICT CAPACITA, to improve workforce participation in the tourism sector through the pandemic. Post-pandemic, the platform continues to support tourism entrepreneurs and businesses on tourism resilience and sustainability issues such as access to sustainable finance and certification. Luxembourg launched the Tourism Academy platform to centralise vocational training related to the tourism sector. Available on the Luxembourg Travel website, it provides a collection of online resources on the latest communication and digital marketing techniques, and how to put these into use for tourism professionals.

Box 2.5. Framework to address future tourism skills and labour challenges in Canada

Canada's Future Skills Framework is designed to strengthen the tourism sector and address the skills and labour challenges. Through a library of competency elements that are easily updated to adapt to the increasing pace of change within today's workplace, the Framework aims to eliminate costly and time-consuming processes associated with updating occupational skills on a job-by-job basis. The Framework provides tourism stakeholders with a better way to align the skills of individuals in the Canadian labour market, minimising gaps and mismatches. It is being informed by ongoing feedback to ensure the Future Skills Competency Framework will best meet the needs of potential users. Canada is actively engaging with employers, Indigenous tourism business representatives and hospitality students nearing the end of their studies to inform this important discussion. It provides a complete picture of the entire sector, making it easier to collect, analyse, and map information.

As part of the recovery from COVID-19, Greece implemented a programme for the upskilling and reskilling of the tourism workforce, funded by the EU's Recovery and Resilience Facility. The programme delivered brief vocational programmes to equip the workforce with the skills needed in the labour market in line with the green and digital transition. Training vouchers to support participation in the programme are expected to be issued to 18 000 beneficiaries by 2025. Greece also announced the creation of the country's first tourism academy in 2023, to offer contemporary tourism education, monitor the needs of the tourism market, and improve employment opportunities in the sector under government supervision.

Other initiatives focus on building a pipeline of workers and supporting students and young people to transition from formal education to the workplace. Türkiye has restructured the education of tourism vocational high schools to provide practical training in tourism facilities in line with the needs of the sector. Similarly, in Canada the tourism sector is included in the Student Work Placement Programme, which has been introduced to create quality work-integrated learning opportunities for students.

Slovenia's strategic Development Partnership for Innovation in Tourism implements a special programme to promote the enrolment of young people in vocational, secondary, and higher education programmes for hospitality and tourism. The programme activities are aimed at young people who are thinking about further education, upskilling, or reskilling as well as their parents, teachers, and school counselling services.

Australia introduced the First Nations Tourism Mentoring Programme, which matches First Nations businesses with skilled and experienced mentors. This programme is designed to support mentees to grow their tourism businesses and achieve their business goals while mentees will have access to expert advice, tailored learning, and culturally respectful industry specialists.

Skills mismatches remain a critical issue for the sector, despite the opportunities for education and learning. Curricula need to keep pace with and meet the ongoing needs of the sector, considering the employing foresight to pre-empt the skills needs in the sector when the student enters the workplace. Building closer linkages between the world of work and educational and training institutions, and more closely incorporating education and training into the workforce system can complement on-the-job learning, including through internships and close collaboration with the private sector in the development and delivery of the curriculum. As part of the Agenda for Tourism Professions, Portugal is implementing the International Tourism Academy which will integrate higher education, vocational education, research and development, and entrepreneurship. Les Roches International School of Hotel Management collaborates with the private sector to provide master classes that inform students about current trends and needs of the sector in line with topics covered in the curriculum.

The changing needs of the sector have seen much consideration given to the curricula of tourism and hospitality training institutions, with many countries undertaking reviews of their existing education systems. Morocco has implemented a training programme aimed at middle managers in the tourism sector, with a new public-private partnership model for vocational training management. This includes efforts to reposition the International Higher Institute of Tourism in Tangier as a reference centre for hotel and tourism management and leading business school, with the creation of six new competency-based programmes. Another vocational training institute, the Ouarzazate Institute, has created four new programmes and adapted one programme also using a competency-based approach. In Germany, the dual vocational education system which comprises training in the vocational school with on-the-job training in the business has proved to be effective over time. To further enhance the attractiveness of this kind of training to prospective students and workers, seven new or updated hospitality professions containing adapted training regulations have been created.

At European level, the EU Pact for Skills in Tourism sets a vision to address current and future challenges by 2030 (Box 2.6). At international level, the UN Tourism Academy Partnership in Education initiative fosters partnerships with educational institutions to develop tailored training programmes. The ILO e-learning module on social justice in rural areas through decent jobs in tourism is part of an online course that provides an opportunity to learn about innovative approaches, tools and methods for promoting decent work and advancing social justice in the rural economy. The Brazil G20 Presidency and the Italy G7 Presidency have also put human capital and skills issues in tourism as priority issues in the respective workstreams in 2024, building on outcomes from the India and Indonesia G20 Presidencies.

Box 2.6. Addressing the future skills needs of tourism across Europe

The EU Pact for Skills in Tourism was implemented as a recovery strategy to implement an upskilling and reskilling framework, maximising the potential of the tourism sector, building resilience and meeting the challenges of the green and digital transition. Launched in 2021, under the broader EU Pact for Skills initiative, the tourism initiative sets a vision of 12 objectives and indicators, to be achieved by 2030 across Europe through a close co-operation between social partners, training and education system, and public authorities. Some of the key objectives include to:

- Improve and extend the skills of the full tourism workforce
- Raise awareness of and access to training for all tourism services
- Provide training and education for 10% of the tourism workforce each year between 2022 and 2030 to tackle the skills gaps in the tourism ecosystem both for the current workforce and new entrants.
- Create more hands-on learning and training through blended concepts
- Increase training activities and participation by 40% of the employed workforce and 80% of the unemployed workforce by 2025
- Detect new and emerging skills through data mining and provide training opportunities to avoid gaps
- Retain current workers and attract new employees to work in tourism
- Develop more stable and better paid contracts due to higher qualification.

Promoting private sector-led workforce initiatives

Private sector-led initiatives provide opportunities to target workforce issues at a more granular level, taking into account the issues on the ground and allowing for tailored solutions. However, government intervention can help to improve operating conditions and leverage existing private sector programmes to make them more accessible across the sector, particularly for SMEs. Addressing structural issues in the tourism workforce through private-public co-operation can help to ensure local implementation, ongoing feedback and adaption of existing initiatives.

International hotel chains and tour operators have taken steps to create better environments by offering support for families and the physical and emotional well-being of workers. While these large businesses have greater capacity to provide these programmes, they provide practical examples of initiatives that could be leveraged for the sector more widely. For example, Marriott provides a comprehensive benefits package to its employees, including healthcare coverage, retirement savings plans, employee assistance programmes, travel discounts and employee well-being support. The TUI Group has sought employee feedback and suggestions on how things can be better done from the ground rather than the head offices and to better understand the best package of benefits for their candidates.

Tourism industry associations can provide opportunities for the private sector to combine resources to tackle existing workforce issues through industry-led initiatives. Restaurants Canada published information for their members on issues including ensuring a positive and inclusive workforce.

Public-private partnerships provide opportunities to target support while leveraging the knowledge of the sector. For example, Switzerland's hotel and catering association, GastroSuisse, launched a five-point plan in 2023 to address workforce shortages by better utilising the domestic workforce. The Swiss Government is providing financial assistance to implement this private sector-led initiative (Box 2.7).

In the United Kingdom, a Hospitality and Tourism Skills Board was set up in 2021 as part of the Hospitality Strategy: Reopening, Recovery, Resilience. The Board's aim is to pursue a co-ordinated, proactive, employer-led approach to recruitment, retention and upskilling, including by developing innovative new recruitment campaigns. The Board is drawn from senior operators and business leaders from across hospitality, tourism and travel, including SMEs.

Box 2.7. Governmental support for a private sector-led initiative in Switzerland

In 2023, GastroSuisse launched a 5-point plan to create more skilled workers in the hospitality sector and better utilise the domestic labour potential. This was formulated in direct response to skills shortages and perceived failures in the existing apprenticeship system, with the benefits recognised by the Swiss Government who have provided additional financial and operational support. The integrated and long-term programme includes:

- Promotion of the image of the industry and the profession.
- Targeted training of entrepreneurs.
- Succession.
- Qualifications for people in professional retraining.
- Increase the attractiveness of working conditions.

The strengths of the initiative are the long-term perspective, bundling of measures, involvement of the companies, adaptability, and innovation and integration of existing programmes that aim to improve working conditions and the perception of the industry. GastroSuisse intends to attract 250 businesses to participate in the training courses and 50 businesses to test the current working conditions in the sector. In May 2024, the project was named "Avanti!" to emphasise the dynamic and future-oriented nature of the measures.

Iceland provides funding for the Tourism Skill Center, with the primary goal of enhancing competence and quality within the Icelandic tourism sector. In collaboration with the Tourism Skill Center, the Icelandic Tourist Board launched a new website in 2023 called "Good to Know." This website serves as an informative hub for the tourism workforce, offering a variety of information and facts about Iceland and the

Icelandic tourism sector. In 2022, the Innovation – Lighthouse Funding in Austria sought innovative projects on new employment models and employee concepts in tourism to address continued workforce challenges for both tourism businesses and destinations. Six innovative projects were selected by a jury of experts, with the winning projects receiving a total of approximately EU 1 million from federal tourism funding and the European Fund for Rural Development.

Adopting a strategic and integrated policy approach to tourism workforce issues

Tourism is a complex sector that spans across many sub-sectors, meaning policy levers often sit beyond tourism policymakers. In the case of the workforce, regulation and policy decisions often reside within labour or employment ministries. Creating tailored policies for the tourism workforce therefore requires co-operation across ministries. However, in many cases, labour laws will be addressed through whole of government actions, or targeted actions with specific subsectors of the tourism sector.

Recognition of the significance of employment for the tourism sector, regional development and socio-cultural ecosystems is evident through the preparation of free-standing tourism workforce analysis and strategies that sit alongside more general tourism strategies and plans. Australia's Visitor Economy Workforce and Skills Interim Action Plan 2023-24 focuses on priorities related to tourism workforce capability by addressing structural challenges and domestic and international workforce supply issues, improving the skills and capability of the tourism workforce and promoting the sector as a career of choice. Across each of the key priorities, the action plan considers opportunities for progress and takes stock of the existing national and state actions and initiatives from the private sector. It includes tourism workforce outcomes like improving the understanding of structural trends or increasing opportunities to enter the sector through internships or industry placements which are underpinned by potential measures.

In Canada, a report on Barriers to Employment and Skills Mismatches examines the key workforce challenges facing the sector in the recovery from COVID-19 including the shift to more flexible work, the declining youth labour market and the need for specialised training for most tourism occupations. It also considers a need to address structural challenges in the tourism workforce, including seasonal employment, immigration constraints and regional development and planning factors such as housing, transportation, and education (Tourism HR Canada, 2022[26]).

The UK's Hospitality Workforce Strategy: Fixing the Crisis provides a framework for collaborative action across the sector and considers the ongoing needs of the sector related to recruitment, skills and training, the sectors image, peoples working lives as well as the infrastructure needed to support the workforce. The Strategy is based on a partnership approach between industry bodies, training and employment stakeholders and the government. Chile's Human Capital Strategic Plan 2023-26 brings together actors from the tourism, hotel and gastronomy sectors to address tourism workforce issues in an integrated approach.

Tourism workforce also needs to be situated within wider strategic thinking and workforce planning. The Morocco Roadmap for Tourism 2023-26 aims to reposition tourism as a key sector in the national economy, with the inclusion of specific tourism employment creation targets, strengthening of human capital across the sector and offering better prospects and careers for young people. Meanwhile, in Colombia and Slovenia the economy-wide national workforce strategies highlight the potential of tourism employment to act as a vehicle for social, political, economic transformation and inclusion.

Addressing tourism workforce issues has also become a more prominent focus in national tourism strategies. There is a growing understanding of the importance of a strong tourism workforce to enable sustainable and resilient development of the tourism sector. Including the tourism workforce as a part of a national approach to tourism development provides opportunities to address structural weaknesses within the wider context but also signals the importance of the workforce to the sector. This can help to bring better recognition to the issues the tourism sector is facing that might be missed in national labour force approaches. Within these national tourism strategies, the tourism workforce is not always a standalone pillar, but often included as a clear goal or action (Box 2.8).

The role of government is to create good framework conditions for education and gainful employment, and may require action on issues beyond the tourism system that impact the tourism workforce. This includes a lack of affordable transport and housing in popular tourism destinations, the need for amenities like childcare to be available during tourism working hours and facilitating the availability of migrant workers. Addressing these issues may require action at national level, but some issues may also be addressed at the local level. In France, for example, the coastal destination of La Baule has undertaken several initiatives to meet the housing needs of seasonal workers. During the 2023 summer season, a former municipal campsite was converted into 80 residences dedicated to seasonal workers while a campaign to connect homeowners and seasonal workers secured housing for a further 32 employees, while units have also been reserved for tourism workers in new social housing projects. More needs to be done to ensure that the needs of tourism workers are integrated into wider government policy setting.

Box 2.8. Prioritisation of workforce in national tourism strategies - selected countries

Addressing tourism workforce issues is a key area of focus to support the strategic development of tourism. Many countries have integrated workforce issues into their national tourism strategies, with a focus on addressing tourism labour and skills shortages as part of a broader approach to tourism development. Targeted actions related to the workforce include:

Malta: The Malta Tourism Strategy 2021-30 aims to strengthen human capital and improve the sector's attractiveness by enhancing continuous training opportunities and improving wage attractiveness relative to competing sectors. To inform this, a survey to understand the skills needs and gaps and perceptions of workers and a campaign to shift the views of potential new workers was undertaken in 2023.

Norway: The National Tourism Strategy 2030 aims to ensure the tourism sector has access to staff with relevant and up-to-date skills. This includes working with the Norwegian Institute for Adult Learning to ensure education meets the needs of workers and businesses.

Switzerland: An action item under the Federal Government Tourism Strategy is to tap into the potential of the tourism labour market. The Swiss Government sees its role as one to encourage co-operation and dialogue but also to provide analysis to support discussion and enable innovative and creative solutions.

United States: Under the 2022 National Travel and Tourism Strategy, the US seeks to attract and retain a diverse workforce, including in customer service positions on federal lands and waters. One of the identified actions is to support and fund local workforce development and entrepreneurship ventures that create and sustain well-paying, quality jobs and boost skills among residents to fill workforce gaps, within applicable laws.

The changing needs and values of workers have seen more emphasis put on the community and the living environment available in addition to the job. Creating liveable tourism destinations could help to address some of the barriers currently seen in the attraction and retention of workers, especially to destinations in rural and remote areas or those that are highly seasonal. Ensuring equitable access to quality public services and infrastructure and providing the right skills and quality job opportunities in regional labour markets are also key recommendations for reducing regional inequalities, but they require co-ordinated and sequenced actions at different government levels (OECD, 2023[19]). Addressing the community needs of workers should be a core consideration as countries look to diversify their tourism offer beyond established destinations.

Tourism is a significant employer of migrant workers, while international workers also play an important role in filling labour and skills needs in many countries. However, these worker flows and pipelines were disrupted in many countries during the pandemic. Several countries have introduced initiatives to restart these worker flows and respond to pressures to access more workers, with tourism continuing to feature as a key sector. For example, in Austria the annual quota for seasonal workers in tourism was increased from 1 200 to 3 000 in 2022 and was further increased to 3 400 in 2023 and to 4 300 in 2024. In addition, new occupations were placed on the shortage list including chefs, housekeepers, hotel clerks and waiters. Other countries also have long-standing programmes in this area, including Canada's Temporary Foreign Worker Program which has been in place for many years and is designed to be responsive to changes in the labour market, helping employers fill labour and skills shortages on a temporary basis, including in the sector.

Better measurement to tackle tourism workforce issues

The importance of timely and granular tourism data to enable evidence-based decision making is well-recognised in the tourism sector (see Chapter 3 for further discussion). A key issue in creating evidence-based policies for the tourism workforce is identifying tourism workers in official statistics. Only a handful of countries have meaningful statistics on employment in the tourism industries (UN Tourism, 2024[27]), and the shortcomings with available employment data was highlighted during the pandemic as many countries lacked access to relevant data to design target policies for tourism workers.

The Tourism Satellite Account, and the OECD Employment Module, provide an internationally accepted methodology for calculating tourism employment in a standardised and comparable way, summing proportions of employees from across nine tourism-related industries. However, the underlying data to prepare these calculations remains a challenge in many countries. The tourism workforce is a complex jigsaw of people working across many industries and geographies, many of whom may not identify as tourism workers, and the high levels of casual and informal workers in the sector means tourism workers are often not captured in official workforce or labour statistics.

Identifying tourism workers and understanding the trends within the sector is essential for evidence-based policy to build a strong and stable workforce. This requires clear definitions and shared understanding with respect to the various employment categories across tourism sub-sectors and the skills levels within them that are applicable to both large corporations and SMEs as an important starting point. It is becoming increasingly recognised that many tourism workforce issues are outside of aggregate estimates like the number of employees, average wages and hours worked.

Work is underway by UN Tourism and ILO to develop a statistical list of tourism occupations as the foundation for data to inform issues related to the tourism labour market, aligned with broader statistical guidance beyond tourism. However, the absence of such clarity in many countries and, internationally between countries, is a major limitation in the development of coherent policy.

Many countries rely on the accommodation and food services subsector as a proxy for tourism, which can be beneficial for identifying core issues, but it also provides a partial view and may skew the analysis of the issues in the tourism sector. Countries have also begun to implement more in-depth surveys and studies to build evidence and better understand the tourism workforce, such as recent in-depth studies of the labour market in tourism conducted in Ireland and Switzerland, at Federal and sub-national level. Other initiatives to better understand the tourism workforce include the development of a quarterly infographic on employment in tourism activities which inputs into the National Tourism Human Capital Model in Chile and environmental scanning and analysis of trends on both the supply and demand sides of tourism and to assess their impact on employment in Colombia.

An increased recognition of the importance of tourism well-being and sentiment has led to the introduction of new data collections in some countries. New Zealand's Voices from the Front-Line Survey and Tourism and Hospitality Workforce Survey are designed to better understand workforce issues with an emphasis on listening to the frequently neglected voices of the tourism workforce itself to better understand the issues faced (Box 2.9). Finland is now gathering qualitative data on tourism employment and employee wellbeing directly from businesses as part of the Sustainable Travel Finland programme, which will be used in the future to develop indicators to help evaluate and develop target setting of the national tourism strategy and its actions regarding tourism employment.

Box 2.9. Building evidence for tourism workforce sentiment in New Zealand

The need to better understand both workers and working conditions saw New Zealand implement two custom tourism employment surveys. The Voices from the Front Line survey asked 40 questions related to tourism work and gathered 396 responses. The survey was aimed at the voices of those who are often overlooked or marginalised voices of employees. The findings highlight unfair and illegal practices but also aim to be the starting point for discussion to improve work experiences and long-term sustainability for the hospitality sector.

The Tourism and Hospitality Workforce Survey is the most detailed survey of tourism and hospitality employees and their employment conditions undertaken in New Zealand, with 902 valid responses covering all sub-sectors of hospitality and tourism industries. The survey findings follow the well-established patterns of concern including low pay, unsatisfactory working conditions, insufficient career progression, and a high level of turnover intention.

Policy considerations to strengthen the tourism workforce

Strengthening the tourism workforce requires addressing real and perceived issues related to pay, working conditions and skills development. The private sector has a key role in creating conditions to attract and retain workers in the sector, while governments and policymakers have an important role to facilitate these initiatives by creating supporting policy conditions. As the sector focuses on addressing the current workforce pressures, policymakers also need to consider the strategic impacts of longer-term changes for both tourism and the workforce, and what that might mean for the needs of workers, businesses, and communities to build a more resilient tourism sector.

Based on the analysis discussed in this chapter, key policy considerations to strengthen the tourism workforce include:

- **Integrate the needs of tourism workers into the wider economic and community development strategies and plans**. More needs to be done to understand and address the needs of workers to make tourism work a more attractive and viable option. This includes factors that occur outside of the job itself including issues related to housing, transport and childcare services which sit outside the mandate of tourism administrations. Addressing these issues effectively requires strong co-ordination across government, horizontally and vertically. Incorporating the specific needs of tourism workers in wider economic, community and workforce development strategies can also encourage greater consideration of the importance of sustainable tourism development and how the benefits can be captured and maximised in local communities.
- **Leverage private sector initiatives to improve working conditions and attract and retain tourism workers.** The private sector has an in-depth understanding of the labour and skills needs at business and sector level, and the barriers to recruiting and retaining workers. Governments have a role to play in ensuring the framework conditions are in place to support and encourage businesses to address issues related to pay, conditions and other factors within their control.

Potential also exists to learn from and leverage private sector initiatives, including large multinational corporations and industry associations, to address workforce issues and implement new training and models of working to improve conditions in the sector. This may include financial or operational support to help extend the benefits of these initiatives across the sector. Supporting the development of local partnerships may also boost the benefits of existing initiatives and improve the attractiveness of the sector through opportunities for career progression and the retention of seasonal workers.

- **Facilitate linkages with and between the private sector and education providers to meet the changing needs of the tourism sector and prepare for the green and digital transitions**. Formal education remains integral for many parts of the tourism workforce, supplemented with on-the-job training to ensure that workers are job-ready. Encouraging collaboration between businesses and the education sector can help to better prepare workers as they enter the workforce and ensure they have the skills needed now and for the future. It will also better align education and skills training with the skills needed in the sector to ensure the tourism sector can benefit from the opportunities created by the green and digital transformations, and help workers navigate the significant impacts of these transformations on labour markets.
- **Support tourism SMEs and workers to adapt to digitalisation and encourage the adoption of digital technology to innovate and ease tourism workforce pressures.** Tourism SMEs are at risk of being left behind in the digital transition, maintaining the burden of manual tasks and impacting their ability to attract and retain a quality workforce. More needs to be done to raise awareness and uptake of digital technologies that can support the tourism workforce including through automated human resource planning and booking systems, digital marketing and artificial intelligence. Providing support to tourism businesses to access finance and ensuring business owners and workers have the tools and skills required to harness these technologies will help keep pace and introduce more innovative business and work practices.
- **Collect and share robust and granular data on tourism employment and workforce issues.** Tourism decision makers need to understand and respond to the changing needs of the sector. This includes developing a better understanding of the nature of work and workforce issues in tourism, and how this is changing. In depth workforce studies and the introduction of employee surveys to capture worker sentiment and working conditions of the tourism workforce provide one approach to building the evidence required to address the key structural issues and policy framework conditions for the sector. Sharing this data in a way that can be used to inform policy decisions is key, also to support the private sector with workforce planning and decision making.

References

Booking.com, Statista.com (2024), *European Accommodation Barometer 2024*, https://www.statista.com/study/168004/2024-european-accommodation-barometer/. [6]

CEDEFOP (2020), *Skills developments and trends in the tourism sector*, https://www.cedefop.europa.eu/en/data-insights/skills-developments-and-trends-tourism-sector#_job_and_skills_demand_in_tourism. [2]

European Commission (2023), *Commission proposes new measures on skills and talent*, https://ec.europa.eu/commission/presscorner/detail/EN/ip_23_5740. [9]

European Commission (2022), *Eurobarometer: Intra-EU labour mobility after the pandemic*, https://europa.eu/eurobarometer/surveys/detail/2671. [12]

ILO (2024), *ILO agreement on living wage definition "a leap forward for social justice"*, https://www.ituc-csi.org/ILO-agreement-on-living-wage-definition#:~:text=The%20new%20definition%20states%20that,work%20performed%20during%20normal%20hours.%E2%80%9D. [23]

ILO (2024), *Realizing decent work in the platform economy*, https://webapps.ilo.org/wcmsp5/groups/public/---ed_norm/---relconf/documents/meetingdocument/wcms_909906.pdf. [13]

ILO (2023), *May they never be deemed 'low skilled' again*, ILO, https://www.ilo.org/wcmsp5/groups/public/---dgreports/---dcomm/---publ/documents/publication/wcms_871016.pdf. [4]

ILO (2022), *Skills development for a just transition*, https://www.ilo.org/wcmsp5/groups/public/---ed_emp/---emp_ent/documents/publication/wcms_860617.pdf. [16]

ILO (2022), *Technical meeting on COVID-19 and sustainable recovery in the tourism sector*, https://www.ilo.org/wcmsp5/groups/public/---ed_dialogue/---sector/documents/meetingdocument/wcms_844312.pdf. [3]

ILO (2022), *The future of work in the tourism sector: Sustainable and safe recover and decent work in the context of the covid-19 pandemic*, https://www.ilo.org/sector/Resources/publications/WCMS_840403/lang--en/index.htm. [8]

ILO (2017), *ILO Guidelines on decent work and socially responsible tourism*, https://www.ilo.org/wcmsp5/groups/public/---ed_dialogue/---sector/documents/normativeinstrument/wcms_546337.pdf. [20]

OECD (2024), *Affordable housing*, https://www.oecd.org/housing/topics/affordable-housing/. [18]

OECD (2024), *OECD Economic Outlook, May 2024*, OECD Publishing, https://doi.org/10.1787/69a0c310-en. [5]

OECD (2023), *Assessing and anticipating skills for the green transition: Unlocking talent for a sustainable future*, Getting Skills Right, OECD Publishing, Paris, https://doi.org/10.1787/28fa0bb5-en. [15]

OECD (2023), *Employment Outlook 2023: Artificial intelligence and jobs*, OECD Publishing, https://doi.org/10.1787/19991266. [14]

OECD (2023), *Living wages in context: A comparative analysis for OECD countries*, OECD Publishing, https://doi.org/10.1787/2e622174-en. [22]

OECD (2023), *Ready for the next crisis? Investing in health system resilience*, OECD Publishing, https://doi.org/10.1787/1e53cf80-en. [7]

OECD (2023), *Regional Outlook 2023: The longstanding geography of inequalities*, OECD Publishing, https://doi.org/10.1787/92cd40a0-en. [19]

OECD (2023), *Retaining talent at all ages*, OECD Publishing, https://doi.org/10.1787/00dbdd06-en. [10]

OECD (2023), *Skills Outlook 2023: Skills for a Resilient Green and Digital Transition*, OECD Publishing, https://doi.org/10.1787/27452f29-en. [25]

OECD (2022), *Coping with the cost of living crisis: Minimum wages in times of rising inflation*, https://www.oecd.org/employment/Minimum-wages-in-times-of-rising-inflation.pdf. [21]

OECD (2022), *Supporting transitions and securing jobs: Social dialogue shaping a stronger recovery from the pandemic*, OECD Publishing, https://www.oecd.org/coronavirus/policy-responses/supporting-transitions-and-securing-jobs-social-dialogue-shaping-a-stronger-recovery-from-the-pandemic-83b6b310/. [17]

OECD (2022), *Tourism Trends and Policies 2022*, OECD Publishing, https://doi.org/10.1787/a8dd3019-en. [1]

OECD (2021), *Preparing the tourism workforce for the digital future*, OECD Publishing, https://doi.org/10.1787/9258d999-en. [24]

Randstad (2022), *Employer brand research 2022: Global report*, https://www.randstad.com/s3fs-media/rscom/public/2023-05/rebr_2022_global_report.pdf. [11]

Tourism HR Canada (2022), *Tourism's double-barrelled labour challenge: Barriers to employment and skills mismatches*, https://tourismhr.ca/labour-market-information/reports/workforce-strategy/tourisms-double-barrelled-labour-challenge-barriers-to-employment-and-skills-mismatches/. [26]

UN Tourism (2024), *Employment and decent work in tourism - ILO and UN Tourism joint project*, https://www.unwto.org/project/employment-and-decent-work-tourism-ilo-unwto-joint-project. [27]

Chapter 3. Building the evidence base for sustainable tourism policies

Recent crises spurred momentum for sustainable tourism and placed a renewed focus on addressing unbalanced tourism development and measuring tourism success differently. The strong rebound in tourism demand has highlighted the need for more and better data to manage the impacts of these tourism flows on destinations, local communities, and the environment. Measuring the economic, environment, and social dimensions of tourism is a significant area of focus at international, national and subnational level. Navigating the different approaches and frameworks and understanding how these fit with the policy needs in countries remains a challenge. This chapter takes stock of the different frameworks and approaches to address data gaps and support the sustainable development of tourism. It highlights the need for further work to develop and implement practical, granular and timely measures linked to the policy needs of destinations to plan and manage tourism sustainably.

Recognition of tourism's contribution to economic and social progress increased significantly in the wake of the crises triggered by the COVID-19 pandemic. The call for the tourism sector to 'build back better' led to increased momentum for sustainable tourism and a renewed focus on addressing unbalanced tourism development. However, the strong rebound in demand and the economic priority to return to pre-COVID levels, has reinforced the need to measure tourism success differently. Evidence-based policy action is needed to strike a better balance between the benefits and costs associated with tourism development and implement a vision for the future of tourism which is better aligned with sustainability principles and the Sustainable Development Goals (SDGs) (OECD, 2021[1]).

Governments at all levels need robust, timely and relevant data to better understand the impacts of tourism on economies, destinations, and local communities, and design targeted and concrete actions and manage the trade-offs to achieve better outcomes. However, the recent crises have revealed shortcomings in existing tourism data, not least with respect to measures to monitor the progress of sustainable tourism development and evaluate the effectiveness of strategies, policies, and programmes.

Improving the evidence base for sustainable tourism policies is not a new area of work. However, the topic has risen high on the policy and data agenda in recent years to support the shift to more sustainable models of tourism. This has resulted in significant work at international, national and subnational levels to better measure the economic, environment, and social dimensions of tourism. While collectively these efforts help to advance this important agenda, navigating the different approaches and frameworks and understanding how these fit with the policy needs in countries remains a challenge.

This chapter takes stock of the different frameworks and approaches to address data gaps and support the sustainable development of tourism. It examines initiatives to measure and monitor the sustainability of tourism, building on work at country level and recent progress on forging international consensus on robust and comparable measures, including the internationally endorsed Statistical Framework for Measuring the Sustainability of Tourism and other initiatives. The chapter considers the need for further work to develop and implement practical, granular and timely measures linked to the specific context and priorities to plan and manage tourism sustainably in different places. The priority policy issues for sustainable tourism development identified from a survey of OECD member and partner countries are presented, stressing the importance of tailoring indicators and data tools to the policy needs of destinations.

Balancing tourism development for a more sustainable future

Sustainable tourism has been defined as tourism that takes full account of its current and future economic, social, and environmental impacts, addressing the needs of visitors, the industry, the environment and host communities (UN Tourism and UNEP, 2005[2]). Significant progress has been made to highlight the importance of sustainable tourism development at all levels of government and in the private sector, including through the integration of tourism into the 2030 Agenda for Sustainable Development (United Nations, 2022[3]). However, more needs to be done to translate this increased recognition into meaningful actions to promote sustainable tourism development and management. This requires the development of strategies and policies for more sustainable tourism, and measurement instruments, indicators and other tools to make the policies work on the ground (UN Tourism and UNEP, 2005[2]).

Sustainable tourism development is now mainstreamed in many national tourism policies, strategies, and plans, setting a path for future programmes and co-ordinated action. Many countries have developed new, or updated existing, tourism strategies and plans to reflect the changed and evolving policy context and priorities post-pandemic (Box 3.1). While the targets in the strategies remain primarily based on the role of tourism as a driver of economic development, broader sustainability targets and indicators to monitor progress are increasingly being embedded in these strategies or subsequently developed as part of the monitoring frameworks, at national and subnational level.

Box 3.1. Mainstreaming sustainability in tourism strategies – selected country examples

Australia: The THRIVE 2030 Strategy for sustainable growth contains over 60 actions including to restore the tourism sector to its pre-pandemic visitor spend of AUD 166 billion by 2024 and AUD 230 billion by 2030, with approximately 40% of this expenditure to go to regional Australia. A key action item has been the development of an industry sustainability framework and toolkit to provide clarity on what sustainability means for the tourism sector, to put forward a vision, goals and priority actions for the sector, and to assist businesses implement and improve sustainability practices.

Colombia: The Tourism Sector Plan 2022-2026 Tourism in Harmony with Life lays out a detailed roadmap to address the fundamental priorities of the tourism sector, with a particular emphasis on sustainability and inclusion. The overarching targets of the plan are to receive 7.5 million tourists over the four-year period and to employ an additional 300 000 people a month (on average) in activities associated with tourism by 2026. Initiatives promoting sustainable tourism seek to: strengthen co-operation; encourage innovation and knowledge exchange; prioritise the well-being of local communities and cultural and natural heritage; and promote sustainable economic development.

France: The Destination France Plan aims to revive and transform tourism by positioning France as the world's leading sustainable destination by 2030. France aims to: raise awareness of environmental issues linked with tourism; extend the tourism season towards 'four seasons'; promote local tourism and enhance dispersal of tourists across the country; and increase the sustainability of accommodation infrastructure and decarbonise transport. The Plan sets out 20 measures across five strategic areas, including a target to invest EUR 44 million to support sustainable tourism infrastructure.

Iceland: The long-term vision Leading in Sustainable Development aims to position Iceland as a leader in sustainable development. The vision is built on four interconnected pillars, economy, community, environment, and visitors, that support the development of a profitable and competitive tourism industry in harmony with country and nation.

Slovenia: The Slovenian Tourism Strategy 2022-28 aims to implement a balanced growth scenario under the principle 'a little more and much better'. The Strategy sets out five goals: increasing the quality and value of 'four season' tourism; increasing the satisfaction of workers and visitors; positioning tourism as a generator of value and sustainable development; decarbonisation; and ensuring a competent and efficient tourism governance structure. To monitor progress, the Strategy defines 14 indicators and 25 measures in total, with targets for 2028.

United States: The National Travel and Tourism Strategy 2022 aims to build a sector that is resilient to natural disasters, public health threats, and the impacts of climate change, and to build a sustainable tourism sector that protects natural resources, supports the tourism economy, and ensures equitable development. The US aims to reach 90 million international arrivals and US 279 billion in tourist expenditure by 2027. The overarching objective is underpinned by four strategic goals: promoting the United States as a travel destination; facilitating travel to and within the United States; ensuring diverse, inclusive, and accessible tourism experiences; fostering resilient and sustainable travel and tourism.

Tourism, more than many other sectors, is highly dependent on the quality of the environment while also impacting it. Growth-oriented tourism models prioritising economic impact often come with unintended negative impacts on the environment and communities and negative economic externalities, including over the longer term. A more balanced model of tourism development and management which considers all three dimensions of sustainability (economic, environmental and social) is needed to ensure that immediate and often short-term economic benefits do not compromise the environment or social fabric of a destination, and, in turn, longer term economic growth.

There is no one-size-fits-all solution to balance tourism development and management. Previous OECD Tourism Committee work has highlighted the need for a robust, timely and disaggregated system of tourism statistics to improve the management of tourism and determine the desired type and scale of tourism appropriate for individual destinations (OECD, 2021[1]). Policies need to consider the specific characteristics of tourism development for each destination, and understanding the trade-offs of different tourism development models is an area that requires more work.

Measuring and monitoring the sustainability of tourism

Measuring and monitoring the sustainability of tourism has been an area of work for over three decades, at country and international level (for example the OECD Indicators for the Integration of Environmental and Sustainability Concerns into Tourism Policies, 2003; the UN Tourism Guidebook on Indicators of Sustainable Development for Tourism Destinations 2004; European Commission's European Tourism Indicators System, 2016; European Commission's EU Tourism Dashboard, 2023; UN Tourism's Statistical Framework for Measuring Sustainable Tourism, 2024). During this time the quality and availability of tourism data has continued to advance, but has typically focused on capturing the economic impacts, guided by the International Recommendations for Tourism Statistics and Tourism Satellite Accounts methodological framework.

The recent endorsement of the Statistical Framework - Measuring the Sustainability of Tourism (SF-MST) by the United Nations Statistics Commission is an important step forward in forging international consensus on the production of reliable and comparable data on the economic, environmental, and social aspects of tourism (UN Tourism, 2023[4]). This UN Tourism-led statistical framework, under the leadership of co-chairs Austria and Spain, provides fundamental concepts, definitions, and data organisation structures for tourism statistics across economic, social, and environmental impacts. Further work is needed to provide methodological guidance to support the concrete implementation of the framework and derive a meaningful set of internationally comparable indicators for sustainable tourism development.

Building on this progress, more work is needed to measure and monitor a wider set of outcomes including social and environmental impacts as well as negative economic externalities not typically accounted for when looking at economic impacts, which can be more challenging to quantify in a consistent and meaningful way. The environmental dimension and related negative economic externalities such as the depletion of natural assets have received more attention of late, also benefiting from wider environmental measurement frameworks like the System of Environmental Economic Accounting (SEEA). However, the measurement of social impacts is lagging. This is in part because the social dimension is often associated with peoples' subjective perceptions, which can be difficult to measure in a comparable way (OECD, 2023[5]).

Considerable progress has been made in recent decades to develop robust and comparable measures for social impacts, including the OECD Well-being Framework. For example, the OECD Indicators for Measuring Well-being and Social Progress and the OECD Better Life Index provide a framework to measure and compare living conditions and quality of life across countries (including housing expenditure, work-life balance, feeling safe walking alone at night) (OECD, 2023[6]).

Potential exists to build on these frameworks and tailor them for the tourism context. Combined with tourism specific measures, like tourism visitation and seasonality, well-being indicators could help to understand and address some core environmental and social challenges for tourism. Further developing these indicators at the sub-national level could provide opportunities to monitor the sustainable development of tourism in popular tourism destinations. The experience of Sweden to adapt the OECD Better Life Index to measure quality of life at municipal level could provide learnings for how the Index could be adapted to also provide a better understanding of the social impact of tourism at destination level.

The strong push to measure and monitor the sustainability of tourism has resulted in many initiatives running concurrently. Together these initiatives are contributing to advancing the agenda. However, navigating this diverse and dynamic body of work can be challenging for policy makers and data practitioners to understand the contribution and purpose of different initiatives and determine where to best focus limited resources for maximum impact. Table 3.1 sets out an overview of the different frameworks that are being used to measure and monitor the sustainable development of tourism, and their associated uses, benefits and challenges.

Table 3.1. Navigating frameworks for the measurement of sustainable tourism

Framework type	Benefits	Challenges	Examples
Statistical framework	Internationally agreed with established statistical concepts Often make sense at a political or strategic scale	Time lag of data, lack of granularity, resources required to calculate, not necessarily relevant for specific issues	Statistical Framework – Measuring Sustainable Tourism (SF-MST), Recommended Methodological Framework – Tourism Satellite Account (RMF:TSA)
Methodological framework	Internationally comparable with established methods linked to the statistical concepts	Not necessarily relevant for specific issues	International Recommendations on Tourism Statistics (IRTS)
Comparable indicator set	Internationally comparable (when indicators are calculated for multiple countries), based on existing and established data	Lack of granularity, not necessarily relevant for specific issues	World Economic Forum Travel and Tourism Development Index, European Tourism Indicator System (ETIS), EU Tourism Dashboard
Targeted Indicator set	Country-specific or targeted specifically to issue, policy and/or strategy	Not necessarily internationally comparable, may not even be comparable between regions	Sustainable Travel Finland, UNWTO-JICA Toolkit of Indicators for Projects

International initiatives to monitor and benchmark the sustainability of tourism

Identifying and implementing indicators to effectively measure and monitor progress has proven challenging. There is currently no internationally agreed set of indicators to support balanced and sustainable tourism development. Drawing on the experiences and insights from existing and ongoing recent initiatives at international and country level provides an opportunity to advance efforts to develop and use indicators for policy making, and provide a basis for valuable comparison and benchmarking between countries (UN Tourism, 2023[4]; European Commission, 2022[7]; European Commission, 2016[8]; ETC/ULS, 2018[9]) (Annex 1: Table A.1).

At the global level, the SF-MST provides a framework from which to derive a core set of international indicators, but further work and practical guidance is now needed on the specific indicators and how to measure them. UN Tourism have proposed an initial set of indicators as part of the wider MST initiative, and it is intended that compilation guidance will be developed to support the production of comparable data and indicators.

At the European level, improving statistics and indicators for tourism is a key pillar of the Agenda for Tourism 2030 and the EU Tourism Transition Pathway, and is the most common topic for pledges and commitments from public and private stakeholders (Council of the European Union, 2022[10]; European Commission, 2022[11]; European Commission, 2023[12]). A range of initiatives are underway to advance this agenda, including the work by Eurostat to develop and implement a set of indicators to measure the sustainability of tourism based on available data, the EU Tourism Dashboard, and the work of the Together for EU Tourism (T4T) expert group, which has a dedicated topic on measuring sustainability, with results to be shared with all stakeholders through a forthcoming Stakeholder Support Platform.

Work is also advancing in the private sector, to develop and implement initiatives to support tourism businesses and destinations in monitoring their levels of sustainability performance, providing performance indicators to provide guidance in measuring compliance with the criteria. For example, the WTTC Travel and Tourism's Global Footprint dashboard provides indicators across all the pillars of environmental, social, economic and the SDGs. Other examples include the World Economic Forum Travel and Tourism Development Index and the Global Sustainable Tourism Council standards for sustainability in travel and tourism (Box 3.2).

Box 3.2. Recent international sustainable tourism indicator frameworks – selected examples

Building on the work to develop and implement these existing frameworks provides an opportunity to accelerate the process of developing indicators. Selected samples of existing international work on indicator frameworks are outlined below.

- **European Tourism Indicators System** – The framework consists of 43 core indicators supplemented by additional indicators. It is a voluntary tool designed to measure the sustainability of European tourism destinations (European Commission, 2016[13]).
- **EU Tourism Dashboard** – Developed in response to the pandemic, the Dashboard presents 19 indicators and 13 descriptors designed to promote and monitor the green and digital transitions and the socio-economic resilience of the tourism sector. The starting point for preparing the indicators has been the identification of data which is available across all EU member states (European Commission, 2023[14]).
- **UN Tourism proposal for a set of indicators to measure and monitor the sustainability of tourism** – Linked with the work to prepare the SF-MST, UN Tourism proposed a set of 30 initial indicators at the 4th Expert Group on Measuring the Sustainability of Tourism in September 2023 (UN Tourism, 2023[15]).
- **World Economic Forum Travel and Tourism Development Index** – Previously focused on competitiveness, the Index was revised with a focus on monitoring the resilience and sustainable development of tourism. A pillar dedicated to 'Travel and Tourism Sustainability' tracks 24 indicators across three themes (environmental sustainability, socioeconomic impact and travel and tourism demand sustainability) (WEF, 2024[16]).
- **World Travel and Tourism Council 'Travel and Tourism's Global Footprint' dashboard** – estimates the economic, social and environmental footprint of the tourism sector globally across 11 core measures and seven of the SDGs related to tourism. The tool allows for benchmarking across countries and international regions, while also providing historical data where available, to allow countries to monitor their own progress (WTTC, 2024[17]).

Existing work to develop and implement indicators provides a platform to build on and accelerate efforts for new data and indicators. An analysis of existing international frameworks (Annex A) shows that as the discussion around sustainable tourism has evolved, so have the measurement frameworks. While most frameworks and indicators are structured around the pillars of economic, environmental and social sustainability, there is considerable diversity in the scope and range of indicators covered which creates challenges for international comparability as well as for decision-makers in destinations (with often limited capacity and resources) to understand which priority issues and indicators to focus on and collect.

In general, the following measures and associated indicators are included in most frameworks:

- Economic measures: for example, seasonality, visitor market share, share of GDP, share of employment, average expenditure, and average length of stay.

- Environmental measures: for example, water and energy consumption, air and greenhouse gas emissions, waste (water and solid), environmental certification and mode of transport.
- Social measures: for example, gender equality, accessibility of tourism sites, satisfaction of the local community, tourist satisfaction, valorisation of culture and heritage.

An important consideration when looking at indicator sets is their interlinked nature. For example, high greenhouse gas emissions not only accelerate climate change, but also impact on the health of communities, and as a result have economic impacts in a variety of areas.

Country initiatives to develop indicators for sustainable planning and management

In many countries work is underway to develop and implement tailored indicator sets and data tools, to better respond to the tourism policy needs and strategic priorities in their country. In some countries these indicator frameworks are standalone tools; other countries have created sustainable tourism monitoring frameworks linked directly to their national tourism strategies. While international indicator frameworks provide a robust set of indicators to measure sustainable tourism development, they may lack the specificity to support national policy priorities and monitor progress. Indicators need to be measured and monitored at the appropriate spatial and temporal scale. They need to be linked to the core policy issues to be effective for decision makers and are only of value when the data exists to measure them.

Many country initiatives draw on work that has already been established in various international frameworks. For example, the Sustainable Tourism Indicator System in Portugal is fundamentally based on the European Tourism Indicator System (ETIS). The 43 economic, social and environmental indicators are linked to concrete targets in Portugal's Tourism Strategy 2027, and cover 11 thematic areas including seasonality, economic benefits, employment, accessibility, pressure, tourist satisfaction, local satisfaction, environmental management, energy management, water management and solid waste management (Box 3.6).

Colombia's National Tourism Information System adopts a comprehensive set of indicators focusing on areas such as tourism seasonality, employment, economic benefits, and environmental impacts. The measures broadly align with international standards and guidelines required by UN Tourism's International Network of Sustainable Tourism Observatories (INSTO) initiative which now counts more than 40 active Observatories globally, and Colombia is exploring the development of additional data, tools, and indicators.

As part of Visit Finland's Sustainable Travel Finland initiative, indicators providing data at business, regional and national level are built from the national sustainable tourism programme and certification scheme to provide visibility to the sustainability of tourism. It is intended that these indicators will help to evaluate and inform the development and implementation of the next tourism strategy (Box 3.3). Costa Rica has seven tourism sustainability indices (30 indicators) to assess the performance of regions with high tourism activity on the national Social Progress Index. Portugal leverages micro-data from the Tourism Companies 360° Initiative where tourism businesses report data on their environmental, social and governance performance, to better understand and design appropriate public policies for the different segments of tourist activity.

To inform tourism decision-making it is necessary to identify and address data gaps using relevant indicators. In Switzerland, a pilot framework of sustainability indicators seeks to combine environmental and social indicators with economic indicators from the TSA, in line with the SF-MST. The economic dimensions include gross value added (GVA) and employment while the environmental factors consider energy use and air emissions across tourism-related sectors. The social dimension will be included in the next cycle as data become available. New Zealand's Sustainable Tourism Explorer identifies 109 measures across five pillars of sustainable tourism. However, data are currently only available for 54 of these measures with work ongoing to compile new data (Box 3.4).

Box 3.3. Creating evidence through the sustainable tourism programme in Finland

Visit Finland has developed the Sustainable Travel Finland (STF) programme for travel companies and regions in Finland. As a part of the programme, national indicators for sustainable tourism have been developed that provide tourism data at a company, regional and national level. In the future, these indicators will help to evaluate and develop target setting of the national tourism strategy and its actions. Indicators are drawn from the data collected from businesses as part of the sustainable tourism certification scheme. New reporting tools have been added to share these data and make them visible for the tourism sector and beyond. This also acts as an opportunity to motivate the sector to make more sustainable choices to achieve common goals. Indicators are compiled based on data collected from businesses, regions, visitor and resident surveys and Statistics Finland. They are structured across four dimensions:

- Destination management: for example, the number of tourism companies participating in the STF programme, share of the destination's residents satisfied with tourism's impact on their place of residence.
- Economic value: for example, the number of education and training courses related to sustainable tourism, share of seasonal workers.
- Social and cultural impact: for example, the number of companies with multilingual communication, share of enterprises providing services from reduced mobility, proportion of companies providing services for the LGBTQ+ community.
- Environmental impact: for example, the share of companies measuring carbon footprint, share of companies actively participating in climate change mitigation measures.

To monitor and transparently communicate progress against the actions and indicators of the programme, Visit Finland published its first annual report State of Sustainable Tourism in May 2023, with the second edition published in June 2024. Based on the results, Visit Finland evaluates which indicators may need more ambitious thresholds, such as the share of companies actively supporting the protection, conservation and maintenance of local biodiversity, which decreased from 67% in 2022, to 41% in 2023 after more ambitious target setting. It also shows where the sector may need more support. The 2022 data indicated that only 27% of tourism businesses measured their carbon footprint. More awareness, competence building, and content was added, which saw the number of businesses measuring their carbon footprint increase to 49% in 2023.

To strengthen the evidence base for sustainable tourism development, Brazil has developed a set of 32 indicators linked to community-based tourism that contribute to the achievement of the SDGs. The set highlights initiatives, actions and investments designed to achieve progress, including through monitoring the number of free training courses offered to communities for qualification in the area of tourism services and products, the number of creative economy incentive programmes and the number of beds offered in accommodation facilities for community members. As socio-economic aspects interact closely with cultural and environmental factors, Brazil intends to measure environmental education for communities and the integration of natural and/or cultural attributes in tourism services and products.

Expert working groups provide an opportunity to address data gaps and create indicators in a collaborative way. In the Netherlands, a National Data Alliance has been created to support evidence-based decision making. The Alliance follows international developments for measuring SDGs and sustainable tourism indicators, and is also developing new indicators to evaluate the social and environmental impact of tourism including the carbon footprint associated with travel to and within the Netherlands.

In Australia, the Industry Data and Expert Analysis (IDEA) Working Group initiated four data and research projects including the Longitudinal Indicators for the Visitor Economy (LIVE) framework. The LIVE framework will be a set of leading and lagging progress indicators for the visitor economy, encompassing social, environmental and economic metrics.

Box 3.4. Developing the Sustainable Tourism Explorer in New Zealand

New Zealand's Sustainable Tourism Explorer was developed by government, private sector and education sector working together. The process began in 2018 by comparing existing measures to the New Zealand Tourism Strategy, the Living Standards Framework and the UN SDGs. The goal was to balance scientific reliability, completeness, and the ongoing economic viability of the tracker while ensuring the Explorer worked well for the target audience.

The initiative identified 109 measures across five pillars of sustainable tourism including the environment, international and domestic visitors, the economy, New Zealanders and our communities and regions. Data are currently only available for 54 of these measures with ongoing work required to compile new data, including on waste management, cultural heritage protection, community attitudes towards tourism, as well as infrastructure investment for resource management and (sustainable) transportation at regional level.

New Zealand's Government partnered with the private sector to improve data sharing across the sector and create and improve key data sets to better measure sustainable tourism impacts. Formal data sharing agreements, new information management systems and new digital infrastructure have been implemented, accompanied by capacity building to provide the skills to develop the systems. The Explorer requires further development, especially to make it easier to use and to fill data gaps.

Informing and evaluating policies and progress towards sustainable tourism

More work is needed to better align indicators with policy issues and build the capacity of policy and decision makers to access and use the information needed to take informed, evidence-based decisions. A recent review of the policy impact of indicator frameworks for sustainable tourism found existing sustainable tourism frameworks are focused on the indicators themselves and raising awareness for sustainable tourism and are less aligned with the policy outcomes (Miller and Torres-Delgado, 2023[18]). This could stem from the tendency for indicators to be defined by the available data rather than beginning with the policy intent. This calls for a shift beyond individual indicators and measures towards a user-focused outcomes approach.

A strong policy perspective with an end user focus may help to better match available data to policy issues and identify priority data gaps to be addressed. This will help to ensure that measures are tailored and meaningful for destinations. Focusing on the priority actions required for change, may help to accelerate the transition to more sustainable models of tourism.

A one-size-fits-all measure or set of measures to monitor all aspects of tourism sustainability in a meaningful way for all destinations would likely include a significant number of indicators with many not relevant for all countries as many destinations face different issues. The experience and evidence from work to develop a common set of agreed indicators supports this, due to the complex nature of tourism and wide range of impacts generated. Focusing on a smaller set of core indicators targeted at a robust set of data that allows for international comparison and benchmarking against core sustainability challenges faced by countries may be a more fruitful approach, supplemented by a selection of indicators tailored to the strategic goals, policy needs and resources of an individual country or destination.

Understanding the policy process, context and goals can help to ensure that evidence is tailored to the needs of decision makers. Policy makers and other users need to be involved from the start and continually consulted throughout the process. This was a clear overarching message at the recent Workshop on Tourism Data Sharing, Integration and Governance organised by the OECD and European Commission. A further key message to emerge was that it is better to measure the right things well, than to try and measure everything.

Capacity and resource constraints continue to inhibit the ability of destinations to consistently develop and monitor data, or even to explore the potential of new and existing data sources from the beginning. Understanding the policy objectives and the measures necessary for decision making, including the granularity and timeliness of the data required, makes it possible to prioritise the set of data to expand and contract based on the resources available. This can also be enabled by understanding and employing the appropriate measurement frameworks.

Addressing policy priorities to promote sustainable tourism

Tourism strategies set out long-term visions to guide sustainable development and provide a good foundation for defining the optimal operating model for tourism. However, understanding what sustainability means for an individual country or destination, and correctly defining the core sustainability priorities and concrete actions to address them is an area where more work is needed.

Beyond national strategies, countries are also prioritising initiatives on several core sustainability issues. It is these priorities or issues that could be used to understand more concretely what is required to create a more sustainable tourism model. An analysis of priority tourism sustainability issues provided in response to a survey of OECD member and partner countries revealed ten common issues:

- **Acceptance and inclusion:** Tourism provides an opportunity for people to experience new cultures and ways of life. Ensuring that destinations and businesses are capable and willing to create an inclusive environment for both workers and visitors (e.g. gender, ethnicity, accessibility needs), can promote economic and social benefits.
- **Biodiversity**: The natural environment remains a key attraction for tourists, but is also impacted by tourism. Reducing the negative impacts of tourism on biodiversity will contribute to ecosystem stability, help build resilience to climate change, contribute to human health and extend the longevity of natural attractions.
- **Circular economy**: Tourism activities generate significant pollution and waste. The increased uptake of circularity principles within tourism can help to reduce waste and pollution, having positive impacts on both the environment and the economy.
- **Community and visitor sentiment:** Local communities often receive the benefits from tourism, but also deal with negative impacts of tourism. Ensuring that local communities are involved in the planning process for tourism can help to improve local acceptance and the experience for visitors, positively impacting both social and economic factors.
- **Decarbonisation of transport:** Tourism is built on the movement of people. Reducing the environmental impact of transport through the development of sustainable aviation fuels and the increased use of public transport and 'soft mobility' options can help to reduce the carbon emissions.
- **Digitalisation**: As in every ecosystem of our economy and our society, digitalisation impacts and transforms tourism (European Commission, 2021[19]). Digital tools for businesses and visitors can help drive productivity and satisfaction, while providing new forms of data and evidence for decision-making.

- **Resilience to shocks**: Shocks, including natural and physical disaster, are expected to become more frequent. To maintain sustainable growth, the tourism sector must minimise the impact of these shocks and build back stronger. Increased resilience can provide stability and improve economic and social benefits of tourism.
- **Tourism concentration**: Destinations are often reliant on both spatial and temporal peaks in tourism. Dispersing tourists to different locations and spreading the tourism season to include shoulder periods can increase the economic benefits while reducing the impact of peak seasons on the community and the environment. Other interventions, such as improving the available infrastructure in a destination, also impact the capacity of a destination to manage visitor flows.
- **Tourism workforce:** As a service sector, tourism is driven by its workforce. Ensuring the tourism sector provides fair and decent work, and helping increase the social, green and digital skills can help to improve the lives of local populations as well as economic benefits.
- **Tourist behaviours:** The impact of tourism is not solely based on numbers, but also on the spatial context tourism takes places in and the way tourists behave. Understanding tourist behaviour and facilitating tourists to make more sustainable choices can have environmental, social and economic benefits.

These issues differ across destinations and should continue to be assessed as not all need to be addressed at the same time or with the same intensity. For example, destinations reliant on coastal tourism are more likely to consider issues like water quality and biodiversity, while island and long-haul destinations identify the need to decarbonise transport. However, several issues are also common across destinations, including seasonality, the spatial dispersal of visitors to less visited areas and the impact of visitors on communities and the natural environment. Table 3.2 provides a breakdown of the priorities by responding country. Work has already begun to address many of these issues through the implementation of new policies and programmes and can provide opportunities for new learning.

Table 3.2. Priority tourism sustainability issues identified by OECD member and partner countries

Key sustainability issues identified	Identifying countries
Acceptance and inclusion	Australia, Brazil, Canada, Finland, Japan, Luxembourg, Romania
Biodiversity	Australia, Austria, Germany, Lithuania, Peru, Poland, Slovenia
Circular economy	Austria, Brazil, Czechia, Germany, Greece, Italy, Japan, Malta, Peru, Poland, Romania, Slovenia, Sweden, Switzerland, Türkiye, United States
Community and visitor sentiment	Australia, Austria, Czechia, France, Iceland, Italy, Japan, Luxembourg, Malta, Romania, Sweden
Decarbonisation of transport	Australia, Brazil, Canada, Finland, France, Germany, Iceland, Italy, Lithuania, New Zealand, Peru, Slovenia, Sweden, Switzerland, Türkiye
Digitalisation	Costa Rica, Estonia, Germany, Greece, Latvia, Luxembourg, Türkiye
Resilience to shocks	Australia, Brazil, Canada, Costa Rica, France, Greece, United States
Tourism concentration	Austria, Brazil, Czech Republic, Greece, Iceland, Italy, Japan, Lithuania, Luxembourg, Malta, New Zealand, Poland, Romania, Slovenia, Switzerland, Türkiye, United Kingdom
Tourism workforce	Australia, Austria, Canada, Costa Rica, Estonia, Finland, Germany, Greece, Iceland, New Zealand, Sweden, Switzerland
Tourist behaviours	Australia, Japan, Lithuania, Poland, Switzerland

Source: OECD country survey.

Strengthening the evidence base for tourism decision-making

Targeted and meaningful policy actions require a strategic approach to developing indicators, tools, and metrics to provide the evidence base for sustainable tourism development and management. Combining the substantial bottom-up analysis of available data with a top-down approach that considers the policy priorities and intent can help to ensure the measures are both available and meaningful at the destination. This integrated, policy-led approach can ensure that indicators are tailored to inform decision making, while implementing targets, thresholds and key performance indicators can help to assess the effectiveness of policy efforts and provide the sector with tangible goals.

Significant work has been undertaken to understand the potential of existing data to measure and monitor the sustainability of tourism, but data gaps still remain. Building on existing work there are opportunities to identify new data sources and products to address these gaps and enable evidence-based policy making, especially by harnessing data created by the digital transition.

Collaborative approaches to tourism policy development could also create new opportunities for data sharing between the public and private sectors, while building the capacity of decision makers to better understand tourism data, including its limitations.

Assessing, selecting, and implementing indicators for sustainable tourism policy

Well-designed indicators can support the development of targeted and effective policies promoting the sustainable development of tourism. These indicators should be reliable, timely and consistent, to inform tourism development and management decisions and monitor progress in delivering sustainable outcomes. There are advantages to focusing, at least initially, on a limited set of practical and achievable indicators which respond to specific policy priorities, bringing focus to the necessary policy requirements within the constraints of often limited resources.

Countries which are well advanced in developing and implementing indicators monitoring the sustainability of tourism have commonly worked closely with policy makers and data professionals from across all levels of government, as well as other relevant actors from the private sector, academia and local communities. This participative approach acknowledges that the process of selecting and agreeing indicators can play an important role in mobilising actors around a common goal and help build capacity to successful implement and use the indicators. It can also help to embed indicators into the policy cycle, form a shared vision and contribute to improved policy coherence.

Under the Plan T - Master Plan for Tourism Austria designed a set of indicators based on data criteria related to availability, timeliness, practicability, and continuity. An initial list of indicators was narrowed down to a short-list of 26 using a working group of experts in data, tourism, and science. A final round of consultation and analysis resulted in a final list of 12 indicators, which are reviewed regularly, with 14 indicators now used (Box 3.5). Similarly, New Zealand's Sustainable Tourism Explorer was developed through a collaborative process with the New Zealand Government adopting a stewardship role in the process (Box 3.4).

Such participative approaches provide an opportunity for the tourism community to work together to define the policy issue, assess available and possible data sources and develop an appropriate measure. The process can have a value beyond the indicator set itself, and result in increased knowledge about the issues from different perspectives and thinking of others. It can also act as a capacity building exercise for the indicator compilers and policy makers as end users to learn about the data and associated challenges and limitations. Furthermore, it can lay the foundation for improved future collaborative actions moving forward (UNEP, 2015[20]).

Collaborative processes help to ensure the indicators are tailored to the needs of policy makers and creates the buy-in and ownership needed to implement and use the indicators. This in turn helps to increase the longevity of the indicators, as well as provide additional data context for the users. This process can also help to improve the data available. For example, in addition to identifying core tourism indicators, Australia's Industry Data and Expert Analysis Working Group was tasked with identifying and making suggestions to improve data collection methods for the identified metrics.

Box 3.5. Monitoring and driving sustainable tourism development in Austria

Under the Plan T – Master Plan for Tourism, Austria has developed a core set of indicators, considering the economic, environmental and social dimensions of sustainability. The indicators were selected through a multi-stakeholder consultation process and are continuously being developed to adapt to changing circumstances and include:

- Tourist arrivals and overnight stays, expenditure, GVA, employment data available from TSA.
- Competitiveness in prices.
- Revenue per available room and fictitious debt repayment period from the Austrian Bank for Tourism Development.
- Share of renewable source of energy in gastronomy and accommodation from Statistics Austria; energy consumption in key tourism sectors.
- Guest satisfaction which is available through the T-MONA guest survey.
- Resident attitude towards tourism/tourism acceptance.
- Number of businesses and destinations certified with the Austrian Eco-label.

The set of indicators is part of Austria's holistic approach to monitor and enact progress on sustainable tourism development at national, regional, destination and enterprise level, which also includes:

- Following a pilot project on Regional Information and Monitoring Systems in two tourism regions, a new publicly accessible dashboard will be launched in the first half of 2024. It is a continuous observation and management tool, also for tourism stakeholders, containing regional data (30 base indicators), ranging from the number of visitors and enterprises to labour market, mobility and environmental data.
- Austrian eco-label for destinations based on evaluation criteria regarding management, socio-economic impact, environmental protection, mobility and culture.
- ESG Data Hub provides nine tourism-specific indicators enabling enterprises to report and access ESG key performance data, aiming to facilitate access to finance and funding and catalyse the fundamental role of the private sector to advance sustainability.
- Quarterly surveys on tourism acceptance of the Austrian resident people implemented at national level which are legally based on the tourism demand and acceptance statistics regulation. As the survey on tourism acceptance is carried out as part of the existing survey on travel behaviour, synergy effects can be achieved both in terms of content and resources. The survey started with the first reference quarter 2024. The ongoing compilation of acceptance statistics aims to record the perceived effects of tourism to provide a holistic picture of the population's attitude towards the phenomenon of tourism and to monitor the development in the long term.

Indicators and evidence used to develop and monitor sustainable tourism policies should continue to be revised and updated to address the priority issues over time. As sustainability practices and data availability evolve, so too should the indicators. This does not only mean adding indicators, but also considering which of the existing indicators are still relevant or should be removed.

Understanding the policy context, and the right level to measure plays a key role in identifying and developing the right indicators for decision making. Focusing only on national and regional level initiatives could lead to the omission of some wider global sustainability issues that need to be addressed at international level (e.g. international aviation). Initiatives like the OECD Database on Air Transport CO_2 Emissions, which contain domestic and international aviation data (passenger and freight flights) for 186 countries and is suitable for both the territorial and the residence approach within the SEEA accounting framework, could help to better monitor emissions from air transport in a complementary and comparable way (OECD, 2023[21]).

Developing tools and metrics to monitor progress

Indicators and data points need to be considered in context to be meaningful and useful. This highlights the importance of adopting targets for indicators, to enable policy makers to monitor whether tourism destinations are moving towards or away from the desired outcome of sustainable developments (Miller and Torres-Delgado, 2023[18]). Sharing evidence such as targets, thresholds, and progress at the national and sub-national level (e.g. through online hubs and dashboards), can help to inform tourism policy and business decision-making and make sustainable development and its benefits, more tangible.

Targets for sustainable tourism measures will vary based on the different context of individual tourism destinations, national, subnational and local, and consider the specific needs or appropriate thresholds for each measure. Determining the appropriate threshold is complex and not static. However, understanding the desired direction the measure should move is a positive start. Providing this context can help decision makers to track progress toward the desired outcome and evaluate the effectiveness of policies and programmes.

While sustainability is more and more mainstreamed in national and subnational tourism strategies and plans in many countries, the targets and key performance indicators set out in these strategies and plans are still typically focused on economic measures (Box 3.1). To engrain sustainable principles in tourism development, there is a need to set out goals and targets in these strategies that encompass all facets of sustainability, looking beyond the historical targets for tourism arrivals and expenditure and focus on the specific needs of the country or destination.

Box 3.6. Setting strategic goals for sustainable tourism development in Portugal

The Tourism Strategy 2027 framed sustainability at the core of tourism policies in Portugal under the vision Tourism as a hub for economic, social and environmental development throughout the territory. The Strategy sets eight strategic goals or targets across the three pillars of sustainability which include:

- Reduce the seasonality index from 36.3% to 33.5% by 2027 (social).
- Double the number of educational qualifications from 30% to 60% (social).
- More than 90% of the resident population consider the impact of tourism on their territory to be positive (social).
- More than 90% of companies adopt energy efficiency measures (environmental).
- More than 90% of companies promote efficient water use in their operations (environmental).
- More than 90% of companies develop efficient waste management actions (environmental).
- Increase overnight stays in Portugal to 80 million in 2027 (economic).
- Increase tourism revenue to EUR 27 billion by 2027 (economic).

This is in addition to the goals for 2023 included in the plan for setting up Regional Tourism Observatories in each of the 7 regional DMOs, in partnership with UN Tourism and its INSTO network, bringing universities and knowledge centres closer to destination management entities.

This is the approach adopted under Portugal's Tourism Strategy 2027, which aims to establish tourism as a hub for economic, social and environmental development throughout the territory, positioning Portugal as one of the most competitive and sustainable tourism destinations in the world. The Strategy incorporates targets across the social, environmental, and economic pillars and puts businesses at the heart of sustainable development (Box 3.6).

Norway's National Tourism Strategy 2030 has an overall goal of "big impact, small footprint" for tourism. The main goals of the Strategy are to enhance value creation and jobs, to help Norway transition to a low-emission society, to help make communities attractive with happy residents and to deliver outstanding customer service to encourage repeat visitation and greater tourist spending. To support these goals, the Strategy commits to a 50% reduction of carbon emissions by 2030 and to reduce annual transport emissions by 10% in addition to revenue and employment targets. Among the initiatives and measures to reach the strategic goals, Norway aims to develop *Klimasmart*, a market development calculator that relates tourist spending to carbon emissions to prioritise low-carbon markets with high spending.

The Slovenian Tourism Strategy 2022-28 looks to set Slovenia as a role model for smart destinations that strengthen and encourage the development of sustainable, boutique, personalised and innovative experiences. To reach a balanced growth model for tourism which focuses on accelerated growth in quality and value add, Slovenia has established 25 impact metrics, each with their own quantitative targets based on a 2019 baseline (Box 3.7).

Box 3.7. Target setting in Slovenia's Tourism Strategy 2022-28

The Slovenian Tourism Strategy 2022-28 defines 14 key impact indicators (25 metrics in total). Building on 2019 baseline data, Slovenia has defined quantitative goals to reach by 2028 for each of the 25 metrics. The target values have been established based on the projected tourism development in Slovenia under a scenario of "A little bit more and a lot better", which emphasises moderate quantitative growth while prioritising enhancements in quality and value added under the motto Across the five objectives, Slovenia for instance aims to:

- Increase the total value added in the core tourism industry from EUR 0.9 billion euros in 2019 to EUR 1.3 billion in 2028 (business and financial aspect).
- Increase the length of stay by 20% (business and financial aspect).
- Improve the average satisfaction of the population with the development of tourism in the destinations included in the Green Scheme from an average score of 3.6 to 4.3 on a scale from 1 to 5 (Societal aspect).
- Increase the number of jobs generated by tourism demand (economic aspect).
- Reduce the Slovenian tourist industry's annual total carbon footprint by at least 1% (environmental and climate aspect).
- Increase the budgets of all destination management boards by 50% (management aspect).

The performance indicators are monitored annually to track progress against the five strategic objectives of the strategy. Indicator compilation relies on multiple data sources including from the Green Scheme managed by the Slovenian Tourist Board, the Statistical Office of the Republic of Slovenia, the Bank of Slovenia and the Slovenian Business Register.

Thresholds are another tool to monitor performance. However, some thresholds may not be quantifiable and may need a more qualitative approach. Overcrowding in destinations has led to an increased focus on understanding the carrying capacity of destinations. Better evidence is needed to anticipate when tourism in a destination is approaching the saturation point and identify effective countermeasures to rebalance the impacts and trade-offs, so the benefits outweigh the costs for host communities, businesses, the environment, and tourists.

Understanding destinations' capacities and determining critical thresholds is increasingly important to manage the trade-offs and pressures that tourism brings on infrastructure, the environment, and the host community. Destination carrying capacity is not a new concept but is the focus of renewed attention as destinations struggle with the impacts from the strong rebound in tourism flows. A recent study suggests that carrying capacity is a fluid concept that cannot be represented by a specific number and that indicators alone may not provide appropriate statements about carrying capacity (ESPON, 2020[22]). It also noted that there was no single way to take specific territorial characteristics of tourist destinations into account when assessing carrying capacity so guidelines needed to be adaptable, while innovative data and visualisations of tourist flows can capture the full picture of local tourism dynamics.

Benchmarking progress within and across countries is often considered a way to monitor progress, providing a common reference point. At European level, the EU Tourism Dashboard provides opportunities for countries and regions to benchmark their progress across 19 common measures and a set of 13 basic descriptors. Where applicable, targets are displayed for measures as well as the positive directional change for data points. These measures are provided in an open-source, online tool that provides a data visualisation at the most granular level possible, both nationally and regionally.

Contextual factors need to be taken into consideration for meaningful benchmarking and target setting. A landlocked, central destination like Switzerland could not meaningfully compare total transport emissions with a remote island destination like New Zealand, or even Malta. In Spain, the four regions of Andalusia, Catalonia, Navarra and the Region of Valencia have developed and piloted a draft set of sustainability indicators, supported by the OECD under the EU-funded Technical Support Instrument. The aim is to compare sustainability performance across all Spanish regions building on common data sources. However, the project has highlighted that direct comparisons can be of limited informative value for regions with different visitor volumes, different types of tourism activity, different geographical characteristics, and different infrastructure. While benchmarking against comparable countries or regions provides opportunities to identify good practice examples and targets, monitoring development over time within one region or country can also be a valuable approach to progress towards sustainable tourism development.

Making data available to inform policy, destination management and business decisions is important to make progress and mobilise further action. The impacts of the pandemic illustrated the importance of having readily available information for decision making, with online dashboards and tools for tourism data and statistics becoming increasingly more available at the international, national and sub-national levels. Slovenia introduced a Daily tourism flows in Slovenia dashboard with published daily data on tourist arrivals and overnight stays in the current year with a three-day delay. The data are published as experimental, as they are subject to change, and do not match official monthly data, but they do provide a timely indication of changing tourism performance.

Addressing sustainability data gaps through traditional methods

Policy and decision makers take decisions based on the data available, which may not be sufficiently robust, timely and relevant to fully understand and address the issue at hand. This can lead to sub-optimal decisions and poorly targeted programmes and actions. Moreover, indicators are only of value when data exists to measure them. Addressing data gaps by focusing of the policy priorities and making the evidence available can support efforts to shift towards a more balanced approach to tourism development and inform decisions considering the trade-offs, economic externalities and interconnectedness of policy issues.

Economic measures are now well established for the tourism sector, but key sustainable tourism policy priorities still lack the data required to enable evidence-based decision-making (*e.g.* acceptance and inclusion, biodiversity, the circular economy, community and visitor sentiment, the decarbonisation of transport and digitalisation). Existing official suffice for the creation of national long-term strategic plans, but more work is required.

Combining different data sources can help enable evidence-based tourism policies. A general issue of the tourism sector is that it is a fragmented sector with many actors having access to limited data connected to their own operations. Within the Austrian National Tourism Data Space several use cases were developed to help address this (*e.g.* energy consumption and mobility). The vision is to rethink the guest experiences and create new business models, better services, seamless experiences as well as to use data for scenario planning (visitor management, seasonal and timely disparity). Through the data space, stakeholders in tourism can use data from various sources including gastronomy, accommodation, mobility, weather, mobile phone companies. It has been developed as a platform for relevant data, applications and visualisations.

The European Commission is working towards developing a common European Tourism Data Space which will provide an opportunity for tourism businesses and public authorities to share data creating opportunities to fill existing data gaps and encourage innovation across the tourism sector.

Countries are also exploring ways to fill the gap in environmental data by linking the TSA to the SEEA. Germany first developed and implemented a comprehensive methodology to link the TSA and SEEA in 2017 which has been integrated into a Tourism Satellite Account–Economy and Environment (TSA-EE). This provides data on the economic impact of the tourism sector as well as tourism-related energy consumption, air emissions, raw material input and the environmental protection expenditure in Germany. This work this has become an area of experimentation for countries with robust TSA and SEEA, data sets including Canada, Saudi Arabia, Switzerland and the United States. UN Tourism developed a technical note for linking the TSA and SEEA in 2018 (UN Tourism, 2018[23]).

In 2023, Croatia developed a methodology to link the TSA and SEEA as part of a comprehensive tourism reform agenda. However, it was found that significant challenges still remained to estimate environmental measures with the existing data, particularly for water flows and solid waste. To address these gaps in the implementation of their Tourism Sustainable Satellite Account, Croatia is undertaking a series of ten bespoke surveys to increase data availability at the national and regional level (Box 3.8). Italy has used a similar approach to derive estimates for the energy and air emissions related to tourism. However, this is only possible from the production perspective and as such misses key consumption inputs like the quantity of fuel used by tourists travelling by car (owned or rented).

The linking of the TSA and the SEEA requires a complex statistical methodology and robust granular data that is not available for all countries or destinations. The use of proxies, while not the complete picture, can help to provide an indication of the environmental progress in the sector. For example, Türkiye has developed a web-based reporting system to monitor and manage the water and energy consumption, waste volume, carbon footprint, and greenhouse gas emission data of accommodation facilities as part of the National Sustainable Tourism Programme. In Norway, CO2rism provides a tool to calculate the CO_2 emissions generated by the transport of tourists to and around Norway.

Countries have been taking steps to better understand the impacts of tourism on local residents and their communities. Resident sentiment and satisfaction surveys are one way to understand the impacts on the local population. Iceland collects survey statistics on the satisfaction of the local residents. Austria recently introduced a new survey that will be issued annually to better understand the impacts of tourism on the local populations.

Spain has implemented an online panel survey with the main goals to develop a simple to understand, easy to implement tourism acceptance/rejection indicator for destinations. The main questions include "On a scale of 1 to 5, in your opinion, how do you think tourism affects your local community?" and "On a scale of 1 to 5, how do you think tourism in your town affects you personally?". This allows Spain to capture both the personal impact and the community impact.

Box 3.8. Using national accounts data to estimate environmental impact of tourism in Croatia

Croatia's National Recovery and Resilience Plan set out a comprehensive reform agenda to promote sustainable tourism planning and development. As part of this ambitious agenda, Croatia undertook work to assess the feasibility of creating a Tourism Sustainable Satellite Account by linking the Tourism Satellite Account (TSA) and System for Environmental Economic Accounting (SEEA) national accounts frameworks. This looks to improve the measurement of the economic and environmental impacts of tourism by providing data related to energy consumption, carbon emissions, water usage and waste production in the tourism sector.

As a foundational principle this methodology utilises the economic share of the tourism sector as calculated in the TSA and applies these proportions to the environmental impact measures available in the SEEA at the sub-sectoral level to estimate the environmental impact of tourism activity. The feasibility study found that the implementation of this approach was possible for air emissions and energy usage at the national level as sufficiently granular data is available from the Croatian SEEA (at two-digit NACE level). Similarly, tourism-induced greenhouse gas emissions, tourism-related pollutant emissions, and tourism-related energy consumption could be calculated, in both absolute terms and intensity. However, indicators related to water consumption, waste generation and environmental protection expenditure require additional data sources.

Croatia will look to extend the Tourism Sustainable Satellite Account methodology to the regional level, with emphasis on the NUTS 3 regions of Adriatic Croatia. The methodology will be extended to include societal data for 10 selected destinations.

Slovenia introduced a survey to measure the local population's satisfaction with tourism as part of the Green Scheme of Slovenian Tourism. As a condition for obtaining the Slovenia Green Destination label, destinations carry out the survey, reflecting the need for granular measurement at sub-national level to respond to needs of the local population. Under the Green Scheme, Slovenia monitors largely qualitative indicators related to destination management, the nature and landscape, environment and climate, culture and tradition, social climate and tourism business operations and communication.

Harnessing the potential of new and alternative data

Official measures based on well-established approaches provide a robust and comparable set of data but can lack the granularity and timeliness required. Countries and the private sector have been exploring the opportunities being presented by new data sources. Data from private sources such as bank and credit card companies or mobile network operators provide new opportunities to monitor the performance and impact of tourism, while administrative data sources also open up new possibilities.

New data sources can help to monitor elements of tourism that have been traditionally difficult to capture, such as events, without the use of surveys which have a widening cost/effectiveness gap. Mobile phone data for example can help to understand the movement patterns of visitors between attractions and accommodation allowing policy makers to take appropriate measures such as adding public transport or soft mobility options. Utilising smart meters in tourism accommodation can provide timely insights in the energy usage of tourists.

Using a combination of these new sources can better equip decision makers to understand not only the economic impacts of tourism but also the social and environmental impacts. This can help consider how to best balance the trade-offs required to make tourism more sustainable. Countries are increasingly moving in the direction to integrate new data sources into the tourism information system, including to strengthen official tourism statistics.

In New Zealand, for example, a pilot is being undertaken to assess how the quality of soundscapes can be monitored by combining data from Global Navigation Satellite System tracking units on the movement of boats and aircraft with sound-modelling software on how sound travels in air and water. Malta meanwhile is using a combination of satellite imaging an artificial technology to map tourism development and monitor the environmental impact. This work is supporting the vision set out in Malta's Tourism Strategy 2021-30 Recover, Rethink, Revitalise and feeding into the development of a set of tailored indicators measuring and monitoring the sustainability of tourism in the country (Box 3.9).

Box 3.9. Using advanced satellite data to monitor tourism trends and impacts in Malta

With a strong rebound of tourism in Malta following the pandemic, the country aims to monitor the impacts of tourism across the country in line with the Sustainable Development Goals. To support the vision set out in Malta's Tourism Strategy 2021-30 Recover, Rethink, Revitalise, Malta is developing a set of sustainability indicators to be monitored by the Malta Tourism Authority and its Observatory. The initiative allows the Ministry for Tourism of Malta to understand and monitor the dynamics and trends of tourism, but also to support the monitoring and implementation of Malta's medium- and long-term tourism strategy.

Malta is incorporating satellite data collected in an interactive dashboard to monitor the environmental impact of tourism in the country. The twelve indicators cover vegetation health, nature and urban green extent, agricultural potential, forest health, water quality (chlorophyll, turbidity, salinity, temperature), urbanisation evolution and its proximity to cultural or natural heritage as well as city air quality. This initiative is a collaboration between Malta Tourism Authority and the tech company Murmuration.

Malta has recognised the use of technologically advanced satellite data as a new innovative addition to the more traditional set of indicators, and the benefits of combining different tools and data sources to inform decision making. The technology has sufficient resolution to understand local differences on a small territory such as the Maltese islands and allows for an assessment of the environmental impact of tourism developments in both residential and natural areas.

The use of new data sources like geospatial data (e.g. mobile positioning or satellite imagery) provide opportunities to effectively map visitors flows. For example, Lithuania have implemented heat maps using mobile positioning data to show the number of visitors at tourism sites. This heat map is publicly available to help those who make decisions based on tourist activity in the area (e.g. tourism service providers) or those who are involved in planning the development of tourist facilities or infrastructure renewal (e.g. local governments). Countries including Australia, Canada, Chile, Costa Rica, Czechia, Hungary, Ireland, Italy, Korea, Lithuania, Netherlands, Poland, Portugal, Saudi Arabia, Slovenia, Spain, Sweden and United Kingdom are exploring mobile positioning data within tourism measurement.

Switzerland used rail ticket data to estimate tourism flows between Swiss cantons which allowed for improved measurement of the regional variation and better inform the local stakeholders. Using this kind of data for estimating tourism flows relies on a large share of tourists using public transport compared to other means of transport, such as cars. Italy is analysing social media data to provide insights into tourists' perceptions, preferences, and experiences while helping to understand the socio-cultural impacts and identifying areas for improvement.

There is also a demand for predictive data concerning future travel. This could allow countries and destinations to plan resources, such as public transport, according to future demand. Countries like Hungary, Italy and Portugal are using internet search analytics for their country or regions to estimate future demand.

New data sources open a wide range of new opportunities to better understand and monitor the impacts of tourism and to evaluate the effectiveness of tourism policies and programmes. However, it is important to use these sources with caution, understanding the current limitations including issues with data quality, coverage, comparability and representativeness as well as issues related to cost and data privacy laws. For example, social media users might not be representative of the entire tourist population, meaning that the social media listening might not represent the true sentiment of tourists or those who search, might not travel. Issues still remain in the definition of tourists within new data sets such as transactions and mobile positioning data. These sources should be used in conjunction with official statistics and continue to be explored as more data becomes available.

Building data literacy and capacity for evidence-based decision making in tourism

In formulating robust and sustainable tourism policies, tourism policy makers increasingly recognise the important role of data-driven approaches in decision-making processes. Understanding the data available is important, and data literacy allows policy makers to critically evaluate the reliability, relevance, and limitations of the information at hand. This enables policy makers to make informed judgements and anticipate potential consequences of policy interventions while also conveying the rationale behind these decisions, articulating the benefits of proposed interventions and to creating greater stakeholder buy-in.

Understanding both the opportunities and limitations of the available data is essential for decision makers. Recognising the capabilities of the data in terms of its coverage, timeliness and relevance to their objectives can help to ensure that decisions are based on sound evidence. At the same time, awareness of the data limitations, including biases and gaps in coverage could help to ensure core issues are addressed in the decision-making process. While there is a growing acceptance of the importance of data and analytical capabilities for decision making, translating this to the tourism environment comes with additional complexities. In Korea, the demand for data literacy training has been increasing as analysis and data services have become more available, especially with the launch of the Korea Tourism Data Lab (Box 3.10). The Korea Tourism Data Lab provided 13 training programmes to 220 novice users in 2023.

Developing the ability to understand and effectively communicate evidence requires dedicated resources, training and capacity building. Access to data, analytical tools and expertise is essential for policy makers to navigate the complexities of evidence-based decision making. Continuous training programmes and capacity building initiatives play an important role in enhancing the data literacy of policy makers. In their communication of their mobility data and tourism dashboards, Lithuania provided training sessions of up to two hours to introduce the dashboards, and participants were asked to try to find the relevant data themselves. In Austria, insufficient data competences were noted as one of the main problems for launching the National Tourism Data Space and as such the Data Stewards Network was launched. This issue was addressed through several training sessions, and they are now advocating a "learning by doing" approach complemented by discussions of the common challenges.

Collaboration and communication between policy makers and statisticians, or others working closely with the data, is important for evidence-based decision making. Policy makers rely on statisticians and data experts to provide accurate, reliable and timely data to inform their decision-making processes. Conversely, statisticians require an understanding of policy objectives and priorities to tailor data collection, analysis and report to meet the needs of policy makers. By fostering collaboration and communication between these two groups, policy decisions can be based on robust evidence, while data-driven insights are effectively translated into actionable policies.

Box 3.10. Building tourism data capacity in Korea

Korea Tourism Data Lab provides official statistics including the Korea Tourism Statistics and the Foreign Tourist Survey, as well as tourism big data. Korea see big data is a complementary tool to official statistics and encourage users to see the tourism trends through big data rather than official figures due to the level of timeliness. Several initiatives have been undertaken to improve the usage of the Data Lab and showcase the possibilities of the available tourism data.

The Korea Tourism Data Lab Best Use Case Contest is held annually to identify how Korea Tourism Data Lab is being used to solve real business problems. In 2023, a total of 53 teams participated, with a tourist start-up *Nolowa Gurye* using the Data Lab to developed tour programmes in seven regions by analysing popular tourist destinations and major attraction factors.

To complement the Data Lab, Korea provides customised support for tourism companies with high growth potential to establish marketing strategies by integrating the data from the Data Lab with company data. In 2023, 15 companies were supported.

User surveys are conducted regularly to understand user needs for new data and analysis services, with customised services for data analysis training offered for users from for beginners to those with advanced technical skills.

Policy considerations to improve the evidence base for sustainable tourism

Optimising the strength and quality of the tourism sector involves shifting to more sustainable practices while addressing structural weaknesses that have impeded the sector in the past. This includes issues linked with seasonality, economic leakage, overdependence and overcrowding, job quality and career prospects. At the same time, actions are needed to accelerate the green tourism transition and ensure that the sector is fully able to benefit from opportunities presented by the digital transition.

Sustainability is now being mainstreamed into tourism strategies, but this needs to be supported by effective policies and implementation structures to develop and manage tourism sustainably, across all levels of government. Delivering on this sustainable tourism agenda requires the development and implementation of policies and programmes that are evidence-based and informed by relevant data. Countries require robust and timely data that is sufficiently disaggregated and comparable to inform the tourism planning, policy and decision-making process. Data is also needed to determine the desired type and scale of tourism appropriate for individual destinations.

Policy considerations to improve the evidence base for sustainable tourism development, include:

- **Considering a policy-led approach to identifying indicators will support evidence-based policies**. Starting with the key policy questions then analysing the data availability and gaps that need to be closed to answer these questions allows for destinations and decision makers to target resources towards prioritised issues. This integrated approach can help to minimise the number of indicators to a core set that can have the greatest impact and deliver the desired outcomes. Understanding the policy goals can also help to ensure that the data selected measures and monitors the issues, understanding the complex and interconnected nature of the tourism sector, and helping to balance the trade-offs required in the policy making process.
- **Addressing the data gaps in the measurement of priority issues for sustainable tourism development**. Tourism data has traditionally focused on the economic impacts of the sector. This has put an emphasis on the economic development, sometimes at the expense of the environment

and local communities. Exploring new opportunities to monitor and measure actions related to the environmental and social issues within the sector could help to accelerate the transition to more sustainable models of tourism. This includes also considering the role of new data beyond the traditional statistical survey measures while taking into account the potential limitations of such sources.

- **Designing a tailored toolkit of indicators, tools and metrics to facilitate evidence-based decision making**. Building on the significant body of existing work on sustainable tourism indicators with new methods being presented by the digital transition can help to align short term actions with long-term strategic goals. Different types of data and tools have different purposes and should be utilised to benefit decision makers. Bringing together robust and internationally comparable data with more targeted, timely and granular measures provides opportunities to create tailored plans for local and regional destinations that align with national and international goals. Measures within the toolkit should be regularly reviewed and assessed to ensure they meet the policy need.
- **Fostering collaborative approaches in the process of designing tools and metrics for the monitoring of tourism**. Bringing both data experts and decision makers together to develop the evidence base for sustainable tourism development can have lasting benefits. Incorporating the policy maker early can allow for more targeted tools that meet the needs of the decision maker, create buy-in for the product, which can help for resources, and builds the capacity of both the policy maker and the data professional. Creating diverse collaboration structures through the development phase, with input from decision makers at all levels, including the private sector, can uncover new sources of information and ensure tools adapted to consider the changing needs of different destinations.
- **Develop the data literacy of decision makers**. Even the best designed tool to measure and monitor sustainable tourism development will be ineffective if decision makers are not able to use it. While collaboration between data and policy experts is necessary to design and implement new data tools and metrics, decision makers (in both policy and the private sector) need to be able to fully digest and utilise these tools to make the right decisions. Increasing the data literacy of decision makers and ensuring that new data initiatives and tools have the appropriate levels of training to understand both the potential and the barriers can help to support more sound policy and business decisions.

References

Council of the European Union (2022), *Council conclusions on a European Agenda for Tourism 2030*, https://data.consilium.europa.eu/doc/document/ST-15441-2022-INIT/en/pdf. [10]

ESPON (2020), *Carrying capacity methodology for tourism*, https://www.espon.eu/sites/default/files/attachments/Tourism_final-report.pdf. [22]

ETC/ULS (2018), *Tourism and the environment - towards a reporting mechanism in Europe*, https://www.eionet.europa.eu/etcs/etc-uls/products/etc-uls-reports/etc-uls-report-01-2018-tourism-and-the-environment-towards-a-reporting-mechanism-in-europe. [9]

European Commission (2023), *EU Tourism Dashboard*, https://tourism-dashboard.ec.europa.eu/?lng=en. [14]

European Commission (2023), *Transition Pathway for Tourism: Summary of stakeholder pledges and commitments published on 31 March 2023*, https://ec.europa.eu/docsroom/documents/54074. [12]

European Commission (2022), *EU Tourism Dashboard*, https://single-market-economy.ec.europa.eu/sectors/tourism/eu-funding-and-businesses/funded-projects/sustainable/indicators_en. [7]

European Commission (2022), *Transition Pathway for Tourism*, Publications Office of the European Union, https://doi.org/10.2873/344425. [11]

European Commission (2021), *The digital transition of tourism*, https://single-market-economy.ec.europa.eu/sectors/tourism/eu-tourism-transition/digital-transition-tourism_en. [19]

European Commission (2016), *European Tourism Indicators System for sustainable destination management*, https://single-market-economy.ec.europa.eu/sectors/tourism/eu-funding-and-businesses/funded-projects/sustainable/indicators_en. [13]

European Commission (2016), *The European Tourism Indicator System - ETIS toolkit for sustainable destination management*, Publications Office of the European Union, https://doi.org/10.2873/983087. [8]

Miller, G. and Torres-Delgado (2023), "Measuring sustainable tourism: a state of the art review of sustainable tourism indicators", *Journal of Sustainable Tourism*, pp. 1-13, https://doi.org/10.1080/09669582.2023.2213859. [18]

OECD (2023), *Air transport CO2 emissions*, https://stats.oecd.org/Index.aspx?DataSetCode=AIRTRANS_CO2. [21]

OECD (2023), *Better Life Index*, https://www.oecdbetterlifeindex.org/#/11111111111. [6]

OECD (2023), *Better Life Index: Life satisfaction*, https://www.oecdbetterlifeindex.org/topics/life-satisfaction/. [5]

OECD (2021), *Managing tourism development of sustainable and inclusive recovery*, OECD Publishing, https://doi.org/10.1787/23071672. [1]

UN Tourism (2023), *Measuring the Sustainability of Tourism*, https://www.unwto.org/tourism-statistics/measuring-sustainability-tourism. [4]

UN Tourism (2023), *Measuring the Sustainability of Tourism (MST): Proposals for a set of indicators*, https://webunwto.s3.eu-west-1.amazonaws.com/s3fs-public/2023-09/MST_Indicators_EG_version_13092023.pdf. [15]

UN Tourism (2018), *Linking the TSA and SEEA: A technical note*, https://seea.un.org/content/linking-tsa-and-seea-technical-note. [23]

UN Tourism and UNEP (2005), *Making tourism more sustainable - A guide for policy makers*, https://www.e-unwto.org/doi/book/10.18111/9789284408214. [2]

UNEP (2015), *Sustainable consumption and production: A handbook for policymakers*, https://www.unep.org/resources/report/sustainable-consumption-and-production-handbook-policymakers. [20]

United Nations (2022), *Sustainable Tourism*, https://sdgs.un.org/topics/sustainable-tourism. [3]

WEF (2024), *Travel and Tourism Development Index*, https://www.weforum.org/publications/travel-tourism-development-index-2024/. [16]

WTTC (2024), *Travel & Tourism's Global Footprint*, https://globaltravelfootprint.wttc.org/. [17]

Annex A.1. International sustainable tourism frameworks

Table A.1. International sustainable tourism frameworks

Indicator framework	Year	Type	Pillars/dimensions	Number of indicators
Tourism Specific Frameworks				
European Environmental Agency - Tourism and Environment Reporting Mechanism [Link]	2013	Reporting mechanism	Focus is on tourism and the environment	19 indicators (within 10 topics)
European Commission: European Tourism Indicators System [Link]	2016	Toolkit for sustainable destination management	1. Destination management 2. Social and cultural impact 3. Economic value 4. Environmental impact	43 core, 13 supplementary
European Commission: EU Tourism Dashboard [Link]	2023	Indicator dashboard	1. Environmental impact 2. Digitalisation 3. Socio-economic vulnerability	19 indicators, 13 basic descriptors
Eurostat - Methodological work on measuring the sustainable development of tourism [Link]	2006	Technical report	1. Environment (main focus) 2. Economic 3. Social	20 indicators
Eurostat - Indicators on sustainability of tourism - Working Group on Tourism Statistics [Link]	2006	Draft indicators for debate	1. Economy (monetary, volume/flows) 2. Labour market 3. Social & cultural 4. Environmental 5. Digitalisation	29 indicators, 11 to be further explored
OECD Indicators for the Integration of Environmental and Sustainability Concerns into Tourism Policies [Link]	2003	Discussion/guidance document	1. Tourism trends and patterns of environmental and social significance 2. Interactions between tourism, environment and social conditions 3. Economic linkages and policy aspects	80 indicators
OECD Indicators for Measuring Competitiveness in Tourism [Link]	2013	Guidance document	1. Tourism performance and impacts 2. Delivering quality and competitive tourism services 3. Attractiveness of destination 4. Policy responses and economic opportunities	11 core indicators, 5 supplementary and 4 for future development
OECD Tourism Paper - Supporting Quality Jobs in Tourism [Link]	2015	Policy paper	Indicators are all either economic or economic/social	11 indicators
OECD Tourism Trends and Policies 2022: Initial ideas for tourism resilience indicators [Link]	2022	Indicator ideas/proposals	1. Social 2. Economic 3. Environment 4. Institutional	29 indicators

Indicator framework	Year	Type	Pillars/dimensions	Number of indicators
UN Tourism 2004: Indicators of Sustainable Development for Tourism Destinations A Guidebook [Link]	2004	Guidance document	Split by issues (e.g. sewage treatment, employment, etc. The issues can be divided into economic, social and environmental	Over 700 indicators
UN Tourism and JICA Achieving the Sustainable Development Goals through Tourism – Toolkit of Indicators for Projects [Link]	2023	Toolkit to measure impact of tourism projects	1. Economic 2. Social 3. Environmental All indicators are linked to the SDG framework (the 17 goals and 169 targets) and a table translating between themes/dimensions and SDGs	Around 500 indicators (3-20 indicators for each of the 104 targets covered)
UN Tourism Statistical Framework for Measuring Sustainable Tourism (SF-MST) [Link]	2024	Statistical framework	1. Economic 2. Environmental 3. Social	
World Economic Forum Travel and Tourism Development Index [Link]	2022	Strategic benchmarking tool (index)	1. Environmental Sustainability 2. Socioeconomic Resilience and Conditions 3. Travel and Tourism Demand Pressure and Impact	29 indicators
World Travel and Tourism Council Environmental and Social Reporting [Link]	2023	Reporting mechanism	Environmental and social reporting	13 indictors linked to the SDGs
Non-tourism specific frameworks				
Measuring and Assessing Job Quality - The OECD Job Quality Framework (2015) [Link]	2015	Framework	1. Earnings 2. Labour Market Security 3. Quality of the Working Environment	10 (4 headline), 1 supplementary
OECD How's Life? 2020 - Measuring Well-being [Link]	2020	Indicator dashboard	11 dimensions of well-being (Income and Wealth, Housing, Work and Job Quality, Health, Knowledge and Skills, Environmental Quality, Subjective Well-being, Safety, Work-Life Balance, Social Connections, Civic Engagement)	36 (headline), 44 supplementary
OECD Regional social and environmental indicators (Edition 2021) [Link]	2021	Statistical database	1. Environment 2. Health 3. Safety 4. Social inclusion 5. Housing	42 indicators
OECD Rethinking Regional Attractiveness in the New Global Environment report: Attractiveness indicators [Link]	2023	Quantitative framework	14 dimensions, across 6 domains of attractiveness (economic attraction, connectedness, visitor appeal, natural environment, resident wellbeing, land use and housing)	54 indicators
UN Sustainable Development Goals (SDGs) [Link]	2016	Framework	17 SDGs (split by 169 targets) that can be split into the pillars of economic, social and environmental	169 targets

Part I OECD country profiles

Australia

Tourism in the economy and outlook

Tourism's contribution to the Australian economy continues to recover from the shock triggered by the COVID-19 pandemic. Tourism accounted for 2.5% of total GDP or AUD 63.0 billion in financial year 2022-23, up from a low of 1.4% of GDP in 2020-21. Prior to the pandemic (2018-19), tourism's share of national GDP was 3.1%. In 2022-23, tourism contributed to 626 400 jobs or 4.1% of total employment, but remains below the 2018-19 record level of 700 900 jobs or 5.1%. Tourism-related exports accounted for 58% of total service exports in 2022-23, up from a low of 38% in 2021-22.

In 2023, Australia recorded 7.2 million international visitor arrivals, or 75.9% of 2019 levels, with steady growth since early 2022. Spending by international tourists reached AUD 27.9 billion, with 242.3 million nights in official accommodation in 2023, recovering to 89% and 88% of 2019 levels, respectively. Australia's top 5 international tourist markets during this period were New Zealand (18%), the United States (9%), the United Kingdom (8%), China (7%), and India (6%).

Domestic overnight trips have seen growth with 112.6 million trips in 2023, sitting 4% below pre-pandemic levels. Total domestic overnight spend for 2023 was AUD 109.3 billion in nominal terms, up 35% on the same period in 2019. The increase in spend is in part attributable to higher prices for travel and related services.

International tourist arrivals are expected to exceed pre-pandemic levels by 2025 to reach 10.2 million. By 2028, international visitation is forecast to be 12.1 million visitors, with spend in Australia of AUD 50.7 billion. Domestic tourism is projected to grow to 128.9 million domestic overnight trips by 2028, up 10% on 2019.

Tourism governance

The Australian Trade and Investment Commission (Austrade) is the federal government agency responsible for tourism policy, programmes, and research. Within Austrade, Tourism Research Australia provides international and domestic tourism data, statistics, and analysis.

Tourism Australia is the government agency responsible for attracting international visitors to the country. Tourism Australia works closely with Australia's state and territory tourism organisations and with key partners to roll out international tourism campaigns and to support the Australian tourism industry to grow tourism.

Austrade works with the Department of Foreign Affairs and Trade to strengthen bilateral tourism relationships and leverage key multilateral tourism bodies. All state and territory governments in Australia incorporate tourism into their portfolios to ensure effective international and domestic tourism promotion and sector development. The Tourism Ministers' Meetings (TMM) bring together tourism ministers from the federal, state and territory governments to discuss tourism policy matters of mutual interest. This work is supported by the Australian Standing Committee on Tourism (ASCOT), which is chaired by Austrade and includes representatives from Tourism Australia, state and territory tourism organisations, and relevant state departments with responsibility for tourism policy. Representatives from the tourism sector and other relevant federal and state departments can be invited to attend ASCOT and TMM meetings, as necessary. Austrade hosts a regular stakeholder engagement forum with a wide range of tourism industry bodies.

A THRIVE 2030 Implementation Advisory Group composed of a mix of industry leaders and government officials' reviews progress against the THRIVE 2030 strategy and provides advice to the Australian Government Minister for Tourism to achieve recovery from the COVID-19 pandemic and long-term sustainable tourism growth.

Tourism Australia's budget allocation was AUD 184.5 million to support its activities during financial year 2023-24.

Australia: Organisational chart of tourism bodies

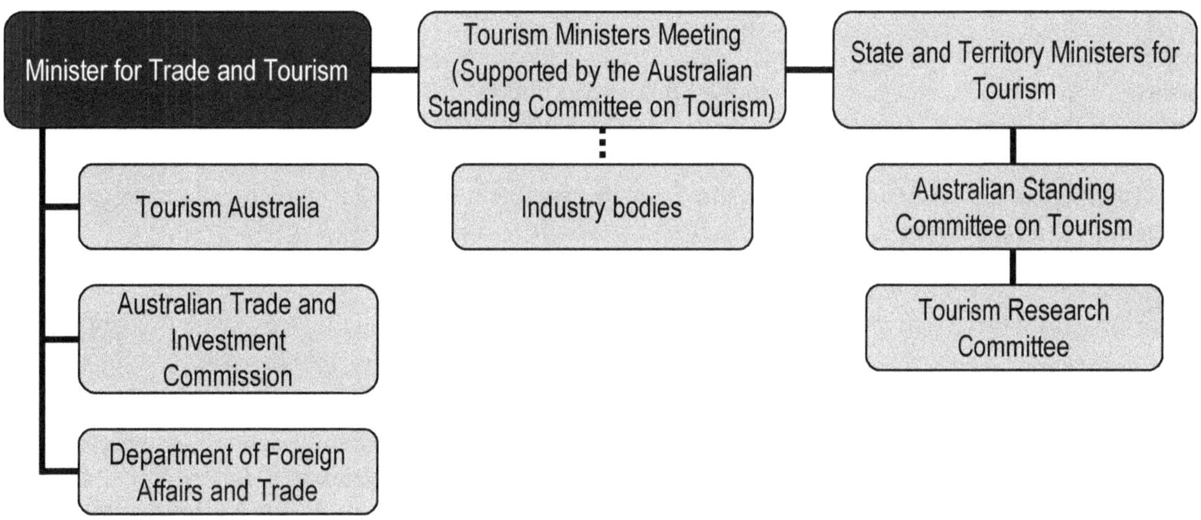

Source: OECD, adapted from the Australian Government, 2024.

Tourism policies and programmes

THRIVE (The Re-Imagined Visitor Economy) 2030 is Australia's national strategy for the long-term sustainable growth of the visitor economy. The Strategy focuses on seven policy priority areas with 64 strategic actions for all levels of government and the tourism sector:

- Deliver success through comprehensive collaboration.
- Improve data and insights.
- Grow a secure and resilient workforce.
- Embrace leading edge business practices.
- Enhance visitor infrastructure.
- Build markets and attract visitors.
- Grow unique and high-quality products, including First Nations experiences.

There are 21 federal government agencies involved in the delivery of the strategy. The priority actions that have been completed are often related to the setting up of the governance structure like appointing advisory councils and establishing working groups. As of May 2024, 22 actions have been completed, 40 actions are underway, and two actions are pending.

The Strategy focuses on the pandemic recovery phase through to the end of 2024. The target to return to pre-pandemic visitor expenditure of AUD 166 billion by December 2024 was exceeded in 2023. The long-term target is to grow the visitor economy to AUD 230 billion by 2030, with regional destinations outside of state and territorial capital cities to comprise approximately 44% of this goal. The Strategy will be reviewed in 2024 to check progress against the targets set and the associated Action Plan; as well as to design the priority actions for the future Consolidation (2025-27) and Growth phases (2028-30) of the Strategy.

As part of the Strategy delivery, Tourism Australia is focusing on rebuilding visitation and spend from key international markets, concentrating on trade and consumer marketing programmes to help the industry return to 2019 levels. This includes actions to maximise the global impact of the Come And Say G'Day campaign, with a campaign launch in China, convert demand by working with airline and key distribution partners; launch a major events strategy which began with the FIFA Women's World Cup hosted by Australia and New Zealand in 2023; promote work and travel around Australia to prospective working holiday makers; elevate and championing Indigenous, sustainable and accessible tourism; and drive consideration and conversion of business events.

In May 2023, the International Diversification Strategy for the Visitor Economy discussion paper was released with the full strategy to be released before the end of 2024. Tourism is also one of 10 priority sectors in the Invested: Australia's Southeast Asia Economic Strategy to 2040, which sets a practical pathway to significantly increase two-way trade and investment between Australia and Southeast Asia. Recommendations are included to expand tourism promotion and build industry capability to meet Southeast Asian demand.

Other key policy responses to challenges and opportunities for Australian tourism include:

- Preparing an Aviation White Paper to set long-term policy for growth and innovation in aviation to ensure efficiency, sustainability, consumer protections, accessibility, and inclusion, ensuring there are appropriately skilled workers within the aviation sector (broader government initiative).
- Supporting visitor economy businesses to implement and improve sustainability practices. A Sustainability Framework, released in late 2023, establishes a national definition and vision for sustainable tourism that considers environmental, cultural, social, and economic factors. The complementary Sustainable Tourism Toolkit provides guidance and advice to assist the large number of micro and small tourism businesses implement sustainability practices.
- Examining workforce issues, including the Employment White Paper, the Migration Strategy, and a parliamentary inquiry into Northern Australia workforce needs. Non-traditional workforces are also being encouraged into the tourism workforce (Box 2.2). Austrade developed a Visitor Economy Workforce and Skills Interim Action Plan to capture workforce capability actions across Australian Government, State and Territory Governments and industry.
- Supporting First Nations communities including through the First Nations Tourism Mentoring Program, launched in February 2023 with a budget of AUD 10 million, and delivered by the National Indigenous Australians Agency. This programme aims to foster the growth of the First Nations tourism sector and embed First Nations culture in the tourism sector.

Statistical Profile

Australia: Domestic, inbound and outbound tourism

	2018	2019	2020	2021	2022
TOURISM FLOWS, THOUSAND					
Domestic tourism					
Total domestic trips	310 166	365 797	236 706	242 543	309 626
Overnight visitors (tourists)	104 822	117 448	72 514	82 074	108 212
Same-day visitors (excursionists)	205 344	248 349	164 192	160 469	201 414
Nights in all types of accommodation	371 528	417 907	275 404	321 109	399 726
Hotels and similar establishments	95 298	101 047	51 589	67 162	106 270
Other collective establishments	94 416	111 905	79 557	90 006	104 781
Private accommodation	181 814	204 955	144 258	163 940	188 675
Inbound tourism					
Total international arrivals	9 246	9 466	1 828	246	3 694
Overnight visitors (tourists)	..	..	..	..	..
Same-day visitors (excursionists)	..	..	..	..	..
Top markets					
New Zealand	1 385	1 434	243	97	698
United Kingdom1	733	716	201	22	399
United States	789	818	189	17	326
India	358	399	84	13	303
Singapore	448	479	58	16	296
Nights in all types of accommodation	273 793	274 477	68 973	16 779	126 098
Hotels and similar establishments	29 232	28 840	..	..	..
Other collective establishments	135 269	138 774	..	..	..
Private accommodation	109 293	106 863	..	..	..
Outbound tourism					
Total international departures	11 061	11 309	2 832	301	5 226
Overnight visitors (tourists)	..	..	..	..	..
Same-day visitors (excursionists)	..	..	..	..	..
Top destinations					
New Zealand	1 437	1 463	439	160	708
Indonesia	1 280	1 401	310	2	612
United States	1 096	1 056	236	17	463
United Kingdom1	663	663	147	15	416
India	393	426	186	12	329
TOURISM RECEIPTS AND EXPENDITURE, MILLION AUD					
Inbound tourism					
Total international receipts	63 253	68 949	38 382	..	..
International travel receipts	60 276	65 484	37 520	22 615	34 755
International passenger transport receipts	2 977	3 197	861	..	..
Outbound tourism					
Total international expenditure	56 853	59 507	11 573	..	..
International travel expenditure	50 043	50 778	11 060	1 570	23 469
International passenger transport expenditure	7 339	7 737	1 742	..	..

.. Not available
1. United Kingdom including, Channel Islands and Isle of Man.
Source: OECD Tourism Statistics (Database).

StatLink https://stat.link/nl7gcu

Australia: Enterprises and employment in tourism

	Number of establishments[1]	Number of persons employed				
	2021	2018	2019	2020	202&	2022
Total	..	700 900	597 800	402 000	442 600	626 400
Tourism industries	358 203	678 200	581 000	391 800	432 900	610 200
Accommodation services for visitors	14 351	85 300	88 900	53 900	61 500	84 400
Hotels and similar establishments	..	..	..	..	..	..
Food and beverage serving industry	96 549	269 100	227 300	188 800	187 500	257 800
Passenger transport	44 831	54 300	46 200	27 400	32 000	41 200
Air passenger transport	5 718	45 000	40 400	24 100	28 000	33 900
Railways passenger transport	85	1 900	..	..	..	..
Road passenger transport	39 028	7 400	5 800	3 300	4 000	7 300
Water passenger transport	..	..	..	..	..	..
Passenger transport supporting services	..	..	..	..	..	..
Transport equipment rental	..	..	..	..	..	..
Travel agencies and other reservation services industry	8 647	35 300	29 100	21 000	31 300	35 300
Cultural industry	19 950	10 700	9 300	6 400	8 500	13 200
Sports and recreation industry	17 115	32 600	29 200	19 000	24 100	38 200
Retail trade of country-specific tourism characteristic goods	156 760	119 900	93 800	72 200	74 700	107 200
Other country-specific tourism industries	..	71 000	57 100	3 100	13 100	32 700
Other industries	..	22 700	16 800	10 200	9 700	16 200

.. Not available
1. Data refer to number of enterprises.
Source: OECD Tourism Statistics (Database).

StatLink https://stat.link/2ondr4

Australia: Internal tourism consumption

Million AUD

	2022		
	Domestic tourism expenditure	Inbound tourism expenditure	Internal tourism consumption
Total	..	..	..
Consumption products	138 423	26 105	164 528
Tourism characteristic products	85 014	12 276	97 290
Accommodation services for visitors	19 313	3 775	23 090
Food and beverage serving services	24 860	2 513	27 373
Passenger transport services	20 850	3 536	24 387
Air passenger transport services	..	..	..
Railways passenger transport services	..	..	..
Road passenger transport services	..	..	..
Water passenger transport services	..	..	..
Passenger transport supporting services	..	..	..
Transport equipment rental services	2 001	557	2 558
Travel agencies and other reservation services industry	8 600	1 130	9 730
Cultural services	..	..	..
Sports and recreation services	9 390	763	10 153
Country-specific tourism characteristic goods	..	..	..
Country-specific tourism characteristic services	..	..	..
Other consumption products	53 408	13 830	67 238
Tourism connected products	52 158	12 889	65 047
Non-tourism related consumption products	1 250	941	2 191
Non-consumption products	..	..	..

.. Not available
Source: OECD Tourism Statistics (Database).

StatLink https://stat.link/yatp09

Austria

Tourism in the economy and outlook

Tourism is an important driver of the Austrian economy. The sector is estimated to have directly contributed EUR 20.3 billion or 4.3% of total GDP in 2023, more than double the amount of 2021 (EUR 8.9 billion) but still short of pre-pandemic levels of EUR 21.9 billion or 5.5% of GDP in 2019.

Austria counted 217 500 employees connected to accommodation and restaurants, contributing to 5.6% of total employment in 2022. International travel receipts reached EUR 19.1 billion in 2022, or 23.9% of total service exports – this is almost double the amount of 2021 (EUR 10.5 billion or 14.8% of service exports) but still below 2019 levels (EUR 22.9 billion or 29.9% of service exports).

The number of international tourist arrivals recorded in all accommodation establishments (commercial and private) in 2023 was 30.9 million, or 97% of 2019 levels. This is up 144% from the lowest of the pandemic, in 2021. Germany remains the top international source market, accounting for 52% of overnight stays, followed by the Netherlands (10%) and Switzerland (4%).

Domestic tourist arrivals in paid accommodation totalled 14.3 million (a 99.9% recovery on 2019 levels), with 39.9 million bednights registered (99.9% on 2019 levels).

Latest forecasts by the Austrian Institute of Economic Research from May 2024 expect around 81.5 million overnights for the summer season 2024, a 3.3% increase compared to the same period in 2019. However, tourism revenue in real terms is expected to stay below 2019 levels, due to continuously high inflation and visitors spending less money.

Tourism governance

At the national level, the Federal Ministry of Labour and Economy is responsible for tourism policy and is overseen by a Parliamentary Committee for Tourism. Legislative and executive responsibility for tourism affairs resides with the nine provinces (*Länder*). Co-ordination between the Ministry and the *Länder* is supported through a Steering Group for Tourism. In addition, the Ministry works with other ministries, departments, institutions, and the private sector on specific topics either via permanent groups, round tables or on a case-by-case basis (e.g. new funding schemes, new legislation affecting tourism).

Austria Tourism, the National Tourist Office, is responsible for market research, brand management, marketing, tourism networking, innovation, and information provision. The Austrian Bank for Tourism Development is a specialised tourism bank acting in a public-private partnership with the Ministry. Statistics Austria collects and disseminates tourism data.

The national tourism administration had a total budget of EUR 65.7 million in 2023. Of this, EUR 28 million was dedicated to financial support for SMEs administered by Austrian Bank for Tourism Development with a further EUR 30.1 million allocated to the Austrian National Tourist Office. The Ministry disbursed EUR 5.8 million through individual subsidies for co-financed tourism projects and service contracts. In addition, SMEs in the tourism sector received EUR 23.3 million from the European Recovery Programme.

In addition to the national budget, all nine *Länder* have tourism budgets to support specific tourism development programmes.

Austria: Organisational chart of tourism bodies

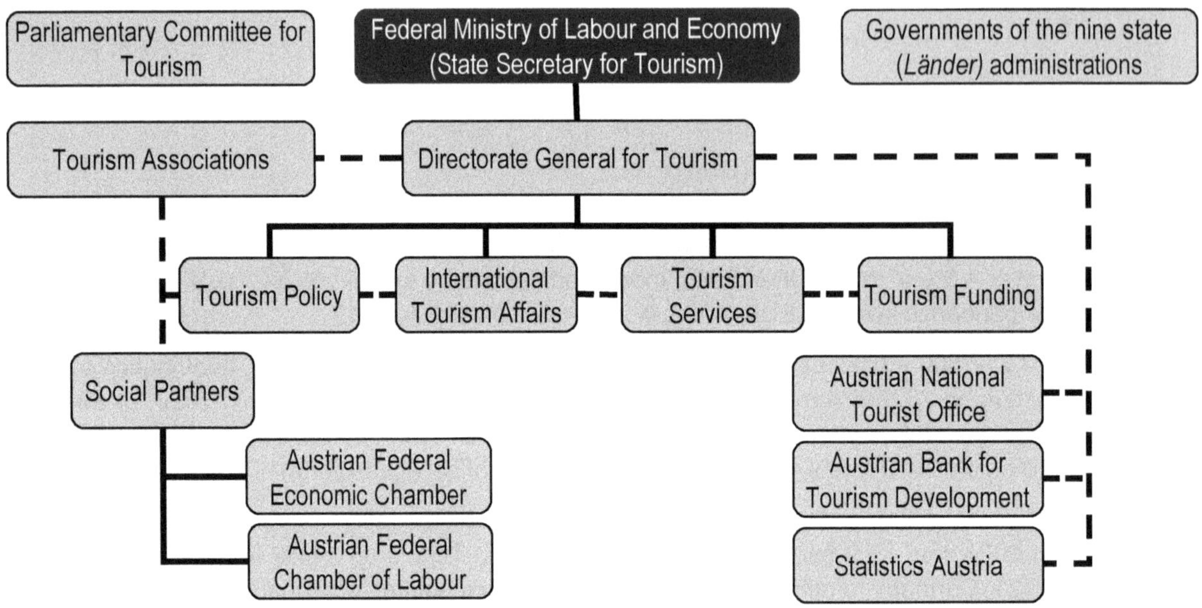

Source: OECD, adapted from the Federal Ministry of Labour and Economy, 2024.

Tourism policies and programmes

Austria's national tourism strategy – the Plan T - Master Plan for Tourism – was launched in spring 2019 and continues to be the base of national tourism policy. The Plan T aims to contribute to the implementation of Agenda 2030 to meet the UN Sustainable Development Goals. The Plan T has nine priority areas, supplemented by specific action plans that outline short-term objectives and respective measures, which for the years 2023-24 include:

- Strengthening the awareness of tourism: actions to further develop tourism indicators to measure success in all dimensions of sustainability (e.g. tourism energy mix, energy consumption, tourism acceptance, inflation/price competitiveness, number of Ecolabel certified enterprises and destinations). Other actions include pooling expertise on policy trends and promoting targeted networking through new formats of stakeholder involvement.
- Establishing a co-operative culture: actions to intensify co-operation with the federal states and political/private stakeholders on sustainability in general, sustainable mobility, digitalisation, financing and tourism marketing.
- Using digital potential: actions to support ongoing development of a Tourism Data Space to collect, exchange and link tourism-relevant data to benefit visitors and businesses and run use cases on visitor management, AI-supported booking/price forecasting, energy efficiency optimisation. Other actions include digitalising the guest registration system and establishing a digital accommodation register; and strengthening digital skills through Austrian National Tourist Office's Data Stewards programme.
- Designing an attractive business environment: actions to improve framework conditions for short-term rentals and support measures for business succession.

- Making training and labour market fit for the future: actions include an online awareness raising campaign Team Tourism = Strong Industry = Your Chance launched in June 2023 to attract and retain staff in the long-term, on social media and a dedicated website. Other actions include developing new curricula for tourism schools and facilitating the entrance of non-EU tourism professionals into the Austrian labour market with the Red-White-Red card and the increase of seasonal quotas.
- Keeping our livelihood sustainable: actions include increasing the number of certified businesses and destinations (with focus on the Austrian Ecolabel) and providing support to the sector on issues such as sustainable tourism mobility and energy efficiency based on a certification strategy and workshops (event series, dedicated platforms, information material, guidelines).
- Creating regional value-added for everybody: actions include the RESY-Dashboard with data on municipal level for various indicators, launched in June 2024. The dashboard is the result of a pilot project with two destinations on implementing regional information and monitoring systems; co-operation with the agricultural sector via a culinary network; and the 2024 edition of Austria's Tourism Innovation Price, which focuses on culinary experiences.
- Further developing tourism marketing: the National Tourist Office has the following main fields of activity: i) communication: current campaign A Summer in Austria – Your Daily Dose of 'Lebensgefühl', marketing initiatives on art and culture (e.g. Feel Austria Festival, influencer trips); ii) co-operation: product development and marketing with stakeholders and Austrian Tourism Day; iii) innovation: AI projects, new B2C and B2B website, focus on sustainability initiatives, market and trend research; and iv) strengthening worldwide network with Austrian embassies and the trade promotion organisation of the Austrian Federal Economic Chamber.
- Making financing and promotion more flexible: includes actions to develop new funding guidelines for tourism SME with a focus on resilience and sustainability (see box below); make use of EU funds for innovative tourism projects; and provide continuous funding support of alpine infrastructure.

New funding guidelines for tourism SMEs in Austria: 'Sustainability bonus' and ESG indicators

In 2023, the Austrian Ministry of Labour and Economy through the Austrian Bank for Tourism Development presented new funding guidelines to support investments by family-run and owner-managed tourism SMEs to strengthen sustainability and financial resilience. The scheme includes subsidised loans and guarantees, along with a 'sustainability bonus' of 7% (max. EUR 350 000) of the investment costs in one of three categories: ecology, staff & regions, digitalisation.

To address tourism intensity and land use issues, the guidelines exclude funding for new buildings in municipalities with over 500.000 overnight stays per tourism year (baseline 2021-22) and projects that increase land surface sealing by over 25%. In 2023, 12 tourism SMEs were granted 'sustainability bonuses' worth a total of EUR 1.7 million.

Moreover, a tourism-specific questionnaire on environment, social and governance (ESG) performance indicators was developed in 2023, for use by banks and businesses to assess their sustainability performance. Information is collected by the public-private bank OeKB Group in its ESG Data Hub. In addition, the Austrian Bank for Tourism Development requires businesses at time of application and during the funding period to report the ESG performance indicators. In the future, the bank plans to publish aggregated ESG data at regular intervals.

Statistical Profile

Austria: Domestic, inbound and outbound tourism

	2018	2019	2020	2021	2022
TOURISM FLOWS, THOUSAND					
Domestic tourism					
Total domestic trips	..	..	..	..	..
Overnight visitors (tourists)	14 033	14 312	9 939	9 416	13 580
Same-day visitors (excursionists)	..	..	..	..	..
Nights in all types of accommodation	39 390	39 944	31 596	29 599	38 881
Hotels and similar establishments	34 201	34 767	25 724	24 577	33 457
Other collective establishments	1 734	1 737	2 267	2 098	2 135
Private accommodation	3 454	3 440	3 605	2 924	3 289
Inbound tourism					
Total international arrivals	..	..	..	..	..
Overnight visitors (tourists)	30 816	31 884	15 091	12 728	26 215
Same-day visitors (excursionists)	..	..	..	..	..
Top markets					
Germany	14 092	14 383	8 550	7 810	13 526
Netherlands	2 001	2 074	1 361	934	2 049
Switzerland and Liechtenstein	1 445	1 451	805	573	1 124
Italy	1 099	1 108	331	335	821
United Kingdom	996	966	304	86	653
Nights in all types of accommodation	110 430	112 765	66 280	49 964	98 031
Hotels and similar establishments	84 078	85 982	47 408	35 753	73 752
Other collective establishments	5 216	5 404	3 735	4 282	5 718
Private accommodation	21 136	21 379	15 137	9 930	18 561
Outbound tourism					
Total international departures	13 646	14 388	5 072	8 628	16 790
Overnight visitors (tourists)	11 043	11 902	3 965	7 522	14 041
Same-day visitors (excursionists)	2 604	2 486	1 108	1 106	2 749
Top destinations					
Germany	2 044	2 559	1 154	1 633	2 379
Italy	2 058	2 269	749	1 994	2 997
Croatia	1 375	1 000	237	845	1 549
Spain	504	629	129	351	752
Greece	322	577	93	469	571
TOURISM RECEIPTS AND EXPENDITURE, MILLION EUR					
Inbound tourism					
Total international receipts	21 404	23 127	13 436	10 168	21 205
International travel receipts	19 559	20 493	12 124	8 836	18 912
International passenger transport receipts	1 845	2 634	1 312	1 332	2 293
Outbound tourism					
Total international expenditure	11 967	12 491	4 518	6 894	12 273
International travel expenditure	10 019	10 364	3 925	6 135	10 591
International passenger transport expenditure	1 948	2 127	593	759	1 682

.. Not available
Source: OECD Tourism Statistics (Database).

StatLink https://stat.link/my54gz

Austria: Enterprises and employment in tourism

	Number of establishments[1]	Number of persons employed				
	2018	2018	2019	2020	2021	2022
Total	..	..	..	..	..	..
Tourism industries	89 544	199 300	205 700	128 600	107 800	..
Accommodation services for visitors	..	130 600	134 700	94 800	79 600	..
Hotels and similar establishments	16 577	..	..	..	..	..
Food and beverage serving industry	31 597	..	..	..	..	..
Passenger transport	12 489	34 500	35 700	11 700	9 000	..
Air passenger transport	169	..	..	..	..	..
Railways passenger transport	32	..	..	..	..	..
Road passenger transport	12 199	..	..	..	..	..
Water passenger transport	89	..	..	..	..	..
Passenger transport supporting services	..	..	..	..	..	..
Transport equipment rental	2 675	..	..	..	..	..
Travel agencies and other reservation services industry	2 488	11 500	11 900	9 900	8 100	..
Cultural industry	21 980	22 700	23 300	12 200	11 000	..
Sports and recreation industry	1 738		..	..	..	..
Retail trade of country-specific tourism characteristic goods	..	..	..	..	..	..
Other country-specific tourism industries	..	..	..	..	..	..
Other industries	..	..	..	..	..	..

.. Not available
1. Data refer to number of enterprises.
Source: OECD Tourism Statistics (Database).

StatLink https://stat.link/3v6cgb

Austria: Internal tourism consumption

Million EUR

	2022		
	Domestic tourism expenditure	Inbound tourism expenditure	Internal tourism consumption
Total	11 113	18 718	30 821
Consumption products	..	..	..
Tourism characteristic products	..	..	..
Accommodation services for visitors	..	..	9 113
Food and beverage serving services	..	..	7 004
Passenger transport services	..	..	5 543
Air passenger transport services	..	..	1 520
Railways passenger transport services	..	..	1 063
Road passenger transport services	..	..	2 890
Water passenger transport services	..	..	69
Passenger transport supporting services	..	..	..
Transport equipment rental services	..	..	151
Travel agencies and other reservation services industry	..	..	404
Cultural services	..	..	3 067
Sports and recreation services	..	..	..
Country-specific tourism characteristic goods	..	..	..
Country-specific tourism characteristic services	..	..	..
Other consumption products	..	..	5 540
Tourism connected products	..	..	..
Non-tourism related consumption products	..	..	..
Non-consumption products	..	..	..

.. Not available
Source: OECD Tourism Statistics (Database).

StatLink https://stat.link/h9giqm

Belgium

Tourism in the economy and outlook

In Belgium, tourism is under the respective authority of three regions: Flanders, Wallonia, and Brussels. This section provides a national overview of the impact of tourism in the country, followed by detail of the respective governance and policy initiatives of the Flanders and Wallonia regions. Travel exports represented 5.0% of total service exports in 2022.

In 2022, Belgium received 5.7 million international tourists in hotel accommodations (84% of 2019 levels), who spent a total of 10.9 million nights in the country. Of this figure, 2.8 million visited Flanders, 2.2 million visited Brussels and 730 000 visited Wallonia. The top three source markets in 2022 were the Netherlands (22%), France (17%) and Germany (11%).

Based on a travel survey, Belgium estimates that 5.8 million domestic trips were taken in 2022 in all types of accommodation. This is 7.4% above 2019 levels.

Flanders Region

Tourism governance

In Flanders, tourism is the responsibility of the Flemish Minister for Justice and Enforcement, Environment and Spatial Development, Energy and Tourism. The Tourism Unit of the Flanders Department of Chancellery and Foreign Affairs is responsible for international tourism policy and relations. Visit Flanders is responsible for the sustainable development and promotion of Flanders as a tourist destination.

The overall public sector budget allocated to tourism remains stable at around EUR 43 million in 2022.

Flanders: Organisational chart of tourism bodies

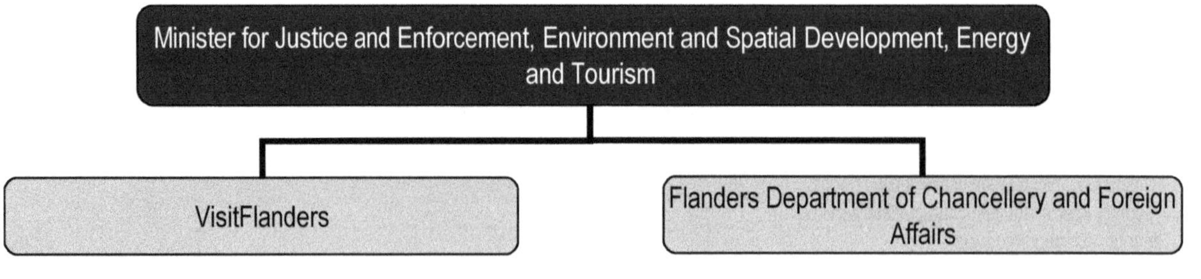

Source: OECD, adapted from the Flanders Department of Chancellery and Foreign Affairs, 2024.

Tourism policies and programmes

Tourism in Flanders is guided by a broader Flemish Resilience 2022-26 regional recovery plan, which has the aim of helping all economic sectors, including tourism, to recover from the economic downturn of the COVID-19 crisis. The Plan has a total budget of approximately EUR 4.3 billion of which EUR 130 million is allocated to tourism. The tourism component of the Plan is centred around investments mainly focused on larger-scale infrastructure and supra-local visitor experiences. At the beginning of 2023, EUR 122 million was attributed to projects, which are all on schedule.

The 2030 long-term strategy for tourism in Flanders is based upon the principles of Travel to Tomorrow, a value-driven vision launched in 2017, built on balance and sustainable tourism principles that also considers quality, creativity, and co-operation. This vision was created in conjunction with the private sector and aims to achieve flourishing communities and vibrant destinations. The Strategy has four main objectives:

- Ensure the demands of the visitor are in balance with the needs of the destination and its residents.
- Connect groups in Flanders to make a more impactful visitor experience.
- Make holidays possible for anyone who experiences barriers.
- Flemish-wide approach that is high-quality and increases the impact.

As part of the Strategy, Flanders launched an updated programme called Everyone Deserves a Holiday in December 2023. Data indicates that 13% of Flemish citizens cannot afford an annual week of holiday due to financial or health reasons. In co-operation with social mediation offices, the programme allows recipients to undertake a holiday at a reduced rate and strengthens the network of organisations who support socially vulnerable groups.

In addition, Visit Flanders has set up an ambitious Sustainability Plan. Launched in 2022, the plan includes 20 indicators to monitor destination management and the business operations of Visit Flanders, with a time horizon of 2030. Key pillars of the plan are inclusiveness and accessibility, transport, communication and access to information, sustainability of the tourism offer and events, liveability, and reduction of greenhouse gas emissions. The goals for 2030 include: increase in the number of tourism businesses certified with a Green Key Label by 44%; make all conference locations accessible to mobility-impaired visitors; reduce greenhouse gas emissions in tourist accommodations by 50%; reduce primary energy consumption of transport operators by 35%; and reduce business travel emissions by 25%.

Wallonia Region

Tourism governance

In Wallonia, tourism is the responsibility of the Minister for Public Service, Tourism, Heritage, and Road Safety. The German-speaking community in Wallonia has made an agreement with Wallonia to manage tourism in its territory. Two main bodies support the Wallonia tourism sector:

- The General Tourism Commission (CGT) is the main tourism administration in Wallonia and focuses on developing quality tourism. It provides support to the sector through advice, recognition, labelling and financial aid.
- Wallonia Belgium Tourism (WBT) is responsible for promoting Walloon tourism in Belgium and foreign markets.

The 2023 Walloon budget allocated to tourism was EUR 67 million.

Wallonia: Organisational chart of tourism bodies

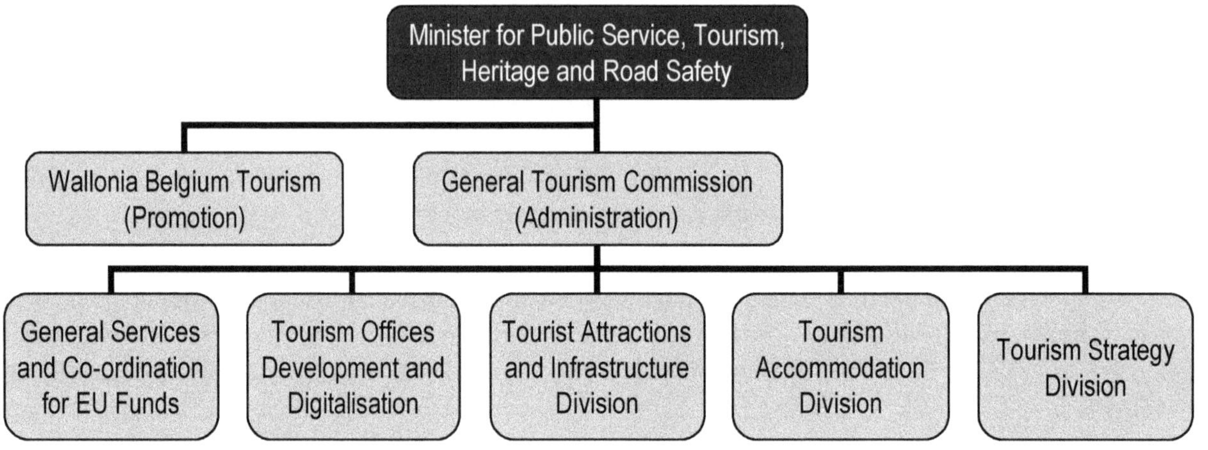

Source: OECD, adapted from the General Tourism Commission of Wallonia, 2024.

Tourism policies and programmes

Tourism in Wallonia is governed by the Wallonia Recovery Plan launched in 2021. In 2022 priority actions to implement the Plan were drafted in partnerships with representative of trade unions, employers and the environment. As part of the Plan, which is partly financed by the European Union, the General Tourism Commission (CGT) launched several projects in 2023:

- A new digital platform and database: CGT and VISITWallonia are preparing the implementation of a transactional platform to connect tourism administrations to tourism operators and organisations (B2B). It is aimed to be a single database for Walloon tourism stakeholders, suitable for tourism authorisations, subsidies, promotion, and other relevant activities. Data and operations will be centralised and visible in real time to authorised stakeholders.
- My Digital Baggage: a digital platform launched in co-operation with CGT, VISITWallonia, Forem Tourisme Competence Centre and other tourism stakeholders, which offer over 3 000 tourist operators targeted tools to develop digital competences and digital offer. Initially, 24 operators participated in the pilot phase of the project. Through this project, Wallonia aims to accelerate digitalisation and resilience of tourism operators, while promoting its tourism offer.
- Developing indicators to measure the social, environmental and accessibility of tourism, in particular on social dimensions. With the current indicators in Wallonia it is not possible to measure the contribution of the tourism sector to dimensions other than Walloon economic development.
- Facilitating participation for anyone living in a difficult social and/or economic situation to explore leisure and tourism activities. Wallonia launched new partnerships to enhance the accessibility of tourism activities. In 2023, more than 2 000 beneficiaries participated and 26 new tourism activity offers were certified in addition to the 16 previously certified in 2021-22.
- Improving the quality of destinations through the continued improvement of the Wallonia Destination Quality (WDQ) approach. WDQ offers workshops encouraging tourism operators to question their mission, vision, and value, as well as concrete tools to support business operations. The aim is to reorganise the tools already available and create new instruments so that each tourism operator aims to strengthen the quality of its services and/or its management.
- Improving the nature tourism offer through a number of projects. This includes improving the brand of Wallonia nature parks, the Biodiversity 360° strategy on sustainable and eco-responsible

development of tourist activities, and exploring the use of digital tools to monitor tourist flows in Walloon natural areas, in particular using big data analysis.

- Increasing the skills and attractiveness of tourism professions (see box below).

Improving data and information to better match tourism employers and workers in Wallonia

Wallonia is undertaking work to improve the labour and skills supply-demand match by creating a common list of tourism professions, skills, and training. Data relating to the tourism sector employment is often scattered and does not enable the different representatives of the sector to speak with one voice. A related challenge is enhancing the value of tourism professions and the attractiveness of the Walloon tourism sector. This initiative aims to address this in a co-ordinated way and two working groups have been launched to support the work:

- Tourism Professions Working Group is developing a list of professions and the associated main skills (knowledge and know-how). The aim is to standardise the wording of job offers, enhance the skills of job seekers in the tourism sector, and improve knowledge tools for the sector. This working group is led by the Forem Tourisme Competence Centre and the General Tourism Commission.
- Statistics Working Group is looking at scoping the tourism sector in terms of jobs, shortfall, temporary unemployment and evolution of demand and job offers through employment market monitoring, analysis, and forecasting service. The aim is to harmonise the approaches used to determine the scope covered by tourism in terms of sectors/professions and structural monitoring projects for tourism professions.

This initiative aims to improve tourism employment by connecting workers and employers, increasing the visibility of the tourism sector as an important sector in Wallonia (based on the number and content of job offers), monitoring in staff shortage and optimising training standards.

Statistical Profile

Belgium: Domestic, inbound and outbound tourism

	2018	2019	2020	2021	2022
TOURISM FLOWS, THOUSAND					
Domestic tourism					
Total domestic trips	..	..	..	..	..
Overnight visitors (tourists)	4 872	5 362	4 284	6 911	5 759
Same-day visitors (excursionists)	18 480	..	..	19 013	..
Nights in all types of accommodation	19 925	18 627	17 407	26 169	20 150
Hotels and similar establishments	11 092	10 376	9 458	16 048	12 286
Other collective establishments	1 666	1 301	1 901	2 742	1 697
Private accommodation	7 166	6 950	6 049	7 379	6 167
Inbound tourism					
Total international arrivals	..	..	..	..	..
Overnight visitors (tourists)	6 700	6 800	1 804	2 313	5 728
Same-day visitors (excursionists)	1 000	..	..	..	..
Top markets					
Netherlands	1 037	1 038	361	611	1 243
France	1 010	1 036	391	571	996
United Kingdom	753	693	136	69	461
Germany	726	756	234	268	633
United States	383	407	62	66	288
Nights in all types of accommodation	..	..	..	..	..
Hotels and similar establishments	12 424	12 669	3 480	4 341	10 916
Other collective establishments	..	..	..	..	..
Private accommodation	..	..	..	..	..
Outbound tourism					
Total international departures	..	..	..	..	..
Overnight visitors (tourists)	15 626	17 322	7 109	8 593	16 005
Same-day visitors (excursionists)	5 458	6 396	3 080	2 280	4 427
Top destinations					
France	4 919	4 780	2 712	3 267	4 979
Netherlands	1 594	2 112	796	844	1 706
Spain	1 797	1 813	550	964	1 929
Germany	945	1 375	465	515	968
Italy	933	1 289	504	636	1 202
TOURISM RECEIPTS AND EXPENDITURE, MILLION EUR					
Inbound tourism					
Total international receipts	8 748	9 402	6 201	6 191	8 264
International travel receipts	7 530	7 894	5 470	5 330	6 585
International passenger transport receipts	1 218	1 508	731	861	1 679
Outbound tourism					
Total international expenditure	17 638	18 707	12 175	13 161	16 884
International travel expenditure	15 655	16 692	11 349	12 407	15 477
International passenger transport expenditure	1 983	2 015	826	754	1 407

.. Not available
Source: OECD Tourism Statistics (Database).

StatLink https://stat.link/y9c2w4

Belgium: Enterprises and employment in tourism

	Number of establishments	Number of persons employed				
	2022	2018	2019	2020	2021	2022
Total	..	..	..	..	..	..
Tourism industries	..	..	378 752	..	..	..
Accommodation services for visitors	10 269..	..	23 969	..	..	..
Hotels and similar establishments	..	..	17 687	..	..	..
Food and beverage serving industry	..	..	185 250	..	..	..
Passenger transport	..	..	75 907	..	..	..
Air passenger transport	..	..	6 132	..	..	..
Railways passenger transport	..	..	30 749	..	..	..
Road passenger transport	..	..	38 787	..	..	..
Water passenger transport	..	..	239	..	..	..
Passenger transport supporting services	..	..	..	..	..	..
Transport equipment rental	..	..	2 828	..	..	..
Travel agencies and other reservation services industry	..	..	7 145	..	..	..
Cultural industry	..	..	41 184	..	..	..
Sports and recreation industry	..	..	34 688	..	..	..
Retail trade of country-specific tourism characteristic goods	..	..	5 175	..	..	..
Other country-specific tourism industries	..	..	2 627	..	..	..
Other industries	..	..	..	..	..	..

.. Not available
Source: OECD Tourism Statistics (Database).

StatLink https://stat.link/d6trcn

Canada

Tourism in the economy and outlook

Tourism is an important part of the Canadian economy, creating jobs and socio-economic growth throughout the country. In 2023, tourism directly contributed CAD 42.7 billion or 1.6% of Canada's total GVA, up from a low of 1.0% in 2020. Tourism GVA has recovered to 98% of pre-pandemic levels of CAD 43.5 billion in 2019 in nominal terms. In 2023, 676 700 jobs were directly supported by tourism, or 3.4% of total employment in Canada. This represents a 35% increase on 2020 (500 300 jobs) and 96% of pre-pandemic levels (704 100 jobs). The visitor economy is one of Canada's top service exports, accounting for 13.3% of total service exports in 2023, up from a low of 3.2% in 2021.

In 2023, Canada recorded over 18.3 million international tourist arrivals, or 83% of 2019 levels. In 2023, spending by international tourists reached CAN 24.1 billion, compared to CAN 6.1 billion in 2020. Total tourism expenditure hit CAD 113.4 billion in 2023, exceeding pre-pandemic levels by 8% in nominal terms. Canada's top three international source markets in 2023 were the United States (70%), the United Kingdom (4%) and France (3%).

Domestic tourism remains an important backbone of tourism in Canada, accounting for 76% of total tourism expenditure. In 2023, the country recorded over 97 million domestic tourist arrivals, 3.6% higher than 2019 levels.

Destination Canada's 2023 Fall Tourism Outlook projects that if Canada's tourism sector continues on the current forecasted trajectory, internal tourism expenditure could surpass CAD 140 billion by 2030.

Tourism governance

In Canada, all levels of government play a role in supporting the tourism sector. The Ministry of Innovation, Science and Economic Development is responsible for tourism policy development at the federal level and collaborates across government on tourism related policies.

Destination Canada is the national destination marketing organisation to promote Canada abroad. As a Crown corporation, it reports to Parliament through the Minister responsible for tourism.

Provincial and territorial governments are responsible for domestic and some international tourism promotion, destination and product development, regulation of accommodation services, and hospitality and tourism education. At the municipal level, tourism activities include marketing, the attraction of meetings and conventions, and the promotion of local festivals and events.

Canada ensures horizontal and vertical co-ordination among the levels of government through the Canadian Council of Tourism Ministers, which annually gathers federal, provincial, and territorial tourism ministers to discuss trends and issues facing Canada's tourism sector and identify collaboration opportunities. The Council has established working groups focused on access to destinations and economic growth.

Though it is difficult to estimate the annual budget for tourism in Canada, under the 2023 Federal Tourism Growth Strategy, notable funding allocations include: CAD 108 million for the Tourism Growth Program, CAD 55 million for the Trans Canada Trail, CAD 20 million for the Indigenous Tourism Fund, and CAD 48.7 million for Destination Canada's efforts to attract business events. In addition, Destination Canada's annual appropriation is CAD 96.5 million.

Canada: Organisational chart of tourism bodies

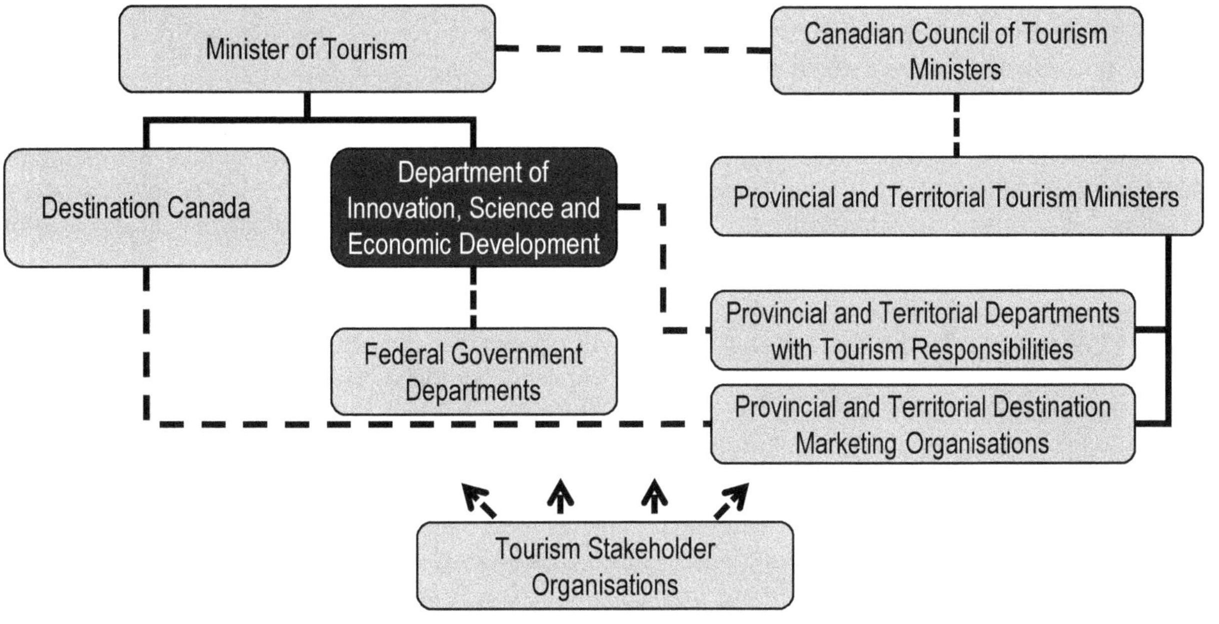

Source: OECD, adapted from Ministry of Innovation, Science and Economic Development, 2024.

Tourism policies and programmes

In 2023, Canada launched a new Federal Tourism Growth Strategy – Canada 365: Welcoming the World, Every Day. It sets out a vision for Canada's tourism sector to increase growth, investment, and stability and help drive Canada's visitor economy to the next level of international success.

The Strategy has set targets to improve Canada's tourism standing internationally. These include increasing tourism's contribution to Canadian GDP by 40% to CAD 61 billion by 2030 and increasing tourism related jobs by 85 000 direct jobs to a total of 790 000 tourism jobs in Canada by 2030.

The Strategy is built on five strategic priorities:

- Invest in tourism assets: Enhance and upgrade tourism assets, in addition to providing support to digitise services and make physical attractions more sustainable and resilient to climate change, offering support to de-risk larger projects, facilitating access to capital, including direct support to businesses and infrastructure investments.
- Embrace recreation and the great outdoors: Facilitate Canadian and international guests' access to natural spaces, helping disperse visitation both seasonally and geographically, to increase tourism sustainability.
- Partner to grow Indigenous tourism: Develop and promote attractions managed by indigenous communities, which offer visitors one-of-a-kind experiences to engage in the sharing of traditional

knowledge, histories, stories, and cultural practices. This allows indigenous communities to assert inherent rights while diversifying their economies for present and future generations.

- Attract more international events: Secure more international events as a four-season driver of travel, bringing more visitors to Canada and extending the tourism season to ensure long-term sustainable growth.
- Improve co-ordination through a Ministerial Tourism Council: Engage Federal Ministers whose mandates and departments include essential policy and programme instruments that impact tourism (e.g. employment and skills, regional and national economic development, parks, transportation, immigration, border services, housing), to implement the Federal Tourism Growth Strategy and ensure a whole-of-government approach to the visitor economy.

The Strategy will be measured against its ability to enhance tourism diversity, support Indigenous tourism, advance Canada's Gender-based analysis, address tourism's environmental impact and support sustainable development goals. The Strategy also seeks to improve Canada's WEF Global Travel and Tourism Development Index ranking from 13th in 2021 to 7th by 2030. To achieve these objectives, several programmes have been launched. These include:

- The Tourism Growth Programme (CAD 108 million over three years), which assists communities, SMEs and non-profit organisations in enhancing local tourism products and experiences. Canada's seven regional development agencies will deliver this programme, through the mandate to promote regional economic development across Canada. The programme, which will run from 2023 to 2026, will help leverage tourism opportunities in communities, including those that are rural and remote, based on regional contexts.
- An expansion of recreation resources and outdoor activities in the Trans Canada Trail (CAD 55 million). This includes funds to maintain, enhance and expand the 28 000 km of trails, connecting rural communities, improving trail infrastructure and enhancing user accessibility. The programme was launched in 2022 and runs over five years.
- The creation of a network of national urban parks in Canada's large urban centres, managed by Parks Canada, via partnerships built on a shared vision to conserve nature, connect people with nature, and advance reconciliation with Indigenous Peoples.
- The Indigenous Tourism Fund (CAD 20 million), launched in 2023 to accelerate the growth of Indigenous tourism in Canada (see box below).
- A CAD 48.7 million investment to support Destination Canada's efforts to attract major international conventions, conferences, and events to Canada.

Actions to strengthen Indigenous tourism partnerships in Canada

Strengthening Indigenous Tourism is a key priority under the new Federal Tourism Growth Strategy. As such, CAD 20 million is being invested in the creation of the Indigenous Tourism Fund to support the Indigenous tourism industry's recovery from the pandemic and to help it position itself for long-term, sustainable growth. Additionally, a portion of the CAD 108 million Tourism Growth Program, announced in the 2023 budget, will further federal government investments in Indigenous tourism experiences through dedicated funding. Before the pandemic, Indigenous tourism was the fastest growing segment in the Canadian tourism market, with significant gains in job creation and contributions to Canada's GDP. However, the Indigenous tourism industry was particularly hard hit by the impact of the COVID-19 pandemic and has been slower to recover than other parts of the tourism sector. The new investments will help meet the growing demand for these unique experiences, so that Indigenous tourism in Canada can continue to sustainably grow and thrive.

Statistical Profile

Canada: Domestic, inbound and outbound tourism

	2018	2019	2020	2021	2022
TOURISM FLOWS, THOUSAND					
Domestic tourism					
Total domestic trips	278 060 |	275 418	..	202 993	258 831
Overnight visitors (tourists)	95 445 |	93 665	..	69 461	90 833
Same-day visitors (excursionists)	182 615 |	181 753	..	133 532	167 998
Nights in all types of accommodation	268 258 |	262 947	..	237 497	282 597
Hotels and similar establishments	..	..	..	..	..
Other collective establishments	..	..	..	..	..
Private accommodation	..	..	..	..	..
Inbound tourism					
Total international arrivals	31 274	32 430	5 068	4 282	17 924
Overnight visitors (tourists)	21 134	22 145	2 960	3 062	12 824
Same-day visitors (excursionists)	10 140	10 284	2 108	1 220	5 100
Top markets					
United States	14 440	15 005	1 929	2 093	9 093
United Kingdom	792	863	96	112	588
China (People's Republic of), mainland	737	708	94	40	64
France	604	663	96	121	463
Germany	406	415	40	54	249
Nights in all types of accommodation	..	..	..	..	..
Hotels and similar establishments	..	..	..	..	..
Other collective establishments	..	..	..	..	..
Private accommodation	..	..	..	..	..
Outbound tourism					
Total international departures	56 340	56 157	14 605	7 906	31 936
Overnight visitors (tourists)	33 440	33 064	8 971	4 954	21 400
Same-day visitors (excursionists)	22 900	23 094	5 634	2 951	10 536
Top destinations					
..	..	..	..	..	..
..	..	..	..	..	..
..	..	..	..	..	..
..	..	..	..	..	..
..	..	..	..	..	..
TOURISM RECEIPTS AND EXPENDITURE, MILLION CAD					
Inbound tourism					
Total international receipts	39 959	44 323	18 894	17 847	..
International travel receipts	35 391	39 547	18 217	18 123	..
International passenger transport receipts	4 568	4 816	780	694	..
Outbound tourism					
Total international expenditure	54 830	57 383	18 739	12 824	..
International travel expenditure	44 740	46 901	16 203	9 895	..
International passenger transport expenditure	10 090	10 482	2 536	1 593	..

.. Not available; | Break in series
Source: OECD Tourism Statistics (Database).

StatLink https://stat.link/kho9wd

Canada: Enterprises and employment in tourism

	Number of establishments	Number of persons employed[1]				
	2022	2018	2019	2020	2021	2022
Total	..	689 900	704 100	500 300	510 500	623 400
Tourism industries	216 602	565 800	578 400	405 000	408 300	505 800
Accommodation services for visitors	22 144	141 100	146 900	95 600	99 100	125 600
Hotels and similar establishments	..	..	..	..	..	..
Food and beverage serving industry	87 526	215 000	219 500	149 500	161 600	198 400
Passenger transport	46 868	91 200	93 100	76 300	63 300	73 500
Air passenger transport	..	..	..	..	..	..
Railways passenger transport	..	..	..	..	..	..
Road passenger transport	..	..	..	..	..	..
Water passenger transport	..	..	..	..	..	..
Passenger transport supporting services	..	..	..	..	..	..
Transport equipment rental	..	..	..	..	..	..
Travel agencies and other reservation services industry	6 804	38 800	39 200	29 200	24 400	30 200
Cultural industry	..	..	..	..	..	..
Sports and recreation industry	53 260	79 700	79 700	54 400	59 800	78 100
Retail trade of country-specific tourism characteristic goods	..	..	..	..	..	..
Other country-specific tourism industries	..	..	..	..	..	..
Other industries	..	124 200	125 700	95 300	102 200	117 600

.. Not available
1. Data refer to number of jobs.
Source: OECD Tourism Statistics (Database).

StatLink https://stat.link/3k1qs4

Canada: Internal tourism consumption

Million CAD

	2022		
	Domestic tourism expenditure	Inbound tourism expenditure	Internal tourism consumption
Total	..	..	..
Consumption products	74 165	19 805	93 970
Tourism characteristic products	45 952	15 082	61 034
Accommodation services for visitors	11 514	5 956	17 470
Food and beverage serving services	11 461	2 738	14 199
Passenger transport services	16 016	4 492	20 508
Air passenger transport services	..	..	..
Railways passenger transport services	..	..	..
Road passenger transport services	..	..	..
Water passenger transport services	..	..	..
Passenger transport supporting services	..	..	..
Transport equipment rental services	..	..	..
Travel agencies and other reservation services industry	1 453	452	1 905
Cultural services	5 508	1 444	6 952
Sports and recreation services	..	..	..
Country-specific tourism characteristic goods	..	..	..
Country-specific tourism characteristic services	..	..	..
Other consumption products	28 213	4 723	32 936
Tourism connected products	..	..	..
Non-tourism related consumption products	..	..	..
Non-consumption products	..	..	..

.. Not available
Source: OECD Tourism Statistics (Database).

StatLink https://stat.link/c3kn9o

Chile

Tourism in the economy and outlook

Tourism is an important sector for the Chilean economy. In 2019, tourism directly contributed CLP 6.5 billion to the economy, or 3.3% of total GDP. Tourism-related industries employed 668 500 people, or 7.5% of total employment in 2019, falling to 461 000 people in 2020 (5.9%). This has since risen to 590 100 people in 2022 (6.7%), but overall numbers of people employed in tourism remains 12% below 2019 levels. In 2023, tourism-related industries employed 620 000 people (6.8% of total employment), 7% below 2019 levels. Tourism is also the second largest services export in the Chilean economy, accounting for 12.0% of total service exports in 2022, up from 1.9% in 2021.

International tourist arrivals reached 3.7 million in 2023, recovering from pandemic low of 190 000 in 2021 but still 17.4% below 2019 levels. The main Chilean inbound markets in 2023 were Argentina (32%), Brazil (13%) and Bolivia (9%).

Domestic tourism is the backbone of tourism demand in Chile and exceeded pre-pandemic levels in 2022, with 61.1 million domestic overnight visitors recorded, 13.7% more than in 2019. Initial figures from 2023 suggest that domestic tourism demand may be softening (7% below 2022 levels) but remains 22% above 2019 levels.

Tourism governance

The Undersecretariat of Tourism of the Ministry of Economy, Development and Tourism fulfils the mission of fostering and promoting the sustainable development of tourism in our country through the definition and co-ordination of public policies on tourism, the articulation of public and private actors in the sector, with the participation of civil society and the consolidation of the institutional system for tourism, in order to generate positive impact on the territories and local communities. It is responsible for the design and implementation of public policies, plans and national tourism strategies. The Committee of Ministers for Tourism and the Advisory Council for Tourism Promotion are the two main co-ordination and consultation mechanisms for tourism at the national and regional levels.

The National Tourism Service (SERNATUR) implements national tourism policies, plans and strategies, under the supervision of and working in conjunction with the Undersecretariat of Tourism. SERNATUR has regional offices in each of Chile's 16 administrative zones (Regions), presided over by a regional Director. It also has local tourism offices in some territories, such as Easter Island, San Pedro de Atacama, Chiloé and Puerto Natales.

Through the regional offices, as a network throughout Chile, SERNATUR co-ordinates activities with relevant actors in the tourism industry, such as the regional governments. These bodies are in charge of the higher administration of the regions. At the regional level, it also works collaboratively with other government agencies, such as the Production Development Corporation (CORFO), which supports entrepreneurship, innovation and competitiveness, and the Technical Cooperation Service (SERCOTEC). Chile has a political-administrative division at the local level called communes or municipalities, with a total of 346 communes nationwide. Of the total number of communes nationwide, 309 have a local tourism office.

A total budget of CLP 34.2 trillion was allocated to the Undersecretariat of Tourism and the National Tourism Service in 2023. Of this amount, 36% was allocated to staffing, and the balance to the implementation of public policy and programmes executed by both institutions. The regional governments and the National Regional Development Fund (FNDR) also provide additional funding for tourism at the regional level, reaching more than CLP 12.5 billion at the national level.

Chile: Organisational chart of tourism bodies

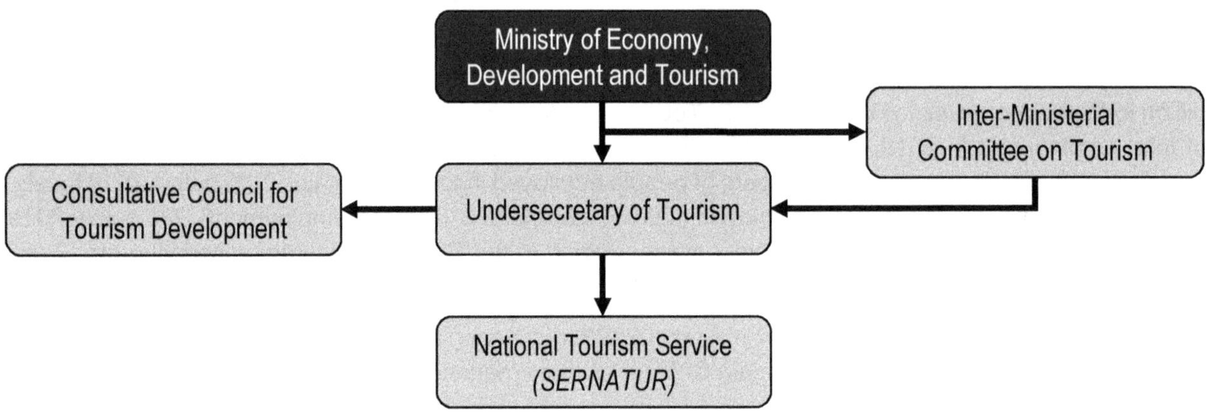

Source: OECD, adapted from the Ministry of Economy, Development and Tourism, 2024.

Tourism policies and programmes

Developed in 2023, the National Strategy for Sustainable Tourism 2035 adopted a participatory approach with 32 face-to-face workshops held in the 16 regions of the country, 3 workshops in island territories (Rapa Nui and Chiloé), 19 online thematic workshops, workshops with unions and other key stakeholders, and interviews with national, regional and local authorities, which brought together 2 277 participants. This strategy is built within the framework of the 2030 Agenda for Sustainable Development, adheres to this commitment and advances towards a vision of sustainability and as a country designs a path for development to harmoniously integrate economic productivity, social improvements and environmental conservation with a regenerative perspective and from this input defines six strategic pillars: sectoral governance; sustainable tourism; positioning and unique experiences; tourism intelligence and planning; high-impact productive ecosystems; and green tourism investment. The Strategy's cross-cutting principles are: decentralisation; equity and inclusion; gender equality; participation; sustainability; and conservation of natural, cultural and gastronomic heritage.

Chile is also implementing an international tourism marketing plan aimed at attracting visitors to Chile in the short, medium and long term, fostering connectivity in the Chilean tourism sector, increasing average spending and promoting new destinations.

Chile supports social tourism with three key initiatives: Family Tourism, Study Tours, and Senior Vacations. These programmes subsidise tourism packages for families, students, and senior citizens, promoting domestic tourism and local economic development. Despite pandemic disruptions, they resumed in 2022, benefiting diverse groups. Future goals include expanding participation, engaging more tourism sectors, and fostering sustainable tourism. These programmes connect various service providers, including travel agencies, transport, lodging, restaurants, tour operators, guides, insurance companies, excursions, handicrafts, wildlife areas, and cultural services, thereby boosting productivity in mid and low seasons.

During the pandemic, travel within the national territory was affected. However, after free mobility was authorised (with COVID-19 health and prevention restrictions), the programmes were reactivated, reaching more than 271 000 overnight stays in 2022.

Recent tourism policies in Chile focus on sustainability and climate resilience. The 2020 Plan for Adaptation to Climate Change in the Tourism Sector aims to enhance the sector's sustainability by 2024 through capacity building and actionable measures requiring collaboration across the industry, host communities, and tourists. As part of the United Nations Framework Convention on Climate Change and the Paris Agreement, the plan will be updated in 2024 to align with Chile's Framework Law on Climate Change. Additionally, the Sustainable Sanitation Systems Programme supports rural tourism microenterprises with technical advice and financing for drinking water and basic sanitation equipment (see box below).

The Biodiversity and Protected Areas Service modifies the legislation on tourism concessions in protected areas. From its entry into force in 2023, it provides for low-impact tourism concessions in protected areas, such as parks and reserves, as long as they are in line with the individual management plans of the protected areas. The Undersecretariat of Tourism may intervene in the protected area planning processes and will be part of the Technical Advisory Committee that will determine the concessions per unit and their concessional income.

The Production Development Corporation has a variety of programmes to improve the competitiveness of companies and territories for the country's different industries with growth potential. In the case of tourism, this entity has made available a series of instruments to promote the governance and productive development of the territories. To date, there is the National Transform Tourism programme, the meso regional programmes of Enotourism, Lagos Rios and Volcanoes and Patagonia Parks, as well as 7 regional programmes for the promotion of tourism.

The PAR Chile Apoya Turismo 2023 programme supports the recovery of micro, small and medium-sized tourism enterprises through financing for training, business plans, consulting, technical assistance, working capital and investment projects. The Programme was launched in March 2023 and can finance up to 100% of tourism-related projects in the 16 regions, with a maximum limit of CLP 3.24 billion.

Sustainable sanitary systems in Chile

Designed by the Undersecretariat of Tourism, in collaboration with the Undersecretariat of Public Health, the Sustainable Sanitation Systems Programme aims to support tourism microenterprises located in rural areas. The programme provides technical advice and financing instruments to enable the sustainable supply of drinking water and basic sanitation equipment in remote areas, through the implementation of rainwater harvesting systems for human consumption, grey water reuse systems, constructed wetlands and dry toilets. Its objective is to improve the quality of rural tourism businesses and the visitor experience, improve conservation conditions in protected areas, and improve the basic conditions of park rangers in these areas. The first initiatives of this programme have included the compilation of alternative and sustainable health technologies in a free digital guide. Delivery of the first project in 2021 provided rainwater for human consumption as part of a tourist lodge on Quehui Island in Chiloé.

Statistical Profile

Chile: Domestic, inbound and outbound tourism

	2018	2019	2020	2021	2022
TOURISM FLOWS, THOUSAND					
Domestic tourism[1]					
Total domestic trips	73 344	74 459	54 425	68 516	85 879
Overnight visitors (tourists)	52 974 e	53 749 p	39 323 p	49 201 p	61 093 p
Same-day visitors (excursionists)	20 370 e	20 711 e	15 102 e	19 315 e	24 787 e
Nights in all types of accommodation	..	..	..	..	..
Hotels and similar establishments	..	..	..	..	..
Other collective establishments	..	..	..	..	..
Private accommodation	..	..	..	..	..
Inbound tourism					
Total international arrivals	6 603	5 431	1 310	192	2 269
Overnight visitors (tourists)	5 723	4 518	1 119	190	2 030
Same-day visitors (excursionists)	880	913	191	2	239
Top markets					
Argentina	2 422	1 435	414	21	652
Brazil	589	542	78	14	247
Bolivia	541	468	133	4	146
Peru	389	411	98	27	183
United States	222	225	62	18	135
Nights in all types of accommodation	..	..	..	..	..
Hotels and similar establishments	..	..	..	..	..
Other collective establishments	..	..	..	..	..
Private accommodation	..	..	..	..	..
Outbound tourism					
Total international departures	4 605	4 091 |	1 162	519	2 366
Overnight visitors (tourists)	3 825	3 346 |	963	514	2 155
Same-day visitors (excursionists)	780	745	198	6	212
Top destinations					
Peru	1 055	1 018 |	..	..	..
Argentina	1 123	996 |	..	..	..
United States	306	295 |	..	..	..
Brazil	301	284 |	..	..	..
Spain	82	..	..	..	..
TOURISM RECEIPTS AND EXPENDITURE, MILLION USD					
Inbound tourism					
Total international receipts	3 937	3 317	841	535	1 907
International travel receipts	2 897	2 303	413	113	1 024
International passenger transport receipts	1 040	1 014	428	422	883
Outbound tourism					
Total international expenditure	3 182	3 191	756	588	2 355
International travel expenditure	2 394	2 459	539	303	1 718
International passenger transport expenditure	788	732	217	285	637

.. Not available; e Estimated value; p Provisional data; | Break in series

1. Trips from demand side surveys; Nights from supply side surveys.

Source: OECD Tourism Statistics (Database).

StatLink https://stat.link/y76vo9

Chile: Enterprises and employment in tourism

	Number of establishments[1]	Number of persons employed[2]				
	2022	2018	2019	2020	2021	2022
Total	194 075	656 p	668 p	461 p	507 p	590 p
Tourism industries	79 237	392 p	397 p	268 p	312 p	369 p
Accommodation services for visitors	14 223	..	..	..	..	..
Hotels and similar establishments	4 351	..	..	..	..	..
Food and beverage serving industry	60 663	..	..	..	..	..
Passenger transport	37 742	114 p	107 p	83 p	82 p	84 p
Air passenger transport	199	..	..	..	..	..
Railways passenger transport	11	..	..	..	..	..
Road passenger transport	37 135	..	..	..	..	..
Water passenger transport	397	..	..	..	..	..
Passenger transport supporting services		150 p	164 p	110 p	112 p	137 p
Transport equipment rental	6 427	..	..	..	..	..
Travel agencies and other reservation services industry	2 975	..	..	..	..	..
Cultural industry	5 312	..	..	..	..	..
Sports and recreation industry	7 953	..	..	..	..	..
Retail trade of country-specific tourism characteristic goods	5 991	..	..	..	..	..
Other country-specific tourism industries		..	..	..	..	..
Other industries	52 789	..	..	..	..	..

.. Not available; p Provisional data

1. Data refer to number of enterprises.
2. Data refer to number of employees.

Source: OECD Tourism Statistics (Database).

StatLink https://stat.link/c1uj6w

Chile: Internal tourism consumption

Million USD

	2022		
	Domestic tourism expenditure	Inbound tourism expenditure	Internal tourism consumption
Total	7 923 e	1 439 e	..
Consumption products	..	..	..
Tourism characteristic products	..	..	..
Accommodation services for visitors	..	..	..
Food and beverage serving services	..	..	..
Passenger transport services	..	..	..
Air passenger transport services	..	..	..
Railways passenger transport services	..	..	..
Road passenger transport services	..	..	..
Water passenger transport services	..	..	..
Passenger transport supporting services	..	..	..
Transport equipment rental services	..	..	..
Travel agencies and other reservation services industry	..	..	..
Cultural services	..	..	..
Sports and recreation services	..	..	..
Country-specific tourism characteristic goods	..	..	..
Country-specific tourism characteristic services	..	..	..
Other consumption products	..	..	..
Tourism connected products	..	..	..
Non-tourism related consumption products	..	..	..
Non-consumption products	..	..	..

.. Not available; e Estimated value

Source: OECD Tourism Statistics (Database).

StatLink https://stat.link/8jvskd

Colombia

Tourism in the economy and outlook

Tourism is an important contributor to the Colombian economy. In 2023, tourism contributed COP 1.4 billion or 2.3% of total GVA, which shows an ongoing recovery since 2020 (1.2%), but is still below 2.6% in 2019. In 2022, tourism supported 709 300 jobs, or 3.2% of total employment; this compares to 3.6% in 2019 and 2.1% in 2020. Travel exports accounted for 44% of total service exports in 2022.

Colombia welcomed 6.1 million international tourist arrivals in 2023, recovering from the pandemic low of 1.4 million in 2020 and exceeding pre-pandemic levels of 4.5 million in 2019. Spending by international tourists reached a total of COP 51 billion in 2023. The main source markets in 2023 were the United States (27%), Ecuador (8%) and Mexico (8%).

Domestic tourism has also surpassed pre-pandemic levels. The number of domestic overnight trips reached 47.4 million in 2023, 2.5% above 2019 (46.3 million). Domestic tourists spent COP 17.7 billion in 2023, or a 7.8% increase on 2019 levels in current prices.

Colombia targets 7.5 million international tourist arrivals and 300 000 additional people employed in tourism-related jobs (passenger transport, accommodation and travel agencies) by 2026.

Tourism governance

The Ministry of Commerce, Industry and Tourism (MINCIT) is responsible for tourism policy in Colombia. Every 4 years it creates the Sectoral Plan for Tourism based on the National Development Plan. An Integrated Destination Management Strategy allows for cross-government co-ordination in the planning and management of activities, resources and stakeholders involved in tourism.

At the national level, MINCIT works with three main organisations: (i) FONTUR: the National Tourism Fund affiliated with the Ministry; (ii) PROCOLOMBIA: the agency charged with international promotion, expansion of Colombian companies, attraction of foreign direct investment, positioning of the country as a tourism destination, and the country's brand; and (iii) Colombia Productiva: helps industry and companies produce better quality services and greater added value to increase productivity and competitiveness.

MINCIT also works with other ministries (e.g. Ministry of Environment and Sustainable Development, Ministry of Culture, National Planning Department) and consults stakeholders and representatives from the private sector on all policies and strategies. At the regional level, tourism activities are decentralised, and implementation is co-ordinated with regional authorities and local communities. Tourism is promoted by local authorities in each territory.

Funding for tourism comes from the general national budget, compulsory contributions from tourism service providers, incomes from tourism properties and brans owned by the government, and from a USD 15 tax on international arrivals by air. In 2023, the Vice-Ministry of Tourism's allocation from the general national budget was COP 3.8 billion, unchanged from 2022. These funds help finance the operations and management of the Vice-Ministry and are primarily used for contractors and travel expenses. The National

Tourism Fund (FONTUR) received COP 194.8 million from the general budget to support the tourism sector's promotion and competitiveness in 2023, up 65% on 2022 levels. In addition, FONTUR's revenue from parafiscal charges, fines, balances, releases, and returns increased by 123.6%, from COP 159.1 million in 2022 to COP 355.8 million in 2023.

Colombia: Organisational chart of tourism bodies

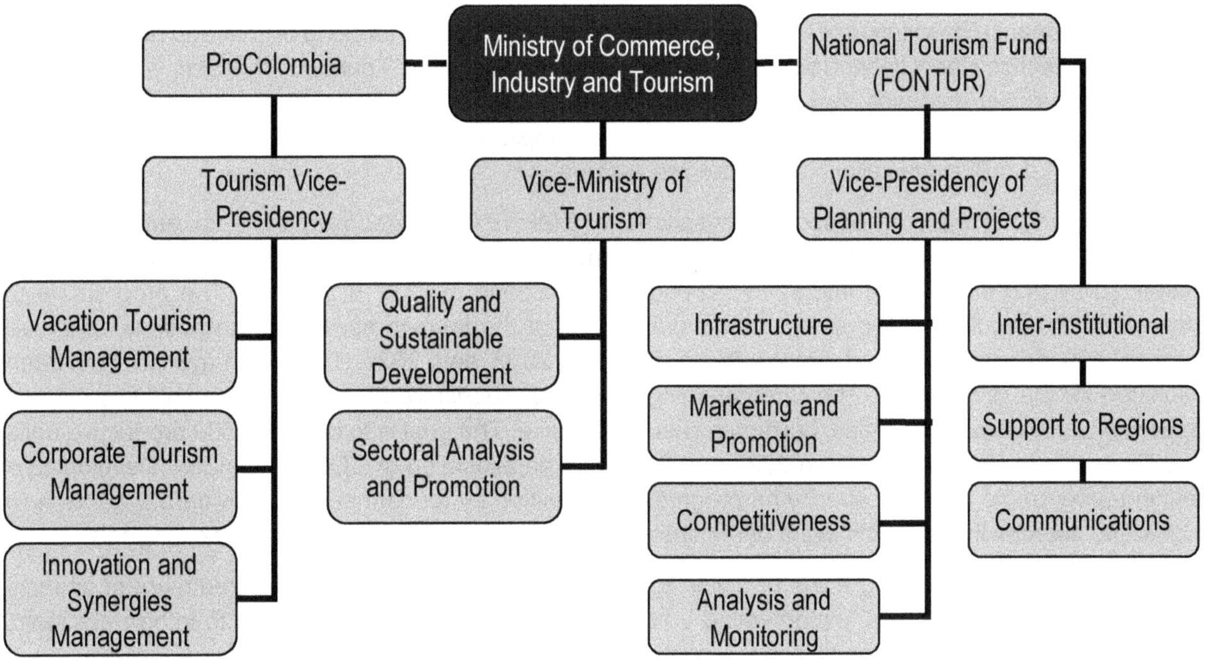

Source: OECD, adapted from the Ministry of Commerce, Industry and Tourism, 2024.

Tourism policies and programmes

The Sectoral Tourism Plan 2022-26 sets out the national strategy guiding tourism development in Colombia. The overall objective is to leverage tourism as a catalyst for economic development, social inclusion, environmental protection, and peacebuilding. The Plan will be measured across targets: by 2026, the goal is to reach 7.5 million international tourists, with an additional 300 000 people employed in tourism-related activities, and 500 tourism-related businesses from Tourism Territories of Peace, 12 subregions affected by armed conflict in Colombia. The main priorities to reach these targets are: economic transition and nature protection; circular economy practices; increasing and promoting community-based and ethnic tourism; fostering innovation and technology; promoting public-private partnerships; improving quality and productivity; fostering infrastructure development; and focusing on inclusivity in the tourism sector.

Linked with the Plan, the Tourism Sustainability Policy 2022-26 sets out Colombia's approach to position the tourism sector as a catalyst for inclusive and sustainable economic progress, protecting the environment while ensuring fair opportunities, community protection, and the preservation of cultural heritage and values. The Policy includes a focus on strengthening information management, consolidating governance, expanding investment and innovation, fostering sustainable management of natural capital, promoting sustainable travel culture, and positioning Colombia as a sustainable tourism destination.

Key programmes and initiatives aim to promote regenerative and circular tourism. They include the adoption of sustainable tourism practices, the use of long-lasting and non-toxic materials, and increasing recycling and reuse in tourism. Partnering with the Ministry of Environment and Sustainable Development,

MINCIT's plans to benefit 2 000 service providers, businesses, and tourist attractions by 2026. This includes technical and financial support to tourism businesses to boost local activities, sustainable practices and green jobs aligned with the renewable energy production model. The initiative also supports communities engaged in tourism activities, focusing on nature tourism to diversify economies based on ethnic groups knowledge and experience. Funding is provided to tourism businesses and the extended supply chain, alongside a tourism leadership programme for women and youth in sustainable tourism.

The responsible Tourism Strategy implementation programme (2022-26) includes prevention of Commercial Sexual Exploitation of Children and Adolescents (CSEC), trafficking of flora and fauna, cultural heritage protection, the Clean Colombia initiative, and Responsible Tourism. The aim is to promote sustainable tourism practices that minimise the negative impact of tourism on local communities and ecosystems. The programme aims to benefit 223,000 people across the tourism ecosystem by 2026. In 2024, COP 11.1 million was allocated for the programme.

The support for community-based organisations – EMPRETUR (2022-26) aims to strengthen the organisational and business capabilities of 74 community-based organisations. This includes fostering sustainability and competitive integration through an allocation of COP 9.1 million. The programme to strengthen the productive and sustainable development of the tourism sectors at the national level will support 430 community-based organisations between 2022 and 2026. COP 21.1 million has been allocated for this programme. The Strengthening tourism in Tourist Territories of Peace initiative creates opportunities for local economies, building a culture of peace. The goal is to integrate 500 productive units into the tourist value chain between 2022 and 2026 with an allocation of COP 12.6 million. Developing a training programme to build capacity on progressive transition by tourism service providers towards new forms and sources that are conscious of the sustainable development of the sector in the long-term.

Other actions include creating a line of action to promote the welfare and dignified treatment of animals used in tourism activities and implementing a National Tourism Information System to inform decisions with reliable data in line with the National Statistical System (see box below).

Strengthening the tourism information system in Colombia

The Sectoral Plan for Tourism 2022-26 underscores the need to implement a National Tourist Information System to enhance integration, supervision, and visualisation tools for the tourism sector, while respecting ecosystems and local communities. Since 2014, the Tourist Information Centre has supported regional systems, but operational and resource management gaps led to an evaluation by the National Administrative Department of Statistics in 2020, determining a complete restructuring.

In 2022, Colombia launched the Directorate of Sectoral Analysis and Promotion, the National Tourism Information Network and the Colombian Tourist Information Portal. The Network oversees national and regional information systems and optimises fund allocation from the National Tourism Fund for tourism information-related projects. The Portal visualises tourism data to support fact-based decisions, and attracts about 3 500 users weekly.

During system implementation, the National Tourism Fund supported projects like the National Urban Economic Census, Tourism (COP 10.7 million), International Travellers Survey (COP 3.7 million), acquisition of data and analytics services (COP 2.1 million), impact evaluation of the Agricultural Scholarships programme (COP 626 million), monthly accommodation survey (COP 581 million), Generation of Sustainable Destinations in Colombia (COP 106 million), Domestic Tourism Spending Survey (COP 5 billion). These investments provide critical insights for informed decision-making in tourism, understanding trends, economic impacts and the effectiveness of programmes and initiatives.

Statistical Profile

Colombia: Domestic, inbound and outbound tourism

	2018	2019	2020	2021	2022 p
TOURISM FLOWS, THOUSAND					
Domestic tourism					
Total domestic trips	81 084	83 856	32 457	48 052	70 955
Overnight visitors (tourists)	45 280	46 279	19 419	29 269	43 567
Same-day visitors (excursionists)	35 804	37 577	13 038	18 782	27 387
Nights in all types of accommodation	219 303	219 816	123 614	163 609	201 214
Hotels and similar establishments	..	..	..	..	..
Other collective establishments	..	..	..	..	..
Private accommodation	..	..	..	..	..
Inbound tourism					
Total international arrivals	4 398	4 531	1 387	2 146	4 721
Overnight visitors (tourists)	..	..	..	..	..
Same-day visitors (excursionists)	..	..	..	..	..
Top markets					
United States	648	705	230	517	904
Ecuador	164	159	38	58	241
Mexico	182	198	52	81	239
Venezuela	399	400	112	182	236
Peru	151	181	48	67	192
Nights in all types of accommodation	..	..	..	..	..
Hotels and similar establishments	..	..	..	..	..
Other collective establishments	..	..	..	..	..
Private accommodation	..	..	..	..	..
Outbound tourism					
Total international departures	4 368	4 479	1 275	3 004	4 931
Overnight visitors (tourists)	..	..	..	..	..
Same-day visitors (excursionists)	..	..	..	..	..
Top destinations					
United States	1 383	1 410	485	1 553	1 576
Mexico	461	499	139	412	830
Spain	427	489	105	223	588
Panama	404	396	103	149	325
Ecuador	300	285	78	55	192
TOURISM RECEIPTS AND EXPENDITURE, MILLION USD					
Inbound tourism					
Total international receipts	6 655	6 785	1 932	3 054	6 948
International travel receipts	5 621	5 682	1 568	2 596	5 919
International passenger transport receipts	1 034	1 102	364	458	1 029
Outbound tourism					
Total international expenditure	5 531	5 658	1 540	3 020	5 014
International travel expenditure	4 784	4 935	1 358	2 626	4 304
International passenger transport expenditure	747	723	182	394	711

.. Not available; p Provisional data
Source: OECD Tourism Statistics (Database).

StatLink https://stat.link/g4v2qw

Colombia: Enterprises and employment in tourism

	Number of establishments	Number of persons employed				
	2022 p	2018	2019	2020	2021 p	2022 p
Total	..	..	..	..	..	..
Tourism industries	82 448	..	..	..	440 160	709 263
Accommodation services for visitors	..	..	..	..	239 157	419 195
Hotels and similar establishments	61 376	..	..	..	..	..
Food and beverage serving industry	1 470	..	..	..	..	..
Passenger transport	..	..	..	..	60 419	96 730
Air passenger transport	..	..	..	..	..	..
Railways passenger transport	..	..	..	..	..	..
Road passenger transport	977	..	..	..	..	..
Water passenger transport	..	..	..	..	..	..
Passenger transport supporting services	..	..	..	..	..	..
Transport equipment rental	408	..	..	..	..	..
Travel agencies and other reservation services industry	12 492	..	..	..	30 016	36 963
Cultural industry	..	..	..	..	..	..
Sports and recreation industry	..	..	..	..	82 956	130 467
Retail trade of country-specific tourism characteristic goods	..	..	..	..	..	..
Other country-specific tourism industries	5 725	..	..	..	27 613	25 908
Other industries	..	..	..	..	..	..

.. Not available; p Provisional data
Source: OECD Tourism Statistics (Database).

StatLink https://stat.link/ptxrgq

Colombia: Internal tourism consumption

Million COP

	2022 p		
	Domestic tourism expenditure	Inbound tourism expenditure	Internal tourism consumption
Total	..	..	..
Consumption products	..	..	..
Tourism characteristic products	15 921 996	44 613 640	60 535 635
Accommodation services for visitors	1 938 757	7 940 851	9 879 608
Food and beverage serving services	5 082 976	10 314 885	15 397 862
Passenger transport services	..	..	..
Air passenger transport services	1 771 305	11 033 261	12 804 566
Railways passenger transport services	..	..	..
Road passenger transport services	1 939 231	4 524 076	6 463 307
Water passenger transport services	..	..	..
Passenger transport supporting services	35 304	0	35 304
Transport equipment rental services	141 217	215 219	356 436
Travel agencies and other reservation services industry	715 472	3 254 575	3 970 047
Cultural services			
Sports and recreation services	2 049 736	6 172 568	8 222 304
Country-specific tourism characteristic goods	2 247 997	1 158 205	3 406 202
Country-specific tourism characteristic services	..	..	..
Other consumption products	..	..	..
Tourism connected products	..	..	..
Non-tourism related consumption products	..	..	..
Non-consumption products	..	..	..

.. Not available; p Provisional data
Source: OECD Tourism Statistics (Database).

StatLink https://stat.link/bv9w0k

Costa Rica

Tourism in the economy and outlook

Tourism is an important economic sector and driver of economic development in Costa Rica. Pre-pandemic, it directly accounted for 4.8% of GDP and 7% of employment. Travel exports represented 36.6% of total service exports in 2019.

In 2022, the sector contributed USD 3.1 million which accounted for almost 40% of exports, and close to 45% of services exports. The Costa Rica Central Bank estimates that tourism contributed CRC 1.1 trillion to the economy in 2023, directly contributing to 5% of GDP. Tourism employment has rebounded in 2022, totalling 169 200 jobs. This corresponds to 99% of 2019 levels.

In 2023, Costa Rica welcomed an estimated 2.5 million international tourist arrivals, recovering from a pandemic low of 1.0 million in 2020, but still at 79.6% of 2019 levels. The largest inbound markets in 2022 were the United States (55%), Europe (20%) and Central America (8%).

The country has one of the longest average stays of any OECD country, at nearly 13.5 nights per trip, and an average expenditure per tourist per trip of close to USD 1 590. Domestic tourism accounts for 15% of total tourism expenditure in Costa Rica.

Costa Rica is targeting 3.8 million international arrivals by 2027, generating USD 4.9 billion in foreign currency. Air connectivity with key source markets will be a key driver of this recovery – 90% of visitors arrive by air. Rising prices linked to energy and transport costs may hit travel demand for long haul travel.

Tourism governance

The Costa Rica Tourism Institute is an autonomous state institution responsible for formulating public policy, as well as designing and executing technical and legal instruments to implement tourism policy. The Tourism Institute is also in charge of drawing up and managing the National Tourism Plan.

The Tourism Institute is in charge of increasing tourism in Costa Rica, promoting the construction and maintenance of tourist accommodation and attractions, branding and promoting the country overseas, and attracting national and foreign investments.

The Institute collaborates with other relevant bodies, including the Ministries of Foreign Relations, Economy and Trade, Transport, Environment and Energy, Health, and Foreign Trade. In particular a co-operation agreement with the Costa Rican Investment Promotion Agency creates a strategic alliance for the promotion and attraction of foreign investment projects for tourism infrastructure.

The Regional Tourism Offices collaborate with the tourism sector by processing the country's quality programmes, such as the Tourism Declaration and the Certificate for Sustainable Tourism, tourist transportation certificates and tourist guide credentials. In addition, they collaborate in the promotion of their regions in the development of international press tours.

The Costa Rican Tourism Institute is financed mainly by revenue from entry and departure taxes and non-tax revenues from rents and leases. Costa Rica's budget allocation to support tourism-related marketing activities in 2024 was USD 31 million.

Costa Rica: Organisational chart of tourism bodies

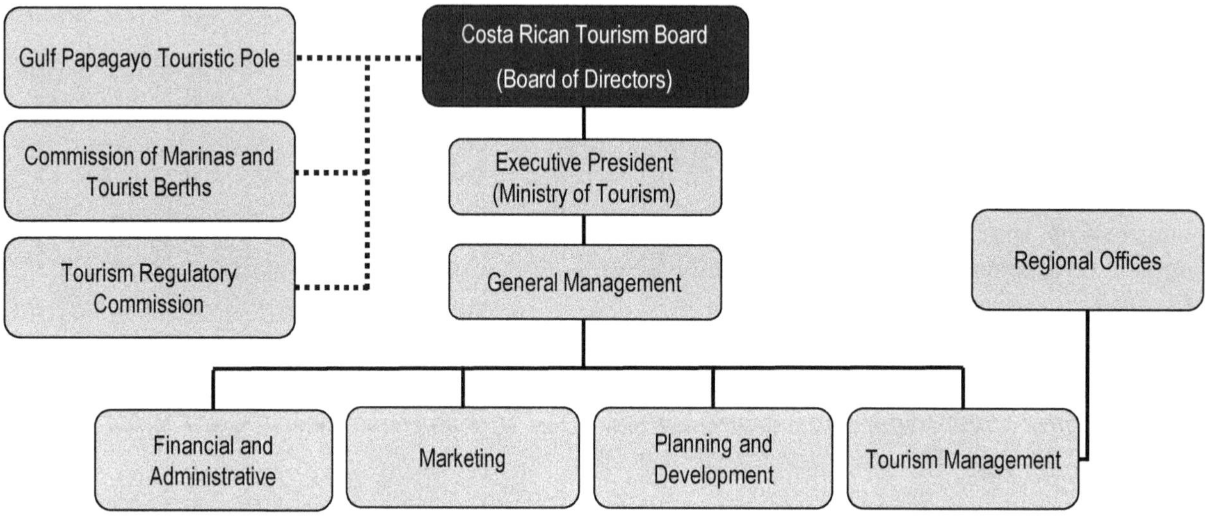

Source: OECD, adapted from Costa Rican Tourism Board, 2024.

Tourism policies and programmes

The National Tourism Development Plan 2022-27 guides the recovery and sustained growth of with a vision to equitably distribute the benefits of tourism so that all Costa Ricans enjoy an improved quality of life. It aims to ensure that tourism continues to be a leading economic sector while both taking advantage of and protecting Costa Rica's natural resources. The Plan sets out a tourism development model based on the three pillars of sustainability, innovation, and inclusiveness, with three main objectives for Costa Rica Tourism:

- Promote a resilient tourism activity that makes sustainable use of tourism and local heritage, with effective destination management plans in place in all 32 Tourism Development Centres by 2027.
- Distribution tourism demand throughout the 32 Tourism Development Centres, to continue to improve the quality of life of communities in different regions.
- Target USD 4.9 billion income from 3.8 million international tourist arrivals by 2027 to maintain tourism as a main engine for the Costa Rican economy.

To deliver these objectives, Costa Rica has developed and implemented several policies and programmes, including:

- Regulations for developments in the Caribbean coastal zone. The Institute is working closely with the heads of local municipalities to promote tourism development while protecting the environment by providing clear rules for investors on tourism development.
- The Destination Management Programme helps develop destinations and Tourism Development Centres in different regions of the country. It assists them to improve their competitiveness and the conditions for tourism development, generating social capital and better living conditions for the inhabitants.

- A free virtual training platform, ICT CAPACITA, to improve workforce participation in the tourism sector. Launched in 2020, the platform trained 13 058 people in the first year. Post-pandemic, the platform continues to support tourism entrepreneurs and businesses on tourism resilience and sustainability issues such as access to sustainable finance and certification.
- The Certification for Sustainable Tourism and Code of Conduct to expand certifications available for tourism businesses. Certifications aim to help maintain a quality service, based on the economic, social, and environmental pillars of sustainability, and a business commitment to the protection of children and adolescents. As of January 2024, almost 150 companies were certified.
- Sofía Network, a platform that provides recommendations and information useful to all women travelling by themselves. It also provides guidance and training for businesses on how to respond in situations where female tourists feel threatened.
- Improving the collection and dissemination of tourism data through monthly reports with variables on seats, flights, and air ticket prices. This information complements the quarterly monitoring of tourist arrivals by port and nationality and the departure of Costa Ricans abroad.
- Establishing new indicators to assess growth in tourism employment. Following the decrease in tourism employment during the pandemic, the aim is to better measure the sector's recovery.
- Developing digital Cultural Tourist Guides for 9 destinations. The digital guides aim to attract visitors to destinations and are available in Spanish and English. They can be downloaded to mobile devices and allow tourists to access information on key sites and areas. So far, 31 of the 32 Tourism Development Centres have their own digital guide.
- A newly updated Social Progress Index to measure the well-being of citizens and monitor social performance, including in tourist destinations, to help Costa Rica reach its targets under the UN SDGs (see box below).

Costa Rica considers its 2023 tourism goals were achieved in three areas: returning to pre-pandemic levels of tourist arrivals by air, increasing the availability of accessible financing mechanisms for small businesses and raising the visibility of the social contribution of tourism. In 2024, the main goal is focusing on tourism infrastructure in protected areas and tourist berths and to continue the implementation of the comprehensive destination management programme while also maintaining successful programmes from 2023.

Measuring the well-being of citizens in Tourism Development Centres in Costa Rica

The Social Progress Index is a tool developed to measure the well-being of citizens which Costa Rica is using to evaluate social progress in tourism destinations, with the perspective to measure tourism as a social phenomenon. The Index uses a new methodology and multidimensional indicators to assess the social sustainability of destinations. It allows Costa Rica to benchmark performance between key tourism destinations and other regions within the country. The target is to reach, or exceed, the level of 70 points in the Social Progress Index over five years. New data will be published in 2024.

The aim of the use of the Index in tourism destinations is to foster the role of tourism as a catalyst for sustainable development within Costa Rica and to meet the UN SDGs. Data collection and comparison commenced again in 2023 across 32 tourism development centres, after it was interrupted by the COVID-19. The data will be used to develop data driven tourism policy across Costa Rica. It is also hoped it will be a catalyst for launching public-private sector collaborations that aim to have a positive impact on local communities.

Statistical Profile

Costa Rica: Domestic, inbound and outbound tourism

	2018	2019	2020	2021	2022
TOURISM FLOWS, THOUSAND					
Domestic tourism					
Total domestic trips	..	..	..	..	..
Overnight visitors (tourists)	..	..	..	..	..
Same-day visitors (excursionists)	..	..	..	..	..
Nights in all types of accommodation	..	..	..	..	..
Hotels and similar establishments	..	..	..	..	..
Other collective establishments	..	..	..	..	..
Private accommodation	..	..	..	..	..
Inbound tourism					
Total international arrivals	3 313	3 378	1 147	1 401	2 650
Overnight visitors (tourists)	3 017	3 139	1 012	1 347	2 350
Same-day visitors (excursionists)	296	239	135	54 |	300 |
Top markets					
United States	1 265	1 335	435	869	1 290
Central America	691	699	202	78	194
Europe	480	501	170	230	470
Canada	217	235	116	53	184
South America	190	196	50	60	111
Nights in all types of accommodation	35 295	39 552	13 054	18 320	31 719
Hotels and similar establishments	..	..	..	..	..
Other collective establishments	..	..	..	..	..
Private accommodation	..	..	..	..	..
Outbound tourism					
Total international departures	..	..	..	..	..
Overnight visitors (tourists)	1 079	1 153	324	588	934
Same-day visitors (excursionists)	..	..	..	..	..
Top destinations					
Central America	583	604	167	222	414
North America	376	418	131	333	380
Panama	301	310	89	128	226
United States	251	280	94	245	234
Nicaragua	141	151	47	44	102
TOURISM RECEIPTS AND EXPENDITURE, MILLION USD					
Inbound tourism					
Total international receipts	4 072	4 340	1 464	1 834	..
International travel receipts	3 769	3 989	1 328	1 717	..
International passenger transport receipts	304	351	136	117	..
Outbound tourism					
Total international expenditure	1 198	1 451	426	764	..
International travel expenditure	838	1 036	243	566	..
International passenger transport expenditure	360	415	183	198	..

..: Not available; | Break in series
Source: OECD Tourism Statistics (Database).

StatLink https://stat.link/dv5ieu

Costa Rica: Enterprises and employment in tourism

	Number of establishments	Number of persons employed				
	2022	2018	2019	2020	2021	2022
Total	..	..	..	..	..	..
Tourism industries	4 392	160 976	170 870	127 570	150 483	169 205
Accommodation services for visitors	..	..	..	..	..	..
Hotels and similar establishments	3 133	27 622	31 743	17 938	24 293	29 602
Food and beverage serving industry	429	99 402	103 099	89 448	100 963	107 393
Passenger transport	..	8 353	6 993	2 744	6 131	3 959
Air passenger transport	17	..	..	..	..	..
Railways passenger transport	..	..	..	..	..	..
Road passenger transport	..	..	..	..	..	..
Water passenger transport	31	..	..	..	..	..
Passenger transport supporting services	..	..	..	..	..	..
Transport equipment rental	55	6 585	6 843	7 052	5 070	4 773
Travel agencies and other reservation services industry	535	6 178	5 025	3 014	2 295	6 730
Cultural industry	..	5 777	8 122	3 746	6 685	9 630
Sports and recreation industry	126	7 059	9 045	3 628	5 046	7 118
Retail trade of country-specific tourism characteristic goods	..	..	..	..	..	..
Other country-specific tourism industries	66	..	..	..	..	..
Other industries	..	..	..	..	..	..

.. Not available
Source: OECD Tourism Statistics (Database).

StatLink https://stat.link/6tl9pd

Czechia

Tourism in the economy and outlook

The tourism economy in Czechia experienced a decade of stable growth before the pandemic hit and recovery is ongoing. Tourism directly contributed CZK 166.5 billion to the Czech economy in 2019, equivalent to 2.9% of total GDP. This fell to a pandemic low of CZK 85.8 billion in 2020, and has since recovered to CZK 150.8 billion or 2.2% of GDP in 2022. Tourism employment accounted for 225 500 people in 2022 or 4.1% of employment. This represents a 4.8% increase from the pandemic low in 2021, which saw 215 200 people or 4.0% of total employment, but is still below 239 500 people in 2019 or 4.4% respectively. In 2022, tourism accounted for 15.0% of tourism exports, still below pre-pandemic levels (24%).

Czechia recorded 9.6 million international tourists at collective accommodation establishments in 2023, up from a pandemic low of 2.6 million in 2021, but still down 12.2% from 2019 levels. The top international inbound markets remained Germany (24%), Slovak Republic (9%), and Poland (8%). International tourism accounted for 49% of tourism expenditure in 2022 (down from 57% in 2019). In contrast to international tourism, domestic overnight trips recorded a strong rebound, recovering to 35.1 million in 2022, or 109% of 2019 levels.

Given the uncertain economic outlook, including Russia's war of aggression against Ukraine, Czechia projects a return to pre-pandemic levels for international tourism in 2026.

Tourism governance

The Ministry of Regional Development is responsible for tourism policy, competitiveness, and legislation in Czechia. The Ministry develops strategic documents and supports tourism via subsidies for public tourism infrastructure, marketing and support to NGOs. The National Collegium of Tourism is the consultative and advisory body of the Minister.

The Ministry, represented by the Tourism Department, co-ordinates with other central government ministries, departments and regions, as well as the private and non-profit sectors on the sustainable development of tourism, including through tourism working groups, roundtables and ad hoc thematic meetings. CzechTourism is the national tourism office in Czechia, a state-funded organisation established by the Ministry and supervised by the Tourism Department. It plays an important role in marketing and co-ordination with regional level organisations.

In recent years, working groups have focused on legislation relevant to tourism, co-ordinating strategic documents, setting up of support systems or action plans. The Ministry participates in the meetings of the Commission of the Council of the Association of Regions for Tourism and the Subcommittee for Tourism of the Chamber of Deputies of the Parliament.

Close co-operation between CzechTourism and regional tourism organisations is subject to the agreed CzechTourism's marketing strategy, which follows the balanced scorecard model and includes the perspectives of both stakeholders and residents. Almost every region has a tourism co-ordinator whose role is to synchronise marketing activities across all public tourism bodies and CzechTourism and provide two-way communication between regional public tourism bodies and CzechTourism at the national level. Twice a year the tourism co-ordinators meet with CzechTourism and delegates of the Ministry. Once a year, the territorial destination management organisations are invited to share knowledge, needs, and information.

The overall 2022 budget for tourism was CZK 1.5 billion of which CZK 382 million was allocated to CzechTourism. The main source of funding for the tourism budget comes from the state budget, but EU Funds also represent an important support mechanism for the sector, particularly for investment in tourism infrastructure. In addition, a local tourism tax is collected by municipalities, but allocation for this is decided locally.

Czechia: Organisational chart of tourism bodies

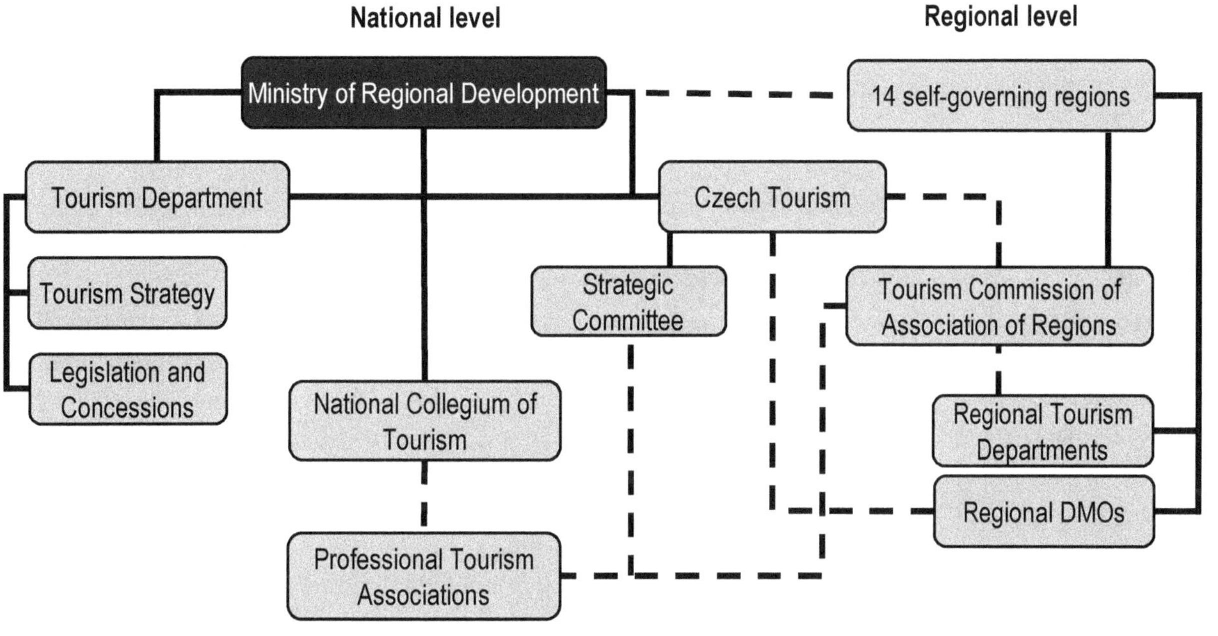

Source: OECD, adapted from the Ministry of Regional Development, 2024.

Tourism policies and programmes

The Tourism Development Strategy 2021-30 sets out the framework underpinning tourism development in Czechia. The Strategy is also a tool to support greater co-ordination and integration of tourism issues into other national strategies and policy areas, including co-operation with relevant Czech ministries through thematic working groups and bilateral meetings. Key priorities to deliver on the agenda set out in the Strategy in the context of structural reforms, and changing the perceptions of tourism within government and the wider public include:

- Ensuring safe and sustainable tourism.
- Using tourism as a tool for regional development.
- Effectively directing the distribution of visitors in destinations.
- Developing targeting and integration of marketing communication.

- Improving the availability and sharing of tourism data and supporting the wholesale digitalisation of the tourism sector.
- Ensuring the availability and quality of employees in tourism.
- Supporting the improvement of tourism service quality.

It is planned to conduct an interim evaluation of the Strategy in 2025, which will be used to adapt and update the Strategy and its targets as required. A final evaluation is planned after its completion in 2030.

To achieve its objectives, a range of annual plans and actions have been implemented. The first Action Plan for 2022-23 focused on restarting tourism and enabling the provision of tourism services. Priorities included improving tourism management and financing systems; developing innovative offers and experiences; stimulating demand; building understanding through research and monitoring; and focusing on people as a key determinant of a quality tourism experience.

The current Action Plan for 2024-25 is based on the need to support the tourism sector recovery, respond to consequences for tourism linked with Russia's war of aggression against Ukraine as well as the broader economic context, including inflation. It is composed of six measures, 12 activities and 26 sub-activities, with a focus on the development of the tourism organisation system, enhancement of data for decision-making, workforce recovery, creation of new tourism offers and support of marketing activities.

CzechTourism developed the Destination Strategy of Czechia for 2021-25 to recapture tourism demand from Europe and North America, post-pandemic. Some marketing efforts will also be channelled towards Korea, India, Latin America and the United Arab Emirates. To attract visitors from these markets, Czechia is promoting Czech traditions, cultural heritage, gastronomy (beer and wine), Czech spa destinations, mountain sports, as well as cultural and sports events.

To attract long-haul markets, Czechia has also invested in opening new direct routes to connect to the Americas and the Asia Pacific region, including to Korea, China and Chinese Taipei. Implemented by CzechTourism, the initiative involves a co-operation analysis with Prague Airport and marketing campaigns in partnership with the respective airlines.

Czechia is developing a new e-Turista platform to serve as a register of all accommodation facilities in the country. The platform, due to be launched in 2025, aims to help reduce the administrative burden on entrepreneurs, provide better tourist data and enable the collection of local tourist fees. Developed by the Ministry of Regional Development, the Register will be compulsory for all types of accommodation facilities, including shared accommodation platforms such as Airbnb, Booking, Expedia Group and Tripadvisor. Implementation of the project requires legislative changes and the development of the system to provide real-time information on the number and composition of domestic and foreign tourists. The information system will serve as an interface for sending mandatory reports to the Foreign Police and other authorities. The register will also serve as a single digital point of contact, in accordance with the recently approved EU regulation on short-term accommodation rentals.

Czechia is preparing to develop indicators to better measure the impacts of tourism and help promote more sustainable tourism. The indicators take draw from the European Tourism Indicators System, the European Environment Agency indicators, and UN Tourism work on indicators of Sustainable Development for Tourism Destinations. The aim is to help measure the impact of tourists on the natural environment, particularly with the increase of domestic demand for active holidays in rural areas. Data from the indicators will form the basis for policy and programme development to counter the impacts.

Statistical Profile

Czechia: Domestic, inbound and outbound tourism

	2018	2019	2020	2021 p	2022 p
TOURISM FLOWS, THOUSAND					
Domestic tourism					
Total domestic trips	85 831	85 867	62 822	71 024	79 405
Overnight visitors (tourists)	31 931	32 287	27 613	30 392	35 099
Same-day visitors (excursionists)	53 901	53 580	35 209	40 632	44 306
Nights in all types of accommodation	119 232	123 750	114 276	120 219	128 463
Hotels and similar establishments	..	..	..	..	..
Other collective establishments	..	..	..	..	..
Private accommodation	..	..	..	..	..
Inbound tourism					
Total international arrivals	36 268	37 202	10 267	10 014	26 592
Overnight visitors (tourists)	14 283	14 651	3 919	3 768	10 219
Same-day visitors (excursionists)	21 986	22 551	6 347	6 246	16 373
Top markets					
..	..	..	..	..	..
..	..	..	..	..	..
..	..	..	..	..	..
..	..	..	..	..	..
..	..	..	..	..	..
Nights in all types of accommodation	46 077	46 617	13 785	12 894	32 823
Hotels and similar establishments	24 427	24 916	6 699	6 067	16 630
Other collective establishments	2 931	2 860	1 035	750	1 870
Private accommodation	18 720	18 842	6 051	6 077	14 323
Outbound tourism					
Total international departures	12 839	12 974	4 049	5 245	11 553
Overnight visitors (tourists)	9 686	9 655	3 140	4 211	8 723
Same-day visitors (excursionists)	3 153	3 319	909	1 034	2 830
Top destinations					
Croatia	813	740	412	607	846
Slovak Republic	1 504	1 357	670	422	1 150
Greece	472	407	..	351	363
Italy	607	605	..	225	519
Austria	676	692	465	..	537
TOURISM RECEIPTS AND EXPENDITURE, MILLION CZK					
Inbound tourism					
Total international receipts	179 957	182 740	89 365	72 764	124 031
International travel receipts	161 717	167 476	83 368	66 838	118 035
International passenger transport receipts	18 240	15 263	5 997	5 925	5 997
Outbound tourism					
Total international expenditure	131 879	138 372	79 847	70 995	117 590
International travel expenditure	129 653	135 042	78 328	69 974	116 033
International passenger transport expenditure	2 226	3 329	1 519	1 021	1 558

.. Not available; p Provisional data
Source: OECD Tourism Statistics (Database).

StatLink https://stat.link/jlxo63

Czechia: Enterprises and employment in tourism

	Number of establishments	Number of persons employed				
	2022	2018	2019	2020	2021	2022p
Total	..	238 337	239 506	220 663	215 233	225 546
Tourism industries	..	234 812	235 969	217 174	211 727	221 988
Accommodation services for visitors	12 306					
Hotels and similar establishments	..	42 560	43 135	36 455	33 029	38 207
Food and beverage serving industry	47 638	68 881	68 692	62 668	62 056	65 087
Passenger transport	..					
Air passenger transport	..	2 216	2 342	1 950	1 703	1 936
Railways passenger transport	..	12 787	12 701	12 406	12 253	12 225
Road passenger transport	..	12 381	12 481	12 312	12 231	12 227
Water passenger transport	..	52	52	45	44	48
Passenger transport supporting services	..	4 291	4 318	4 163	4 015	4 178
Transport equipment rental	..	140	143	139	137	139
Travel agencies and other reservation services industry	..	13 861	14 041	10 250	9 431	10 146
Cultural industry	..	12 492	12 511	11 935	11 659	11 955
Sports and recreation industry	..	2 835	2 831	2 702	2 642	2 670
Retail trade of country-specific tourism characteristic goods	..					
Other country-specific tourism industries	..	62 316	62 723	62 150	62 526	63 168
Other industries	..	3 524	3 537	3 488	3 506	3 558

.. Not available; p Provisional data
Source: OECD Tourism Statistics (Database).

StatLink https://stat.link/n8bs3d

Czechia: Internal tourism consumption

Million CZK

	2022 p		
	Domestic tourism expenditure	Inbound tourism expenditure	Internal tourism consumption
Total	..	..	..
Consumption products	136 317	139 511	285 925
Tourism characteristic products	89 882	89 176	189 155
Accommodation services for visitors	19 453	27 400	56 951
Food and beverage serving services	26 671	27 874	54 545
Passenger transport services	18 451	25 294	43 745
Air passenger transport services	10 854	22 282	33 136
Railways passenger transport services	1 240	856	2 096
Road passenger transport services	6 202	2 156	8 358
Water passenger transport services	155	.	155
Passenger transport supporting services	4 496	3 175	7 671
Transport equipment rental services	310	425	735
Travel agencies and other reservation services industry	9 695	742	10 436
Cultural services	6 753	3 499	10 252
Sports and recreation services	3 039	767	3 806
Country-specific tourism characteristic goods			..
Country-specific tourism characteristic services	1 013		1 013
Other consumption products	46 435	50 335	96 770
Tourism connected products	46 435	50 335	96 770
Non-tourism related consumption products	..	..	..
Non-consumption products	..	..	..

.. Not available; p Provisional data
Source: OECD Tourism Statistics (Database).

StatLink https://stat.link/7jl8gk

Denmark

Tourism in the economy and outlook

Tourism is a significant contributor to the Danish economy. Tourism directly contributed DKK 45.6 billion or 1.8% of total GVA in 2022, almost recovering to 2019 levels (DKK 46.9 billion or 2.3% of total GVA). Correspondingly, the sector directly contributed 1.8% of GDP and 3.3% total of employment in Denmark (compared to 2.3 and 3.7% in 2019, respectively). Tourism accounted for 7.0% of service exports in 2022.

In 2023, Denmark recorded 32.2 million international overnights spent at commercial accommodation establishments (111.5% of 2019 levels) and 30.8 million domestic overnights (113.3% of 2019 levels), resulting in a record of 63.0 million total tourist overnights in 2023. In 2022, the four most important international source markets were Germany (32%), Norway (10%), Sweden (10%) and the Netherlands (6%). While arrivals from European markets and the United States are above 2019 levels, long haul markets, especially from Asia, have not recovered.

In 2022, total tourism expenditure hit DKK 152.6 billion, which equates to a 11.5% growth from 2019 in current prices. Domestic tourism expenditure contributed DKK 86.9 billion or 57% of total expenditure.

After recovering to pre-pandemic levels in 2022, Danish tourism is now looking to build on this recovery for sustainable growth in 2024 and beyond. Based on development in accommodation statistics and prices, total tourism expenditure in 2023 is estimated to DKK 163.9 billion.

Tourism governance

At the time of writing, responsibility for tourism development in Denmark is moving from the Ministry of Industry, Business and Financial Affairs to the Ministry of Urban, Rural, and Ecclesiastical Affairs. The Danish Tourism Advisory Board advises the Danish National Tourism Forum on opportunities and challenges to Danish tourism and supports the Ministry in setting the strategic direction for tourism in the country. Chaired by the Deputy Permanent Secretary of the Ministry, the Forum gathers members from other ministries, industry representatives and civil society and publishes a yearly status report on the tourism sector in Denmark.

VisitDenmark manages the international marketing of tourism, and is also responsible for market research, analysis and monitoring trends and activities. It works closely with three other tourism promotion and destination management organisations – the Danish Coastal and Nature Tourism which works to develop tourism outside major cities, MeetDenmark which focuses on developing business tourism, and Wonderful Copenhagen which hosts the Danish Metropolitan Tourism Organisation and is responsible for developing tourism in the capital city.

Across the country, 19 decentralised DMOs support local tourism businesses and tourism development initiatives to develop strong and coherent tourism destinations. The DMOs are primarily funded by municipalities and collaborate closely with VisitDenmark on international marketing activities. The DMOs are guided by the national tourism strategy which also serves as a framework for allocating national funds for specific projects on an application basis.

In 2024, the four national tourism organisations received a combined budget of DKK 218.7 million in base funding. This included DKK 138.6 million for VisitDenmark, DKK 28.7 million for the National Tourism Development Organisations, and DKK 49.4 million to Wonderful Copenhagen. The Danish Government has recently proposed to allocate a total additional DKK 100 million to tourism between 2024-27, spread equally across each year. There are also several funding pools open to tourism organisations to receive grants.

Denmark: Organisational chart of tourism bodies

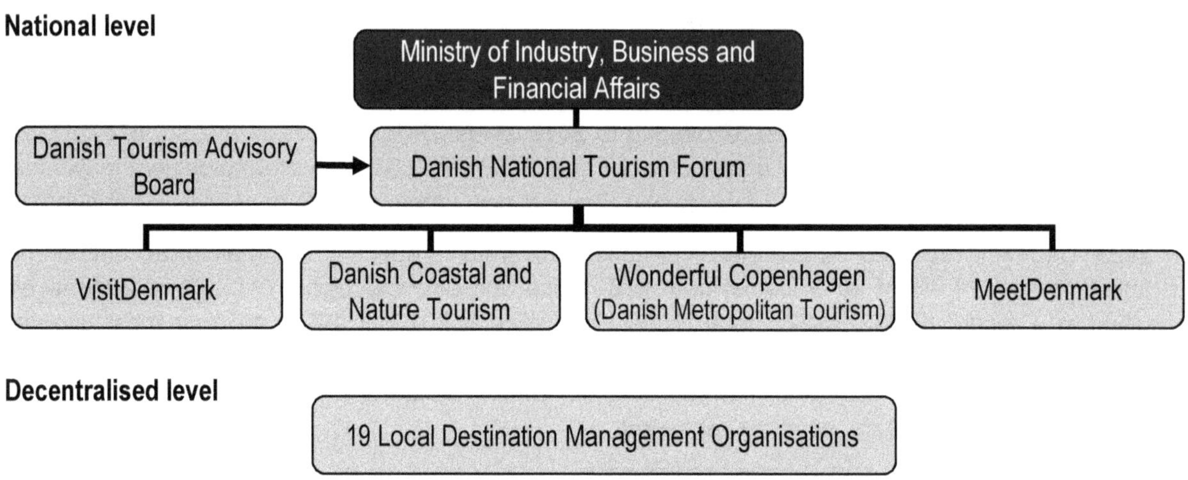

Note: At the time of writing, tourism is transitioning from the Ministry of Industry, Business and Financial Affairs to the Ministry of Urban, Rural, and Ecclesiastical Affairs.
Source: OECD, adapted from Ministry of Industry, Business and Financial Affairs, 2024.

Tourism policies and programmes

The National Strategy for Sustainable Growth in Tourism provides the strategic guiding framework for tourism in Denmark for 2030 with 9 overall targets for sustainable tourism development across the dimensions of economic, social and environmental sustainability.

The Strategy recognises that building a successful and future-proof tourism sector requires a broad cross-dimensional focus within all tourism business areas (nature, business and metropolitan). Released in 2022 and covering the period to 2030, the Strategy is to being updated in 2024.

The key challenges faced by Danish tourism the Strategy seeks to:

- Foster and measure the transition to more sustainable tourism in Denmark across all three dimensions (social, economic, and environmental).
- Address shortage of skilled and unskilled labour, which is a fundamental barrier to the sustainable growth of the sector.
- Boost private investment in accommodation and attractions outside the major cities, where investment has decreased, despite a growing demand for nature and coastal tourism in Denmark.

Five development tracks are included in the Strategy, to be achieved by 2030: (i) Returning international tourism to Denmark as soon as possible; (ii) Ensuring the recovery of urban tourism is sustainable; (iii) Establishing Denmark as an attractive destination for business and conferencing tourism; (iv) Taking advantage of new potentials and opportunities; (v) Following and adapting to the changing preferences of tourists.

To achieve these objectives, several programmes have been developed and implemented. A comprehensive Comeback Copenhagen Plan to recover tourism and create a local and authentic experience for visitors in the city was launched in 2021 and will run until 2025. The Plan has four overall ambitions backed by specific initiatives to deliver: bringing tourists and tourism revenue back on the growth-track, adjusting to attract new target markets, with a focus on the Danish domestic market and nearby markets, tourism for the benefit of the entire capital, and sustainable tourism behaviour as a key competitive factor. The Plan is currently in the latter stages of implementation, with overnight tourist stays increasing 18.2% in 2023 compared to 2019, and 10.8% compared to 2022.

The national brand The Land of Everyday Wonder is also being further developed by strengthening its role at the local level and helping DMOs align local branding accordingly. All publicly funded sub-national DMOs with international marketing campaigns must use the brand Land of Everyday Wonder. By early 2024, there were 50 international campaigns using this brand with a 25 further in planning.

A total funding of DKK 175 million for public tourism infrastructure, including harbourfronts and pathways, was allocated in two tranches: DKK 110 million in November 2023 and the remainder by the end of 2024. The Danish Board of Business Development has allocated the funding for projects outside major cities to attract private tourism investment. To increase regional development, Denmark has also launched a new national data platform in 2023, which aims to support tourism decision making and provide better data to DMOs (see box below).

Additionally, a comprehensive plan for the sustainable development of business tourism in Denmark was launched in 2022. The plan features 11 initiatives and includes development programmes for companies to enhance the sustainability of tourism businesses. As of early 2024, 58 businesses had participated in these programmes and reported positive results.

Connect data to decisions through a new national data platform in Denmark

In May 2023, VisitDenmark, Danish Coastal and Nature Tourism, NTT DATA Business and the West Denmark DMOs launched a new national data platform for tourism to provide DMOs and partners with data and tools to support decision-making. By connecting various data sources and combining data, tourism stakeholders can gain new insights into tourist behaviour and make better business decisions.

The platform handles the data in a responsible way. DMOs gain access to shared knowledge and data on the number of nights, attractions and visitor numbers. In the long run, this will enable DMOs to draw on the experiences of other destinations and compare local results with new relevant benchmarks. Furthermore, DMOs can store and use data that only they will be able to access. The platform couples data from both public and commercials sources (e.g, VISA, telecom companies). DMOs will therefore be able to create tailor-made knowledge-solutions that the actors at destination-level were previously unable to access. The national platform builds on the project Destination Digital, which began on Rømø island and has since scaled up to encompass the entire west coast via Destination Nordvestkysten, Destination Vesterhavet and Destination Vadehavskysten, with NTT DATA Business Solutions and Danish Coastal and Nature Tourism as partners.

By the end of 2023, all Danish DMOs were connected to the platform. Companies are also expected to be connected by 2024. As of early 2024, the different actors involved in the project were working on the release of the dashboard and data products.

Statistical Profile

Denmark: Domestic, inbound and outbound tourism

	2018	2019	2020	2021	2022
TOURISM FLOWS, THOUSAND					
Domestic tourism					
Total domestic trips	63 160	68 895	62 265	62 625	61 554
Overnight visitors (tourists)	16 619	18 865	17 919	20 002	20 472
Same-day visitors (excursionists)	46 541	50 030	44 346	42 624	41 082
Nights in all types of accommodation	67 017	75 472 |	80 661 |e	86 948	81 526
Hotels and similar establishments	20 334	21 643	22 833	28 247	25 908
Other collective establishments	9 789	8 441	9 484	10 455	9 393
Private accommodation	36 894	45 389	48 344	48 246	46 224
Inbound tourism					
Total international arrivals	30 089 e	32 065 |e	16 031 e	18 372	31 530
Overnight visitors (tourists)	12 749 e	14 725 |e	6 229 e	7 555	14 190
Same-day visitors (excursionists)	17 340 e	17 340 |e	9 802 e	10 817 e	17 340 e
Top markets					
Germany	3452 e	3 964	2 548	2 755	4 472
Norway	1886 e	1 517	593	539	1 465
Sweden	1572 e	1 483	514	639	1 424
United States	942 e	1 039	250	452	772
Netherlands	780 e	712	345	594	854
Nights in all types of accommodation	55 931	58 006	31 179	35 823	59 760
Hotels and similar establishments	29 306	31 240	16 547	17 450	31 994
Other collective establishments	4 584	3 743	2 530	2 774	4 742
Private accommodation	22 041 e	23 024	12 102	15 598	23 024
Outbound tourism					
Total international departures					
Overnight visitors (tourists)	7 475 e	9 088	4 230	3 182	6 043
Same-day visitors (excursionists)					
Top destinations					
..					
..					
..					
..					
..					
TOURISM RECEIPTS AND EXPENDITURE, MILLION DKK					
Inbound tourism					
Total international receipts	73 702	74 072	31 440	34 719	75 630
International travel receipts	57 533	57 701	25 917	28 144	63 124
International passenger transport receipts	16 169	16 371	5 524	6 575	12 506
Outbound tourism					
Total international expenditure	79 016	80 050	40 299	51 548	69 852
International travel expenditure	66 574	66 717	36 081	46 802	59 875
International passenger transport expenditure	12 442	13 333	4 218	4 746	9 977

.. Not available; e Estimated value; | Break in series
Source: OECD Tourism Statistics (Database).

StatLink https://stat.link/kdvh97

Denmark: Enterprises and employment in tourism

	Number of establishments[1]	Number of persons employed				
	2022	2018	2019	2020	2021	2022
Total	..	..	..	..	..	..
Tourism industries	24 913	267 140	273 199	253 694	247 854	279 005
Accommodation services for visitors	1 995	21 370	21 940	18 384	17 859	22 918
Hotels and similar establishments	912	..	..	..	..	
Food and beverage serving industry	14 515	119 601	123 092	114 010	113 722	130 420
Passenger transport	4 358	55 723	56 169	53 390	50 655	52 924
Air passenger transport	89	4 320	3 757	5 171	2 798	2 274
Railways passenger transport	117	6 074	6 058	6 031	5 871	5 801
Road passenger transport	4 043	25 439	25 855	22 708	22 085	23 434
Water passenger transport	109	19 893	20 499	19 480	19 900	21 414
Passenger transport supporting services	5	..	..	..	..	
Transport equipment rental	268	..	..	..	..	
Travel agencies and other reservation services industry	598	6 746	6 824	5 432	4 073	5 056
Cultural industry	1 091	29 419	65 174	62 478	61 545	67 687
Sports and recreation industry	2 083	34 281		..	..	..
Retail trade of country-specific tourism characteristic goods	..	..	..	..	..	..
Other country-specific tourism industries	..	..	..	..	..	..
Other industries	..	..	..	..	..	..

.. Not available; f Forecast value

1. Data refer to number of enterprises.

Source: OECD Tourism Statistics (Database).

StatLink https://stat.link/53pr0x

Denmark: Internal tourism consumption

Million DKK

	2022		
	Domestic tourism expenditure	Inbound tourism expenditure	Internal tourism consumption
Total	..	..	..
Consumption products	86 913	65 695	152 609
Tourism characteristic products	54 263	32 648	86 911
Accommodation services for visitors	12 548	10 339	22 887
Food and beverage serving services	13 239	9 608	22 847
Passenger transport services	17 682	7 753	25 435
Air passenger transport services	11 820	3 043	14 863
Railways passenger transport services	257	513	770
Road passenger transport services	799	1 270	2 069
Water passenger transport services	4 806	2 927	7 733
Passenger transport supporting services	1 311	949	2 260
Transport equipment rental services	1 532	1 473	3 005
Travel agencies and other reservation services industry	2 581	707	3 288
Cultural services	5 285	1 723	7 009
Sports and recreation services	..	..	..
Country-specific tourism characteristic goods	..	..	..
Country-specific tourism characteristic services	84	96	180
Other consumption products	32 650	33 047	65 698
Tourism connected products	21 451	17 858	39 309
Non-tourism related consumption products	11 199	15 189	26 389
Non-consumption products	..	..	..

.. Not available

Source: OECD Tourism Statistics (Database).

StatLink https://stat.link/le8wht

Estonia

Tourism in the economy and outlook

Tourism is an important contributor to the Estonian economy, with travel and passenger transport services responsible for 16% of all services exports in 2023. In 2022, tourism accounted for 3.7% of GDP of the Estonian economy (compared to 5.4% in 2019). Tourism-related industries accounted for 7.1% of total employment in 2022 (back at the level of 7.1% in 2019).

In 2023, Estonia welcomed 2.4 million international overnight visitors. This is significantly up on the pandemic low of 801 200 in 2021, but is still 27% below 2019 levels. The top three international source markets were Finland (43%), Latvia (15%) and Germany (5%).

Domestic travel is also recovering but similarly remains below 2019 levels. In 2023, 3.2 million domestic overnight trips were recorded in Estonia, up on the pandemic low of 2.1 million in 2020 but still 7.3% lower than in 2019. However, if the number of nights spent on domestic trips in commercial accommodation establishments is considered, domestic tourism fully recovered, reaching 3.1 million overnights in 2023 compared to 2.7 million in 2019.

International tourism might not return to pre-pandemic levels by 2025 due to a drastic drop in tourists from Russia after the escalation of Russia's war of aggression against Ukraine and a slowdown in the economies of Estonia's neighbouring countries and main trade partners, which could further delay the recovery of international tourism.

Tourism governance

The Ministry of Economic Affairs and Communications co-ordinates national tourism policy in close co-operation with department of tourism (Visit Estonia) in the Joint organisation of KredEx and Enterprise Estonia. Other bodies regularly involved in tourism policy development and implementation include the Estonian Travel and Tourism Association, the Estonian Hotel and Restaurant Association, Estonian Rural Tourism, the Estonian Spa Association, and the Estonian Convention Bureau. The Consumer Protection and Technical Regulatory Authority is the main supervisory authority for tourism.

Visit Estonia is responsible for tourism policy implementation and has a key role in strengthening the network of destination management organisations (DMO) and co-ordinating tourism product development and customer journey experience activities. In 2021, Visit Estonia began a phased reform of DMO structures, to enhance the strategic vision and co-operation with destinations (see box below).

Regional county development centres located in all 15 Estonian counties offer free advisory services to enterprises, local government, non-profit associations and foundations. Visit Estonia has specialist partners in DMOs that offer data management services for every county. Larger cities also have their own tourism development structures.

In 2023, EUR 21.1 million was allocated to tourism, of which EUR 15.8 million from the state budget – EUR 3.5 million for developing competitiveness and increasing added value of Estonian tourism businesses, products, and destinations; EUR 9.4 million for a smart data-driven tourism marketing programme; EUR 2.8 million for targeted financing; EUR 100 000 for software integration and connectivity support in the tourism sector – and EUR 5.3 million from EU funds.

Estonia: Organisational chart of tourism bodies

Source: OECD, adapted from the Ministry of Economic Affairs and Communications, 2024.

Tourism policies and programmes

The Tourism Strategy 2022-25 guides tourism policy in Estonia and targets a more adaptable, resilient and sustainable tourism economy by 2025, with strategic goals set out in three priority areas:

- Product and destination development: become a sustainable tourism destination that offers visitors a diverse and unique travel experience in all seasons.
- Restoration of demand: exceed pre-crisis levels of number of tourists and export of tourism services.
- Ensuring connectivity: be well-connected to the main markets and have easily accessible tourism products and services, both physically and virtually.

To achieve these objectives, the Strategy prioritises longer stays and higher spending per visitor over increasing the number of international arrivals. This strategic shift also aims to enhance the sustainability of tourism and generate greater added value.

Co-operation with key stakeholders is fundamental to delivering on the Strategy, with a number of models and approaches being taken to strengthen engagement with business associations, transport carriers and entry points to Estonia (focusing on air and sea ports), and other key partners through the Tourism Council, which gathers at the Ministry of Economic Affairs and Communications to discuss current topics in tourism.

Tourism in Estonia had already exceeded the targets set out in the Strategy by the end of 2023. However, given the new geopolitical and economic challenges facing Estonia, the Tourism Council decided not to amend the target levels in 2023-24. However, Estonia remains committed to fulfilling the vision for tourism set out in the Strategy. Connectivity remains a crucial issue, as well as upskilling the workforce.

In addition to the Tourism Strategy 2022-25, Estonia is currently drafting a 2035 long-term vision for tourism. Recognising tourism's interconnected nature with other sectors, Estonia adopted a multi-level approach, including workshops, surveys, interviews, and validation seminars, to engage stakeholders in developing its long-term vision using Strategic Foresight (Box 1.2).

To support the implementation of the Tourism Strategy 2022-25, several tourism programmes have been launched. For example, Estonia commissioned a study entitled Transition to Sustainable Tourism in

Estonia: Current Situation, Preconditions, Impact, Investment and Support Needs for the Tourism Sector. A Tourism Sustainability Action Plan was created at the end of 2023, based on policy recommendations. The Action Plan requires collaboration between government and non-government stakeholders to ensure sustainability is integrated into the Estonian tourism offering.

Other initiatives include the Tourism Digital Mentoring Alongside Digitalisation Roadmap which aims to increase digital literacy and digital uptake within tourism businesses, through mentoring and the creation of a digital roadmap. Each company will be required to contribute 10% of the cost of the mentoring over a five-month period. In return, they will receive training in digital marketing and a roadmap catered to their business to help achieve greater profitability and efficiency over a three-year period.

The Integration and Interface Support for Tourism Sector Software support scheme aims to assist in the digitalisation and automation of work processes for tourism service providers. The support enables the adoption of software, such as implementing new resource management software, and allows the integration of various software systems. The application process for the support opened in November 2023 and applications can be submitted continuously. The budget totals EUR 1.9 million, and businesses can benefit from a EUR 20 000 maximum grant, if they contribute with at least 30% of self-financing.

Optimising the structure of Destination Management Organisations in Estonia

In 2021 Visit Estonia launched a phased reform of the country's destination management organisation (DMOs) structures. The reform aims to consolidate the approximately 40 DMOs to a maximum of eight state-supported DMOs on a voluntary basis to allow for more regional specialisation, greater strategic vision, and co-operation within and between destinations. The large number of small DMOs often resulted in duplicated efforts while operating within constrained budgets. Consolidating the human and financial resources and competences into few but stronger DMOs will help to better manage the destination. The new DMOs structures aim to also guide entrepreneurs and become a strong partner for the public sector in planning marketing and development activities and investments.

In 2024, there are seven DMOs in Estonia. DMOs are based on a public/private partnership model with strong collaboration between the sectors and they cover all 15 counties as well the capital city of Tallinn that is a separate DMO. Representatives from both the public and private sectors are involved in the planning and implementation of joint activities of the DMOs. DMO territory and Lead Partner are appointed by the country development organisations, DMO Lead Partner can be a local government or its subsidiary, a foundation, or a non-profit organisation. For example, the Southern Estonia DMO was established by the Southern Estonia Tourism Cluster within the Tartumaa Tourism Foundation, encompassing tourism businesses, networks, and regional development centres. The Southern Estonia DMO collaborates with the city and county of Tartu, as well as the counties of Põlva and Võru, and the municipalities of Jõgeva, Mustvee, Otepää, and Valga. Official collaboration began on January 1, 2023, with the lead partner being the Tartumaa Tourism Foundation.

To foster the creation of robust DMOs in Estonia, financial support from the State is necessary. Visit Estonia finances development actions of DMOs, calculating sums based on tourism volume and co-operation potential of respective areas. DMOs are expected to provide at least 30% of self-financing in the first year of action, raising up to 40% for the second year and to 50% for the following years.

Statistical Profile

Estonia: Domestic, inbound and outbound tourism

	2018	2019	2020	2021	2022
TOURISM FLOWS, THOUSAND					
Domestic tourism[1]					
Total domestic trips	12 616	..	..	7 466	..
Overnight visitors (tourists)	4 399	3 486	2 136	2 267	2 640
Same-day visitors (excursionists)	8 217	..	..	5 200	..
Nights in all types of accommodation	2 456	2 591	2 270	2 716	3 032
Hotels and similar establishments	2 455	2 590	2 268	2 715	3 028
Other collective establishments	1	2	2	1	4
Private accommodation	..	..	..	..	..
Inbound tourism[2]					
Total international arrivals	6 033	6 103	1 695	1 302	3 497
Overnight visitors (tourists)	3 226	3 336	1 023	801	2 166
Same-day visitors (excursionists)	2 807	2 766	673	500	1 331
Top markets					
Finland	1 145	1 130	419	215	862
Latvia	298	320	178	138	334
Russia	464	463	112	44	117
Germany	245	269	56	67	115
Sweden	119	129	19	30	59
Nights in all types of accommodation	4 175	4 376	1 404	1 283	2 919
Hotels and similar establishments	4 164	4 362	1 399	1 280	2 908
Other collective establishments	11	13	5	3	11
Private accommodation	..	..	..	..	..
Outbound tourism					
Total international departures	3 607	3 641	1 335	1 226	2 690
Overnight visitors (tourists)	3 088	3 116	1 151	1 050	2 243
Same-day visitors (excursionists)	520	525	184	176	447
Top destinations					
Finland	520	513	273	214	487
Latvia	301	288	200	81	398
Germany	213	213	87	74	175
Sweden	219	215	74	75	160
Russia	255	268	56	54	103
TOURISM RECEIPTS AND EXPENDITURE, MILLION EUR					
Inbound tourism					
Total international receipts	1 974	2 060	732	769	1 561
International travel receipts	1 510	1 552	524	538	1 215
International passenger transport receipts	464	508	209	231	346
Outbound tourism					
Total international expenditure	1 397	1 616	598	681	1 332
International travel expenditure	1 241	1 381	526	587	1 115
International passenger transport expenditure	156	235	73	94	217

.. Not available

1. Trips from demand side surveys; Nights from supply side surveys.

2. Arrivals from demand side surveys; Nights from supply side surveys.

Source: OECD Tourism Statistics (Database).

StatLink https://stat.link/v273rk

Estonia: Enterprises and employment in tourism

	Number of establishments	Number of persons employed				
	2022	2018	2019	2020	2021	2022
Total	..	..	..	..	..	..
Tourism industries	..	..	..	..	..	..
Accommodation services for visitors	1 337	7 100	7 000	5 600	..	..
Hotels and similar establishments	..	..	..	..	..	..
Food and beverage serving industry	..	17 900	19 600	16 804	..	..
Passenger transport	..	..	..	..	..	..
Air passenger transport	..	..	..	..	..	..
Railways passenger transport	..	..	..	..	..	..
Road passenger transport	..	..	..	..	..	..
Water passenger transport	..	..	..	..	..	..
Passenger transport supporting services	..	..	..	..	..	..
Transport equipment rental	..	..	..	..	..	..
Travel agencies and other reservation services industry	..	1 800	1 900	1 600	..	..
Cultural industry	..	..		..	..	..
Sports and recreation industry	..	..	..	..	..	..
Retail trade of country-specific tourism characteristic goods	..	..	..	..	..	..
Other country-specific tourism industries	..	..	..	..	..	..
Other industries	..	..	..	..	..	..

.. Not available
Source: OECD Tourism Statistics (Database).

StatLink https://stat.link/x2cdbe

Estonia: Internal tourism consumption

Million EUR

	2017		
	Domestic tourism expenditure	Inbound tourism expenditure	Internal tourism consumption
Total	..	..	..
Consumption products	269	1 721	2 359
Tourism characteristic products	236	1 130	1 706
Accommodation services for visitors	72	298	511
Food and beverage serving services	49	370	419
Passenger transport services	54	306	534
Air passenger transport services	29	97	178
Railways passenger transport services	2	1	7
Road passenger transport services	9	28	66
Water passenger transport services	13	166	239
Passenger transport supporting services	..	9	9
Transport equipment rental services	0.3	4	34
Travel agencies and other reservation services industry	51	71	140
Cultural services	4	65	69
Sports and recreation services	2	11	13
Country-specific tourism characteristic goods	..	..	..
Country-specific tourism characteristic services	5	10	21
Other consumption products	33	591	654
Tourism connected products	18	47	85
Non-tourism related consumption products	15	544	569
Non-consumption products	..	..	..

.. Not available
Source: OECD Tourism Statistics (Database).

StatLink https://stat.link/3jp04a

Finland

Tourism in the economy and outlook

Tourism is an important economic sector in Finland. Before the pandemic, tourism was one of the fastest growing sectors of service exports in Finland, with inbound tourism expenditure increasing faster than other service exports at an annual rate of approximately 11% from 2016 to 2019. In 2022, tourism directly accounted for EUR 4.1 billion or 1.8% of GVA, clearly up on the pandemic low of EUR 2.9 billion in 2020, but below 2019 levels of EUR 5.7 billion or 2.7% of GVA. In 2022, the tourism sector directly provided 119 600 full-time equivalent jobs or 5.1% of total employment (compared to 133 200 jobs and 5.8% of total employment in 2019). The Finnish tourism sector continues to suffer from lack of skilled workforce.

Tourist accommodations in Finland recorded 5.8 million international overnight stays in 2023, 18.5% fewer than in 2019. According to estimations, international revenues in 2022 grew to EUR 3.3 billion, approximately 62% of the peak in 2019 in current prices. Germany (12%), Sweden (12%) and the United Kingdom (9%) were the largest international source markets in 2022, with European markets accounting for 78% of international tourism revenues (excluding passenger transport).

Domestic tourism has held up well during the pandemic. Finland recorded 27.1 million domestic tourist arrivals in 2022, slightly below pre-pandemic levels of 29.3 million. Finland predicts international arrivals will return to pre-pandemic levels by 2025, having taken longer to recover due to Russia's war of aggression against Ukraine.

Tourism governance

The Ministry of Economic Affairs and Employment is responsible for tourism policy development and support, drafting legislation and maintaining international relations regarding tourism. In developing the sector, the Ministry collaborates closely with other ministries.

A High-Level Working Group on Tourism established in 2021 supports the implementation of tourism policy and preparation on tourism-related matters at the ministry level. Composed of ministries that are of key importance to the tourism sector, regional councils, state administrations, regional tourism organisations, tourism businesses, trade unions, and research and educational institutions and organisations, the Working Group is chaired by the Minister of Economic Affairs. It continues the work of the unofficial Inter-Ministerial Working Group on Tourism (MiniMatka) which had previously operated under the chair of the Ministry for over 20 years.

The national tourism organisation Visit Finland is a unit of Business Finland which gathers all the services related to the promotion of innovation funding, exports, investment and tourism. Funded by the state budget, Visit Finland is responsible for promoting Finland as a destination and supporting Finnish tourism businesses to develop and operate in international markets. Regional Councils provide support for tourism development projects, general marketing, advisory services, training and research in Finland's 19 regions. Finland has a total of 15 Centres for Economic Development, Transport and the Environment

(ELY Centres), which are tasked with promoting regional competitiveness, well-being and sustainable development and curbing climate change. They offer financial, advisory, consulting and training services to tourism businesses, grant investment support and manage matters related to their local infrastructure.

For 2024, the Parliament through the Ministry of Economic Affairs and Employment allocated EUR 9.8 million to Business Finland's tourism promotion and development actions, namely to Visit Finland. Between 2021-24, Business Finland received approximately EUR 12 million from Finland's national Recovery and Resilience Plan. The organisation has been given responsibility to implement the tourism-specific investment included in the plan.

Finland: Organisational chart of tourism bodies

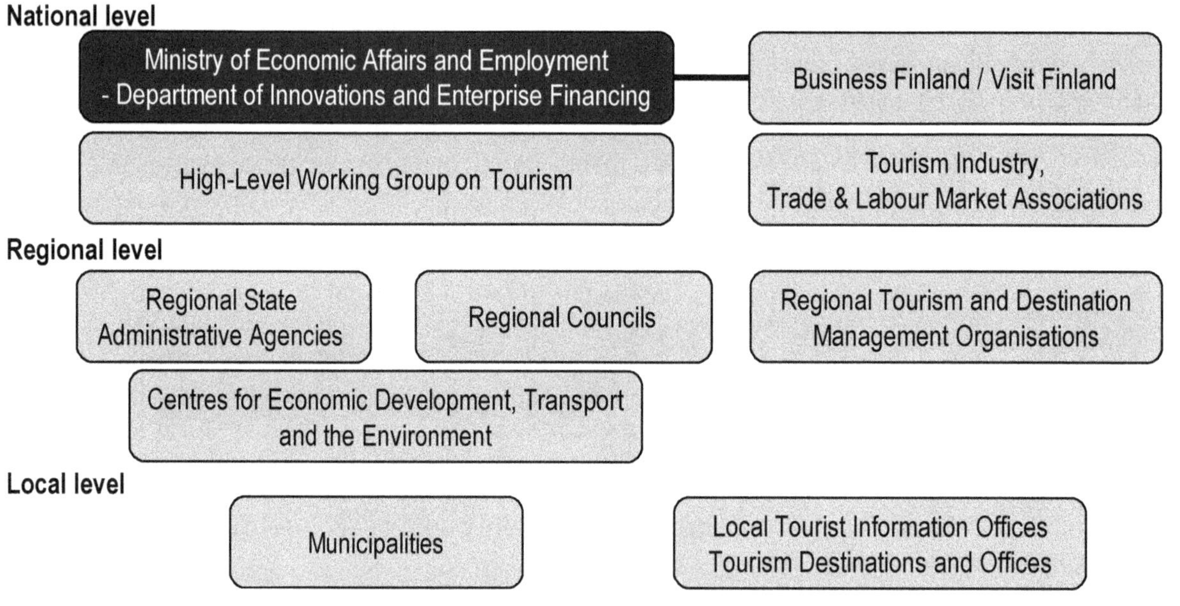

Source: OECD, adapted from the Ministry of Economic Affairs and Employment, 2024.

Tourism policies and programmes

Finland's National Tourism Strategy, Achieving More Together - Sustainable Growth and Renewal in Finnish Tourism 2022-28, guides tourism policy and programme development in Finland. The Strategy was originally launched in 2019 and updated in 2022 to better reflect the changing operational environment, including following the COVID-19 pandemic and Russia's war of aggression against Ukraine. The High-Level Working Group on Tourism played a key role in designing the update. The updated Strategy identifies four priorities to facilitate sustainable growth and renewal in the tourism sector, including: (i) supporting sustainable development; (ii) responding to the digital transformation; (iii) improving accessibility; and (iv) ensuring an operating environment that supports competitiveness. The objective is for Finland to become the most sustainably growing tourism destination in the Nordic countries.

An action plan for the years 2022-23 supported the implementation of the Strategy, with a broad range of targeted actions and goals requiring collaboration of many actors, including tourism businesses, destinations, regions, funding authorities and ministries. Actions were implemented within the resources made available by central government spending limits and budgets, with no specific budget allocation for the implementation phase. The monitoring of Finland's National Tourism Strategy and Action Plan occur collectively, with specific measurements every two years. A monitoring report on the implementation of the 2022–23 Action Plan will be published in early autumn 2024. Based on the monitoring results, updates to the Strategy and subsequent Action Plan, will be made, if necessary.

Key tourism policy priorities include supporting sustainable development of tourism businesses and destinations, strengthening climate action, clarifying legislation on short-term rentals to correspond to the current practices and needs, and supporting knowledge-based management at the national and regional level. These priorities are translated into programmes such as the Sustainable Travel Finland Programme, launched in 2020 following a successful pilot in 2018-19. Visit Finland works closely with the Finnish tourism businesses and regions, including to develop and report national indicators for sustainable tourism. According to the results of the first State of Sustainable Tourism report launched in 2023, tourism businesses and destinations have high engagement in environmental protection and climate action, but less focus on social impacts. Therefore, Visit Finland will prioritise activities and advancements in diversity, equity, and inclusion in 2024. The indicators are visualised in a real-time online dashboard and will inform the evaluation and updated target setting for the National Tourism Strategy and supporting actions in 2024. The programme also aims to gather qualitative data on tourism employment which will help to evaluate and develop setting targets for the Strategy and Action Plans regarding tourism workforce issues.

Visit Finland published its Climate Action Plan in November 2023 to provide tourism businesses, tourism destinations and Visit Finland with a pathway to systematically reducing emissions from tourism. A 2024 progress report will include a roadmap to help preserve natural environments, seek ways to use nature-based solutions to regenerate nature and increase the positive impacts of tourism. In addition, almost 70 Finnish tourism organisations have signed the Glasgow Declaration on Climate Action in Tourism. All signatories are required to provide climate action plans for decreasing their CO2 emissions.

Additionally, the Ministries of the Environment, Justice and Economic Affairs and Employment have started to map the current legislation framework to identify the needs for a legislative update. The conditions for short-term rentals will be regulated while making available better methods to address problems. Finland launched a new border survey in 2023. The open data is updated monthly (see box below). While additional monitoring efforts at the national level are challenging, some destinations have developed monitoring systems including dashboards and analysis methods and knowledge-based models to enhance decision-making at the destination level.

New border survey collecting and sharing monthly tourism statistics in Finland

The new Visit Finland Border Survey was launched in March 2023 to measure the number of arrivals, spending, carbon footprint and segmentation of international tourists in Finland. The survey aims to fill key tourism data gaps and provide monthly open data updates for tourism stakeholders. The survey will provide data for international arrivals, tourism receipts and the travel item for the balance of payments.

Data is collected via face-to-face interviews conducted at airports and major seaports and harbours, covering more than 90% of international air and sea passengers. Land border crossings are currently excluded from the survey. Statistics Finland and commercial partners Norstat Finland and TAK assist Visit Finland in collecting and disseminating the data. The research is financed by the EU's Resilience and Recovery Facility (RRF), which supports development measures for sustainable and digital growth in the tourism sector. Survey results are published at Visit Finland's statistical database. A new approach involves publishing the interview data as open data online for detailed analysis, dashboards, and commercial and scientific use.

Statistical Profile

Finland: Domestic, inbound and outbound tourism

	2018	2019	2020	2021	2022
TOURISM FLOWS, THOUSAND					
Domestic tourism					
Total domestic trips	45 280	..	..	61 300	..
Overnight visitors (tourists)	29 130	29 320	23 340	29 380	27 100
Same-day visitors (excursionists)	16 160	..	..	31 920	..
Nights in all types of accommodation	78 360	81 760	90 240	102 260	90 950
Hotels and similar establishments	13 360	12 920	8 370	9 930	10 780
Other collective establishments	10 940	10 720	13 230	14 210	14 870
Private accommodation	54 060	58 120	68 640	78 120	65 300
Inbound tourism					
Total international arrivals	..	..	..	..	..
Overnight visitors (tourists)	3 224	3 290	896	807	2 127
Same-day visitors (excursionists)	..	..	..	..	..
Top markets					
Germany	304	313	96	106	263
Sweden	323	320	56	85	246
United Kingdom	230	220	52	89	184
United States	139	143	41	43	130
France	106	120	42	41	110
Nights in all types of accommodation	6 843	7 056	2 291	2 085	4 975
Hotels and similar establishments	6 505	6 695	2 155	1 968	4 711
Other collective establishments	337	361	136	117	264
Private accommodation	..	..	..	..	..
Outbound tourism					
Total international departures	10 480	10 440	2 690	2 260	6 780
Overnight visitors (tourists)	9 450	9 410	2 330	1 800	6 180
Same-day visitors (excursionists)	1 030	1 030	360	460	600
Top destinations					
Estonia	1 670	1 600	620	390	1 190
Sweden	1 780	1 770	430	420	1 110
Spain	880	790	270	230	600
Greece	260	260	..	..	310
Germany	500	610	..	..	290
TOURISM RECEIPTS AND EXPENDITURE, MILLION EUR					
Inbound tourism					
Total international receipts	4 883	5 000	1 562	926	3 133
International travel receipts	3 103	3 328	1 107	926	2 136
International passenger transport receipts	1 780	1 672	455	..	997
Outbound tourism					
Total international expenditure	6 127	5 919	1 705	1 186	4 618
International travel expenditure	5 152	5 074	1 468	1 186	4 158
International passenger transport expenditure	975	845	237	..	460

.. Not available
Source: OECD Tourism Statistics (Database).

StatLink https://stat.link/9zxyb0

Finland: Enterprises and employment in tourism

	Number of establishments	Number of persons employed				
	2022	2018	2019	2020	2021	2022 p
Total	..	..	..	..	..	..
Tourism industries	49 234	129 600	133 200	108 800	109 600	119 600
Accommodation services for visitors	3 481	14 000	14 300	11 500	11 800	14 300
Hotels and similar establishments	1 233	..	..	..	..	..
Food and beverage serving industry	15 016	65 900	68 300	56 300	58 300	62 200
Passenger transport	9 242	34 300	34 500	27 100	25 500	27 600
Air passenger transport	121	4 100	3 900	2 000	1 700	2 800
Railways passenger transport	45	4 400	4 600	4 500	3 600	3 700
Road passenger transport	8 733	20 700	20 800	16 800	17 000	17 500
Water passenger transport	343	5 100	5 200	3 800	3 200	3 600
Passenger transport supporting services		..	..	..	..	..
Transport equipment rental	864	1 500	1 600	1 400	1 500	1 600
Travel agencies and other reservation services industry	2 465	1 900	2 000	1 500	1 200	1 600
Cultural industry	10 504	5 200	5 800	4 900	5 400	5 900
Sports and recreation industry	7 662	6 800	6 700	6 100	5 900	6 400
Retail trade of country-specific tourism characteristic goods	..	..	..	..	..	..
Other country-specific tourism industries	..	..	..	..	..	..
Other industries	..	..	..	..	..	..

.. Not available; p Provisional data
Source: OECD Tourism Statistics (Database).

StatLink https://stat.link/d8ek6w

Finland: Internal tourism consumption

Million EUR

	2021		
	Domestic tourism expenditure	Inbound tourism expenditure	Internal tourism consumption
Total	8 246	1 303	11 345
Consumption products	7 918	1 298	11 012
Tourism characteristic products	4 087	931	6 639
Accommodation services for visitors	875	190	2 195
Food and beverage serving services	1 230	262	1 492
Passenger transport services	1 042	369	1 867
Air passenger transport services	263	244	694
Railways passenger transport services	157	7	194
Road passenger transport services	415	46	699
Water passenger transport services	207	72	280
Passenger transport supporting services	..	.	.
Transport equipment rental services	184	5	195
Travel agencies and other reservation services industry	96	5	131
Cultural services	231	55	286
Sports and recreation services	429	45	474
Country-specific tourism characteristic goods	.	.	.
Country-specific tourism characteristic services	.	.	.
Other consumption products	3 831	367	4 372
Tourism connected products	1 527	41	1 742
Non-tourism related consumption products	2 304	326	2 630
Non-consumption products	328	5	333

.. Not available
Source: OECD Tourism Statistics (Database).

StatLink https://stat.link/4j316l

France

Tourism in the economy and outlook

Tourism is a significant contributor to the French economy. Its structural importance can be measured in two ways, on the one hand, by domestic tourism consumption (which amounts to approximately 7.5% of GDP) and, on the other hand, by the share of tourism sectors in added value total (which represents, excluding crisis episodes, around 4% of GDP). In 2022, direct tourism employment amounted to 1.5 million jobs, up from 1.3 million in 2020, representing 7.7% of total employment.

International tourism demand has returned to pre-pandemic levels in France. Revenues from international tourism, which fell to EUR 28.5 billion in 2020, have recovered well, reaching EUR 56.7 billion in 2022, similar to 2019 levels in current prices. Provisional data indicates that for 2023, total revenue have reached EUR 63.5 billion. Tourism contributes positively to the balance of payments, with the tourism balance recording an increase from EUR 3.4 billion in 2020 to EUR 18.5 billion in 2023 (compared to EUR 11.6 billion in 2019). France recorded 98 million international tourist arrivals in 2023 (according to provisional estimates from Atout France), up from 90.9 million in 2019, and 41.7 million in 2020. European countries remain the main international source markets in France, accounting for over 83.3% of international arrivals. German tourists constitute the leading international clientele, with more than 16% of total arrivals in 2022.

Domestic tourism remains a major component of tourist demand. It structurally represents two-thirds of tourism consumption in France and constituted an important factor for the sector's resilience during the COVID-19 crisis.

For 2024, France expects more international arrivals boosted by the Olympics and Paralympics Games in Paris.

Tourism governance

The Ministry for the Economy, with the Directorate General for Enterprise (DGE), is responsible for tourism at the national level in France. For tourism, being a transversal economic sector, co-ordination with other inter-ministerial departments is of great importance and this is carried out in particular by the Inter-ministerial Tourism Council. Dialogue between administrations and representatives of private actors also takes place within the Tourism Sector Committee (CFT) established in 2019 and relaunched in 2022 to bring together public and private parties to guide tourism development post-pandemic.

Tourism is a shared competence in France: all levels of sub-national government are involved in tourism policy development and implementation. Each regional council, with the support of the Regional Tourism Committee (CRT), co-ordinates public and private initiatives in the field of tourism development, information and promotion, including actions on international markets. They also collect, process and disseminate local data relating to tourism in each region. Departmental councils can set up Departmental Tourism Committees (CDT) focusing on structuring the offer and supporting the stakeholders involved. At municipal authority level, responsibility for tourism has largely been transferred from municipalities to Public Inter-municipal Co-operation Establishments (EPCI).

The overall budgetary allocation for tourism from State and local authorities is difficult to calculate as it includes the contributions of several ministerial departments. In 2022, the combined budget of the Regional Tourism Committees was EUR 140 million, while the Departmental Tourism Committee received EUR 222 million. Further, EUR 822 million was allocated for local tourism information offices.

France: Organisational chart of tourism bodies

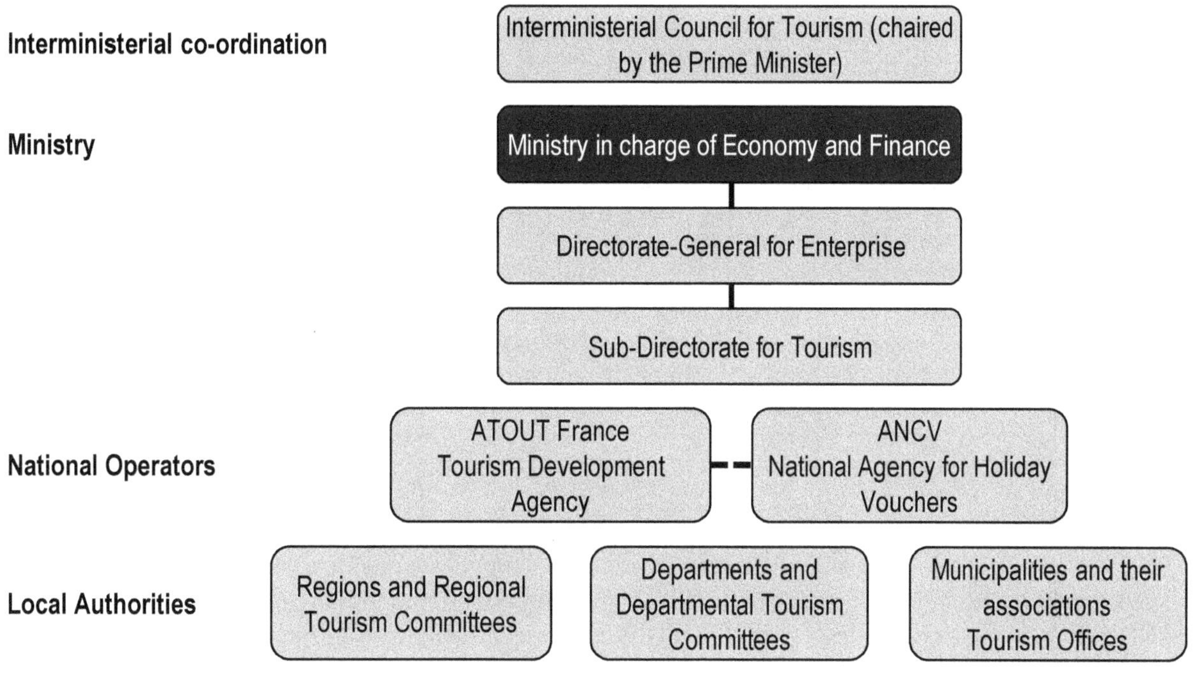

Source: OECD, adapted from the Directorate-General for Enterprise, 2024.

Tourism policies and programmes

The national long-term strategy for tourism, the Destination France Plan, was launched in November 2021 and is organised under five main pillars: (i) Winning over and winning back talent; (ii) Strengthening the sector's resilience and supporting the drive to improve the quality of its offering; (iii) Promoting and developing France's tourism assets; (iv) Meeting the challenges of transforming the tourism sector; (v) Promoting France as a destination and consolidating its market share.

The Plan mobilises more than EUR 1.9 billion from 2022 to 2024, to position France as a leading sustainable tourism destination by 2030. By the end of 2023, more than EUR 1.2 billion had been committed to the Plan’s measures, including stimulus loans.

Among the measures planned by the Destination France Plan, certain areas can be highlighted. Major sporting events, such as the 2023 Rugby World Cup and the 2024 Olympic and Paralympic Games are promoted, involving a wide range of public and private actors. France aims to build on the legacy of these events to boost visitor numbers and tourism revenue over the long-term, relying on the modern image sporting events can highlight and on the great visibility the events will bring to certain territories.

France is also revising and modernising laws and regulations in the tourism sector. For example, the classification standards for tourism accommodation are regularly updated, to include sustainability criteria. To improve the balance between short-term rentals and the current housing stock, France aims to enhance the collection and transmission of data on accommodation from rental platforms to local authorities in 2024.

This includes setting up a platform for centralising the exchange of information between digital operators and local authorities (provided for in the bill to secure and regulate the digital space). France will also adapt its law to meet the new European regulation on short-term rentals.

In 2022-23, a national campaign was organised by the Ministry for the Economy to promote tourism jobs. The Directorate General for Enterprise also organised the first Tourism Careers Week, which included more than 1 300 events across France. The aim was to make the tourism sector more appealing to young people and jobseekers. After a successful first edition, a second edition of the event was held in March 2024. The Directorate has also worked with the tourism sector to draw up a multi-year plan for seasonal workers (2023-25), which includes 15 commitments.

In 2023, France's national tourism development agency, Atout France, carried out the Horizons 2040 study, which formalises four scenarios for the future of tourism in France. These scenarios aim to guide the development of tourism policies in France and provide useful insights for tourism stakeholders.

France has initiated several programmes to support its commitment to sustainable tourism. Among these actions is the creation of a table of sustainable tourism indicators, which will enrich the statistics provided by the France Tourism Observation portal managed by Atout France. The measures also include the greening of all tourist accommodation classification benchmarks (hotels, campsites, etc.) and actions undertaken with tourism professionals to better distribute tourist flows and avoid overcrowding-related issues in tourist destinations (see box below).

Promoting a better distribution of tourist flows in France

To contribute to the sustainability and acceptance of tourism, France aims to avoid the phenomena of overcrowding. A balanced distribution of tourist flows throughout the territory is needed, especially as 80% of tourism is concentrated in just 20% of the territory annually. Key actions include:

- Encouraging tourism activities in sparsely populated areas. This includes the promotion of slow tourism and tourism based on showcasing traditional know-how and crafts. Destination France has dedicated EUR 13 million in funding to support these two new initiatives.
- Increasing the availability of consulting services to help professionals to diversify the tourist offer in rural destinations and in mountain resorts to move towards more attractive, more diversified tourism, and better distributed over time. EUR 331 million has been allocated under the Mountain Futures Plan and EUR 55 million under the Destination France Plan.
- Stepping up investment to develop low-carbon mobility projects. The Mountain Futures Plan provides for the reinstatement of 1 000 km of mountain trails (EUR 10 million) and the introduction of engineering support to improve mobility (EUR 10 million). Destination France is strengthening the France Seaview programme with the repair and tourist promotion of 1 200 km of coastal paths, after which a total of 7 000 km of coastal paths will be open to the public.
- Launching France's National Strategy for Managing Tourist Flows in June 2023. It aims to preserve the balance between the development of the local economic fabric, and the sustainability and preservation of tourist sites. It is structured around four lines: i) disseminating a common understanding of the management of tourist flows; ii) raising awareness among stakeholders and users regarding the management of tourist flows; iii) measuring tourist flows and impacts to better manage them; and iv) support territories in managing flows. The Strategy involves creating a national observatory for major tourist sites, measuring the acceptability of tourist flows amongst locals and raising awareness among tourists and influencers.

Statistical Profile

France: Domestic, inbound and outbound tourism

	2018	2019	2020	2021	2022
TOURISM FLOWS, THOUSAND					
Domestic tourism					
Total domestic trips	268 152	299 315 |	212 547	252 240	274 644
Overnight visitors (tourists)	189 755	207 624 |	152 119	187 321	201 310
Same-day visitors (excursionists)	78 397	91 691 |	60 428	64 919	73 335
Nights in all types of accommodation	897 591	921 767 |	768 138	865 396	889 900
Hotels and similar establishments	..	306 077 |	235 128	277 539	285 398
Other collective establishments	..	87 991 |	64 311	77 925	80 132
Private accommodation	..	527 698 |	468 699	509 932	524 371
Inbound tourism					
Total international arrivals	211 998	217 877	117 109	141 297	230 675
Overnight visitors (tourists)	89 322	90 914	41 684	48 395	93 196
Same-day visitors (excursionists)	122 676	126 963	75 424	92 902	137 478
Top markets					
United Kingdom	13 008	12 403	4 560	3 263	11 303
Germany	12 272	13 606	6 447	7 515	14 083
Belgium	10 507	11 854	7 203	8 314	12 192
Italy	6 963	7 419	3 277	3 359	8 023
Switzerland	6 772	6 506	3 657	4 750	8 433
Nights in all types of accommodation	596 784	619 887	298 289	375 456	..
Hotels and similar establishments	..	..	..	..	..
Other collective establishments	..	..	..	..	..
Private accommodation	..	..	..	..	..
Outbound tourism					
Total international departures	48 069	52 542 |	20 803	21 366	39 484
Overnight visitors (tourists)	30 509	38 301 |	11 461	13 108	28 085
Same-day visitors (excursionists)	17 560	14 241 |	9 342	8 258	11 399
Top destinations					
Spain	4 526	6 175 |	1 652	2 990	..
Italy	3 311	3 847 |	1 149	1 556	..
Great Britain + Ireland	1 804	2 577 |	596	250	..
Belgium + Luxembourg	1 727	2 012 |	998	931	..
Portugal	1 627	1 906 |	642	876	..
TOURISM RECEIPTS AND EXPENDITURE, MILLION EUR					
Inbound tourism					
Total international receipts	61 555	63 313	31 303	37 973	64 488
International travel receipts	55 490	56 730	28 510	34 498	56 670
International passenger transport receipts	6 065	6 583	2 793	3 475	7 818
Outbound tourism					
Total international expenditure	50 164	53 407	27 589	33 081	45 864
International travel expenditure	41 978	45 148	25 151	30 473	39 221
International passenger transport expenditure	8 186	8 259	2 438	2 608	6 643

.. Not available; | Break in series
Source: OECD Tourism Statistics (Database).

StatLink https://stat.link/7aus3b

France: Enterprises and employment in tourism

	Number of establishments[1]	Number of persons employed[2]				
	2022 p	2018	2019	2020	2021	2022
Total	..	1 736 392	1 792 001	1 618 282	1 534 176	..
Tourism industries	264 514	1 720 695	1 792 001	1 618 282	1 534 176	..
Accommodation services for visitors	52 128	361 227	372 326	325 679	366 237	..
Hotels and similar establishments	19 117	184 638	190 044	152 036	179 527	..
Food and beverage serving industry	174 451	852 500	901 384	819 395	940 740	..
Passenger transport	6 508	290 254	290 574	268 351	..	..
Air passenger transport	494	60 143	60 402	55 924	54 287	..
Railways passenger transport	1 659	100 129	96 568	85 365	83 951	..
Road passenger transport	3 639	120 002	123 225	117 856	118 791	..
Water passenger transport	716	9 980	10 379	9 206	9 757	..
Passenger transport supporting services	..	..	..	..	..	..
Transport equipment rental	3 271	18 715	19 232	18 107	19 545	..
Travel agencies and other reservation services industry	7 330	45 772	47 582	40 952	41 308	..
Cultural industry	1 375	25 660	26 337	24 368	26 151	..
Sports and recreation industry	19 451	126 567	134 566	121 430	140 195	..
Retail trade of country-specific tourism characteristic goods	..	..	..	..	..	..
Other country-specific tourism industries	..	..	..	..	..	..
Other industries	..	15 697	..	..	..	..

.. Not available; p Provisional data
1. Data refer to number of enterprises.
2. Data refer to number of employees.
Source: OECD Tourism Statistics (Database).

StatLink https://stat.link/g1sev3

France: Internal tourism consumption

Million EUR

	2021		
	Domestic tourism expenditure	Inbound tourism expenditure	Internal tourism consumption
Total	78 200	37 800	137 600
Consumption products	..	..	..
Tourism characteristic products	46 900	26 100	94 600
Accommodation services for visitors	15 100	12 900	49 600
Food and beverage serving services	8 000	4 900	12 900
Passenger transport services	16 200	5 700	21 900
Air passenger transport services	4 900	2 600	7 500
Railways passenger transport services	5 400	700	6 100
Road passenger transport services	1 200	900	2 100
Water passenger transport services	200	200	400
Passenger transport supporting services	..	..	..
Transport equipment rental services	4 300	1 200	5 500
Travel agencies and other reservation services industry	3 300	400	3 700
Cultural services	800	500	1 300
Sports and recreation services	3 500	1 700	5 200
Country-specific tourism characteristic goods	..	..	..
Country-specific tourism characteristic services	..	..	..
Other consumption products	31 300	11 700	43 000
Tourism connected products	..	..	..
Non-tourism related consumption products	..	..	..
Non-consumption products	..	..	..

.. Not available
Source: OECD Tourism Statistics (Database).

StatLink https://stat.link/ak61ny

Germany

Tourism in the economy and outlook

Tourism is an important economic sector in Germany and recovery is ongoing. In 2020, during the COVID-19 pandemic, tourism directly contributed EUR 73.0 billion to the economy, accounting for 2.4% of GVA. This was down from 4.0% in 2019. Tourism directly employed 1.9 million people in 2022 or 4.1% of total employment. This was 0.6% below 2019 levels. As tourism is recovering, German companies are facing difficulties to fill vacancies with adequate staff, since many employees have permanently migrated to other sectors. Travel exports accounted for 7.3% of total service exports in 2022, still below 2019 levels of 11.4%.

International tourism is rebounding but remains below pre-pandemic levels. Germany welcomed 34.8 million international tourists in 2023. This represents an ongoing recovery from the pandemic low of 11.7 million in 2021 but remains 12.0% below 2019 levels. Germany's top three international source markets in 2023 were the Netherlands (14%), Switzerland (9%) and the United States (8%). Domestic tourism is a significant contributor to German tourism and has recovered more quickly. In 2023, Germany recorded 148.5 million domestic overnight visitors in commercial accommodation, just 2% below 2019 levels. Germany's tourism sector anticipates a strong 2024, building on continued tourism recovery in 2023.

Tourism governance

The Federal Minister for Economic Affairs and Climate Action has lead responsibility for tourism policy development. The Minister is supported by the Advisory Council on Tourism Issues, which brings together government, businesses, academia, and other tourism stakeholders. The Federal Government Co-ordinator for the Maritime Economy and Tourism is responsible for co-ordinating tourism policy within the Federal Government and the German Parliament, particularly with the Parliamentary Tourism Committee. They also co-operate with tourism stakeholders and represent the country in international tourism fora.

Tourism policy in Germany is governed by a complex structure of responsibilities: On the federal level, several ministries are involved in issues which concern tourism as a cross-sectoral industry. Apart from this, the federal government only plays a co-ordinating role in tourism whereas the 16 Federal States (*Länder*) are responsible for developing, shaping and promoting tourism policy. Their ministries are charged with designing, implementing and funding policies to promote local tourism development. Each federal state has a destination management organisation that represents the interests of subnational organisations. Local tourism offices co-ordinate the work of tourism SMEs, promote product design and undertake relevant marketing activities. The Joint Federal/*Länder* Scheme for the Improvement of Regional Economic Structures (GRW) is the central instrument of the Federal Government's regional policy, which includes tourism development as a key pillar. GRW project funding is provided in the form of investments in trade and industry, which includes tourism (e.g. tourism spatial planning and public tourist facilities).

For 2023, the budget allocated by the Ministry to the German National Tourist Board was EUR 40.6 million (compared to EUR 39 million in 2022). The National Tourist Board also received funds from services and membership fees, amounting to EUR 3.9 million in 2023. These funds finance national tourism promotion abroad; domestic tourism promotion is carried out by each Federal State. In addition, the Ministry had a EUR 3 million budget in 2023 for selected projects to enhance performance in the tourism sector.

The Joint Federal/*Länder* Scheme for the Improvement of Regional Economic Structures (GRW) budget allocated to tourism was EUR 1.4 billion for 2018-22, divided evenly between federal and *Länder* contributions. Funds allocated to tourism corresponded to 21.9% of the entire GRW funds across all sectors approved in this period, which highlights the importance of tourism. In addition to public funds, revenue is also generated from spa tourism and accommodation taxes.

Germany: Organisational chart of tourism bodies

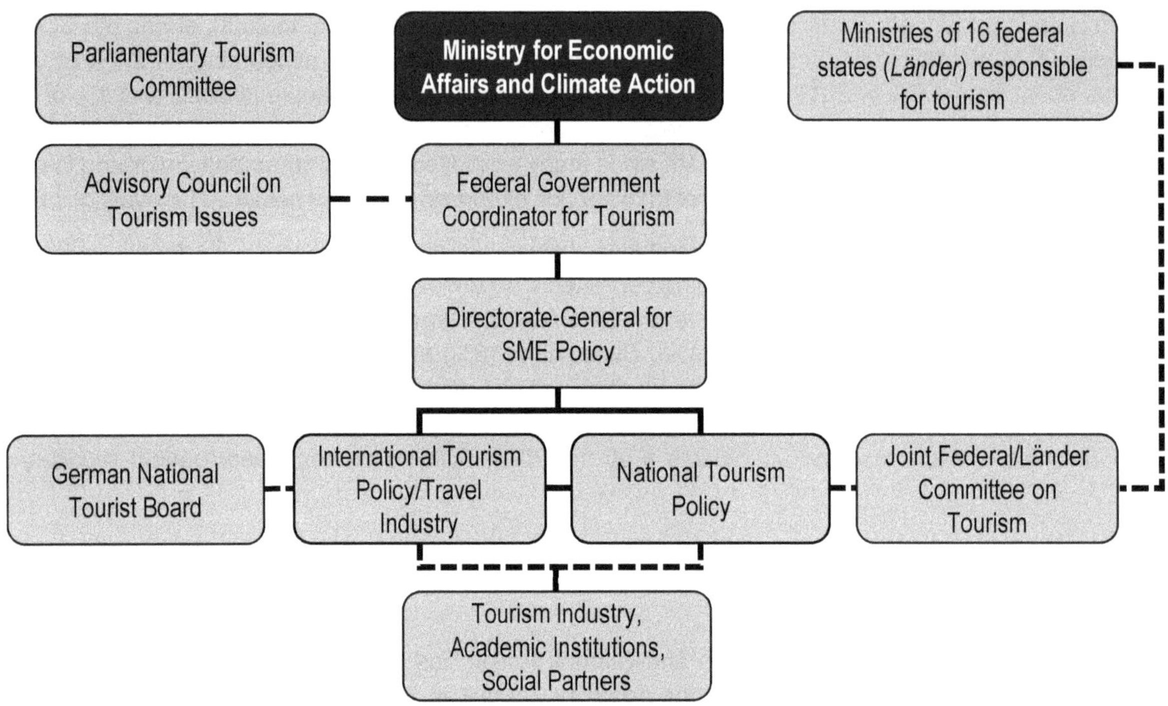

Source: OECD, adapted from the Ministry for Economic Affairs and Climate Action, 2024.

Tourism policies and programmes

Since 2022, the Federal Government has been further enhancing the National Tourism Strategy to strengthen the economy, prepare the sector for the future and support post-crisis recovery. The Strategy addresses four key challenges in the German tourism sector: climate neutrality and nature protection; recruiting and securing staff; digitalisation; and competitive tourism.

The Strategy invites all stakeholders to contribute initiatives around these topics. A National Platform for the Future of Tourism was established to collect these initiatives and connect central tourism stakeholders from Federal and State governments, the industry and academia in a long-term dialogue on the future issues of tourism. The online platform, in place until at least the end of 2025, aims to support stakeholders to work together, create synergies between different initiatives and raise awareness of best practices.

The overarching objectives of the Strategy, supported by the Future of Tourism platform, are to (i) strengthen sustainable growth of tourism companies; (ii) ensure that the tourism sector makes a relevant contribution to climate neutrality by 2045; (iii) promote the needs-based expansion and interconnectedness of tourism mobility; (iv) work towards international quality leadership in tourism products, infrastructure, and services; (v) achieve maximum efficiency in service provision and administrative processes; (vi) stimulate social and ecological responsibility both nationally and internationally by making tourism integrative, inclusive and barrier-free; (vii) strengthen resilience in national and international tourism; (viii) increase acceptance of tourism by local communities; (ix) strengthen the environment and nature as a basis for tourism; (x) conserve natural resources; (xi) strengthen regional value creation.

Additionally, the tourism sector benefits from several cross-sectoral and sector-specific initiatives. The LIFT funding programme aims to improve performance, promote innovation and activate tourism SMEs and destinations to deal with future tourism issues. The objective is to develop future-proofed, applicable solutions to make tourism sustainable and ensure the sector contributes to sustainable development.The Federal Statistical Office of Germany compiles an extended Tourism Satellite Account–Economy and Environment (TSA-EE) since 2019, providing data on the tourism sector's economic impact in Germany (tourism-related output, gross value added and tourism employment) as well as tourism-related energy consumption, air emissions, raw material input and environmental protection expenditures at federal level.

The Centre of Excellence for the Green Transition of Tourism supports the tourism industry on its way to climate neutrality and sustainable transformation by sharing knowledge on climate-friendly and resource-saving innovations. The German Climate Fund for Tourism is part of the National Climate Initiative, a Federal project which supports measurable actions that reduce GHG emissions. The Fund is currently piloted, supported with a grant of EUR 1.5 million. It aims to enable the industry to develop, implement and document effective GHG reductions in line with the national climate action targets. Decarbonisation workshops are used to formulate feasible long-term reduction targets for the sector. Model solutions for the reduction of emissions by tourism service providers and destinations will then be developed and tested.

In May 2020, Germany published a study on the Climate Information System that assists tourism regions in adapting to future climate changes. In addition, an action guideline for destination management has been developed to support adaptation to climate change as a strategic process. Also, a new data dashboard developed by the German National Tourist Board aims to support the sustainable development of tourism (see box below). The Federal Competition for Sustainable Tourism Destinations awards active regions in sustainable tourism to show other regions to improve the quality of tourism offers. Last held in 2022-23, the competition encourages tourism organisations and associations, as well as visitors, to adopt sustainable development principles.

Data dashboard on sustainable travel trends in Germany

A new data dashboard developed by the German National Tourist Board aims to support the sustainable development of tourism. Launched in September 2023, the new dashboard has an ecological focus and presents market-specific economic key figures. It complements the Inbound Travel Trends Germany Dashboard which was successfully launched in October 2021.

The dashboard supports users with detailed information from three angles: (i) the general attitude of consumers from source markets towards sustainability, climate protection and their interest in sustainable travel; (ii) the perception of Germany as a destination and its positioning in the European competition; and (iii) the current travel behaviour from a sustainable perspective, including the relevance of multi-destination trips, length of stay, tourism density and CO2-equivalent emissions for transport.

The combination of the two dashboards provides tourism stakeholders with an efficient and quick overview of relevant data to further adjust their business activities from a sustainability perspective. The initiative is largely funded by the German Federal Government.

Statistical Profile

Germany: Domestic, inbound and outbound tourism

	2018	2019	2020	2021	2022
TOURISM FLOWS, THOUSAND					
Domestic tourism					
Total domestic trips	726 728	..	..	622 827	..
Overnight visitors (tourists)	159 338	160 985	109 296	129 491	135 069
Same-day visitors (excursionists)	567 391	..	..	493 336	..
Nights in all types of accommodation	587 419	588 870	456 020	513 745	531 717
Hotels and similar establishments	235 441	236 481	122 744	148 135	183 211
Other collective establishments	136 487	139 356	123 829	137 128	149 183
Private accommodation	215 491	213 033	209 447	228 482	199 324
Inbound tourism					
Total international arrivals	..	..	..	..	..
Overnight visitors (tourists)	38 748	39 563	12 449	11 688	28 463
Same-day visitors (excursionists)	..	..	..	..	..
Top markets					
Netherlands	4 717	4 820	2 282	2 038	4 494
Switzerland	3 311	3 399	1 404	1 208	2 762
United States	2 969	3 057	594	701	2 321
Austria	2 064	2 116	820	842	1 718
United Kingdom	2 679	2 552	648	359	1 577
Nights in all types of accommodation	86 962	89 261	31 733	30 732	67 616
Hotels and similar establishments	82 167	84 568	29 562	29 094	63 734
Other collective establishments	4 794	4 693	2 171	1 638	3 883
Private accommodation	..	..	..	..	..
Outbound tourism					
Total international departures	208 172	212 143	103 117	100 720	168 698
Overnight visitors (tourists)	108 542	99 533	36 867	48 667	86 623
Same-day visitors (excursionists)	99 630	112 610	66 250	52 053	82 075
Top destinations					
Austria	14 396	11 718	7 494	7 252	11 908
Italy	13 573	11 633	4 151	7 552	12 064
Netherlands	11 672	10 985	2 716	5 414	9 468
Spain	7 413	7 091	4 082	3 459	5 783
France	6 143	6 468	2 653	3 383	6 075
TOURISM RECEIPTS AND EXPENDITURE, MILLION EUR					
Inbound tourism					
Total international receipts	51 085	37 620	19 472	19 208	30 505
International travel receipts	36 391	37 344	19 351	18 827	29 959
International passenger transport receipts	14 694	276	121	381	546
Outbound tourism					
Total international expenditure	88 142	83 346	34 060	43 150	85 779
International travel expenditure	80 934	83 292	34 029	43 150	85 204
International passenger transport expenditure	7 208	54	31	..	575

.. Not available
Source: OECD Tourism Statistics (Database).

StatLink https://stat.link/6jmhlg

Germany: Enterprises and employment in tourism

	Number of establishments[2]	Number of persons employed				
	2021	2018	2019	2020	2021	2022
Total	..	..	..	..	..	..
Tourism industries	235 619	2 179 830	2 145 026	1 546 927	1 778 520	..
Accommodation services for visitors	..	1 806	1 752	1 335	1 144	..
Hotels and similar establishments[1]	29 410	..	..	..	..	..
Food and beverage serving industry	172 315	1 517 082	1 493 927	999 938	1 456 955	..
Passenger transport	..	..	..	..	..	..
Air passenger transport	550	58 380	59 568	59 167	54 733	..
Railways passenger transport	24	..	..	..	..	..
Road passenger transport	22 650	482 486	469 768	399 433	186 527	..
Water passenger transport	488	10 007	9 742	..	8 754	..
Passenger transport supporting services	..	..	..	..	..	..
Transport equipment rental	..	..	..	..	..	..
Travel agencies and other reservation services industry	10 182	110 069	110 269	87 054	79 161	..
Cultural industry	..	..	..	..	..	..
Sports and recreation industry	..	..	..	..	..	..
Retail trade of country-specific tourism characteristic goods	..	..	..	..	..	..
Other country-specific tourism industries	..	..	..	..	..	..
Other industries	..	..	..	..	..	..

.. Not available
1. Data for hotels and similar establishments refer to number of establishments.
2. Data refer to number of enterprises.
Source: OECD Tourism Statistics (Database).

StatLink https://stat.link/0vtjue

Germany: Internal tourism consumption

Million EUR

	2020		
	Domestic tourism expenditure	Inbound tourism expenditure	Internal tourism consumption
Total	..	..	..
Consumption products	140 514	22 655	197 783
Tourism characteristic products	84 184	16 857	117 119
Accommodation services for visitors	18 853	7 135	30 196
Food and beverage serving services	31 509	6 335	37 844
Passenger transport services	16 533	2 884	19 417
Air passenger transport services	4 711	1 745	6 456
Railways passenger transport services	2 481	240	2 721
Road passenger transport services	8 442	477	8 918
Water passenger transport services	899	422	1 321
Passenger transport supporting services	..	..	..
Transport equipment rental services	1 617	157	1 774
Travel agencies and other reservation services industry	3 854	268	4 122
Cultural services	..	..	..
Sports and recreation services	11 818	79	23 766
Country-specific tourism characteristic goods	..	..	..
Country-specific tourism characteristic services	..	..	..
Other consumption products	56 330	5 798	80 664
Tourism connected products	21 249	1 414	22 663
Non-tourism related consumption products	35 081	4 384	58 002
Non-consumption products	..	..	..

.. Not available
Source: OECD Tourism Statistics (Database).

StatLink https://stat.link/5z4e8i

Greece

Tourism in the economy and outlook

Tourism is vital to the Greek economy and has recovered strongly. The sector directly contributed EUR 12.9 billion to the economy in 2022, equivalent to 7.1% of total GVA. This reflects the significant recovery from the pandemic low of EUR 6.4 billion in 2020 (4.4% of total GVA) and brings the sector back in line with pre-pandemic levels. Tourism employment directly accounted for 13.6% of total Greek workforce in 2022, still down from 14.4% in 2019.

International tourism accounted for 23.1 million or 73.5% of arrivals in accommodation establishments in 2022. In total, Greece welcomed 29.9 million international visitors in 2022, showing a strong recovery but still 12.1% below 2019 levels. In 2022, travel receipts totalled EUR 17.7 billion, down by only 2.8% in current prices compared with 2019. The top source markets are the United Kingdom (15%), Germany (15%) and France (6%), with international visitor arrivals from these three markets surpassing pre-pandemic levels in 2022. Particularly arrivals from the United Kingdom rose to 4.5 million, an increase of 28% compared to 2019. Domestic tourism continues to grow in Greece. In 2022, 6.0 million overnight domestic tourists were recorded, 15.6% above 2019 levels.

Tourism governance

The Ministry of Tourism is responsible for Greece's tourism policy and international marketing strategy, legislative reform, tourism planning and national government co-operation. The Ministry also implements tourism education and training programmes to improve the quality and competitiveness of Greek tourism. The General Secretariat of Co-ordination co-ordinates the implementation of public policies, resolves any disagreements between co-competent Ministries, checks the compatibility of the proposed regulations with government policy, prepares recommendations for monitoring the implementation of government policies to the Council of Ministers and proposes horizontal policies.

The implementation of the marketing strategy is carried out by the Greek National Tourism Organisation (GNTO), which operates a network of offices overseas. The Hellenic Chamber of Hotels is the Government's statutory advisor on tourism, as well as the competent authority responsible for the official classification of main tourist accommodation. The Greek Tourism Confederation (SETE) aims at bringing together the tourism entrepreneurship of Greece as the official body of the tourism private sector. SETE is actively involved in the public dialogue and is collaborating with the State and the regional authorities, to promote and facilitate investment opportunities and ensure the business competitiveness of the sector.

The Ministry of Tourism operates 14 Regional Tourist Offices, responsible for licensing, conducting quality control of tourism services and imposing administrative sanctions on tourism businesses. Local administrations (regions and municipalities) develop and implement programmes and activities for tourism development and promotion in the areas under their jurisdiction. All promotional activity is aligned with the national tourism promotion strategy. The budget for the Ministry of Tourism in Greece in 2023 was EUR 86.7 million, 31% lower than in 2022 (EUR 125.6 million). In 2023, the Greek National Tourism

Organisation was granted EUR 12.0 million of this overall standard budget, supplemented by another EUR 21 million from the public investments program. In 2022, this was EUR 11.6 million and EUR 18 million.

Greece: Organisational Chart of Tourism Bodies

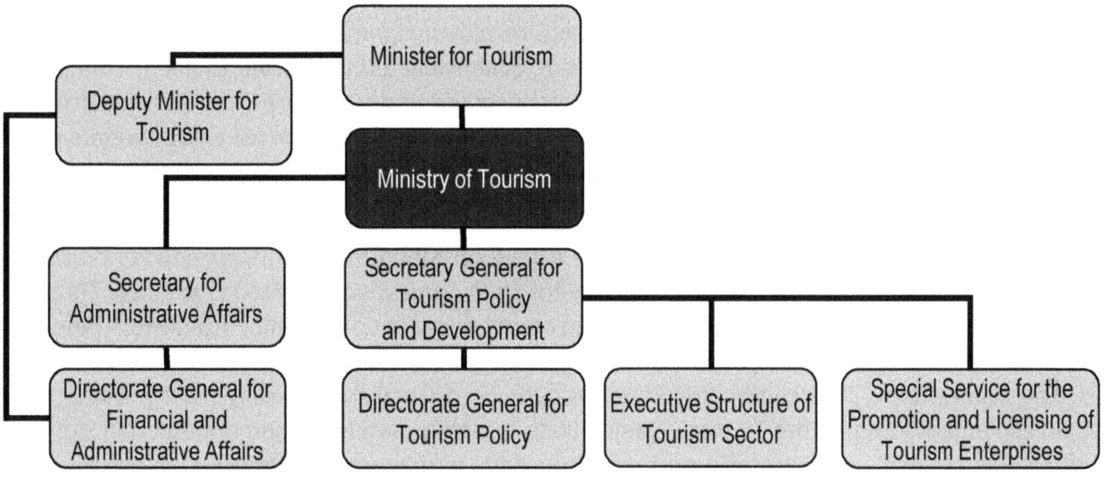

Source: OECD, adapted from the Ministry of Tourism, 2024.

Tourism policies and programmes

Greek tourism is guided by National Action Plans for Tourism. Since 2020, Greece has launched annual action plans focused on addressing the top three challenges for tourism in Greece, to build tourism resilience and leveraging opportunities from the green and digital transition: (i) Managing tourist flows and seasonality in flagship destinations, (ii) Developing national tourism products, (iii) Upgrading and modernising tourism education and training, and attracting and retaining the tourism workforce.

The 2024 Action Plan for Tourism is in line with the EU Transition Pathway for Tourism and the UN 2030 Agenda 2030. It focuses on promoting the Greek tourism brand and national tourism product portfolio abroad, enhancing bilateral and multilateral tourism co-operation, and reducing seasonality and raising per capita spending. To achieve this, Greece is building a strategic framework for the development of inbound tourism, strengthening the share of two new target markets outside the EU, and developing promotion action plans focusing on specific long-haul source markets. Upgrading and modernising the framework for tourism education and training as well as upskilling and reskilling the tourism workforce is also a priority for the 2024 Action Plan. A project funded by the EU Recovery and Resilience Facility will be undertaken in 2024-25 to upskill and reskill tourism workers through 250-hour vocational programmes. The project aims to equip 18 000 workers with the skills needed in the labour market, in line with the green and digital transition of the sector.

The digital transition of the tourism sector is a priority of the 2024 Action Plan. Initiatives include the digital transformation of the Ministry of Tourism and Greek National Tourism Organisation, with the creation of a user-friendly portal for citizens, entrepreneurs and tourists to access information from the Ministry. The My Digital Tourism platform aims to streamline processes and encourage investment in tourism. It will facilitate the submission of documents for licensing tourism businesses, the filing of tourist complaints, the inspections of tourism businesses and investigation of complaints, the collection of statistical data on tourist accommodation via a subsystem for recording arrivals and departures and will provide information on legislation and procedures to establish and operate a tourism business. The platform is expected to be fully operational by the second quarter of 2025 and to benefit over 100 000 businesses.

To improve the competitiveness, diversify and upgrade the national tourism product, the 2024 Action Plan also envisages initiatives to: enhance the regulatory framework for product development in special interest tourism; adapt the institutional framework regarding the licensing of tourist ports, to create an interconnected system for Agri-Food, Gastronomy and Tourism; upgrade mountain tourism infrastructure; and develop other niche tourism products (e.g. diving, religious/pilgrimage tourism, sports tourism, rural tourism, outdoor activities, health and wellness tourism, accessible tourism, silver tourism).Tourism for All 2024-25 programme aims to strengthen domestic tourism demand. Actions refer to modernising the institutional framework regulating the relations between tourist accommodation service providers and their customers, defining functional specifications for awarding the Glamping Label as well as special awards for facilities open to visitors, tourist destinations and tourism businesses.

To enhance tourism development, Greece enacted a Law on Model Tourism Destinations of Integrated Management and Destination Management and Marketing Organisations (DMMOs) in 2021. Through the development of a network of DMMOs Greece aims to create a stable co-operation framework between the public and private sectors, ensuring continuity in the promotion of tourism products and the quality of service. The framework is financed by the EU's Recovery and Resilience Facility (RRF). Under the law, Greece is also establishing Model Tourism Destinations for Integrated Management that can significantly contribute to the country's tourist profile and require special management. Destinations are expected to apply for the designation (see box below).

To enhance tourism data, Greece is working to create a National Sustainable Tourism Observatory and implement a Tourism Satellite Account (TSA). A pilot TSA exercise was conducted in 2017 and the full TSA is scheduled to be available by the end of 2025. Greece is also working to measure indicators of sustainable tourism development at the national and regional spatial scale. The Ministry of Tourism has also been selected by the EU to participate in the Crisis Management and Governance in Tourism project, which aims to improve the EU tourism ecosystem governance by making it more **resilient** and better prepared for managing and mitigating crises. Greece is also being supported by the EU Technical Support Instrument to run a project aiming to support the tourism ecosystem, towards a more sustainable, resilient and digital tourism.

Designation of Model Tourism Destinations of Integrated Management in Greece

The 2021 law on Model Tourism Destinations of Integrated Management, Destination Management and Marketing Organisations (DMMOs), Thermal Springs and regulations to enhance tourism development establishes for the first time the legal basis for destination management and marketing activity in Greece, to improve the country's tourism governance framework.

One of the three primary initiatives introduced under the law was to establish the designation of Model Tourism Destination of Integrated Management. The Ministry introduced this designation to recognise those destinations that can significantly contribute to the country's tourist profile and due to their natural environment and particular characteristics, require careful planning and monitoring to ensure long-term success. To receive the designation as a Model Tourism Destination, the relevant local government organisation applies to the Ministry, which in turn formulates a recommendation to the Minister.

The initiative is intended to support a sustainable model of tourism development. Applications for designation as a Model Tourism Destination are assessed against a set of core criteria (currently 38) covering six categories: i) Special characteristics; ii) Infrastructure and services; iii) Accessibility; iv) Data and characteristics of tourist activity; v) Sustainable destination management, vi) Possibilities for future sustainable development.

Statistical Profile

Greece: Domestic, inbound and outbound tourism

	2018	2019	2020	2021	2022
TOURISM FLOWS, THOUSAND					
Domestic tourism[1]					
Total domestic trips	26 301	27 879	23 507	21 899	21 682
Overnight visitors (tourists)	5 691	5 180	4 448	4 831	5 990
Same-day visitors (excursionists)	20 610	22 699	19 059	17 069	15 692
Nights in all types of accommodation	24 064	23 623	12 277	14 963	21 196
Hotels and similar establishments	23 209	22 682	11 685	14 360	20 407
Other collective establishments	855	941	593	603	789
Private accommodation	..	..	..	..	..
Inbound tourism					
Total international arrivals	33 072	34 005	7 406	15 246	29 876
Overnight visitors (tourists)	..	..	..	..	..
Same-day visitors (excursionists)	..	..	..	..	..
Top markets					
United Kingdom	2 943	3 499	1 069	1 591	4 485
Germany	4 381	4 026	1 526	3 001	4 352
Bulgaria	3 135	3 883	663	762	1 812
France	1 524	1 542	469	1 175	1 758
Italy	1 667	1 553	373	806	1 413
Nights in all types of accommodation	230 726	236 547	64 172	133 735	220 213
Hotels and similar establishments	..	..	..	..	..
Other collective establishments	..	..	..	..	..
Private accommodation	..	..	..	..	..
Outbound tourism					
Total international departures	7 961	7 848	2 324	2 026	5 094
Overnight visitors (tourists)	..	..	..	..	..
Same-day visitors (excursionists)	..	..	..	..	..
Top destinations					
North Macedonia	1 352	1 138	343	174	877
Bulgaria	2 371	1 916	617	212	862
Türkiye	967	1 091	123	149	479
Italy	405	438	146	184	407
Germany	500	584	227	225	378
TOURISM RECEIPTS AND EXPENDITURE, MILLION EUR					
Inbound tourism					
Total international receipts	18 444	20 618	5 353	11 621	19 552
International travel receipts	16 086	18 179	4 319	10 503	17 676
International passenger transport receipts	2 359	2 439	1 034	1 119	1 875
Outbound tourism					
Total international expenditure	3 314	3 764	1 321	1 891	3 411
International travel expenditure	2 191	2 744	793	1 113	1 925
International passenger transport expenditure	1 123	1 021	528	778	1 487

.. Not available

1. Trips from demand side surveys; Nights from supply side surveys.

Source: OECD Tourism Statistics (Database).

StatLink https://stat.link/3s2o5v

Greece: Enterprises and employment in tourism

	Number of establishments	Number of persons employed				
	2022	2018	2019	2020	2021	2022
Total	..	..	..	..	..	..
Tourism industries	91 230	541 285	564 003	535 801	509 037	564 852
Accommodation services for visitors	62 420	100 442	99 494	75 312	92 395	107 696
Hotels and similar establishments	9 716	94 700	93 635	69 635	84 689	96 462
Food and beverage serving industry	..	266 227	287 398	273 443	239 031	280 113
Passenger transport	..	99 643	99 748	105 346	104 301	92 761
Air passenger transport	..	4 712	3 804	5 840	8 592	4 100
Railways passenger transport	..	87 027	87 404	59 153	73 534	86 138
Road passenger transport	11 890	2 000	2 322	3 943	2 756	2 111
Water passenger transport	..	63 740	62 783	65 912	55 033	47 579
Passenger transport supporting services	..	..	..	..	..	..
Transport equipment rental	..	6 094	7 224	5 244	4 186	4 729
Travel agencies and other reservation services industry	7 094	14 136	15 251	17 483	16 456	18 111
Cultural industry	..	17 638	19 443	17 985	17 062	17 940
Sports and recreation industry	..	37 106	35 444	40 990	35 606	43 502
Retail trade of country-specific tourism characteristic goods	..	..	..	..	..	..
Other country-specific tourism industries	110	..	..	..	..	..
Other industries	..	..	..	..	..	..

.. Not available
Source: OECD Tourism Statistics (Database).

StatLink https://stat.link/01amsw

Hungary

Tourism in the economy and outlook

Tourism is a key sector of the Hungarian economy, having grown at a significantly higher rate than the overall economic growth in the decade leading up to the COVID-19 pandemic. The total gross value added of tourism industries was 6.2% in 2022, compared to 6.8% in 2019. Tourism was also a major source of employment in 2021, accounting for 383 700 jobs, or 8.7% of national employment (down from 421 000 in 2019). Travel exports accounted for 18.4% of the total service exports, below 2019 levels (24.2%).

Hungary welcomed 12.2 million international tourists in 2023 (76% of 2019 levels). International travel receipts reached HUF 3.0 billion, which equates to 92% of 2019 levels in current prices. The top three source markets in 2022 for Hungary were Germany (14%), Austria (10%) and Romania (7%).

Domestic tourism has recovered faster, with 12.8 million domestic overnight trips recorded in 2023 (90% of 2019 levels). Domestic tourism expenditure in 2022 was responsible for 30% of tourism expenditure in Hungary.

Tourism governance

Since 2024, the new Ministry for National Economy is responsible for tourism policy. The Prime Minister's Office (formerly responsible for tourism policy) remain responsible for active, eco and wine tourism, while the new Ministry for National Economy takes over responsibility for health tourism, in co-operation with the Minister for Health. The Ministry of Foreign Affairs and Trade is responsible for bilateral, regional, and international tourism co-ordination, while responsibility for sport tourism sits with the Ministry of Defence and heritage tourism with the Ministry of Construction and Investment.

The Hungarian Tourism Agency is responsible for the management of the Hungarian tourism sector at national and regional level. The Agency manages tourism strategy development, tourism products development and management, central marketing, international sales, communication campaigns and the co-ordination of specific tourism developments.

Work is underway to create a new destination management services network, to ensure effective communication between local and central levels and within the destination to promote a destination-based approach to product development and successful market entry. Led by the Hungary Tourism Agency, the new model aims to implement unified management and support the co-operation of local stakeholders to achieve a shared vision for Hungarian destinations.

The Hungarian Government will contribute HUF 150 billion in the annual central budget to tourism over four years to 2027, broken down as follows: HUF 30 billion in 2024, HUF 45 billion in 2025, HUF 60 billion in 2026 and HUF 15 billion in 2027.

Hungary: Organisational chart of tourism bodies

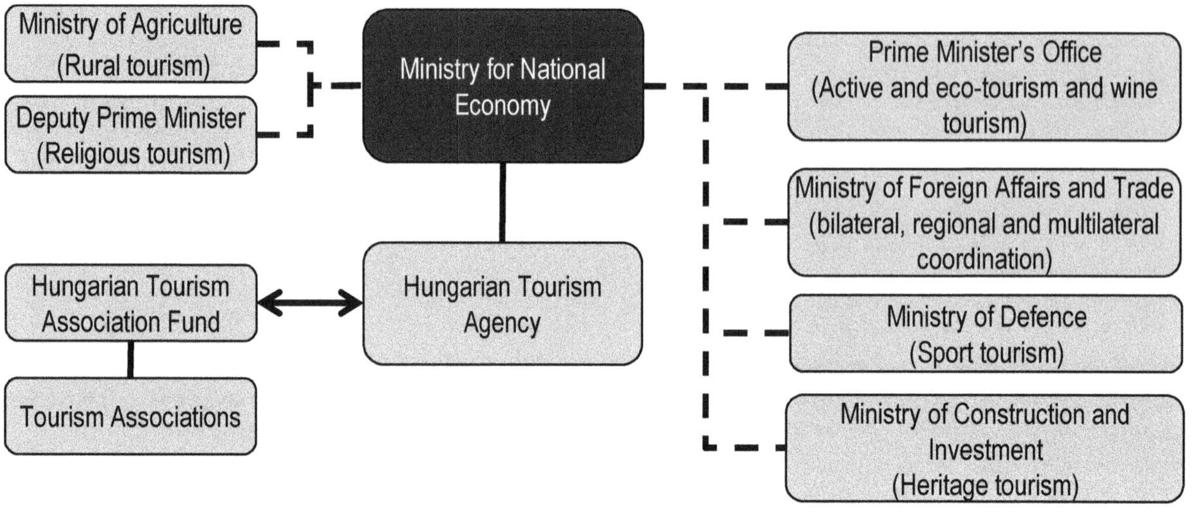

Source: OECD, adapted from the Hungarian Tourism Agency, 2024.

Tourism policies and programmes

The National Tourism Development Strategy 2030 - Tourism 2.0 guides tourism policy and programme development in Hungary. The Strategy was updated in 2021 to respond to the unique challenges of the COVID-19 pandemic and set out the direction and priorities for tourism in Hungary to 2030, with key objectives to:

- Complement the previous supply and product-based approach with a strong demand and needs-based approach. The focus of the strategy is shifting from development to marketing, with a well-developed understanding of international and domestic market segment needs, used for marketing, sales and future development.
- Define a new model of governance whereby sectoral governance is complemented at the destination level. The new network of destination management organisations links central management with the tourism regions.
- Strengthen the role of the Hungarian Tourism Agency in education and career-path shaping to help improve the quality of the workforce.
- Utilise digital solutions to accompany and support the travel process. Sectoral interests also need to play an active role in developing and connecting digital solutions to improve the guest experience and understanding the opportunities of big data by looking in detail at sub-sectors, such as hospitality and the labour market.
- Promote sustainability as a strategic objective, channelled through sector-based interests to involve actors across all sectors. Sustainability considerations are reflected in product development at the destination level through the introduction of a sustainability trademark and priority development for sustainable and ecotourism attractions (e.g. national park visitor centres and water recreation sites). This will help lay the foundations for a sustainable profile for tourism in Hungary.

The specific targets of the Strategy are to increase the total number of guest nights in Hungary to 50 million by 2030 (up 20% on 2019 levels), to be generated by 20 million tourists with an equal distribution of domestic and international tourists and spread between Budapest and rural destinations. A further aim is for Hungary to be the most popular Central European tourist destination.

To meet the objectives of the Strategy and to achieve sustainable growth, Hungary is developing and implementing several policies and programmes. The update the Széchenyi Leisure Card (SZÉP Card) aims to increase domestic consumption and encourage domestic tourism. Employees have been encouraged to use the funds on the cards by a one-off fee of 15% on unused balances accumulated on the cards for at least a year. The government also permitted employers to transfer a one-off amount of up to HUF 200 000 to SZÉP Cards on top of the current HUF 450 000 recreational allowance, during a 4-month period in 2024. The SZÉP Card will continue to be available as a fringe benefit in Hungary, with a reduced public tax rate.

Created in 2019, the National Tourism Data Supply Centre is an electronic tourism registration and administration system. The administration of accommodation facilities is handled through the online platform, which provides online statistical data on a daily basis.

In April 2023, Hungary reintroduced the Tourism Development Contribution, after suspending it during the pandemic to provide financial support and alleviate the administrative burden for tourism businesses. The contribution collects revenues from catering and commercial accommodation providers to reinvest in tourism. To strengthen the competitiveness of tourism, the VAT on commercial accommodation services has been reduced from 18% to 5% since 2020. A digital tourist tax declaration for accommodation providers was also introduced. The mandatory use of paper guest books was abolished, eliminating the double record-keeping obligation for accommodation providers, and making it faster for guests to check-in.

The manufacturing programme has been extended to the tourism sector. This initiative helps 1 445 accommodation and catering businesses registered to the programme to reduce the costs of utilities, particularly energy. It also supports SMEs to invest in energy efficiency and retain their workforce through binding commitments. In addition to the utility allowance, it was possible to apply for a non-repayable grant to supplement the loan for energy efficiency investments. Businesses who benefited from the programme had to pledge to keep at least 90% of their staff employed until the end of 2023 and commit to invest in energy efficiency by the end of 2024 at the latest.

A national accommodation rating system was introduced in 2022, to align with international standards and respond to visitor expectations (see box below).

Introduction of a national accommodation rating system in Hungary

Hungary introduced a new star rating system for tourist accommodations to respond to international visitor expectations. For each type of accommodation, a rating system has been developed based on the Hotelstars Union criteria, an HOTREC-backed association which harmonises hotel classification standards across Europe.

The system will be phased in over several years, with an initial free certification to spread adoption in Hungary. Since 2022, Hungarian accommodation establishments must comply with the requirements published by the certification body to continue their activities.

This star rating system ensures that ratings are comprehensible and transparent, providing a fair market operation. It protects consistently high-quality accommodations and enhances competition by making performance measurable and comparable. A searchable database will allow consumers to verify ratings, preventing misleading practices.

The digital platform is part of a broader strategic plan to digitise the sector. Future steps include the integration of certified accommodations into online sales platforms. Digitalisation will assist DMOs, municipalities and tax authorities in the collection of data and taxes from tourism businesses.

Statistical Profile

Hungary: Domestic, inbound and outbound tourism

	2018	2019	2020	2021	2022
TOURISM FLOWS, THOUSAND					
Domestic tourism					
Total domestic trips	48 310	47 923	29 932	38 810	45 511
Overnight visitors (tourists)	14 386	14 249	8 919	10 183	12 499
Same-day visitors (excursionists)	33 924	33 674	21 013	28 628	33 013
Nights in all types of accommodation	45 910	45 032	30 883	33 185	36 810
Hotels and similar establishments	..	..	..	..	..
Other collective establishments	..	..	..	..	..
Private accommodation	25 041	23 775	18 362	20 016	19 340
Inbound tourism[1]					
Total international arrivals	55 462	58 619	29 057	33 050	42 965
Overnight visitors (tourists)	16 766	15 949	6 624	6 973	11 731
Same-day visitors (excursionists)	38 696	42 670	22 433	26 077	31 233
Top markets					
Slovak Republic	10 000	10 072	5 606	5 216	8 941
Romania	11 898	13 249	6 733	8 026	7 597
Austria	8 523	9 053	5 167	5 140	7 382
Germany	3 202	3 075	1 371	2 269	2 930
Poland	2 425	2 435	1 193	1 438	1 757
Nights in all types of accommodation	20 162	20 794	5 035	7 628	17 316
Hotels and similar establishments	13 094	13 413	3 126	4 342	10 138
Other collective establishments	2 246	2 339	648	1 156	2 226
Private accommodation	4 822	5 042	1 261	2 129	4 952
Outbound tourism					
Total international departures	19 248	20 722	8 782	8 753	13 969
Overnight visitors (tourists)	7 771	8 318	2 762	3 101	5 909
Same-day visitors (excursionists)	11 477	12 404	6 019	5 653	8 060
Top destinations					
Austria	840	701	356	364	1 533
Germany	943	938	356	394	860
Slovak Republic	883	841	416	213	466
Croatia	523	470	216	268	348
Czechia	649	463	158	156	348
TOURISM RECEIPTS AND EXPENDITURE, MILLION HUF					
Inbound tourism					
Total international receipts	2 608 871	2 979 032	1 290 984	1 729 106	3 390 058
International travel receipts	1 870 832	2 123 363	987 083	1 262 779	2 109 992
International passenger transport receipts	738 039	855 669	303 902	466 327	1 280 066
Outbound tourism					
Total international expenditure	877 872	976 583	407 134	522 149	1 167 883
International travel expenditure	715 494	799 100	356 203	440 155	898 793
International passenger transport expenditure	162 379	177 484	50 931	81 994	269 090

..: Not available

1. Arrivals from demand side surveys; Nights from supply side surveys.

Source: OECD Tourism Statistics (Database).

StatLink https://stat.link/hsk2yp

Hungary: Enterprises and employment in tourism

	Number of establishments[1]	Number of persons employed				
	2022	2018	2019	2020	2021	2022
Total	..	..	..	..	..	..
Tourism industries	195 726	412 674	421 036	398 052	383 737	..
Accommodation services for visitors	40 463	41 486	44 305	32 702	29 861	..
Hotels and similar establishments	2 219	35 201	..	..	..	..
Food and beverage serving industry	32 855	131 214	134 382	130 120	125 927	..
Passenger transport	..	91 674	104 110	94 227	89 369	..
Air passenger transport	128	..	..	..	..	..
Railways passenger transport	4	29 386	37 236	32 384	36 647	..
Road passenger transport	10 111	55 229	55 980	53 358	48 220	..
Water passenger transport	181	..	..	..	..	..
Passenger transport supporting services	5 296	30 772	24 753	24 391	25 116	..
Transport equipment rental	4 847	..	..	..	..	..
Travel agencies and other reservation services industry	3 117	6 298	6 683	..	..	..
Cultural industry	46 341	43 468	41 673	43 266	43 593	..
Sports and recreation industry	20 707	33 598	36 361	38 014	34 011	..
Retail trade of country-specific tourism characteristic goods	..	..	..	..	..	..
Other country-specific tourism industries	29 457	31 837	26 778	26 452	29 406	..
Other industries	..	..	..	..	..	..

.. Not available

1. Data refer to number of enterprises.

Source: OECD Tourism Statistics (Database).

StatLink https://stat.link/gr7ihf

Hungary: Internal tourism consumption

Million HUF

	2021		
	Domestic tourism expenditure	Inbound tourism expenditure	Internal tourism consumption
Total	..	..	..
Consumption products	545 639	1 249 954	1 795 593
Tourism characteristic products	328 263	601 306	929 568
Accommodation services for visitors	134 449	169 726	304 176
Food and beverage serving services	124 134	132 934	257 068
Passenger transport services	22 802	76 434	99 236
Air passenger transport services	14 743	65 254	79 997
Railways passenger transport services	4 219	1 086	5 305
Road passenger transport services	3 840	9 561	13 401
Water passenger transport services	0	533	533
Passenger transport supporting services	2 410	8 493	10 902
Transport equipment rental services	213	802	1 015
Travel agencies and other reservation services industry	11 364	3 513	14 876
Cultural services	9 806	14 927	24 733
Sports and recreation services	21 456	96 128	117 584
Country-specific tourism characteristic goods	..	..	..
Country-specific tourism characteristic services	1 628	98 349	99 977
Other consumption products	217 376	648 648	866 025
Tourism connected products	207 253	556 021	763 274
Non-tourism related consumption products	10 123	92 628	102 751
Non-consumption products	..	..	..

.. Not available

Source: OECD Tourism Statistics (Database).

StatLink https://stat.link/31h60o

Iceland

Tourism in the economy and outlook

Following two challenging years in 2020 and 2021, tourism reclaimed its position as Iceland's top foreign exchange-generating export industry in 2022. Tourism and passenger transportation together generated ISK 455 billion in international receipts in 2022, equivalent to 26% of total export revenue and 60% of total service exports (49% in 2019). The sector directly contributed ISK 293.0 billion in 2022 or 7.8% to the country's GDP (compared to 8.4% in 2019) and accounted for almost 26 000 jobs or 12% of the workforce (28 800 in 2019).

Iceland welcomed 2.2 million international tourist arrivals in 2023, 30.4% above 2022 levels and 11.1% above 2019 levels. In 2023, the top three source markets were the United States (29%), the United Kingdom (13%), and Germany (6%).

Iceland recorded 1.3 million domestic tourists in 2022, 79% above 2019 levels. Around 84% of the Icelandic population travelled domestically in 2023, a similar number as in recent years.

Forecasts for 2024 anticipate 2.2 million international tourist arrivals. Growth is expected to continue in 2025, with 2.3 million international tourists, followed by 2.35 million in 2026.

Tourism governance

The Ministry of Culture and Business Affairs is responsible for developing tourism policy and co-ordinating the work of governmental bodies in Iceland. The Department of Business Affairs and Tourism is the lead department and oversees the operation and performance of the Icelandic Tourist Board.

The Icelandic Tourist Board is responsible for the implementation of government tourism policy, planning and support for regional development, licencing and monitoring of licenced activities, data collection, processing and presentation, safety, quality and consumer protection in relation to tourism, and administration of the Tourist Site Protection Fund and Route Development Fund.

The Tourism Council serves as an advisory body to the Minister and is composed of representatives from the ministries of finance, environment, and infrastructure, as well the Icelandic Association of Local Authorities and the Icelandic Travel Industry Association.

Visit Iceland is the official destination marketing organisation. It is part of Business Iceland, a public-private partnership established to promote Icelandic exports, foreign direct investments, and Iceland as a tourism destination.

Local municipalities are responsible for planning and management of many visitor attractions. With the support of the Icelandic Regional Development Institute, associations of municipalities operate development agencies which deliver tourism projects. Destination management organisations in each region are public-private entities responsible for developing and implementing regional destination management plans and co-ordinating tourism priorities. They do this in collaboration with stakeholders, including Business Iceland and the Icelandic Tourist Board, which provides financial support.

The general overall budget allocated to tourism in 2022 was ISK 2.28 billion. In 2023, this was increased to ISK 2.38 billion, allocated as follows: ISK 724 million to the Icelandic Tourist Board; ISK 588 million to the Tourist Site Protection Fund; and ISK 1.065 million to tourism services, of which ISK 300 million was dedicated to marketing and promotion.

Iceland: Organisational chart of tourism bodies

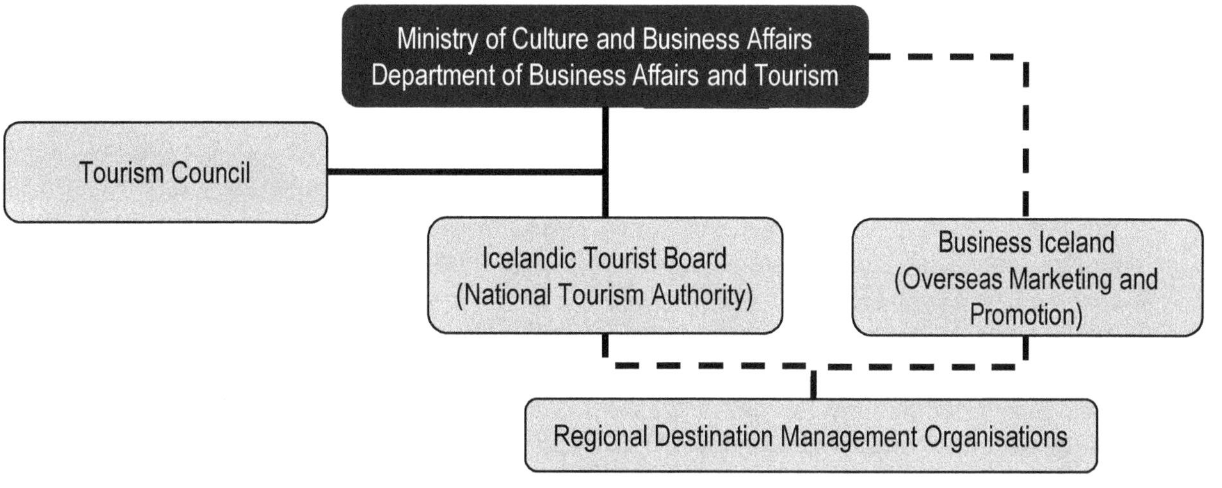

Source: OECD, adapted from the Ministry of Culture and Business Affairs, 2024.

Tourism policies and programmes

Iceland's policy framework, Leading in Sustainable Development, Icelandic Tourism 2030, guides tourism policy development in Iceland, with the implementation of an action-oriented strategy underway. Originally developed in 2019, the framework was updated in early 2023 and aims to position the country as a leading sustainable tourism destination, fostering a profitable and competitive tourism industry in harmony with its country and its people. The framework is organised around four main guiding principles for the sustainable development of tourism in Iceland:

- Profitability above tourist numbers.
- Benefits for locals in all regions.
- Unique experiences, quality, and professionalism.
- A balance between utilisation and nature conservation.

Under the leadership of the Ministry of Culture and Business Affairs, seven expert working groups were assembled to implement the framework, formulating recommendations for specific actions for an updated Tourism Action Plan. The Action Plan was approved by Parliament in June 2024, following extensive public and private sector consultation. Until the implementation of the new Action Plan is fully underway, Iceland's Government remains committed to improving tourism through the following programmes:

- Tourism Impact Assessment: A management tool relying on defined sustainability indicators to regularly evaluate the impact of tourism across the environment, infrastructure, society, and economy. To maximise its utility, the Tourism Impact Assessment requires ongoing development and is currently undergoing revision, as part of the efforts related to the Action Plan.

- Tourist Site Protection Fund and the Icelandic Route Development Fund: Funds are allocated to support destination development, aligned with the goal of distributing tourists more evenly throughout the country. This approach aims to ease the strain on popular tourism destinations, while benefiting both the industry and residents. A working group has been established to undertake a thorough review of the Tourist Site Protection Fund's objectives and functions.
- Tourism Skill Centre: Funded by the Ministry of Culture and Business Affairs, the Centre aims to promote competence and quality in the tourism industry in Iceland. Two ongoing initiatives until 2025 include the Training for the Future and Co-operation with regional destination agencies. The aim is to provide consultation and assistance to business managers in establishing targeted training programmes and monitor their effectiveness. The methodology, presentation materials, and digital tools, developed by the Centre are to be implemented in individual businesses through training provider partners. Funding for this work is sponsored by vocational education funds, as part of collective agreements. Performance evaluations will be undertaken in 2025.
- Co-operation with regional destination agencies: The goal is to foster co-operation to enhance the competence and professionalism of managers and staff, contributing to increased quality, a positive image, and profitability in the sector. This collaboration aims to keep the Tourism Skills Centre connected to grassroots discussions. Partnerships, contracts, and collaborative partnerships have been established. In 2024, co-operation will be strengthened through a needs analysis and digital tools. In 2025, performance evaluations will be undertaken.
- Car rental operators legislative update: In June 2023, a new legislation took effect, abolishing the requirements for car rental operators to have a fixed establishment. The impact of the legislation, along with other legislative changes in the tourism industry in 2022 following the OECD's competition assessment of the country's tourism sector (see box below), has contributed to a more flexible environment for tourism related business and aims to create new employment opportunities, higher productivity, and stronger economic growth in the coming years.

Review of tourism and infrastructure legislation for flexible business environments in Iceland

The Icelandic tourism and construction industries hold significant macroeconomic importance and play a pivotal role in providing employment to a substantial portion of the population. In 2019, the Ministry of Culture and Business Affairs (previously the Ministry of Industries and Innovation) requested the OECD to conduct a competitive assessment of the regulatory framework, governing both the Icelandic construction industry and the tourism sector. The assessment involved screening the legislation in both sectors using the OECD's Competition Assessment Toolkit. Under the assessment, 632 legal texts were reviewed resulting in 121 recommendations for change directly related to the tourism sector. In 2021 the Ministry of Culture and Business Affairs responded to all but three of the 121 OECD recommendations. The impact of these legislative and regulation changes, such as abolishing prescriptive accommodation standards and requirements for car rentals to have fixed establishment, has contributed to a more flexible environment for tourism related business. The OECD estimated that the implementation of the OECD recommendations for both sectors combined could generate more than EUR 200 million in benefits per year, around 1% of Iceland's GDP.

Statistical Profile

Iceland: Domestic, inbound and outbound tourism

	2018	2019	2020	2021	2022
TOURISM FLOWS, THOUSAND					
Domestic tourism					
Total domestic trips	..	..	..	..	..
Overnight visitors (tourists)	701	699	890	1 191	1 253
Same-day visitors (excursionists)	..	..	..	..	..
Nights in all types of accommodation	1 105	1 090	1 468	1 939	1 968
Hotels and similar establishments	661	581	745	1 097	1 206
Other collective establishments	402	450	586	726	641
Private accommodation	42	59	137	116	122
Inbound tourism[1]					
Total international arrivals	..	2 598	489	717	1 886
Overnight visitors (tourists)	2 316	2 202	486	698	1 715
Same-day visitors (excursionists)	..	189	2	19	171
Top markets					
United States	695	464	53	227	458
United Kingdom	298	262	102	54	230
Nordic countries	165	149	39	41	133
Germany	139	132	44	64	132
France	97	98	28	37	89
Nights in all types of accommodation	7 444	7 317	1 828	3 072	6 579
Hotels and similar establishments	5 200	5 211	1 275	2 142	4 645
Other collective establishments	1 519	1 389	367	702	1 425
Private accommodation	724	716	186	228	509
Outbound tourism					
Total international departures	..	..	..	..	..
Overnight visitors (tourists)	668	631	133	219	587
Same-day visitors (excursionists)	..	..	..	..	..
Top destinations					
..	..	..	..	..	..
..	..	..	..	..	..
..	..	..	..	..	..
..	..	..	..	..	..
..	..	..	..	..	..
TOURISM RECEIPTS AND EXPENDITURE, MILLION ISK					
Inbound tourism					
Total international receipts	520 129	469 951	112 928	203 183	454 514
International travel receipts	338 026	330 364	86 740	165 375	336 170
International passenger transport receipts	182 103	139 586	26 188	37 808	118 344
Outbound tourism					
Total international expenditure	207 322	203 449	73 724	101 607	217 400
International travel expenditure	183 305	185 122	70 802	96 336	204 897
International passenger transport expenditure	24 018	18 327	2 922	5 270	12 503

.. Not available

1. Arrivals from demand side surveys; Nights from supply side surveys.

Source: OECD Tourism Statistics (Database).

StatLink https://stat.link/3wdaj2

Iceland: Enterprises and employment in tourism

	Number of establishments[1]	Number of persons employed[2]				
	2022	2018	2019	2020	2021	2022
Total	..	..	..	..	..	
Tourism industries	2 313	30 474	28 813	20 426	20 258	25 976
Accommodation services for visitors	674	6 768	6 663	4 051	4 076	6 206
Hotels and similar establishments	469	6 228	6 147	3 722	3 713	5 716
Food and beverage serving industry	624	9 815	9 269	7 286	8 163	10 064
Passenger transport	200	7 438	6 484	4 637	3 780	3 674
Air passenger transport	16	..	..	..	..	..
Railways passenger transport	0	..	..	..	..	..
Road passenger transport	163	..	..	..	..	..
Water passenger transport	21	..	..	..	..	..
Passenger transport supporting services	..	1 931	1 609	1 231	1 167	1 491
Transport equipment rental	62	1 210	1 131	793	774	1 098
Travel agencies and other reservation services industry	560	2 948	2 830	1 679	1 608	2 545
Cultural industry	55	559	550	532	522	582
Sports and recreation industry	112	791	839	720	737	823
Retail trade of country-specific tourism characteristic goods	..	..	..	..	..	..
Other country-specific tourism industries	26	946	1 047	730	598	985
Other industries	..	..	..	..	..	..

.. Not available
1. Data refer to number of employers.
2. Data refer to number of employees.
Source: OECD Tourism Statistics (Database).

StatLink https://stat.link/fqrp20

Iceland: Internal tourism consumption

Million ISK

	2022 e		
	Domestic tourism expenditure	Inbound tourism expenditure	Internal tourism consumption
Total	244 942	390 438	646 641
Consumption products	..	..	..
Tourism characteristic products	204 192	324 795	540 196
Accommodation services for visitors	52 046	91 324	143 684
Food and beverage serving services	24 606	47 756	72 553
Passenger transport services	..	..	..
Air passenger transport services	27 216	73 372	103 154
Railways passenger transport services	..	..	..
Road passenger transport services	1 468	10 049	12 069
Water passenger transport services	577	2 532	3 239
Passenger transport supporting services	..	..	..
Transport equipment rental services	10 312	41 224	51 698
Travel agencies and other reservation services industry	62 368	42 112	104 861
Cultural services	7 968	3 701	11 669
Sports and recreation services	17 632	12 727	30 359
Country-specific tourism characteristic goods	..	..	..
Country-specific tourism characteristic services	..	..	6 911
Other consumption products	40 750	65 643	106 445
Tourism connected products	..	..	..
Non-tourism related consumption products	40 750	65 643	106 445
Non-consumption products	..	..	..

.. Not available; e Estimated value
Source: OECD Tourism Statistics (Database).

StatLink https://stat.link/h562gl

Ireland

Tourism in the economy and outlook

Tourism plays a significant role in the Irish economy. Before the pandemic, tourism directly contributed EUR 15.5 billion or 4.4% of total GDP and employed 284 800 people in tourism related sectors, or 12.3% of national employment.

Official data on international tourism performance is unavailable for the period 2020-23 due to the suspension of data collection between March 2020 and April 2023. The Irish Tourism Industry Confederation estimates that 7 million international tourists visited Ireland in 2022, representing a recovery to 73% of 2019 levels. This aligns with Tourism Ireland estimates that overseas tourist arrivals to the island of Ireland in 2022 reached 75% of 2019 levels. Ireland recorded 5.1 million visitors from April to December 2023, and the total expenditure by international visitors reached EUR 5.2 billion.

Irish residents took 14.3 million domestic overnight trips and 12.6 million outbound overnight trips in 2023. Total domestic nights decreased slightly at 33.0 million in 2023, compared with 34.2 million in 2022.

Ireland expects a 5.5% increase in revenue associated with overseas tourist visits as well as a 6.0% increase in revenue associated with domestic tourist trips in 2024. International arrivals are expected to return to pre-pandemic levels by 2025 or 2026.

Tourism governance

The Tourism Division of the Department of Tourism, Culture, Arts, Gaeltacht, Sport and Media sets national tourism policy in Ireland, providing the strategic direction to support the sustainable growth of the sector. Fáilte Ireland and Tourism Ireland operate under the responsibility of the Department to administer national tourism policy, while the Hospitality and Tourism Forum provides a platform for structured engagement between the tourism industry, agencies and relevant government departments.

Fáilte Ireland is the National Tourism Development Authority. It supports tourism businesses to better manage and market their products and services and develop experiences in line with Fáilte Ireland's brands. It works with other state agencies and representative bodies at local and national levels and is responsible for promoting Ireland as a domestic holiday destination and managing a network of tourist information centres throughout the country.

Tourism Ireland Ltd is responsible for marketing Ireland and Northern Ireland as a holiday and business tourism destination overseas. It is funded by the Department for the Economy in Northern Ireland and by the Department of Tourism, Culture, Arts, Gaeltacht, Sport and Media in Ireland.

Local authorities have an officer responsible for co-ordinating tourism development in each authority area. City and county councils have Tourism Statements of Strategy alongside work programmes of investment and promotion implemented by the local authority and its partners. They work closely with Fáilte Ireland to develop public tourism infrastructure and organise local events.

In 2022, EUR 288.5 million was allocated for tourism, up from EUR 220.9 million in 2021. In 2023, EUR 15 million in additional funding was secured for marketing Ireland overseas and EUR 15 million was allocated to a range of industry initiatives, including increasing domestic marketing, continuing Fáilte Ireland's work in the area of sustainability, and hosting the American College Football Classic. A further EUR 36.5 million was provided to fund tourism product development in line with the National Development Plan.

Ireland: Organisational chart of tourism bodies

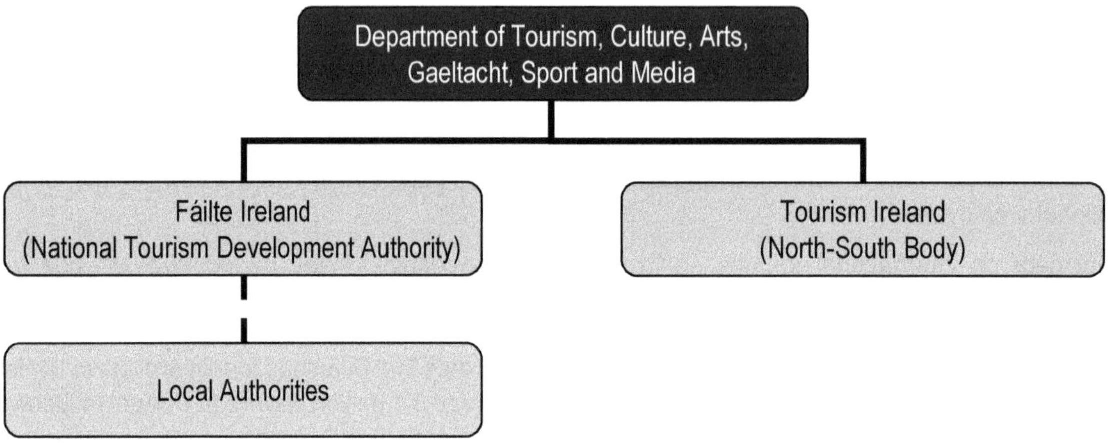

Source: OECD, adapted from the Department of Tourism, Culture, Arts, Gaeltacht, Sport and Media, 2024.

Tourism policies and programmes

Ireland's policy statement People, Place and Policy – Growing Tourism to 2025 guides the development of tourism to deliver on three headline targets to increase tourism revenues, jobs and overseas visits by 2025. A Sustainable Tourism Working Group established to support the implementation of the policy set out Guiding Principles for Sustainable Tourism Development in Ireland, together with a suite of Actions to Promote Sustainable Tourism Practices 2021-23 (see box below).

A new national tourism policy was initiated in 2022 to help mainstream sustainable economic development across the country. It prioritises environmental protection, with a focus on reducing seasonality, to ensure a thriving tourism sector by 2030, consistent with climate change commitments. Initial consultations with key stakeholders were completed in 2023, and in early 2024, an online survey was launched seeking the views of the public to help finalise the Framework. Matters raised in the survey are being fully considered in the finalising of the policy framework, which is due to be published soon. The final policy framework will focus on tourism workforce, innovation, product development, regional distribution, seasonality and the impact of broader Government and international decisions, aiming to increase sustainability through the promotion of sustainable travel options, like greenways, blueways and walking holidays, and improving biodiversity.

In addition to the national policy framework, Fáilte Ireland has launched four new Regional Tourism Development Strategies 2023-27 for Ireland's Ancient East, Wild Atlantic Way, Hidden Heartlands and Dublin, which provide a framework for sustainable tourism development across Ireland. The strategies are implemented across all regions through local area action plans, or Destination and Experience Development Plans. The collaborative plans involve all local stakeholders, with ownership of actions assigned to various parties.

Ireland has prioritised several actions to enhance tourism employment and skills in the country (see Box 2.3). Launched in 2022, the Employer Excellence programme helps participating businesses improve their employer practices and enhance their reputation as excellent employers. This was supported by learniFI, a new learning management system launched by Fáilte Ireland in 2023, offering online courses to support the development of careers in tourism, the Transition Year Work Placement Programme, giving secondary school students a high-quality work placement in tourism, and the Tourism and Hospitality Careers Oversight Group, a public-private sector initiative focusing on recruitment and retention strategies.

Additionally, the National Skills Strategy 2025 Ireland's Future includes a new suite of third-level education programmes to encourage the retention and recruitment of talent for the tourism and hospitality sector. The online skills-focused programmes provide tourism and hospitality employees with access to qualifications that help advance their careers in the sector.

Fáilte Ireland has also started working on a new digitalisation strategy for the tourism sector, building in the success of the Digital that Delivers programme, which helps tourism businesses increase their online presence. The programme includes a focus on emerging technologies like Generative AI, Augmented Reality and Virtual Reality and will support over 700 businesses by 2026, resulting in additional economic activity of EUR 408 million over a 10-year period.

The Shared Island Initiative Report 2022 – Action on a Shared Future outlines the second year of the Shared Island Initiative, demonstrating the Government's commitment to engage with all communities and traditions to build a shared future on the island. An online Shared Island Dialogue on Tourism brought together tourism agencies, organisations, interest groups and civil society to assess tourism co-operation and explore future economic opportunities for Ireland and Northern Ireland.

Additionally, Ireland will receive up to EUR 84.5 million from the EU Just Transition Fund over the period to 2027 to support areas heavily dependent on carbon-intensive activities to diversify their economy. Ireland benefited from a total budget of EUR 169 million for this project, of which EUR 68 million are allocated to tourism initiatives, such as regenerative tourism projects in communities impacted by the decline in peat production, planning for sustainable tourism and a climate action roadmap.

Implementing sustainable tourism practices in Ireland

A Sustainable Tourism Working Group was established to develop a sustainable tourism policy based on Actions to Promote Sustainable Tourism Practices 2021-23, which includes 31 concrete actions to help mainstream sustainable economic development for the Irish tourism sector.

Fáilte Ireland launched the Climate Action Roadmap in 2022 along with a series of guides explaining sustainable tourism, setting out actions to reduce carbon emissions, illustrated by case studies that demonstrate the benefits of adopting sustainable practices. The guides cover the following key areas; energy management, water management, waste management, biodiversity, how to tell your climate action story, carbon offsetting and how to run climate-friendly meetings, events and festivals.

A Bespoke Carbon Calculator was also launched by Fáilte Ireland in 2022 to help tourists and businesses measure and understand their carbon footprint, set targets for emission reductions and benchmark with themselves over time and other tourism businesses.

Statistical Profile

Ireland: Domestic, inbound and outbound tourism

	2018	2019	2020	2021	2022
TOURISM FLOWS, THOUSAND					
Domestic tourism					
Total domestic trips	..	..	..	..	..
Overnight visitors (tourists)	10 919	11 621	7 721	5 663	13 274
Same-day visitors (excursionists)	..	..	..	..	..
Nights in all types of accommodation	28 393	29 469	23 518	17 886	34 236
Hotels and similar establishments	..	..	..	..	..
Other collective establishments	..	..	..	..	..
Private accommodation	..	..	..	..	..
Inbound tourism					
Total international arrivals	..	..	..	..	..
Overnight visitors (tourists)	9 273	9 353	..	..	..
Same-day visitors (excursionists)	..	..	..	..	..
Top markets					
Great Britain	3 253	3 269	..	..	..
Other Europe	2 203	2 321	..	..	..
United States and Canada	1 924	1 863	..	..	..
Germany	755	723	..	..	..
France	521	529			
Nights in all types of accommodation	..	..	..	..	..
Hotels and similar establishments	..	..	..	..	..
Other collective establishments	..	..	..	..	..
Private accommodation	..	..	..	..	..
Outbound tourism					
Total international departures	8 276	8 814	2 417 e	2 314	10 077
Overnight visitors (tourists)	8 085	8 620	2 365 e	2 276	8 787
Same-day visitors (excursionists)	191	194	52 e	38	1 290
Top destinations					
..	..	..	..	..	..
..	..	..	..	..	..
..	..	..	..	..	..
..	..	..	..	..	..
..	..	..	..	..	..
TOURISM RECEIPTS AND EXPENDITURE, MILLION EUR					
Inbound tourism					
Total international receipts	13 015	13 297	4 116	4 450	13 678
International travel receipts	5 796	5 787	2 095	2 272	6 686
International passenger transport receipts	7 219	7 510	2 021	2 178	6 992
Outbound tourism					
Total international expenditure	6 557	7 459	2 358	2 257	8 102
International travel expenditure	6 474	7 375	2 277	2 166	8 053
International passenger transport expenditure	83	84	81	91	49

.. Not available; e Estimated value
Source: OECD Tourism Statistics (Database).

StatLink https://stat.link/nt3hpq

Ireland: Enterprises and employment in tourism

	Number of establishments[1]	Number of persons employed				
	2021	2018	2019	2020	2021 p	2022
Total	..	..	..	..	..	..
Tourism industries	45 265	233 524	284 838	196 210	202 349	..
Accommodation services for visitors	17 862	175 591	210 697	138 012	147 320	..
Hotels and similar establishments	..	..	..	..	..	..
Food and beverage serving industry	..	..	..	..	..	..
Passenger transport	13 798	22 684	25 792	23 247	22 571	..
Air passenger transport	..	..	..	..	..	..
Railways passenger transport	..	..	..	..	..	..
Road passenger transport	..	..	..	..	..	..
Water passenger transport	..	..	..	..	..	..
Passenger transport supporting services	..	..	..	..	..	..
Transport equipment rental	..	..	..	..	..	..
Travel agencies and other reservation services industry	1 372	8 632	10 070	7 104	5 976	..
Cultural industry	12 233	26 617	38 279	27 847	26 482	..
Sports and recreation industry	..	..	..	..	..	..
Retail trade of country-specific tourism characteristic goods	..	..	..	..	..	..
Other country-specific tourism industries	..	..	..	..	..	..
Other industries	..	..	..	..	..	..

.. Not available; p Provisional data
1. Data refer to number of enterprises.
Source: OECD Tourism Statistics (Database).

StatLink https://stat.link/cylo7h

Ireland: Internal tourism consumption

Million EUR

	2007		
	Domestic tourism expenditure	Inbound tourism expenditure	Internal tourism consumption
Total	..	..	..
Consumption products	**3 142**	**3 637**	**6 779**
Tourism characteristic products	2 337	2 875	5 212
Accommodation services for visitors	228	672	900
Food and beverage serving services	983	932	1 915
Passenger transport services	762	1 062	1 824
Air passenger transport services	..	..	..
Railways passenger transport services	..	..	..
Road passenger transport services	..	..	..
Water passenger transport services	..	..	..
Passenger transport supporting services	..	..	..
Transport equipment rental services	..	..	..
Travel agencies and other reservation services industry	155	12	167
Cultural services	209	197	406
Sports and recreation services	..	..	..
Country-specific tourism characteristic goods	..	..	..
Country-specific tourism characteristic services	..	..	..
Other consumption products	805	762	1 567
Tourism connected products	..	..	..
Non-tourism related consumption products	..	..	..
Non-consumption products	..	..	..

.. Not available
Source: OECD Tourism Statistics (Database).

StatLink https://stat.link/c1ixnh

Israel

Tourism in the economy and outlook

In 2022, tourism contributed ILS 29.8 billion to the economy accounting for 1.9% of GVA, up from a low of ILS 9.6 billion or 0.7% of GVA in 2020. Prior to the pandemic, tourism's share of national GVA was 2.6%. Direct tourism employment was estimated at 135 500 jobs, or 3.2% of total employment. This was still 9.6% below 2019 levels, but up 25% compared to 108 200 jobs in 2021. Travel exports accounted for 6.3% of total service exports in 2022, less than half of the pre-pandemic levels of 13.3%.

Israel recorded 2.7 million international tourist arrivals in 2022, a recovery of 59% compared to 2019 levels, but a significant increase compared to 402 000 arrivals in 2021. The top three international source countries were the United States (30%), France (9%) and the United Kingdom (7%).

Domestic tourism is a key driver of demand in Israel and was resilient in the aftermath of the COVID-19 pandemic. In 2022, Israel registered a new record of 9.4 million domestic tourists and 20.1 million domestic nights. This represented a 16.1% increase in domestic nights spent on 2019 levels.

Tourism governance

The Ministry of Tourism (IMOT) is the national government entity responsible for steering tourism policy and the sector. The Ministry continuously engages with all parts of the tourism sector, putting particular emphasis on emergency support programmes for hotels and inbound tour operators and preparing SMEs for the recovery of domestic and inbound tourism. The Ministry co-operates with other relevant ministries, authorities, and agencies on an ad-hoc basis and within the framework of joint steering committees.

Large local authorities usually co-ordinate tourism policies with national policy, particularly in relation to domestic and inbound marketing activities. Smaller, mainly rural authorities, tend to cluster into regional tourism destination management organisations (DMOs) to develop more coherent products and enable more effective branding and marketing policies. The Ministry has a continuous working relationship with regional DMOs and tourism departments, and co-ordinates marketing, product development and regional branding.

The Ministry also assists local authorities in tourism development research and feasibility studies, especially for infrastructure development and zoning. The Ministry organises professional coaching and training programmes in product development and marketing for SMEs, with the active participation of regional DMOs.

The total tourism budget for Israel in 2023 was ILS 615 million down from ILS 735 million in 2022 and down from ILS 1.1 billion in 2019. The tourism budget is divided into three main areas of activity:

- Development of accommodation through grants to hotels: ILS 130 million in 2023, down from ILS 170 million in 2022.
- Development of public tourism infrastructures: ILS 215 million in 2023, down from ILS 265 million in 2022.
- Marketing: ILS 130 million in 2023, down from 180 million in 2022.

Israel: Organisational chart of tourism bodies

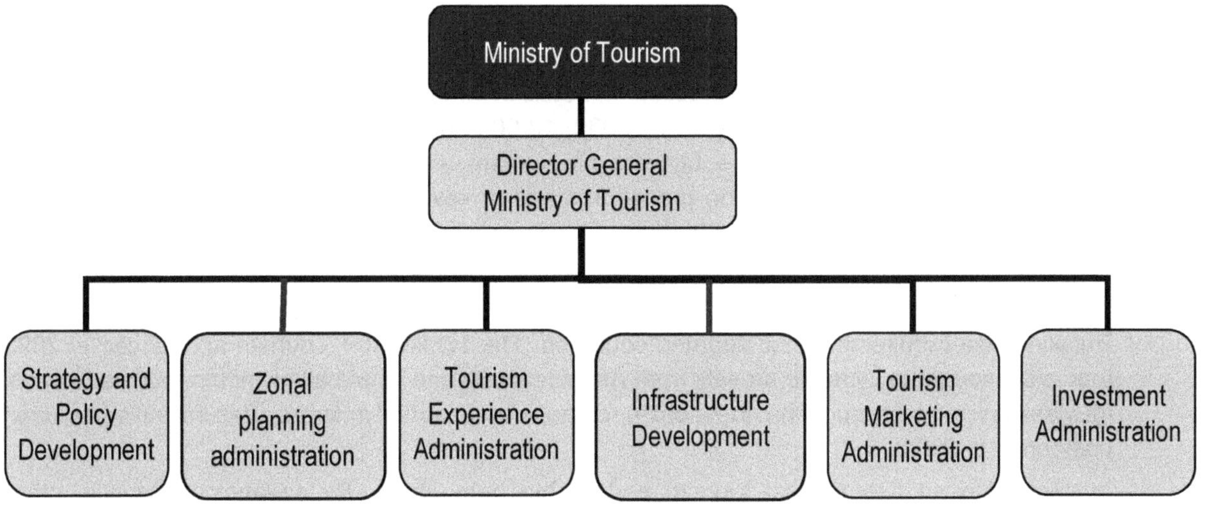

Source: OECD, adapted from the Ministry of Tourism, 2024.

Tourism policies and programmes

In 2023, Israel launched its new long-term tourism strategy. The strategy sets a target of welcoming 7 million international tourists annually by 2030 and analyses all the different aspects of the 'tourism world', from creating products, marketing them, to enhancing the entire tourist experience. The strategy has outlined five major targets for the coming years:

- Increasing tourism travel to Israel and its revenues.
- Developing new diversified, competitive, and sustainable tourism products.
- Improving the value for money and tourist satisfaction.
- Strengthening the supporting infrastructure in the Ministry.
- Promoting and strengthening the human resources in the tourism industry.

For each target, Israel has established several long-term goals, such as improving the impact on the economy through domestic tourism. Each year, Israel establishes a work plan consisting of numerous assignments, linked to specific goals and targets. All assignments are prioritised based on their impact on the success of the long-term target, the likelihood of success, and the office's ability to influence the mission's success.

The work plan for 2024 includes: i) promoting investment to accelerate expansion of accommodation offerings and increasing diversification, ii) infrastructure development including implementation of the national zoning plan, infrastructure development from leading brands, re-investing in upgrading content in existing infrastructures and positioning the Ministry of Tourism as an initiating partner, iii) focus marketing on competitive brands, integrating domestic tourism as part of the product development and managing seasonality, and iv) improving tourist satisfaction. The internal priorities include develop working processes, forums, and promoting an organisational culture change, which will help the brand and product managers work synergistically. Products will be promoted based on the brand priorities and strategy.

Israel initiated tourism programmes to facilitate economic recovery and bolster the rebound of international tourists. However, the development of those projects has been slowed and stopped as a result of the security situation. Initiatives include:

- Launching a fund for the promotion of international film and TV productions. In June 2022, Israel launched the ILS 45 million programme to encourage the production of international film and TV series in Israel. The programme would enable production companies to claim up to 30% of their expenses back if they filmed in Israel. The programme aimed to highlight the natural beauty and historical significance of Israel through the media.
- Increasing investment in, and construction of, hotels in Israel. To reach Israel's goal of welcoming 7 million international tourists per year by 2030, 12 000 additional hotel rooms would need to be added to the existing stock. The Ministry of Tourism aims to accelerate the pace of hotel construction by shortening planning procedures and by reviewing city construction plans. These measures will add to those taken in 2022 to diversify and increase supply, which include adjusting the height limit for hotel construction to add additional rooms in Eilat, and creating dedicated camping and glamping complexes.
- Relaxing visa requirements for targeted countries. The Minister for Tourism announced in 2023 that Israel sought to increase arrivals from Asian markets and would allow Indian tourists to apply for visas online and reduce the questioning methods upon arrival in Israel. This initiative has been postponed to 2024.
- Implementing an international tourism partnership programme. By advancing ties with other countries, Israel's Ministry of Tourism is increasing the number of international tourists. These partnerships are seeking to increase the two-way flow of tourists and particularly focus on the younger tourists.
- Increasing the number of direct international flights to Israel. In 2023, new direct routes with Australia, Ireland, Japan, Korea, and the United States were launched. The increase in direct flights aims to better connect Israel to the world and encourage more international visitors.

However, the development of those projects has been slowed and stopped as a result of the security situation with international tourism remaining down on pre-pandemic levels in Israel. The Israeli authorities have informed the Secretariat that the terrorist attacks of 7 October 2023 and the subsequent war have hit Israel's tourism economy hard, bringing international tourism to a halt (down 33.9% in 2023). This is impacting exports and economy growth in the country more widely (OECD, 2024). Uncertainty about the evolution of these geopolitical conflicts and tensions has impacted international and domestic tourism alike, and a number of other services have been negatively impacted as well, such as tourism human resources and accommodations.

Statistical Profile

Israel: Domestic, inbound and outbound tourism

	2018	2019	2020	2021	2022
TOURISM FLOWS, THOUSAND					
Domestic tourism					
Total domestic trips	..	..	..	..	..
Overnight visitors (tourists)	8 071	8 243	3 941	8 575	9 360
Same-day visitors (excursionists)	..	..	..	..	..
Nights in all types of accommodation	17 105	17 341	8 943	18 422	20 141
Hotels and similar establishments	14 482	14 589	7 474	15 585	17 019
Other collective establishments	2 005	2 142	999	2 138	2 426
Private accommodation	618	609	470	700	695
Inbound tourism[1]					
Total international arrivals	4 390	4 905	887	402	2 851
Overnight visitors (tourists)	4 121	4 552	832	397	2 675
Same-day visitors (excursionists)	269	353	56	6	176
Top markets					
United States	898	1 008	206	149	811
France	346	377	59	42	236
Russian Federation	316	394	60	14	163
Germany	263	306	52	17	151
United Kingdom	218	260	47	32	178
Nights in all types of accommodation	13 862	14 420	2 609	1 059	8 137
Hotels and similar establishments	13 018	13 621	2 474	866	7 599
Other collective establishments	770	735	120	178	498
Private accommodation	75	64	16	15	41
Outbound tourism					
Total international departures	8 473	9 179	1 544	3 022	8 432
Overnight visitors (tourists)	..	..	..	..	..
Same-day visitors (excursionists)	..	..	..	..	..
Top destinations					
..	..	..	..	..	..
..	..	..	..	..	..
..	..	..	..	..	..
..	..	..	..	..	..
..	..	..	..	..	..
TOURISM RECEIPTS AND EXPENDITURE, MILLION USD					
Inbound tourism					
Total international receipts	8 048	8 439	2 661	2 517	..
International travel receipts	7 225	7 620	2 500	2 217	..
International passenger transport receipts	823	839	161	216	..
Outbound tourism					
Total international expenditure	9 975	10 390	2 175	3 889	..
International travel expenditure	7 878	8 154	1 804	3 233	..
International passenger transport expenditure	2 097	2 236	371	656	..

.. Not available

1. Arrivals from demand side surveys. Nights from supply side surveys.

Source: OECD Tourism Statistics (Database).

StatLink https://stat.link/d6jkct

Israel: Enterprises and employment in tourism

	Number of establishments	Number of persons employed				
	2022	2018	2019	2020	2021	2022
Total	..	141 140	149 900	117 670	108 174	135 540
Tourism industries	18 460	137 550	146 100	113 610	104 274	130 870
Accommodation services for visitors	1 678	45 000	46 500	24 400	27 500	43 500
Hotels and similar establishments	633	..	..	..	..	..
Food and beverage serving industry	14 666	15 790	16 200	12 690	13 000	16 130
Passenger transport	..	18 080	20 760	18 920	14 300	16 420
Air passenger transport	..	12 900	15 130	13 660	9 630	11 240
Railways passenger transport	..	..	..	..	..	..
Road passenger transport	..	5 180	5 630	5 260	4 670	5 180
Water passenger transport	..	..	..	..	..	..
Passenger transport supporting services	..	..	..	..	..	..
Transport equipment rental	..	5 490	5 950	6 290	5 160	4 900
Travel agencies and other reservation services industry	1 483	20 330	19 610	16 650	11 530	17 150
Cultural industry	..	..	..	..	..	..
Sports and recreation industry	..	12 250	16 220	14 950	12 872	12 280
Retail trade of country-specific tourism characteristic goods	..	20 610	20 860	19 710	19 912	20 490
Other country-specific tourism industries	..	..	..	..	..	..
Other industries	..	3 590	3 840	4 010	3 900	4 670

.. Not available
Source: OECD Tourism Statistics (Database).

StatLink https://stat.link/xmvi45

Israel: Internal tourism consumption

Million ILS

	2022		
	Domestic tourism expenditure	Inbound tourism expenditure	Internal tourism consumption
Total	..	..	..
Consumption products	**31 424**	**17 376**	**48 800**
Tourism characteristic products	..	..	..
Accommodation services for visitors	..	..	..
Food and beverage serving services	..	..	..
Passenger transport services	..	..	..
Air passenger transport services	..	..	..
Railways passenger transport services	..	..	..
Road passenger transport services	..	..	..
Water passenger transport services	..	..	..
Passenger transport supporting services	..	..	..
Transport equipment rental services	..	..	..
Travel agencies and other reservation services industry	..	..	..
Cultural services	..	..	..
Sports and recreation services	..	..	..
Country-specific tourism characteristic goods	..	..	..
Country-specific tourism characteristic services	..	..	..
Other consumption products	..	..	..
Tourism connected products	..	..	..
Non-tourism related consumption products	..	..	..
Non-consumption products	..	..	..

.. Not available
Source: OECD Tourism Statistics (Database).

StatLink https://stat.link/2o6x7h

Italy

Tourism in the economy and outlook

Tourism is an important driver of economic development in Italy and has recovered strongly in recent years. The sector directly accounted for 6.2% of GVA in 2019. Tourism directly employed 2.1 million people in 2019, contributing 8.9% of total employment in 2019. Travel exports represented 36.3% of total service exports in 2022, almost back to the pre-pandemic levels of 40.5% and a significant increase compared to the pandemic low of 23.3% in 2020.

In 2022, Italy received 49.8 million inbound tourists, 77.2% of 2019 levels, and a 98% increase compared to the pandemic low of 25.2 million arrivals in 2020. The top three international source markets were Germany (20%), United States (11%) and France (9%).

Domestic tourism is an important part of the Italian tourism sector, with 44 million overnight domestic trips in 2022. This represented an increase of 18.3% on 2021 levels, and accounts for 81.1% of 2019's pre-pandemic levels.

Tourism governance

The Ministry of Tourism plays is responsible for national strategic co-ordination, development plan implementation, promotion of initiatives to enhance tourism offerings, and assistance mechanism planning for tourists and plays a leading role in innovation.

The Ministry supports and supervises the National Agency for Tourism, which oversees the promotion and marketing of the national image and brand, and *Club Alpino Italiano*, responsible for promoting mountaineering, the conservation and study of the Italian Alps. The National Agency for Tourism actively collaborates with tourism stakeholders through periodic meetings to continuously improve the sector.

The Italian Constitution devolves several key competences to regional governments. However, central and regional authorities collaborate through agreements, jointly exercising regulatory powers on numerous issues concerning tourism. Each region has legislative authority to adopt triennial plans with annual programmes outlining responsibilities, objectives and guidelines for tourism management. Strategic collaboration between central authorities and local institutions is co-ordinated through the Unified Conference.

The budget for tourism in Italy in 2023 was EUR 421.3 million, 53% higher than in the previous year. This derives from the joint effects of an increase in current expenses (EUR 66.7 million) and an increase in capital expenses (EUR 79.3 million). The Adjustment Act has increased the budget appropriations by about EUR 1.4 million. Approximately EUR 42 million of the overall budget if allocated to specialised agencies such as the National Agency for Tourism and *Club Alpino Italiano*.

Additional resources have been allocated as relief measures to mitigate the negative impact of natural disasters affecting tourism destinations. These include EUR 10 million for the flood emergency in Emilia Romagna and EUR 15 million for the bushfire emergency in Sicily and Sardinia in 2023.

Italy: Organisational chart of tourism bodies

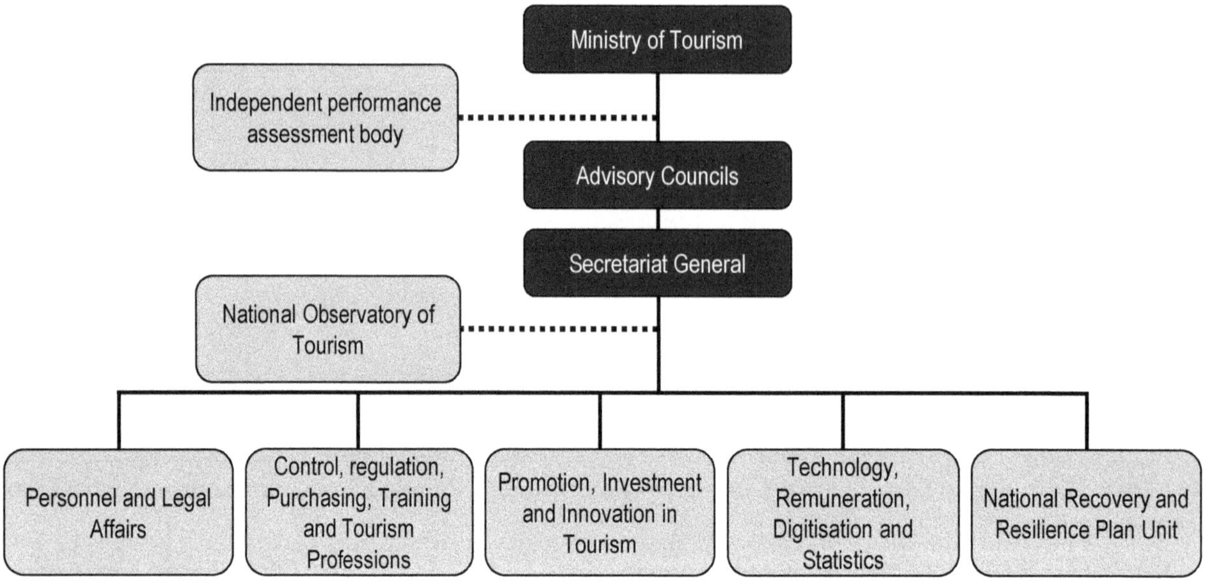

Source: OECD, adapted from the Italian Ministry of Tourism, 2024

Tourism policies and programmes

In 2022, Italy developed a new Strategic Plan for Tourism 2023-27. The Plan is based on five strategic pillars:

- Governance;
- Sustainability;
- Innovation;
- Quality, safety and inclusion;
- Education and tourism careers.

The strategic pillars are declined into key issues defined by the Ministry of Tourism that include environmental conservation and climate change resilience; cultural heritage preservation and community involvement; diversification of the touristic offer both in time and space; and promotion of responsible travel behaviours.

Other major concerns addressed by the Plan are improving timeliness, quality and coherence of tourism statistics to complement and strengthen existing statistical approaches to support tourism policy making; strengthen digital tools and accessibility to improve tourists' travel experience; tacking tourism workforce issues; and collaborating with tourism stakeholders to implement the Strategic Plan.

To tackle these issues, Italy aims to establish a robust decision-making process between State and regional authorities to ensure swift action, even during emergencies. The Ministry intends to enhance tourism's role in the economy by co-operating with other relevant Ministries, including those responsible for sport, culture, education, sea, environment, Made in Italy, economy, transports, and foreign affairs. To integrate tourism into the broader economy, the following strategies are being developed:

- Italicares Project Platform, supported by the 2022 National Tourism Fund, which will promote a relationship between health and tourism

- The 2023 law for Delegations to the Government on Policies in Favour of the Elderly, focused on ensuring and enhancing essential levels of social services and psychophysical health, while also promoting wellness tourism and encouraging slow, sustainable tourism for the elderly
- National Sea Plan 2023-25 to help shape strategic and operational directives on maritime issues that affect tourism.

The Strategic Plan seeks to foster digital change in the tourism ecosystem and its supply chain, strengthening the value of networks through a process of sharing the best experiences and encouraging the transition from traditional to an innovative tourism model. This also includes adapting towards a circular model to achieve sustainable growth in line with EU Green Deal objectives. Additionally, the Plan also wishes to enhance Italy’s international reputation as a safe and inclusive destination by offering a diversified, resilient, and secure tourism experience. Finally, it also aims to promote lesser-known destinations year-round, reducing the effects of overtourism and ensuring long-term economic benefits.

Several initiatives have been launched to achieve these objectives. The tax-free shopping initiative lowers the minimum economic threshold to access the service, promoting Made in Italy products and supporting local craftsmanship, to boost the recovery of the national tourism industry and enhance Italy's international appeal.

- The fund for sustainable tourism allocated EUR 5 million in 2023 and EUR 10 million in 2024 and 2025, to mitigate overcrowding, create innovative itineraries, and de-seasonalise destinations. The fund will identify intermodal routes using electric transport and support accommodation facilities and tourism businesses in obtaining sustainability certifications.
- The fund to encourage and improve the professionalism and competitiveness of workers in the tourism sector, allocated EUR 5 million in 2023 and EUR 8 million in 2024 and 2025 to retrain existing personnel, provide training to new professionals and integrate senior professionals into the tourism market.
- A memorandum of understanding with the Ministry of Internal Affairs addresses the transitional programming of entry flows for non-EU seasonal and non-seasonal workers, to reduce pressure on tourism recruitment issues. Additionally, a tax break for night shifts and public holiday work for tourism sector employees aims at renew interest in tourism careers, particularly targeting young workers.
- Funds for small municipalities with a tourist vocation, amounting to EUR 10 million in 2023 and EUR 12 million in 2024 and 2025, finance projects in municipalities with fewer than 5 000 inhabitants. These projects focus on innovations in accessibility, mobility, urban regeneration and environmental sustainability.

An integrated digital platform, the Tourism Digital Hub, aims to support innovation and digitisation in Italian tourism businesses, and provide better information on the distribution of tourist flows. The platform will include the development of a data lake and artificial intelligence models to analyse user behaviour online.

Other initiatives include financial incentives through tax breaks, funds, and loans to support SMEs and encourage recovery and investments, a fund to enhance UNESCO touristic destinations and initiatives for the relaunch of mountain tourism through infrastructural adjustments, modernisation, and maintenance of cableway and snowmaking facilities, along with the promotion of mountain products. Participation in major events such as conventions, exhibitions, entertainment, and sports happenings is being prioritised to strengthen the Italy and Made in Italy brands worldwide.

Statistical Profile

Italy: Domestic, inbound and outbound tourism

	2018	2019	2020	2021	2022
TOURISM FLOWS, THOUSAND					
Domestic tourism[1]					
Total domestic trips	145 307	132 858	74 654	73 000	90 259
Overnight visitors (tourists)	62 861	54 253	34 130	37 183	43 996
Same-day visitors (excursionists)	82 446	78 604	40 524	35 817	46 264
Nights in all types of accommodation	..	..	..	..	..
Hotels and similar establishments	..	..	..	..	..
Other collective establishments	..	..	..	..	..
Private accommodation	194 501	172 981	134 573	155 955	161 465
Inbound tourism					
Total international arrivals	93 229	95 399	38 419	40 186	74 317
Overnight visitors (tourists)	61 567	64 513	25 190	26 888	49 811
Same-day visitors (excursionists)	31 661	30 886	13 229	13 298	24 506
Top markets					
Germany	13 518	13 951	5 161	4 604	10 179
France	7 641	7 978	3 687	3 910	5 667
United Kingdom	5 659	6 006	1 756	909	4 446
Austria	4 020	4 309	2 034	2 488	3 014
United States	3 694	3 946	526	706	2 464
Nights in all types of accommodation	384 426	398 963	182 214	208 525	354 239
Hotels and similar establishments	177 738	175 649	54 228	53 537	116 428
Other collective establishments	66 547	73 335	25 543	32 700	55 572
Private accommodation	140 141	149 980	102 444	122 288	182 240
Outbound tourism					
Total international departures	61 195	62 207	21 448	17 588	46 695
Overnight visitors (tourists)	33 347	34 703	11 960	12 354	24 970
Same-day visitors (excursionists)	27 848	27 505	9 489	5 234	21 725
Top destinations					
France	5 787	5 631	2 522	2 667	3 743
Spain	3 567	3 694	943	1 648	3 487
Germany	3 048	3 517	1 396	1 155	2 075
Austria	2 191	2 327	1 025	709	1 084
United Kingdom	1 788	1 823	614	259	1 170
TOURISM RECEIPTS AND EXPENDITURE, MILLION EUR					
Inbound tourism					
Total international receipts	43 860	46 440	17 708	21 595	45 366
International travel receipts	41 712	44 302	17 332	21 266	44 254
International passenger transport receipts	2 148	2 138	376	329	1 112
Outbound tourism					
Total international expenditure	31 972	33 896	11 455	14 538	31 296
International travel expenditure	25 485	27 100	9 577	12 645	26 029
International passenger transport expenditure	6 487	6 796	1 878	1 893	5 267

.. Not available

1. Trips and nights from demand side surveys.

Source: OECD Tourism Statistics (Database).

StatLink https://stat.link/f8lisa

Italy: Enterprises and employment in tourism

	Number of establishments	Number of persons employed				
	2022	2018	2019	2020	2021	2022
Total	..	..	..	..	..	..
Tourism industries	..	..	2 136 578	..	..	..
Accommodation services for visitors	220 457	.	524 528	.	.	.
Hotels and similar establishments	217 889	.	315 698	.	.	.
Food and beverage serving industry	..	.	1 080 934	.	.	.
Passenger transport	..	.	184 591	.	.	.
Air passenger transport	..	.	15 172	.	.	.
Railways passenger transport	..	.	31 001	.	.	.
Road passenger transport	..	.	96 887	.	.	.
Water passenger transport	..	.	41 531	.	.	.
Passenger transport supporting services	..	.	..	.	.	.
Transport equipment rental	..	.	12 948	.	.	.
Travel agencies and other reservation services industry	..	.	52 051	.	.	.
Cultural industry	..	.	135 758	.	.	.
Sports and recreation industry	..	.	145 768	.	.	.
Retail trade of country-specific tourism characteristic goods	..	.	..	.	.	.
Other country-specific tourism industries	..	.	..	.	.	.
Other industries	..	..	..	..	..	..

.. Not available
Source: OECD Tourism Statistics (Database).

StatLink https://stat.link/ljpaq3

Italy: Internal tourism consumption

Million EUR

	2019		
	Domestic tourism expenditure	Inbound tourism expenditure	Internal tourism consumption
Total	..	..	..
Consumption products	**71 589**	**55 437**	**164 012**
Tourism characteristic products	55 313	42 195	134 328
Accommodation services for visitors	16 438	16 951	59 863
Food and beverage serving services	12 169	10 683	23 913
Passenger transport services	9 665	3 404	17 440
Air passenger transport services	3 543	1 810	8 381
Railways passenger transport services	2 038	360	3 295
Road passenger transport services	2 020	790	3 256
Water passenger transport services	2 064	444	2 508
Passenger transport supporting services	..	..	..
Transport equipment rental services	432	616	1 455
Travel agencies and other reservation services industry	3 528	515	6 673
Cultural services	411	585	1 744
Sports and recreation services	1 319	1 878	4 325
Country-specific tourism characteristic goods	11 351	7 564	18 915
Country-specific tourism characteristic services	..	..	..
Other consumption products	16 277	13 242	29 684
Tourism connected products	..	..	..
Non-tourism related consumption products	..	..	..
Non-consumption products	..	..	..

.. Not available
Source: OECD Tourism Statistics (Database).

StatLink https://stat.link/rpyldg

Japan

Tourism in the economy and outlook

Tourism remains a pillar of Japan's growth strategy and is an important driver of regional development. However, the sector is still recovering from the COVID-19 pandemic. In 2021, tourism accounted for 0.6% of GDP and contributed 6 million jobs to the economy, or 8.8% of total employment. This is lower than in 2019, when tourism accounted for 2.0% of GDP and 9.7% of employment. In 2022, travel exports represented 5.5% of total service exports, up from the pandemic low of 2.8% in 2021, but still 22% down from pre-pandemic levels.

Japan was still impacted by travel restrictions through most of 2022, when the country recorded 3.8 million international tourist arrivals. Although this was a significant increase compared to the pandemic low of 245 000 international tourist arrivals in 2021, it only represented 12% of 2019 levels. In 2023, Japan showed signals towards an international tourism recovery, with 25.1 million tourists, 79% of 2019 levels. The top three source countries in 2023 were Korea (28%), Chinese Taipei (17%) and China (10%). This is a change from 2019 when China was the top source market (30%).

The domestic market remains an important driver of Japanese tourism. In 2022, a total of 232.5 million domestic tourist arrivals were recorded, up from the pandemic low of 141.8 million but still 74.6% of 2019 levels.

Tourism governance

Established as an external bureau of the Ministry of Land, Infrastructure, Transport and Tourism, the Japan Tourism Agency takes a leading role in tourism policy, tourism development and the promotion of Japan as a tourist destination. The Agency is also responsible for co-ordinating efforts between public and private tourism stakeholders and favouring the development of tourism destinations.

A Ministerial Council for the Promotion of Japan as a Tourism-Oriented Country was established in 2013 to unify government efforts on tourism. The Council is presided by the Prime Minister and attended by all Cabinet ministers.

The Japan National Tourism Organisation is under the jurisdiction of the Japan Tourism Agency and acts as the official tourism bureau in the country. The National Tourism Organisation promotes Japan as a tourism destination abroad, provides information to foreign tourists, and conducts actions to encourage visits to Japan.

In addition, the nine District Transport Bureaus, which are local branches of the Ministry of Land, Infrastructure, Transport and Tourism, conduct tourism-related operations, in co-operation with local governments and private stakeholders to promote tourism throughout their areas of jurisdiction. Tourism departments in each District Transport Bureau focus on developing tourist-friendly environments and creating regional circuits for tourists. Additionally, together with the Japan Tourism Agency, they offer consultation services to local stakeholders on tourism initiatives for regional revitalisation.

The supplementary budget for Fiscal Year 2023 was JPY 68.9 billion. This included JPY 18.4 billion to attract foreign visitors to local regions, JPY 20 billion to add value to tourist destinations and tourism industries, and JPY 30.5 billion to prevent and restrain overtourism and promote sustainable tourism.

Japan: Organisational chart of tourism bodies

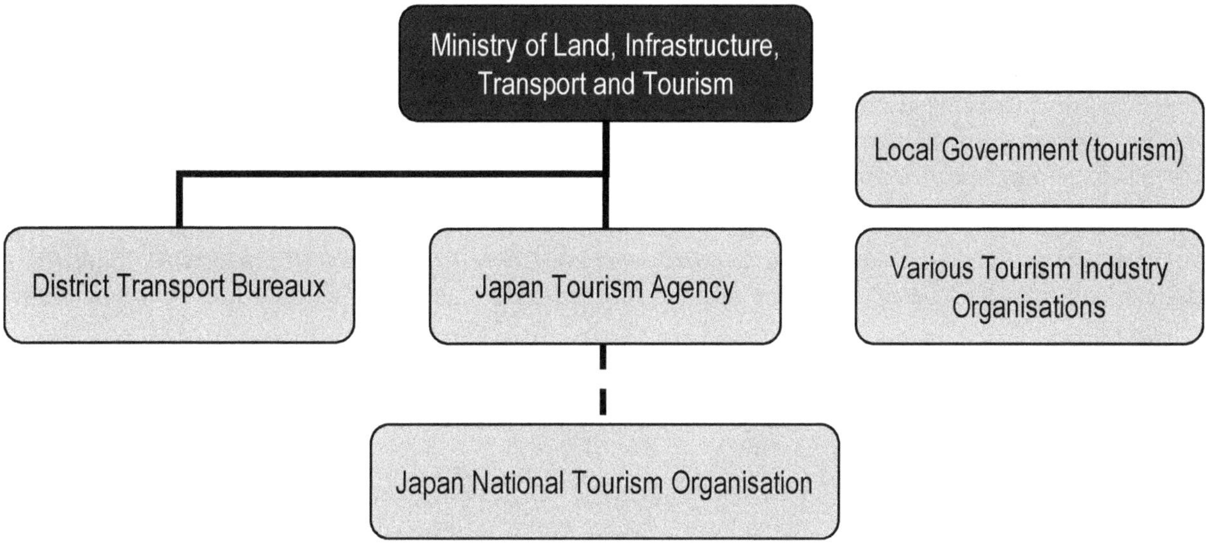

Source: OECD, adapted from the Ministry of Land, Infrastructure, Transport and Tourism, 2024.

Tourism policies and programmes

In 2023, Japan approved the new Tourism Nation Promotion Basic Plan, a three-year plan that aims to revitalise the tourism sector after the pandemic, focusing on sustainable tourism development. The Plan is structured around three key pillars: developing a sustainable tourism destination, recovering inbound travel and expanding the domestic market.

With the new Plan, Japan is focused on developing high value-added tourism products, to increase inbound tourism expenditure per capita to JPY 200 000, a 25% increase from pre-pandemic levels in current prices. In 2022-23, Japan allocated JPY 158.2 billion for the revitalisation of high value-added tourism destinations, programmes for digitalisation within the tourism sector, developing a sustainable tourism workforce and promoting sustainable tourism.

The Japan Sustainable Tourism Standard for Destinations helps promote the development of sustainable tourism destinations in the country. Based on international sustainability standards, these guidelines serve as a tool for local governments and Destination Management Organisations to engage in sustainable regional management through data measurement and medium-term planning, balancing the interests of travellers and local residents. As of April 2024, 35 regions used the Sustainable Tourism Standard. The goal is to have 100 regions using it by 2025.

In 2023, Japan also designated 11 Japanese destinations as Model Tourist Destinations for Creating Luxury Inbound Tourist Destinations in Regional Areas. The initiative aims to encourage international tourists to explore Japan beyond its metropolitan areas, and to attract more wealthy visitors to rural areas. Japan characterises the Model Tourist Destinations as places where tourists can experience nature, history and culture that are unique to Japan.

While domestic and international tourism demand are rapidly recovering in many Japanese destinations, concerns about the impact of overcrowding and bad tourist behaviour on the daily lives of residents increase. Tourist satisfaction has decreased in certain areas, in particular those with high tourist concentrations. To address these issues, relevant ministries and agencies have convened a task force to compile a package of measures to prevent and curb overtourism, such as improving the receiving environment, preventing manner violation and attracting more visitors to rural areas. Japan is also adopting crisis planning into tourism management. The Japan Tourism Agency has published national guidelines and a manual on preparing tourism crisis management plans to protect international visitors during crises (see box below).

Strategic initiatives to achieve recovery of inbound travel are valued at JPY 51.2 billion. They include the Open the Treasure of Japan! project, which supports tourism stakeholders develop special experiences for visitors, refinement of tourism resources and environment around the country, strategic promotion of Travels to Japan, and development of high value-added tourism destinations for inbound tourism in regional areas.

To encourage the expansion of the domestic market, JPY 21.6 billion was allocated to develop destinations, with a focus on workation promotion, accessible tourism for all, and a second hometown initiative.

Building resilience through crisis planning in Japan

The Japan Tourism Agency has published national guidelines and a manual on preparing tourism crisis management plans to protect international visitors during crises. Many local authorities lack the resources, including budget, staff, and multilingual capabilities, to handle foreign visitors in the event of a crisis. Additionally, few local authorities and tourism-related businesses have disaster regulations, which highlights the need to strengthen skills for responding to foreign tourists in emergencies.

The Guidelines for Preparing Manuals to Address the Needs of Foreign Tourists in the Event of a Crisis provide policies for specific responses by administrative organisations and businesses. Based on these guidelines, a detailed manual for tourism crisis management plans was published, offering key points and summaries for those handling disasters on site. A symposium was also held to promote the initiative, open to tourism stakeholders across all levels of government and members of the private sector.

As part of the APEC Tourism Working Group activities, a Tourism Crisis Management Communication Plan was developed for Asia-Pacific countries. The Plan outlines how to collect information from within an organisation and relevant authorities during a crisis, provide unified information to tourists and the media, facilitate the dissemination of information and promote recovery.

Statistical Profile

Japan: Domestic, inbound and outbound tourism

	2018	2019	2020	2021	2022
TOURISM FLOWS, THOUSAND					
Domestic tourism[1]					
Total domestic trips	561 779	587 103	293 408	268 208	417 854
Overnight visitors (tourists)	291 052	311 624	160 703	141 768	232 467
Same-day visitors (excursionists)	270 727	275 478	132 705	126 440	185 387
Nights in all types of accommodation	443 726	480 265	311 309	313 457	433 956
Hotels and similar establishments	435 959	472 615	307 462	310 784	430 023
Other collective establishments	7 767	7 650	3 847	2 673	3 933
Private accommodation	..	..	..	..	..
Inbound tourism[2]					
Total international arrivals	31 192	31 882	4 116	246	3 832
Overnight visitors (tourists)	..	..	..	..	..
Same-day visitors (excursionists)	..	..	..	..	..
Top markets					
Korea	7 539	5 585	488	19	1 013
Chinese Taipei	4 757	4 891	694	5	331
United States	1 526	1 724	219	20	324
Vietnam	..	..	..	27	284
Hong Kong, China	2 208	2 291	346	1	269
Nights in all types of accommodation	94 275	115 656	20 345	4 317	16 503
Hotels and similar establishments	93 892	115 297	20 100	4 276	16 473
Other collective establishments	383	359	245	41	30
Private accommodation	..	..	..	..	..
Outbound tourism					
Total international departures	18 954	20 081	3 174	512	2 772
Overnight visitors (tourists)	..	..	..	..	..
Same-day visitors (excursionists)	..	..	..	..	..
Top destinations					
..	..	..	..	..	..
..	..	..	..	..	..
..	..	..	..	..	..
..	..	..	..	..	..
..	..	..	..	..	..
TOURISM RECEIPTS AND EXPENDITURE, MILLION JPY					
Inbound tourism					
Total international receipts	4 999 529	5 364 344	1 228 716	587 797	1 444 993
International travel receipts	4 648 362	5 020 374	1 142 541	533 559	1 214 733
International passenger transport receipts	351 168	343 970	86 174	54 237	230 260
Outbound tourism					
Total international expenditure	3 104 607	3 175 483	729 893	360 914	784 009
International travel expenditure	2 232 381	2 318 068	587 350	310 842	590 569
International passenger transport expenditure	872 226	857 416	142 544	50 072	193 439

.. Not available

1. Trips from demand side surveys; Nights from supply side surveys.
2. Arrivals from demand side surveys; Nights from supply side surveys.

Source: OECD Tourism Statistics (Database).

StatLink https://stat.link/0qhtsl

Japan: Enterprises and employment in tourism

	Number of establishments[1]	Number of persons employed				
	2016	2018	2019	2020	2021	2022
Total	..	..	..	..	..	..
Tourism industries	**796 440**	6 450 000	6 640 000	6 310 000	6 010 000	..
Accommodation services for visitors	..	..	..	..	..	..
Hotels and similar establishments	48 963	640 000	670 000	610 000	540 000	..
Food and beverage serving industry	590 847	3 590 000	3 580 000	3 350 000	3 220 000	..
Passenger transport	33 571	920 000	840 000	820 000	810 000	..
Air passenger transport	922	60 000	50 000	50 000	60 000	..
Railways passenger transport	4 277	240 000	240 000	250 000	260 000	..
Road passenger transport	23 028	560 000	490 000	460 000	430 000	..
Water passenger transport	5 344	60 000	60 000	60 000	60 000	..
Passenger transport supporting services	66 772	650 000	680 000	690 000	670 000	..
Transport equipment rental	..	..	..	..	..	..
Travel agencies and other reservation services industry	..	..	..	..	..	..
Cultural industry	..	..	..	..	..	..
Sports and recreation industry	56 287	670 000	870 000	840 000	770 000	..
Retail trade of country-specific tourism characteristic goods	..	..	..	..	..	..
Other country-specific tourism industries	..	..	..	..	..	..
Other industries	..	..	..	..	..	..

.. Not available

1. Data refer to number of enterprises.

Source: OECD Tourism Statistics (Database).

StatLink https://stat.link/y3dsa7

Japan: Internal tourism consumption

Million JPY

	2021		
	Domestic tourism expenditure	Inbound tourism expenditure	Internal tourism consumption
Total	..	..	..
Consumption products	9 268 000	572 000	10 298 000
Tourism characteristic products	5 270 000	410 000	6 137 000
Accommodation services for visitors	1 992 000	160 000	2 609 000
Food and beverage serving services	1 250 000	125 000	1 376 000
Passenger transport services	1 399 000	107 000	1 508 000
Air passenger transport services	450 000	56 000	507 000
Railways passenger transport services	776 000	42 000	818 000
Road passenger transport services	132 000	9 000	141 000
Water passenger transport services	41 000	..	42 000
Passenger transport supporting services	..	..	..
Transport equipment rental services	165 000	6 000	172 000
Travel agencies and other reservation services industry	50 000	2 000	52 000
Cultural services	130 000	3 000	134 000
Sports and recreation services	283 000	5 000	288 000
Country-specific tourism characteristic goods	..	..	..
Country-specific tourism characteristic services	..	..	..
Other consumption products	3 998 000	162 000	4 160 000
Tourism connected products	3 672 000	151 000	3 823 000
Non-tourism related consumption products	326 000	11 000	337 000
Non-consumption products	..	..	..

.. Not available

Source: OECD Tourism Statistics (Database).

StatLink https://stat.link/4pzlqn

Korea

Tourism in the economy and outlook

Tourism in Korea was heavily affected by the pandemic but is showing positive signs of recovery. In 2022, tourism-related businesses employed 198 600 people, representing 0.7% of the total employment (compared to 275 600 in 2019 and the pandemic low of 191 000 jobs in 2020). In 2023, travel exports represented 12.3% of total service exports, above the pandemic low of 9.0% in 2021 and but still below pre-pandemic level of 20% in 2019.

International overnight visitors totalled 3.2 million in 2022. This is showing a strong recovery compared to 967 000 in 2021, but remains 82% below 2019 levels (17.5 million). The three main international source markets were the United States (17%), Japan (9%) and China (7%), whereas traditionally China (34%) and Japan (19%) were the main pre-pandemic international source markets. Korea recorded a stronger 2023, receiving approximately 11.0 million international tourists, equivalent to 63% of 2019 levels.

Domestic tourism in Korea remains an important source of revenue, however, it is increasingly challenged by a strong outbound demand and insufficient local tourism attractions in multiple destinations. In 2022, domestic overnight tourists totalled 116.6 million, which is 28% below 2019 levels, but 33% higher than the pandemic low in 2021.

Korea projects a robust tourism recovery and sustained growth in the next few years and is anticipated to reach pre-pandemic levels of international tourist arrivals by 2025.

Tourism governance

The Ministry of Culture, Sports, and Tourism (MCST) of the Republic of Korea is responsible for shaping and implementing tourism policies. The Ministry has two main tourism directorates and collaborates closely with key entities such as the Korea Tourism Organisation (KTO) and the Korea Culture and Tourism Institute (KCTI) to drive research, formulate policies, and promote Korea as a destination.

The Ministry operates in co-ordination with the National Tourism Strategy Meeting, chaired by the Prime Minister. This strategic platform facilitates the harmonisation of tourism policies across various ministries, government agencies, the tourism industry, and relevant organisations. The inclusion of representatives from the tourism sector and related organisations fosters a collaborative approach, allowing diverse perspectives to shape policy discussions.

At the regional level, local governments, supported by the Ministry, autonomously formulate and execute their tourism policies. This approach emphasises the importance of tailoring strategies to the distinctive characteristics of each region, promoting diverse tourist attractions, and developing essential tourism infrastructure.

The 2023 tourism budget for Korea was KRW 1.2 trillion, distributed across different accounts. The general account comprises a total of KRW 2.4 billion, the special account for balanced development is allocated KRW 170 billion, and the tourism fund receives the majority with KR846.5 billion. These funds are allocated in the form of loans, investments, and subsidies.

Korea: Organisational chart of tourism bodies

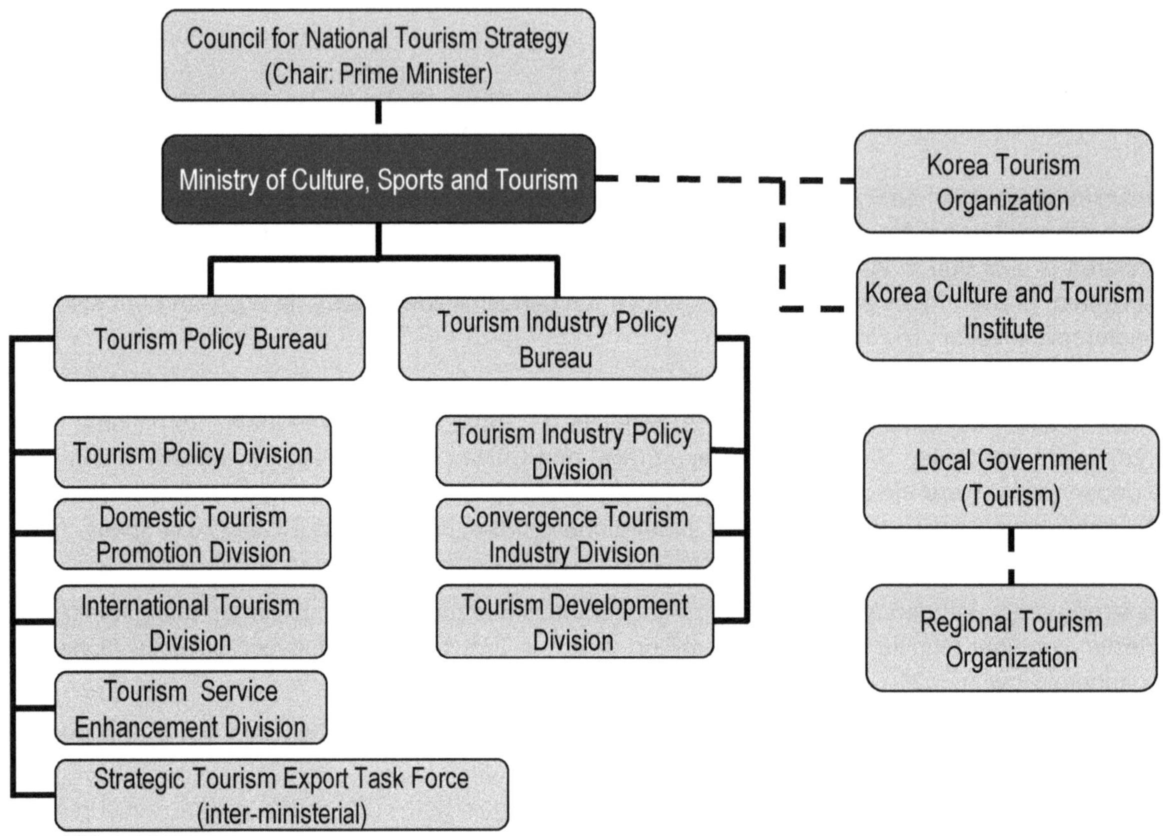

Source: OECD, adapted from the Ministry of Culture, Sports and Tourism, 2024.

Tourism policies and programmes

The Tourism Promotion Master Plan 2023-27 drives tourism policies and programmes in Korea. Its objective is to position the country as an attractive destination with a strong emphasis on K-Culture. The strategy underscores four main pillars to enhance Korea's appeal as a global tourism destination:

- Creating an attractive destination for international visitors.
- Innovating the tourism industry together with local communities.
- Domestic tourism growing hand in hand with the people.
- Achieving an era of local tourism where visitors stay longer and visit more often.

The Tourism Promotion Master Plan lays a foundation for a dynamic and resilient tourism sector, aligned with the evolving needs of visitors and the industry itself. The Master Plan sets out clear targets for the tourism sector to be achieved by 2027, including reaching 30 million international arrivals, USD 30 billion in tourism revenue, 15 days of domestic travel for Koreans and KRW 50 trillion in spending by domestic tourists.

The Master Plan focuses on four key strategies:

- Promoting the charms of K-tourism to attract diverse markets from around the world.
- Fostering innovation in the tourism sector by easing regulations and laying the foundations to lead the industry into the future.
- Building a sustainable tourism ecosystem that encourages domestic tourism.
- Developing tourism models that incentivise longer stays.

To support the implementation of the Master Plan and to meet its objectives, Korea is implementing key tourism initiatives on digital transformation, venture development and local tourism.

Korea has initiated a comprehensive digital transformation programme for tourism businesses to support the sector remain competitive in a digital world. The Smart Meetings, Incentives, Conferences and Exhibitions Industry (MICE) Activation programme implemented by the Korean MICE bureau under the Korean Tourism Organisation focuses on strengthening SMEs in the MICE industry by connecting them with digital experts. In 2023, KRW 6.34 billion in vouchers were awarded to SMEs enrolled in the programme. Additionally, the Korea Tourism Data Lab platform provides since 2021 access to private data, promoting granular analysis for customised tourism products and addressing issues like overcrowding. In 2023, KRW 12.600 million were allocated by the government.

On tourism venture development, Korea launched the Innovation Voucher in 2020 to help tourism businesses create digital and virtual offerings for visitors. The programme financially supports startups with innovative ideas for digitalisation and aims to create additional digital tourism jobs. In 2023, 140 companies were supported at different stages, including on funding, education, consulting, and promotion. In addition, the Tourism Business Connection Week facilitated discussions between investors and startups, fostering collaboration and attracting investments. In 2023, a total of KRW 5.94 billion in vouchers was awarded. In 2020, Korea launched the International Tourism City programme, which aims to promote destinations outside Seoul to international tourists, given that 80% do not venture outside the capital during their stays. Four destinations were labelled Regional Tourism Hub Cities and given a unique local tourism brand. To stimulate domestic tourism and tourism dispersion, Korea launched the Digital Tourism Residency Card project. After a successful trial in 2022, the project is expanding in 2024. This innovative card, which can be acquired online, encourages longer stays in areas facing population decline to foster economic growth. (see box below).

A Digital Tourism Card to stimulate regional development in Korea

Korea has launched the Digital Tourism Residency Card to attract people to regions facing population decline and foster economic growth. The country has been experiencing natural population declines, affecting 66% of cities and counties. This has a negative impact on local communities, however, tourism could offer an opportunity to revitalise those areas.

The initiative aims to make people more interested in, and connected to, depopulated areas of Korea through tourism. The goal is to encourage tourists to visit these regions more often and stay longer. Tourists can apply for an 'honorary resident card' through websites and mobile apps. With a QR code, they can enjoy discounts on accommodations, meals, experiences, and more in tourist areas. The card was initially reserved to Korean residents but was expanded to include international tourists during a one-year trial in 2024. After a successful trial in 2022, the ambition is to expand the card to 40 areas in 2024. In 2022, 41 467 cards were issued and two areas benefited from the programme. This increased to 399 071 cards to 15 areas in 2023.

Statistical Profile

Korea: Domestic, inbound and outbound tourism

	2018	2019	2020	2021	2022
TOURISM FLOWS, THOUSAND					
Domestic tourism					
Total domestic trips	311 153 |	344 750	225 199	245 127	283 722
Overnight visitors (tourists)	163 204 |	162 376	88 450	87 785	116 589
Same-day visitors (excursionists)	147 949 |	182 374	136 749	157 342	167 133
Nights in all types of accommodation	408 941 |	403 336	211 127	207 379	276 770
Hotels and similar establishments	12 845	13 324	9 630	15 224	18 171
Other collective establishments	..	..	..	..	..
Private accommodation	..	..	..	..	..
Inbound tourism					
Total international arrivals	15 347	17 503	2 519	967	3 198
Overnight visitors (tourists)	..	..	..	..	..
Same-day visitors (excursionists)	..	..	..	..	..
Top markets					
China (People's Republic of)	4 790	6 023	686	170	227
Japan	2 949	3 272	431	15	297
Chinese Taipei	1 115	1 260	167	4	73
United States	968	1 044	220	204	544
Hong Kong (China)	684	695	89	1	61
Nights in all types of accommodation	10 726	6 802	1 378	1 641	4 009
Hotels and similar establishments	..	..	..	..	..
Other collective establishments	..	..	..	..	..
Private accommodation	..	..	..	..	..
Outbound tourism					
Total international departures	28 696	28 714	4 276	1 223	6 554
Overnight visitors (tourists)	..	..	..	..	..
Same-day visitors (excursionists)	..	..	..	..	..
Top destinations					
..	..	..	..	..	..
..	..	..	..	..	..
..	..	..	..	..	..
..	..	..	..	..	..
..	..	..	..	..	..
TOURISM RECEIPTS AND EXPENDITURE, MILLION USD					
Inbound tourism					
Total international receipts	23 104	25 457	11 524	11 432	14 967
International travel receipts	18 567	20 867	10 276	10 804	12 462
International passenger transport receipts	4 537	4 589	1 248	628	2 505
Outbound tourism					
Total international expenditure	38 022	35 340	16 647	18 343	22 267
International travel expenditure	35 133	32 739	16 092	17 829	20 831
International passenger transport expenditure	2 889	2 600	555	514	1 436

.. Not available; | Break in series
Source: OECD Tourism Statistics (Database).

StatLink https://stat.link/l8ipcb

Korea: Enterprises and employment in tourism

	Number of establishments	Number of persons employed[1]				
	2021	2018	2019	2020	2021	2022
Total	..	..	..	..	..	..
Tourism industries	33 553	267 561	275 619	191 005 p|	195 280	198 626
Accommodation services for visitors	2 372	69 926	70 658	49 930	56 320	59 154
Hotels and similar establishments	..	..	..	..	..	..
Food and beverage serving industry	3 337	32 785	35 644	26 446	26 812	27 995
Passenger transport	..	..	..	..	..	..
Air passenger transport	..	..	..	..	..	..
Railways passenger transport	..	..	..	..	..	..
Road passenger transport	..	..	..	..	..	..
Water passenger transport	..	..	..	..	..	..
Passenger transport supporting services	..	..	..	..	..	..
Transport equipment rental	..	..	..	..	..	..
Travel agencies and other reservation services industry	17 433	99 077	103 311	61 784	56 009	50 493
Cultural industry	..	..	..	..	..	..
Sports and recreation industry	9 210	56 673	55 771	44 462	47 727.	51 952
Retail trade of country-specific tourism characteristic goods	..	..	..	..	..	..
Other country-specific tourism industries	1 201	9 100	10 235	8 383	8 413	9 031
Other industries	..	..	..	..	..	..

.. Not available; p Provisional data; | Break in series
1. Data refer to number of employees.
Source: OECD Tourism Statistics (Database).

StatLink https://stat.link/64exob

Korea: Internal tourism consumption
Million KRW

	2019 p		
	Domestic tourism expenditure	Inbound tourism expenditure	Internal tourism consumption
Total	57 088 564	30 467 398	96 139 553
Consumption products	56 611 040	30 369 552	95 564 182
Tourism characteristic products	55 129 470	26 652 595	89 138 991
Accommodation services for visitors	6 152 958	4 917 722	11 100 697
Food and beverage serving services	17 047 188	3 909 557	20 956 745
Passenger transport services	7 846 449	7 070 601	14 917 050
Air passenger transport services	5 785 402	5 320 402	11 105 804
Railways passenger transport services	795 512	697 066	1 492 578
Road passenger transport services	1 069 258	1 025 983	2 095 241
Water passenger transport services	196 277	27 150	223 427
Passenger transport supporting services	0	0	0
Transport equipment rental services	9 857 849	624 362	10 482 211
Travel agencies and other reservation services industry	1 269 650	6 336	1 275 986
Cultural services	1 503 970	226 659	1 730 629
Sports and recreation services	995 422	1 842 295	2 843 333
Country-specific tourism characteristic goods	10 455 985	7 649 733	25 427 011
Country-specific tourism characteristic services	0	405 331	405 331
Other consumption products	1 481 570	3 716 957	6 425 191
Tourism connected products	327 000	2 503 795	4 057 459
Non-tourism related consumption products	1 154 570	1 213 162	2 367 732
Non-consumption products	477 524	97 846	575 370

.. Not available; p Provisional data
Source: OECD Tourism Statistics (Database).

StatLink https://stat.link/2gwkhr

Latvia

Tourism in the economy and outlook

Tourism is a driver of the Latvian economy, but recent crises, including the proximity of Russia's war of aggression against Ukraine, the rise in consumer prices, and strong seasonality, have resulted in a slow post-pandemic recovery.

2022 was a year of growth and renewal for the Latvian tourism industry. Employment in tourism-related sectors represented 7.2% of the total workforce, equivalent to 63 400 jobs in 2022, down 16.1% from 75 600 jobs in 2019. Travel exports represented 14.5% of total service exports (EUR 1.1 billion) in 2022, still below the pre-pandemic share of 16.2%. However, an absolute increase in nominal terms was recorded, surpassing pre-pandemic levels, and for the first time, travel exports exceeded EUR 1 billion.

In 2023, Latvia recorded 2.4 million tourists in commercial accommodation, a 12.1% increase on 2022, but still 14.4% below 2019 levels, when 2.85 million tourists stayed in official establishments. Inbound tourism has taken longer to recover: 1.4 million inbound tourists stayed in commercial accommodation establishments in 2023. This represents a 22% increase on 2022, but is still 29% below 2019. Total nights spent by inbound tourists has also grown 22% compared to 2022, totalling 2.6 million nights at commercial accommodation establishments in 2023, for an average of 1.9 nights per tourist. The top international markets in 2023 were Germany, the Baltic States (Lithuania and Estonia), Nordic countries (Sweden, Finland and Norway). In the same year, the number of visitors from neighbouring countries surpassed pre-pandemic levels – Lithuania had a 23% increase compared to 2019, and Estonia, a 6.1% increase.

In contrast, domestic tourism has fully recovered in Latvia. In 2023, the country recorded 2.9 million domestic overnight trips, which is 16.2% above pre-pandemic levels, and significantly higher than the pandemic low of 1.4 million trips in 2020.

Tourism governance

The Ministry of Economics is responsible for developing national tourism policy and organising and co-ordinating its implementation. The Ministry supervises the Investment and Development Agency of Latvia, which is responsible for implementing tourism policy and promoting Latvia domestically and abroad.

To promote the development of the tourism sector, the Ministry of Economics and the Investment and Development Agency of Latvia co-operate with several organisations through the Latvian Tourism Consultative Council. The Council is composed of members from the public and private sector, including representatives from several ministries and non-governmental organisations related to tourism.

Tourism development strategies and plans are also undertaken at regional and local levels, by planning regions or regional tourism associations, as well as local municipalities. Tourism development clusters also have specific development plans.

The Investment and Development Agency of Latvia was also responsible for implementing the promotion of international competitiveness programme (until 2023), co-financed by the European Regional

Development Fund, which supports tourism entrepreneurs in various marketing activities. In 2023, the total budget for tourism marketing was EUR 3.86 million from the European Regional Development Fund and EUR 750 000 from the state budget, including administrative costs. In 2024, EUR 3.72 million have been allocated specifically for marketing activities, including administrative costs from the state budget. In addition, various support programmes are available for the representatives of the industry, such as the support for the development of new tourism products, which runs until end 2029 with a total funding of EUR 6.4 million.

Latvia: Organisational chart of tourism bodies

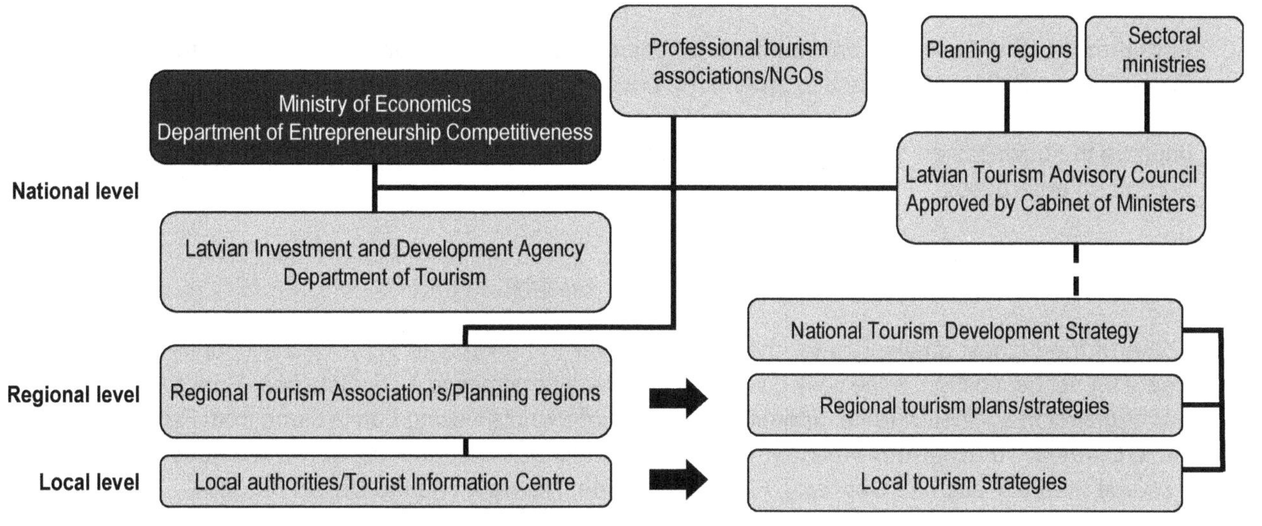

Source: OECD, adapted from the Ministry of Economics, 2024.

Tourism policies and programmes

Multiple national plans drive tourism policy development in Latvia. This includes the National Development Plan 2021-27 (NDP2027), the National Industrial Policy Guidelines 2021-27, the Latvian Tourism and Event Industry Export Promotion Strategy 2023-27 and the Latvian Tourism Marketing Strategy 2021-27.

The National Development Plan 2021-27 sets tourism development as a priority for Latvia's economy. The National Industrial Policy Guidelines for 2021-27 aim to strengthen the export capacity of the Latvian tourism sector, emphasising the need to create new internationally competitive tourism products to increase competitiveness and quality.

The Latvian Tourism and Event Industry Export Promotion Strategy 2023-27 aims to increase Latvia's tourism exports to EUR 1.5 billion in 2027. Latvia also uses funding from the EU to enhance the export capacity of the tourism sector and increase the country's competitiveness abroad. Currently, the Ministry has developed two action plans for the export promotion strategy of the tourism and event industry:

- Ensuring the international recognition of Latvian tourism (see box below).
- Business and event tourism export promotion.

Several policies have been identified to help implement plans and meet targets. These include developing products and destinations through the creation of innovative tourism offerings, focusing on increasing the added value of offerings, creating co-operation opportunities for tourism providers and strengthening skills of entrepreneurs in the sector.

Effective marketing activities are also being created to promote Latvia as a tourism destination, showcasing the uniqueness of Latvian tourism offerings. The Latvian Tourism Marketing Strategy 2021-27 stipulates that promotion efforts should focus on business, health, cultural and nature tourism products. Tourism marketing actions include participating in tourism roadshows abroad, developing advertising campaigns for international target markets, organising visits for journalists and social media content creators, as well as tourism operators and business event organisers, and conducting tourism market research.

To better understand tourist behaviour and expenditure, Latvia has transitioned from border surveys to foreign payment card data collected by the Bank of Latvia. This shift provides more precise analyses, allowing the discovery and investment in new niches and the expansion of tourism offerings to a broader market.

Furthermore, the business environment is being improved through amendments to the regulatory framework. In 2024, Latvia plans to amend the Law on Tourism, the system of provision and monitoring of complex tourism services, the regulation of short-term rental accommodation, and other objectives to improve the business environment, including the implementation of measures to reduce the administrative burden on enterprises.

Actions to improve Latvia's image as a tourism destination in times of geopolitical unrest

One of the biggest challenges for the tourism sector in Latvia is to improve the country's image as a safe tourist destination, especially due to the country's proximity to a conflict zone. Prior to Russia's war of aggression against Ukraine, approximately 30% of tourists visiting Latvia came from Russia, Belarus, and Ukraine. To achieve pre-pandemic levels in terms of tourist arrivals, Latvia will need to target new source markets, such as Germany, Finland, Sweden, Norway, and the United Kingdom.

To attract these markets, Latvia aims to improve tourist information, promote Latvia as a safe destination and enhance competitiveness and attractiveness. This includes prioritising the development and digitalisation of the sector to offer high quality services at a competitive price. In 2023, the Latvian Tourism and Events Export Promotion Strategy for 2023-27 was developed in collaboration with the Latvian Tourism Advisory Council.

The Strategy is complemented by the Latvian Tourism Marketing Strategy for 2021-27, which co-ordinates foreign tourism marketing activities. The Strategy was developed within the Marketing and Product Development Subgroup of the Latvian Tourism Advisory Council with extensive consultation with relevant stakeholders or their representatives.

Latvia also looks at targeting food tourism. In 2023, Michelin launched its first guide of Latvia, including over 20 restaurant recommendations.

Statistical Profile

Latvia: Domestic, inbound and outbound tourism

	2018	2019	2020	2021	2022
TOURISM FLOWS, THOUSAND					
Domestic tourism					
Total domestic trips	10 948	10 416	6 153	8 282	9 296
Overnight visitors (tourists)	2 584	2 501	1 367	2 392	2 828
Same-day visitors (excursionists)	8 365	7 915	4 786	5 890	6 468
Nights in all types of accommodation	5 514	5 792	4 083	6 604	7 198
Hotels and similar establishments	478	538	477	759	752
Other collective establishments	508	676	542	856	823
Private accommodation	4 528	4 577	3 065	4 989	5 622
Inbound tourism					
Total international arrivals	7 775	8 342	3 204	1 937	..
Overnight visitors (tourists)	1 946	1 935	636	478	..
Same-day visitors (excursionists)	5 829	6 408	2 568	1 459	..
Top markets					
Lithuania	275	309	205	66	..
Germany	260	245	44	48	..
Russian Federation	244	298	85	76	..
Estonia	176	210	90	45	..
Sweden	91	40	13	13	..
Nights in all types of accommodation	7 864	8 266	2 872	2 847	..
Hotels and similar establishments	3 049	3 549	757	390	..
Other collective establishments	395	320	424	596	..
Private accommodation	4 419	4 397	1 691	1 861	..
Outbound tourism					
Total international departures	2 176	2 384	689	629	1 729
Overnight visitors (tourists)	1 368	1 480	432	512	1 303
Same-day visitors (excursionists)	807	904	258	117	426
Top destinations					
Estonia	206	161	90	83	236
Lithuania	157	166	54	31	154
Russia	117	102	..	..	..
Sweden	100	100	..	30	31
Germany	80	98	48	27	37
TOURISM RECEIPTS AND EXPENDITURE, MILLION EUR					
Inbound tourism					
Total international receipts	1 381	1 412	825	848	1 683
International travel receipts	896	907	698	634	1 050
International passenger transport receipts	485	505	127	214	633
Outbound tourism					
Total international expenditure	857	871	554	712	1 148
International travel expenditure	660	669	486	625	960
International passenger transport expenditure	197	202	68	87	188

.. Not available
Source: OECD Tourism Statistics (Database).

StatLink https://stat.link/2ti08g

Latvia: Enterprises and employment in tourism

	Number of establishments	Number of persons employed				
	2022	2018	2019	2020	2021	2022
Total	..	..	..	..	..	..
Tourism industries	16 427	77 100	75 600	68 300	61 200	63 400
Accommodation services for visitors	1 584	5 600	6 600	6 300	4 600	4 800
Hotels and similar establishments	494	4 500	5 400	5 000	3 000	3 700
Food and beverage serving industry	4 639	26 700	25 500	23 300	21 200	21 900
Passenger transport	1 801	16 800	13 600	11 300	12 000	11 900
Air passenger transport	19	2 200 e	..	..	..	..
Railways passenger transport	41	2 700	2 100	..	..	..
Road passenger transport	1 709	10 900	9 500	8 000	8 200	7 800
Water passenger transport	32	..	..	..	..	..
Passenger transport supporting services	..	..	..	..	..	..
Transport equipment rental	895	..	..	..	..	..
Travel agencies and other reservation services industry	808	2 500	2 000	2 100	..	..
Cultural industry	2 449	11 500	12 600	13 000	11 600	12 500
Sports and recreation industry	4 251	13 700	15 000	11 600	9 900	9 400
Retail trade of country-specific tourism characteristic goods	..	..	..	..	..	..
Other country-specific tourism industries	..	..	..	..	..	..
Other industries	..	..	..	..	..	..

.. Not available; e Estimated value
Source: OECD Tourism Statistics (Database).

StatLink https://stat.link/sakb7z

Lithuania

Tourism in the economy and outlook

Lithuania has faced numerous challenges, including Russia's war of aggression against Ukraine, which has directly impacted the destination's resilience and safety image. In 2022 tourism directly generated EUR 1.3 billion, or 2.2% of the country's GVA. This is an increase compared to the pandemic low of 1.7% in 2020, but below the pre-pandemic level of 2.9%. In 2022, the tourism sector accounted for 47 100 jobs, representing 4.5% of total employment in the country. Travel exports reached EUR 1.7 billion, or 8.5% of total service exports in 2023 and has surpassed travel export in 2019 by 25%.

Lithuania recorded 1.4 million tourist arrivals at accommodation establishments in 2023, representing a growth of 19% compared to 2022, or 71% of the level in 2019. At the same time Lithuania's domestic market saw strong growth in 2023 with 2.6 million domestic overnight trips at, an increase of 25% compared to 2019. Lithuania is now focused on strengthening domestic tourism by increasing the length of stay.

The fall-out from Russia's war of aggression against Ukraine continues to impact Lithuania. The country expects to reach 2019 levels by 2025.

Tourism governance

Responsibility for tourism in Lithuania is spread across three public bodies. The Ministry of the Economy and Innovation is responsible for tourism policy and international co-operation. Lithuania Travel, a public company established in 2019, conducts marketing and tourism promotion actions for international and domestic markets. Its main goal is to promote Lithuania as a tourism destination, developing inbound and local tourism in the country. The State Consumer Rights Protection Authority is responsible for the supervision of tourism service providers.

The Tourism Council, an advisory body of the Ministry of Economy, was renewed in 2023. Its members include tourism-related ministries and tourism business associations, chaired by the Vice-Minister of the Economy and Innovation. At local level, municipalities and Local Tourism Information Centres are responsible for tourism. The Chamber for Tourism of the Republic of Lithuania is the main tourism business organisation in the country. The Chamber represents 11 leading tourism business associations.

The State budget for tourism in 2023 was EUR 9 million. Lithuania Travel's budget increased to EUR 5.8 million from EUR 2.9 million in 2022.

Lithuania: Organisational chart of tourism bodies

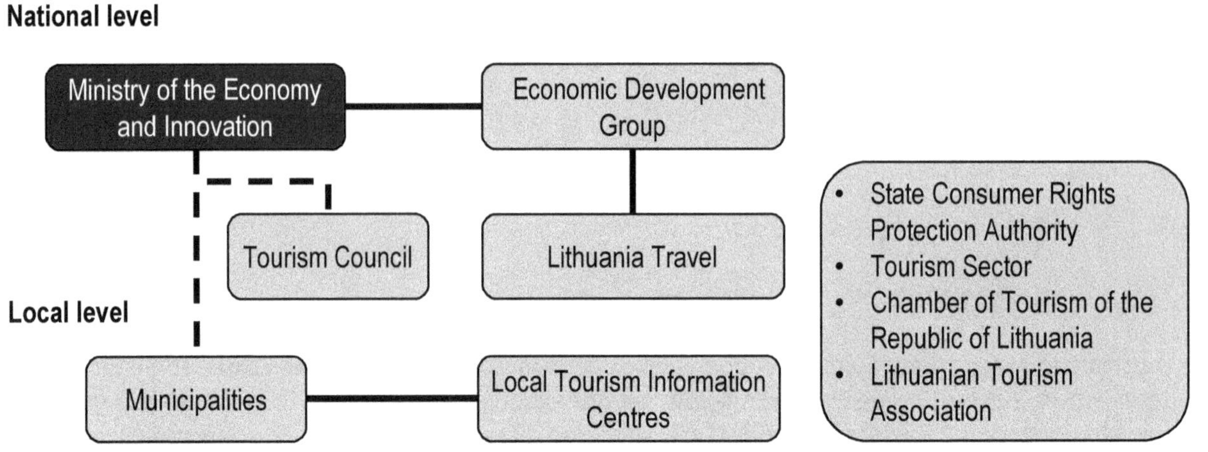

Source: OECD, adapted from the Ministry of the Economy and Innovation, 2023.

Tourism policies and programmes

Lithuania is strengthening its policies at national and regional levels to maintain its vigour and continue to drive tourism development. This is despite the ongoing impacts of the COVID-19 pandemic, Russia's war of aggression against Ukraine, with a spillover effect to most neighbouring tourism markets, and the uncertain global economic situation.

In June 2024, Lithuania adopted a National Tourism Pathway 2030, a collaborative effort between the public and private sector to develop Lithuania's tourism economy until 2030. The aim is to increase the tourism sector's competitiveness and pursue the objectives set out in the National Progress Plan. The main goals are to accelerate the transformation of the tourism sector and develop tourism infrastructure and marketing tools. The Pathway also aims to address issues related to connectivity and accessibility, the country's image as a tourist destination, skills for the tourism workforce, tourism infrastructure investment and the quality of tourism services through innovation and digitalisation.

The National Tourism Information System aims to better connect tourists and service providers in a one-stop shop as well as collect data for public and private sector use. This system will be automated, gathering data from natural objects, landmarks, cultural heritage sites and tourism services and will incorporate mobile phone data. The information will be visible and accessible on the Lithuania travel website, allowing users to create personal touristic routes or making travel packages for tour operators. By reducing the administrative burden on service providers, the website aims to promote a more transparent hospitality sector that employs data driven decision making to produce more sustainable tourism services in regions and prolong tourist stays. Ultimately this will increase tourism's contribution to the Lithuanian economy.

Lithuania is also expanding the Tourism Data Dashboard to monitor the tourism sector. The Dashboard shows publicly available and systematised accommodation, employment and balance of payments data as well as import and export data provided by Statistics Lithuania, linked to the Travel Tech Sandbox.

The Dashboard also features statistical indicators describing the mobility patterns of foreign travellers visiting Lithuania, based on passive mobile positioning data. The indicators are calculated and analysed to improve the travel experience of tourists, to promote investments in local businesses creating new tourism services or products as well as to improve the current tourism infrastructure, and to optimise the efficiency of Lithuania Travel's operations. Mobile data can cover all foreign visitors, not just those using tourist accommodation, which provides a comprehensive overview for decision-makers. Interpreting this data requires basic knowledge of mobile data principles and comes with challenges such as accuracy issues, limited granularity, and high costs. The trial data was based on one mobile network operator's data from the period of May to October 2021 and April to August 2022. The next stage was to provide a continuous full-year data timeline from September 2022 to August 2023. The project is carried out by the national tourism development agency Lithuania Travel in collaboration with multiple telephone companies.

Lithuania has also passed law amendments to better support the tourism sector. These include the Law on Sustainable Resorts and Resort Territories (see box below) and the Law on State Debt to help tourism providers access and afford insurance. The amendments to this law stipulate that the guarantor institution may provide guarantees to cover part of the insurance or guarantee benefit paid by the insurance company under a suretyship insurance contract or by a financial institution under a granted financial guarantee to the tour operator established in the Republic of Lithuania.

Tools are also being developed to help the tourism sector. The E-business model tool will support tourism providers with e-business solutions, while the Retraining of Enterprise Workers tool and the Innovative Checks tool will finance the purchase of publishing, voice-reading, translation, photography, filming, design and communication services for tourism companies.

Lithuania's Law on the sustainable development of resorts and resort areas

In 2023, Lithuania adopted the Law on the Sustainable Development of Resorts and Resort Territories underlining the importance of health and wellness for the country's tourism development and the need to support their green transition.

The new law aims to provide the legal framework and the economic conditions necessary to ensure the sustainability of resorts and spa areas in the long-term. This includes the responsible use of natural resources, mainly water springs, and conditions to reduce resort areas strong seasonality, fostering domestic tourism year-round. Lithuania currently has four resorts and five resort territories that have been designated under the law. There is a possibility to apply for the status of the resort or resort territory.

On health tourism, Lithuania also works collaboratively with European Health Insurance Funds (2011/24/ EU on patients' rights in cross-border healthcare). Further, in September 2024 Lithuania will host the ESPA Annual Congress, a multi-dimensional event for all business partners of the SPA industry. The Annual Congress includes B2B meetings, the ESPA Innovation Awards, strategic thinking and knowledge sharing about the SPA industry and resorts of Europe.

Statistical Profile

Lithuania: Domestic, inbound and outbound tourism

	2018	2019	2020	2021	2022
TOURISM FLOWS, THOUSAND					
Domestic tourism[1]					
Total domestic trips	14 678	14 785	11 389	11 593	12 842
Overnight visitors (tourists)	2 641	2 827	2 438	3 090	3 595
Same-day visitors (excursionists)	12 037	11 958	8 951	8 503	9 247
Nights in all types of accommodation	4 355	4 804	3 812	4 360	5 459
Hotels and similar establishments	4 285	4 717	3 758	4 239	5 367
Other collective establishments	70	87	55	121	92
Private accommodation	..	..	..	..	..
Inbound tourism[2]					
Total international arrivals	6 115	6 150	2 284	2 096	4 725
Overnight visitors (tourists)	2 825	2 875	937	948	2 169
Same-day visitors (excursionists)	3 291	3 275	1 348	1 148	2 556
Top markets					
Germany	242	243	113	81	174
Belarus	443	424	103	67	163
Poland	250	248	89	108	282
Latvia	362	357	86	180	409
Estonia	83	89	77	56	152
Nights in all types of accommodation	3 737	4 143	1 120	1 183	2 614
Hotels and similar establishments	3 695	4 091	1 104	1 167	2 591
Other collective establishments	42	51	16	15	24
Private accommodation	..	..	..	..	..
Outbound tourism					
Total international departures	4 703	4 882	1 643	1 743	3 999
Overnight visitors (tourists)	2 244	2 347	682	830	1 919
Same-day visitors (excursionists)	2 458	2 534	961	913	2 079
Top destinations					
Latvia	250	260	118	111	179
Poland	169	178	61	89	181
Germany	132	146	58	54	121
United Kingdom	215	217	57	45	144
Türkiye	150	166	3	91	195
TOURISM RECEIPTS AND EXPENDITURE, MILLION EUR					
Inbound tourism					
Total international receipts	1 503	1 442	581	573	1 278
International travel receipts	1 274	1 333	507	499	1 127
International passenger transport receipts	229	109	74	74	151
Outbound tourism					
Total international expenditure	1 361	1 420	523	573	1 342
International travel expenditure	1 186	1 241	475	491	1 177
International passenger transport expenditure	175	180	48	83	165

.. Not available

1. Trips from demand side surveys; Nights from supply side surveys.
2. Arrivals from demand side surveys; Nights from supply side surveys.

Source: OECD Tourism Statistics (Database).

StatLink https://stat.link/d41kwz

Lithuania: Enterprises and employment in tourism

	Number of establishments[2]	Number of persons employed				
	2021	2018	2019	2020	2021 p	2022
Total	..	..	..	..	..	..
Tourism industries	24 881	49 090	51 388	44 356	45 471	..
Accommodation services for visitors[1]	4 361	14 856	14 889	13 187	12 943	..
Hotels and similar establishments	630	14 856	14 889	13 187	12 943	..
Food and beverage serving industry	4 130	14 785	15 660	15 192	16 350	..
Passenger transport	11 023	8 548	7 883	7 042	6 362	..
Air passenger transport	198	943	1 042	791	567	..
Railways passenger transport	1	185	96	19	51	..
Road passenger transport	10 779	7 405	6 738	6 227	5 703	..
Water passenger transport	45	15	7	5	41	..
Passenger transport supporting services	..	638	840	364	401	..
Transport equipment rental	1 135	525	673	626	815	..
Travel agencies and other reservation services industry	1 032	3 212	4 628	2 801	2 484	..
Cultural industry	1 107	3 709	4 255	3 154	3 436	..
Sports and recreation industry	2 093	2 816	2 560	1 990	2 680	..
Retail trade of country-specific tourism characteristic goods	..	..	..	..	..	..
Other country-specific tourism industries	..	..	..	..	..	..
Other industries	..	..	..	..	..	..

.. Not available; p Provisional data
1. Data for accommodation service for visitors refer to number of establishments.
2. Data refer to number of enterprises.
Source: OECD Tourism Statistics (Database).

StatLink https://stat.link/u0vmgy

Lithuania: Internal tourism consumption
Million EUR

	2021		
	Domestic tourism expenditure	Inbound tourism expenditure	Internal tourism consumption
Total	..	..	..
Consumption products	1 036	798	1 834
Tourism characteristic products	571	496	1 067
Accommodation services for visitors	157	68	225
Food and beverage serving services	131	274	405
Passenger transport services	118	39	158
Air passenger transport services	68	29	97
Railways passenger transport services	13	0	13
Road passenger transport services	35	10	45
Water passenger transport services	2	1	3
Passenger transport supporting services	26	16	42
Transport equipment rental services	96	64	160
Travel agencies and other reservation services industry	29	1	31
Cultural services	7	22	29
Sports and recreation services	7	12	18
Country-specific tourism characteristic goods	..	..	..
Country-specific tourism characteristic services	..	..	..
Other consumption products	465	302	767
Tourism connected products	..	..	..
Non-tourism related consumption products	..	..	..
Non-consumption products	..	..	..

.. Not available
Source: OECD Tourism Statistics (Database).

StatLink https://stat.link/yvfxtb

Luxembourg

Tourism in the economy and outlook

Tourism provides economic benefits to the Luxembourg economy. In 2021, tourism directly generated EUR 548 million or 0.8% of Luxembourg's total GDP, down from 1.2% of GDP in 2019. Tourism provided 38 000 direct jobs in 2021, or 7.9% of total employment, which is below the 8.4% of the workforce in 2019. Travel exports represented 3.7% of total service exports (EUR 5.1 billion) in 2022, down from 4.6% in 2019.

In 2022, Luxembourg returned to 97% of pre-pandemic levels in terms of inbound tourism, with 1.0 million international tourists staying in registered tourism accommodation. European tourists are the driving force of inbound tourism in Luxembourg, representing 70% of international visitors. The three main international markets in 2022 were the Netherlands (22%), Belgium (18%) and Germany (17%).

Luxembourg has witnessed an increase in domestic tourism during and after the pandemic. In 2022, 155 000 domestic tourist trips were recorded, 13.2% more than in 2021, and 25% more than in 2019.

Tourism governance

Tourism policy in Luxembourg is the responsibility of the Ministry of the Economy, SMEs, Energy and Tourism. The General Directorate of Tourism is responsible for regulations, and awards grants to associations that aim to improve tourism products and the quality of residents' lives. The General Directorate of Tourism also implements policies to optimise the national tourism offer, through developing tourism labels, providing promotional opportunities and maintaining close relationships with international partners.

Luxembourg for Tourism is responsible for tourism marketing and for promoting Luxembourg as a destination. The organisation is largely financed by the state with support from regional tourist offices, professional associations and private actors.

Regional tourist offices are members of Luxembourg for Tourism and are represented at the national level. The regional tourist offices have the mission of co-ordinating local stakeholders and developing the regional tourism offer. The capital of Luxembourg City has its own tourist structure, the Luxembourg City Tourist Office. The Luxembourg Convention Bureau is an economic interest group, which is the dedicated body for developing the MICE sector.

In 2023, the total budget allocated for tourism in Luxembourg was EUR 31.8 million, which includes EUR 3 million for regional DMO's and EUR 6 million for Luxembourg for Tourism.

Luxembourg: Organisational chart of tourism bodies

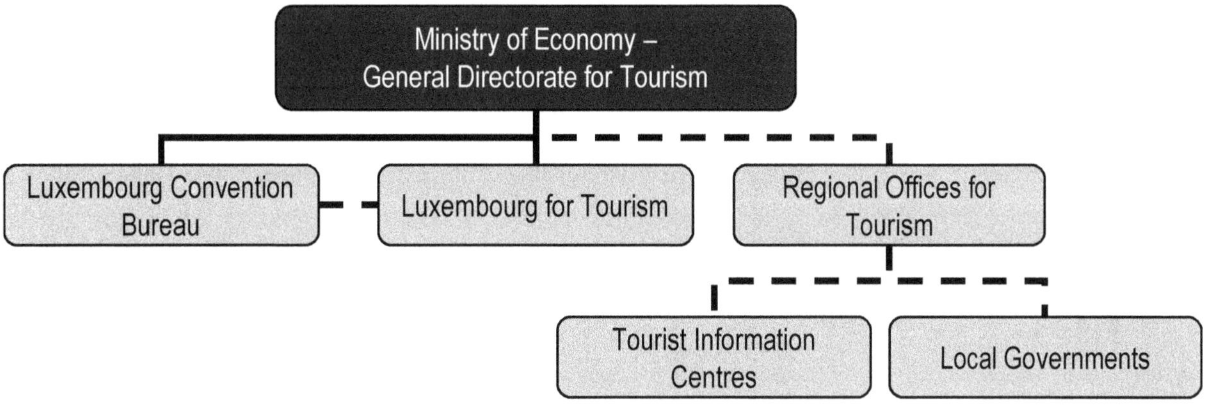

Source: OECD, adapted from the Ministry of Economy, 2024.

Tourism policies and programmes

In 2022, Luxembourg developed a new tourism strategy named People, Regions, and Economy to guide tourism stakeholders in their decision-making. The long-term Strategy is intended to provide enduring guidance. It focuses on improving the quality of life for residents, ensuring visitor satisfaction and strengthening the tourism economy. To promote tourism in line with these objectives, the new Strategy has defined six central areas of action:

- A modern tourism offer rich in experiences: adapting the existing tourism offer to current needs, particularly in outdoor, gastronomy and cultural tourism.
- Attractive and resilient tourism businesses: encouraging investment and improving the attractiveness of the sector for qualified staff.
- A sustainable and accessible, quality of stay for all: considering the ecological, economic, social and cultural dimensions of sustainability in the tourism offer, which will improve the quality of life of tourists, residents and cross-border commuters.
- Inclusive and user-oriented digitalisation: continuing to promote existing digitalisation initiatives. Digitalisation is seen as a basic requirement for a modern tourism offer in Luxembourg.
- Collaboration based on trust and strong networks: establishing close co-operation between stakeholders in the tourism sector, to encourage constructive exchange while involving the public.
- Targeted implementation: monitoring the implementation of strategic objectives. Luxemburg for Tourism collects a variety of statistical data from different sources and performs market surveys on a range of topics, such as customer satisfaction. The data collection process is continually updated and improved and serves as the basis for assessing the success of the strategy implementation. The aim is to collect the most important tourism data on an ongoing basis.

Luxembourg also launched the Business Events 2030 strategy in 2023. This initiative is targeted at the professional events segment (including conferences, congresses, conventions, exhibitions, trade fairs, corporate events, incentives and special events) which is an important sub-sector for tourism and where Luxembourg sees significant development potential. The Strategy was developed in close consultation with local and international representatives of the business events sector. It identifies new opportunities to help stakeholders make the right choices when it comes to investing, organising and adapting their services to new trends.

Luxembourg has launched several initiatives to enhance its tourism sector, in line with the new tourism strategy. A national campaign launched in 2021, that brings together events and activities, which give visibility and showcase the wealth and diversity of tourist assets in Luxembourg, across all regions (see box below). The Velosummer programme is the result of a joint effort by the General Directorate of Tourism and the Ministry of Mobility and Public Works. During the event, launched in 2020, over 500km of roads are closed to motorised traffic in August, allowing cyclists to enjoy traffic-free routes and encouraging active tourism in the country. A learning platform is being established to centralise professional training related to the tourism sector and to enhance the value of tourism-related jobs. Additionally, managing tourist flows is critical to avoid overcrowding and dissatisfaction among visitors and residents. Mobile phone data analysis helps track overall visitor movements, while gamification challenges at various tourist sites aim to direct visitors to lesser known and less crowded locations.

Campaign to enhance tourism dispersion in Luxembourg

The national campaign Luxembourg, that's vacation (*Lëtzebuerg, dat ass Vakanz)* launched in 2021, brings together events and activities, which create visibility and showcase the wealth and diversity of tourist assets in Luxembourg, across all regions. This campaign is undertaken to help meet the objectives of the strategy, such as managing tourism flows and improving the quality of life for residents.

In 2023 the theme was Active Tourism, in collaboration with regional tourist offices. The campaign was launched in Luxembourg City with national and regional tourism stands and highlighted the importance of local producers and products. It targets residents of the Grand Duchy, cross-border commuters as well as international tourists to make them aware of tourist attractions throughout the country.

The campaign's theme varies annually and is following the guidelines of the national tourism strategy. For instance, in 2024, the focus is on cultural tourism. The campaign targets both residents and non-residents, promoting a more sustainable and resilient form of tourism by encouraging resident participation. It invites locals and visitors to engage in authentic experiences, discover unique cultural and historical sites, and partake in diverse events and activities.

Statistical Profile

Luxembourg: Domestic, inbound and outbound tourism

	2018	2019	2020	2021	2022
TOURISM FLOWS, THOUSAND					
Domestic tourism					
Total domestic trips	..	..	..	..	..
Overnight visitors (tourists)	121	124	130	137	155
Same-day visitors (excursionists)	..	..	..	..	..
Nights in all types of accommodation	346	348	307	351	392
Hotels and similar establishments	254	256	236	250	308
Other collective establishments	92	91	71	102	84
Private accommodation	..	..	..	..	..
Inbound tourism					
Total international arrivals	..	..	..	..	..
Overnight visitors (tourists)	1 018	1 041	525	615	1 013
Same-day visitors (excursionists)	..	..	..	..	..
Top markets					
Belgium	208	207	116	137	181
Netherlands	170	188	105	133	223
Germany	148	149	74	114	172
France	136	134	71	109	137
United Kingdom	66	66	32	9	45
Nights in all types of accommodation	2 575	2 505	1 210	1 523	2 404
Hotels and similar establishments	1 715	1 652	752	940	1 538
Other collective establishments	860	853	458	583	866
Private accommodation	..	..	..	..	..
Outbound tourism					
Total international departures	4 063	4 063	2 452	2 759	5 005
Overnight visitors (tourists)	2 510	2 548	1 460	1 814	2 819
Same-day visitors (excursionists)	1 554	1 515	992	944	2 186
Top destinations					
France	490	494	379	464	647
Germany	330	373	201	218	357
Belgium	208	218	177	194	257
Portugal	..	..	..	..	238
Italy	232	212	100	139	230
TOURISM RECEIPTS AND EXPENDITURE, MILLION EUR					
Inbound tourism					
Total international receipts	4 947	5 235	4 094	5 030	5 551
International travel receipts	4 481	4 764	3 828	4 714	5 144
International passenger transport receipts	466	471	266	316	407
Outbound tourism					
Total international expenditure	2 849	3 278	1 863	3 280	3 296
International travel expenditure	2 790	3 224	1 819	3 223	3 233
International passenger transport expenditure	59	54	44	57	63

.. Not available
Source: OECD Tourism Statistics (Database).

StatLink https://stat.link/dnsgbe

Luxembourg: Enterprises and employment in tourism

	Number of establishments	Number of persons employed				
	2021	2018	2019	2020	2021	2022
Total	..	..	..	..	..	..
Tourism industries	..	37 484	38 984	38 432	38 298	..
Accommodation services for visitors	..	3 591	3 615	3 426	3 285	..
Hotels and similar establishments	223	3 097	3 102	2 898	2 722	..
Food and beverage serving industry	..	17 609	18 238	17 827	17 621	..
Passenger transport	..	11 208	11 634	11 678	11 748	..
Air passenger transport	..	3 293	3 347	3 304	3 186	..
Railways passenger transport	..	3 367	3 497	3 627	3 721	..
Road passenger transport	..	4 506	4 727	4 698	4 791	..
Water passenger transport	..	42	63	49	49	..
Passenger transport supporting services	..	..	..	..	..	..
Transport equipment rental	..	454	476	468	508	..
Travel agencies and other reservation services industry	..	602	685	649	572	..
Cultural industry	..	1 988	2 251	2 334	2 444	..
Sports and recreation industry	..	2 033	2 084	2 049	2 121	..
Retail trade of country-specific tourism characteristic goods	..	..	..	..	..	..
Other country-specific tourism industries	..	..	..	..	..	..
Other industries	..	..	..	..	..	..

.. Not available
Source: OECD Tourism Statistics (Database).

StatLink https://stat.link/qp4wbk

Luxembourg: Internal tourism consumption

Million EUR

	2021		
	Domestic tourism expenditure	Inbound tourism expenditure	Internal tourism consumption
Total	..	..	..
Consumption products	517	3 263	3 817
Tourism characteristic products	360	524	914
Accommodation services for visitors	74	223	320
Food and beverage serving services	92	142	234
Passenger transport services	51	42	93
Air passenger transport services	29	40	68
Railways passenger transport services	0	33	33
Road passenger transport services	51	6	57
Water passenger transport services	0	3	3
Passenger transport supporting services	..	..	..
Transport equipment rental services	6	8	13
Travel agencies and other reservation services industry	78	0	84
Cultural services	31	70	101
Sports and recreation services	..	..	..
Country-specific tourism characteristic goods	..	..	..
Country-specific tourism characteristic services	..	..	..
Other consumption products	157	2 738	2 904
Tourism connected products	..	..	..
Non-tourism related consumption products	..	..	..
Non-consumption products	..	..	..

.. Not available
Source: OECD Tourism Statistics (Database).

StatLink https://stat.link/tv7385

Mexico

Tourism in the economy and outlook

Tourism is an important contributor to the Mexican economy. In 2022, tourism directly contributed MXN 2.4 billion to the Mexican economy, accounting for 8.5% of total GDP, above the pre-pandemic levels of 8.4% in 2019.Tourism directly employed 2.8 million people and accounted for 7.1% of the total workforce in 2022, which is above the 6.6% share in 2019. Travel exports reached MXN 58.0 billion, representing 58.3% of total service exports in 2022, compared to 59.2% in 2019.

In 2023, Mexico received 42.2 million international tourists, which indicates a strong recovery from the COVID-19 pandemic low of 24.3 million tourists in 2020, but is still 6.4% below 2019 levels. The top markets in 2023 were the United States (32%), Canada (6%) and the United Kingdom (1%).

Domestic tourism is an important contributor to the tourism sector. In 2022, Mexico recorded 98.0 million domestic overnight trips, which is 96% of 2019 levels, and up compared to the pandemic low of 48.0 million trips in 2020.

Tourism governance

The Ministry of Tourism is responsible for leading the design and implementation of public policies to strengthen tourism development. This includes promoting innovation in the sector, improving the quality of tourism services and the competitiveness of national tourism, and promoting strategies that articulate governmental priorities and contribute to the sustainable and inclusive growth of tourism. FONATUR is Mexico's agency for the development of tourism investment.

Three co-ordination mechanisms contribute to formulating strategies and actions to achieve a comprehensive development of national tourism activity. These mechanisms are:

- The Executive Tourism Commission, an inter-ministerial body whose purpose is to fully understand and resolve tourism-related matters.
- The Tourism Advisory Council, whose purpose is to suggest strategic responses and co-ordinate actions with the agencies of the Federal Government, with the full participation of the public and private sectors, to achieve comprehensive development of tourism activity.
- The National Tourism Conference, a co-ordinating body between the three levels of government, is in charge of establishing the policy, planning and programming of tourist activity throughout Mexico.

In the Ministry of Tourism, the Great Council for tourism sustainability has been established. The Council brings together more than 130 participants from across government, international organisations, civil society, indigenous communities, social enterprises, private companies and academia.

The total tourism budget in 2023 was MXN 2.6 billion.

Mexico: Organisational chart of tourism bodies

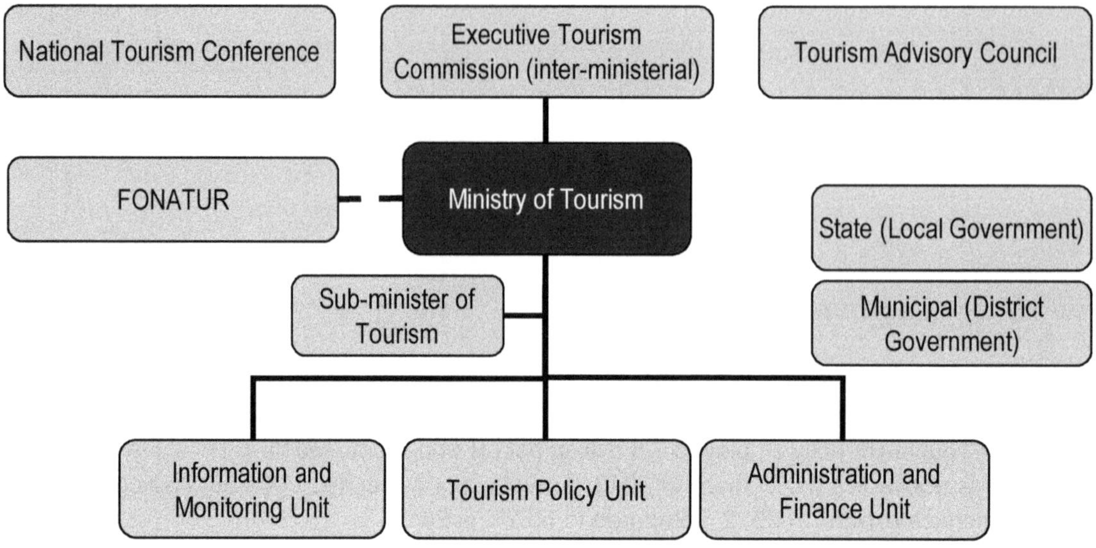

Source: OECD, adapted from the Ministry of Tourism, 2024.

Tourism policies and programmes

The Tourism Sectorial Programme 2020-24 (PROSECTUR) is the framework guiding national tourism policy in Mexico and relates to the National Development Plan 2019-24. PROSECTUR contains four priority objectives:

- Guarantee a social approach and respect for human rights in tourism.
- Promote the balanced development of tourism destinations.
- Strengthen the diversification of tourism markets at national and international levels.
- Promote sustainable tourism.

PROSECTUR involves the social, ethical and economic redevelopment of destinations. The goal is for tourism to permeate all regions, destinations and communities as a tool for social integration and reconciliation to create well-being for all. A report for the 2020 fiscal year listed the progress towards the priority objectives and well-being goals contained in the PROSECTUR framework. The programme will end in 2024 and as of 2023, the 110 actions were 98% complete.

Tourism is closely guided by the Sustainable Tourism Strategy 2030 which aims to make Mexico's destinations a benchmark for sustainable, resilient tourism, encouraging sustainable consumption and production value chains, local communities' engagement, and biodiversity preservation. It prioritises the achievement of the UN Sustainable Development Goals in the tourism economy, with the long-term aim that future generations can continue to benefit from natural resources that attract tourists. The measures supporting this strategy include:

- Promoting sustainable mobility and zero emissions tourism. Under this action, bicycle lanes are developed to connect local communities where visitors can travel to natural and cultural destinations. For example, *Ciclovía Maya*, the largest tourist bikeway in the world, will connect and integrate economic activities for dozens of local communities in the Yucatan Peninsula.
- Creating solutions for the integrated management of solid waste for the goal of zero waste. This includes implementing local models for integrated solid waste management, seeking to generate zero waste and creating destinations free of single-use plastics.

- Investing in and promoting the sustainable tourism offer. This will be done on multi-channels and new innovative marketing platforms, seeking virtual and physical presence in national and international spaces and events.

To meet the objectives in the strategies and to strengthen the Mexican tourism economy further, several programmes have been initiated. A Tourism Planning System is being developed with a tourism sector prospective exercise to create better co-ordination between all tourism stakeholders. This will analyse the current state of the sector, establish a database of work in progress and provide recommendations for the future.

The *Kuxatur* project consists in developing sustainable tourism zones to facilitate biodiversity conservation, focusing on coastal ecosystems. The initiative is associated with the Indigenous People's Programme and integrates local communities to enhance capacity building and local sustainable development (see box below).

The Secretary of Tourism Development of Yucatán (SEFOTUR), UNESCO in Mexico, Airbnb, and the Union of Community Tourism Cooperatives have also launched a programme for the Capacity Enhancement for Community Tourism in Yucatán and to promote a fairer distribution of tourism benefits. This scheme aims to strengthen the capacities of local communities in heritage management, sustainability, and the development of authentic tours and activities. The programme is the first of its kind in Mexico and will start in Yucatán. It will benefit tourism co-operatives, collectives, and family-based grassroots enterprises directly by providing training in cultural and natural heritage, community tourism management, promotion, and the development of sustainable tourism products.

Establishing sustainable tourism development zones in Mexico

Mexico aims to mainstream biodiversity conservation, with an emphasis on biodiversity-rich coastal ecosystems. Under the project *Kuxatur* (which translates to 'Living Tourism' in the Mayan language), action is undertaken to enhance nature tourism through the design and implementation of innovative sustainable tourism policies and models. The goal of *Kuxatur* is to integrate local communities into tourism policy development, capacity building and implementing sustainable tourism targets. Mexico's Indigenous People's Programme is integrated in this initiative and will be critical to its success.

Kuxatur will lay the foundation for sustainable tourism by 2025 by establishing sustainable tourism development zones. The areas of Maya Ka'an, Quintana Roo, in the Yucatan Peninsula, the Huatulco-Chacahua Corridor, in Oaxaca, and La Paz, Sierra la Laguna and Los Cabos, in Baja California will serve as pilot regions for the project and will function as tangible and replicable models. Each region benefits from unique ecosystems and cultural heritage, established conservation efforts and potential for sustainable tourism development.

Statistical Profile

Mexico: Domestic, inbound and outbound tourism

	2018	2019	2020	2021	2022
TOURISM FLOWS, THOUSAND					
Domestic tourism					
Total domestic trips	..	..	..	..	..
Overnight visitors (tourists)	100 445	101 749	48 042	76 565	98 013
Same-day visitors (excursionists)	..	..	..	..	..
Nights in all types of accommodation	..	..	..	..	..
Hotels and similar establishments	166 707	174 610	83 122	134 822	172 429
Other collective establishments	..	..	..	..	..
Private accommodation	..	..	..	..	..
Inbound tourism					
Total international arrivals	96 497	97 406	51 128	55 301	65 994
Overnight visitors (tourists)	41 313	45 024	24 284	31 860	38 326
Same-day visitors (excursionists)	55 184	52 382	26 845	23 441	27 669
Top markets					
United States	10 496	10 511	5 151	10 240	13 001
Canada	2 155	2 310	976	504	1 759
Spain	591	581	104	125	566
France	386	392	100	221	366
United Kingdom	287	305	116	157	295
Nights in all types of accommodation	..	..	..	..	..
Hotels and similar establishments	93 323	97 151	43 614	70 992	103 877
Other collective establishments	..	..	..	..	..
Private accommodation	..	..	..	..	..
Outbound tourism					
Total international departures	86 280	82 752	36 056	32 978	41 891
Overnight visitors (tourists)	19 748	19 810	7 345	11 685	13 750
Same-day visitors (excursionists)	66 531	62 942	28 710	21 292	28 140
Top destinations					
..	..	..	..	..	..
..	..	..	..	..	..
..	..	..	..	..	..
..	..	..	..	..	..
..	..	..	..	..	..
TOURISM RECEIPTS AND EXPENDITURE, MILLION USD					
Inbound tourism					
Total international receipts	26 044	27 126	12 133	21 509	30 398
International travel receipts	22 526	24 573	10 996	19 765	28 017
International passenger transport receipts	3 518	2 553	1 137	1 743	2 381
Outbound tourism					
Total international expenditure	14 074	12 300	4 240	6 798	9 634
International travel expenditure	11 230	9 881	3 475	5 147	7 054
International passenger transport expenditure	2 844	2 419	765	1 652	2 580

.. Not available.
Source: OECD Tourism Statistics (Database).

StatLink https://stat.link/hgjv4u

Mexico: Enterprises and employment in tourism

	Number of establishments	Number of persons employed				
	2021	2018	2019	2020	2021 p	2022 p
Total	..	2 522 320	2 613 864	2 325 187	2 532 581	2 814 979
Tourism industries	114 098	1 846 426	1 948 476	1 726 411	1 852 053	2 065 220
Accommodation services for visitors	..	283 951	286 130	311 170	335 824	348 039
Hotels and similar establishments	25 497	283 951	286 130	311 170	335 824	348 039
Food and beverage serving industry	80 198	691 592	708 015	584 451	644 476	754 999
Passenger transport	..	605 224	608 387	526 401	554 311	615 221
Air passenger transport	..	41 042	41 384	37 699	46 419	63 752
Railways passenger transport	..	1 212	1 213	1 177	1 302	1 632
Road passenger transport	..	559 329	562 097	485 731	504 250	546 906
Water passenger transport	..	3 641	3 693	1 794	2 340	2 931
Passenger transport supporting services	..	5 055	4 867	4 132	4 700	5 884
Transport equipment rental	..	8 002	8 352	7 634	7 855	8 492
Travel agencies and other reservation services industry	8 403	27 101	26 577	22 663	25 581	27 085
Cultural industry	..	34 221	34 237	27 964	30 515	36 260
Sports and recreation industry	..	64 305	62 256	52 763	55 338	60 965
Retail trade of country-specific tourism characteristic goods	..	126 975	209 655	189 233	193 453	208 275
Other country-specific tourism industries	..	..	..	..	..	..
Other industries	..	675 894	665 388	598 776	680 528	749 759

.. Not available; p Provisional data
Source: OECD Tourism Statistics (Database).

StatLink https://stat.link/pvsd7c

Mexico: Internal tourism consumption

Million MXN

	2022 p		
	Domestic tourism expenditure	Inbound tourism expenditure	Internal tourism consumption
Total	..	..	..
Consumption products	3 135 125	691 035	3 826 160
Tourism characteristic products	2 811 528	679 922	3 491 450
Accommodation services for visitors	465 094	192 402	657 497
Food and beverage serving services	560 865	167 992	728 858
Passenger transport services	846 373	91 357	937 730
Air passenger transport services	409 373	47 827	457 200
Railways passenger transport services	8 103	0	8 103
Road passenger transport services	410 899	43 530	454 429
Water passenger transport services	17 998	0	17 998
Passenger transport supporting services	56 564	2 109	58 673
Transport equipment rental services	23 192	0	23 192
Travel agencies and other reservation services industry	29 108	717	29 825
Cultural services	13 974	30 024	43 998
Sports and recreation services	21 678	50 245	71 923
Country-specific tourism characteristic goods	794 680	145 075	939 755
Country-specific tourism characteristic services	..	..	..
Other consumption products	323 597	11 113	334 710
Tourism connected products	..	..	..
Non-tourism related consumption products	..	..	..
Non-consumption products	..	..	..

.. Not available; p Provisional data
Source: OECD Tourism Statistics (Database).

StatLink https://stat.link/65tayr

Netherlands

Tourism in the economy and outlook

Tourism is an important contributor to the Dutch economy and has recovered towards pre-pandemic levels. In 2022, tourism contributed for EUR 31.7 billion in nominal terms, or 3.7% of total GVA of the Netherlands. This remains lower than in 2019 (4.4% of total GDP) but is a significant increase from the pandemic-low of 2.3% in 2020. The tourism sector provided 452 000 jobs in 2022 (or 5.5% of total employment), which is still below 2019 levels (496 000 jobs and 6.4% of total employment). Travel exports represented 8.1% of total service exports in 2022 and have thus recovered above the pre-pandemic level of 7.2% in 2019.

In 2022, the Netherlands welcomed 16.6 million international tourists in commercial accommodation establishments, which is equivalent to 82% of the pre-pandemic levels. The top international source markets were Germany (37%), Belgium (14%) and the United States (10%).

The contribution of domestic tourists increased following the COVID-19 pandemic, with a record high of 29.4 million domestic tourists in commercial accommodation establishments in 2022, a 14% increase on 2019 levels. Domestic tourism expenditure amounted to EUR 57.7 million in nominal terms, or 62.6% of total tourism expenditure.

Tourism governance

The Ministry of Economic Affairs and Climate Policy is responsible for tourism at national level and acts as a first contact point within government for tourism industry associations and stakeholders.

The Netherlands Board of Tourism and Conventions is the national destination management organisation and works on the country's tourism positioning, development, and marketing, in close collaboration with public and private sector stakeholders. Their aim is to turn the Netherlands into a liveable, popular, and valuable destination for residents, visitors and businesses.

Regional and local authorities are responsible for tourism policy at their respective levels, often with their own strategy or a joint strategy with other municipalities. They receive and distribute funding locally and are responsible for marketing nationally and internationally and undertaking product development.

Destination Nederland, founded in 2022, is a network and industry organisation of local destination and city marketing organisations in the Netherlands. The network aims to strengthen destination management and marketing, through knowledge, and increase the Netherlands appeal as a destination to visit and stay, for residents, visitors and companies.

During the COVID-19 crisis, the national government, together with stakeholders in the sector, created a national Taskforce on Leisure and Tourism. The purpose of this taskforce is to strengthen co-operation between the various parties in the tourism sector. Currently an evaluation of the taskforce is underway to determine if the governance structure can be reorganised for greater effectiveness. Tourism significantly impacts diverse policy areas, for which other ministries and government levels share responsibility. These areas include spatial planning, agriculture, infrastructure, and culture. Research is being conducted into a new form of governance that requires more commitment from various departments. A renewed taskforce is expected to be set up in 2024. The Centre of Expertise Leisure, Tourism & Hospitality is a collaboration between universities of applied sciences in the field of tourism. The aim is to stimulate public-private partnerships in knowledge and research to encourage collaboration between education, industry and government.

The Netherlands Board of Tourism and Conventions is partially funded by the Ministry of Economic Affairs. In 2023, a total of EUR 10.1 million was allocated by the Ministry to the Board, in addition to third-party funding for specific projects. There is no budget allocated for tourism at the national level.

The Netherlands: Organisational chart of tourism bodies

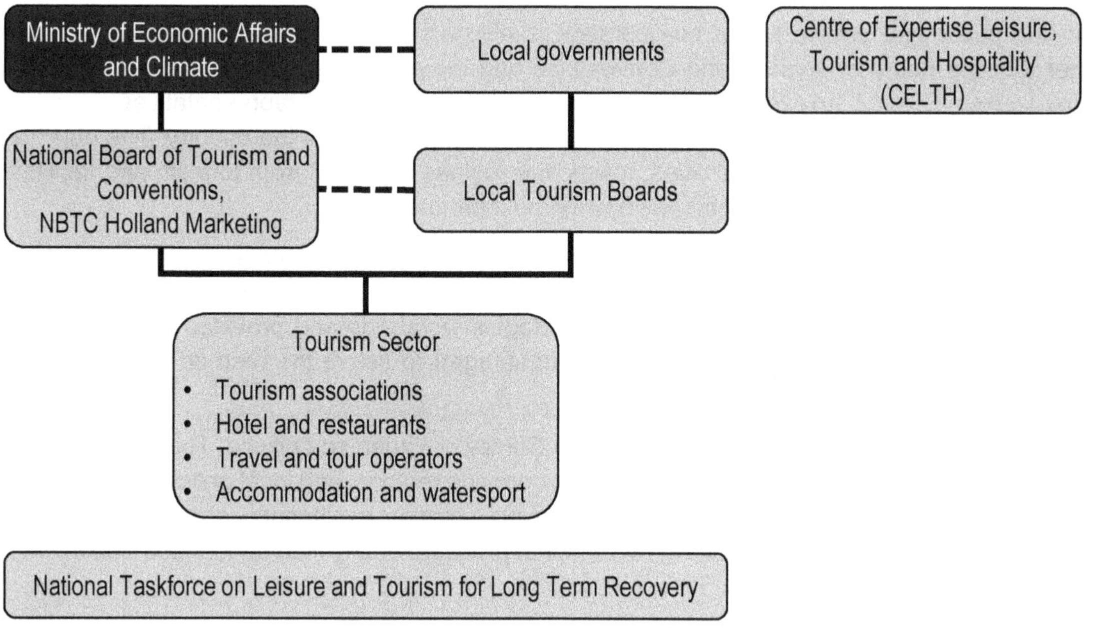

Source: OECD, adapted from Ministry of Economic Affairs and Climate, 2024

Tourism policies and programmes

Tourism in the Netherlands is guided by the long-term strategy Perspective 2030. The Strategy was developed in 2019 with the objective that every Dutch citizen should be able to benefit from tourism. Achieving the ambition of Perspective 2030 requires a switch from promoting destinations to developing destinations and making visitor flows more manageable. The Strategy is based on five strategic pillars:

- Creating more benefits than burdens from tourism.
- Making the Netherlands attractive by positioning different attractive destinations.
- Promoting accessibility and reachable tourist destinations.
- Enhancing sustainable tourism with less waste and pollution.
- Building a hospitable experience for visitors.

The Netherlands Board of Tourism and Conventions, the Ministry of Economic Affairs and Climate Policy, and the provinces created a taskforce to review and update the Action Plan for tourism. Current work focuses on destination management, sustainability, spatial planning and tourism, and tourism workforce issues. The updated Action Plan is expected to be released by mid-2024.

The three main policy goals of the Ministry are still:

- Supporting sustainable development of tourism.
- Enhancing co-operation across and between different levels of government.
- Supporting the tourism sector by focusing on opportunities for sustainability, entrepreneurship, innovation and digitisation.

The Netherlands has begun to pay more attention to the sustainable development and climate change as the strong growth in tourism number has led to increasingly negative impacts. The new Action Plan will focus on climate adaptation and addressing climate and sustainability challenges. This will move the focus away from simply promoting the Netherlands as a tourism destination.

Nationwide public and private sector co-operation is also a priority for the Netherlands. The Ministry, together with the Board of Tourism and Conventions and the provinces, organised three editions of the National Tourism Summit, an event that brought together a broad group of representatives of the business community, tourist organisations and government bodies from all parts of the country. The objective was to work on a joint approach to enable cities, towns and regions to benefit from tourism and facilitate peer learning. Due to its success, the Summit will now be held annually.

To foster balanced tourism that incorporates the interests of residents, businesses, and visitors, the Centre of Expertise Leisure, Tourism & Hospitality, the Board of Tourism and Conventions, and the statistical office have conducted a review of existing methodologies worldwide and provided insights into tourism balance. All destinations in the Netherlands are encouraged to select the method that best suits their specific needs.

Additionally, new guidelines were developed by the Centre of Expertise Leisure, Tourism and Hospitality on Space for Recreation and Tourism. The guidelines provide regional and local policymakers with actions to integrate tourism and recreation into spatial planning, creating multifunctional landscapes that serve both residents and tourists amidst growing recreational pressure and limited space (see box below).

Better integrating tourism into spatial planning in the Netherlands

The 12 Dutch provinces commissioned new Space for Recreation and Tourism guidelines, which were released by the Centre of Expertise Leisure, Tourism and Hospitality in 2023. The guidelines provide insights for those working on tourism policy at the regional and local level as to the actions that can be taken in the recreation and tourism sectors to create local landscapes to best serve both residents and tourists. Thinking in terms of leisure landscapes is essential because the population is growing, and recreational pressure is increasing, so every landscape is potentially also a leisure landscape, whether it concerns the urban landscape, the rural environment, or the areas in between.

The green recreational space has decreased, and domestic and international visitors have increased, which is expected to continue. To address this, both recreation and tourism have been integrated into planning and spatial policy. The Netherlands faces the dual challenge of scarce physical space and limited budgets, so smart planning is needed to optimise investments and to create multifunctional places that are of value to residents and visitors.

Statistical Profile

Netherlands: Domestic, inbound and outbound tourism

	2018	2019	2020	2021	2022
TOURISM FLOWS, THOUSAND					
Domestic tourism					
Total domestic trips	..	..	..	..	..
Overnight visitors (tourists)	18 341	17 989	16 958	21 664	16 498
Same-day visitors (excursionists)	864 762	..	..	49 199	..
Nights in all types of accommodation	101 873	88 237	88 665	99 654	73 401
Hotels and similar establishments	12 573	11 579	12 687	15 064	13 339
Other collective establishments	58 137	57 255	57 978	73 092	53 087
Private accommodation	31 163	19 403	18 000	11 497	6 975
Inbound tourism					
Total international arrivals	..	..	..	..	..
Overnight visitors (tourists)	18 780	20 129	7 265	6 248	16 582
Same-day visitors (excursionists)	..	..	..	..	..
Top markets					
Germany	5 689	6 175	3 283	2 471	6 143
Belgium	2 398	2 507	1 102	1 100	2 251
United Kingdom	2 212	2 402	595	209	1 429
United States	2 072	2 181	384	350	1 618
Asia	1 360	1 473	253	240	731
Nights in all types of accommodation	47 002	51 750	21 372	18 615	48 160
Hotels and similar establishments	41 721	45 848	17 990	15 657	41 654
Other collective establishments	5 282	5 902	3 383	2 958	6 506
Private accommodation	..	..	..	..	..
Outbound tourism					
Total international departures	..	..	..	..	
Overnight visitors (tourists)	22 277	22 925	11 719	10 670	19 435
Same-day visitors (excursionists)	13 791	12 709	5 038	3 940	7 981
Top destinations					
Germany	3 789	3 734	2 570	1 574	2 857
France	2 876	2 692	1 517	2 032	2 912
Spain	2 621	2 583	993	1 096	2 028
Belgium	1 579	1 787	1 030	1 113	1 956
Italy	1 440	1 322	533	970	1 511
TOURISM RECEIPTS AND EXPENDITURE, MILLION EUR					
Inbound tourism					
Total international receipts	22 529	23 962	10 847	13 070	28 359
International travel receipts	16 236	17 624	8 729	10 714	22 844
International passenger transport receipts	6 293	6 339	2 118	2 357	5 515
Outbound tourism					
Total international expenditure	22 188	23 553	8 185	8 691	20 066
International travel expenditure	19 287	20 656	7 281	8 006	17 874
International passenger transport expenditure	2 901	2 898	904	686	2 192

.. Not available
Source: OECD Tourism Statistics (Database).

StatLink https://stat.link/iay3l1

Netherlands: Enterprises and employment in tourism

	Number of establishments	Number of persons employed				
	2022 p	2018	2019	2020 p	2021 p	2022 p
Total	..	479 000	496 000	419 000	401 000	452 000
Tourism industries	217 600	..	..	..	..	..
Accommodation services for visitors	10 710	..	..	..	..	..
Hotels and similar establishments	5 800	..	..	..	..	..
Food and beverage serving industry	57 885	..	..	..	..	..
Passenger transport	13 665	..	..	..	..	..
Air passenger transport	335	..	..	..	..	..
Railways passenger transport	20	..	..	..	..	..
Road passenger transport	12 030	..	..	..	..	..
Water passenger transport	1 280	..	..	..	..	..
Passenger transport supporting services	6 550	..	..	..	..	..
Transport equipment rental	1 230	..	..	..	..	..
Travel agencies and other reservation services industry	6 065	..	..	..	..	..
Cultural industry	97 600	..	..	..	..	..
Sports and recreation industry	23 895	..	..	..	..	..
Retail trade of country-specific tourism characteristic goods	..	..	..	..	..	..
Other country-specific tourism industries	..	..	..	..	..	..
Other industries	..	..	..	..	..	..

.. Not available; p Provisional data
Source: OECD Tourism Statistics (Database).

StatLink https://stat.link/ohdgij

Netherlands: Internal tourism consumption

Million EUR

	2022		
	Domestic tourism expenditure	Inbound tourism expenditure	Internal tourism consumption
Total	57 665	34 474	95 835
Consumption products	..	..	..
Tourism characteristic products	..	..	..
Accommodation services for visitors	..	..	..
Food and beverage serving services	..	..	..
Passenger transport services	..	..	..
Air passenger transport services	..	..	..
Railways passenger transport services	..	..	..
Road passenger transport services	..	..	..
Water passenger transport services	..	..	..
Passenger transport supporting services	..	..	..
Transport equipment rental services	..	..	..
Travel agencies and other reservation services industry	..	..	..
Cultural services	..	..	..
Sports and recreation services	..	..	..
Country-specific tourism characteristic goods	..	..	..
Country-specific tourism characteristic services	..	..	..
Other consumption products	..	..	..
Tourism connected products	..	..	..
Non-tourism related consumption products	..	..	..
Non-consumption products	..	..	..

.. Not available
Source: OECD Tourism Statistics (Database).

StatLink https://stat.link/5comy8

New Zealand

Tourism in the economy and outlook

In the financial year ended March 2022, tourism generated NZD 10 billion, directly contributing to 3.1% of total GVA, compared to 5.4% pre-pandemic. Tourism directly employed 128 000 people in 2022, accounting for 4.7% of total employment. This was 42% down on 2019 levels. Travel exports represented 4.4% of total service exports in 2022, significantly lower than the pre-pandemic level of 58%, but also lower than the levels in 2020 (48%) and 2021 (29%).

Despite current high costs of intercontinental travel, New Zealand has experienced a strong rebound in international visitors since reopening its borders in 2022. In 2022, there were 1.4 million international visitors (37% of pre-COVID 2019 levels), accounting for NZD 5.5 billion in nominal terms. New Zealand's top three markets in 2022 were Australia (60%), the United States (8%) and the United Kingdom (6%). The Chinese market has not yet recovered, accounting for 1% of international tourist arrivals in 2022 compared to 11% in 2019.

New Zealand recorded 25.8 million domestic guest nights in all means of accommodation in 2022 (113% of pre-pandemic 2018 levels), accounting for NZD 21 billion in nominal terms. Domestic tourism grew significantly during the pandemic but is waning, as outbound tourism demand increases, and the country faces persistently high annual inflation rates. Data for 2023 indicates tourism expenditure has returned to 2019 in nominal terms, with total tourism expenditure at NZD 30 billion in the year ending September 2023, 0.3% below the same period in 2019.

Tourism governance

The Ministry of Business, Innovation and Employment advises the national government on creating balanced growth in the tourism sector. The Ministry works closely with other government agencies whose portfolios intersect with the tourism sector, including the Department of Conservation, the Department of Internal Affairs, responsible for local government, the Ministry for Culture and Heritage, and the Ministry of Transport. Tourism New Zealand, a public body, is responsible for marketing the country as a visitor destination internationally, in partnership with industry and regional tourism organisations.

Local and regional authorities provide tourism-related infrastructure and local planning frameworks to help communities grow and manage local tourism challenges. Regional Tourism Organisations are responsible for promoting their destinations and, in recent years, have taken the lead in co-ordinating local stakeholders to develop Destination Management Plans. Vertical co-ordination is achieved through shared understanding of key strategic documents, relationships with key destinations, and regular discussions between the Ministry and Regional Tourism New Zealand and/or Local Government New Zealand.

The New Zealand Government Budget for the tourism portfolio for the 2023-24 financial year is NZD 227 million. Budget 2023 shifted focus towards addressing long-term problems and opportunities while supporting balanced growth as opposed to recovery as seen in Budget 2022. This includes specific funding for Tourism New Zealand to promote the country as a business and visitor destination

(NZD 112 million), for the Ministry functions (policy, data and fund management) (NZD 11 million), and a one-off fund for the Innovation Programme for Tourism Recovery (NZD 54 million). Regional Tourism Organisations are largely funded and governed by local authorities, with many of them receiving additional funding from other sources, including central government, annual membership fees from local industry, and industry partnership funding.

New Zealand: Organisational chart of tourism bodies

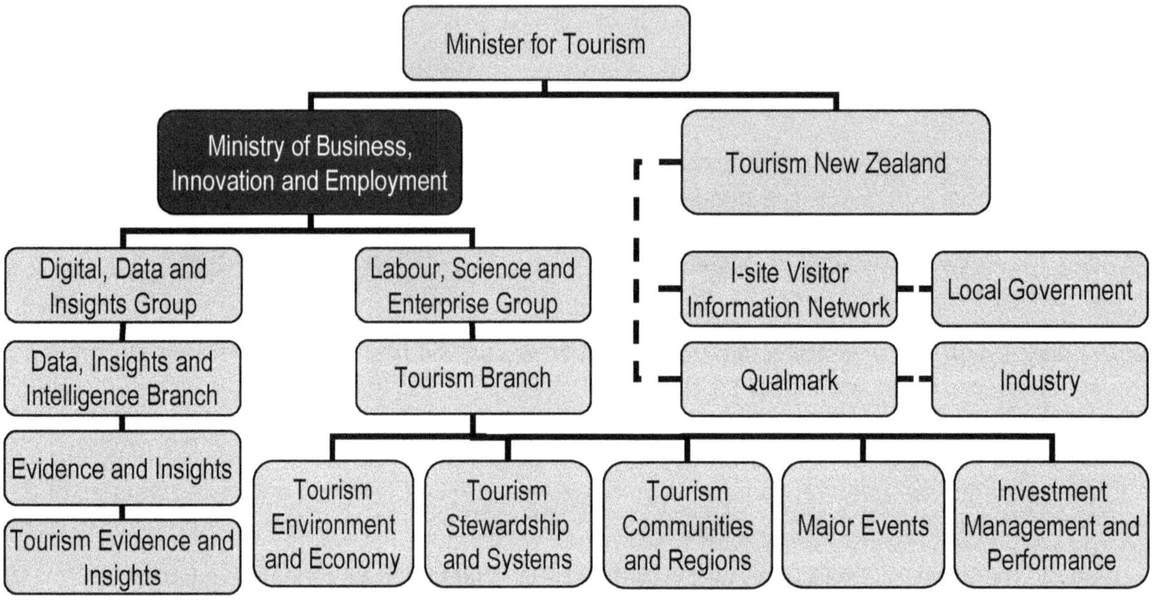

Source: OECD, adapted from the Ministry of Business, Innovation and Employment, 2024.

Tourism policies and programmes

The New Zealand-Aotearoa Government Tourism Strategy, published in 2019, sets out a stewardship role for the government to ensure tourism enriches New Zealand through more productive, sustainable and inclusive growth, building better partnerships with Māori tourism enterprise, *iwi, hapū and tangata whenua*.

New Zealand's Tourism Strategy focuses on five key areas: the Economy, International and domestic Visitors, the Environment, New Zealanders and its communities, and regions. In addition to growing the value of international tourism while managing social license and within environmental constraints, and co-ordination across the tourism system to improve tourism outcomes, current policy priorities include:

- Long-term Sustainable Funding Mechanisms, including implementing the International Visitor Conservation and Tourism Levy and accompanied strategic investment plan. A revised investment plan was produced in 2023 to focus government tourism spending on nationally significant investments and projects that provide a co-ordinated approach to address shared tourism system changes, including consultation with the private sector.
- Setting local agendas for destination management through collaborative Destination Management Plans in each region to uphold a positive social licence. Funding from the COVID-19 recovery funding has enabled all 31 Regional Tourism Organisations to complete a tailored Destination Management Plan. The plans are agreed by tourism businesses, locals, including local Māori communities, local government, and other stakeholders. Initial plans were funded by central government, and implementation will be undertaken locally, including resourcing.

- Better data and insight, including implementing the Tourism Data Domain Plan, identifying future trends that could impact on the tourism system and co-ordinate and share data and insight to support the industry.

This builds on recent work undertaken as part of the Tourism Industry Transformation Plan, a partnership between the Government and the tourism industry, workers and Māori that aims to build a regenerative tourism system that gives back more to people, communities and the environment than it takes. The Better Work phase focused on addressing key system issues facing the tourism workforce, including addressing pay and conditions, demand fluctuations, firm maturity and scale, and skill gaps. This resulted in the publication of the Better Work Action Plan in March 2023. This work was accompanied by the Tourism and hospitality Workforce Survey undertaken in 2022 to better understand the issues for the tourism workforce. The second phase of the Tourism Transformation Plan focussed on the environment with a draft action plan published in June 2023. To measure and monitor the sustainability of the tourism ecosystem, New Zealand have introduced the Sustainable Tourism Explorer. Data is collected, or is planned to be collected, on a range of topics such as waste management, quality of visitor experience, tourism demand, amenities and facilities, and regions' reliance on tourism. However, a key issue with tourism data relating to sustainability is that many measures have not, or cannot, be quantified.

A Tourism Data Leadership Group was formed, including representatives from industry and academia, to create a collaborative forum to identify the information needs of the diverse set of tourism data users (industry, central and local government, communities, iwi, interest groups, academics and commentators), communicate those needs to the wide range of stakeholders, and support the implementation of possible solutions, including the provision of data and insights to users.

New Zealand has also taken action to regulate impacts of freedom camping (see box below).

Reforms to manage the impact of freedom camping in New Zealand

Over the last two decades, New Zealand has seen a significant increase in the number of domestic and international visitors participating in freedom camping. However, there have been growing concerns over the cumulative impact of freedom campers on the natural environment, access to local amenities, and social licence. Freedom campers, who stay in vehicles that are not self-contained and therefore cannot dispose of their waste appropriately, have presented a particular concern.

In June 2023, the Self-contained Motor Vehicles Legislation Act was passed to address issues with vehicle-based camping. The main changes were: (i) The establishment of a regulatory system for the certification of self-contained vehicles, including a new regulator; (ii) Vehicles are required to have a fixed toilet to be certified as self-contained; (iii) Vehicle-based freedom campers are required to use a certified self-contained vehicle when they stay on local authority land; (iv) The strengthening of the infringement system, with a broader range of offences and higher infringement fees for some offences; and (v) The introduction of an exemption for people experiencing homelessness from freedom camping-related sanctions.

The new regulator has been operating since the end of 2023, including the management of a digital register where details of certified vehicles are stored, and is accessible to enforcement agencies. The 2023-24 summer is the first where the new rules apply. The introduction of self-containment certification requirements is being phased in over two years.

Statistical Profile

New Zealand: Domestic, inbound and outbound tourism

	2018	2019	2020	2021	2022
TOURISM FLOWS, THOUSAND					
Domestic tourism					
Total domestic trips	..	..	..	..	..
Overnight visitors (tourists)	..	..	..	..	..
Same-day visitors (excursionists)	..	..	..	..	..
Nights in all types of accommodation	22 778	..	..	23 640	25 773
Hotels and similar establishments	17 279	..	..	15 349	17 549
Other collective establishments	5 499	..	..	8 291	8 224
Private accommodation	..	..	..	..	..
Inbound tourism[1]					
Total international arrivals	3 858	3 888	996	207	1 434
Overnight visitors (tourists)	3 686	3 702	949	205	1 389
Same-day visitors (excursionists)	172	186	48	2	45
Top markets					
Australia	1 411	1 538	360	160	829
China	441	407	59	2	17
United States	338	368	125	5	110
United Kingdom	232	232	94	6	88
Japan	96	98	26	1	13
Nights in all types of accommodation	17 589	..	..	1 370	4 849
Hotels and similar establishments	14 723	..	..	1 214	3 907
Other collective establishments	2 867	..	..	156	942
Private accommodation	..	..	..	..	..
Outbound tourism					
Total international departures	3 045	3 225	511	234	1 629
Overnight visitors (tourists)	..	..	..	..	..
Same-day visitors (excursionists)	..	..	..	..	..
Top destinations					
Australia	..	..	..	..	..
United States	..	..	..	..	..
Fiji	..	..	..	..	..
China (People's Republic of)	..	..	..	..	..
United Kingdom	..	..	..	..	..
TOURISM RECEIPTS AND EXPENDITURE, MILLION NZD					
Inbound tourism					
Total international receipts	17 504	17 920	10 809	..	..
International travel receipts	15 717	15 988	8 869	4 052	786
International passenger transport receipts	1 787	1 932	1 940	..	..
Outbound tourism					
Total international expenditure	8 232	8 280	4 004	..	..
International travel expenditure	6 670	6 527	339	1 641	447
International passenger transport expenditure	1 562	1 753	1 777	..	..

.. Not available

1. Arrivals from demand side surveys; Nights from supply side surveys.

Source: OECD Tourism Statistics (Database).

StatLink https://stat.link/y4hcjv

New Zealand: Enterprises and employment in tourism

	Number of establishments	Number of persons employed				
	2022	2018	2019	2020	2021	2022
Total	..	221 046	219 867	219 093	141 517	127 980
Tourism industries	..	181 593	180 975	179 883	110 878	99 750
Accommodation services for visitors	5 931	28 920	28 761	27 411	14 982	11 502
Hotels and similar establishments	..	..	..	..	..	..
Food and beverage serving industry	18 300	63 525	62 202	62 205	36 708	33 378
Passenger transport	..	10 224	14 907	15 174	10 752	9 942
Air passenger transport	387	10 224	10 677	10 812	7 218	6 969
Railways passenger transport	3	..	..	..	..	..
Road passenger transport	8 337	..	..	..	..	..
Water passenger transport	186	..	..	..	..	..
Passenger transport supporting services	..	16 731	12 669	13 173	8 130	6 006
Transport equipment rental	1 578	4 500	4 488	4 404	3 492	3 144
Travel agencies and other reservation services industry	1 560	..	..	..	..	..
Cultural industry	4 131	8 307	8 598	8 625	5 547	4 617
Sports and recreation industry	6 633	..	..	..	..	..
Retail trade of country-specific tourism characteristic goods	..	34 479	33 480	32 649	22 500	22 851
Other country-specific tourism industries	..	14 907	15 870	16 239	8 667	8 313
Other industries	..	39 453	38 895	39 210	30 639	28 230

.. Not available
Source: OECD Tourism Statistics (Database).

StatLink https://stat.link/uy6fx7

New Zealand: Internal tourism consumption

Million NZD

	2021 p		
	Domestic tourism expenditure	Inbound tourism expenditure	Internal tourism consumption
Total	..	..	..
Consumption products	22 390	1 331	23 722
Tourism characteristic products	9 287	752	10 042
Accommodation services for visitors	1 492	283	1 776
Food and beverage serving services	2 371	249	2 621
Passenger transport services	4 553	220	4 774
Air passenger transport services	2 306	147	2 454
Railways passenger transport services	..	..	..
Road passenger transport services	..	..	..
Water passenger transport services	..	..	..
Passenger transport supporting services	..	..	..
Transport equipment rental services	..	..	..
Travel agencies and other reservation services industry	..	..	..
Cultural services	..	..	..
Sports and recreation services	..	..	..
Country-specific tourism characteristic goods	871	0	871
Country-specific tourism characteristic services	..	..	..
Other consumption products	12 012	496	12 504
Tourism connected products	..	..	..
Non-tourism related consumption products	..	..	..
Non-consumption products	..	..	..

.. Not available; p Provisional data
Source: OECD Tourism Statistics (Database).

StatLink https://stat.link/yrfqio

Norway

Tourism in the economy and outlook

Prior to the pandemic, the economic contribution of the tourism sector in Norway had increased considerably, reaching NOK 127.4 billion in 2019 and representing 3.6% of total GDP. Tourism also became a significant employer, particularly in rural areas, providing over 182 800 full-time jobs, or 7.4% of national employment. In 2022, travel exports represented 10.6% of total service exports, compared to 13.5% in 2019, and a pandemic low of 4.7% in 2021.

International tourism has recovered strongly. In 2022, Norway recorded 5.0 million international tourist arrivals in commercial accommodation establishments, representing a 247% increase compared to 2021 but remaining 15.3% below 2019 levels. In 2023, Norway recorded 11 million international overnight stays in commercial accommodation establishments, thus surpassing the level in 2019 by 4%. The top source markets in 2023 were Germany (21%), United States (10%) and Sweden (10%).

Domestic tourism for both leisure and business purposes dominates the tourism sector in Norway, accounting for 25.9 million domestic nights in commercial accommodation in 2023, or 70% of all commercial accommodation. This is 6% above 2019 levels.

Tourism governance

The Ministry of Trade, Industry and Fisheries is responsible for developing and regulating tourism. The Ministry co-operates closely with other ministries on tourism issues, including:

- The Ministry of Local Government and Regional Development who provides oversight of regional and local authorities promoting tourism development. They are responsible for planning and regulating infrastructure, utilities, national parks and natural and cultural heritage attractions.
- The Ministry of Climate and Environment and the Ministry of Transport who develop policies for a more sustainable tourism sector.
- The Ministry of Agriculture and Food who promotes co-operation between farmers and food producers, restaurants and other sectors of the tourism industry.

Innovation Norway is the country's national tourism organisation and is responsible for meeting economic growth targets for tourism and international marketing. It is primarily funded by the Ministry of Trade, Industry and Fisheries but also receives funding from other ministries. Regional reform initiated in 2020 gave the counties renewed roles and wider tourism responsibilities and is expected to provide a more efficient framework to solve cross-sectoral and cross-regional challenges to benefit the tourism industry.

In 2024, Innovation Norway will receive a total of NOK 195 million for its tourism work. Innovation Norway allocates travel and tourism companies loans, grants, and guarantees. In 2022, a total of NOK 164 million NOK was allocated in pledges from Innovation Norway to the tourism industry.

Norway: Organisational chart of tourism bodies

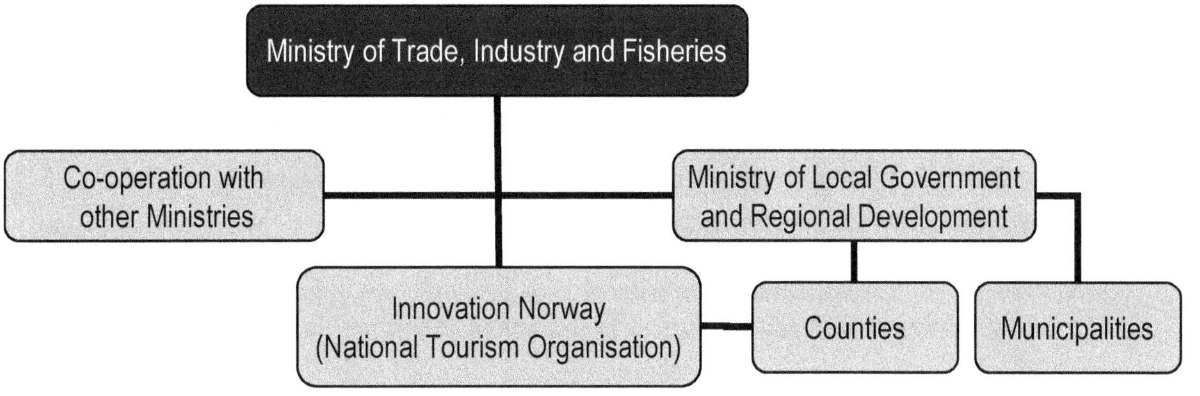

Source: OECD, adapted from the Ministry of Trade, Industry and Fisheries, 2024

Tourism policies and programmes

The National Tourism Strategy 2030 - Big impact, small footprint was published in 2021 and provides the long-term strategy set and monitored by Innovation Norway. The Strategy sets out 23 policy measures to ensure the development of a more sustainable and profitable tourism sector by 2030 to assist post-pandemic recovery and to respond to changing tourism trends. The goals and targets for the Strategy include:

- Increasing value creation and helping create jobs in Norway by increasing the export value of consumption by NOK 20 billion by 2030, increasing the number of tourism-related jobs in Norway by 25% by 2030.
- Supporting Norway to become a low-emissions society by reducing greenhouse gas emissions in the local tourist industry by 50% by 2030 and reducing the carbon footprint resulting from visitors' transport to/from/around Norway by 10% a year, using 2019 as a base.
- Supporting the creation of attractive local communities and happy residents.
- Delivering customer value that customers are willing to pay more for and make repeat purchases to increase consumption by 25% by 2030.

A new Roadmap for the Tourism Industry was presented by the Ministry in February 2024. The Roadmap outlines the government's progress and sets three main ambitions: increasing profitability, promoting sustainability, and supporting local communities. It includes 43 initiatives aimed at enhancing the sector's competitiveness, reducing its environmental impact, and developing sustainable destinations and strategic international marketing. The Roadmap was informed by input from industry organisations, the Sami Parliament, the National Tourism Strategy 2030 and the Destinations Committee's report (see box below). These sources provided valuable insights and recommendations for shaping a more sustainable and attractive tourism industry in Norway.

To address long-term challenges of the Norwegian Tourism sector, such as a low share of high value-added tourism products, strong seasonality, a lack of co-operation between destinations, and, more recently, overtourism in certain destinations, the government is developing several measures, led by Re-start Reiseliv 2021-24 – a programme to help tourism rebuild post-pandemic. It focuses on increased resources for product development, marketing and recruitment, including through:

- Reiseliv 2030 – a strategy group which will provide proposals on prioritised research and innovation activities to make the tourism sector less seasonal, increase value creation and contribute to the green transition. The strategy group submitted its final report to the Ministry of Trade, Industry and Fisheries in June 2024.

- The development of a climate-smart digital calculator that links data on CO2 emissions from transportation, and tourism expenditure from the various tourist markets. The goal is to permit informed strategic choices by tourism stakeholders so the sector can meet the target of a 10% annual reduction in total greenhouse gas emissions from commercial tourism activity. The project was initiated in 2022 and the tool will be available to all parts of Norwegian tourism.
- Innovation Norway was commissioned by the Ministry of Trade, Industry and Fisheries to formulate a proposal for a national recognition scheme for local and regional guides, tour leaders and mountain guides, in co-operation with outdoor organisations. The proposal was submitted to the Ministry of Trade, Industry and Fisheries in December 2023, and is now being assessed and followed up.

A new model for destination development and visitor management in Norway

A Committee for destination development and visitor management was appointed in autumn 2021 to undertake a comprehensive review of relevant framework conditions for the development of tourism activity in Norwegian municipalities as part of the National Tourism Strategy 2030. The Committee assessed and, if appropriate, proposed adjustments to regulations, structures and/or financing models, to support the Strategy's objective of more environmentally, socially and economically sustainable tourism.

The Committee report, submitted in March 2023, proposed a new model for the organisation of sustainable Norwegian destinations, consisting of:

- Establishing a destination management team that is adapted to local conditions and anchored in the municipalities.
- Conducting strategic visitor management and managing the development and operation of public goods at each destination based on a broadly rooted visitor strategy.
- Financing the work on destination management, visitor management and public goods through a visitor contribution that is collected nationally, but managed regionally and locally.

The Committee report provides an important knowledge base for all actors who have a role in destination development to strengthen their work for a more sustainable tourism in Norway.

The Committee proposed several action items for sustainable destination development, and made recommendations related to visitor management, destination management, public benefit financing, accessibility and cruise tourism. A key message in the report is that tourism must be developed in a way that creates attractive local communities for residents and visitors. The Committee believes that destination development must take place through systematic work involving local authorities, the industry and the voices of the local community. The Government is currently assessing the Committee's recommendations and how these should be followed up.

Statistical Profile

Norway: Domestic, inbound and outbound tourism

	2018	2019	2020	2021	2022
TOURISM FLOWS, THOUSAND					
Domestic tourism					
Total domestic trips	..	..	..	..	..
Overnight visitors (tourists)	18 970	14 710	16 580	20 450	21 790
Same-day visitors (excursionists)	..	..	..	..	..
Nights in all types of accommodation	63 280	48 030	66 650	80 100	77 270
Hotels and similar establishments	11 480	10 810	8 850	10 200	14 360
Other collective establishments	15 220	5 480	10 480	11 060	9 590
Private accommodation	36 580	31 740	47 320	58 840	53 320
Inbound tourism					
Total international arrivals	..	..	..	..	..
Overnight visitors (tourists)	5 688	5 879	1 387	1 435	4 979
Same-day visitors (excursionists)	..	..	..	..	..
Top markets					
Germany	1 150	1 041	258	362	1 113
Sweden	623	574	158	166	495
United States	487	555	105	112	461
Netherlands	435	429	83	112	556
Denmark	371	319	219	109	340
Nights in all types of accommodation	10 138	10 701	3 318	3 310	9 813
Hotels and similar establishments	8 065	8 472	2 689	2 500	7 255
Other collective establishments	2 073	2 230	629	809	2 559
Private accommodation	..	..	..	..	..
Outbound tourism					
Total international departures	16 530	18 624	3 203	3 699	13 028
Overnight visitors (tourists)	8 120	9 070	1 745	2 027	7 372
Same-day visitors (excursionists)	8 410	9 554	1 458	1 672	5 656
Top destinations					
Sweden	1 361	1 918	239	587	1 527
Spain	1 170	1 225	216	266	1 139
Denmark	882	1 017	224	284	843
United Kingdom	638	661	166	79	460
Germany	563	548	112	188	418
TOURISM RECEIPTS AND EXPENDITURE, MILLION NOK					
Inbound tourism					
Total international receipts	59 235	61 891	14 729	20 768	62 594
International travel receipts	48 214	51 520	17 127	16 649	52 609
International passenger transport receipts	11 022	10 369	3 233	4 119	9 984
Outbound tourism					
Total international expenditure	149 039	155 626	42 161	37 774	143 448
International travel expenditure	138 842	145 315	39 543	35 289	134 911
International passenger transport expenditure	10 196	10 311	2 619	2 485	8 537

.. Not available
Source: OECD Tourism Statistics (Database).

StatLink https://stat.link/e2k8th

Norway: Enterprises and employment in tourism

	Number of establishments	Number of persons employed				
	2021	2018	2019	2020	2021	2022
Total	..	..	..	..	..	..
Tourism industries	27 004	179 000	182 800	165 700	..	..
Accommodation services for visitors	3 474	24 500	24 900	20 300	..	..
Hotels and similar establishments	1 466	..	..	..	..	..
Food and beverage serving industry	12 559	56 500	57 200	51 800	..	..
Passenger transport	7 598	51 100	51 700	48 300	..	..
Air passenger transport	131	6 200	6 300	5 500	..	..
Railways passenger transport	63	3 800	3 800	4 000	..	..
Road passenger transport	6 979	29 800	30 100	27 900	..	..
Water passenger transport	425	11 300	11 500	10 900	..	..
Passenger transport supporting services	..	..	..	..	..	..
Transport equipment rental	692	7 400	7 700	7 500	..	..
Travel agencies and other reservation services industry	2 681	5 700	5 800	4 300	..	..
Cultural industry	..	23 400	25 000	23 800	..	..
Sports and recreation industry	..	10 400	10 500	9 700	..	..
Retail trade of country-specific tourism characteristic goods	..	..	..	..	..	..
Other country-specific tourism industries	..	..	..	..	..	..
Other industries	..	..	..	..	..	..

.. Not available
Source: OECD Tourism Statistics (Database).

StatLink https://stat.link/ki1ljx

Norway: Internal tourism consumption

Million NOK

	2020		
	Domestic tourism expenditure	Inbound tourism expenditure	Internal tourism consumption
Total	..	..	..
Consumption products	110 704	19 046	129 750
Tourism characteristic products	54 223	10 339	64 562
Accommodation services for visitors	10 184	3 039	13 223
Food and beverage serving services	17 277	3 448	20 725
Passenger transport services	17 073	3 014	20 087
Air passenger transport services	11 129	1 700	12 829
Railways passenger transport services	881	182	1 063
Road passenger transport services	2 271	224	2 495
Water passenger transport services	2 792	908	3 700
Passenger transport supporting services	..	..	..
Transport equipment rental services	313	135	448
Travel agencies and other reservation services industry	6 792	130	6 922
Cultural services	626	80	706
Sports and recreation services	1 958	493	2 451
Country-specific tourism characteristic goods	..	..	..
Country-specific tourism characteristic services	..	..	..
Other consumption products	56 481	8 707	65 188
Tourism connected products	..	..	..
Non-tourism related consumption products	..	..	..
Non-consumption products	..	..	..

.. Not available
Source: OECD Tourism Statistics (Database).

StatLink https://stat.link/dkqb27

Poland

Tourism in the economy and outlook

Tourism is an important driver of the Polish economy. In 2022, the total value of the tourism economy in Poland was estimated at PLN 131.4 billion, or 4.3% of Poland's GDP (accounting for direct and indirect impacts). The total value of the tourism economy in 2022 represented an increase of 43% in nominal terms since 2021, but this was still 7.3% below the pre-pandemic level. In 2022, 215 900 people were employed in the accommodation services sector, an increase of 10% compared to 2020, and 4% above 2019 levels. Travel exports reached PLN 64.6 billion, or 15.2% of total service exports in 2022.

International tourism has seen a strong recovery in Poland, with 15.9 million international tourists in 2022, but it remains 25% below 2019 levels. Germany remains the largest source market, accounting for 33% of international tourism, followed by Ukraine (22%), and Belarus (5%).

Domestic tourism remains an essential part of the sector. In 2022, Polish residents made 51.7 million domestic overnight trips, 3.4% above 2019 levels, and accounted for 76% of total overnight visitors. Poland counted 11.7 million outbound trips, 13.3% below 2019 levels.

At the beginning of Russia's war of aggression against Ukraine in 2022, Poland experienced a decline in bookings across the country. Due to the persisting uncertainty of the multiple crises, international arrivals are projected to reach near pre-pandemic levels by the end of 2024, with the possibility of exceeding this level in 2025.

Tourism governance

The Ministry of Sport and Tourism is responsible for tourism-related matters, including the sector's management, legislation and regulation in Poland. The Ministry also supervises the Polish Tourism Organisation, responsible for marketing and promotion of Poland as a tourist destination and ensuring the development and operation of the Polish tourist information system. The organisation has 16 international offices, located in established and emerging markets, and co-operates with the tourist organisations and others involved in promoting and developing tourism at the regional level.

At the regional level, tourism development is the responsibility of regional and local governments. Regional Tourism Organisations collaborate between local governments, particularly at the provincial level, and tourism sector representatives. Joint activities focus on the development of products and the tourist information system, consumer marketing, domestic and international promotion, and infrastructure development and modernisation. There are approximately 130 local tourist organisations in Poland.

The Minister of Sport and Tourism established the Tourism Experts Council for tourism development in Poland. The council is made up of experts and practitioners and designed to support continued initiatives for the pandemic recovery.

The tourism budget in Poland has been increasing. In 2023, tourism was allocated PLN 110.3 million, including PLN 84.5 million for the Polish Tourism Organisation. This represents a total increase of 53%

compared to 2022, when the tourism budget was PLN 71.9 million and the Polish Tourism Organisation received PLN 60.2 million.

Poland: Organisational chart of tourism bodies

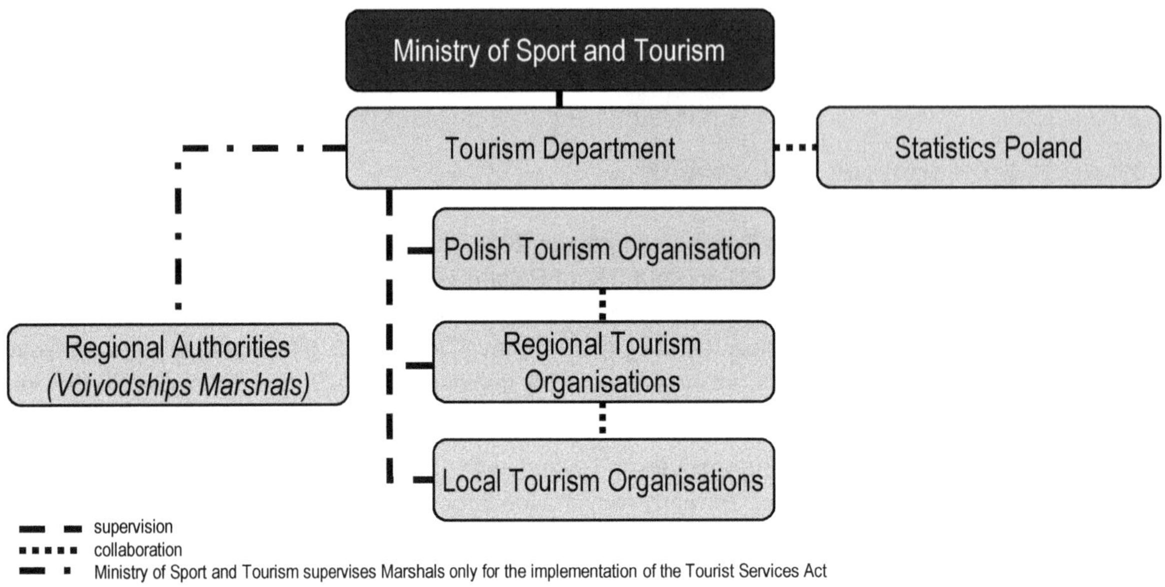

Source: OECD, adapted from the Sport and Tourism, 2024.

Tourism policies and programmes

Poland is currently working on a new long-term strategy a blueprint of effective instruments, solutions and mechanisms for state intervention will be developed, providing an effective response to potential crises and ensuring sustainable and stable tourism development. This strategy will replace the existing long-term tourism strategy which set targets until 2020. Preparatory work has begun and will focus on diagnosis, evaluation and recommendations, however, given the context's complexity and the anticipated challenges, the strategy has yet to be finalised.

The Strategy will be developed in co-operation with key tourism stakeholders, including, the Polish Tourism Organisation, Central Statistical Office, Regional Tourism Organisations, entrepreneurs in the tourism industry, Trade Associations. Work is also underway to ensure appropriate legislative solutions to support these objectives.

It is anticipated that the new strategy will focus on the key issues of:

- Digitalisation and technological innovation
- Climate-resilient and environmentally sustainable services - sustainable tourism and ecotourism
- Development of inbound tourism
- Development of social tourism
- Modern ways of collecting and managing tourism data
- Activities for the promotion and development of Polish tourism
- Increasing resilience to future crises.

While developing a new long-term strategy, Poland continues to support tourism through several key programmes. The Tourism Reimbursement Fund, established in September 2020, aims to prevent business bankruptcies within the tourism sector and has distributed nearly PLN 300 million to over 100 000 beneficiaries. The Tourism Aid Fund provides loans to tour operators for event cancellations due to extraordinary circumstances and has been utilised twice in response to global geopolitical tensions.

A social tourism programme promotes tourism for the elderly, children from orphanages, children with disabilities and their caretakers, and includes training for those working with people with special needs. This programme received over PLN 6.5 million in 2023, with approximately PLN 5 million planned for 2024.

Another programme focuses on promoting physical activity by renovating and establishing new hiking trails, with PLN 2 million in funding for 2023 and PLN 3 million planned for 2024. The System of Public Registers in Tourism aims to provide reliable information to tourists and professionals, verify legally operating accommodation facilities, enhance digitalisation, and strengthen domestic tourism post-COVID.

Additionally, the Polish Tourism Brands Project aims to create a catalogue of attractive Polish regions and tourist routes, with nine brands currently participating and three new brands to be announced in early 2024. The catalogue will be professionally managed and promoted to foster tourism development in the selected areas.

Statistical Profile

Poland: Domestic, inbound and outbound tourism

	2018	2019	2020	2021	2022
TOURISM FLOWS, THOUSAND					
Domestic tourism					
Total domestic trips	95 973	..	..	80 671	51 702
Overnight visitors (tourists)	47 736	50 018	38 570	46 278	51 702
Same-day visitors (excursionists)	48 237	..	..	34 393	
Nights in all types of accommodation	224 767	233 660	182 815	220 111	241 626
Hotels and similar establishments	47 324	51 912	35 922	42 969	54 496
Other collective establishments	71 902	76 020	52 508	70 937	78 454
Private accommodation	105 541	105 728	94 385	106 206	108 676
Inbound tourism					
Total international arrivals	85 947	88 515	51 076	51 026	71 814
Overnight visitors (tourists)	19 623	21 158	8 418	9 722	15 948
Same-day visitors (excursionists)	66 324	67 356	42 658	41 304	55 867
Top markets					
Germany	6 704	7 067	3 426	3 630	5 219
Ukraine	2 038	2 596	1 021	1 496	3 462
Russia	919	955	238	..	..
United Kingdom	919	1 002	360	389	699
Belarus	793	807	391	490	735
Nights in all types of accommodation	122 065	131 988	57 306	64 531	103 351
Hotels and similar establishments	47 195	52 979	20 637	21 467	31 830
Other collective establishments	13 781	15 849	4 946	4 920	8 865
Private accommodation	61 089	63 160	31 723	38 144	62 655
Outbound tourism					
Total international departures	48 615	50 558	26 893	24 220	33 748
Overnight visitors (tourists)	12 747	13 545	6 187	6 813	11 742
Same-day visitors (excursionists)	35 868	37 013	20 706	17 407	22 006
Top destinations					
Germany	2 438	2 523	1 603	1 797	2 419
Italy	1 055	1 114	393	383	1 047
United Kingdom	1 031	1 100	437	..	749
Czechia	762	790	410	383	..
Greece	752	857	..	451	801
TOURISM RECEIPTS AND EXPENDITURE, MILLION PLN					
Inbound tourism					
Total international receipts	56 775	61 514	34 333	39 260	73 530
International travel receipts	50 613	53 802	31 975	35 163	64 623
International passenger transport receipts	6 162	7 712	2 358	4 097	8 907
Outbound tourism					
Total international expenditure	37 970	39 279	21 884	23 588	36 951
International travel expenditure	34 759	35 653	20 536	22 224	34 238
International passenger transport expenditure	3 211	3 626	1 348	1 364	2 713

.. Not available
Source: OECD Tourism Statistics (Database).

StatLink https://stat.link/exm641

Poland: Enterprises and employment in tourism

	Number of establishments	Number of persons employed[1]				
	2023	2018	2019	2020	2021	2022
Total	..	..	..	..	..	..
Tourism industries	17 261	..	..	..	..	..
Accommodation services for visitors	9 809	195 675	208 257	195 539	198 693	215 877
Hotels and similar establishments	3 982	..	..	..	..	..
Food and beverage serving industry	7 452	..	..	..	..	..
Passenger transport	..	..	..	..	..	..
Air passenger transport	..	..	..	..	..	..
Railways passenger transport	..	..	..	..	..	..
Road passenger transport	..	..	..	..	..	..
Water passenger transport	..	..	..	..	..	..
Passenger transport supporting services	..	..	..	..	..	..
Transport equipment rental	..	..	..	..	..	..
Travel agencies and other reservation services industry	..	..	..	..	..	..
Cultural industry	..	..	..	..	..	..
Sports and recreation industry	..	..	..	..	..	..
Retail trade of country-specific tourism characteristic goods	..	..	..	..	..	..
Other country-specific tourism industries	..	..	..	..	..	..
Other industries	..	..	..	..	..	..

.. Not available
1. Data refer to number of employees.
Source: OECD Tourism Statistics (Database).

StatLink https://stat.link/lyr38g

Poland: Internal tourism consumption

Million PLN

	2015		
	Domestic tourism expenditure	Inbound tourism expenditure	Internal tourism consumption
Total	..	..	..
Consumption products	**21 420**	**36 750**	**65 099**
Tourism characteristic products	15 411	12 854	31 500
Accommodation services for visitors	4 853	3 320	10 244
Food and beverage serving services	4 874	4 328	9 202
Passenger transport services	3 066	2 825	6 599
Air passenger transport services	2 058	1 897	4 121
Railways passenger transport services	219	113	697
Road passenger transport services	783	724	1 685
Water passenger transport services	6	91	97
Passenger transport supporting services	..	..	..
Transport equipment rental services	167	0	547
Travel agencies and other reservation services industry	2 031	458	2 566
Cultural services	419	1 923	2 342
Sports and recreation services	..	..	..
Country-specific tourism characteristic goods	..	..	..
Country-specific tourism characteristic services	..	..	..
Other consumption products	6 009	23 896	33 600
Tourism connected products	..	..	..
Non-tourism related consumption products	..	..	..
Non-consumption products	..	..	..

.. Not available
Source: OECD Tourism Statistics (Database).

StatLink https://stat.link/tcbf1p

Portugal

Tourism in the economy and outlook

Tourism is a fundamental economic activity for wealth generation and employment in Portugal and the 2023 data reaffirm this importance. In 2023, travel exports reached EUR **25.1** billion, representing 48.6% of total service exports in 2023 and directly contributed to 9.5% of GDP. Activities related to accommodation and food services employed 328 800 people in 2023, which accounted for 6% of total employment in Portugal.

Portugal recorded a total of 77.2 million overnight stays in 2023, which represents an increase of 10.7% compared to the same period last year. From this, 53.8 million overnight stays were from international visitors. The top markets were United Kingdom (18%), Germany (11%), Spain (10%), France (9%) and the United States (9%). Domestic tourism is also a strong contributor to the Portuguese economy, with 23.4 million overnight stays in 2023, 2.1% above 2022 levels.

Tourism governance

The Secretary of State for Tourism sits within the Ministry of Economy. Turismo de Portugal is the national tourism authority and responds to the Secretary of State for Tourism. It is responsible for national tourism policy, promotion, training, investment, valuation and sustainability of tourism activities.

At regional level, Portugal has five Regional Tourism Bodies which act as destination management organisations with financial and administrative autonomy. These regional bodies are responsible for domestic promotion and product development. There are also two Regional Directorates for Tourism covering the autonomous regions of Madeira and the Azores, with political and administrative autonomy.

Turismo de Portugal develops and implements international promotion initiatives in co-ordination with seven Regional Tourism Promotion Agencies. The regional promotion agencies are non-profit, private law associations with Regional Tourism Body and private sector membership. They have a formal contractual relationship with Turismo de Portugal for developing promotional activities in international markets.

The total budget of Turismo de Portugal in 2023 was EUR 407.2 million (operating costs and overheads included), of which half came from the dedicated taxes (gambling tax) with the remaining coming from EU Structural Funds and other public funding sources.

Portugal: Organisational chart of tourism bodies

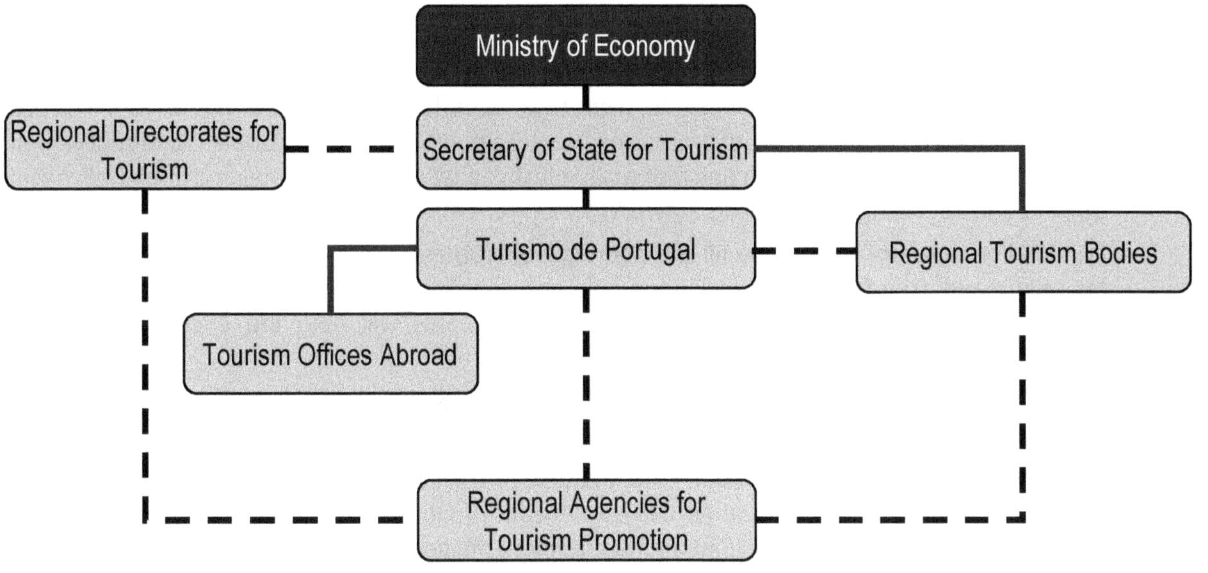

Source: OECD, adapted from Turismo de Portugal, 2024.

Tourism policies and programmes

Tourism in Portugal is guided by the 2027 Tourism Strategy. The Strategy is a ten-year plan launched in 2017, which aims to drive economic, social and environmental development throughout the country. The strategy is built around the following goals:

- Offer a strategic framework to be used as a guideline for national tourism for the next 10 years.
- Ensure stability and acceptance of commitments regarding the strategic options for national tourism.
- Promote integration of sectoral policies.
- Generate ongoing joint action between tourism stakeholders.
- Act with a sense of strategy in the present and in the short to medium-term.

To achieve the goals of the Strategy, shorter-term action plans have been built, including the Action Plan Reactivate Tourism | Building the Future and the Sustainable Tourism Plan 2020-23.

The Action Plan aims to encourage the recovery of the national tourism sector. It has four axes - supporting companies, promoting safety, generating business and building a future - and is fully integrated with the objectives of the Recovery and Resilience Plan, and the Portugal 2030 Strategy. The Action Plan is composed of specific and measurable actions that, in the short, medium and long-term, aim to transform the sector to create more value, significantly contributing to GDP growth and a fairer distribution of wealth. This plan sets the target of exceeding EUR 27 billion in tourist receipts by 2027.

Several programmes have been launched to meet the objectives and targets of the Action Plan, including:

- *Empresas Turismo 360º*, or Tourism Companies 360°, which encourages companies to undertake sustainability reporting. The programme provides technical support for companies to integrate ESG measures based on performance. This programme was developed in partnership with the private sector and the banking system and is supported by a dedicated platform (Forest) for businesses to report their ESG performance.

- A revision of Executive orders on Tourist Accommodation and Local Accommodation, including mandatory sustainability requirements focusing on energy efficiency, water efficiency and waste management, as well as an inclusion of sustainability criteria into tourism specific financing instruments managed by *Turismo de Portugal*.
- The Agenda for the Tourism Professions, a strategic agenda made up of 20 measures to increase qualifications, the attractiveness of professions and the number of professionals. To attract workers and promote growth, the agenda has four main initiatives: attracting and retaining talent, increasing training and knowledge, generating networks amongst similar sectors and promoting diversity.
- Immigration agreements to help fill the shortage of workers in the tourism sector. Portugal has recently made an agreement with Portuguese speaking countries, to facilitate mobility between member countries, through a simplified visa regime. This will help the sector fill additional vacancies.
- The Tourism Agenda for the Inland Territory will invest in companies, qualifying professionals and projecting the interior and its offer (see box below).
- The creation of Regional Tourism Observatories in each of the seven regional DMOs, in partnership with the UNWTO and its INSTO network of Observatories, bringing universities and knowledge centres closer to destination management entities.

At the end of 2023, Portugal launched a new international marketing campaign, *#It's not tourism. It's futourism*. It is a campaign that sets 12 New Year's resolutions to meet the changing needs for the tourist of the future and aims to mobilise people to change their way of travel. This campaign is aligned with the national strategy and calls on everyone to join Visit Portugal on a transformative journey towards a more inclusive, sustainable, and responsible tourism. The #Futourism movement, invites future tourists to turn their trips into more authentic and sustainable experiences, resulting in a positive impact for territories, the environment, and the communities.

Promoting the geographic dispersion of tourism in Portugal

In 2021, 82% of total accommodation capacity and 90% of total tourist demand was concentrated in Portugal's coastal destinations. This unbalanced dispersion of demand creates obstacles to achieving a sustainable and balanced growth in the tourism sector and leads to economic inequality in other inland regions.

The Tourism Agenda for the Inland Territory was launched in early 2023 and aims to boost the tourism sector in inland Portugal to act as a catalyst for the cohesion and economic development of low-density territories. This Agenda consists of initiatives aimed at connecting territories, enhancing resources, investing in companies and the tourism offer with a package of approximately EUR 200 million.

In 2023, the Interior and Tourism Microcredit financing lines were made available to boost investment to encourage tourism. Future credit lines also include EUR 35 million for business creation and expansion in inland regions and EUR 50 million allocated to allow access to 80% interest-free loans, as well as a realisation premium of up to 30% of non-refundable funds. Additional measures are also being introduced to support: the internationalisation of companies, employment, internships and events.

Campaigns are planned for inland destinations for domestic and international markets, to mobilise operators, institutions and the community.

Statistical Profile

Portugal: Domestic, inbound and outbound tourism

	2018	2019	2020	2021	2022
TOURISM FLOWS, THOUSAND					
Domestic tourism[1]					
Total domestic trips	..	..	..	..	..
Overnight visitors (tourists)	19 593	21 363	13 730	16 506	22 627
Same-day visitors (excursionists)	..	..	..	..	..
Nights in all types of accommodation	24 719	26 115	16 875	22 486	27 488
Hotels and similar establishments	16 048	16 815	10 751	14 867	18 329
Other collective establishments	5 741	6 047	4 293	5 140	6 082
Private accommodation	2 930	3 252	1 831	2 479	3 077
Inbound tourism					
Total international arrivals	..	..	..	..	..
Overnight visitors (tourists)	16 186	17 283	4 208	6 345	16 308
Same-day visitors (excursionists)	..	..	..	..	..
Top markets					
Spain	2 238	2 463	878	1 259	2 365
United Kingdom	2 127	2 220	492	720	2 179
France	1 851	1 816	518	841	1 742
Germany	1 756	1 704	497	655	1 654
Netherlands	692	672	205	356	750
Nights in all types of accommodation	50 480	51 708	13 409	20 122	49 686
Hotels and similar establishments	40 514	41 178	10 178	15 320	38 910
Other collective establishments	3 586	3 581	1 486	1 974	3 999
Private accommodation	6 380	6 948	1 744	2 828	6 777
Outbound tourism					
Total international departures	..	..	..	..	..
Overnight visitors (tourists)	2 486	3 100	680	1 012	4 897
Same-day visitors (excursionists)	..	..	..	..	..
Top destinations					
..	..	..	..	..	..
..	..	..	..	..	..
..	..	..	..	..	..
..	..	..	..	..	..
..	..	..	..	..	..
TOURISM RECEIPTS AND EXPENDITURE, MILLION EUR					
Inbound tourism					
Total international receipts	20 699	21 997	9 218	11 777	25 286
International travel receipts	17 054	18 291	7 716	10 064	21 141
International passenger transport receipts	3 645	3 706	1 502	1 713	4 145
Outbound tourism					
Total international expenditure	5 458	6 101	3 091	3 997	6 478
International travel expenditure	4 584	5 124	2 743	3 574	5 533
International passenger transport expenditure	874	977	348	423	945

.. Not available

1. Trips from demand side surveys; Nights from supply side surveys.

Source: OECD Tourism Statistics (Database).

StatLink https://stat.link/5ln382

Portugal: Enterprises and employment in tourism

	Number of establishments[1]	Number of persons employed				
	2021	2018	2019	2020	2021	2022
Total	138 776	..	..	..	..	..
Tourism industries	133 793	..	..	..	..	..
Accommodation services for visitors	39 212	107 590	115 803	103 555	101 416	..
Hotels and similar establishments	..	..	..	..	..	..
Food and beverage serving industry	71 882	267 477	283 438	262 340	257 573	..
Passenger transport	18 583	54 617	..	..	..	..
Air passenger transport	96	..	..	..	..	..
Railways passenger transport	2	..	..	..	..	..
Road passenger transport	18 250	54 617	..	41 621	40 737	..
Water passenger transport	235	..	..	..	..	..
Passenger transport supporting services	..	..	..	..	..	..
Transport equipment rental	..	..	..	..	..	..
Travel agencies and other reservation services industry	4 116	14 254	15 022	13 439	12 213	..
Cultural industry	..	..	..	..	..	..
Sports and recreation industry	..	..	..	..	..	..
Retail trade of country-specific tourism characteristic goods	..	..	..	..	..	..
Other country-specific tourism industries	..	..	..	..	..	..
Other industries	4 983	..	11 116	10 664	10 575	..

.. Not available
1. Data refer to number of enterprises.
Source: OECD Tourism Statistics (Database).

StatLink https://stat.link/cdj74z

Portugal: Internal tourism consumption

Million EUR

	2020		
	Domestic tourism expenditure	Inbound tourism expenditure	Internal tourism consumption
Total	..	..	..
Consumption products	6 562	8 593	16 847
Tourism characteristic products	5 087	6 420	27 456
Accommodation services for visitors	1 822	2 242	5 273
Food and beverage serving services	1 503	2 405	3 908
Passenger transport services	659	1 544	2 360
Air passenger transport services	89	985	1 110
Railways passenger transport services	78	12	190
Road passenger transport services	266	160	431
Water passenger transport services	31	12	60
Passenger transport supporting services	..	..	..
Transport equipment rental services	195	375	570
Travel agencies and other reservation services industry	223	38	260
Cultural services	25	72	252
Sports and recreation services	485	108	603
Country-specific tourism characteristic goods	..	..	..
Country-specific tourism characteristic services	370	12	393
Other consumption products	1 476	2 173	3 745
Tourism connected products	284	652	945
Non-tourism related consumption products	1 191	1 521	2 800
Non-consumption products	..	..	..

.. Not available
Source: OECD Tourism Statistics (Database).

StatLink https://stat.link/sm7wjl

Slovak Republic

Tourism in the economy and outlook

Tourism is an important lever for regional development in the Slovak Republic and has become a strategic sector to the national economy. In 2021, tourism directly generated EUR 1.4 billion in GDP, or 1,4% of the national GDP, down from 2.8% in 2019. Tourism accounted for 165 000 jobs in the economy (down from 185 000 in 2019). Travel exports were EUR 1.3 billion in 2022 and represented 10.7% of total service exports but remain significantly lower than the pre-pandemic level of 26%.

Post-pandemic, the number of visitors to the Slovak Republic is recovering. In 2023, total visitors are 11% below pre-pandemic levels, totaling 5.7 million domestic and international tourists in commercial accommodation. In 2023, the Slovak Republic recorded 2.1 million international tourists in commercial accommodation, which corresponds to a 31% increase compared with 2022 but is still 16% below 2019 figures. The key markets are the Czechia (34%), followed by Poland (13%) and Germany (7%). As for domestic tourism, 3.6 million domestic tourists were recorded in commercial accommodation in 2023, 8.0% below 2019 levels.

The Slovak Republic predicts that in 2024 international visitor numbers will slightly increase. Tourism demand is expected to return to 2019 levels by 2026.

Tourism governance

The new Ministry of Tourism and Sports of the Slovak Republic was established in February 2024, shifting tourism responsibilities from the Ministry of Transport. Tourism responsibilities have been split into two sections, state policy and destination management. The Ministry of Tourism and Sports co-operates with other ministries through participation in various committees dealing with issues impacting tourism, including the Working Group to Co-ordinate the Presentation of Slovakia Abroad, the Interdepartmental Commission of the Geo Parks Network, the Impact and Adaptation Steering Group, and the Working Group of the Government Council for Vocational Education and Training.

The Ministry established Slovakia Travel in 2021 as the National Tourism Organisation responsible for tourism marketing and promotion as well as a tourism data centre. The Slovak Tourism Association, composed of representatives of the main tourism organisations, promotes co-operation in the sector and advises on legislative changes.

At local and regional levels, tourism associations contribute to quality improvement, professional training, and the sharing of best practices. The Slovak Republic also delegates tourism responsibilities to self-governing bodies in eight regions and municipalities. Local and regional destination management organisations (DMOs) are responsible for developing tourism products and promotion. There are 39 local and 8 regional DMOs in the Slovak Republic.

The ministerial budget for direct support of the tourism sector was EUR 9.2 million in 2023, an increase from EUR 8.6 million in 2022. This budget is allocated for subsidies to local and regional DMOs, mainly for marketing, product development and tourism infrastructure, and has steadily increased since 2018. Additional funding for the tourism sector includes the budget for Slovakia Travel, which amounted to EUR 21 million in 2023 for marketing campaigns aimed at domestic and international markets and promotional activities.

Slovak Republic: Organisational chart of tourism bodies

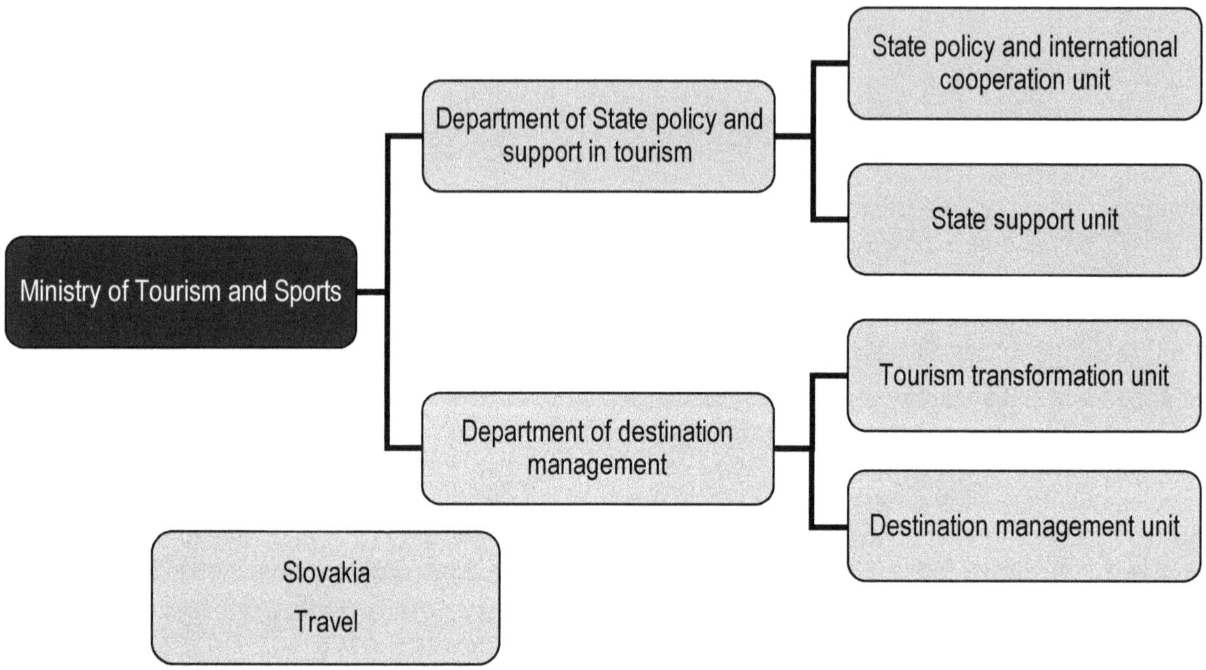

Source: OECD, adapted from the Ministry of Tourism and Sports, 2024

Tourism policies and programmes

In 2024, the Slovak Republic is finalising the National Sustainable Tourism Strategy for 2035. The new Strategy aims to increase the competitiveness of tourism, better use its potential, balance regional disparities and create new jobs. It sets priorities and goals to improve digitalisation, social sustainability and resilience in the tourism sector. The new Ministry of Tourism and Sports of the Slovak Republic will focus on important areas for sustainable development across the tourism sector, including:

- A competitive tourism sector that is ready for green and digital transformation.
- Durable destinations which can provide quality stays for visitors and quality of life for residents.
- A functional and flexible tourism management model.

The Slovak Republic will launch new information channels nationwide, through regional tourism offices, the national tourism board, municipalities and private entities. Under the 2035 strategy, the Slovak Republic will also set new tourism communication channels between national and international stakeholders, especially in EU countries.

Key tourism programmes and initiatives recently implemented in the Slovak Republic include:

- Lowering the Value Added Tax (VAT) for gastronomy and selected leisure services such as wellness centres, aqua parks and ski resorts from 20% to 10% in January 2023.
- Creating a tourism fund to support all tourism stakeholders.

- Implementing an eVisitor system to improve data collection and data sharing. This initiative will provide better access to accommodation providers' registrar and guest data to enhance national security and enforce effective tax collection, while also helping enhance the digitalisation of the tourism sector and collecting real time data to support governance and decision making at the local and national level. It is a large-scale project with several stages of implementation being undertaken in collaboration with partner countries who have successfully implemented similar initiatives (see box below).

Implementing an e-Visitor monitoring system in the Slovak Republic

The e-Visitor initiative will create a database system that can publish visitor data in an external environment with export capabilities. It will be designed to integrate with Central Registry of Public Administration Reference Data Information System and provide a portal solution (extensive identity management) and an analytical layer.

Advantages of the e-Visitor system include:

- Contributing to the digitalisation of the collection of accommodation fees and making their collection and reporting more efficient;
- Reducing the administrative burden on accommodation providers;
- Providing unified data collection and relevant information on visitation in the Slovak Republic with the required granularity (e.g. gender, nationality, age);
- Integrating the required data into various institutions through existing databases;
- Creating online reports to understand tourism in the country with real-time data.

A feasibility study is currently being prepared for the e-Visitor initiative, with the financing, scheduling and materials still being discussed. The goal of the study is to provide an independent assessment of the project, examining all attributes of the proposed project including the economic, financial, and legal aspects of the implementation. This information will provide the foundation of the project documentation for the next phases in accordance with Decree No. 401/2023. A Steering Committee is being formed to support the initiative. Communication is also being undertaken regarding the placement of the public administration information system into cloud environments accessible to the state.

Statistical Profile

Slovak Republic: Domestic, inbound and outbound tourism

	2018	2019	2020	2021	2022
TOURISM FLOWS, THOUSAND					
Domestic tourism					
Total domestic trips	3 340	3 958	2 356	2 149	3 541
Overnight visitors (tourists)	3 340	3 958	2 356	2 149	3 541
Same-day visitors (excursionists)	..	..	..	..	..
Nights in all types of accommodation	9 819	11 453	7 443	6 704	9 984
Hotels and similar establishments	9 501	11 047	7 054	6 340	..
Other collective establishments	128	131	140	151	..
Private accommodation	189	275	249	213	..
Inbound tourism					
Total international arrivals	2 256	2 475	854	576	1 757
Overnight visitors (tourists)	2 256	2 475	854	576	1 757
Same-day visitors (excursionists)	..	..	..	..	..
Top markets					
Czech Republic	702	777	378	230	..
Poland	226	240	116	59	..
Germany	178	182	63	53	..
Hungary	112	124	43	28	..
Austria	100	97	31	26	..
Nights in all types of accommodation	5 696	6 251	2 348	1 465	4 237
Hotels and similar establishments	5 345	5 855	2 121	1 358	..
Other collective establishments	214	193	123	67	..
Private accommodation	138	203	104	41	..
Outbound tourism					
Total international departures	8 321	9 669	1 996	..	..
Overnight visitors (tourists)	5 313	5 971	1 180	..	..
Same-day visitors (excursionists)	3 008	3 699	815	..	..
Top destinations					
Czech Republic	1 060	1 281	323	384	..
Croatia	440	423	122	309	..
Italy	257	295	..	46	..
Austria	309	351	82	99	..
Hungary	308	240	52	101	..
TOURISM RECEIPTS AND EXPENDITURE, MILLION EUR					
Inbound tourism					
Total international receipts	2 817	2 996	1 162	1 001	1 427
International travel receipts	2 710	2 861	1 132	941	1 291
International passenger transport receipts	107	134	31	59	135
Outbound tourism					
Total international expenditure	2 403	2 501	1 171	1 313	2 278
International travel expenditure	2 225	2 313	1 111	1 257	2 135
International passenger transport expenditure	178	188	61	56	143

.. Not available

Source: OECD Tourism Statistics (Database).

StatLink https://stat.link/20w46q

Slovak Republic: Enterprises and employment in tourism

	Number of establishments[1]	Number of persons employed				
	2021	2018	2019	2020	2021	2022
Total	..	..	..	..	..	..
Tourism industries	45 388	177 638	184 891	170 510	164 622	..
Accommodation services for visitors	3 721	17 998	18 384	15 709	15 281	..
Hotels and similar establishments	..	..	..	..	..	..
Food and beverage serving industry	14 221	70 032	74 540	70 237	66 848	..
Passenger transport	2 853	26 476	26 635	25 317	24 748	..
Air passenger transport	..	..	..	..	..	..
Railways passenger transport	..	..	..	..	..	..
Road passenger transport	..	..	..	..	..	..
Water passenger transport	..	..	..	..	..	..
Passenger transport supporting services	..	..	..	..	..	..
Transport equipment rental	570	1 402	1 501	1 488	1 452	..
Travel agencies and other reservation services industry	1 386	3 327	3 386	2 538	2 296	..
Cultural industry	2 573	10 152	10 475	10 122	10 104	..
Sports and recreation industry	5 054	18 932	19 844	17 090	16 377	..
Retail trade of country-specific tourism characteristic goods	..	..	..	..	..	..
Other country-specific tourism industries	15 010	29 319	30 126	28 009	27 516	..
Other industries	..	..	..	..	..	..

.. Not available
1. Data refer to number of enterprises.
Source: OECD Tourism Statistics (Database).

StatLink https://stat.link/m0lekf

Slovak Republic: Internal tourism consumption

Million EUR

	2021		
	Domestic tourism expenditure	Inbound tourism expenditure	Internal tourism consumption
Total	..	..	..
Consumption products	1 383	565	3 028
Tourism characteristic products	922	366	2 368
Accommodation services for visitors	242	129	511
Food and beverage serving services	311	126	441
Passenger transport services	185	21	722
Air passenger transport services	..	..	..
Railways passenger transport services	..	..	..
Road passenger transport services	..	..	..
Water passenger transport services	..	..	..
Passenger transport supporting services	..	..	..
Transport equipment rental services	13	15	28
Travel agencies and other reservation services industry	51	3	55
Cultural services	10	6	180
Sports and recreation services	50	27	161
Country-specific tourism characteristic goods	28	19	47
Country-specific tourism characteristic services	34	22	225
Other consumption products	461	199	660
Tourism connected products	..	..	..
Non-tourism related consumption products	..	..	..
Non-consumption products	..	..	..

.. Not available
Source: OECD Tourism Statistics (Database).

StatLink https://stat.link/sq2cil

Slovenia

Tourism in the economy and outlook

Tourism is a key contributor to the Slovenian economy. Travel exports represented 28% of total services exports (or almost EUR 3.3 billion) in 2023 but remained below the pre-pandemic levels of 33%. Tourism-related industries employed almost 69 600 persons in 2023, accounting for 7.4% of the total workforce and increased by 0.5% compared to 2019. Tourism is continuing to recover after its direct contribution to national GDP fell to 3.3% in 2020, down from 5.4% in 2019.

In 2023, Slovenia saw almost 4.7 million international visitors at commercial accommodation establishments, representing 99% of pre-pandemic levels. The top international source markets in Slovenia were Germany (15%), Italy (11%) and Austria (9%). International tourism accounted for almost 11.6 million overnight stays, a 244% increase compared to the pandemic low in 2020. Domestic tourism performs strongly in Slovenia. In 2023, 1.5 million domestic tourists and almost 4.6 million overnight stays were recorded at commercial accommodation establishments, returning to pre-pandemic levels after a surge in domestic tourism from 2020 to 2022.

Tourism governance

The Ministry of Economy, Tourism and Sport was established in 2022, with the Tourism Directorate, the responsible governmental body for tourism policy and its implementation. The Tourism Directorate is divided into the Division for Tourism Development and the Division for Business Environment in Tourism.

The Ministry assures the legal framework for better tourism governance and stimulates the business environment for tourism SMEs, encourages co-operation between public and private stakeholders, and ensures the effective management of the tourism budget.

The Tourism Council, established by the Ministry, consists of government and industry representatives and is the main political body for co-ordinating tourism policy. The Ministry co-operates and consults with the Tourist and Catering Chamber, the Chamber of Crafts and Entrepreneurs and the Tourist Association of Slovenia and other representatives of the tourism sector. The Tourist Association of Slovenia is a national non-governmental organisation comprised of more than 600 local tourism associations.

The Slovenian Tourist Board is a public agency responsible for the marketing of Slovenia's tourist products and services as well as the programme for enhancing the sustainable development of Slovenian tourism. The Tourism Board acts on an annual work programme funded by the national tourism budget for tourism, and is responsible for programme activities related to collecting and sharing data to support the green and digital transformation of tourism, conducting research and surveys, tourism marketing and knowledge promotion, developing products and strengthening destinations management by supporting networking in the tourism ecosystem.

The entire State tourism budget dedicated to tourism in 2023 amounted to EUR 32. 2 million of which EUR 17.7 million were allocated to the STB working programme implementation. The national budget for 2023 represents a 65% increase compared to the previous year, resulting from the implementation of the Slovenian Tourism Strategy 2022-28. In addition, the EU allocated EUR 217 million to the development of tourism until 2029 as part of the National Resilience and Recovery Plan and the EU Cohesion package for Slovenia.

Slovenia: Organisational chart of tourism bodies

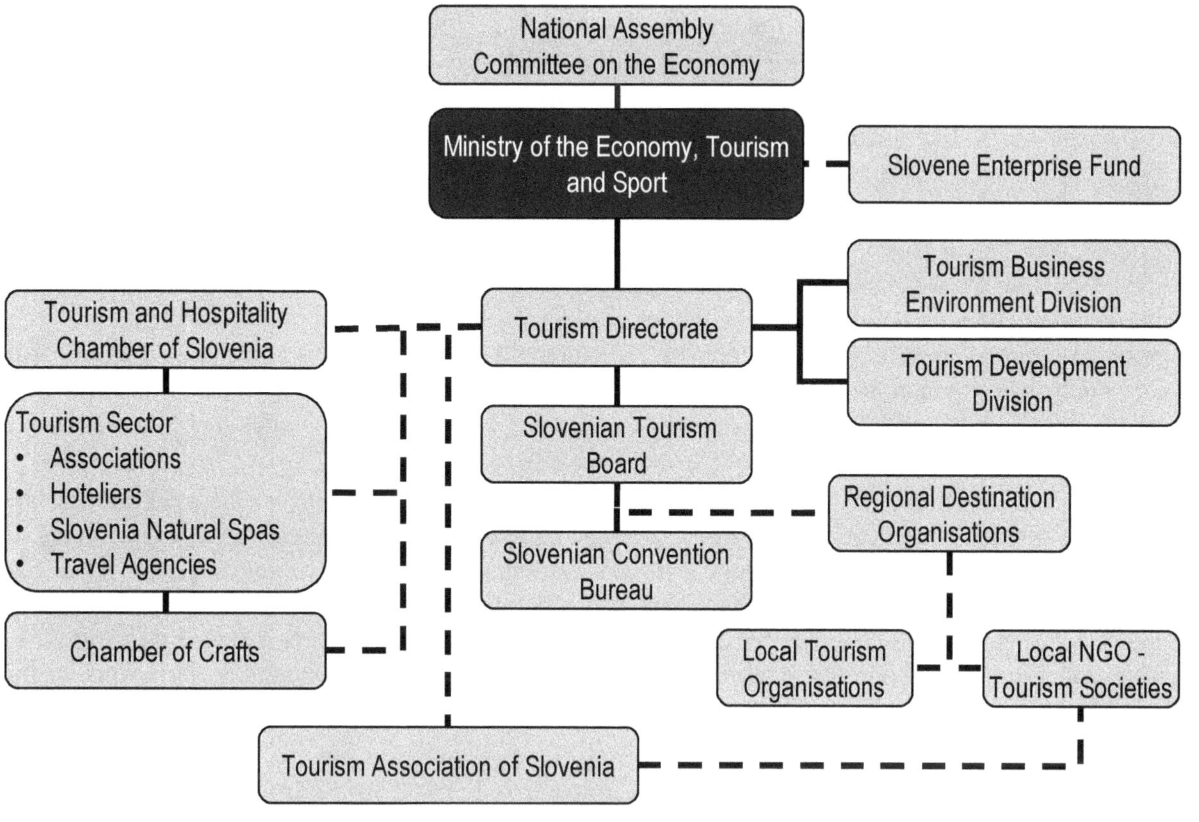

Source: OECD, adapted from the Ministry of the Economy, Tourism and Sport, 2024.

Tourism policies and programmes

The Slovenian Tourism Strategy 2022-28 aims to address the gaps tourism destinations and tourism providers face related to the adaption to the green transition, digitalisation and the rapid change in tourists needs and expectation in a post-pandemic context. The Strategy promotes the country's key strategic objective to become a green boutique destination with high value-added for satisfied tourists and locals. The Strategy comprises five pillars:

- Providing safe, sustainable, and attractive experiences.
- Mitigating the effects of the crisis and adjustment of businesses.
- Understanding new consumer needs and new market segmentation.
- Maximising the use of digital technology.
- Building sustainable relationships with businesses, tourists, and local communities.

The Strategy focuses on green tourism and particularly emphasises environmental sustainability and tourism carbon footprint reduction. The green transformation of enterprises and destinations will be achieved through a series of programmes and measures, including:

- The Green scheme of Slovenian tourism with the certification system Slovenia Green. In the first half of 2024, Slovenia Green certificates (first awarded in 2015) were approved for 60 destinations, 159 accommodation providers, 68 restaurants, four nature parks, nine tourist agencies, 13 attractions and two beaches. The Slovenia Green scheme and the green and sustainable indicators are continually revised to ensure they are fit for purpose.
- New assessment and measurement methods for green certification will be introduced, according to the new set of sustainable indicators. These will be introduced within the National Tourism Information Centre (NIS) by the end of 2024 and shared with the wider public in 2025 (see box below).
- A database to monitor actual green progress of individual destinations and providers, will be established. The database will enable comparison and benchmarking between providers and destinations through destination dashboards.

The promotion of work, jobs and careers in tourism remains a priority for Slovenia. In 2023, the Tourism Workforce and Career Opportunities Programme is implemented in co-operation with the Ministry, the Tourism Board and private sector associations. Under the programme, a special career portal named I create experiences was established. The portal presents education and apprenticeship opportunities, aggregates information on employer incentives, scholarships, job vacancies and includes a calendar of events such as education promotion events, career fairs and careers competitions. The portal also highlights the experiences of successful individuals who chose a career in tourism or hospitality and succeeded in both their personal and professional lives (see chapter 2).

The Strategic Development Partnership for Innovation in Tourism also implements a special programme to promote the enrolment of young people in vocational, secondary, and higher education programmes for hospitality and tourism. The programme aims to increase the volume of tourism and hospitality professionals and enhance the workforce skills to strengthen the resilience of the sector. The programme activities are aimed at young people who consider further education, upskilling, or reskilling as well as their parents, teachers, and school counselling services. The programme sits under the framework of the national campaign My Slovenia, which promotes key institutions and its activities participating in the tourism ecosystem.

A National Information Hub for Tourism in Slovenia

The new National Tourism Information Hub (NIS) is part of a horizontal development policy led by the Slovenian government in the field of digitalisation. This on-going project, managed by the Slovenian Tourist Board, aims to create a unique data hub where local, national, and international tourism-relevant data will be collected and processed, to enable and ease data-driven decision-making. NIS will focus on accelerating green and digital transition and upgrading the Green Scheme of Slovenian tourism.

The implementation of a comprehensive information hub began at the end of 2022 and is expected to be completed by the end of 2025. The project covers two parallel phases: (i) Implementing a modern digital analytical tool for measuring the impacts of tourism on all leading Slovene tourism destinations, to foster the industry's sustainable transition; and (ii) Measuring tourism flows in leading destinations and managing the geographical distribution of tourism development in a more sustainable way.

The prototype development phase with the analysis of data sources, preparation of functional specifications, implementation design and architectural scheme for the NIS hub has been carried out and completed in 2023. The implementation phase is due to be commenced in 2024. Due to the complexity of the project, experts from several fields, such as information technology experts, data analytics, experts on artificial intelligence and machine learning, will participate in the implementation phase.

Statistical Profile

Slovenia: Domestic, inbound and outbound tourism

	2018	2019	2020	2021	2022
TOURISM FLOWS, THOUSAND					
Domestic tourism[1]					
Total domestic trips	..	..	..	..	..
Overnight visitors (tourists)	1 508	1 528	1 849	2 171	1 933
Same-day visitors (excursionists)	..	..	..	..	..
Nights in all types of accommodation	4 519	4 405	5 850	6 457	5 507
Hotels and similar establishments	3 934	3 815	4 983	5 630	4 808
Other collective establishments	584	589	867	826	699
Private accommodation	..	..	..	..	..
Inbound tourism					
Total international arrivals	..	..	..	..	..
Overnight visitors (tourists)	4 425	4 702	1 216	1 832	3 936
Same-day visitors (excursionists)	..	..	..	..	..
Top markets					
Italy	599	597	159	162	434
Germany	506	585	289	414	681
Austria	382	396	143	171	363
Croatia	219	235	82	63	214
Netherlands	185	187	45	108	203
Nights in all types of accommodation	11 176	11 371	3 354	4 794	10 075
Hotels and similar establishments	9 826	9 923	2 802	3 844	8 421
Other collective establishments	1 350	1 448	552	950	1 654
Private accommodation	..	..	..	..	..
Outbound tourism					
Total international departures	5 409	6 049	1 892	3 030	4 727
Overnight visitors (tourists)	3 188	3 170	1 138	2 123	3 161
Same-day visitors (excursionists)	2 221	2 879	754	907	1 566
Top destinations					
Croatia	1 732	1 572	817	1 274	1 720
Italy	236	289	87 e	120	265
Austria	204	189	50 e	79 e	117
Germany	191	140	..	62 e	78 e
Bosnia and Herzegovina	142	200	..	183	251
TOURISM RECEIPTS AND EXPENDITURE, MILLION EUR					
Inbound tourism					
Total international receipts	2 870	2 998	1 279	1 726	3 021
International travel receipts	2 704	2 843	1 237	1 685	2 972
International passenger transport receipts	166	155	41	41	49
Outbound tourism					
Total international expenditure	1 585	1 583	838	1 206	1 761
International travel expenditure	1 483	1 500	805	1 173	1 733
International passenger transport expenditure	103	83	33	33	28

.. Not available; e Estimated value

1. Source: supply side survey.

Source: OECD Tourism Statistics (Database).

StatLink https://stat.link/6hm7t2

Slovenia: Enterprises and employment in tourism

	Number of establishments[1]	Number of persons employed				
	2021	2018	2019	2020	2021	2022
Total	..	..	..	..	..	..
Tourism industries	30 298	68 150	69 253	62 058	66 354	68 096
Accommodation services for visitors	9 606	17 570	17 796	14 251	16 396	16 616
Hotels and similar establishments	5 126	10 235	10 378	8 870	10 871	9 623
Food and beverage serving industry	7 437	25 322	26 106	22 588	24 693	25 354
Passenger transport	1 123	5 826	5 420	4 778	4 696	4 895
Air passenger transport	142	736	302	291	312	296
Railways passenger transport	1	c	c	c	c	c
Road passenger transport	916	4 430	4 449	3 846	3 767	3 946
Water passenger transport	64	c	c	c	c	c
Passenger transport supporting services	445	3 126	3 191	5 078	4 965	5 120
Transport equipment rental	333	469	489	457	474	492
Travel agencies and other reservation services industry	931	2 257	2 368	1 683	1 791	2 007
Cultural industry	6 240	8 197	8 372	8 263	8 278	8 310
Sports and recreation industry	4 183	5 383	5 511	4 960	5 061	5 302
Retail trade of country-specific tourism characteristic goods	..	..	..	..	..	..
Other country-specific tourism industries	..	..	..	..	..	..
Other industries	..	..	..	..	..	..

.. Not available; c Confidential data
1. Data refer to number of enterprises.
Source: OECD Tourism Statistics (Database).

StatLink https://stat.link/9lqtuj

Slovenia: Internal tourism consumption

Million EUR

	2020		
	Domestic tourism expenditure	Inbound tourism expenditure	Internal tourism consumption
Total	..	..	..
Consumption products	**1 326**	**1 506**	**2 908**
Tourism characteristic products	928	627	1 632
Accommodation services for visitors	263	246	555
Food and beverage serving services	295	190	486
Passenger transport services	189	55	244
Air passenger transport services	..	..	..
Railways passenger transport services	..	..	..
Road passenger transport services	..	..	..
Water passenger transport services	..	..	..
Passenger transport supporting services	..	..	..
Transport equipment rental services	..	..	..
Travel agencies and other reservation services industry	27	12	39
Cultural services	70	11	112
Sports and recreation services	84	112	197
Country-specific tourism characteristic goods	..	..	..
Country-specific tourism characteristic services	..	..	..
Other consumption products	398	879	1 277
Tourism connected products	..	..	..
Non-tourism related consumption products	..	..	..
Non-consumption products	..	..	..

.. Not available
Source: OECD Tourism Statistics (Database).

StatLink https://stat.link/5uqx3d

Spain

Tourism in the economy and outlook

Tourism is a key sector of the Spanish economy and an outstanding driver of socio-economic development. In 2022, tourism employed 2.6 million people, which represented 12.9% of the total workforce, and remained only 1.5% below 2019. Travel exports represented 44% of total service exports in 2022, still below the pre-pandemic level of 51%, but significantly above the pandemic low of 21% in 2020. Tourism is still recovering after the impacts of the COVID-19 pandemic, which reduced tourism's direct contribution to GDP from 12.4%, or EUR 155 billion in 2019, to 5.5% in 2020.

In 2023, international tourist arrivals reached 85.0 million, up 1.8% from 83.5 million international arrivals in 2019. International tourist expenditure increased 25% compared to 2022, reaching EUR 108.8 billion. The top three source markets in 2023 were the United Kingdom (17.3 million arrivals, a 14.2% increase compared to 2022), France (11.8 million arrivals, a 16.5% increase compared to 2022) and Germany (nearly 11 million arrivals, a 12.5% increase compared to 2022). Domestic tourism has continued to recover, with 124.5 million domestic tourist arrivals in 2022, up 15.6% compared to 2021. However, it still remains below the 2019 levels of 137.2 million domestic tourists.

Tourism governance

The Ministry of Industry and Tourism has been responsible for tourism since 2018. The State Secretariat for Tourism and the General Direction of Tourism Policies are responsible for defining, developing, co-ordinating and implementing tourism policy within the remit of central government's responsibility, as well as related institutions at national and international levels. The State Secretariat co-ordinates three organisations at the national level. SEGITTUR, the organisation for innovation and management of tourism technology, is a public sector body responsible for the development of new technologies in the Spanish tourism industry in both public and private sectors. It researches and manages technology, knowledge and innovation to enhance the competitiveness, quality and sustainability of all aspects of tourism. Turespaña is an autonomous body attached to the Ministry, responsible for carrying out the international tourism marketing and promotion of Spain abroad. It uses a network of 33 international tourism offices that support the implementation of the agreed marketing plan. Paradores de Turismo is a public company that runs a state-owned hotel network of 97 establishments located in historic sites, national parks or protected areas.

Co-ordinating mechanisms between the central and regional administrations and with the private sector play an important role in decision-making and co-ordination of different Spanish tourism policies. These bodies have neither a specific budget nor staff. They are all chaired by the Minister, or the State Secretariat for Tourism, which provides secretariat services. The Sectoral Tourism Conference is a collegiate, advisory and executive co-ordination body chaired by the Minister for Tourism, bringing together central government and autonomous region representatives to discuss key tourism policies and regulations. The Spanish Tourism Council is an advisory body which gathers tourism authorities at all levels and private sector stakeholders. The Inter-Ministerial Committee for Tourism includes representatives from national ministries responsible for tourism-related matters. The Advisory Council of Turespaña, comprising 11 members from the public and private sector, assists in defining and implementing strategies to market Spain abroad.

The State Secretariat for Tourism had an overall budget of EUR 1.08 billion in 2024, of which 75% was financed by Next Generation EU and the European Recovery Fund, to support the ongoing implementation of the Recovery, Transformation and Resilience Plan for Tourism. The remaining EUR 270 million comes from the Public general budget.

Spain: Organisational chart of tourism bodies

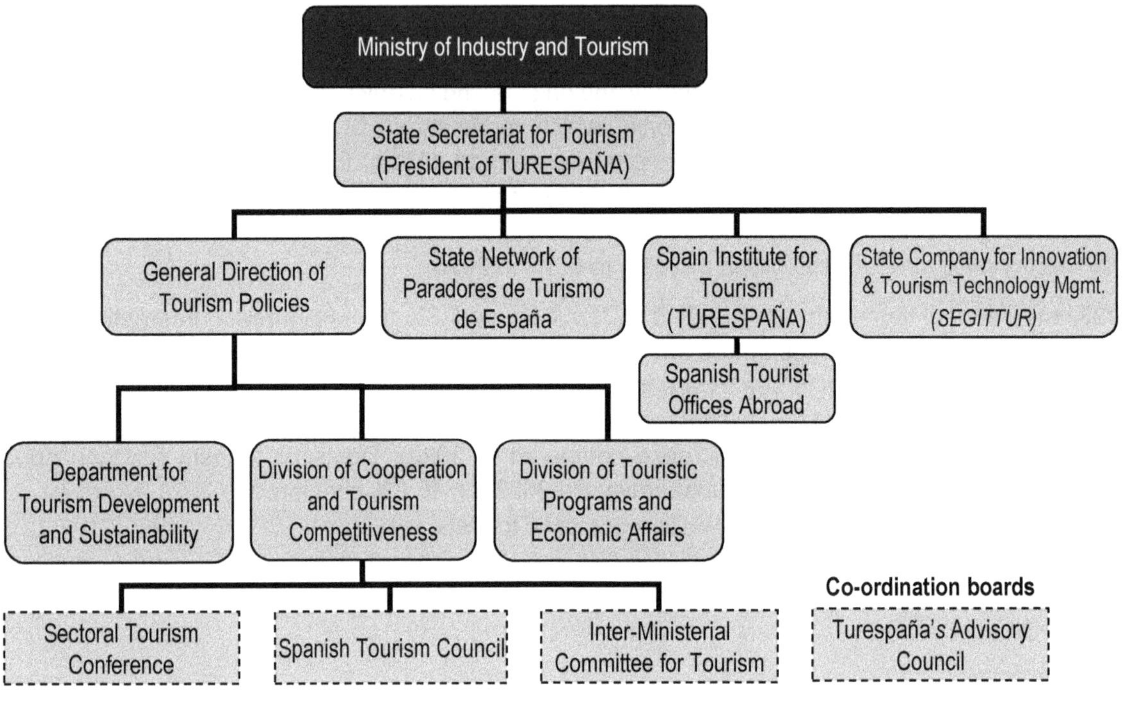

Source: OECD, adapted from Ministry of Industry & Tourism, 2024.

Tourism policies and programmes

Spain has a core objective to transform and modernise the tourism sector by increasing its competitiveness and resilience. The overall aim is to recover to pre-COVID-19 levels but also build a tourism model which is more sustainable, diversified and profitable. Policy initiatives to support the recovery are organised into four main pillars: actions on tourism sustainability, promoting digitisation and new intelligence, a Tourism Resilience Strategy for the Canary and Balearic Islands and the autonomous cities of Ceuta and Melilla, and actions to build competitiveness.

Spain has defined a range of strategic areas, encouraging investments in innovation, energy efficiency and green transition as well as enhancing the effectiveness of policies supporting research. Further actions include sustaining the economy, supporting employment and skills development, improving access to digital learning and broader digitalisation. The Tourism Sustainability Strategy aims to strengthen the environmental, socio-economic and regional sustainability of tourism and targets tourist destinations, social partners and private operators to stimulate:

- Green transition – actions on environmental restoration, management and public use of protected natural areas, the implementation of tourism certification systems, the implementation of circular economy measures and investment in cycling / walking paths.

- Energy efficiency – actions to reduce CO2 emissions in buildings, public infrastructure and services, implement environmental technologies and improve urban environments.
- Digital transformation – actions to digitalise services for tourists at destinations, develop the digital footprint of destinations and improve tourism demand management (see box below).
- Competitiveness transformation – improving local tourism infrastructures and fostering job creation through the development of new tourism products relating to culture, nature, gastronomy, traditional crafts and industrial tourism services.

In 2022 Spain started a multiannual programme to rehabilitate historical heritage buildings in the frame of the Recovery, Transformation and Resilience Plan for Tourism. The budget for 2024 is EUR 208 million.

The Tourism Resilience Strategy for the extra-peninsular territories (Canary and Balearic Islands and Ceuta and Melilla) will improve the competitiveness and capacity of these territories to adapt to changes in international markets. These regional strategies have been approved by the national government and include investment in public infrastructure, environmental management and waste treatment, reinforcement of public services, training (especially youth training) linked to the tourism sector, development of alternative tourism products, incentives to facilitate the connectivity of these territories and for tourism companies to operate outside the high season, and development of new tourism products aligned with the Sustainable Tourism Strategy. Spain is also implementing specific actions to build competitiveness across the country. The Sectoral Conference established gastronomy and wine in 2022-23.

As part of the plan to modernise and enhance competitiveness of the tourism sector, the National Food and Wine Tourism Plan aims to convert the body of knowledge, know-how, arts and crafts that enable healthy eating and drinking into sustainable and integrated tourism experiences throughout the territory. The National Plan is structured around: food and wine destinations (EUR 51.4 million), Spain Tourism Experiences Programme (EUR 10 million and EUR 5 million for additional actions), and an international promotion programme (EUR 2.2 million). Its objectives are developed around the product, process and culture, involving the entire value chain by: (i) promoting Spanish food and wine destinations by financing destination sustainability plans; (ii) generating sustainable and diverse gastronomic tourism experiences; (iii) improving training of workers in the food and wine tourism value chain, enhancing their digital skills and sustainability; (iv) collecting existing practices that give meaning to the concept of Spanish gastronomy in an accessible and open space to generate a differential message and building stories to inspire other initiatives in the country, and (v) deepening the use of gastronomy and wine as a pillar for tourism promotion of Spain abroad.

Digitisation and Intelligence Programme

The Digitisation and Intelligence Programme aims to enable destinations and the tourism sector to develop smart destination platforms that provide tourists with interoperable public and private services. This will be complemented with the development of a Tourist Intelligence System and a set of initiatives to boost the Spanish Smart Destinations Network. The actions will support digital solutions based on artificial intelligence and provide financing for the development of industrial data spaces and the promotion of digital innovation in the tourism sector.

Spain is co-funding projects to foster digitalisation on both tourism destinations within the Spanish Smart Destinations Network and tourism companies as part of the Recovery, Transformation and Resilience Plan for Tourism. In 2024, Spain expects to spend EUR 104 million to implement artificial intelligence in tourism businesses, and EUR 96 million to foster the development of intelligent platforms at tourist destinations.

Statistical Profile

Spain: Domestic, inbound and outbound tourism

	2018	2019	2020	2021	2022
TOURISM FLOWS, THOUSAND					
Domestic tourism					
Total domestic trips	425 452	394 810	235 089	320 698	330 698
Overnight visitors (tourists)	139 931	137 191	74 750	107 727	124 490
Same-day visitors (excursionists)	285 521	257 619	160 340	212 971	206 207
Nights in all types of accommodation	507 739	510 938	353 020	441 404	490 028
Hotels and similar establishments	90 648	93 696	38 001	67 638	92 607
Other collective establishments	35 713	33 081	23 661	32 199	35 801
Private accommodation	381 378	384 161	291 358	341 567	361 620
Inbound tourism					
Total international arrivals	124 456	126 170	36 410	51 631	104 968
Overnight visitors (tourists)	82 808	83 509	18 933	31 181	71 659
Same-day visitors (excursionists)	41 647	42 661	17 477	20 451	33 309
Top markets					
United Kingdom	18 524	18 012	3 150	5 823	15 122
France	11 415	11 158	2 391	5 209	10 096
Germany	11 293	11 147	3 888	4 303	9 769
Nordic Countries	5 804	5 530	1 175	2 049	4 291
Italy	4 389	4 535	947	1 840	4 011
Nights in all types of accommodation	616 715	594 018	147 986	253 985	537 612
Hotels and similar establishments	287 884	287 764	57 065	108 424	257 976
Other collective establishments	35 599	34 093	7 942	14 832	32 029
Private accommodation	293 233	272 161	82 979	130 729	247 607
Outbound tourism					
Total international departures	19 750	20 097	5 610	7 557	16 087
Overnight visitors (tourists)	16 424	17 126	4 314	6 032	13 589
Same-day visitors (excursionists)	3 326	2 971	1 296	1 525	2 498
Top destinations					
France	2 410	2 560	691	1 102	2 500
Portugal	2 282	2 355	796	1 066	1 777
Italy	1 860	1 895	328	761	1 614
United Kingdom	1 465	1 487	332	218	1 081
Andorra	851	860	441	555	646
TOURISM RECEIPTS AND EXPENDITURE, MILLION EUR					
Inbound tourism					
Total international receipts	69 168	71 202	16 202	29 198	69 219
International travel receipts	69 168	71 167	16 203	29 198	69 219
International passenger transport receipts	..	..	..	..	..
Outbound tourism					
Total international expenditure	22 395	24 813	7 573	10 667	20 816
International travel expenditure	22 395	24 813	7 572	10 667	20 816
International passenger transport expenditure	..	..	..	..	..

.. Not available
Source: OECD Tourism Statistics (Database).

StatLink https://stat.link/ef2863

Spain: Enterprises and employment in tourism

	Number of establishments	Number of persons employed				
	2022	2018	2019	2020	2021	2022
Total	..	..	..	..	..	..
Tourism industries	694 734	2 604 899	2 673 520	2 333 736	2 367 560	2 633 751
Accommodation services for visitors	200 538	409 208	407 804	318 697	317 858	417 499
Hotels and similar establishments	17 635	361 444	360 134	276 236	271 613	368 052
Food and beverage serving industry	265 992	1 298 528	1 307 576	1 113 390	1 144 229	1 222 867
Passenger transport	64 833	281 328	317 596	288 436	265 383	281 952
Air passenger transport	235	43 196	52 334	44 275	46 061	50 338
Railways passenger transport	90	26 791	24 794	21 709	27 098	21 259
Road passenger transport	63 709	199 190	231 537	213 837	185 814	204 206
Water passenger transport	799	12 151	8 932	8 613	6 410	6 148
Passenger transport supporting services	24 657	..	..	..	..	..
Transport equipment rental	9 148	215 580	232 442	242 114	255 530	279 087
Travel agencies and other reservation services industry	17 136	78 698	70 119	63 124	66 315	69 310
Cultural industry	51 572	112 674	115 887	105 101	102 125	115 641
Sports and recreation industry	60 858	208 884	222 096	202 875	216 121	247 395
Retail trade of country-specific tourism characteristic goods	..	..	..	..	..	..
Other country-specific tourism industries	..	..	..	..	..	..
Other industries	..	..	..	..	..	..

.. Not available
Source: OECD Tourism Statistics (Database).

StatLink https://stat.link/m0i8c2

Spain: Internal tourism consumption

Million EUR

	2021		
	Domestic tourism expenditure	Inbound tourism expenditure	Internal tourism consumption
Total	..	..	..
Consumption products	55 321	34 992	107 219
Tourism characteristic products	46 808	23 415	87 129
Accommodation services for visitors	16 298	10 755	41 125
Food and beverage serving services	17 125	4 516	21 721
Passenger transport services	5 870	2 031	9 472
Air passenger transport services	3 038	1 183	5 182
Railways passenger transport services	983	169	1 392
Road passenger transport services	1 294	640	2 101
Water passenger transport services	556	39	798
Passenger transport supporting services	..	..	..
Transport equipment rental services	89	638	728
Travel agencies and other reservation services industry	4 042	217	4 423
Cultural services	727	2 407	3 514
Sports and recreation services	2 656	2 852	6 145
Country-specific tourism characteristic goods	..	..	..
Country-specific tourism characteristic services	..	..	..
Other consumption products	8 513	11 577	20 090
Tourism connected products	..	..	..
Non-tourism related consumption products	8 513	11 577	20 090
Non-consumption products	..	..	..

.. Not available
Source: OECD Tourism Statistics (Database).

StatLink https://stat.link/fc72r9

Sweden

Tourism in the economy and outlook

Tourism is an important economic driver for the Swedish economy, but it was significantly impacted by successive crises. In 2021, tourism contributed SEK 105 billion or 1.9% of GDP, compared to 2.4% in 2019. On average,101 000 people were employed in tourism in 2021, equating to 94 303 full-time jobs. This is a decrease of 3.4% compared to the previous year, and 18.9% below the level in 2019. Travel exports are recovering, reaching SEK 91.4 billion or 9.4% of total service exports in 2022. While the tourism share of services exports increased compared to 2020 (6.2% of services exports), it remained below the pre-pandemic level of 11.8%.

In 2023, Sweden registered 16.5 million international tourist nights in commercial accommodation establishments. This is an 11.3% increase from 2022 but is still 1.2% below 2019 levels. The mounting cost-of-living is seen as an obstacle to fully recover to pre-pandemic levels. The three main source markets in 2023 were Germany (5%), Norway (5%), and Denmark (3%).

Domestic tourism fell by 1.9% in 2023 compared to the previous year, with 51.4 million domestic nights recorded at commercial accommodation establishments. The figure is 3.2% above 2019 levels.

Tourism governance

The Swedish Agency for Economic and Regional Growth, Tillväxtverket, is responsible for tourism at the national level. Visit Sweden is the government body which markets Sweden as a tourist destination internationally. Both organisations report to the Ministry of Climate and Enterprise.

Tillväxtverket develops, implements, and supports knowledge-based initiatives and activities to promote tourism sector development and entrepreneurship. The Agency is also responsible for official tourism statistics, including the production and dissemination of knowledge on tourism and its effects on the Swedish economy. It collaborates with other government agencies related to tourism.

A regional tourism network is established, organised and run at the regional level. The network is an important tool for communication and collaboration with industry organisations and national stakeholders. Tourism is prioritised and high on the agenda in many municipalities and regions. The Swedish Association of Local Authorities and Regions, an umbrella organisation for local and regional authorities, offers them support and services through networking platforms, knowledge reports, and conferences, among other activities.

Swedish Embassies play a central role in promoting Sweden abroad. In collaboration with these embassies, the Swedish Institute co-ordinates a Team Sweden group to promote international positive interest and confidence in Sweden. Aligned with the foreign trade strategy, their objective is to strengthen Sweden's position as a global leader and strategic partner in innovation, knowledge and trade. Visit Sweden's assignment is part of the work to promote Sweden abroad.

Visit Sweden was allocated SEK 105 million in 2023 while Tillväxtverket was not allocated any additional budget for tourism activities. Significant resources have also been allocated to tourism through regional and EU funds.

Sweden: Organisational chart of tourism bodies

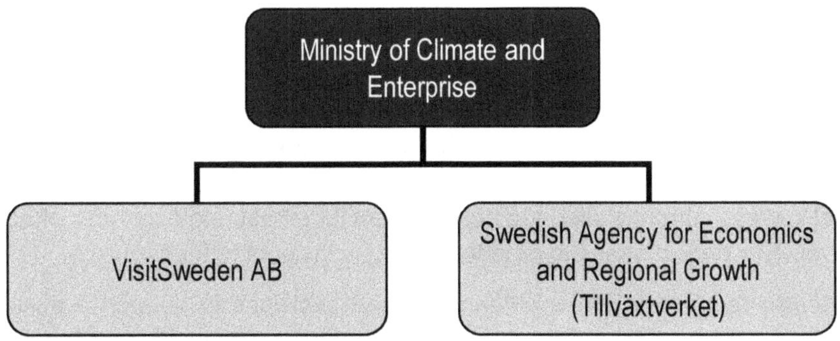

Source: OECD, adapted from the Ministry of Climate and Enterprise, 2024.

Tourism policies and programmes

The long-term strategy for Swedish tourism was presented by the former government in October 2021. It has not been formally repealed but is no longer actively in use. A new tourism policy goal was accepted by the Parliament in 2022 but was formally repealed in January 2024. Tourism policy is now part of the economic policy goal. The Swedish government and the tourism sector remain committed to rebuilding and boosting the sector despite the lack of an overarching strategy. Sweden has several initiatives which currently support tourism.

To help develop more robust tourism data and statistics, the agency for Economic and Regional Growth was allocated SEK 150 million for data and statistics and to support the transition towards sustainable tourism in 2021 and 2022. The funding was used to create better models for data and statistics, provide suggestions for indicators to measure sustainable tourism, develop products with a special focus on nature-based tourism, strengthen digitalisation, and create methods to develop attractive places for residents and visitors. As part of the efforts to improve tourism data, Sweden is leading a Nordic collaboration on payment card transaction data (see box below).

Between 2021 and 2024, SEK 100 million will be distributed to almost 40 projects across Sweden to support infrastructure investments for recreation and tourism in rural areas such as trails for hiking and mountain biking. This programme will result in more and better trails that benefit residents, visitors, and businesses.

The Smarter Together platform was created in collaboration with the Agency for Economic and Regional Growth, Visit Sweden and the regions of Sweden, aiming to build better capacity for destinations, local authorities and regions. In 2023, the platform focused on skills and training, transport, knowledge sharing and innovation both in public sector and in the tourism industry.

Workforce and skills shortage became a pressing issue for tourism and a priority to the government, as one-quarter of the Swedish tourism workforce moved to other sectors during the COVID-19 pandemic. This has been partly restored. However, it remains a challenge for the tourism industry. Tillväxtverkets published eight reports analysing the issue, concluding that recruitment potential largely lies among those who are currently out of the labour market.

The pandemic also led to an increased interest in nature and outdoor tourism, which has continued to grow. Initiatives to promote and strengthen this segment, have included the production of a report and articles which provide insights on the trends, development opportunities and target markets in nature tourism. This report was distributed to various stakeholders. Tillväxtverkets also financed the attendance to the Adventure Travel World Summit in 2022 for nature tourism companies and regional promotion actors.

Better and more granular tourism data for Sweden and the Nordics

Sweden is leading a Nordic collaboration project to use payment card transaction data (Visa and Mastercard) to integrate data into the national Tourism Satellite Account (TSA). This method provides more precise estimation and granularity of tourism data and allows for a shorter delivery time at a lower cost. The manual surveys currently used are not sufficient for measuring economic effects from tourism on a regional level. This project uses big data to bring new insights to tourism.

Accurate data is also required to make evidence-based decisions to support a sustainable tourism development and a green transition of the tourism sector in the stakeholder system at all levels. The Nordic collaboration project also addresses the statistics and data needed for a sustainable tourism policy development such as the implementation of a Tourism Sustainability Satellite Account (linking the Tourism Satellite Account and the System of Environmental Economic Accounting).

The project, launched in 2022, is funded until the end of 2024, with hopes to secure further Nordic funding until 2025 so that the new TSA model can be fully operational in Nordic countries by 2026.

Statistical Profile

Sweden: Domestic, inbound and outbound tourism

	2018	2019	2020	2021	2022
TOURISM FLOWS, THOUSAND					
Domestic tourism[1]					
Total domestic trips	55 880	56 171	128 792 |	122 669	143 700
Overnight visitors (tourists)	35 686	36 891	49 831 |	51 185	62 334
Same-day visitors (excursionists)	20 194	19 280	78 961 |	71 484	81 366
Nights in all types of accommodation	47 852	49 849	38 122	46 946	52 420
Hotels and similar establishments	33 075	34 712	23 135	29 742	35 931
Other collective establishments	12 096	12 483	12 235	13 790	13 027
Private accommodation	2 681	2 654	2 752	3 414	3 462
Inbound tourism					
Total international arrivals	..	..	..	..	..
Overnight visitors (tourists)	7 440	7 616	1 957	2 990	6 629
Same-day visitors (excursionists)	..	..	..	..	..
Top markets					
..	..	..	..	..	..
..	..	..	..	..	..
..	..	..	..	..	..
..	..	..	..	..	..
..	..	..	..	..	..
Nights in all types of accommodation	17 310	17 504	5 173	7 266	15 333
Hotels and similar establishments	11 720	11 716	3 851	4 846	9 859
Other collective establishments	3 949	4 246	577	1 659	4 104
Private accommodation	1 642	1 541	746	761	1 371
Outbound tourism					
Total international departures	19 939	19 061	6 081 |	7 615	..
Overnight visitors (tourists)	18 855	18 000	4 225 |	5 767	..
Same-day visitors (excursionists)	1 084	1 061	1 856 |	1 848	..
Top destinations					
..	..	..	..	..	..
..	..	..	..	..	..
..	..	..	..	..	..
..	..	..	..	..	..
..	..	..	..	..	..
TOURISM RECEIPTS AND EXPENDITURE, MILLION SEK					
Inbound tourism					
Total international receipts	102 581	104 222	44 529	58 683	106 341
International travel receipts	87 027	86 948	40 055	52 362	91 407
International passenger transport receipts	15 554	17 274	4 474	6 321	14 934
Outbound tourism					
Total international expenditure	159 621	162 002	62 585	79 524	145 970
International travel expenditure	136 477	135 876	56 826	72 242	125 067
International passenger transport expenditure	23 144	26 125	5 759	7 282	20 903

.. Not available; | Break in series

1. Trips from demand side surveys; Nights from supply side surveys..

Source: OECD Tourism Statistics (Database).

StatLink https://stat.link/ltb8kh

Sweden: Enterprises and employment in tourism

	Number of establishments[1]	Number of persons employed				
	2021	2018	2019	2020	2021	2022
Total	..	116 286	116 278	97 650	94 303	..
Tourism industries	..	73 590	73 076	65 183	61 882	..
Accommodation services for visitors	..	30 592	28 987	23 657	25 201	..
Hotels and similar establishments	2 160	..	..	..	..	..
Food and beverage serving industry	..	18 411	17 809	15 003	15 489	..
Passenger transport	..	12 400	12 894	13 123	8 932	..
Air passenger transport	..	4 341	4 719	7 594	3 757	..
Railways passenger transport	..	2 779	1 958	2 101	2 169	..
Road passenger transport	..	3 486	3 491	2 720	2 273	..
Water passenger transport	..	1 794	2 726	708	733	..
Passenger transport supporting services	..	..	..	..	..	..
Transport equipment rental	..	818	987	1 013	924	..
Travel agencies and other reservation services industry	..	6 922	7 796	7 625	7 058	..
Cultural industry	..	2 439	2 508	2 891	2 550	..
Sports and recreation industry	..	2 008	2 095	1 871	1 728	..
Retail trade of country-specific tourism characteristic goods	..	..	..	..	..	..
Other country-specific tourism industries	..	..	..	..	..	..
Other industries	..	42 696	43 202	32 467	32 421	..

.. Not available
1. Data refer to number of enterprises.
Source: OECD Tourism Statistics (Database).

StatLink https://stat.link/mdr79f

Sweden: Internal tourism consumption

Million SEK

	2021		
	Domestic tourism expenditure	Inbound tourism expenditure	Internal tourism consumption
Total	..	..	..
Consumption products	191 746	57 093	248 838
Tourism characteristic products	131 005	27 108	158 113
Accommodation services for visitors	56 511	7 819	64 330
Food and beverage serving services	20 567	6 630	27 197
Passenger transport services	24 534	7 788	32 322
Air passenger transport services	9 173	3 770	12 943
Railways passenger transport services	1 800	779	2 579
Road passenger transport services	11 648	1 292	12 940
Water passenger transport services	1 912	1 947	3 859
Passenger transport supporting services	..	..	..
Transport equipment rental services	5 649	1 840	7 489
Travel agencies and other reservation services industry	10 564	1 331	11 895
Cultural services	10 188	519	10 707
Sports and recreation services	2 992	1 181	4 173
Country-specific tourism characteristic goods	0	0	0
Country-specific tourism characteristic services	0	0	0
Other consumption products	60 740	29 985	90 725
Tourism connected products	..	..	..
Non-tourism related consumption products	..	..	..
Non-consumption products	..	..	..

.. Not available
Source: OECD Tourism Statistics (Database).

StatLink https://stat.link/4u6g7t

Switzerland

Tourism in the economy and outlook

Tourism is an important contributor to the Swiss economy, directly accounting for 2.6% of Swiss GVA and employing 166 627 people (full-time equivalents), or 3.9% of the total workforce in 2022. Travel exports represented 11.4% of total service exports in 2022, recovering from 7.9% in 2020. From an economic perspective, the tourism sector has yet to recover to pre-pandemic levels, when it accounted for 2.9% of total GVA, 4.2% of employment and 13.7% of services exports.

International tourism continues to recover towards pre-pandemic levels in Switzerland. International tourist arrivals at commercial accommodation establishments rose to 9.2 million in 2022, double the number of arrivals in 2021, and 87.5% of 2019 levels. Data for 2023 shows an increase of 19.2% compared to 2022, a historic high.

In 2023, Switzerland's top three source markets were Germany (22%), United States (13%) and Great Britain (9%). European visitors accounted for 16.8 million overnight stays, which represented an 8.3% increase compared to 2022. Demand from the United States was high while demand from Asia is starting to recover from the COVID-19 pandemic.

Domestic demand was down slightly in 2023 with domestic visitors staying more than 30 million nights in hotels and similar establishments yearly. This represents a significant increase compared to pre-pandemic levels, 11.8% above 2019.

Switzerland expects the total number of overnight stays in Summer 2024 to be above 2019 levels by 24.2 million. This is attributed to the recovery in overseas markets, particularly the United States and Asian countries, and domestic demand, which is expected to decline slightly but is still above pre-pandemic levels.

Tourism governance

The State Secretariat for Economic Affairs (SECO), in collaboration with numerous national and regional level political bodies, is responsible for designing and implementing Switzerland's tourism policy. SECO enforces the Federal Act on the Promotion of Innovation, Co-operation and Knowledge Building in Tourism (Innotour) and supervises two organisations tasked with implementing tourism-related measures: Switzerland Tourism carries out marketing activities, and the Swiss Society for Hotel Credit supports investment in the accommodation sector.

Each canton has a tourism office which carries out cantonal level promotion. The Swiss Tourism Forum facilitates a close exchange between the central government, the cantons and tourism stakeholders. The central government and the cantons promote the mountain region, urban and rural areas and the border regions.

For the years 2024-27, the overall federal contribution to Switzerland Tourism will be CHF 233 million. CHF 45 million in regular funds are available over the same period via Innotour to promote innovation in tourism, of which CHF 15 million will be used as part of a COVID-19 recovery programme. The promotional activities of the Swiss Society for Hotel Credit are based on a federal loan of CHF 236 million and the New Regional Policy framework provides around CHF 200 million in loans for investment and CHF 200 million for contributions (subsidies) to projects with regional economic impact.

Switzerland: Organisational chart of tourism bodies

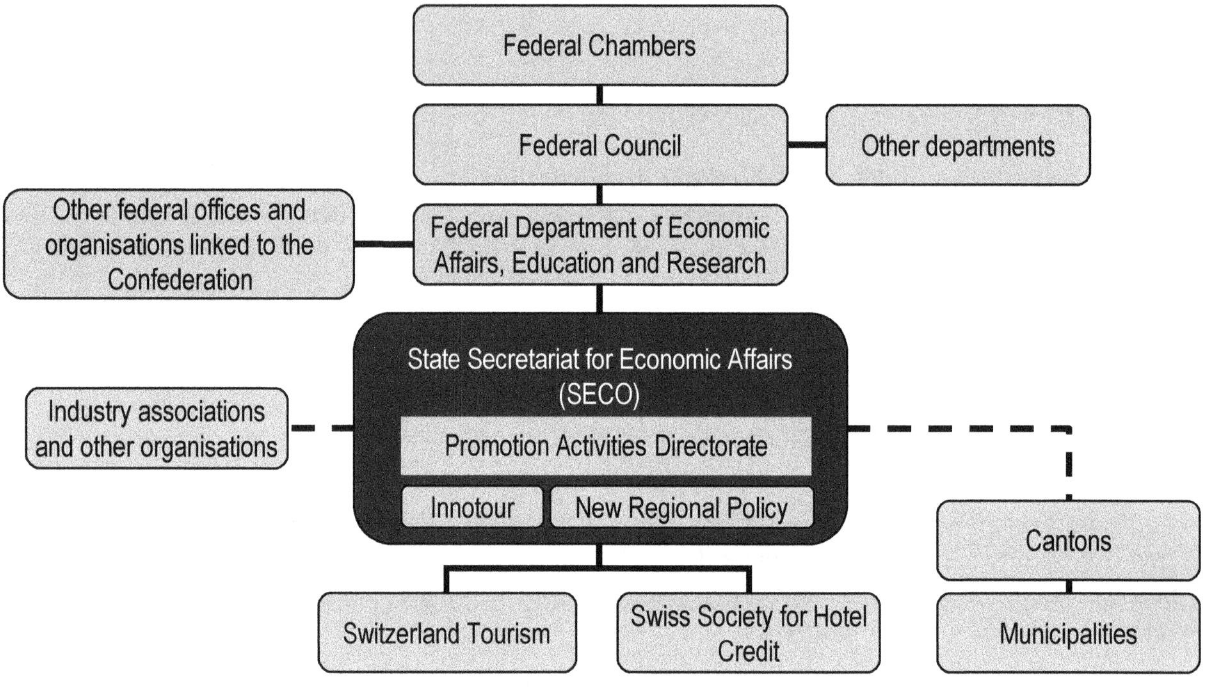

Source: OECD, adapted from the State Secretariat for Economic Affairs, 2024.

Tourism policies and programmes

The Tourism Strategy of the Swiss Confederation was published in 2021 as the government's long-term vision for tourism in Switzerland. The main objectives of the strategy are to improve the framework conditions, promote entrepreneurship, take advantage of opportunities offered by digitalisation, and enhance the attractiveness of tourism products and Switzerland's market presence. The next report on the implementation and the strategic orientation of the Swiss Confederation's tourism policy will be published in 2026.

Each objective is supplemented by three action items, with 15 action items in total. Unlike objectives, action items are not final and can be amended and extended as needed to achieve the objectives. This aims to ensure that the Federal Government's Tourism Strategy is agile and capable of both action and reaction. Action items have a medium to long-term horizon but may run indefinitely. Some action items tackle ongoing tasks under the Tourism Strategy.

Sustainable development and employment are two of the top priorities of Switzerland's tourism strategy:

- Sustainable development: As part of the Federal Government's Tourism Strategy, the Swiss Tourism Federation launched the Competence Center for Sustainability in Swiss Tourism (KONA) with the support of Switzerland Tourism and the Innotour funding instrument in 2022. KONA aims to make Swiss tourism a leader in sustainability by initiating and implementing projects and providing a central contact point for sustainability issues in Swiss tourism. New funding guidelines for tourist accommodation SMEs are prepared (see box below).

- Labour market: A study was conducted to investigate labour market movements in tourism before, during and after the COVID-19 pandemic and found that the labour market in the tourism sector is very flexible (and recovered quickly from the COVID-19 downturn). However, many of the concerns prior to COVID-19 were still inhibiting the sector from attracting workers (*e.g.* the impact of shift work on family life, negative image of the sector, lack of attractive salary, lack of contemporary leadership culture). The study concluded that there was a higher-than-average probability of workers leaving the sector and retaining workers remains a major challenge. To counteract this problem, the *5 Punkte Plan* by GastroSuisse was launched as part of the promotional programme Innotour, with the aim of having a significant positive impact on the image of the sector and attracting new talent to the sector.

Additional policy initiatives include the *Motion 21.3743 Stöckli* which aims to strengthen Innotour and instructs the Federal Council to prioritise funding for projects that promote digitisation and sustainability and the *Motion 21.4426 Gmür-Schönenberger* which instructs the Federal Council to support the implementation of a digital reporting to government on commercial accommodation of guests.

New funding guidelines for Swiss accommodation facilities: Sustainability bonus

Motion 19.3234 Stöckli aims to create a modern act for tourist accommodation across Switzerland that will be implemented by the Swiss Society for Hotel Credit. The programme will support the renovation of accommodation facilities in the Alpine region and seasonal tourist areas. This motion is set to address the prioritisation of renovating and modernising guest accommodation, with a focus on energy efficiency.

Funding will be limited to accommodation upgrades that meet strict energy efficiency standards and is restricted to existing accommodation, with new construction excluded. Accommodation facilities that have met energy efficiency standards will receive a subsidy towards their next tourism investment within a ten-year period, reflecting investment cycles in the building industry.

A public consultation was conducted on the revision of the law in 2024. Implementation is expected to begin in 2026 and will have a budget of approximately CHF 195 million, subject to funding approval.

Statistical Profile

Switzerland: Domestic, inbound and outbound tourism

	2018	2019	2020	2021	2022
TOURISM FLOWS, THOUSAND					
Domestic tourism[1]					
Total domestic trips	80 020	78 317	62 951 |	88 996	67 473
Overnight visitors (tourists)	8 201	7 765	8 319 |	9 077	8 513
Same-day visitors (excursionists)	71 819	70 551	54 632 |	79 919	58 960
Nights in all types of accommodation	28 610	29 391	28 293	34 344	33 446
Hotels and similar establishments	26 198	26 841	24 880	29 949	30 165
Other collective establishments	2 412	2 550	3 413	4 394	3 281
Private accommodation	..	..	..	..	..
Inbound tourism					
Total international arrivals	..	..	..	..	..
Overnight visitors (tourists)	11 715	11 818	3 690	4 390	9 160
Same-day visitors (excursionists)	..	..	..	..	..
Top markets					
Germany	2 216	2 220	1 219	1 455	2 128
China (People's Republic of) and Hong Kong (China)	1 135	1 141	77	17	87
United States	1 118	1 219	167	279	1 145
France	826	831	489	627	866
United Kingdom	820	818	224	140	653
Nights in all types of accommodation	26 748	26 843	10 221	11 541	22 194
Hotels and similar establishments	25 579	25 636	9 460	10 521	20 639
Other collective establishments	1 168	1 207	761	1 019	1 555
Private accommodation	..	..	..	..	..
Outbound tourism					
Total international departures	26 397	21 360	8 319 |	11 127	17 943
Overnight visitors (tourists)	16 735	14 622	6 813 |	7 188	12 539
Same-day visitors (excursionists)	9 662	6 737	1 506 |	3 940	5 404
Top destinations					
Germany	3 135	2 816	1 474 |	1 197	2 075
Italy	2 964	2 594	1 487 |	1 439	2 730
France	2 441	1 885	1 178 |	1 014	1 653
Austria	1 078	940	629 |	351	923
..	..	..	..	..	..
TOURISM RECEIPTS AND EXPENDITURE, MILLION CHF					
Inbound tourism					
Total international receipts	20 820	21 118	9 416	11 054	..
International travel receipts	17 592	17 837	8 511	10 070	16 564
International passenger transport receipts	3 229	3 280	906	984	..
Outbound tourism					
Total international expenditure	20 985	20 963	9 751	11 578	..
International travel expenditure	18 650	18 635	8 974	10 675	16 771
International passenger transport expenditure	2 334	2 328	776	903	..

.. Not available; | Break in series

1. Trips from demand side surveys; Nights from supply side surveys.

Source: OECD Tourism Statistics (Database).

StatLink https://stat.link/mzpo3q

Switzerland: Enterprises and employment in tourism

	Number of establishments	Number of persons employed				
	2022	2018	2019	2020	2021	2022 p
Total	..	174 514	174 220	149 903	161 524	166 627
Tourism industries	..	141 772	141 065	116 643	128 285	132 772
Accommodation services for visitors	35 662	36 409	35 747	30 573	34 967	38 711
Hotels and similar establishments	4 498	32 962	32 185	27 074	31 352	34 769
Food and beverage serving industry	..	46 384	45 061	30 860	39 129	37 239
Passenger transport	..	26 820	27 950	27 449	26 821	27 684
Air passenger transport	..	8 677	9 082	8 463	7 571	7 678
Railways passenger transport	..	13 037	13 414	13 538	13 656	14 251
Road passenger transport	..	4 212	4 427	4 373	4 429	4 574
Water passenger transport	..	894	1 027	1 075	1 165	1 182
Passenger transport supporting services	..	6 044	6 157	5 737	5 273	5 589
Transport equipment rental	..	644	583	524	528	543
Travel agencies and other reservation services industry	..	13 555	13 435	10 672	10 121	10 408
Cultural industry	..	3 953	3 987	3 872	3 917	4 290
Sports and recreation industry	..	5 774	5 903	5 773	5 980	6 333
Retail trade of country-specific tourism characteristic goods	..	..	..	..	..	
Other country-specific tourism industries	..	2 190	2 242	1 182	1 549	1 974
Other industries	..	32 742	33 155	33 259	33 239	33 855

.. Not available; p Provisional data
Source: OECD Tourism Statistics (Database).

StatLink https://stat.link/5sq7ur

Switzerland: Internal tourism consumption

Million CHF

	2017		
	Domestic tourism expenditure	Inbound tourism expenditure	Internal tourism consumption
Total	23 827	17 156	46 072
Consumption products	18 999	14 281	38 369
Tourism characteristic products	16 483	12 249	33 420
Accommodation services for visitors	2 684	2 856	9 567
Food and beverage serving services	3 318	3 147	6 465
Passenger transport services	5 911	4 220	10 424
Air passenger transport services	3 845	2 792	6 637
Railways passenger transport services	1 361	851	2 504
Road passenger transport services	623	519	1 142
Water passenger transport services	82	59	141
Passenger transport supporting services	453	371	824
Transport equipment rental services	220	210	430
Travel agencies and other reservation services industry	1 254	186	1 592
Cultural services	473	169	858
Sports and recreation services	1 630	987	2 617
Country-specific tourism characteristic goods	..	..	..
Country-specific tourism characteristic services	540	103	643
Other consumption products	7 345	4 907	12 653
Tourism connected products	2 517	2 032	4 950
Non-tourism related consumption products	4 828	2 875	7 703
Non-consumption products	..	..	..

.. Not available
Source: OECD Tourism Statistics (Database).

StatLink https://stat.link/gk13rx

Türkiye

Tourism in the economy and outlook

Despite several local crises and natural disasters, tourism has made a quick recovery from the COVID-19 pandemic downturn and remains a key contributor to Türkiye's economy. In 2022, tourism represented 4.4% of GDP and direct tourism-related employment accounted for 2.9% of the workforce, or 885 000 people. This is an increase compared to the 2.4% share in 2021, but still below 3.3% in 2019. Travel exports represented 45.7% of total service exports in 2022, above the pre-pandemic level of 44.4%. In 2023, tourism represented 5.0% of GDP.

In 2022, the number of international tourist arrivals recovered to 98.6% of pre-pandemic levels reaching 51.4 million. The top three source markets were Germany (11%), Russia (10%) and the United Kingdom (6%). Tourism revenue reached USD 49.8 billion in 2022. In 2023, the number of international tourist arrivals reached to 56.7 million. The top three source markets were Russia (11%), Germany (10.7%) and United Kingdom (6.5%).

Domestic tourism was more significantly affected by the pandemic and has yet to recover. In 2022, Türkiye recorded 52.3 million domestic tourists, which remains 33% below 2019.

As 2023, the number of foreign visitors to Türkiye were 55.2 million and as 2023 tourism revenues in Türkiye reached USD 55.9 billion. Compared 2022, the number of foreign visitors increased by 9,32% and tourism revenue increased by 12%. Türkiye aims to achieve strong tourism growth by 2028, including nearly 80 million arrivals and USD 100 billion in revenue.

Tourism governance

In Türkiye, the Ministry of Culture and Tourism is responsible for tourism policy. Its duties are to investigate, develop, protect, maintain, evaluate, disseminate and promote tourism.

The Türkiye Tourism Promotion and Development Agency is responsible for promoting Türkiye as a brand and a popular destination to both domestic and international tourism markets; discovering, developing and promoting natural, cultural and heritage assets; boosting the tourism capacity of Türkiye, increasing tourism investments in the national economy and raising the quality of service through communication and marketing activities. Operating under the auspices of the Ministry of Culture and Tourism, the Agency is subject to private law provisions. Türkiye has 81 Provincial Culture and Tourism offices that work to conserve the historical, cultural and natural heritage, diversify tourism, and promote their regions through cultural events, festivals and fairs.

The Ministry works closely with the Association of Turkish Travel Agencies, Touristic Hotels and Investors Association, Hoteliers Federation, Turkish Tourism Investors Association and the Union of Tourist Guides' Chambers to plan tourism and address specific issues. The investment Office of the Presidency of the Republic of Türkiye also promotes Türkiye's investment opportunities to the global business community and assists investors.

Türkiye: Organisational chart of tourism bodies

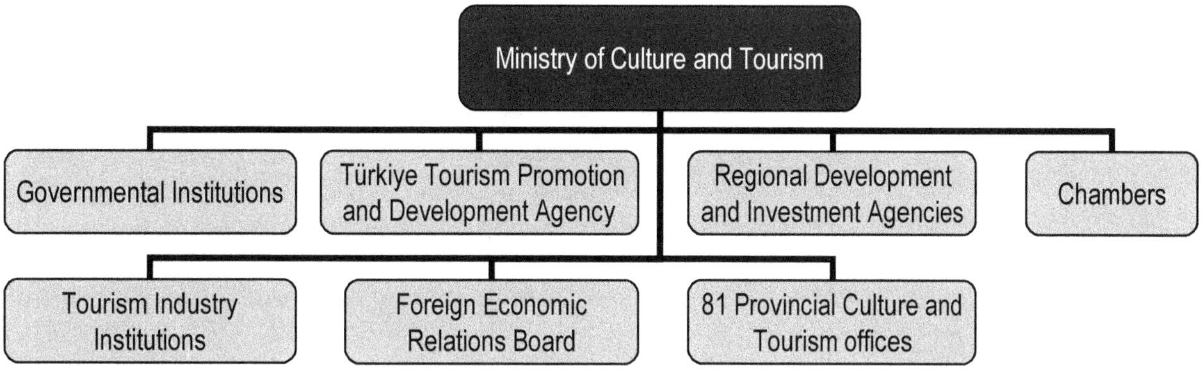

Source: OECD, adapted from the Ministry of Culture and Tourism, 2024.

Tourism policies and programmes

In 2023, Türkiye launched a new tourism master plan (12th Development Plan) for 2024-28. The plan serves as a comprehensive roadmap for achieving sustainable and inclusive tourism growth in Türkiye through safe mobility, green transformation, sustainability, crisis management, a more resilient sector, inclusivity, and digital transformation. Global branding and promotion activities will continue to increase annually, with a budget of USD 225 million allocated for marketing communications until 2028. Türkiye will have a total of nine destination brands and 20 product sub-brands to bring Türkiye Tourism to the world.

The National Türkiye Sustainable Tourism Programme was developed ensure the sustainable growth of the tourism sector and to develop a common sustainability approach at international level for Turkish tourism industry with the participation and support of all tourism stakeholders. The Programme aims to improve sustainable management, socio-economic and cultural sustainability, and environmental sustainability in the tourism sector. Through the programme, the water and energy consumption, waste volume, carbon footprint, and greenhouse gas emission data of accommodation facilities are monitored, with all accommodation facilities in Türkiye required to fully comply with the Global Sustainable Tourism Council (GSTC) standards by 2030. To achieve this target, Türkiye has a three-year partnership agreement with the GSTC (see box below). First of all, Türkiye Sustainable Tourism Criteria prepared for accommodation facilities which has been recognised according to the GSTC standards, with the Programme granted the Acknowledged status. Türkiye's Sustainable Tourism Programme also contributes to supporting the UN Sustainable Development Goals and complies with legal regulations and commitments such as the Paris Climate Agreement while maintaining the competitiveness of the tourism sector.

The legal directive n. 2022/2, was published on November 15, 2022, and requires all accommodation facilities to obtain at least a Stage 1 Verification in the Sustainable Tourism Programme by December 31, 2023. This initiative has transitioned sustainability from a voluntary concept to a mandatory approach. Currently, Türkiye has more than 17 800 hotels and more than 1.6 million beds which have received Sustainable Tourism Verifications and Certificates.

The Province Promotion and Development Programme, aims to enhance local development by undertaking a long-term transformation of the Destination Management Office model. This was developed with the participation of governments, private sector institutions, and civil society organisations to enhance the tourism potential of all 81 provinces. Türkiye aims to create increase the visibility of destinations in the digital world, to create a sustainable and learning destination working model, and to strengthen branding processes through more effective promotion of destinations nationally and internationally.

Mainstreaming tourism sustainability certification in Türkiye

In 2022, Türkiye signed a three-year partnership agreement with the Global Sustainable Tourism Council to help deliver its National Sustainable Tourism Programme – the first partnership of its type at a government level.

The programme aims to increase resiliency and inclusivity through responsible and sustainable policies, and to be in full compliance with all international standards by 2030. It also seeks to ensure the sustainable growth of the tourism sector and to develop a shared understanding of Turkish tourism through the participation of all tourism stakeholders, with Accommodation facilities are the primary focus.

The Programme is planned to transition through three stages and is set to be completed by 2030. The first stage requires accommodation facilities to adhere to 30% of the defined standards before December 2023. By 2025, the target will increase to 70%, followed by all facilities becoming Sustainable Tourism Certified by 2030.

By June 2024, 17 811 accommodation facilities had been verified and certified - 16 790 accommodation facilities had successfully met the criteria and attained the 1st Stage Verification, 1 facility had achieved the 2nd Stage Verification and 1 020 had obtained 3rd Stage Verification.

Statistical Profile

Türkiye: Domestic, inbound and outbound tourism

	2018	2019	2020	2021	2022
TOURISM FLOWS, THOUSAND					
Domestic tourism					
Total domestic trips	126 446	124 639	67 142	75 883	76 567
Overnight visitors (tourists)	78 523	78 202	42 847	52 774	52 327
Same-day visitors (excursionists)	47 923	46 437	24 295	23 109	24 240
Nights in all types of accommodation	633 721	637 070	469 091	458 872	426 579
Hotels and similar establishments	55 815	51 633	23 569	41 654	39 967
Other collective establishments	19 116	19 087	9 926	16 480	15 049
Private accommodation	558 790	566 350	435 596	400 738	371 563
Inbound tourism[1]					
Total international arrivals	46 113	51 747	15 971	30 039	51 388
Overnight visitors (tourists)	45 768	51 192	15 894	29 925	50 453
Same-day visitors (excursionists)	345	555	77	114	935
Top markets					
Russian Federation	5 954	6 996	2 117	4 684	5 193
Germany	4 464	4 993	1 119	3 083	5 581
United Kingdom	2 220	2 504	821	387	3 254
Bulgaria	2 383	2 710	1 242	1 402	2 878
Georgia	2 002	2 103	408	290	1 514
Nights in all types of accommodation	112 245	132 808	40 093	93 124	148 553
Hotels and similar establishments	112 226	132 776	40 083	93 093	148 506
Other collective establishments	19	32	10	31	47
Private accommodation	..	..	..	..	..
Outbound tourism					
Total international departures	8 389	9 653	2 243	2 738	7 267
Overnight visitors (tourists)	..	..	..	..	
Same-day visitors (excursionists)	..	..	..	..	
Top destinations					
Europe not specified	1 359	1 499	..	480	1 214
Bulgaria	751	1 085	..	285	623
Iraq	853	977	..	366	786
Georgia	701	1 000	..	202	615
Greece	783	804	..	63	412
TOURISM RECEIPTS AND EXPENDITURE, MILLION USD					
Inbound tourism					
Total international receipts	37 175	41 291	13 567	28 790	..
International travel receipts	25 243	29 813	10 190	21 087	41 702
International passenger transport receipts	11 932	11 478	3 377	7 702	..
Outbound tourism					
Total international expenditure	5 003	5 259	1 436	2 109	..
International travel expenditure	4 601	4 108	1 066	1 672	4 092
International passenger transport expenditure	402	1 151	370	437	..

.. Not available

1. Arrivals from demand side surveys; Nights from supply side surveys.

Source: OECD Tourism Statistics (Database).

StatLink https://stat.link/oyqwn8

Türkiye: Enterprises and employment in tourism

	Number of establishments[1]	Number of persons employed				
	2022	2018	2019	2020	2021	2022
Total	..	..	..	..	..	..
Tourism industries	..	..	935 000	627 000	697 000	885 000
Accommodation services for visitors	28 008	..	367 000	289 000	308 000	366 000
Hotels and similar establishments	24 577	..				
Food and beverage serving industry	285 641	..	279 000	139 000	164 000	256 000
Passenger transport	..	..	206 000	145 000	153 000	170 000
Air passenger transport	248	..	..	..	..	..
Railways passenger transport	..	..	..	..	..	..
Road passenger transport	173 539	..	..	..	..	..
Water passenger transport	3 947	..	..	..	..	..
Passenger transport supporting services	..	..	..	..	..	..
Transport equipment rental	12 376	..	2 000	1 000	2 000	2 000
Travel agencies and other reservation services industry	13 371	..	51 000	41 000	56 000	62 000
Cultural industry	6 726	..	24 000	9 000	9 000	20 000
Sports and recreation industry	18 645	..	6 000	3 000	5 000	9 000
Retail trade of country-specific tourism characteristic goods	..	..	..	..	..	..
Other country-specific tourism industries	..	..	..	..	..	..
Other industries	..	..	..	..	..	..

.. Not available; c Confidential data
1. Data refer to number of enterprises.
Source: OECD Tourism Statistics (Database).

StatLink https://stat.link/jt9axf

Türkiye: Internal tourism consumption

Million TRY

	2022		
	Domestic tourism expenditure	Inbound tourism expenditure	Internal tourism consumption
Total	..	..	..
Consumption products	..	..	..
Tourism characteristic products	..	..	..
Accommodation services for visitors	31 677	144 997	176 674
Food and beverage serving services	33 451	125 726	159 177
Passenger transport services	108 502	409 363	517 865
Air passenger transport services	..	..	..
Railways passenger transport services	..	..	..
Road passenger transport services	..	..	..
Water passenger transport services	..	..	..
Passenger transport supporting services	..	..	..
Transport equipment rental services	744	8 472	9 217
Travel agencies and other reservation services industry	26 036	37 672	63 708
Cultural services	1 466	16 784	18 250
Sports and recreation services	773	3 853	4 626
Country-specific tourism characteristic goods	..	..	..
Country-specific tourism characteristic services	..	..	..
Other consumption products	..	..	..
Tourism connected products	..	..	..
Non-tourism related consumption products	79 012	282 839	361 851
Non-consumption products	..	..	..

.. Not available
Source: OECD Tourism Statistics (Database).

StatLink https://stat.link/r80tpz

United Kingdom

Tourism in the economy and outlook

Tourism is a driver of economic growth for the United Kingdom. In 2021, the sector contributed GBP 15.9 billion in nominal terms to the United Kingdom economy accounting for 0.8% of GVA, compared to 3.7% in 2019. The journey to recovery has not been linear. For example, in March 2023, the number of businesses in the tourism industry had increased by 12 530 (4.2%) compared to March 2019, but had decreased by 9 965 (3.1%) compared to March 2022. Continued recovery saw travel exports represent 12.9% of total service exports in 2022, above the pandemic low of 7.3% in 2020, but still below the pre-pandemic level of 14.0%.

The United Kingdom recorded 38.0 million international arrivals in 2023, 7% below 2019 levels but up 21% compared to 2022 levels, with international tourist spend estimated at GBP 31.1 billion. The top three source markets were the United States (5 122), France (3 172) and Germany (2 957). There has been a strong visitor rebound from the United States but traditionally active markets such as China remain behind.

With regards to domestic tourism, the United Kingdom recorded 117.3 million arrivals from domestic tourists in 2023, 7% below 2022 levels. In Q3 2023, 35.7 million domestic overnight trips were taken within Great Britain, down 4% compared to Q3 in 2022. Visitors spent a total of GBP 6.3 billion in Q1 2023.

Tourism governance

The Department for Culture, Media and Sport is responsible for tourism policy development in the United Kingdom. The Tourism Industry Council is a collaborative forum consisting of government and industry members and is the government's key tourism stakeholder engagement forum. The forum's four key delivery priorities are: events; inclusivity and accessibility; international competitiveness and demand; and sustainability. An inter-ministerial group for Tourism, chaired by the Secretary of State for the Department and supported by the Minister for Tourism, brings together all government departments with policy interest or responsibility for tourism.

Destination Management Organisations have been renamed as Local Visitor Economy Partnerships (LVEPs), as part of the recommendations the government is taking forward from an independent review of destination management organisations released in August 2021 (the 'de Bois' review). These LVEPs will provide local governance leadership in tourism destinations across the United Kingdom - collaboratively working with local, regional and national stakeholders on shared priorities and targets. Other recommendations from this review aimed to strengthen the structure and coherence of the regional tourism landscape in the United Kingdom and better support regional areas to attract and manage tourists.

The budget allocated to tourism through the British Tourist Authority in 2023-24 was GBP 50.7 million.

United Kingdom: Organisational chart of tourism bodies

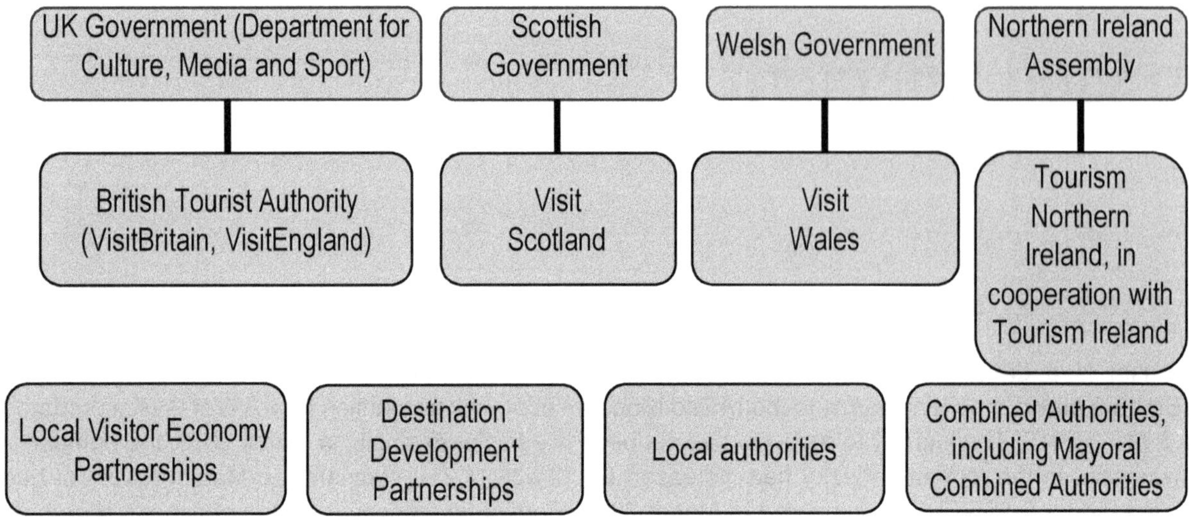

Source: OECD, adapted from the Department for Culture, Media and Sport, 2024.

Tourism policies and programmes

The UK Tourism Recovery Plan was launched in 2021 and sets out the role that the United Kingdom government will play in assisting and accelerating the tourism sector's recovery. The plan outlines six key aims and objectives which include:

- A swift recovery back to 2019 levels of tourism volume and visitor expenditure.
- To see the benefits of tourism shared across every nation and region as tourism recovers and then exceeds 2019 levels.
- To build back better with a more productive, innovative and resilient tourism industry.
- For tourism to contribute to the enhancement and conservation of the United Kingdom's cultural, natural and historic heritage and minimise damage to the environment.
- Providing an inclusive and accessible tourism offer that is open to all.
- For the UK to be a leading European country for business events.

The Plan included targets for domestic overnight trips to recover to 99 million with GBP 19 billion in spend by the end of 2022, and 41 million international visitors spending GBP 28 billion by the end of 2023. This aim was underpinned by activities to reopen safely, support businesses and stimulate demand.

By the end of 2022, domestic overnight trips exceeded this target - welcoming 126 million with GBP 33 billion in spend. In contrast, international visitors came to a total of 31.2 million, spending GBP 26.5 billion.

The Government works closely with the devolved administrations - Scottish and Welsh governments and the Northern Irish Executive - to improve tourism for the whole of the United Kingdom. Each of the devolved administrations has their own recovery strategy and the UK Government supports their efforts, collaborating on shared initiatives.

To meet the objectives of the Recovery Plan, the United Kingdom government has launched several initiatives. Nationally supported and strategic Local Visitor Economy Partnerships (LVEPs) will replace Destination Management Organisations, providing robust local leadership and governance in tourism destinations (see box below).

A registration scheme for short-term rentals in England will be implemented through the Levelling Up and Regeneration Bill. The consultation for the design of the scheme was undertaken in 2023 and it will be operationalised soon.

Over GBP 1.5 billion in grants and loans will be provided to approximately 5 000 organisations through the Culture Recovery Fund, to fund heritage sites in the United Kingdom. Additional funding will be provided through the Towns Fund (worth GBP 3.6 billion in total), the United Kingdom Shared Prosperity Fund (GBP 2.6 billion), the Getting Building Fund (GBP 900 million), and the United Kingdom Community Renewal Fund (GBP 220 million). The Levelling Up Fund (worth GBP 4.8 billion in total) supports a significant number of projects across the United Kingdom that have a visitor economy element or focus.

Investment in transport infrastructure and connectivity is crucial to underpin the success of the United Kingdom tourism sector. VisitBritain's Gateway Innovation Fund will provide grants to deliver international marketing activity for a specific inbound gateway or region. The United Kingdom continues to invest in and renew the rail and bus networks, with over GBP 35 billion of rail investment between 2022-23 and 2024-25. The United Kingdom have also published a framework and plan for achieving net zero aviation by 2050.

Work to develop the United Kingdom's approach to accessibility and inclusion has focused on actions to build on existing best practice and toolkits, such as the National Accessible Scheme, and examine existing access limitations in tourism services based on different protected characteristics. These have been undertaken with consultation through the Tourism Industry Council Working Group on Inclusivity and Accessibility, the Disability & Accessibility Ambassador, England's Inclusive Tourism Action Group, and other stakeholders.

Additionally, the Ministerial Advocacy Programme will be enhanced by increasing Ministerial attendance at business events and letters of support for event bids, evaluating the case for expanding the VisitBritain Business Events Growth Programme and working with the Tourism Industry Council Working Group to produce a strategy for sustainable business events in line with the broader Sustainable Tourism Plan.

Restructuring destination management in the United Kingdom

The United Kingdom continues to implement key recommendations from the de Bois Review of Destination Management Organisations. The UK Government recognises that DMOs are a vital part of England's tourism landscape, and that it is necessary to transform the landscape at a local level to address long-running concerns about the structure, funding models and fragmentation.

VisitEngland is responsible for developing and administering a new accreditation scheme, with support from the United Kingdom government (GBP 1.8 million between 2022 and 2025). Under the new accreditation scheme, successful DMOs will be given Local Visitor Economy Partnership (LVEPs) status. As of June 2024, 33 LVEPs had been accredited.

A Destination Development Partnership (DDP) model is being piloted in the Northeast of England, led by the NewcastleGateshead Initiative, supported by GBP 2.25 million in funding. The government will award one partnership multi-year funding and the opportunity to focus on activities that ensure their region remains sustainable, competitive and responsive to challenges such as boosting skills, accessibility and levelling up.

Statistical Profile

United Kingdom: Domestic, inbound and outbound tourism

	2018	2019	2020	2021	2022
TOURISM FLOWS, THOUSAND					
Domestic tourism					
Total domestic trips	1 821 600	1 775 780	..	710 200	1 212 000
Overnight visitors (tourists)	118 600	122 780	..	86 200	126 000
Same-day visitors (excursionists)	1 703 000	1 653 000	..	624 000	1 086 000
Nights in all types of accommodation	208 054	220 812	..	302 600	383 300
Hotels and similar establishments	144 261	161 881	..	..	..
Other collective establishments	63 793	58 931	..	..	..
Private accommodation	..	..	..	..	..
Inbound tourism					
Total international arrivals	40 283	40 857	11 101	6 384	31 244
Overnight visitors (tourists)	38 664	39 418	..	6 287	30 741
Same-day visitors (excursionists)	1 619	1 439	..	97	503
Top markets					
United States	..	..	..	699	..
Ireland	..	..	..	685	..
France	..	..	..	610	..
Spain	..	..	..	492	..
Germany	..	..	..	388	..
Nights in all types of accommodation	139 759	158 335	..	93 522	262 864
Hotels and similar establishments	135 996	155 280	..	..	..
Other collective establishments	3 763	3 055	..	..	..
Private accommodation	..	..	..	..	..
Outbound tourism					
Total international departures	90 571	93 086	23 827	19 142	70 950
Overnight visitors (tourists)	88 759	91 592	..	19 037	70 589
Same-day visitors (excursionists)	1 811	1 494	..	105	361
Top destinations					
Spain	..	..	..	4 232	..
France	..	..	..	1 598	..
Portugal	..	..	..	1 159	..
Greece	..	..	..	1 132	..
Ireland	..	..	..	1 057	..
TOURISM RECEIPTS AND EXPENDITURE, MILLION GBP					
Inbound tourism					
Total international receipts	54 598	58 299	25 259	29 163	60 371
International travel receipts	43 803	47 506	22 809	27 442	53 064
International passenger transport receipts	10 795	10 793	2 450	1 721	7 307
Outbound tourism					
Total international expenditure	77 030	80 868	24 636	27 200	86 307
International travel expenditure	64 188	67 850	20 798	23 909	73 779
International passenger transport expenditure	12 842	13 018	3 838	3 291	12 528

.. Not available
Source: OECD Tourism Statistics (Database).

StatLink https://stat.link/s4q3w7

United Kingdom: Enterprises and employment in tourism

	Number of establishments[1]	Number of persons employed				
	2020 e	2018	2019	2020	2021	2022
Total	..	1 547 496	2 165 000	1 108 000	..	..
Tourism industries	241 490	1 115 496	1 742 000	917 000	..	..
Accommodation services for visitors	18 530	378 000	424 000	207 000	..	..
Hotels and similar establishments	..	..	..	..	..	..
Food and beverage serving industry	144 719	404 000	421 000	251 000	..	..
Passenger transport	14 356	105 000	120 000	106 000	..	..
Air passenger transport	461	31 000	34 000	38 000	..	..
Railways passenger transport	73	30 000	30 000	32 000	..	..
Road passenger transport	13 101	43 000	55 000	35 000	..	..
Water passenger transport	721	1 000	1 000	1 000	..	..
Passenger transport supporting services	..	..	..	..	..	..
Transport equipment rental	3 934	4 000	8 000	3 000	..	..
Travel agencies and other reservation services industry	8 670	55 000	71 000	42 000	..	..
Cultural industry	29 880	82 000	85 000	46 000	..	..
Sports and recreation industry	17 198	87 000	119 000	71 000	..	..
Retail trade of country-specific tourism characteristic goods	..	..	..	..	..	..
Other country-specific tourism industries	4 203	496	494 000	191 000	..	..
Other industries	..	432 000	423 000	191 000	..	..

.. Not available; e Estimated value
1. Data refer to number of enterprises.
Source: OECD Tourism Statistics (Database).

StatLink https://stat.link/o024xw

United Kingdom: Internal tourism consumption

Million GBP

	2020 e		
	Domestic tourism expenditure	Inbound tourism expenditure	Internal tourism consumption
Total	..	..	..
Consumption products	62 930	6 912	71 614
Tourism characteristic products	41 327	3 629	44 956
Accommodation services for visitors	5 596	1 447	7 042
Food and beverage serving services	15 912	1 002	16 913
Passenger transport services	10 257	963	11 221
Air passenger transport services	6 406	661	7 068
Railways passenger transport services	2 067	92	2 159
Road passenger transport services	1 282	137	1 418
Water passenger transport services	503	73	576
Passenger transport supporting services	..	..	..
Transport equipment rental services	1 763	46	1 810
Travel agencies and other reservation services industry	1 530	29	1 559
Cultural services	2 668	57	2 725
Sports and recreation services	3 423	50	3 473
Country-specific tourism characteristic goods	..	..	..
Country-specific tourism characteristic services	178	36	213
Other consumption products	21 602	3 283	26 658
Tourism connected products	..	..	
Non-tourism related consumption products	..	..	..
Non-consumption products	..	..	..

.. Not available; e Estimated value
Source: OECD Tourism Statistics (Database).

StatLink https://stat.link/h3m7ua

United States

Tourism in the economy and outlook

The travel and tourism sector is a critical driver of economic growth and employment in the United States. In 2022, the sector generated USD 764 billion in GVA (value added) and directly employed 6.6 million people. This means tourism directly accounted for 3.0% of national GVA and 4.2% of the total workforce. This period was still impeded by the impacts of COVID-19, so remains below the 2019 high of 7.3 million jobs. The recovery in international tourism has continued, and in 2023 travel exports of USD 213 billion represented 21.3% of total service exports, down from 26.8% in 2019, but a significant increase compared to the pandemic low of 10.5% in 2021.

Recovery from the pandemic has been uneven across the United States, with some destinations taking much longer to recover, while others have already surpassed 2019 levels: overseas visitation to 8 states and one U.S. territory surpassed 2019 visitation in 2023, while visitation remained under 60% of 2019 levels of visitation in 5 states and 2 U.S. territories. In 2023, the United States recorded 66.5 million international tourist arrivals, up 246% from the pandemic low of 19.2 million in 2020, but still at 84% of 2019 levels. The top five source markets were Canada (31%), Mexico (22%), United Kingdom (6%), and Germany and India each at 3%.

Domestic tourism is key to tourism in the United States. Domestic travellers took an estimated 2.3 billion person-trips and spent USD 943 billion in nominal terms in 2023, down from USD 992 billion in 2019, according to the US Travel Association Winter 2024 Forecast.

The United States' National Travel and Tourism Office forecast expects total international visitation to reach 77.7 million in 2024, 85.2 million in 2025 (surpassing the 79.4 million of 2019), and 91.1 million in 2026, before reaching 96.8 million in 2028.

Tourism governance

Travel and tourism in the United States is highly decentralised. Public authorities manage tourism at the national, state, regional and local levels. These include the federal government, state governments, and destination marketing organisations (DMOs).

The U.S. Travel and Tourism Advisory Board consists of up to 32 private-sector tourism representatives from businesses and organisations appointed by the Secretary of Commerce to provide policy input on key sector issues. The Tourism Policy Council is an inter-agency council established by law to ensure the nation's travel and tourism interests are considered in federal decision-making, co-ordinating national policies and programmes that have a significant effect on international travel and tourism, recreation, and national heritage resources. The Policy Council reviews and considers the Advisory Board recommendations and provides additional insight from the public sector perspective on issues affecting travel and tourism nationally.

The National Travel and Tourism Office (NTTO), within Department of Commerce, serves as the central point of contact within the federal government. NTTO is the source of official tourism statistics to inform public policy and private sector business decisions. NTTO is also the official government liaison to the Corporation for Travel Promotion, operating as Brand USA, a non-profit corporation that promotes travel to the United States. Brand USA's Board of Directors is appointed by the Secretary of Commerce.

NTTO is allocated resources from a congressional appropriation to the Department of Commerce and sells research reports and data to generate additional operating revenues, while inter-agency agreements also generate funds. NTTO's operational budget for FY2023 was approximately USD 6.9 million. NTTO also approves up to USD 100 million from the Travel Promotion Fund for use by Brand USA, which is supported by a portion of the fees charged for the Electronic System for Travel Authorisation, paid by international travellers coming from countries participating in the visa waiver programme. In December 2022, The United States Congress passed the Visit America Act which, among other things, establishes the role of the Assistant Secretary for Travel and Tourism at the United States Department of Commerce. The implementation of the act is under discussion.

United States: Organisational chart of tourism bodies

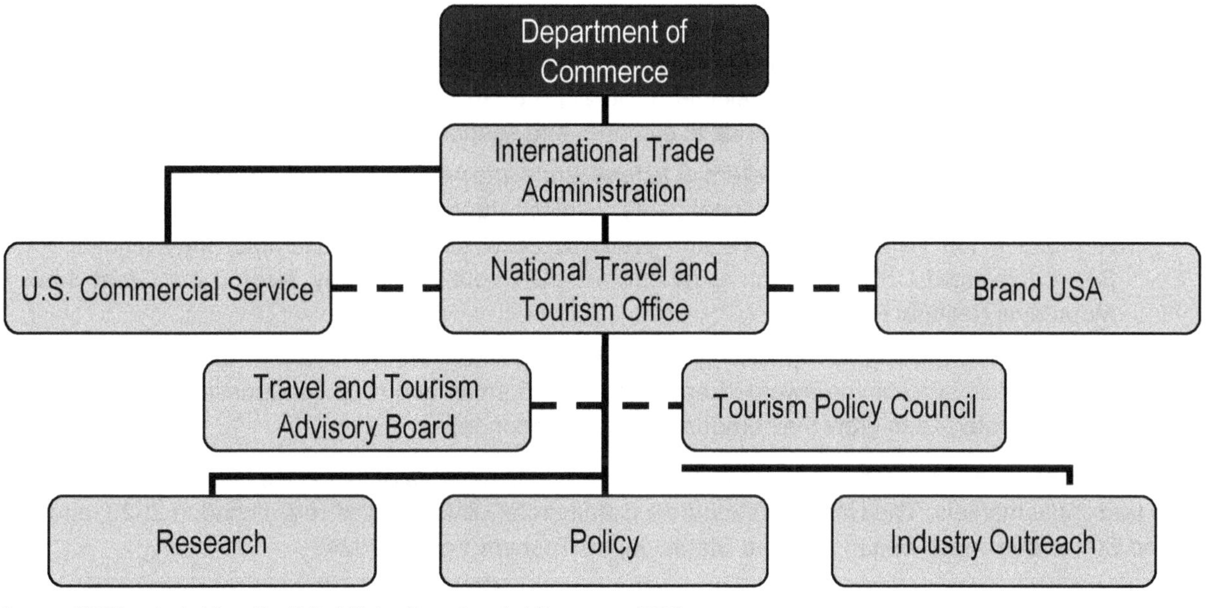

Source: OECD, adapted from the United States Department of Commerce, 2024.

Tourism policies and programmes

The 2022 National Travel and Tourism Strategy is the guiding document for tourism development in the United States. The Strategy set an overarching goal of attracting 90 million visitors, who are estimated to spend USD 279 billion annually by 2027. The United States is taking a holistic approach to tourism development to foster growth while addressing the challenges that accompany it. The Strategy is divided into four pillars: promoting the United States; facilitating travel to and within the United States; ensuring diverse, inclusive, and accessible travel and tourism; and fostering resilient and sustainable travel and tourism. In the first year of the strategy implementation, progress has been made through:

- Supporting communities in recovery: The American Rescue Plan supported travel, tourism, and outdoor recreation communities whose economies were hard hit by the pandemic (valued at USD 750 million). Competitive grant funding worth USD 240 million was distributed across 126 awards and are expected to generate USD 1.1 billion in private investment and create or save approximately 10 000 jobs. More than 50% of these awards are expected to benefit historically underserved communities and populations.

- Driving visitation to the United States from top markets: 21 US Embassies have created strategic Tourism Country Plans, in collaboration with the Federal Government, to promote travel to the United States.
- Helping communities prepare for extreme weather and climate changes and protecting travel and tourism assets: A USD 2.6 billion framework was developed to invest in climate resilience and coastal communities funded by from the Inflation Reduction Act. The funding will also support critical improvements and accessibility services at visitor centres within the National Marine Sanctuary System.
- Facilitating travel by issuing visas at record pace: In 2023, more than 10.4 million non-immigrant visas were issued globally, surpassing any high-water mark in recent history. US embassies and consulates issued 20% more than in 2019. Today, more people can travel to the United States than ever before (see box below).
- Supporting Native American communities: In partnership with the American Indian Alaska Native Tourism Association, USD 990 000 in grants were provided to six tribes to develop recreation and tourism infrastructure and/or technical assistance in Native American communities over two years.
- Enhancing secure travel and travel experience: Biometric exiting at airports has been expanded through public-private partnerships with the airlines and airports to enhance security and the travel experience. Biometric exit is available at 50 airports and over 500 million travellers have been processed through facial biometrics at air, land, and seaports.
- Expanding accessibility for travellers at federal lands and waters: Reparation and improvements to infrastructure and facilities in national parks, wildlife refuges and other sites has been undertaken to improve the visitor experience and enhance accessibility. For example, the National Park Service invested USD 31 million to rehabilitate the Foothills Parkway West in the Great Smoky Mountains National Park.
- Strengthening economic opportunities for communities: the Recreation Economy for Rural Communities programme awarded assistance to 25 small and rural communities in 17 states to identify strategies to grow their outdoor recreation economies.

Under the continued implementation of the Strategy, an additional area of focus has been to regain visitors from traditional markets. The United States-India Commercial Dialogue was relaunched in 2023, and the United States and Japan began a United States-Japan Tourism Year in 2024.

Improving visa processing in the United States

The United States expanded the authority for consular officers to waive the in-person interview requirement for certain low-risk non-immigrant visa applicants. In fiscal year 2023, nearly 40% of the 10.4 million travellers who received U.S. non-immigrant visas did not require an in-person interview. The interview waiver authority allows posts with higher interview wait times to focus on applicants who must appear in person. Demand remains at historic levels in some countries, contributing to lengthy appointment wait times even as the United States issued record numbers of visas in countries like Mexico, Brazil, India, and Colombia. U.S. embassies and consulates have significantly reduced appointment wait times in most markets over the past year. Technology continues to be leveraged to streamline visa processing and improve the US travel experience. The Visa Office is developing a digital visa authorisation that could be issued in place of the traditional visa foil printed and affixed in the applicant's passport.

Statistical Profile

United States: Domestic, inbound and outbound tourism

	2018	2019	2020	2021	2022
TOURISM FLOWS, THOUSAND					
Domestic tourism					
Total domestic trips	2 278 000	2 318 000	1 580 000	2 040 000	2 300 000
Overnight visitors (tourists)	..	..	..	..	..
Same-day visitors (excursionists)	..	..	..	..	..
Nights in all types of accommodation	..	..	..	..	..
Hotels and similar establishments	1 694 889	1 749 542	1 331 737	1 821 203	1 851 402
Other collective establishments	..	..	..	..	..
Private accommodation	..	..	..	..	..
Inbound tourism					
Total international arrivals	169 325	165 477	53 557	46 524	89 470
Overnight visitors (tourists)	79 746	79 442	19 212	22 280	50 870
Same-day visitors (excursionists)	89 579	86 035	34 345	24 244	38 600
Top markets					
Canada	21 475	20 720	4 809	2 529	14 382
Mexico	18 387	18 328	6 809	10 576	12 535
United Kingdom	4 659	4 780	730	461	3 466
Germany	2 062	2 064	294	249	1 481
France	1 767	1 844	298	222	1 318
Nights in all types of accommodation	405 682	411 164	95 783	95 783	435 103
Hotels and similar establishments	212 207	215 359	38 765	38 765	227 898
Other collective establishments	18 546	17 227	3 445	3 445	18 230
Private accommodation	174 930	178 578	53 573	53 573	188 975
Outbound tourism					
Total international departures	148 083	158 092	61 703	70 891	102 524
Overnight visitors (tourists)	93 137	99 755	33 499	49 097	80 730
Same-day visitors (excursionists)	54 946	58 336	28 203	21 794	21 794
Top destinations					
Mexico	36 923	39 942	21 729	28 789	33 540
Canada	14 440	14 994	1 929	2 093	9 088
United Kingdom	3 927	3 943	620	747	3 734
France	3 021	3 140	366	710	3 086
Dominican Republic	2 882	2 957	1 014	2 805	2 707
TOURISM RECEIPTS AND EXPENDITURE, MILLION USD					
Inbound tourism					
Total international receipts	241 985	239 064	84 296	84 169	165 460
International travel receipts	200 724	198 982	72 479	71 411	136 869
International passenger transport receipts	41 261	40 082	11 817	12 758	28 591
Outbound tourism					
Total international expenditure	176 395	184 785	47 075	74 544	161 941
International travel expenditure	125 717	131 990	33 704	56 697	115 312
International passenger transport expenditure	50 678	52 795	13 371	17 847	46 629

.. Not available
Source: OECD Tourism Statistics (Database).

StatLink https://stat.link/1xc34d

United States: Enterprises and employment in tourism

	Number of establishments	Number of persons employed				
	2021 p	2018	2019	2020	2021 p	2022
Total	..	6 103 000	6 070 000	3 466 000	4 807 000	6 647 000 |
Tourism industries	912 696	5 316 000	5 282 000	3 049 000	3 571 000	4 860 000 |
Accommodation services for visitors	67 354	1 537 000	1 565 000	1 001 000	1 083 000	1 333 000 |
Hotels and similar establishments	59 596	..	..	..	..	..
Food and beverage serving industry	666 409	1 776 000	1 701 000	877 000	1 607 000	1 820 000 |
Passenger transport	24 260	795 000	818 000	544 000	154 000	744 000 |
Air passenger transport	4 344	594 000	618 000	450 000	16 000	571 000 |
Railways passenger transport	..	9 000	9 000	3 000	4 000	5 000 |
Road passenger transport	16 988	154 000	147 000	74 000	121 000	151 000 |
Water passenger transport	2 928	38 000	44 000	17 000	13 000	16 000 |
Passenger transport supporting services	..	312 000	319 000	227 000	170 000	311 000 |
Transport equipment rental	15 891	113 000	128 000	149 000	143 000	20 000 |
Travel agencies and other reservation services industry	20 710	204 000	203 000	23 000	30 000	161 000 |
Cultural industry	18 221	48 000	43 000	29 000	34 000	38 000 |
Sports and recreation industry	99 851	531 000	505 000	199 000	350 000	433 000 |
Retail trade of country-specific tourism characteristic goods	..	..	..	..	..	..
Other country-specific tourism industries	..	..	..	..	..	..
Other industries	..	787 000	788 000	417 000	1 236 000	1 787 000 |

.. Not available; p Provisional data, | Break in series
Source: OECD Tourism Statistics (Database).

StatLink https://stat.link/9lympo

United States: Internal tourism consumption

Million USD

	2021		
	Domestic tourism expenditure	Inbound tourism expenditure	Internal tourism consumption
Total	588 559	31 692	39 015 145
Consumption products	882 049	49 299	44 412 686
Tourism characteristic products	820 486	41 892	2 912 373
Accommodation services for visitors	186 764	9 146	195 909
Food and beverage serving services	168 330	9 021	1 182 340
Passenger transport services	185 373	12 348	238 533
Air passenger transport services	158 856	12 054	170 910
Railways passenger transport services	984	..	984
Road passenger transport services	19 685	223	60 230
Water passenger transport services	5 848	71	6 409
Passenger transport supporting services	105 614	7 123	792 767
Transport equipment rental services	43 931	452	56 924
Travel agencies and other reservation services industry	61 599	477	66 748
Cultural services	15 732	936	76 506
Sports and recreation services	53 143	2 389	302 646
Country-specific tourism characteristic goods	..	..	..
Country-specific tourism characteristic services	..	..	..
Other consumption products	61 563	7 407	41 500 313
Tourism connected products	61 563	7 407	5 270 839
Non-tourism related consumption products	..	..	36 229 474
Non-consumption products	..	..	..

.. Not available
Source: OECD Tourism Statistics (Database).

StatLink https://stat.link/40htm6

Part II Partner country profiles

Brazil

Tourism in the economy and outlook

Tourism is an important economic sector in Brazil and offers strong untapped growth potential as it recovers from the shock of the COVID-19 pandemic. Travel and Tourism supported 2.14 million formal jobs in 2022, or 4.0% of total employment. This is slightly below 2019 levels, when the sector accounted for 2.19 million jobs.

In 2023, Brazil recorded 5.9 million international overnight visitors. This represents a 63% increase in 2022 (3.6 million) but remains 7.2% below 2019 levels. Spending by international tourists accounted for USD 6.9 billion in 2023, exceeding pre-pandemic levels in nominal terms by 15.2%. The top international inbound markets are Argentina (32%), the United States (11%), Chile (8%) and Paraguay (7%).

Data on domestic tourism is available since 2020. Brazil recorded 9.6 million domestic overnight tourists in 2020, which fell slightly to 9.3 million in 2021.

International tourist arrivals are expected to exceed pre-pandemic levels in 2024, with arrivals in the first half of the year already up 1.9% compared to the same period in 2019.

Tourism governance

The Ministry of Tourism is the federal authority in charge of tourism policy in Brazil. Among its attributions, the Ministry oversees and evaluates tourism programmes, promotes Brazil as a tourism destination, stimulates innovation, entrepreneurship, and investment in the tourism sector, fosters financing programmes and access to credit through the General Tourism Fund, and inspects tourism service providers.

The Ministry of Tourism also collaborates with other ministries to formulate policies and programmes aimed at improving infrastructure, generating employment and income, and dealing with crises, resilience and climate action in tourism destinations. Since 2023, the reinstated Ministry of Culture handles the cultural agenda, allowing the Ministry of Tourism to concentrate solely on tourism matters.

Embratur, the Brazilian Agency for the International Promotion of Tourism, is a national organisation whose objective is to design, develop and implement actions for promoting Brazilian tourism products, services and destinations abroad, supervised by the Ministry of Tourism. Additionally, the Tourism National Council is an organism formed by high level members and authorities from the executive branch, entities from various segments related to the travel industry and strategic players from the private and public sector, whose decisions are taken collectively.

Tourism is a shared competence in Brazil, designed and implemented at national, state and municipal levels. The Ministry of Tourism collaborates directly with regional and local authorities through its policies, as well as through collegial bodies established within the structure of the Ministry or created by federal entities.

Brazil: Organisational chart of tourism bodies

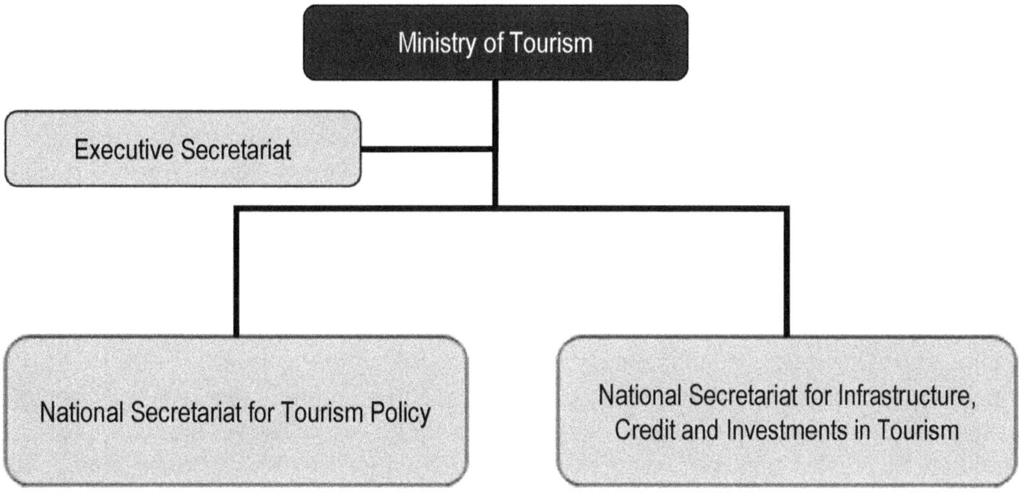

Source: OECD, adapted from the Ministry of Tourism, 2024.

Tourism policies and programmes

In January 2024, the National Tourism Council validated the National Tourism Plan 2024-27, outlining a roadmap for tourism development in Brazil. The new Plan was developed by the Ministry of Tourism in close collaboration with public and private organisations, universities, unions and associations, and included public hearings and consultations to ensure the participation of multiple stakeholders across the tourism sector.

The Plan is structured around three key pillars on development – social and guarantee of rights, economic and socio-environment sustainability, and defence of democracy and reconstruction of the State and sovereignty – and sets bold tourist arrivals targets: by 2027, Brazil aims to welcome 8.1 million international tourists, consolidating its position as the largest tourist economy in South America, and 150 million domestic tourists.

Several programmes have been implemented to support recovery and growth of the tourism sector in Brazil. The Emergency Programme for the Resumption of the Events Sector, launched in 2021, introduced significant tax incentives benefiting 30 segments of the cultural, tourism and entertainment sectors, including a BRL 15 billion limit for tax incentives. FUNGETUR, a funding programme for the construction sector, released BRL 1.2 billion in 2023 for over 1 000 tourism-related projects, while CADASTUR, a registration system for tourism service providers, supports nearly 160 000 subscribers benefit from FUNGETUR funds. The Regionalisation Programme registered over 3 000 cities on the Tourism Map online platform to facilitate public policy and investment development.

The Ministry has also created an online platform, investment.tourism, to promote investments and stimulate new businesses in the tourism sector. Institutions and entrepreneurs are also encouraged by the Ministry to participate in major tourism trade shows and events throughout the country focused on real estate investments to promote their innovative projects. The Smart Tourism Destinations programme awarded certifications to 21 destinations that enhanced experiences for both tourists and residents (see box below).

To enhance tourism mobility, the Traveller Support Points programme was launched, inaugurating essential service areas for travellers on major highways, following the increase in motorway travel since the COVID-19 pandemic. The Ministry of Tourism also improved active tourism trails, mapping over 100 towns and 18 cycle routes, with 3 500 km of signposted trails, particularly within national parks.

To foster sustainable tourism, several initiatives were implemented. In 2023, 42 Brazilian beaches received the Blue Flag Certification, an international eco-label based on water quality, waste management and biodiversity conservation. In partnership with the Ministry of Environment and the Institute for Biodiversity Conservation, the Ministry of Tourism is supporting visitation structuring in conservation units through a partnerships and investments programme. In 2019, feasibility studies for four national parks were conducted, leading to continued concession processes with the National Bank for Economic and Social Development, with further studies underway. Further, the Marine Spatial Planning initiative collects and georeferences tourism activities along Brazil's coasts. Committed to promoting sustainability and reducing conflicts, the initiative includes data on diving spots, shipwrecks, beaches, and other significant marine sites, aiming to streamline environmental licensing and plan for climate change adaptations.

To increase social inclusion through tourism, the Ministry of Tourism launched, in partnership with the Federal Fluminense University, the Original Brazil Experiences programme, which developed 40 tourism products involving indigenous and quilombola communities. Three programmes were launched to promote domestic tourism. Discover Civic Brazil, launched in 2023, encouraged students, teachers, and researchers to visit Brasília and the capital's historical sites. Discover Brazil: Make it Happen aims to facilitate credit access for tourism packages, tickets, accommodation, theme park tickets, among other travel services, and Discover Brazil by Flying partnered with airlines to stimulate domestic travel.

Culture and heritage are also a priority for tourism development in Brazil. The Tourism Management of World Cultural and Natural Heritage initiative, co-ordinates the Interministerial Committee to develop, organise, and promote tourism segments related to Brazil's UNESCO World Heritage sites. The REVIVE Programme complements this by requalifying unused assets through private investments, enabling their tourist use and contributing to the economic and social development of their regions. Two cities, Rio de Janeiro and Penedo, joined the UNESCO Creative Cities Network, with the support of the Ministry of Tourism, and are now labelled Creative Cities for Literature and Cinema.

Creating smart tourism destinations in Brazil

In 2022, the Ministry of Tourism launched the Smart Tourism Destinations Brazil programme. Ten pilot destinations actively working to enhance their tourism experience were awarded the Smart Tourism Destination certification in transformation.

The certification process involves meeting 105 specific requirements across nine strategic pillars: Governance, Innovation, Sustainability, Mobility and Transportation, Accessibility, Safety, Technology, Creativity, and Promotion and Marketing.

In 2023, 11 additional destinations earned the same certification. The programme aims to make destinations more sustainable, accessible, technological, creative, and safe while improving governance and mobility. In 2024, the goal is to certify all qualifying destinations, provide special training across Brazil, and conduct inspections to ensure the implementation of Transformation Plans.

Statistical Profile

Brazil: Domestic, inbound and outbound tourism

	2018	2019	2020	2021	2022
TOURISM FLOWS, THOUSAND					
Domestic tourism					
Total domestic trips	..	..	13 302	12 247	..
Overnight visitors (tourists)	..	..	9 637	9 256	..
Same-day visitors (excursionists)	..	..	3 665	2 991	..
Nights in all types of accommodation	..	..	..	..	..
Hotels and similar establishments	..	..	..	..	..
Other collective establishments	..	..	..	..	..
Private accommodation	..	..	..	..	..
Inbound tourism					
Total international arrivals	..	..	..	..	..
Overnight visitors (tourists)	6 621	6 353	2 146	746	3 630
Same-day visitors (excursionists)	..	..	..	..	..
Top markets					
Argentina	2 498	1 955	888	67	1 033
United States	539	591	172	132	441
Paraguay	357	407	123	132	308
Chile	387	392	131	47	202
Uruguay	348	365	114	12	180
Nights in all types of accommodation	..	..	..	..	..
Hotels and similar establishments	..	..	..	..	..
Other collective establishments	..	..	..	..	..
Private accommodation	..	..	..	..	..
Outbound tourism					
Total international departures	..	..	..	..	..
Overnight visitors (tourists)	10 733	..	..	..	..
Same-day visitors (excursionists)	..	..	..	..	..
Top destinations					
United States	2 209	..	..	..	..
Portugal	1 117	..	..	..	..
Argentina	947	..	..	..	..
Chile	589	..	..	..	..
Spain	559	..	..	..	..
TOURISM RECEIPTS AND EXPENDITURE, MILLION USD					
Inbound tourism					
Total international receipts	6 323	6 127	3 099	3 005	4 968
International travel receipts	5 921	5 995	3 044	2 947	4 952
International passenger transport receipts	403	132	55	58	16
Outbound tourism					
Total international expenditure	22 229	21 178	6 490	6 252	15 426
International travel expenditure	18 266	17 593	5 394	5 250	12 185
International passenger transport expenditure	3 963	3 585	1 096	1 002	3 241

.. Not available
Source: OECD Tourism Statistics (Database).

StatLink https://stat.link/9m0g6t

Brazil: Enterprises and employment in tourism

	Number of establishments[1]	Number of persons employed[2]				
	2020	2018	2019	2020	2021	2022
Total	..	..	..	..	..	..
Tourism industries	260 834	2 133 822	2 192 235	1 693 074	1 793 996	2 138 612
Accommodation services for visitors	30 721	315 481	318 114	271 902	302 104	338 000
Hotels and similar establishments	..	..	..	..	..	..
Food and beverage serving industry	189 286	1 233 881	1 271 932	1 051 147	1 106 747	1 346 872
Passenger transport	14 073	453 943	420 919	219 417	222 463	258 384
Air passenger transport	649	50 136	55 057	46 389	47 959	50 313
Railways passenger transport	..	..	..	..	..	..
Road passenger transport	12 808	355 246	358 222	165 576	167 443	198 904
Water passenger transport	616	7 935	7 640	7 452	7 061	9 167
Passenger transport supporting services	..	..	..	..	..	..
Transport equipment rental	5 585	40 626	48 839	54 376	63 495	69 932
Travel agencies and other reservation services industry	12 437	90 968	92 865	46 600	47 121	61 257
Cultural industry	8 732	39 549	39 566	49 632	52 066	64 167
Sports and recreation industry	..	..	..	..	..	..
Retail trade of country-specific tourism characteristic goods	..	..	..	..	..	..
Other country-specific tourism industries	..	..	..	..	..	..
Other industries	..	..	..	..	..	..

.. Not available
1. Data refer to number of enterprises.
2. Data refer to number of jobs.
Source: OECD Tourism Statistics (Database).

StatLink https://stat.link/23xy4m

Bulgaria

Tourism in the economy and outlook

Tourism is an important source of employment and foreign exchange earnings in Bulgaria. In 2021, tourism contributed to 201 000 jobs in the country, 14.9% below 2019 levels.

International tourism recovery continued in 2023. Bulgaria recorded 3.6 million international visitors in commercial accommodation. This represents an 18% increase in 2022, when the country recorded 3.1 million visitors, but is still 11% below 2019 levels. The top three source countries in 2023 were Romania (24%), Poland (8%) and Germany (8%).

Domestic tourism experienced a quick recovery in Bulgaria. In 2022, 4.6 million domestic trips were recorded in commercial accommodation, a 10.5% increase compared to 2019. Provisional data for 2023 shows a continued growth in domestic tourism, with over 5 million domestic trips in commercial accommodation, or a 22% increase on pre-pandemic levels.

Tourism governance

The Ministry of Tourism is responsible for implementing tourism policy at national level. This includes the National Strategy for Sustainable Development of Tourism in the Republic of Bulgaria 2014-30 with an Action plan, strategies for the development of different tourism segments, short-term programmes and plans, and regulation of the tourism sector. The Ministry is also in charge of international marketing, co-ordinating the implementation of national marketing strategies, overseeing regional marketing strategies, and co-ordinating the implementation of tourism activities from other ministries and institutions. The national tourism policy is formulated by the Council of Ministers.

The National Tourism Council is the consultative body operating under the authority of the Ministry of Tourism. Its members include representatives from tourism-related ministries as well as national, regional and local tourism associations as well as branch and product associations, transport operators and consumer bodies.

Regional authorities are in charge of implementing the national tourism policy at regional level. Their responsibilities include devising regional strategies, implementing tourism development programmes, as well as supporting the programmes of national authorities, regional tourism management organisations and tourism development associations.

Nine Regional Tourism Management Organisations were established to co-ordinate tourism activities, comprising tourism associations, municipal and regional representatives, scientific organisations, institutes and schools in the field of tourism, consumer associations and other stakeholders. Their main goal is to reduce regional disparities by creating strong regional brands and specialised tourism products based on local resources. At the local level, municipal administrations are responsible for tourism development. The municipal council adopts a tourism development programme for the municipality aligned with the regional strategy, marketing strategy and following local tourism resources and needs.

In 2023, the tourism budget allocated to the Ministry of Tourism was BGN 28.2 million. This amount is comprised of subsidies from the state budget, registration fees for tourism activities, certification and categorisation of tourism sites, revenue from fines and penalties imposed under the Tourism Act, funds from international programmes, donations, grants and other sources defined by law.

Bulgaria: Organisational chart of tourism bodies

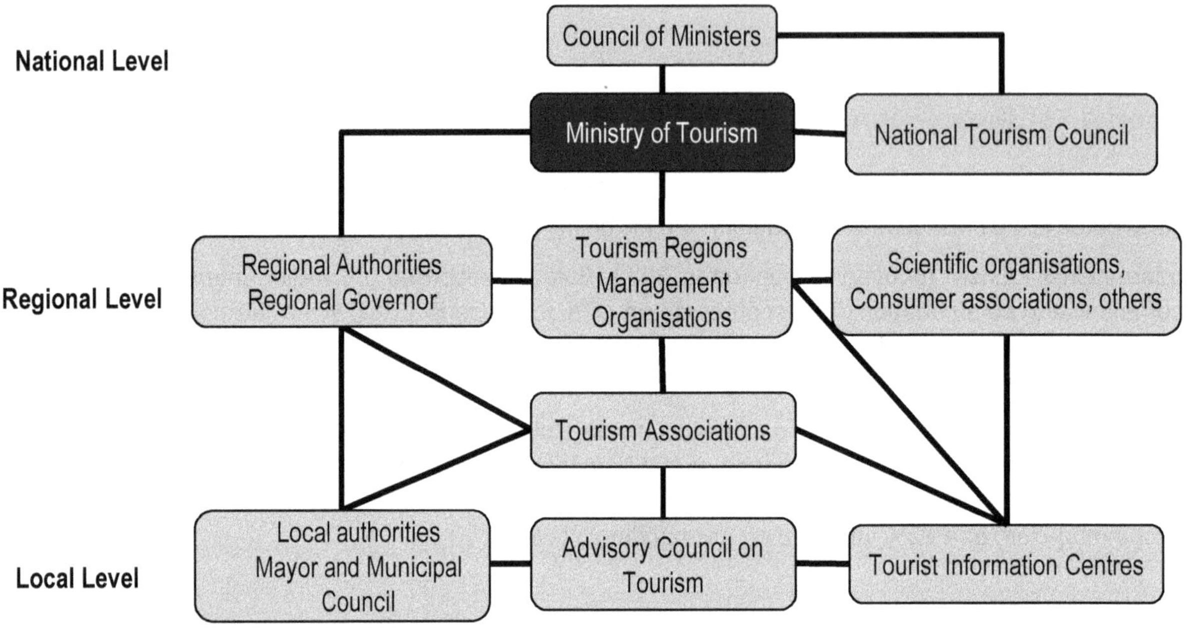

Source: OECD, adapted from the Ministry of Tourism, 2024.

Tourism policies and programmes

Tourism policy is guided by the National Strategy for Sustainable Development of Tourism in the Republic of Bulgaria 2014-30. The Strategy aims to strengthen the competitiveness and efficiency of the tourism sector in Bulgaria using the resources in a sustainable way, in line with market requirements and consumer expectations for sustainable tourism development. These include: (i) Diversifying national tourism products; (ii) Promoting quality services and protecting the rights and safety of consumers; (iii) Ensuring effective co-ordination between the institutions and integrating tourism into related sectoral policies; (iv) Making Bulgaria a leading tourism development destination; (v) Raising awareness of Bulgaria's year-round rich tourism offerings; and (vi) Marketing the destination effectively.

In 2023, the Ministry of Tourism completed a mid-term evaluation of the Strategy and prepared an action plan for its implementation until 2025. The evaluation led to updates in the Strategy to address key issues in Bulgarian tourism and support the country's green and digital transitions. The focus until 2025 includes increasing tourism sector competitiveness, improving tourism data collection and sharing, promoting sustainable management at regional level and enhancing digitalisation for SMEs.

The main policy responses and initiatives to tackle the challenges for the sector include the Tourism Guarantee Fund, created by the Bulgarian government to protect consumers in the event of insolvency of tour operators due to force majeure.

Providing the sector with trained personnel to meet the ever-increasing demands of tourists is one of the biggest challenges facing the Bulgarian tourism industry. As popularity declines, there are less people interested in working in the sector. Several measures are in development, including, the adaptation of curricula and dual education programmes and campaign with the Association of the secondary restaurateur and hotelier schools aimed at raising awareness and increasing the image of tourism professions among the young people. At the moment in a process of implementation is revision of the List of the professions (incl. in the field of tourism), which will lead to revision and adaptation of the curricula in order to better respond to the needs of the business and the level of tourism development.

In the final phase of the elaboration are the amendments of the Ordinance for dual education. The amendments are aimed at improving the model of the dual education. Some of the changes that would be useful for the tourist industry, are allowing flexibility for changing daily to dual form of education and seasonal implementation of dual training, based on a training schedule, prepared by the business.

In 2022, Bulgaria launched an aid programme to support Ukrainians displaced by Russia's war of aggression against Ukraine. Co-ordinated by the Ministry of Tourism and a special ad hoc working group, the programme allocated hotels and other accommodation facilities for those seeking temporary protection (see box below).

Decentralisation for regional tourism marketing and promotion on the municipal level is also an important policy development. The Ministry of Tourism developed a targeted programme to support the promotion of the Black Sea municipalities, which allowed foreign tour operators, airports and municipalities to join efforts in promoting the Black Sea region, with an active and goal-oriented partnership.

Bulgaria is also developing programmes to support digitalisation and innovation in the tourism industry. This includes a strategic document for digitalisation of the sector, expected to be finalised by the end of 2024. Additionally, the country is also focusing on controlling air and water quality and achieving sustainable waste and water management, crisis management, stimulating tourism investment and climate change adaptation.

Bolstering the Bulgarian tourism industry by supporting Ukrainians in need

Russia's war of aggression against Ukraine heavily impacted Bulgaria's tourism sector following the COVID-19 crisis, yet the sector quickly provided targeted aid for Ukrainians seeking temporary protection. While supporting Ukrainians in need, the initiative helped the sector rebound and bolstered the tourism workforce in Bulgaria after the pandemic. In 2022, Bulgaria launched an aid programme to support Ukrainians displaced as a result of Russia's war of aggression against Ukraine. Hotels and other accommodation facilities were allocated through the Ministry of Tourism and a special ad hoc working group within the Council of Ministers for persons seeking temporary protection in the Republic of Bulgaria. The programme provided accommodation, food and entertainment for both children and adults, and allowed families and close relatives to be placed together in the same facilities.

Accommodation facilities were utilised year-round including in low and shoulder tourist seasons. More than 400 000 Ukrainian citizens were accommodated from March 2022 to December 2023 and a total of BGN 250 million was allocated in the 2022 and 2023 budgets. As a result of the programme, tourism businesses have year-round demand and over 3 500 Ukrainian citizens have transitioned to work in the tourism sector. Once Ukrainians are employed, they are no longer eligible to benefit from the aid. All Ukrainian citizens who participated in the programme were registered in the Bulgarian Unified Tourist Information System but were exempted from the tourism statistical data.

Statistical Profile

Bulgaria: Domestic, inbound and outbound tourism

	2018	2019	2020	2021	2022
TOURISM FLOWS, THOUSAND					
Domestic tourism[1]					
Total domestic trips	6 529	6 833	4 485	5 711	6 397
Overnight visitors (tourists)	4 151	4 702	2 995	3 871	4 132
Same-day visitors (excursionists)	2 378	2 131	1 490	1 840	2 266
Nights in all types of accommodation	9 096	9 675	7 312	9 627	11 286
Hotels and similar establishments	..	..	..	..	..
Other collective establishments	..	..	..	..	..
Private accommodation	..	..	..	..	..
Inbound tourism[2]					
Total international arrivals	12 368	12 552	4 973	7 188	10 888
Overnight visitors (tourists)	..	..	..	..	..
Same-day visitors (excursionists)	..	..	..	..	..
Top markets					
Romania	1 377	1 287	626	822	1 250
Greece	1 116	1 168	271	259	807
Türkiye	625	649	332	401	579
Germany	850	761	138	288	471
Republic of North Macedonia	560	554	169	175	303
Nights in all types of accommodation	17 749	17 480	4 656	7 994	12 887
Hotels and similar establishments	..	..	..	..	..
Other collective establishments	..	..	..	..	..
Private accommodation	..	..	..	..	..
Outbound tourism[3]					
Total international departures	6 699	7 007	3 973	5 182	7 252
Overnight visitors (tourists)	..	..	..	..	..
Same-day visitors (excursionists)	..	..	..	..	..
Top destinations					
Türkiye	1 516	1 622	..	..	..
Greece	1 403	1 461	..	..	..
Republic of North Macedonia	416	429	..	..	..
Romania	523	554	..	..	..
Serbia	494	515	..	..	..
TOURISM RECEIPTS AND EXPENDITURE, MILLION USD					
Inbound tourism					
Total international receipts	5 099	4 840	1 847	2 741	3 754
International travel receipts	4 501	4 294	1 693	2 483	3 413
International passenger transport receipts	599	546	154	257	341
Outbound tourism					
Total international expenditure	2 247	2 196	1 253	1 520	1 840
International travel expenditure	1 870	1 826	1 039	1 291	1 550
International passenger transport expenditure	377	370	214	229	290

.. Not available

1. Trips from demand side surveys. Nights from supply side surveys.
2. Arrivals from demand side surveys; Nights from supply side surveys. Data for top markets refer to the number of arrivals of foreign visitors (overnight visitors and same - day visitors) without transit

3 data include overnight and same-day departures.

Source: OECD Tourism Statistics (Database).

StatLink https://stat.link/woqs3u

Bulgaria: Enterprises and employment in tourism

	Number of establishments[1]	Number of persons employed				
	2021 p	2018 p	2019 p	2020 p	2021 p	2022
Total	..	..	..	..	..	..
Tourism industries	..	..	..	..	..	..
Accommodation services for visitors	29 475	82 646	84 373	68 370	73 530	..
Hotels and similar establishments	4 506	43 633	44 810	29 207	33 629	..
Food and beverage serving industry	18 921	93 796	94 354	77 237	79 551	..
Passenger transport	4 536	22 634	22 497	20 908	19 542	..
Air passenger transport	56	1 865	2 042	1 744	1 493	..
Railways passenger transport	..	5 831	5 853	5 705	..	..
Road passenger transport	4 450	14 573	14 213	13 158	12 461	..
Water passenger transport	30	365	389	301	..	..
Passenger transport supporting services						..
Transport equipment rental	2 129	2 818	3 002	2 891	2 729	..
Travel agencies and other reservation services industry	1 691	6 421	6 214	4 506	4 269	..
Cultural industry	1 194	1 744	1 914	1 635	1 752	..
Sports and recreation industry	3 682	23 980	23 940	19 036	19 615	..
Retail trade of country-specific tourism characteristic goods	..	..	..	..	..	..
Other country-specific tourism industries	..	..	..	..	..	..
Other industries	..	..	..	..	..	..

.. Not available; p Provisional data
1. Data refer to number of enterprises.
Source: OECD Tourism Statistics (Database).

StatLink https://stat.link/ipqohe

Bulgaria: Internal tourism consumption

Million BGN

	2021		
	Domestic tourism expenditure	Inbound tourism expenditure	Internal tourism consumption
Total	..	..	..
Consumption products	1 271	4 444	..
Tourism characteristic products	1 268	3 606	..
Accommodation services for visitors	607	1 403	..
Food and beverage serving services	456	1 351	..
Passenger transport services	196	602	..
Air passenger transport services	..	..	..
Railways passenger transport services	..	..	..
Road passenger transport services	..	..	..
Water passenger transport services	..	..	..
Passenger transport supporting services	..	..	..
Transport equipment rental services	..	..	..
Travel agencies and other reservation services industry	6	163	..
Cultural services	1	25	..
Sports and recreation services	1	63	..
Country-specific tourism characteristic goods	..	..	..
Country-specific tourism characteristic services	..	..	..
Other consumption products	3	837	..
Tourism connected products	..	..	..
Non-tourism related consumption products	..	..	..
Non-consumption products	..	..	..

.. Not available
Source: OECD Tourism Statistics (Database).

StatLink https://stat.link/9z7u0q

Croatia

Tourism in the economy and outlook

Tourism is critical to the Croatian economy. In 2022, the sector accounted for 66.6% of service exports, the largest export category of the country, and directly provided 91 400 jobs or 6.5% of total employment. This is an increase from the pandemic-low of 78 500 jobs in 2020, but remains 6% below 2019 levels (91 500 jobs). In 2023, the sector accounted for 65.4% of service exports and provided 98 400 jobs or 6.8% of total employment. In 2019, tourism contributed EUR 5.1 billion or 11.3% of GVA.

In 2022, Croatia recorded 15.3 million international tourists in commercial accommodation, or 88.3% of 2019 levels, up from 5.5 million in 2020. This accounted for EUR 13.1 billion in international tourism revenues, a 24% increase on 2019 levels. The top markets in 2022 were Germany (21%), Austria (9%) and Slovenia (9%).

In 2023, Croatia joined the Schengen area and the Eurozone, enabling more European tourists to travel faster, facilitating price and service quality comparisons and eliminating uncertainties regarding exchange rate. The country recorded 17 million international tourist arrivals, a 10% increase on 2022 levels.

Domestic tourism accounted for 2.6 million tourists in commercial accommodations in 2023. This represents a 7.6% increase on 2022, and a 10.8% increase on pre-pandemic levels.

Tourism governance

The Ministry of Tourism and Sport is responsible for tourism in Croatia. The Ministry regularly co-operates with the Chamber of Economy, the Chamber of Trades and Crafts and professional associations in the tourism and hospitality sectors. The Croatian National Tourist Board reports to the Ministry and is in charge of tourism promotion.

At the regional level, 20 county administrative offices, and the city of Zagreb, have tourism departments responsible for accommodation classification and permits for tourism-related services. In addition, 280 local tourist offices are responsible for developing tourist products and providing tourism information, under guidance from regional tourism offices.

The Ministry of Tourism and Sport, collaborates with other ministries, state and private organisations to shape common policies. Collaboration examples include:

- The Ministry of Regional Development and EU Funds: loans and benefits for entrepreneurs and the implementation of EU operational programmes.
- The Ministry of Maritime Affairs, Transport and Infrastructure: extending certificates in national navigation, concession fees and charges in ports.
- The Ministry of Physical Planning, Construction and State Assets: renting business premises owned by Croatia.

- The ACI Club (Croatia's marine tourism company): fee payments in large marinas, including exemptions and instalments.

The Ministry of Tourism and Sport's budget increased from EUR 13.5 million in 2022 to EUR 20.4 million in 2023, due to the expansion of the Ministry's activities and projects.

Croatia: Organisational chart of tourism bodies

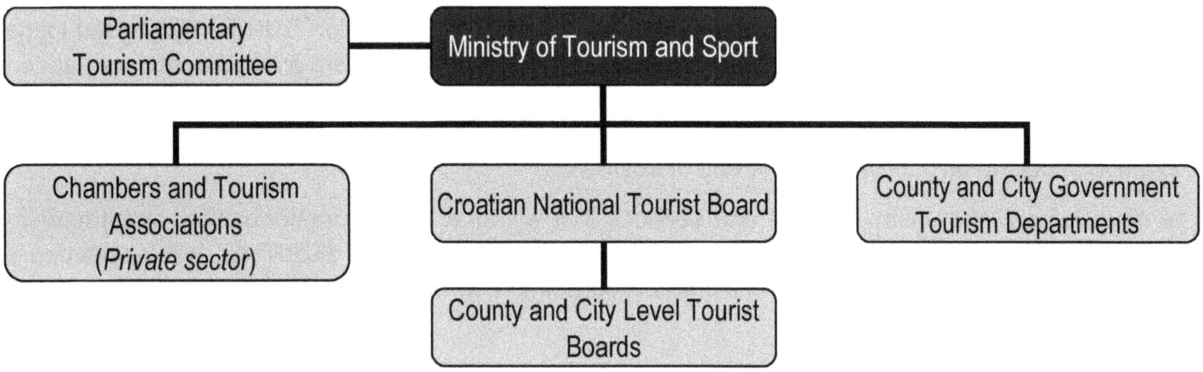

Source: OECD, adapted from the Ministry of Tourism, 2024.

Tourism policies and programmes

The Sustainable Tourism Development Strategy 2030, the National Plan for the Development of Sustainable Tourism 2027 and the Action Plan for the Implementation of the National Plan 2025 offer a strategic oversight of tourism in Croatia. The Strategy 2030 was launched at the end of 2022, and defines four key strategic goals for sustainable tourism development: year-round and more regionally balanced tourism; tourism with preserved environment, space and climate; competitive and innovative tourism; and sustainable tourism. In the long-term, the Strategy 2030 aims to maintain Croatia as one of Europe's leading tourist destinations for safety, quality, added value, sustainability and innovation. In 2025, the Strategy will be formally evaluated to identify implementation gaps and, based on the assessment results, make necessary adjustments if changes are required.

The Strategy 2030 is funded through the State Budget of the Republic of Croatia, the National Budget Recovery and Resilience Plan 2021-26, the Competitiveness and Cohesion Programme 2021-27, the Effective Human Resources 2021-27 Programme, the Integrated Territorial Programme 2021-27 and EU funded programmes.

Several plans support the strategy. The 3-year Action Plan for the Implementation of the National Sustainable Tourism Development Plan 2027 was adopted in 2023 to implement specific goals for tourism through concrete measures. Additionally, the Croatian Tourism Act, which entered into force on 1 January 2024, creates a framework for tourism development management based on data and metrics, to preserve resources and space, guarantee the satisfaction and quality of life of the population in tourist destinations, while ensuring the competitiveness of Croatian tourism on the global market. The Strategic Marketing and Operational Plan of Croatian Tourism was developed in 2023 to better position Croatia on international markets. Regional and local marketing plans will also be developed, and activities will be carried out in the next four years with a focus on promoting tourist attractions that can contribute to reducing seasonality and more balanced tourism development, while setting Croatia's image as a high-value tourist destination.

In 2022, Croatia launched a public call to promote the green and digital transition of public tourism infrastructure and to develop public tourism infrastructure beyond the main tourist and coastal areas, with a budget of 123 million EUR. Another public call, with 165 million EUR, was launched to enhance sustainability and support the green and digital transition of tourism entrepreneurs. As part of the reform of tourism, Croatia improved the Satellite Accounts System in the area of sustainability (Box 3.8).

Educational programmes to strengthen capacities for resilient and sustainable tourism are being implemented, in particular programmes targeting the unemployed and employees in state administrations and tourist boards, with a budget of 1.3 million EUR. The implementation phase will be running until the end of 2025.

The Competitiveness and Cohesion Programme 2021-27 allocated 90 million EUR for subsidised loans for SMEs to encourage competitiveness and develop green and digital tourism products with more added value. Additional 40 million EUR will be allocated for public tourism infrastructure, health, and active tourism products, contributing to social inclusion and sustainable development. The public calls are being prepared and are expected to be published by the end of 2024.

The development of tourism products and services that will enable equal opportunities, adapt tourism infrastructure and adapt business processes to the needs of people with disabilities, will be granted 7 million EUR by the Effective Human Resources Programme 2021-27. The public call is expected to be published in 2025.

Every year, the Ministry of Tourism and Sport launches a small support programme to increase competitiveness in the tourism sector, financed by the State budget, for the green and digital transition of micro, small and medium-sized businesses. In 2023, 221 tourism businesses received 2.57 million EUR in grants, while a new public call was published in 2024.

Statistical Profile

Croatia: Domestic, inbound and outbound tourism

	2018	2019	2020	2021	2022
TOURISM FLOWS, THOUSAND					
Domestic tourism					
Total domestic trips	8 166	10 445	6 183	6 974	7 122
Overnight visitors (tourists)	3 197	3 708	2 510	3 278	3 148
Same-day visitors (excursionists)	4 969	6 737	3 673	3 696	3 974
Nights in all types of accommodation	17 581	20 712	15 341	19 200	19 464
Hotels and similar establishments	1 524	1 725	1 037	2 844	3 354
Other collective establishments	583	738	274	974	1 064
Private accommodation	15 474	18 249	14 029	15 381	15 046
Inbound tourism					
Total international arrivals	..	..	..	..	..
Overnight visitors (tourists)	16 645	17 353	5 545	10 641	15 324
Same-day visitors (excursionists)	..	..	..	..	..
Top markets					
Germany	2 784	2 881	1 480	2 737	3 281
Austria	1 370	1 385	355	1 026	1 453
Slovenia	1 364	1 426	769	995	1 419
Italy	1 148	1 175	228	417	908
Czechia	755	742	481	721	835
Nights in all types of accommodation	83 175	84 148	35 379	62 848	82 288
Hotels and similar establishments	29 319	29 707	7 890	17 423	25 829
Other collective establishments	18 380	18 183	8 228	16 301	20 220
Private accommodation	35 477	36 258	19 261	29 123	36 239
Outbound tourism					
Total international departures	2 980	3 500	678	907	2 005
Overnight visitors (tourists)	2 058	2 255	493	639	1 351
Same-day visitors (excursionists)	922	1 245	185	268	653
Top destinations					
Bosnia and Herzegovina	390	455	122	214	341
Germany	326	303	86	87	141
Italy	213	238	27	40	113
Slovenia	171	190	57	63	109
Austria	166	197	63	36	108
TOURISM RECEIPTS AND EXPENDITURE, MILLION USD					
Inbound tourism					
Total international receipts	11 442	12 020	5 486	10 924	14 007
International travel receipts	11 220	11 798	5 422	10 803	13 810
International passenger transport receipts	222	222	64	121	197
Outbound tourism					
Total international expenditure	1 742	1 809	790	1 128	1 499
International travel expenditure	1 695	1 763	777	1 108	1 460
International passenger transport expenditure	47	46	14	20	39

.. Not available
Source: OECD Tourism Statistics (Database).

StatLink https://stat.link/pmb4zn

Croatia: Enterprises and employment in tourism

	Number of establishments[1]	Number of persons employed[2]				
	2021	2018	2019	2020	2021	2022
Total	..	..	..	..	..	..
Tourism industries	22 830	86 646	91 608	78 485	80 223	91 398
Accommodation services for visitors	3 655	41 826	44 326	35 071	36 204	42 767
Hotels and similar establishments	1 254	..	..	..	..	..
Food and beverage serving industry	17 446	38 678	41 011	38 198	39 486	43 719
Passenger transport	5 299	..	..	..	..	..
Air passenger transport	17	..	..	..	..	..
Railways passenger transport	..	..	..	..	..	..
Road passenger transport	4 128	..	..	..	..	..
Water passenger transport	1 154	..	..	..	..	..
Passenger transport supporting services	..	..	..	..	..	..
Transport equipment rental	..	..	..	..	..	..
Travel agencies and other reservation services industry	1 729	6 142	6 271	5 216	4 533	4 912
Cultural industry	..	..	..	..	..	..
Sports and recreation industry	..	..	..	..	..	..
Retail trade of country-specific tourism characteristic goods	..	..	..	..	..	..
Other country-specific tourism industries	..	..	..	..	..	..
Other industries	..	..	..	..	..	..

.. Not available
1. Data refer to number of enterprises.
2. Data refer to number of employees.
Source: OECD Tourism Statistics (Database).

StatLink https://stat.link/kopt84

Croatia: Internal tourism consumption

Million EUR

	2019		
	Domestic tourism expenditure	Inbound tourism expenditure	Internal tourism consumption
Total	..	..	..
Consumption products	1 575	10 517	12 372
Tourism characteristic products	1 497	9 681	11 458
Accommodation services for visitors	201	3 276	3 757
Food and beverage serving services	284	2 123	2 407
Passenger transport services	459	377	835
Air passenger transport services	99	110	209
Railways passenger transport services	27	12	39
Road passenger transport services	305	75	380
Water passenger transport services	28	180	208
Passenger transport supporting services	..	..	..
Transport equipment rental services	..	..	..
Travel agencies and other reservation services industry	91	370	461
Cultural services	109	726	834
Sports and recreation services	..	..	..
Country-specific tourism characteristic goods	..	..	..
Country-specific tourism characteristic services	353	2 810	3 163
Other consumption products	78	836	914
Tourism connected products	..	..	..
Non-tourism related consumption products	..	..	..
Non-consumption products	..	..	..

.. Not available
Source: OECD Tourism Statistics (Database).

StatLink https://stat.link/e8rzf9

Indonesia

Tourism in the economy and outlook

Tourism is a key driver of economic growth, regional development and employment in Indonesia. In 2022, the tourism sector contributed approximately USD 6.8 billion in foreign exchange earnings, and accounted for 3.6% of the country's GDP. This is still down from 5% in 2019, but up from the pandemic-low of 2.2% in 2020. In the same year, tourism provided employment for approximately 22.9 million people or 16.9% of total employment. This was up 0.8% compared to 2019.

In 2023, Indonesia recorded 11.7 million international overnight visitors, or 73% of 2019 levels (16.1 million visitors). This was up 98% compared to 2022. The top source markets in 2023 were Malaysia (16%), Singapore (12%) and Australia (12%). Further, the recovery in 2023 boosted tourism receipts. In 2023, foreign exchange earnings reached USD 14 billion, more than double the level in 2022.

Domestic tourism plays an important role in Indonesia and has regularly increased in recent years. In 2023, the country recorded 825.8 million domestic overnight visitors, a 14% increase compared to 2019.

Indonesia forecasts that the number of international tourist arrivals will vary between 10.4 million and 14.3 million in 2024, and tourism receipts are expected to reach between USD 10.5 million and USD 13.1 million.

Tourism governance

The Ministry of Tourism and Creative Economy is responsible for tourism in Indonesia. The Ministry collaborates regularly with various stakeholders, such as the ministries of Health, Foreign Affairs and Communication and Information to develop tourism and the creative economy. The Ministry also collaborates regularly with the Ministry of Public Works and Housing in the development of tourism destinations, especially in Indonesia's super-priority and priority tourism destinations.

The Co-ordinating Ministry for Maritime and Investment has a Deputy of Tourism and Creative Economy responsible for co-ordinating and synchronising the formulation, decision-making process, and implementation of tourism and creative economy policies with related ministries and agencies, especially the Ministry of Tourism and Creative Economy.

In 2023, Indonesia's national budget allocated IDR 3.38 trillion to tourism, a decrease from IDR 3.59 trillion in 2022. This was supplemented by the Special Allocation Fund for Tourism Infrastructure of IDR 0.45 trillion (up from IDR 0.31 trillion in 2022) and the Special Allocation Fund for Tourism Infrastructure of IDR 133.3 billion (a IDR 9.8 billion increase compared to 2022).

Indonesia: Organisational chart of tourism bodies

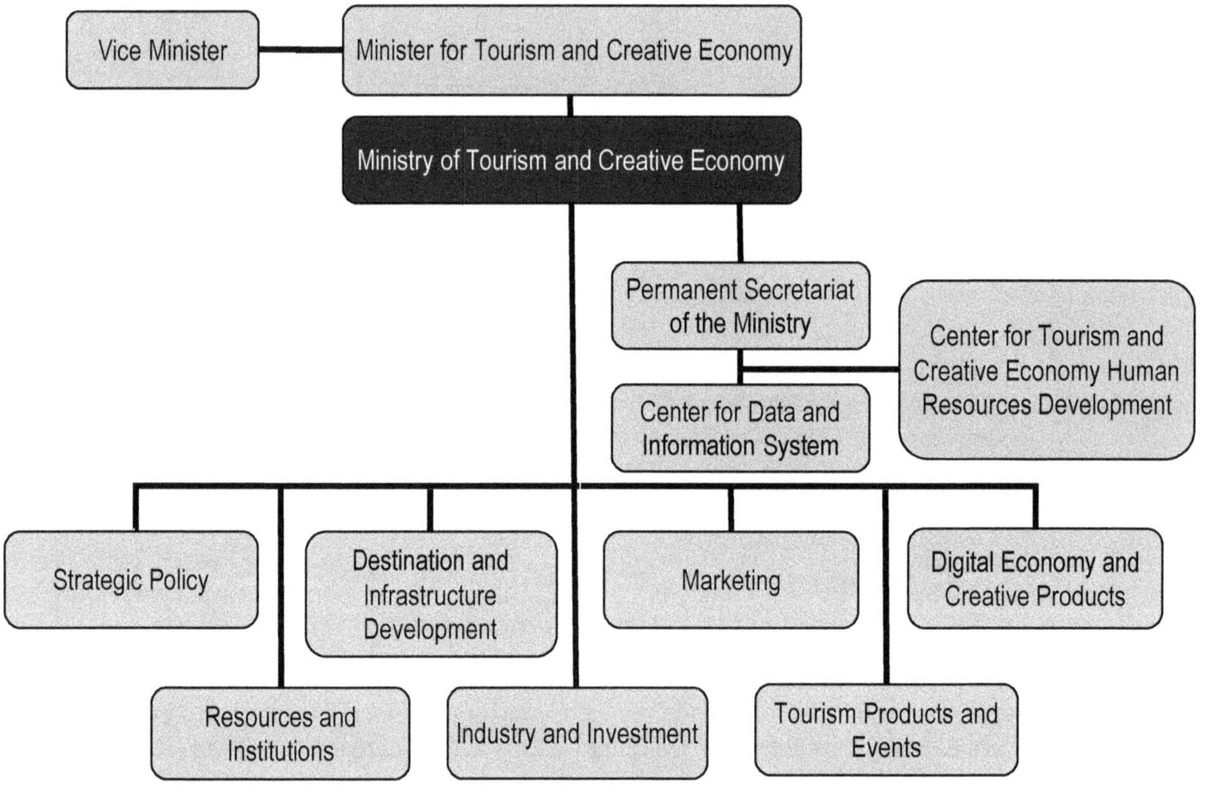

Source: OECD, adapted from the Ministry of Tourism and Creative Economy, 2024.

Tourism policies and programmes

Tourism growth and development in Indonesia are guided by the country's long-term tourism strategy, the Institutional Framework for Tourism Policy Development, which establishes the following priorities:

- Increase destination competitiveness in the form of quality tourism products and services, with implementation focused on Super Priority Tourism Destinations.
- Support the upskilling and reskilling of the tourism workforce, marketing, the crisis management programme, and the MICE sector.
- Increase domestic tourism, with the Proud to Travel in Indonesia campaign, which promotes several attractive destinations.
- Restore leading tourism destinations such as Bali, Batam-Bintan and Bandung.
- Develop tourism villages by optimising the potential of the creative economy as a driver of community economy.

Indonesia has committed to a phased and structured approach for tourism recovery, aligned with three core principles: productivity, inclusivity, and sustainability. This approach is divided in three phases:

- 2020-21 - Resiliency: to manage crises effectively and mitigate their impact on the sector, the Indonesian government implemented the Crisis Management for Tourism Destinations Cleanliness, Health, Safety, and Environmental Sustainability programme. The programme prioritised domestic tourism and developed contingency plans for evacuation, emergency response protocols, and communication. The Ministry worked closely with the National Disaster Management Agency and Indonesia's National Search and Rescue Agency.

- 2022-23 - Recovery: to accelerate recovery and improve productivity within the tourism and creative economy sectors, Indonesia designated Super Priority Tourism Destinations, key drivers of growth with a pivotal role in revitalising the tourism sector. Indonesia also established a Tourism Ecosystem designed to nurture these selected destinations. Under the National Medium-Term Plan 2020-24, ten Priority Tourism Destinations, of which five are Super Priority Tourism Destinations, benefit from the development of supporting roads, ports, airports, pioneering tourism destinations, tourism villages. The programme also includes developing tourism products, improving the creative economy ecosystem, and developing human resources in each location.
- 2024-25 - Preparing for Adaptive and Sustainable Destinations: The flagship initiative during this period involves further improving the Super Priority Tourism Destinations to ensure environmentally conscious, socially responsible, and economically resilient growth.

To respond to the challenges and capitalise on the opportunities under the recovery phase, six segments are being prioritised: (i) Bleisure: to capitalise on the increase of remote working, attracting digital nomads and business travellers; (ii) Ecotourism and adventure: this includes nature and environmental-related tourism with a growing number of destinations and operators are committed to low carbon as well as Blue, Green, and Circular Economy; (iii) Health tourism: a special economic zone has been designated to support comprehensive health tourism for visitors seeking wide range of medical treatments; (iv) Heritage and culture: to prioritise tangible and intangible cultural products and attractions in tourist destinations; (v) Gastronomy tourism; (vi) Tourism villages: to offer a holistic tourism experience while educating tourists on culture and sustainability (see box below).

Responsible and sustainable tourism villages in Indonesia

With potential to accelerate the recovery of sustainable tourism and increase economic growth, Indonesia's tourism villages programme aims to strengthen the industry's readiness to improve sustainable tourism practices, train a professional staff, supply high-quality tourism products, and adhere to strict health procedures. The programme helps preserve the natural environment and support local communities, and tourism villages offer a holistic tourism experience, combining culture, nature, and education.

There are several government-initiated tourism village development programmes, such as the Tourism Awareness Campaign 5.0, the Indonesian Tourism Village Awards, and the Sustainable Tourism Village Certification. These programmes aim to develop tourism villages through areas like limited to human resources development, collaboration with Corporate Social Responsibility programmes, support for tourism and creative economy businesses and financial literacy programmes. It also provides capacity building in areas, such as homestay management, tourism products and travel patterns development, tourism job certification, financial management, food and beverage preparation production and packaging training, setting local businesses, guiding training and fostering collaboration across ministries, institutions, and the private sector for the development of tourism villages.

As of June 2024, 6 024 tourism villages have been registered in the platform, above the target of 6 000 businesses by 2024. Benefits include increasing local tourism during the pandemic by 30%, increasing global competitiveness, economic improvements and mapping creative economy potential. To further promote the initiative, Indonesia has been holding the Tourism Village Awards annually since 2021.

Statistical Profile

Indonesia: Domestic, inbound and outbound tourism

	2018	2019	2020	2021	2022
TOURISM FLOWS, THOUSAND					
Domestic tourism					
Total domestic trips	..	722 159	524 571	613 299	734 865
Overnight visitors (tourists)	303 404	354 353	364 698	406 242	497 334
Same-day visitors (excursionists)	..	367 805	159 873	207 058	237 531
Nights in all types of accommodation	..	306 556	378 006	449 310	..
Hotels and similar establishments		55 390	117 609	185 971	..
Other collective establishments	..	16 032	36 668	36 664	..
Private accommodation	..	235 135	223 730	226 675	..
Inbound tourism					
Total international arrivals	15 810	16 107	4 053	1 558	5 889
Overnight visitors (tourists)	13 396	15 455	3 981	1 546	5 761
Same-day visitors (excursionists)	2 414	652	72	11	128
Top markets					
China (People's Republic of)	2 139	2 072	240	55	169
Singapore	1 769	1 934	280	19	737
Malaysia	2 503	2 981	980	481	1 213
Australia	1 301	1 387	256	3	655
India	595	657	112	7	282
Nights in all types of accommodation	..	..	..	..	..
Hotels and similar establishments	..	..	..	..	..
Other collective establishments	..	..	..	..	..
Private accommodation	..	..	..	..	..
Outbound tourism					
Total international departures	9 468	11 689	2 918	1 711	3 541
Overnight visitors (tourists)	..	..	..	503	3 379
Same-day visitors (excursionists)	..	..	..	1 208	162
Top destinations					
	..	..	..	..	..
	..	..	..	..	..
	..	..	..	..	..
	..	..	..	..	..
	..	..	..	..	..
TOURISM RECEIPTS AND EXPENDITURE, MILLION USD					
Inbound tourism					
Total international receipts	17 915	18 405	3 602	548	..
International travel receipts	16 426	16 911	3 382	521	6 719
International passenger transport receipts	1 489	1 494	221	27	..
Outbound tourism					
Total international expenditure	13 171	14 449	2 075	516	..
International travel expenditure	10 314	11 308	1 748	472	6 288
International passenger transport expenditure	2 857	3 141	327	45	..

.. Not available

Source: OECD Tourism Statistics (Database).

StatLink https://stat.link/by6njs

Indonesia: Enterprises and employment in tourism

	Number of establishments[1]	Number of persons employed				
	2022	2018	2019	2020	2021	2022 p
Total	..	..	..	..	..	..
Tourism industries	..	..	..	..	..	..
Accommodation services for visitors	..	..	..	..	..	..
Hotels and similar establishments	28 800	408 565	407 292	348 270	186 643	339 224
Food and beverage serving industry	..	..	8 016 863		..	..
Passenger transport	..	..	21 535	15 428	..	..
Air passenger transport	..	..	..	..	..	..
Railways passenger transport	..	..	..	..	..	..
Road passenger transport	..	..	..	..	..	..
Water passenger transport	..	..	..	..	..	..
Passenger transport supporting services	..	..	..	..	..	..
Transport equipment rental	..	..	..	..	..	..
Travel agencies and other reservation services industry	..	..	86 770	65 112	..	..
Cultural industry	..	..	117 092	98 539	..	..
Sports and recreation industry	..	..	..	..	..	..
Retail trade of country-specific tourism characteristic goods	..	..	..	..	..	..
Other country-specific tourism industries	..	..	..	..	..	..
Other industries	..	..	..	..	..	..

.. Not available

1. Data refer to number of enterprises.

Source: OECD Tourism Statistics (Database).

StatLink https://stat.link/69e7qw

Indonesia: Internal tourism consumption

Million IDR

	2020		
	Domestic tourism expenditure	Inbound tourism expenditure	Internal tourism consumption
Total	..	..	..
Consumption products	674 507 316	71 080 512	745 587 827
Tourism characteristic products	653 262 094	62 301 195	715 563 290
Accommodation services for visitors	114 514 144	24 197 504	138 711 648
Food and beverage serving services	207 484 990	16 666 223	224 151 212
Passenger transport services	241 889 120	8 749 838	250 638 958
Air passenger transport services	215 827 566	5 765 994	221 593 560
Railways passenger transport services	732 433	162 310	894 743
Road passenger transport services	16 007 808	1 587 083	17 594 892
Water passenger transport services	9 321 312	1 234 450	10 555 762
Passenger transport supporting services	..	..	..
Transport equipment rental services	22 213 587	461 108	22 674 695
Travel agencies and other reservation services industry	4 630 045	613 839	5 243 884
Cultural services	13 872 288	1 833 053	15 705 341
Sports and recreation services	..	..	..
Country-specific tourism characteristic goods	44 131 761	5 660 575	49 792 336
Country-specific tourism characteristic services	4 526 160	4 119 055	8 645 215
Other consumption products	21 245 221	8 779 316	30 024 538
Tourism connected products	..	..	..
Non-tourism related consumption products	..	..	..
Non-consumption products	..	..	..

.. Not available

Source: OECD Tourism Statistics (Database).

StatLink https://stat.link/8w39ab

Malta

Tourism in the economy and outlook

Tourism is an essential contributor to the Maltese economy. In 2023, total international tourist expenditure reached the record figure of EUR 2.7 billion. Tourism is estimated to have contributed 10.2% to GDP in 2023, based on the GDP identity from the expenditure side. In 2022, the tourism sector directly supported 48 000 jobs, or 16.9% of total employment. This represents an 18.2% increase on 2019, when the sector directly accounted for 40 500 jobs.

The disruption caused by the COVID-19 pandemic during the years 2020-22 was followed by a strong recovery in 2023, culminating in a record 3.0 million international tourists. Top source markets for the year 2023 were Italy (18%), followed closely by the United Kingdom (18%) and France (10%).

Domestic tourism increased during the pandemic. Malta recorded over 360 000 domestic overnight tourists in 2020, compared to 240 000 in 2019. Domestic tourism increased in 2021, with a record of 390 000 overnight tourists and stabilised in 2022 at 370 000 tourists.

Tourism governance

As of January 2024, the Ministry for Tourism and Public Cleanliness is responsible for tourism. Its mission is to establish and execute tourism policies based on the principles of sustainable development. The Ministry strives to improve Malta's competitiveness by working with various stakeholders to ensure that products, services and value reach levels that enable both the island of Malta and Gozo to improve the seasonal spread of tourism and its economic benefits.

Malta Tourism Authority is the destination management organisation under the Ministry's remit, responsible for promoting Malta as a tourist destination, advising the government on tourism operations and issuing licences under the relevant legislation. Malta Tourism Authority also caters for the needs of the islands of Gozo and Comino, liaising with the Ministry for Gozo, the Gozo Tourism Association, which represents Gozitan tourism stakeholders, and the Gozo Regional Development Authority.

The actual amounts spent in 2022 for tourism-related activities under the Ministry for Tourism and Public Cleanliness and its entities amounted to around EUR 145.9 million from national funds and around EUR 2.2 million from EU funds. The estimated allocation for the year 2023 amounted to EUR 145.3 million from national funds and EUR 2.6 million from EU funds.

Malta: Organisational chart of tourism bodies

Source: OECD, adapted from the Ministry of Tourism, 2024.

Tourism policies and programmes

Tourism policy in Malta is guided by the national strategy Recover, Rethink, Revitalise for the years 2021-30, which aims to continue post-pandemic recovery, to rethink tourism growth models by incorporating sustainable development and climate policy, and to revitalise the tourism sector by developing niche markets. The Strategy's key priorities are: (i) an upskilled tourism workforce; (ii) modernised infrastructure; (iii) updated tourism legislation; (iv) stronger potential for digitalisation; (v) continued development of Malta's airline connectivity, and (iv) an innovative approach towards responding to new travel trends.

Efforts to implement the Strategy began immediately after its publication. The Malta Tourism Observatory was set up in September 2022, to oversee the delivery of the strategy and to operate within the framework of UN Tourism's International Network of Sustainable Tourism Observatories. The Observatory plays a vital role in the Maltese tourism and hospitality industry by collecting, analysing, and disseminating data and insights about tourism activities in Malta, with multifaceted tasks and functions impacting the tourism sector. The Observatory also collaborates with relevant stakeholders to ensure broad participation in the Strategy's implementation.

To diversify markets and extend the tourism season, Malta is focusing on adventure tourism, wellness tourism, and cultural experiences. The diving industry, for example, is an important niche in Malta, which attracts adventure-seekers all year long. Divers search for new underwater attractions, and the Hephaestus tanker will serve as a new artificial reef, expected to attract sea life and act as a nursery for smaller fish. The Visit Malta official website is also promoting the island as a wellness destination, displaying its natural characteristics and wellness tourism products.

To improve the culture experience, foreign tourism employees in Malta receive general knowledge training of the Maltese archipelago, its history, heritage sites, local customs and gastronomy. Several cultural tours have been offered to foreign workers in the tourism industry. Participants received a complete cultural training experience, with in-house training on Maltese culture, including a presentation on Maltese language, indigenous traditions and local food.

To strengthen the local tourism offering, Malta Tourism Authority is actively identifying lesser-known areas for tourism revitalisation. The Tourism Authority is also updating the eco-certification label for tourism accommodations to promote sustainable practices across the Maltese Islands, and signed memorandums of understanding with Green Key International and the Global Sustainable Tourism Council in December 2023.

Tackling overtourism in Malta

Overtourism is a significant tourism policy challenge faced by small island states like Malta. The surge in visitors during peak season can cause negative impacts on the environment, infrastructure strain, cultural degradation, and an overall decline in the quality of life for residents.

To mitigate the impacts of overtourism and ensure sustainable tourism development, Malta aims to implement a multifaceted policy reform that promotes responsible tourism and seeks to distribute the benefits of tourism more equitably. Therefore, the country has developed an outline for reform:

- **Carrying capacity assessment and visitor management:** Malta is preparing to conduct a thorough assessment to determine the island's carrying capacity for sustainable tourism. This exercise will be conducted based on a set of sustainable tourism indicators instead of a Carrying Capacity Assessment. Malta will also develop strategies to manage visitor flows and limit arrivals during peak season.
- **Promote off-peak tourism:** Malta is incentivising off-peak tourism through year-round marketing campaigns. Malta Tourism Authority's marketing campaign uses a mix of digital, out of home, online and print, B2B and B2C activities aimed at encouraging bookings based on a call to action. Off-peak advertising is generally highly niche-focused.
- **Environmental sustainability initiatives:** Malta encourages responsible behaviour among tourists, such as waste reduction, respect for local culture, and conservation of natural resources. The Tourism Authority is engaged in the creation of the coastal-climate vulnerability strategy for Malta.
- **Diversification of tourism offerings:** To reduce pressure on popular destinations, Malta is promoting other aspects of the island. Along with the University of Malta, the Tourism Authority organised a lecture series to foster diving, which has become an important pillar of tourism in Malta.
- **Infrastructure and carrying capacity monitoring:** Malta is investing in improving infrastructure and regularly monitoring the island's carrying capacity, using data analysis and technological solutions to manage visitor flows and make informed decisions regarding resource allocation and future tourism development.

By adopting these policies, Malta aims to transition towards a more sustainable and resilient tourism sector that balances the economic benefits of tourism with the preservation of its natural and cultural heritage.

Statistical Profile

Malta: Domestic, inbound and outbound tourism

	2018	2019	2020	2021	2022
TOURISM FLOWS, THOUSAND					
Domestic tourism					
Total domestic trips	..	..	..	..	..
Overnight visitors (tourists)	245	237	360	389	369
Same-day visitors (excursionists)	..	..	..	..	..
Nights in all types of accommodation	650	618	1 064	1 081	994
Hotels and similar establishments	164	145	150	197	207
Other collective establishments	..	..	..	..	..
Private accommodation	486	473	914	884	787
Inbound tourism					
Total international arrivals	3 153	3 383	717	984	2 704
Overnight visitors (tourists)	2 599	2 753	659	968	2 287
Same-day visitors (excursionists)	554	629	59	132	417
Top markets					
France	213	239	71	134	258
Germany	227	212	72	97	169
Italy	391	393	94	128	398
Spain	99	116	27	36	87
United Kingdom	641	650	136	214	427
Nights in all types of accommodation	18 570	19 339	5 227	8 390	16 608
Hotels and similar establishments	10 082	10 069	2 362	6 534	13 810
Other collective establishments	..	..	..	..	
Private accommodation	8 488	9 270	2 865	1 855	2 798
Outbound tourism					
Total international departures	728	774	218	344	694
Overnight visitors (tourists)	667	707	197	303	602
Same-day visitors (excursionists)	61	67	21	41	93
Top destinations					
Italy	212	214	67	119	227
United Kingdom	119	126	29	26	65
Spain	38	45	10	21	36
France	28	28	8	12	35
Germany	42	38	11	11	22
TOURISM RECEIPTS AND EXPENDITURE, MILLION USD					
Inbound tourism					
Total international receipts	1 848	1 897	392	772	1 841
International travel receipts	1 848	1 897	392	772	1 841
International passenger transport receipts	..	..	..	..	..
Outbound tourism					
Total international expenditure	518	530	127	240	476
International travel expenditure	518	530	127	240	476
International passenger transport expenditure	..	..	..	..	..

.. Not available
Source: OECD Tourism Statistics (Database).

StatLink https://stat.link/wetm62

Malta: Enterprises and employment in tourism

	Number of establishments[1]	Number of persons employed				
	2022	2018	2019	2020	2021	2022
Total	..	..	..	..	..	..
Tourism industries	8 873	33 997	40 568	40 722	40 070	47 956
Accommodation services for visitors	919	7 547	7 723	6 584	6 489	8 697
Hotels and similar establishments	272	..	..	..	..	..
Food and beverage serving industry	2 471	7 215	9 945	9 786	8 163	10 111
Passenger transport	1 999	4 128	4 594	6 051	5 977	7 006
Air passenger transport	40	1 563	1 073 e	1 490	2 250	2 358
Railways passenger transport	0	..	..	..	..	..
Road passenger transport	1 822	1 769	2 927	3 934	2 952	3 474
Water passenger transport	137	797	594 e	627 e	776 e	1 174 e
Passenger transport supporting services	729	2 473	2 983	3 454	4 172	4 843
Transport equipment rental	147	683	1 050	361 e	291 e	924 e
Travel agencies and other reservation services industry	468	1 228	1 349	1 427	1 163 e	1 179
Cultural industry	1 654	8 708	11 052	11 517	12 881	13 165
Sports and recreation industry	486	2 014	1 871	1 542	933 e	2 031
Retail trade of country-specific tourism characteristic goods	..	..	..	..	..	..
Other country-specific tourism industries	..	..	..	..	..	..
Other industries	..	..	..	..	..	..

.. Not available; e Estimated value
1. Data refer to number of enterprises.
Source: OECD Tourism Statistics (Database).

StatLink https://stat.link/za5tw1

Malta: Internal tourism consumption

Million EUR

	2010		
	Domestic tourism expenditure	Inbound tourism expenditure	Internal tourism consumption
Total	..	..	..
Consumption products	**112**	**1 033**	**1 150**
Tourism characteristic products	99	859	963
Accommodation services for visitors	7	232	243
Food and beverage serving services	17	258	275
Passenger transport services	31	256	287
Air passenger transport services	29	231	260
Railways passenger transport services	..	..	..
Road passenger transport services	2	25	26
Water passenger transport services	..	..	..
Passenger transport supporting services	..	..	..
Transport equipment rental services	0	19	19
Travel agencies and other reservation services industry	44	36	80
Cultural services	0	13	13
Sports and recreation services	0	23	23
Country-specific tourism characteristic goods	..	..	..
Country-specific tourism characteristic services	..	..	..
Other consumption products	13	174	187
Tourism connected products	4	104	108
Non-tourism related consumption products	9	70	79
Non-consumption products	..	..	..

.. Not available
Source: OECD Tourism Statistics (Database).

StatLink https://stat.link/irzbmx

Montenegro

Tourism in the economy and outlook

Tourism is strategic to Montenegro's economy, accounting for an important share of the country's GDP and employment. According to estimates from WTTC, the total contribution of tourism reached EUR 1.4 billion or 26% of total GDP in 2023, including wider effects from investment, the supply chain and induced income impacts, while the sector supported 55 000 jobs or 25.6% of total employment in 2022. Taking direct impacts only, tourism's contribution to GDP is expected to grow by 4.1% per year to EUR 658.4 billion (9.1% of GDP) from 2023 to 2033

The country recorded 2.0 million international tourists in commercial accommodation in 2022. This remains 18.9% below 2019 levels but shows a strong recovery from the pandemic low of 351 000 in 2020. The top three international markets in 2022 were Serbia (21%), Bosnia and Herzegovina (10%) and Russia (8%).

Domestic tourism represents a small component of overall visitor overnight stays in Montenegro. Commercial accommodation establishments in Montenegro recorded 528 000 domestic nights (10.0% above 2019 levels) which contrasts with 3.7 million international nights for the same period.

Due to a strong increase in tourism demand at the beginning of 2023, international overnight tourist arrivals returned to 2019 levels by the end of the year.

Tourism governance

The Ministry of Tourism, Ecology, Sustainable Development and Northern Region Development is responsible for tourism policy in Montenegro. The National Tourism Organisation of Montenegro and local tourism organisations also have a leading role in defining development policies in tourism, destination management and creating a tourism product.

Montenegro will also establish a National Tourism Council. The Council's main task is to strengthen tourism as a sector, both nationally and abroad. The Council will design and implement activities of importance for all entities in the country in the field of tourism and complementary branches, as well as raise standards in the sector to enhance Montenegro's position as a tourism destination, strengthening the economy through better integration of tourism and other industries, creating a stable business environment to foster investment in the tourism sector and greater tourist satisfaction. The Council will have a role in controlling the implementation of the strategies and programmes, and will include representatives of the private sector, which would further strengthen public-private partnerships and the role of the private sector in making strategic decisions in the field of tourism.

To improve the business and investment environment at a local level, Montenegro is scoping the introduction of a destination management model to strengthen public-private partnerships and encourage better vertical co-ordination within government. Also important to the Montenegro tourism governance structure are the Public Enterprise National Parks of Montenegro, which manages 7.7% of land in Montenegro, and the Public Enterprise for Coastal Zone, which manages approximately 300 km of beaches.

Through the 2023 Action Plan, to achieve operational goals in tourism, a total of EUR 19.5 million was allocated, of which EUR 18.1 million are dedicated to investment projects planned within the Capital Budget (Tourist activity), EUR 1.2 million originate from the current budget (MERT) and EUR 185 000 from donor sources.

Montenegro: Organisational chart of tourism bodies

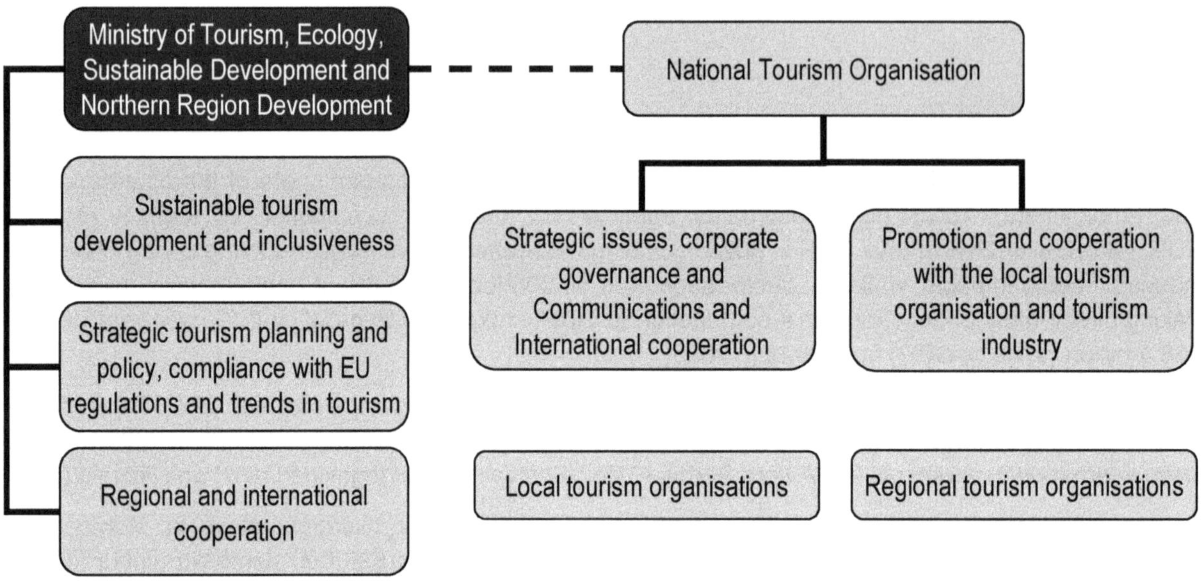

Source: OECD, adapted from the Ministry of Tourism, Ecology, Sustainable Development and Northern Region Development, 2024.

Tourism policies and programmes

Sustainable tourism development is key for Montenegro and has been included as a priority in the Government Programme of Economic Reforms. The Strategy for the Development of Tourism in Montenegro 2022-25 translates this goal into measures, guiding the country's tourism policy. The Strategy centres around sustainable, inclusive, smart, green and responsible tourism development, with a particular focus on addressing the challenges of seasonality and mass tourism. The Strategy includes seven key operational goals to improve the areas below:

- Regulatory framework in tourism to formalise tourism turnover;
- Tourism infrastructure;
- Quality and quantity of accommodation capacities;
- Quality of diversified tourism products;
- Human resources, knowledge and skills in tourism;
- Development of digital, innovative solutions and new technologies in tourism;
- Development of Montenegro as a globally recognised tourism destination.

To reduce the environmental impact of tourism, several initiatives will be undertaken. These include developing sustainable capacities and services, adhering to international eco-standards such as eco-labels SafeTravel, Green Key, and Blue Flag, improving energy efficiency, and applying circular economy principles in hospitality businesses. Additionally, the Ministry of Tourism, Ecology, Sustainable Development and Northern Region Development became a Member of the Global Sustainable Tourism Council in 2023.

To diversify tourism offers, efforts are focused on eco and rural tourism, sports-recreational and adventure activities, health and cultural tourism, and tourism in national parks and protected areas. Activities such as hiking, biking, and panoramic routes aim to satisfy modern tourists' desires for nature stays and small-scale accommodations, promoting local family farms and non-urban areas.

The National Cultural Development Programme 2023-27 aims to establish a professional, efficient, and connected cultural sector, strengthening the non-institutional sector for culture. For 2023-24, a total of EUR 1.8 million was allocated to implement the cultural activities listed in the programme.

The Rural Tourism Development Programme of Montenegro 2023-25 aims to diversify and develop an authentic rural tourist offer in Montenegro, improving living standards and reducing migration from rural areas. Key objectives include attracting young people to rural tourism, preserving heritage, improving the quality and quantity of rural tourism offerings, sustainably managing natural resources, increasing the use of EU funds to rural tourism, and enhancing digitisation and promotion. The programme also focuses on fostering associations for better market conditions and adapting national legislation to support rural tourism. The Ministry of Economic Development and Tourism has allocated EUR 75 000 for 2023, with further funding planned for 2024 and 2025.

The Health Tourism Development Programme of Montenegro 2021-23 outlines goals such as establishing a framework for medical tourism development, enhancing Montenegro's international competitiveness in health tourism, and strengthening the capacities of the Dr. Simo Milosevic Institute, along with education and implementation monitoring systems. The total budget allocated to the programme is EUR 1.2 million, with EUR 1.1 million sourced from loans and EUR 105 000 from the national budget.

These efforts collectively aim to make Montenegro a sustainable tourist destination with year-round offerings, balanced regional development, and a preserved environment.

Montenegro: Domestic, inbound and outbound tourism

	2018	2019	2020	2021	2022
TOURISM FLOWS, THOUSAND					
Domestic tourism					
Total domestic trips	..	..	..	..	..
Overnight visitors (tourists)	..	..	..	..	..
Same-day visitors (excursionists)	..	..	..	..	..
Nights in all types of accommodation	..	..	..	..	..
Hotels and similar establishments	445	480	342	376	528
Other collective establishments	1	1	1	0	1
Private accommodation	41	42	18	73	33
Inbound tourism					
Total international arrivals	..	..	..	..	..
Overnight visitors (tourists)	2 077	2 510	351	1 554	2 036
Same-day visitors (excursionists)	..	..	..	..	..
Top markets					
Serbia	409	403	58	429	435
Russia	338	385	39	108	170
Bosnia and Herzegovina	194	204	50	215	211
Germany	90	164	18	71	152
France	77	90	10	36	76
Nights in all types of accommodation	..	..	..	..	..
Hotels and similar establishments	3 732	4 168	601	2 547	3 749
Other collective establishments	31	33	1	26	38
Private accommodation	8 680	9 733	1 625	6 851	8 080
Outbound tourism					
Total international departures	..	..	..	..	..
Overnight visitors (tourists)	..	..	..	..	..
Same-day visitors (excursionists)	..	..	..	..	..
Top destinations					
..	..	..	..	..	..
..	..	..	..	..	..
..	..	..	..	..	..
..	..	..	..	..	..
..	..	..	..	..	..
TOURISM RECEIPTS AND EXPENDITURE, MILLION USD					
Inbound tourism					
Total international receipts	1 224	1 277	180	903	..
International travel receipts	1 171	1 225	166	895	1 080
International passenger transport receipts	53	52	14	8	..
Outbound tourism					
Total international expenditure	74	72	38	58	..
International travel expenditure	68	58	30	42	59
International passenger transport expenditure	5	14	8	15	..

.. Not available
Source: OECD Tourism Statistics (Database).

StatLink https://stat.link/uhr0fc

Montenegro: Enterprises and employment in tourism

	Number of establishments	Number of persons employed				
	2022	2018	2019	2020	2021	2022
Total	..	..	..	..	..	..
Tourism industries	..	..	..	..	..	..
Accommodation services for visitors	..	7 102	8 020	5 508	6 469	9 423
Hotels and similar establishments	..	6 094	6 850	4 527	5 335	8 090
Food and beverage serving industry	..	9 444	10 965	8 399	9 416	12 789
Passenger transport	..	..	..	..	..	
Air passenger transport	..	442	436	407	97	179
Railways passenger transport	..	1 347	1 330	1 232	1 226	936
Road passenger transport	..	1 813	2 311	1 960	1 917	2 200
Water passenger transport	..	208	280	216	219	283
Passenger transport supporting services	..	..	..	..	..	
Transport equipment rental	..	531	592	515	532	668
Travel agencies and other reservation services industry	..	1 458	1 667	1 261	1 279	1 719
Cultural industry	..	548	551	528	595	989
Sports and recreation industry	..	3 192	3 468	3 133	3 124	3 809
Retail trade of country-specific tourism characteristic goods	..	..	..	..	..	..
Other country-specific tourism industries	..	..	..	..	..	..
Other industries	..	..	..	..	..	..

.. Not available
Source: OECD Tourism Statistics (Database).

StatLink https://stat.link/dlu63f

Morocco

Tourism in the economy and outlook

Tourism is an essential pillar for socio-economic development in Morocco. In 2022, Morocco experienced a 3.4% GDP growth, with a 14% rise in export services, largely driven by the good performance of the tourism sector which accounts for 47% of Morocco's service exports. In 2019, tourism directly contributed MAD 81.4 billion to the economy, representing 7.1% of the national GDP. The sector is also an important driver for employment in Morocco, providing 565 000 direct jobs in 2019, equating to 5.0% of the total workforce in the country.

In 2023, Morocco welcomed 14.5 million international tourists, marking a significant 34% increase compared to 2022 and surpassing 2019 levels by 12%. The top three source markets were France (14%), Spain (9%), and the United Kingdom (5%).

Domestic tourism is also a significant revenue stream in Morocco and has rebounded quicker than international tourism. In 2023, Morocco recorded 3.9 million domestic tourists, marking an 11% increase compared to 2022 and a 9% rise from 2019 levels.

Tourism governance

The Department of Tourism sits within the Ministry of Tourism, Handicrafts, and Social and Solidarity Economy and is responsible for developing and implementing government policy on tourism, supporting the sector's workforce and overseeing the public agencies involved in tourism.

The Department of Tourism operates with dual responsibilities at national and regional levels through its decentralised services. The Department oversees the management of regional public services, as well as the implementation of public policies and engages in the development and execution of tourism related programmes and projects at regional level. Decentralised services ensure the execution of directives and decisions from the national government authorities to whom they report and carry out programmes and projects at the local or provincial level.

The Moroccan National Tourism Office is tasked with promoting and marketing Morocco as a destination both domestically and abroad. The Moroccan Agency for Tourism Development is the public body in charge of tourism development in Morocco. The Agency actively implements the objectives of the Moroccan tourism strategy by conceptualising tourism projects. This includes identifying potential sites for tourism development, securing land, conducting market research and feasibility studies, promoting investment opportunities and enhancing private initiatives and public-private partnerships.

In 2023, the Department of Tourism's budget totalled MAD 736 million, allocated as follows: MAD 182 million for central administration and external services, MAD 300 million for the Moroccan National Tourism Office, and MAD 254 million for the Moroccan Agency for Tourism Development.

Morocco: Organisational chart of tourism bodies

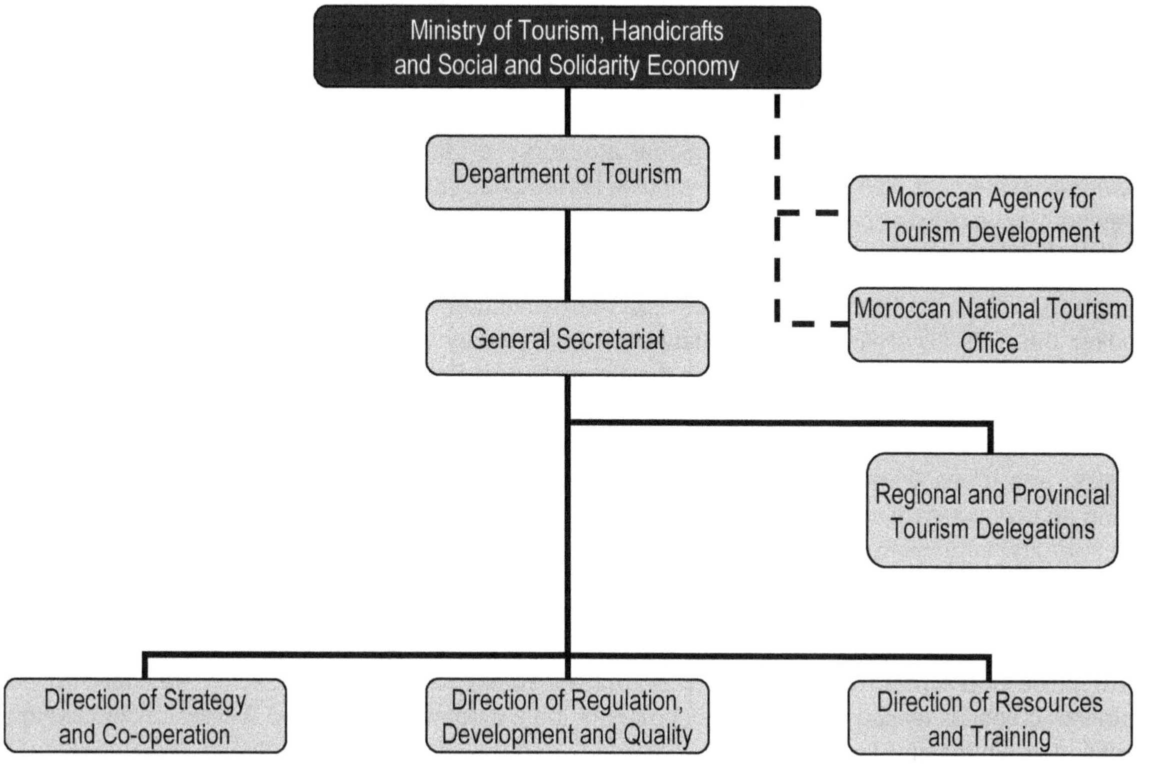

Source: OECD, adapted from the Ministry of Tourism, Handicrafts and Social and Solidarity Economy, 2024.

Tourism policies and programmes

Tourism policy in Morocco is steered by the Roadmap for the Tourism Sector 2023-26, a strategic plan designed to elevate the tourism sector's contribution to the national economy and foster a resilient and integrated industry. Launched in 2023, this ambitious policy is backed by a substantial financial envelope of MAD 6.1 billion and will be executed over the 2023-26 period. The Roadmap outlines three primary objectives to be achieved by the end of 2026:

- Attracting 17.5 million tourists.
- Generating MAD 120 billion in foreign currency.
- Creating 200 000 new job opportunities.

This strategy marks a paradigm shift, transitioning from a destination-focused approach to a client experience-oriented model. The roadmap is structured around 9 thematic sectors and 5 cross-cutting sectors, and is supported by 6 strategic levers which are as follows:

- Developing a plan to double air capacity
- Strengthening promotion and marketing efforts with particular emphasis on digitalisation
- Diversifying cultural and entertainment products
- Rehabilitating hotels and expanding accommodation options and capacities
- Strengthening human capital through an attractive training framework
- Strengthening the Tourism Observatory of Morocco

In order to ensure the success of the Roadmap, a new governance system has been put in place through the creation of a National Interministerial Tourism Commission, chaired by the Head of Government and composed of the signatory parties, as well as two national commissions which are the Aviation Commission and the Supply/Demand Product Commission, and twelve commissions for the follow-up of regional plans, chaired by the Walis of each region.

A central structure of animation and regional structures of animation are also included in the new governance system, as well as local level impulse laboratories whose mission is providing an institutional framework for dialogue between the public and private sectors, each of them consisting of a multidisciplinary team (see box below).

To implement the priorities outlined in the 2023-26 Roadmap, Morocco introduced several initiatives, including the GO SIYAHA programme launched in February 2024. This programme, developed in collaboration with the National Agency for the Promotion of Small and Medium-sized Enterprises and industry professionals, aims to support 1 700 tourism enterprises with a total budget of MAD 720 million by 2026. GO SIYAHA encompasses three distinct sub-programmes: investment support, technical expertise, and green development. Each sub-programme is tailored to foster growth in specific areas, creating an ecosystem of innovative, dynamic, and eco-friendly tourism enterprises.

Promoting public-private partnerships in Morocco

The impulse laboratories, pillars of the new 2023-26 Roadmap for the Tourism Sector, are public-private partnership entities tasked with the development of the 9 thematic sectors and 5 cross-cutting sectors identified within the new tourism policy.

The mission of the impulse laboratories is structured around four main objectives which are as follows:

- Identifying of the prerequisites necessary to facilitate the development of each target sector, namely in terms of infrastructure, public financing, and regulations to be adapted.
- Establishing launch plans for the driving projects to be initiated for each sector.
- Preparing public-private agreements to develop target sectors.
- Elaborating specific action plans for each target sector, each cluster, each priority region, as well as for each driving project.

The establishment of the 10 impulse laboratories is currently underway. So far, two regional action plans have been signed, the first one for the Fès-Meknès Region in January 2024 and the second one for the Béni Mellal - Khénifra Region in February 2024.

Statistical Profile

Morocco: Domestic, inbound and outbound tourism

	2018	2019	2020	2021	2022
TOURISM FLOWS, THOUSAND					
Domestic tourism					
Total domestic trips	..	..	..	..	..
Overnight visitors (tourists)	3 247	3 547	1 442	2 764	3 504
Same-day visitors (excursionists)	..	..	..		..
Nights in all types of accommodation	..	..	..	..	..
Hotels and similar establishments	7 166	7 833	3 509	6 376	7 939
Other collective establishments	..	..	..	..	..
Private accommodation	..	..	..	..	..
Inbound tourism					
Total international arrivals	..	..	..	..	..
Overnight visitors (tourists)	12 289	12 933	2 778	3 722	10 869
Same-day visitors (excursionists)	..	..	..	..	..
Top markets					
France	1 844	1 991	412	494	1 505
Spain	814	881	200	99	902
Germany	394	413	79	39	171
United Kingdom	511	551	113	56	482
Belgium	274	272	41	65	173
Nights in all types of accommodation	147 790	..	..	..	..
Hotels and similar establishments	16 866	17 415	3 480	2 816	11 069
Other collective establishments	30 953	..	..	..	..
Private accommodation	99 971	..	..	..	..
Outbound tourism					
Total international departures	..	..	..	..	
Overnight visitors (tourists)	1 923	2 009	738	643	2 021
Same-day visitors (excursionists)	..	..	..	..	
Top destinations					
..	..	..	..	..	..
..	..	..	..	..	..
..	..	..	..	..	..
..	..	..	..	..	..
..	..	..	..	..	..
TOURISM RECEIPTS AND EXPENDITURE, MILLION USD					
Inbound tourism					
Total international receipts	9 520	9 949	4 513	4 670	10 414
International travel receipts	7 774	8 187	3 847	3 840	9 063
International passenger transport receipts	1 746	1 762	666	830	1 352
Outbound tourism					
Total international expenditure	2 988	3 103	1 509	1 707	2 494
International travel expenditure	1 976	2 176	1 113	1 205	1 883
International passenger transport expenditure	1 011	926	396	502	611

.. Not available
Source: OECD Tourism Statistics (Database).

StatLink https://stat.link/reul1w

Morocco: Enterprises and employment in tourism

	Number of establishments	Number of persons employed				
	2022	2018 e	2019 e	2020	2021	2022
Total	..	550 000	565 000	..	..	..
Tourism industries	6 327	424 000	435 800	..	..	..
Accommodation services for visitors	..	..	..	..	..	..
Hotels and similar establishments	4 650	140 000	144 000	..	..	..
Food and beverage serving industry	..	90 000	92 500	..	..	..
Passenger transport	..	37 000	38 000	..	..	..
Air passenger transport	..	..	..	..	..	..
Railways passenger transport	..	..	..	..	..	..
Road passenger transport	..	..	..	..	..	..
Water passenger transport	..	..	..	..	..	..
Passenger transport supporting services	..	..	..	..	..	..
Transport equipment rental	..	..	..	..	..	..
Travel agencies and other reservation services industry	1 677	24 000	24 600	..	..	..
Cultural industry	..	10 000	10 300	..	..	..
Sports and recreation industry	..	3 000	3 100	..	..	..
Retail trade of country-specific tourism characteristic goods	..	120 000	123 300	..	..	..
Other country-specific tourism industries	..	..	..	..	..	..
Other industries	..	126 000	129 200	..	..	..

.. Not available; e Estimated value
Source: OECD Tourism Statistics (Database).

StatLink https://stat.link/mx7a25

Morocco: Internal tourism consumption

Million MAD

	2014		
	Domestic tourism expenditure	Inbound tourism expenditure	Internal tourism consumption
Total	..	..	..
Consumption products	**32 000**	**73 508**	**105 508**
Tourism characteristic products	21 648	53 666	75 315
Accommodation services for visitors	6 196	11 962	18 158
Food and beverage serving services	5 318	10 088	15 406
Passenger transport services	4 868	14 212	19 080
Air passenger transport services	..	..	..
Railways passenger transport services	..	..	..
Road passenger transport services	..	..	..
Water passenger transport services	..	..	..
Passenger transport supporting services	..	..	..
Transport equipment rental services	122	..	122
Travel agencies and other reservation services industry	43	1 100	1 143
Cultural services	106	1 017	1 123
Sports and recreation services	2 416	8 032	10 449
Country-specific tourism characteristic goods	2 580	7 256	9 836
Country-specific tourism characteristic services	..	..	..
Other consumption products	10 352	19 841	30 193
Tourism connected products	..	..	..
Non-tourism related consumption products	10 352	19 841	30 193
Non-consumption products	..	..	..

.. Not available
Source: OECD Tourism Statistics (Database).

StatLink https://stat.link/8eh5vl

Peru

Tourism in the economy and outlook

Tourism is an important economic contributor in Peru and has started to recover after the COVID-19 pandemic. In 2023, tourism directly contributed PEN 25 billion to the economy, representing 2.5% of total GDP in Peru. This is still 14% below 2019 figures, when tourism contributed 3.9% of GDP, but represents a 136% increase from the pandemic low in 2020. The sector generated 1.2 million jobs (direct and indirect) in 2023, 21% below 2019 levels.

In 2023, Peru recorded 2.5 million international tourist arrivals. This represents a significant increase compared to the pandemic low of 444 000 in 2021, but it remains 42% below 2019 levels. The top three international markets in 2023 were Chile (24%), the United States (19%), and Ecuador (9%), similar to 2019, when Chile (27%) was the largest source market, followed by the United States (18%).

As with inbound tourism, domestic tourism also shows signs of post-pandemic recovery. Peru recorded 37.2 million domestic tourist arrivals in 2023, an 159% increase compared to the pandemic low in 2020, but still 23% below pre-pandemic levels. Peru predicts that international tourism arrivals will surpass pre-pandemic levels by 2026.

Tourism governance

The Ministry of Foreign Trade and Tourism is the tourism sector's lead political and administrative authority. Its role is to define, direct, execute and co-ordinate the country's foreign trade and tourism policy in harmony with the general policy of Peru. The Vice Ministry for Tourism, part of the Ministry, oversees the General Directorate of Tourism Development Policy, responsible for implementing, evaluating and supervising tourism policy. The Directorate also formulates and implements actions to improve the quality of tourism services, its environmental management, tourism facilitation, tourist protection, and the promotion of culture. The Vice Ministry for Tourism also oversees the General Directorates of Research and Studies on Tourism and Handicrafts, Tourism Strategy, Crafts, and Casino Games and Slot Machines.

The Ministry has two Specialised Advisory Bodies, the Tourism Advisory Committee and the National Council for Handicraft Development. The Tourism Training Centre and the Exports and the Tourism Promotion Board of Peru are also attached to the Ministry and operate Peru's Commercial Offices Abroad.

Regional governments are responsible for formulating, approving and executing policies relating to the development of regional tourist activity, qualification of regional tourist service providers, and co-ordination with local governments on tourism activities. They also maintain and update directories of tourism service providers, tourism resources, and regional events calendars.

At the national level, the total budget for tourism in 2023 was PEN 652.9 million, which represents a strong increase from PEN 204.6 million in 2022. The budget was split into PEN 267.7 million granted to the Ministry of Foreign Trade and Tourism, PEN 24.8 million for the Tourism Training Centre, and PEN 360.4 million to the Commission for the Promotion of Peru for Export and Tourism.

Peru: Organisational chart of tourism bodies

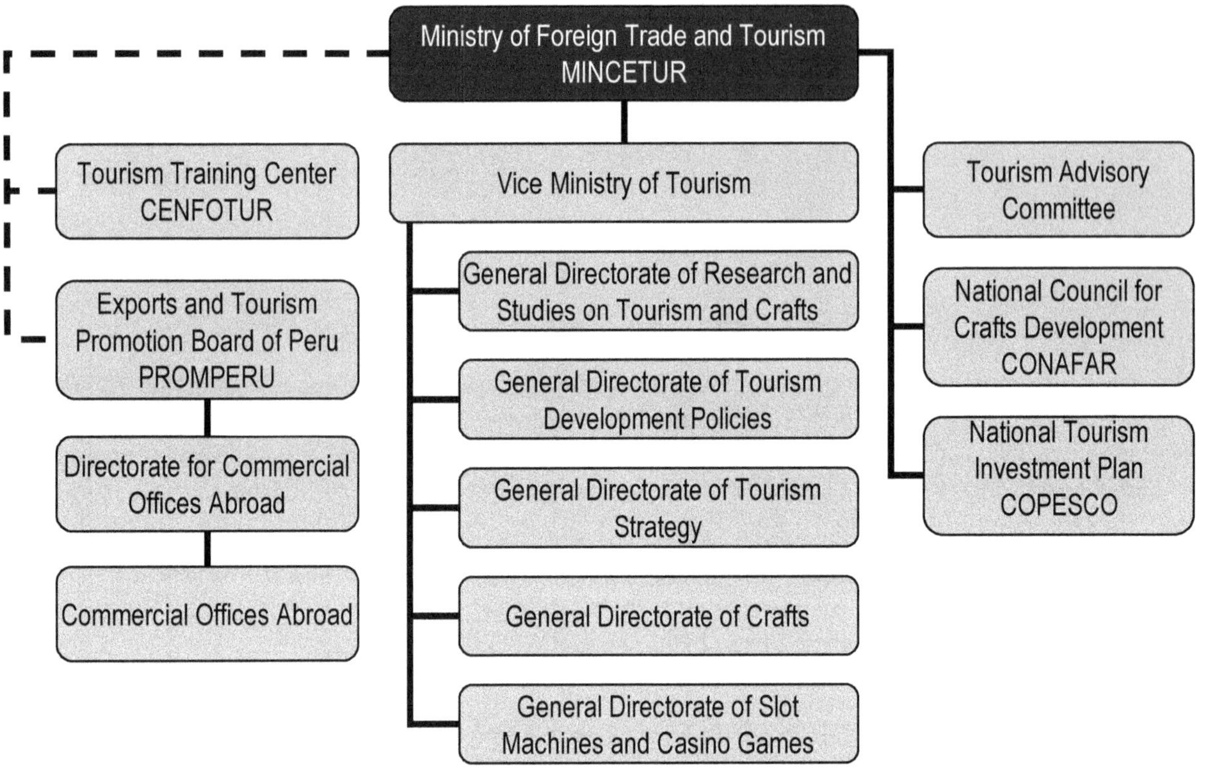

Source: OECD, adapted from the Ministry of Foreign Trade and Tourism, 2024.

Tourism policies and programmes

In 2016, Peru launched a 10-year strategy, PENTUR 2016-25, which focused on increasing international arrivals. Following the COVID-19 pandemic, the country approved the National Tourism Sector Reactivation Strategy 2022-25 to address the challenges faced by the Peruvian tourism sector. In 2024, Peru initiated the development of a new tourism strategy which seeks to be a guiding document for all tourism stakeholders and integrate the needs of the tourism sector in the agenda and operational plans of all relevant sectors. The new strategy will adopt a multisectoral and participatory approach and will be developed in consultation with different stakeholders at the national and regional level through workshops and interviews. It is expected that the national tourism policy will be available by the end of 2024.

The current strategy aims to promote the reactivation of the tourism sector in Peru by creating unique and biosecure tourist experiences based on the country's natural resources and ancestral culture, focusing on inclusivity and sustainability. Several initiatives have been launched under the strategy, such as the Guide of Regional Tourism Marketing Plans, developed by PROMPERÚ in agreement with the Swiss Import Promotion Programme, or the Peru Carbon Footprint Scheme, which had 29 hotels registered by end 2023, demonstrating their commitment to reducing greenhouse gas emissions.

Additionally, the Programme to Stimulate Business Competitiveness offers courses focused on sales, marketing, finance, innovation, among others, aimed at strengthening the competitiveness of micro, small, and medium-sized tourism enterprises. As of 2024, over 300 tourism businesses benefited from the initiative. The Virtual Classroom, launched in 2021, is the first e-learning platform of the Peruvian State specialised in the travel and tourism sector, aimed at entrepreneurs, academia, and individuals interested in accessing training in commercial management and destination management in tourism. As of 2024, over 15 000 users had registered nationwide, benefiting from over 80 free educational courses.

The Economic Reactivation Plan supports the recovery of all national productive sectors, allocating a PEN 500 million budget to tourism. This funding aims to improve airport runways and taxiways, enhance safety and service quality for tourists at airports, invest in tourist circuits like Machu Picchu, Kuelap, and Colca Canyon, and refund VAT on goods purchased by foreign tourists.

Aligned with the objectives of the PENTUR 2016-25, Peru has developed initiatives to enhance social tourism. The Social Tourism Initiative works to diversify tourism offerings in Peru through guiding instruments, capacity strengthening, design of innovative and accessible tourism products and services, and the development of tools to facilitate the approach of demand to accessible, safe, and quality offerings. The initiative is underpinned by the Guidelines for the Development of Social Tourism in Peru (2020) and Tourism for All, which has been used to promote 25 accessible and inclusive tourism experiences in cities and regional areas. Accessibility training and awareness sessions for over 1 200 people on were provided. In 2023, the V Social Tourism Forum was held in Lima to create a space for the exchange of international experiences in Social Tourism management, as well as the generation of networks that enhance its development. Under the Tourism Entrepreneurship Initiative, a national public competition was organised to select and grant subsidies to individuals and legal entities, including micro and small businesses related to the tourism industry (see box below).

The Charming Villages Initiative recognised nine towns with tourist potential, highlighting authentic and unique natural and cultural attributes to diversify Peru's tourism offerings, enhance visitor experience, boost the local economy, promote heritage conservation, and improve the quality of life for locals. The empowerment and commitment of local governments and participation of local stakeholders in tourism planning are taken into consideration to award destinations with the label. In 2023, local providers received training in business management, good handling practices, and natural and cultural heritage conservation.

The National Strategic Plan for Handicrafts 2019-29 outlines four areas of focus to promote the competitiveness of Peruvian handicrafts, including development of offerings with an entrepreneurial vision, access to profitable markets, management of critical risks in the handicraft activity, and strategic leadership for competitiveness. The Plan complements other measures developed and implemented to improve tourism in Peru.

Supporting formal employment and economic recovery for the Peruvian tourism sector

The Tourism Entrepreneurship programme tackles the challenge of the informal economy and the share of formal employment in Peru's tourism sector. The programme generates between five direct and ten indirect jobs per beneficiary. The Ministry's competitive fund supports tourism service providers through an annual national public competition that grants financing to legal entities, entrepreneurs, and micro and small tourism businesses. The programme aims to revitalise and promote tourism-related private companies, diversifying the country's tourism offerings.

The programme has been strengthened to mitigate the COVID-19 pandemic impacts. By the end of 2023, it allocated PEN 8.6 million to 108 winning beneficiaries nationwide. In its previous nine editions, the initiative has attracted over 25 000 tourism service providers and benefited more than 8 300 winners, distributing PEN 136.8 million. Beneficiaries of grants included 397 accommodation services providers, 286 food services providers, 640 tour operators or travel agencies, 27 associations, 117 artisanal companies, 4 738 artisans, and 2 040 tourist guides. These funds have significantly contributed to the economic recovery of the sector.

Statistical Profile

Peru: Domestic, inbound and outbound tourism

	2018	2019	2020	2021	2022
TOURISM FLOWS, THOUSAND					
Domestic tourism					
Total domestic trips	128 839	134 995	47 070	..	..
Overnight visitors (tourists)	46 517	48 575	14 370	16 496	27 102
Same-day visitors (excursionists)	82 322	86 420	32 700	..	..
Nights in all types of accommodation	273 000	291 600	43 109	65 985	159 903
Hotels and similar establishments	..	..	..	..	..
Other collective establishments	..	..	..	..	..
Private accommodation	..	..	..	..	..
Inbound tourism[1]					
Total international arrivals	5 385	5 275	1 119	444	2 278
Overnight visitors (tourists)	4 419	4 372	897	444	2 009
Same-day visitors (excursionists)	965	903	222	..	269
Top markets					
Chile	1 159	1 196	288	37	366
United States	641	657	128	177	465
Ecuador	293	339	67	10	157
Colombia	219	224	49	41	133
Bolivia	159	189	52	4	98
Nights in all types of accommodation	44 194	43 718	..	..	..
Hotels and similar establishments	14 302	14 796	3 415	3 573	9 123
Other collective establishments	..	..	..	..	..
Private accommodation	..	..	..	..	..
Outbound tourism					
Total international departures	3 435	3 634	893	617	2 350
Overnight visitors (tourists)	3 078	3 275	791	617	2 119
Same-day visitors (excursionists)	357	359	102	..	231
Top destinations					
Chile	1 373	1 417	334	36	529
United States	294	325	89	269	322
Colombia	135	177	44	38	202
Spain	160	184	42	70	194
Bolivia	284	291	70	4	137
TOURISM RECEIPTS AND EXPENDITURE, MILLION USD					
Inbound tourism					
Total international receipts	4 505	4 703	1 002	1 042	2 938
International travel receipts	3 557	3 738	776	688	2 137
International passenger transport receipts	947	965	226	355	801
Outbound tourism					
Total international expenditure	3 352	3 627	938	1 521	2 953
International travel expenditure	2 604	2 775	733	1 149	2 345
International passenger transport expenditure	749	853	205	372	608

.. Not available
1. Arrivals from demand side surveys; Nights from supply side surveys.
Source: OECD Tourism Statistics (Database).

StatLink https://stat.link/ndumr7

Peru: Enterprises and employment in tourism

	Number of establishments	Number of persons employed				
	2022	2018	2019 e	2020 e	2021	2022
Total	..	700 367	725 980	353 552	..	..
Tourism industries	..	..	..	..	..	..
Accommodation services for visitors	..	..	..	..	..	..
Hotels and similar establishments	26 729	80 044	81 964	40 741	..	..
Food and beverage serving industry	305 892	236 632	252 152	125 284	..	..
Passenger transport	..	..	..	..	..	..
Air passenger transport	..	4 799	4 982	2 443	..	..
Railways passenger transport	..	..	..	..	..	..
Road passenger transport	..	139 745	143 582	71 127	..	..
Water passenger transport	..	711	721	362	..	..
Passenger transport supporting services	..	..	..	..	..	..
Transport equipment rental	..	..	..	..	..	..
Travel agencies and other reservation services industry	17 499	28 047	28 781	14 420	..	..
Cultural industry	..	20 373	20 708	10 369	..	..
Sports and recreation industry	..	15 466	15 843	7 872	..	..
Retail trade of country-specific tourism characteristic goods	..	..	..	..	..	..
Other country-specific tourism industries	..	53 744	55 033	27 355	..	..
Other industries	..	120 806	122 214	53 579	..	..

.. Not available; e Estimated value
Source: OECD Tourism Statistics (Database).

StatLink https://stat.link/apo0q8

Peru: Internal tourism consumption
Million PEN

	2020 e		
	Domestic tourism expenditure	Inbound tourism expenditure	Internal tourism consumption
Total	..	..	..
Consumption products	**11 700**	**3 500**	**17 300**
Tourism characteristic products	..	..	..
Accommodation services for visitors	..	..	..
Food and beverage serving services	..	..	..
Passenger transport services	..	..	..
Air passenger transport services	..	..	..
Railways passenger transport services	..	..	..
Road passenger transport services	..	..	..
Water passenger transport services	..	..	..
Passenger transport supporting services	..	..	..
Transport equipment rental services	..	..	..
Travel agencies and other reservation services industry	..	..	..
Cultural services	..	..	..
Sports and recreation services	..	..	..
Country-specific tourism characteristic goods	..	..	..
Country-specific tourism characteristic services	..	..	..
Other consumption products	..	..	..
Tourism connected products	..	..	..
Non-tourism related consumption products	..	..	..
Non-consumption products	..	..	..

.. Not available; e Estimated value
Source: OECD Tourism Statistics (Database).

StatLink https://stat.link/firsyt

Romania

Tourism in the economy and outlook

Tourism plays an important role in the Romanian economy. In 2021, tourism directly accounted for RON 18.8 billion, representing 1.6% of GDP. This shows a slight recovery from the pandemic low of RON 16.8 million but remains 40% below pre-pandemic levels. In 2021, the tourism sector directly accounted for 6.1% of total employment in Romania, representing 340 200 jobs. This was still considerably lower than 2019 levels, when tourism accounted for 412 600 jobs.

In 2023, Romania recorded 2.1 million international overnight visitors in commercial accommodation establishments. This is a strong recovery compared to the pandemic low of 450 000 international tourists in 2020, but it is still 21% below the pre-pandemic level in 2019. The three main source markets in 2023 were Germany (10%), Italy (9%) and Israel (7%).

Domestic tourism remains a critical component of Romanian tourism. In 2023, Romania recorded 11.6 million domestic overnight visitors in commercial accommodation establishments, 9.0% above pre-pandemic levels and 6.7% above 2022.

Tourism governance

The Ministry of Economy, Entrepreneurship and Tourism is responsible for tourism in Romania. The main tourism-related fields of activity include:

- Developing and implementing national and sectoral tourism strategies.
- Promoting Romania as a tourism destination domestically and abroad.
- Developing destinations and tourism products.
- Developing tourism-related infrastructure.
- Authorising and controlling tourism services.
- Representing Romania in international tourism organisations.

The Consultative Council for Tourism includes representatives of central and local administrations, the private sector, academia, associations for different tourism sectors or destinations in Romania, and cultural institutions of national interest. In 2022, Romania established the National Tourist Brand Council, which includes representatives of the public and private sectors, to co-ordinate tourism promotion activities.

Local administrations collaborate with the Ministry to implement tourism policies. At the local level, tourism associations bring together interested parties to contribute to tourism development. Additionally, 17 territorial representatives of the Ministry work with local partners to help implement national tourism policies. Establishing Destination Management Organisations is a priority for the Ministry (see box below). 21 DMOs have already been certified in Romania, one at regional level, two at county level and 18 at local level.

In 2024, the tourism budget including the programme for tourism marketing and promotion and the programme for the development of tourist destinations, forms and products decreased from RON 120 million to RON 55 million. The marketing budget increased by 27% but the product development budget decreased by 68%.

Romania: Organisational chart of tourism bodies

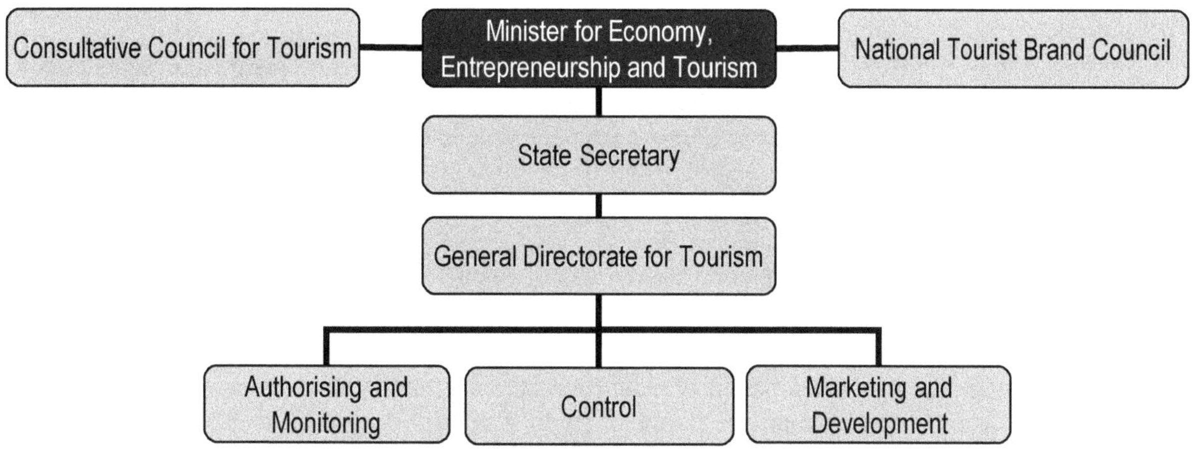

Note: The chart shows the section for tourism within the Ministry of Economy, Entrepreneurship and Tourism
Source: OECD, adapted Ministry of Economy, Entrepreneurship and Tourism, 2024.

Tourism policies and programmes

The National Tourism Development Strategy 2023-35, developed with support from the World Bank, aims to make Romania a renowned, high-quality, year-round tourism destination by 2035. The Strategy focuses on the country's unique cultural and natural heritage, and high-quality services. The Strategy was under consultation with the public and the Consultative Council for Tourism in 2023, and at time of writing is going through inter-ministerial approval processes. The Governing Plan 2023-24 outlines government priorities and objectives for the strategy implementation, focusing on developing tourism destinations through public-private partnerships, enhancing Romania's notoriety abroad, promoting ecotourism, attracting investments, simplifying authorisation systems, protecting tourists and businesses, improving digitalisation and supporting entrepreneurs. Several initiatives have been established to support implementation of the Governing Plan including state aid schemes to support the private sector in developing spa resorts, incoming tourism, and participating in tourism promotion events abroad alongside the Ministry.

The Ministry has created a voluntary national system for labelling cultural-touristic routes, developed by tourism and culture organisations or local public authorities, to meet the increasing demand for experiential and personalised tourism. Currently, 154 cultural-touristic routes of local, regional and national level have been labelled.

The Operational Programme for Administrative Capacity (SIPOCA) project aims to analyse, improve, and update the legal framework in the field of tourism. The project's general objective is to optimise the decision-making process and increase the efficiency of ministry activities by systemising and improving tourism legislation to fulfil strategic objectives according to the institutional mandate.

To promote sustainable tourism practices, Romania participates in international contests that award remarkable tourist destinations such as the Best Tourism Villages award by UN Tourism. The country also awards outstanding beaches with the Blue Flag label and designates ecotourism destinations. To support domestic tourism, Romania implemented a travel voucher system. These vouchers, which can only be used in Romania and are valid for one year, have been successful over the past few years and continue to receive funding.

The National Recovery and Resilience Plan includes a chapter dedicated to tourism and culture, with key initiatives including the development of Destination Management Organisations, the creation and promotion of 12 cultural touristic routes, the creation and modernisation of nine museums and memorials, and the development of cycling tourism.

Additional sectoral strategies developed in Romania include:

- The National Strategy for Ecotourism Development 2019-29 aims to create the conditions for ecotourism development in natural protected areas by developing a network of certified ecotourism destinations and creating competitive ecotourism products for both national and international markets. Based on the National Strategy for Ecotourism Development, the Ministry, together with other institutions and organisations from Romania, such as the Ministry of Environment, Waters and Forests, the National Institute for Research and Development in Tourism and the Ecotourism Association of Romania, developed a system to evaluate ecotourism destinations in Romania, based on the Global Criteria for Sustainable Tourism (GSTC) and the European Ecotourism Standard (EETLS). To date, six tourism destinations have received this recognition.
- The Strategy for the Development of Spa Tourism, launched in 2019, promotes an innovative approach combining public-private partnerships to support the development of a wide variety of health tourism-related products, with a focus on green, sustainable projects. The Strategy will be implemented through a dedicated action plan.

Strengthening local governance through Destination Management Organisations in Romania

Romania's National Recovery and Resilience Plan aims to enhance the competitiveness of rural and less-visited tourist destinations. A key component of the Strategy involves the establishment of Destination Management Organisations (DMOs).

As part of the EU Structural Reform Support Programme, Romania formalised a legal framework for DMOs in the country. These organisations function as partnerships between administrative-territorial unit(s) of the destination with payers of special taxes for tourism promotion and/or other entities which pay a membership fee.

To obtain the certification, DMOs at local level must meet specific criteria. They must be designated as a tourist resort of local or national interest, or possess a minimum of 100 beds in authorised accommodation facilities. Additionally, a draft strategy for tourism development and marketing, and an action plan, should be drafted and subjected to approval by the DMO management. These documents can also be elaborated and approved within one year from the DMO certification. At least one member of the DMO must hold a Tourism Destination Manager diploma, a postgraduate qualification designed to equip DMOs with a common knowledge base. The course is supported by tourism organisations and bodies at the national level, such as the Federation of Romanian Tourism Employers, the Federation of Tourist Promotion Associations in Romania, the Federation of Hotel Industry in Romania, and the Alliance for Tourism. Finally, the DMO must possess a minimum budget equivalent to EUR 30 000 in RON. The requirements are slightly different for the DMO at county and regional level. There is also specified the general framework for the national level DMO.

As of 2024, Romania boasts 21 certified DMOs, encompassing regional (1), county (2) and local (18) levels. The National Recovery and Resilience Plan aims to expand this network by establishing a total of eight regional DMOs.

Statistical Profile

Romania: Domestic, inbound and outbound tourism

	2018	2019	2020	2021	2022
TOURISM FLOWS, THOUSAND					
Domestic tourism					
Total domestic trips	10 109	10 691	5 945	9 326	10 914
Overnight visitors (tourists)	10 109	10 691	5 945	9 326	10 914
Same-day visitors (excursionists)	..	..	..	..	..
Nights in all types of accommodation	23 315	24 795	13 582	20 823	23 378
Hotels and similar establishments	16 543	17 446	9 224	13 276	14 993
Other collective establishments	6 772	7 349	4 357	7 547	8 385
Private accommodation	..	..	..	..	..
Inbound tourism					
Total international arrivals	2 797	2 684	454	879	1 674
Overnight visitors (tourists)	2 797	2 684	454	879	1 674
Same-day visitors (excursionists)	..	..	..	..	..
Top markets					
Germany	327	298	57	111	183
Israel	278	235	29	52	160
Italy	241	223	40	77	132
United States	166	162	22	47	107
France	172	155	30	58	89
Nights in all types of accommodation	5 330	5 291	997	1 925	3 667
Hotels and similar establishments	4 560	4 544	888	1 718	3 337
Other collective establishments	769	747	109	207	329
Private accommodation	..	..	..	..	..
Outbound tourism					
Total international departures	10 469	13 651	4 267	8 237	10 895
Overnight visitors (tourists)	10 361	13 515	4 237	8 182	10 724
Same-day visitors (excursionists)	108	136	30	55	170
Top destinations					
Türkiye	197	315	68	193	325
Bulgaria	164	209	106	194	202
Greece	161	130	46	75	141
Spain	71	..	..	..	34
Italy	69	44	..	13	24
TOURISM RECEIPTS AND EXPENDITURE, MILLION USD					
Inbound tourism					
Total international receipts	3 834	4 183	1 580	3 509	5 072
International travel receipts	3 396	3 578	1 436	3 299	4 704
International passenger transport receipts	438	605	144	210	368
Outbound tourism					
Total international expenditure	6 105	7 161	3 521	6 021	8 858
International travel expenditure	5 339	6 001	3 077	5 230	7 762
International passenger transport expenditure	766	1 159	444	790	1 097

.. Not available value
Source: OECD Tourism Statistics (Database).

StatLink https://stat.link/3xyzrs

Romania: Enterprises and employment in tourism

	Number of establishments[1]	Number of persons employed[2]				
	2020	2018	2019	2020	2021	2022
Total	..	..	..	..	..	..
Tourism industries	51 294	409 881	412 649	393 427	340 217	..
Accommodation services for visitors	7 650	43 686	40 910	40 849	44 889	..
Hotels and similar establishments	7 650	36 954	35 511	36 947	41 771	..
Food and beverage serving industry	18 031	156 669	163 335	146 888	132 835	..
Passenger transport	12 446	152 623	146 191	143 973	105 815	..
Air passenger transport	72	6 626	6 884	5 208	6 198	..
Railways passenger transport	43	35 010	30 649	31 185	26 519	..
Road passenger transport	12 220	108 754	104 650	102 069	70 172	..
Water passenger transport	111	2 233	4 008	5 511	2 926	..
Passenger transport supporting services	..	..	..	..		..
Transport equipment rental	793	914	1 078	2 607	1 017	..
Travel agencies and other reservation services industry	2 177	11 993	13 718	12 570	10 714	..
Cultural industry	1 243	18 961	15 714	13 968	10 416	..
Sports and recreation industry	5 564	25 035	31 703	32 572	34 531	..
Retail trade of country-specific tourism characteristic goods	3 390	..	..	..	..	..
Other country-specific tourism industries	..	..	..	..	..	..
Other industries	..	..	..	..	..	..

.. Not available
1. Data refer to number of enterprises.
2. Data refer to number of employees.
Source: OECD Tourism Statistics (Database).

StatLink https://stat.link/k0vngd

Romania: Internal tourism consumption

Million RON

	2020		
	Domestic tourism expenditure	Inbound tourism expenditure	Internal tourism consumption
Total	..	..	..
Consumption products	1 793	33 694	35 661
Tourism characteristic products	1 616	29 961	31 736
Accommodation services for visitors	583	5 790	6 508
Food and beverage serving services	426	10 765	11 215
Passenger transport services	264	8 245	8 508
Air passenger transport services	4	2 008	2 012
Railways passenger transport services	2	302	304
Road passenger transport services	257	5 894	6 150
Water passenger transport services	1	41	42
Passenger transport supporting services	..	..	..
Transport equipment rental services	50	221	271
Travel agencies and other reservation services industry	..	2 421	2 421
Cultural services	57	513	570
Sports and recreation services	55	786	842
Country-specific tourism characteristic goods	108	375	482
Country-specific tourism characteristic services	74	846	920
Other consumption products	177	3 733	3 925
Tourism connected products	..	..	..
Non-tourism related consumption products	..	..	..
Non-consumption products	..	73	73

.. Not available
Source: OECD Tourism Statistics (Database).

StatLink https://stat.link/dwkumr

Saudi Arabia

Tourism in the economy and outlook

Tourism is one of Saudi Arabia's fastest growing sectors and is seen as essential in the country's economic diversification, employment, and sustainable development. In 2022, tourism was estimated to have directly contributed 3.4% to the country's GDP, almost matching the 3.6% share recorded in 2019. Preliminary estimates for 2023 indicate this share to be between 4.0% and 4.4%, exceeding 2019 levels. The number of direct tourism jobs reached 925 000 in 2023, comprising 5.8% of total employees in the Saudi economy, up 62% from 2019 levels.

In 2023, inbound tourism reached a peak of 27.4 million international tourist arrivals, a 65% rise compared to 2022, and a 56% increase compared to 2019. This surge resulted in inbound tourism receipts amounting to SAR 141.2 billion, reflecting a corresponding 44% increase from 2022 and 37% from 2019. Leisure tourism emerged as one of the primary drivers of inbound tourism growth, witnessing a substantial increase from 1.1 million tourists in 2019 to 2.5 million in 2022, and further escalating to 6.2 million tourists in 2023.

Domestic tourism also demonstrated significant growth, recording 81.9 million overnight domestic tourists in 2023, representing a 5% increase over 2022 and 71% over 2019. This surge in domestic tourism generated revenues totalling SAR 114.4 billion, surpassing figures from 2022 and 2019, by 7% and 87% respectively.

Saudi Arabia welcomed more than 100 million inbound and domestic tourists in 2023, seven years ahead of the initial timeline set by Saudi Vision 2030, representing significant growth compared to pre pandemic levels. This has spurred Saudi Arabia to adjust its earlier goal with a more ambitious target of hosting 150 million tourists by 2030.

Tourism governance

The Ministry of Tourism is responsible for defining tourism policy and regulating the tourism sector in Saudi Arabia, and focuses on strategy, regulations, destination development, human capital development, and investment attraction.

The Ministry co-ordinates with other government entities on tourism policy development through several mechanisms, including memorandums of understanding, joint committees and regular meetings with other ministries. The Ministry also engages with the private sector on tourism policy development through several mechanisms, including public-private partnerships, tourism councils and industry surveys.

The Ministry is supported by the Saudi Tourism Authority, in charge of branding, marketing and promotional efforts with different travel agencies and tour operators. The Tourism Development Fund is in charge of funding iconic projects and supporting the private sector to develop offerings and accommodations. The General Commission for Tourism and National Heritage is responsible for developing and preserving Saudi Arabia's cultural heritage.

The tourism policy ecosystem works closely with all the relevant government entities, such as the Ministry of Foreign Affairs, Ministry of Interior, Ministry of Transport, Ministry of Electricity, Water and Agriculture, through a government body called the Tourism Development Committee, where major cross-governmental initiatives are discussed and monitored.

Governance has also been put in place to manage the development of the tourism sector through the Regional Tourism Development Committee, which gathers provincial administration, regional development entities, the different entities in charge of developing sites and destinations, and professional associations.

Regional development authorities play a crucial role in developing and promoting tourism destinations. They are responsible for ensuring that the necessary infrastructure and services are in place to support the industry. The Royal Commission for Al-Ula is tasked with developing the Al-Ula region as a world-class tourist destination, while the Madinah Development Authority launched a project to enhance the tourism experience for visitors by redesigning and upgrading major streets and public realm areas of the city.

Saudi Arabia: Organisational chart of tourism bodies

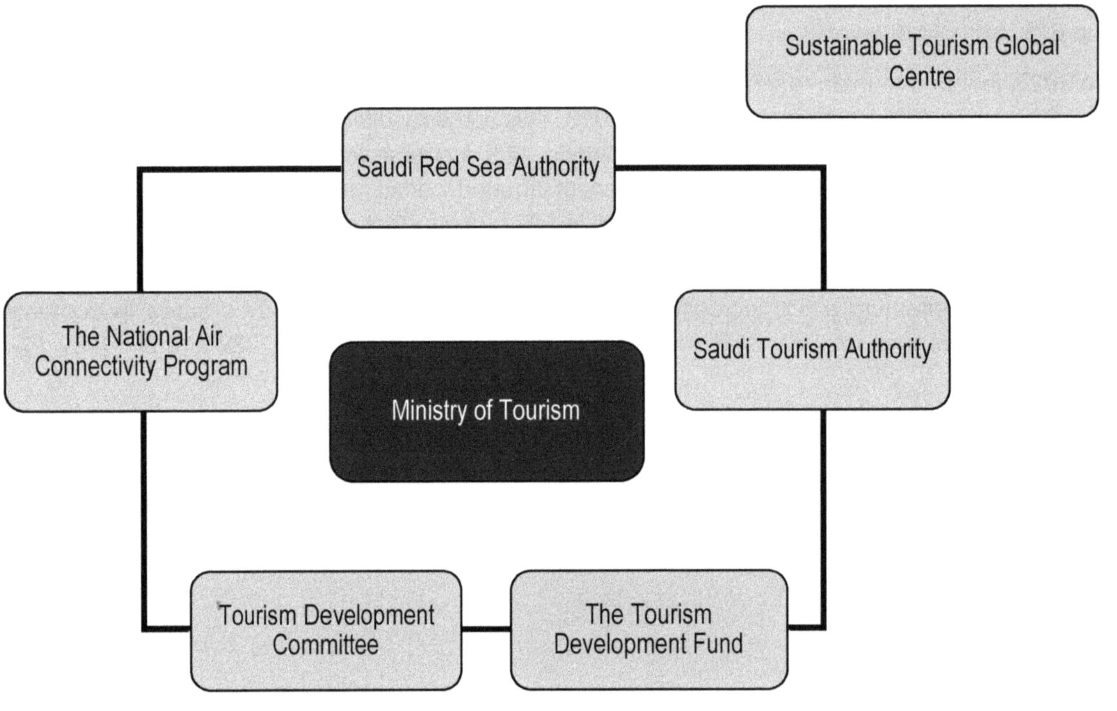

Source: OECD, adapted from Ministry of Tourism, 2024.

Tourism policies and programmes

Since the Vision 2030 strategy was launched, the Kingdom of Saudi Arabia has taken a wide range of steps to strengthen the role of the tourism sector as a driver of local economic growth. In 2019, the government announced the National Tourism Strategy, under the banner of Vision 2030. Tourism contributes to three of the key Vision 2030 objectives:

- Strengthen Islamic and national identity by facilitating hosting of more than 37 million Hajj and Umrah visitors and enrich their experience.
- Support the diversification efforts of the economy by increasing the contribution of the private sector and attracting Foreign Direct Investment, to reach 2030 targets of 10% contribution to GDP and creating 1.6 million jobs.
- Enhance government effectiveness through unlocking the potential of the non-oil sector.

To measure progress, three-year action plans have been implemented. The first three-year action plan ran from 2019-22 to address the complex and dynamic development of the tourism sector and identify key gaps. Over the years, the tourism sector has matured, and the National Tourism Strategy has become a platform for regulation and policy reforms to set up the tourism sector in the Kingdom of Saudi Arabia.

Phase 2 of the Strategy will be implemented from 2024-26, aiming to strengthen the Kingdom of Saudi Arabia's position as a leading tourism destination. While Phase 2 is under development, a number of policy and programmes have been continued or implemented, including:

- Regulating the use of technology in the Saudi tourism sector. This includes regulating the use of online travel platforms, and ensuring that tourists have access to accurate and reliable information about tourism products and services.
- Promoting tourism investment through developing new investment incentives, and making it easier for foreign investors to do business in Saudi Arabia.
- Developing tourism giga projects, including Neom, Red Sea, Qiddiya and Diriyah.
- Protecting the environment and cultural heritage through developing new regulations to govern tourism activities in sensitive areas, and supporting the restoration and preservation of cultural heritage sites.
- Establishing the Tourism Development Fund in 2020 to provide financial support for tourism projects. With a SAR 160 billion (USD 43 billion) budget over a ten-year period, the fund finances projects that have an important economic impact and focus on long-term sustainability.
- Establishing the Sustainable Tourism Global Centre (STGC) which focuses on renewable energy alternatives and developing innovative methods to curtail food and water waste.

The Ministry of Tourism issued the Tourism Law, which provides a comprehensive framework for the development and regulation of the tourism sector. The law covers a wide range of topics, including tourism licensing, tourism products and services, and the rights and obligations of tourists (see box below).

A new tourism law in Saudi Arabia

In 2022, the Ministry of Tourism implemented a new policy reform to regulate all tourism activities, including Online Travel Agencies and tour guides. This reform aims to ensure that all tourism activities have regulatory coverage and enhance the management and oversight of the tourism industry.

The new tourism law is a key driver for achieving Vision 2030's goals. It aims to better organise the tourism sector and improve the quality of services in the country. The new tourism law contains provisions to address the current situation such as licensing provisions, financial fees, licensee obligations, inspection details and the sanctions. In addition, the law also ensures that any tourism activities that may develop in the future are included through a partnership with The Sandbox.

The new tourism law has been developed to be more flexible, in line with international best practices, attracting local and foreign investment in the tourism sector to Saudi Arabia. The new law includes penalties for anyone who violates its provisions.

Statistical Profile

Saudi Arabia: Domestic, inbound and outbound tourism

	2018	2019	2020	2021	2022
TOURISM FLOWS, THOUSAND					
Domestic tourism					
Total domestic trips	46 512	53 074	48 399	108 129	125 817
Overnight visitors (tourists)	43 255	47 805	42 107	63 834	77 837
Same-day visitors (excursionists)	3 256	5 269	6 292	44 295	47 980
Nights in all types of accommodation	232 122	268 751	228 538	353 331	369 606
Hotels and similar establishments	140 452	155 540	121 909	161 334	205 161
Other collective establishments	9 034	7 874	4 900	6 057	5 022
Private accommodation	82 637	105 337	101 730	185 940	159 424
Inbound tourism					
Total international arrivals	17 570	20 292	4 882	3 869	18 256
Overnight visitors (tourists)	15 334	17 526	4 138	3 477	16 638
Same-day visitors (excursionists)	2 236	2 767	744	392	1 618
Top markets					
Bahrain	574	511	100	240	2 178
Kuwait	1 993	2 132	629	623	1 948
Egypt	800	1 100	432	308	1 463
Pakistan	2 177	2 211	483	258	1 407
Indonesia	1 375	1 429	293	11	1 228
Nights in all types of accommodation	173 929	189 036	37 824	31 771	270 728
Hotels and similar establishments	153 005	164 526	30 447	16 081	153 744
Other collective establishments	5 298	1 011	119	210	8 043
Private accommodation	15 626	23 499	7 258	15 480	108 941
Outbound tourism					
Total international departures	27 425	27 196	6 657	10 682	24 264
Overnight visitors (tourists)	19 751	19 010	4 839	8 415	16 882
Same-day visitors (excursionists)	7 674	8 186	1 819	2 266	7 381
Top destinations					
Bahrain	3 957	3 907	588	1 282	2 931
UAE	3 262	3 125	792	1 189	2 644
Egypt	2 459	2 352	751	1 366	2 076
Kuwait	2 498	2 447	567	887	1 952
Jordan	1 462	1 417	336	713	1 579
TOURISM RECEIPTS AND EXPENDITURE, MILLION USD					
Inbound tourism					
Total international receipts	16 974	19 849	4 646	4 639	26 517
International travel receipts	13 790	16 431	4 036	3 817	23 475
International passenger transport receipts	3 184	3 418	610	822	3 042
Outbound tourism					
Total international expenditure	17 939	16 415	9 379	13 130	18 662
International travel expenditure	16 651	15 140	8 843	12 176	15 914
International passenger transport expenditure	1 288	1 275	536	954	2 748

.. Not available
Source: OECD Tourism Statistics (Database).

StatLink https://stat.link/rkg06i

Saudi Arabia: Enterprises and employment in tourism

	Number of establishments[1]	Number of persons employed				
	2022	2018	2019	2020	2021	2022
Total	..	..	..	..	..	..
Tourism industries	121 779	552 556	571 152	683 178	762 957	880 140
Accommodation services for visitors	12 451	118 941	124 676	94 660	98 492	110 095
Hotels and similar establishments	..	..	..	..	..	..
Food and beverage serving industry	88 938	298 487	306 508	455 168	520 643	608 722
Passenger transport	2 832	69 855	72 441	50 875	45 282	44 124
Air passenger transport	94	28 232	29 547	21 578	20 106	18 118
Railways passenger transport	4	1 655	1 716	2 298	282	14
Road passenger transport	2 560	39 669	40 860	26 253	23 823	24 896
Water passenger transport	174	299	319	746	1 071	1 096
Passenger transport supporting services	..	..	..	..	..	..
Transport equipment rental	968	21 084	21 868	11 897	13 447	16 030
Travel agencies and other reservation services industry	2 071	25 560	26 327	14 793	15 771	19 892
Cultural industry	406	2 256	2 339	3 029	4 710	4 699
Sports and recreation industry	1 515	13 359	13 843	8 544	10 046	11 323
Retail trade of country-specific tourism characteristic goods	11 170	..	..	36 979	43 877	52 576
Other country-specific tourism industries	1 432	3 014	3 150	7 233	10 689	12 679
Other industries	..	..	..	..	..	..

.. Not available
1. Data refer to number of enterprises.
Source: OECD Tourism Statistics (Database).

StatLink https://stat.link/syz6v0

Saudi Arabia: Internal tourism consumption

Million SAR

	2022		
	Domestic tourism expenditure	Inbound tourism expenditure	Internal tourism consumption
Total	..	..	..
Consumption products	137 175	103 515	250 252
Tourism characteristic products	101 918	70 695	172 612
Accommodation services for visitors	27 230	28 323	55 554
Food and beverage serving services	40 134	18 151	58 285
Passenger transport services	23 095	17 818	40 912
Air passenger transport services	16 490	11 565	28 054
Railways passenger transport services	332	240	573
Road passenger transport services	6 229	6 013	12 243
Water passenger transport services	43	0	43
Passenger transport supporting services	..	..	0
Transport equipment rental services	3 990	120	4 110
Travel agencies and other reservation services industry	1 284	3 136	4 419
Cultural services	2 474	944	3 418
Sports and recreation services	3 711	2 203	5 914
Country-specific tourism characteristic goods	..	..	
Country-specific tourism characteristic services	..	..	
Other consumption products	35 257	32 820	77 640
Tourism connected products	..	..	..
Non-tourism related consumption products	..	..	..
Non-consumption products	..	..	..

.. Not available
Source: OECD Tourism Statistics (Database).

StatLink https://stat.link/t5s937

Serbia

Tourism in the economy and outlook

Tourism is an important contributor to the economy in Serbia, and has recovered following the COVID-19 pandemic. In 2022, accommodation services directly contributed RSD 25 915 million to the Serbian economy or 0.4% of total GDP. The Statistical Office of Serbia recorded approximately 154 000 jobs within tourism industries, which represents 6.7% of total employment. This is an increase of 10 000 tourism jobs compared to 2019.

In 2023, Serbia registered 2.1 million international tourist arrivals at official accommodation establishments. This represents an increase of 16% compared to the year 2019. The top three source markets were Türkiye (9%), Russian Federation (8%) and Bosnia and Herzegovina (7%).

Domestic tourism is essential for the tourism sector in Serbia, with 2.1 million overnight domestic tourists recorded at official accommodation establishments in 2023, 12% above the level in 2019.

Serbia projects a total of 4.5 million arrivals at official accommodation establishments and approximately 14 million overnight stays in 2024.

Tourism governance

The Ministry of Tourism and Youth is responsible for tourism affairs, dealing with all aspects of tourism strategy, policy, promotion, and development. The Ministry provides direct and indirect support to regional and local authorities, including incentive programmes for tourism development projects such as infrastructure, promotion, education, and training, and supporting local governments and regional development agencies with jointly funded projects.

The Ministry co-operates closely with other ministries, particularly the Ministry of Culture on international bilateral co-operation and the development of cultural routes, the Ministry of Agriculture on the development of rural tourism and the support instruments in the field of rural development, the Ministry of Environmental Protection on sustainable tourism development, and the Ministry of Health. The Ministry works closely with the private sector and is active in regional initiatives and programmes and projects from international organisations.

The Tourist Organisation of Serbia carries out promotional activities internationally. Regional and local tourist organisations are closely integrated into promotional activities. The Provincial Secretariat for Economy and Tourism in the Autonomous Province of Vojvodina is responsible for managing tourism development, in accordance with the Tourism Development Strategy and the Law on Tourism of the Republic of Serbia.

In 2023 the total tourism budget was RSD 4.9 billion. This included RSD 2.7 billion for infrastructure projects, RSD 1.7 billion for promotional projects, and RSD 500 million for the National Tourism Organisation.

Serbia: Organisational chart of tourism bodies

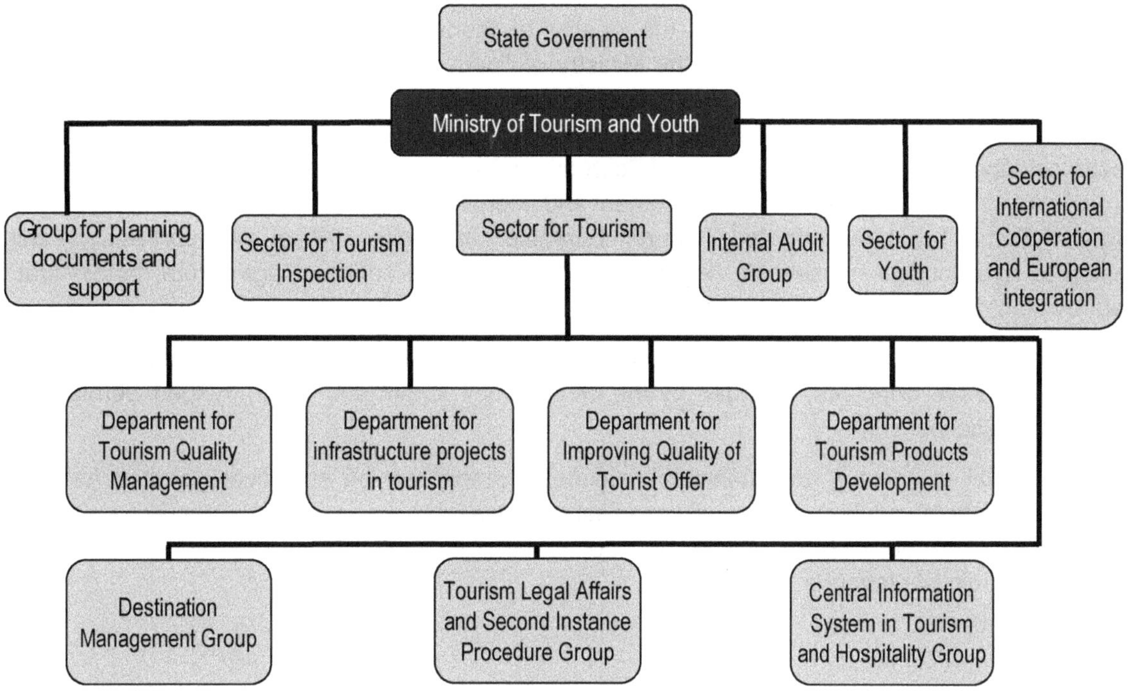

Source: OECD, adapted from the Ministry of Tourism and Youth, 2024

Tourism policies and programmes

Serbian tourism is guided by the Tourism Development Strategy 2016-25. The Strategy is implemented through a mixture of strategic master plans, a strategic marketing plan, a product development programme, and spatial and urban plans. The Tourism Development Strategy also establishes a competitive arena for the business sector in Serbian tourism.

Serbia is in the final stages of drafting a new strategy for tourism development. The main objectives of the strategy are to manage tourism more efficiently, attract investments, increase employment and create attractive tourism products and offerings based on sustainability principles.

To implement the strategy, several programmes have been implemented, with a particular focus on rural and regional tourism development. Lessons learned from the pandemic include the importance of developing tourism in smaller rural areas. Positive rural impacts in Serbia were seen including increased employment of women in rural areas, encouraged entrepreneurship, and boosted tourism employment, like local guides, national park rangers, and food suppliers. This revealed the necessity to involve residents in the creation of local tourist offerings where possible.

The Ministry of Tourism and Youth supports the development of rural and village tourism through incentive funds. In addition to funds allocated for events organised in rural areas, the Development Fund approves favourable credit resources to enhance the quality of tourism offerings in rural tourism. In 2023, RSD 17.7 million was allocated. In 2024, the Ministry of Tourism and Youth will pass a law to allow the allocation of non-refundable funds to rural tourist households, with a 20% co-founding arrangement, to repair and construct accommodation facilities, improve landscaping, upgrade tourism facilities, and increase catering in rural areas. At the end of February 2024, the regulation on the conditions, method of awarding and using incentives for the development and improvement of rural tourism and hospitality in the territory of Serbia has been adopted. Non-reimbursable funds with 10% of own participation will be allocated to rural tourism households (legal entities and physical entities - agricultural farms) that are engaged in the development of rural tourism.

To continue supporting domestic tourism, Serbia has extended the use of travel vouchers in 2023 and 2024. In 2022, travel vouchers, provided by the Ministry of Tourism and Youth, helped Serbia reach a record in domestic tourism.

In 2024, national criteria for sustainable tourism development will be specifically crafted for Serbian destinations, the hotel industry, and travel organisers. Serbia will be supported by the Global Council for Sustainable Tourism. Serbia is also finalising its tourism digitalisation programme to present the Serbian tourism offer on digital platforms.

Statistical Profile

Serbia: Domestic, inbound and outbound tourism

	2018	2019	2020	2021	2022
TOURISM FLOWS, THOUSAND					
Domestic tourism					
Total domestic trips	1 720	1 843	1 374	1 720	2 096
Overnight visitors (tourists)	1 720	1 843	1 374	1 720	2 096
Same-day visitors (excursionists)	..	..	..	..	..
Nights in all types of accommodation	5 678	6 063	4 937	5 733	7 306
Hotels and similar establishments	4 624	4 916	3 572	4 327	4 991
Other collective establishments	48	35	18	21	25
Private accommodation	1 006	1 112	1 347	1 385	2 290
Inbound tourism					
Total international arrivals	1 711	1 847	446	871	1 773
Overnight visitors (tourists)	1 711	1 847	446	871	1 773
Same-day visitors (excursionists)	..	..	..	..	..
Top markets					
Bosnia and Herzegovina	121	136	51	103	149
Montenegro	82	90	26	59	81
China (People's Republic of)	102	145	18	16	33
Croatia	94	104	27	39	90
Türkiye	97	108	25	49	126
Nights in all types of accommodation	3 658	4 010	1 265	2 430	4 939
Hotels and similar establishments	3 416	3 761	1 201	2 290	3 860
Other collective establishments	24	20	1	9	17
Private accommodation	218	229	63	131	1 062
Outbound tourism					
Total international departures	..	..	..	..	..
Overnight visitors (tourists)	..	..	..	..	..
Same-day visitors (excursionists)	..	..	..	..	..
Top destinations					
..	..	..	..	..	..
..	..	..	..	..	..
..	..	..	..	..	..
..	..	..	..	..	..
..	..	..	..	..	..
TOURISM RECEIPTS AND EXPENDITURE, MILLION USD					
Inbound tourism					
Total international receipts	1 941	2 001	1 430	2 172	2 592
International travel receipts	1 547	1 604	1 245	1 882	2 592
International passenger transport receipts	394	396	185	290	..
Outbound tourism					
Total international expenditure	1 837	1 999	1 178	1 718	2 459
International travel expenditure	1 643	1 806	1 115	1 617	2 459
International passenger transport expenditure	194	194	64	101	..

.. Not available
Source: OECD Tourism Statistics (Database).

StatLink https://stat.link/ay8q4e

Serbia: Enterprises and employment in tourism

	Number of establishments[1]	Number of persons employed				
	2022	2018	2019	2020	2021	2022
Total	..	..	..	..	..	..
Tourism industries	63 399	138 947	143 724	149 106	149 932	153 711
Accommodation services for visitors	4 846	21 681	23 308	24 619	24 795	26 240
Hotels and similar establishments	1 995	12 035	12 768	13 361	13 056	14 127
Food and beverage serving industry	27 773	61 348	63 961	66 159	67 316	68 291
Passenger transport	17 940	20 964	20 065	20 428	19 802	19 710
Air passenger transport	52	1 431	1 414	1 498	1 286	1 405
Railways passenger transport	2	1 593	1 398	2 370	2 404	2 447
Road passenger transport	17 827	17 881	17 183	16 489	16 042	15 792
Water passenger transport	59	59	70	71	70	66
Passenger transport supporting services	..	..	..	..	..	
Transport equipment rental	654	1 022	1 025	1 115	1 164	1 337
Travel agencies and other reservation services industry	1 703	4 689	4 782	4 457	3 408	3 474
Cultural industry	4 133	12 442	12 799	12 855	13 021	13 453
Sports and recreation industry	6 350	16 801	17 784	19 473	20 426	21 206
Retail trade of country-specific tourism characteristic goods	..	..	..	..	..	..
Other country-specific tourism industries	..	..	..	..	..	..
Other industries	..	..	..	..	..	..

.. Not available

1. Data refer to number of enterprises.

Source: OECD Tourism Statistics (Database).

StatLink https://stat.link/685l9z

South Africa

Tourism in the economy and outlook

Tourism plays a significant role in the South African economy and remains a priority sector to respond to socio-economic challenges in the country. In 2022, tourism directly contributed an estimated ZAR 234.7 billion to the South African economy, accounting for 3.5% of GDP, which is slightly below the share in 2019 which was 3.7%. Tourism directly contributed a total of 733 400 jobs to the economy accounting for 4.7% of the total workforce, down by 6% compared to 2019.

International tourist arrivals totalled 8.5 million in 2023, 17% below 2019 levels. The top three source markets in terms of international arrivals were Zimbabwe (25% of total arrivals), Mozambique (16%) and Lesotho (14%). International tourism expenditure in 2023 reached ZAR 70.9 billion, showing a strong recovery from the ZAR 35.9 billion in 2020, but still down on the peak of ZAR 121.5 billion in 2019.

South Africa's domestic tourism played an important role in the country's economic rebound, with a peak of 37.9 million domestic tourists in 2023, which is 33% above 2019 levels. Domestic tourism expenditure amounted to ZAR 99 billion in 2022, 177% higher than in 2019.

Tourism governance

Tourism is a concurrent function in South Africa's Constitution, meaning that all three levels of government (national, provincial and local) have jurisdiction and direct responsibility in developing and implementing tourism policy. The Ministry of Tourism is the executive authority for national tourism policy and accounts to Parliament on tourism development in the country. It oversees South African Tourism, the national tourism organisation which markets South Africa internationally, and the Department of Tourism, responsible for promoting the inclusive growth of tourism through research, policy, destination development, international relations and sector support services. The Department of Tourism co-ordinates the activities of public and private sector stakeholders through the National Tourism Stakeholder Forum, the Tourism Leadership Dialogue and other stakeholder engagement sessions. Horizontal co-ordination is pursued through bilateral engagement and co-operation with key ministries on areas such as visa policy, air connectivity and licensing. The Department of Tourism participates in international engagements, multilateral organisations, and in bilateral relations through signed memoranda of understanding with key countries in Africa, Middle East and the rest of the world.

Provincial and local governments have responsibility for tourism development regionally. At provincial level, a Member of the Executive Council in each of South Africa's nine provinces is charged with responsibility for tourism. The Minister of Tourism and the Executive Councils co-ordinate and align strategic performance plans, priorities, and objectives, through the MINMEC intergovernmental forum. At local level, a municipality led by the Member of Mayoral Committee responsible for local economic development is charged with the responsibility for tourism development. The Tourism Business Council of South Africa is an umbrella organisation gathering private sector stakeholders. It plays an active role in tourism policy advocacy and takes part in the National Tourism Stakeholder Forum.

The total allocated budget for 2023-24 is ZAR 2.524 billion, which represents a 0.9% increase compared to 2022-23. In 2023-24, corporate management was allocated ZAR 324.9 million; tourism research, policy and international relations (including South African Tourism, the Department of Tourism's only entity) were allocated ZAR 1435.2 million; destination development, ZAR 401.1 million; and tourism sector support services, ZAR 363 000.

South Africa: Organisational chart of tourism bodies

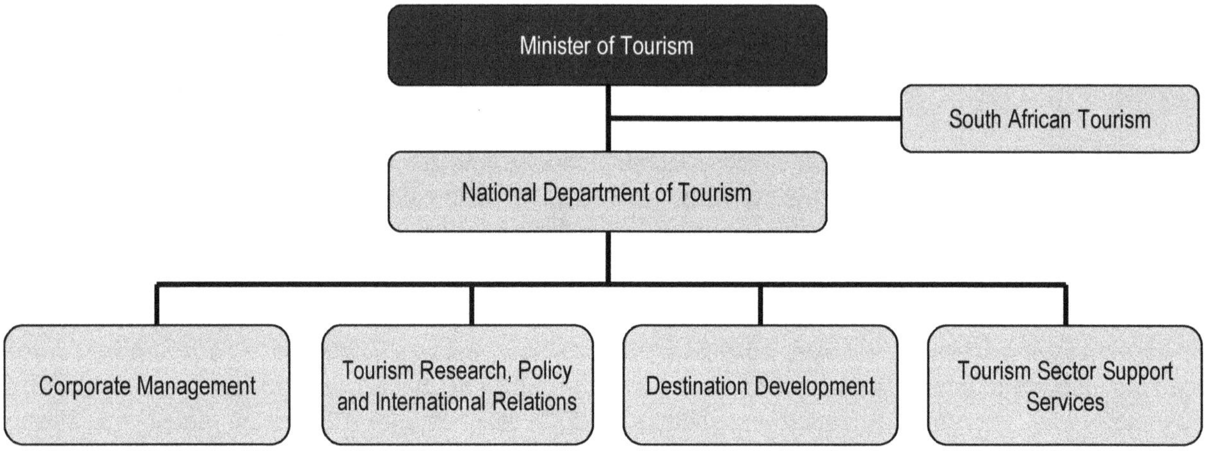

Source: OECD, adapted from the Department of Tourism, 2024.

Tourism policies and programmes

Tourism development and growth is guided by the National Tourism Sector Strategy, 2016-26. The Strategy aims to promote rapid and inclusive tourism development, focusing on South Africa's competitive edge in nature, culture, and heritage, underpinned by *Ubuntu* and supported by innovation and service excellence. The plan sets out clear targets for 2026 and key economic performance indicators, which are: increase direct tourism GDP to ZAR 302 billion; increase total (direct and indirect) contribution to GDP to ZAR 941 billion; increase the number of direct jobs supported by the sector to 1 million jobs; increase the number of total jobs supported by the sector to 2.2 million jobs; increase tourism export earnings to ZAR 359 billion and increase in capital investment to ZAR 148 billion for international, regional and domestic tourism.

To support the Strategy after the COVID-19 pandemic, the Tourism Sector Master Plan was launched in September 2023. The Master Plan adjusts the Tourism Sector Recovery Plan timeframes and seeks to continue to monitor the implementation of strategic interventions until 2026.

The Master Plan is anchored on three interlinked strategic themes: protect and rejuvenate supply, reignite demand and strengthen enabling capability for long term sustainability. Within these pillars, there are seven strategic interventions that address key areas of focus. These interventions include: enhancing education and skills development, promoting entrepreneurship and economic growth, improving infrastructure and connectivity, fostering social cohesion and well-being, preserving the environment and natural resources, strengthening governance and institutions, and promoting regional co-operation.

The Master Plan is aligned to the country's broader Economic Recovery and Reconstruction Plan, contributing to the infrastructure development, mass public employment, green economy interventions, the inclusion of women and youth, and skills development. An annual performance statement is conducted to measure the Master Plan's progress.

Various policies and programmes directly contribute to the tourism recovery in South Africa. These include:

- Infrastructure programme: South Africa implements infrastructure maintenance and renovation projects in several provinces, particularly in provincial and national parks. These seek to ensure maintenance of tourism infrastructure to provide quality services to visitors. As part of route development, community-based tourism projects have been implemented to ensure inclusivity and promote transformation of the tourism sector in South Africa. There are 29 community tourism projects currently being implemented as part of destination enhancement and route development to diversify tourism offerings and visitor experience in identified priority areas. The projects contribute to uplifting rural communities, grow domestic tourism, job creation and small medium, and micro-enterprise development.
- Capacity building programme: South Africa implements a large-scale skills development programme where especially women and young people are trained in various skills initiatives which include professional cookery; recognition of prior learning for chefs; sommelier and wine service training; food safety assurers; hospitality service training; resource efficiency; safety monitors programme; National Tourism Career Expo and the executive development programme for women. These initiatives aim to ensure the workforce skills are aligned with the industry's needs. Most of the programmes are funded through the Expanded Public Works Programme of government, which supports employment and job creation interventions. At least 4 000 participants are targeted for these initiatives on an annual basis.
- Incentives: Under the broader Tourism Incentive Programme, which has a budget allocation of ZAR 225.7 million for the 2023/24 financial year, financial incentive and support programmes are offered to stimulate sector transformation, enterprise growth, operational sustainability, job creation and an enhanced visitor experience. Targeted multi-year programmes include the Market Access Support Programme to expose small tourism enterprises at international, regional and domestic trade platforms; the Tourism Grading Support Programme to encourage participation in the country's tourism grading system; the Green Tourism Incentive Programme to encourage investment in more energy and water efficiency systems to facilitate more sustainable operations; and the Tourism Equity Fund and Tourism Transformation Fund as two blended finance support mechanisms to encourage capital investment that will stimulate sector transformation through more inclusive enterprise ownership.

The Tourism Green Paper Review of South Africa

South Africa has published the Green Paper policy that seeks to develop and promote sustainable tourism in the country. The Green Paper on the development and promotion of tourism in South Africa was approved by Cabinet for public consultation. Comments received from the public consultation process were analysed, and subsequently the Green Paper was updated. The Minister of Tourism endorsed the finalised Tourism White Paper for tabling at Government Clusters for concurrence and Cabinet Meetings for approval.

Policy reform is being undertaken to create an enabling regulatory environment for technological development in tourism; promoting an inclusive sector through empowerment initiatives; instilling a whole-of-government approach to tourism development; ensuring an intelligence-based tourism safety initiative and developing a comprehensive crisis management framework to guide crisis management in tourism. The Green Paper was developed in response to concerns raised in the economic survey of South Africa conducted by Treasury with the support of OECD. The survey found more could be done to elevate South African tourism to its full potential and utilising resources.

Statistical Profile

South Africa: Domestic, inbound and outbound tourism

	2018	2019	2020	2021	2022
TOURISM FLOWS, THOUSAND					
Domestic tourism					
Total domestic trips	133 650	264 980	125 077	83 597	210 394
Overnight visitors (tourists)	17 650	28 456	17 038	14 837	34 029
Same-day visitors (excursionists)	116 000	236 524	108 039	68 760	176 366
Nights in all types of accommodation	69 300	94 144	56 808	51 185	118 646
Hotels and similar establishments	..	..	..	..	..
Other collective establishments	..	..	..	..	..
Private accommodation	..	..	..	..	..
Inbound tourism					
Total international arrivals	15 004	14 797	3 886	2 664	7 342
Overnight visitors (tourists)	10 472	10 228	2 802	2 256	5 698
Same-day visitors (excursionists)	4 532	4 569	1 084	408	1 644
Top markets					
Zimbabwe	2 209	2 259	685	411	1 234
Lesotho	1 739	1 563	449	355	836
Mozambique	1 361	1 333	423	523	944
Swaziland	884	918	215	178	404
United Kingdom	431	436	132	46	283
Nights in all types of accommodation	..	..	..	..	..
Hotels and similar establishments	..	..	..	..	..
Other collective establishments	..	..	..	..	..
Private accommodation	..	..	..	..	..
Outbound tourism					
Total international departures	6 015	6 076	1 624	1 624	3 731
Overnight visitors (tourists)	..	..	..	..	..
Same-day visitors (excursionists)	..	..	..	..	..
Top destinations					
..	..	..	..	..	..
..	..	..	..	..	..
..	..	..	..	..	..
..	..	..	..	..	..
..	..	..	..	..	..
TOURISM RECEIPTS AND EXPENDITURE, MILLION USD					
Inbound tourism					
Total international receipts	9 789	9 064	2 717	2 113	4 738
International travel receipts	8 989	8 390	2 607	2 108	4 738
International passenger transport receipts	800	674	109	5	..
Outbound tourism					
Total international expenditure	6 017	5 551	1 466	1 669	2 220
International travel expenditure	3 402	3 141	928	991	2 220
International passenger transport expenditure	2 615	2 410	538	678	..

.. Not available
Source: OECD Tourism Statistics (Database).

StatLink https://stat.link/5yenzs

South Africa: Enterprises and employment in tourism

	Number of establishments	Number of persons employed[1]				
	2022	2018	2019	2020	2021	2022
Total	..	..	..	..	..	..
Tourism industries	55 228	623 515	777 686	454 114	492 561	733 384
Accommodation services for visitors	12 063	125 757	118 128	93 366	86 514	118 422
Hotels and similar establishments	3 504	..	..	..	..	
Food and beverage serving industry	22 500	97 051	144 225	76 182	87 916	133 765
Passenger transport	7 254	211 348	276 908	157 147	193 889	262 415
Air passenger transport	1 354	29 037	28 540	20 262	9 462	20 075
Railways passenger transport	38	4 819	6 318	2 981	3 318	5 782
Road passenger transport	5 531	174 778	241 670	133 591	180 409	232 194
Water passenger transport	331	2 714	380	313	700	4 364
Passenger transport supporting services	..	..	..	..	..	..
Transport equipment rental	451	11 424	10 009	8 050	4 655	8 103
Travel agencies and other reservation services industry	2 361	31 318	32 536	24 041	23 443	23 099
Cultural industry	5 630	18 605	19 627	10 892	12 860	27 912
Sports and recreation industry	4 969	9 543	17 678	11 379	12 125	17 221
Retail trade of country-specific tourism characteristic goods	..	118 469	158 575	73 056	71 159	142 447
Other country-specific tourism industries	..	..	..	..	..	..
Other industries	..	..	..	..	..	..

.. Not available
1. Data refer to number of jobs.
Source: OECD Tourism Statistics (Database).

StatLink https://stat.link/auxm7f

South Africa: Internal tourism consumption

Million ZAR

	2022		
	Domestic tourism expenditure	Inbound tourism expenditure	Internal tourism consumption
Total	..	..	..
Consumption products	435 756	71 087	506 843
Tourism characteristic products	267 103	48 570	315 673
Accommodation services for visitors	35 378	11 009	46 387
Food and beverage serving services	51 941	10 184	62 125
Passenger transport services	123 773	16 582	140 355
Air passenger transport services	47 725	3 984	51 709
Railways passenger transport services	671	95	766
Road passenger transport services	57 823	11 934	69 757
Water passenger transport services	2 396	212	2 608
Passenger transport supporting services	..	..	..
Transport equipment rental services	15 159	357	15 515
Travel agencies and other reservation services industry	18 924	2 869	21 793
Cultural services	8 790	3 396	12 186
Sports and recreation services	28 297	4 530	32 827
Country-specific tourism characteristic goods	..	..	..
Country-specific tourism characteristic services	..	..	..
Other consumption products	168 653	22 518	191 170
Tourism connected products	37 191	10 957	48 148
Non-tourism related consumption products	131 462	11 561	143 022
Non-consumption products	..	..	..

.. Not available
Source: OECD Tourism Statistics (Database).

StatLink https://stat.link/5alhfy

www.ingramcontent.com/pod-product-compliance
Lightning Source LLC
Chambersburg PA
CBHW061158240926
51846CB00006B/1048
* 9 7 8 9 2 6 4 3 2 2 5 9 2 *